Happy Christmas, Ellis,

love from

Judith, Ian &

Christopher.

FLASHMAN'S FIRST OMNIBUS

Flashman's First Omnibus

FLASHMAN
ROYAL FLASH
FLASH FOR FREEDOM!

Edited and arranged by
GEORGE MACDONALD FRASER

Barrie & Jenkins, London

For

KATH

Barrie & Jenkins Ltd
3 Fitzroy Square, London W 1 P 6 JD

An imprint of the Hutchinson Publishing Group

London Melbourne Sydney Auckland
Wellington Johannesburg and agencies
throughout the world

Flashman
First published 1969
© George MacDonald Fraser 1969

Royal Flash
First published 1970
© George MacDonald Fraser 1970

Flash for Freedom!
First published 1971
© George MacDonald Fraser 1971

This edition first published 1979

Printed and bound in Great Britain
by McCorquodale (Newton) Ltd,
Newton-le-Willows, Lancashire

ISBN 0 214 20672 6

CONTENTS

One fine summer evening Flashman had been regaling himself on gin-punch, at Brownsover; and, having exceeded his usual limits, started home uproarious. He fell in with a friend or two coming back from bathing, proposed a glass of beer, to which they assented, the weather being hot, and they thirsty souls, and unaware of the quantity of drink which Flashman had already on board. The short result was, that Flashy became beastly drunk. They tried to get him along, but couldn't; so they chartered a hurdle and two men to carry him. One of the masters came upon them, and they naturally enough fled. The flight of the rest excited the master's suspicions, and the good angel of the fags incited him to examine the freight, and, after examination, to convoy the hurdle himself up to the School-house; and the Doctor, who had long had his eye on Flashman, arranged for his withdrawal next morning.

—THOMAS HUGHES, *Tom Brown's Schooldays.*

FLASHMAN

From The Flashman Papers
1839–1842

Explanatory Note

The great mass of manuscript known as the Flashman Papers was discovered during a sale of household furniture at Ashby, Leicestershire, in 1965. The papers were subsequently claimed by Mr Paget Morrison, of Durban, South Africa, the nearest known living relative of their author.

A point of major literary interest about the papers is that they clearly identify Flashman, the school bully of Thomas Hughes' *Tom Brown's Schooldays*, with the celebrated Victorian soldier of the same name. The papers are, in fact, Harry Flashman's personal memoirs from the day of his expulsion from Rugby School in the late 1830's to the early years of the present century. He appears to have written them some time between 1900 and 1905, when he must have been over eighty. It is possible that he dictated them.

The papers, which had apparently lain untouched for fifty years, in a tea chest, until they were found in the Ashby sale-room, were carefully wrapped in oilskin covers. From correspondence found in the first packet, it is evident that their original discovery by his relatives in 1915 after the great soldier's death caused considerable consternation; they seem to have been unanimously against publication of their kinsman's autobiography—one can readily understand why—and the only wonder is that the manuscript was not destroyed.

Fortunately, it was preserved, and what follows is the content of the first packet, covering Flashman's early adventures. I have no reason to doubt that it is a completely truthful account; where Flashman touches on historical fact he is almost invariably accurate, and readers can judge whether he is to be believed or not on more personal matters.

Mr Paget Morrison, knowing of my interest in this and related subjects, asked me to edit the papers. Beyond correcting some minor spelling errors, however, there has been no editing to do.

Flashman had a better sense of narrative than I have, and I have confined myself to the addition of a few historical notes.

The quotation from *Tom Brown's Schooldays* was pasted to the top page of the first packet; it had evidently been cut from the original edition of 1856.

G.M.F.

Hughes got it wrong, in one important detail. You will have read, in *Tom Brown,* how I was expelled from Rugby School for drunkenness, which is true enough, but when Hughes alleges that this was the result of my deliberately pouring beer on top of gin-punch, he is in error. I knew better than to mix my drinks, even at seventeen.

I mention this, not in self-defence, but in the interests of strict truth. This story will be completely truthful; I am breaking the habit of eighty years. Why shouldn't I? When a man is as old as I am, and knows himself thoroughly for what he was and is, he doesn't care much. I'm not ashamed, you see; never was—and I have enough of what Society would consider the credit side of the ledger—a knighthood, a Victoria Cross, high rank, and some popular fame. So I can look at the picture above my desk, of the young officer in Cardigan's Hussars; tall, masterful, and roughly handsome I was in those days (even Hughes allowed that I was big and strong, and had considerable powers of being pleasant), and say that it is the portrait of a scoundrel, a liar, a cheat, a thief, a coward—and, oh yes, a toady. Hughes said more or less all these things, and his description was pretty fair, except in matters of detail such as the one I've mentioned. But he was more concerned to preach a sermon than to give facts.

But I am concerned with facts, and since many of them are discreditable to me, you can rest assured they are true.

At all events, Hughes was wrong in saying I suggested beer. It was Speedicut who ordered it up, and I had drunk it (on top of all those gin-punches) before I knew what I was properly doing. That finished me; I was really drunk then—"beastly drunk," says Hughes, and he's right—and when they got me out of the "Grapes" I could hardly see, let alone walk. They bundled me into a sedan, and then a beak hove in sight and Speedicut lived up to his name and bolted. I was left sprawling in the chair, and up came the master and saw me. It was old Rufton, one of Arnold's housemasters.

"Good God!" he said. "It's one of our boys—drunk!"

I can still see him goggling at me, with his great pale gooseberry eyes and white whiskers. He tried to rouse me, but he might as well have tried to wake a corpse. I just lay and giggled at him. Finally he lost his temper, and banged the top of the chair with his cane and shouted:

"Take him up, chairmen! Take him to the School! He shall go before the Doctor for this!"

So they bore me off in procession, with old Rufton raging behind about disgusting excesses and the wages of sin, and old Thomas and the chairmen took me to the hospital, which was appropriate, and left me on a bed to sober up. It didn't take me long, I can tell you, as soon as my mind was clear enough to think what would come of it. You know what Arnold was like, if you have read Hughes, and he had no use for me at the best of times. The least I could expect was a flogging before the school.

That was enough to set me in a blue funk, at the very thought, but what I was really afraid of was Arnold himself.

They left me in the hospital perhaps two hours, and then old Thomas came to say the Doctor wanted to see me. I followed him downstairs and across to the School-house, with the fags peeping round corners and telling each other that the brute Flashy had fallen at last, and old Thomas knocked at the Doctor's door, and the voice crying "Come in!" sounded like the crack of doom to me.

He was standing before the fireplace, with his hands behind looping up his coat-tails, and a face like a Turk at a christening. He had eyes like sabre-points, and his face was pale and carried that disgusted look that he kept for these occasions. Even with the liquor still working on me a little I was as scared in that minute as I've ever been in my life—and when you have ridden into a Russian battery at Balaclava and been chained in an Afghan dungeon waiting for the torturers, as I have, you know what fear means. I still feel uneasy when I think of him, and he's been dead sixty years.

He was live enough then. He stood silent a moment, to let me stew a little. Then:

"Flashman," says he, "there are many moments in a school-master's life when he must make a decision, and afterwards wonder whether he was right or not. I have made a decision, and for once I am in no doubt that I *am* right. I have observed you for several years now, with increasing concern. You have been an evil influence in the school. That you are a bully, I know; that you are untruthful, I have long suspected; that you are deceitful and mean, I have feared; but that you had fallen so low as to be a drunkard—that, at least, I never imagined. I have looked in the past for some signs of improvement in you, some spark of grace, some ray of hope that my work here had not, in your case, been unsuccessful. It has not come, and this is the final infamy. Have you anything to say?"

He had me blubbering by this time; I mumbled something about being sorry.

"If I thought for one moment," says he, "that you *were* sorry, that you had it in you to show *true* repentance, I might hesitate from the step that I am about to take. But I know you too well, Flashman. You must leave Rugby tomorrow."

If I had had my wits about me I suppose I should have thought this was no bad news, but with Arnold thundering I lost my head.

"But, sir," I said, still blubbering, "it will break my mother's heart!"

He went pale as a ghost, and I fell back. I thought he was going to hit me.

"Blasphemous wretch!" he cried—he had a great pulpit trick with phrases like those—"your mother has been dead these many years, and do you dare to plead her name—a name that should be sacred to you—in defence of your abominations? You have killed any spark of pity I had for you!"

"My father—"

"Your father," says he, "will know how to deal with you. I hardly think," he added, with a look, "that his heart will be broken." He knew something of my father, you see, and probably thought we were a pretty pair.

He stood there drumming his fingers behind him a moment, and then he said, in a different voice:

"You are a sorry creature, Flashman. I have failed in you. But even to you I must say, this is not the end. You cannot continue here, but you are young, Flashman, and there is time yet. Though your sins be as red as crimson, yet shall they be as white as snow. You have fallen very low, but you can be raised up again...."

I haven't a good memory for sermons, and he went on like this for some time, like the pious old hypocrite that he was. For he was a hypocrite, I think, like most of his generation. Either that or he was more foolish than he looked, for he was wasting his piety on me. But he never realised it.

Anyway, he gave me a fine holy harangue, about how through repentance I might be saved—which I've never believed, by the way. I've repented a good deal in my time, and had good cause, but I was never ass enough to suppose it mended anything. But I've learned to swim with the tide when I have to, so I let him pray over me, and when he had finished I left his study a good deal happier than when I went in. I had escaped flogging, which was the main thing; leaving Rugby I didn't mind a button. I never much cared for the place, and the supposed disgrace of expulsion I didn't even think about. (They had me back a few years ago to present prizes; nothing was said about expulsion *then*, which shows that they are just as big hypocrites now as they were in Arnold's day. I made a speech, too; on Courage, of all things.)

I left the school next morning, in the gig, with my box on top, and they were damned glad to see me go, I expect. Certainly the fags were; I'd given them toco in my time. And who should be at the gate (to gloat, I thought at first, but it turned out otherwise) but the bold Scud East. He even offered me his hand.

"I'm sorry, Flashman," he said.

I asked him what he had to be sorry for, and damned his impudence.

"Sorry you're being expelled," says he.

"You're a liar," says I. "And damn your sorrow, too."

He looked at me, and then turned on his heel and walked off. But I know now that I misjudged him then; he *was* sorry, heaven knows why. He'd no cause to love me, and if I had been him I'd have been throwing my cap in the air and hurrahing. But he was soft: one of Arnold's sturdy fools, manly little chaps, of course, and full of virtue, the kind that schoolmasters love. Yes, he was a fool then, and a fool twenty years later, when he died in the dust at Cawnpore with a Sepoy's bayonet in his back. Honest Scud East; that was all that his gallant goodness did for *him*.

I didn't linger on the way home. I knew my father was in London, and I wanted to get over as soon as I could the painful business of telling him I had been kicked out of Rugby. So I decided to ride to town, letting my bags follow, and hired a horse accordingly at the "George". I am one of those who rode as soon as he walked—indeed, horsemanship and my trick of picking up foreign tongues have been the only things in which you could say I was born gifted, and very useful they have been.

So I rode to town, puzzling over how my father would take the good news. He was an odd fish, the guv'nor, and he and I had always been wary of each other. He was a nabob's grandson, you see, old Jack Flashman having made a fortune in America out of slaves and rum, and piracy, too, I shouldn't wonder, and buying the place in Leicestershire where we have lived ever since. But for all their moneybags, the Flashmans were never the thing—"the coarse streak showed through, generation after generation, like dung beneath a rosebush," as Greville said. In other words, while other nabob families tried to make themselves pass for quality, ours didn't, because we couldn't. My own father was the first to marry well, for my mother was related to the Pagets, who as everyone knows sit on the right hand of God. As a consequence he kept an eye on me to see if I gave myself airs; before mother died he never saw much of me, being too busy at the clubs or in the House or hunting—foxes sometimes, but women mostly—but after that he had to take some interest in his heir, and we grew to know and mistrust each other.

He was a decent enough fellow in his way, I suppose, pretty rough and with the devil's own temper, but well enough liked in his set, which was country-squire with enough money to pass in the West End. He enjoyed some lingering fame through having gone a number of rounds with Cribb, in his youth, though it's my belief that Champion Tom went easy with him because of his cash. He lived half in town, half in country now, and kept an expensive house, but he was out of politics, having been sent to the knacker's yard at Reform. He was still occupied, though, what with brandy and the tables, and hunting—both kinds.

I was feeling pretty uneasy, then, when I ran up the steps and hammered on the front door. Oswald, the butler, raised a great cry when he saw who it was, because it was nowhere near the end of the half, and this brought other servants: they scented scandal, no doubt.

"My father's home?" I asked, giving Oswald my coat and straightening my neck-cloth.

"Your father, to be sure, Mr Harry," cried Oswald, all smiles. "In the saloon this minute!" He threw open the door, and cried out: "Mr Harry's home, sir!"

My father had been sprawled on a settee, but he jumped up when he saw me. He had a glass in his hand and his face was flushed, but since both those things were usual it was hard to say whether he was drunk or not. He stared at me, and then greeted the prodigal with:

"What the hell are you doing here?"

At most times this kind of welcome would have taken me aback, but not now. There was a woman in the room, and she distracted my attention. She was a tall, handsome, hussy-looking piece, with brown hair piled up on her head and a come-and-catch-me look in her eye. "This is the new one," I thought, for you got used to his string of madames; they changed as fast as the sentries at St James'.

She was looking at me with a lazy, half-amused smile that sent a shiver up my back at the same time as it made me conscious of the schoolboy cut of my clothes. But it stiffened me, too, all in an instant, so that I answered his question pat:

"I've been expelled," I said, as cool as I could.

"Expelled? D'ye mean thrown out? What the devil for, sir?'

"Drunkenness, mainly."

"Mainly? Good God!" He was going purple. He looked from the woman back to me, as though seeking enlightenment. She seemed much amused by it, but seeing the old fellow in danger of explosion I made haste to explain what had happened. I was truthful enough, except that I made rather more of my interview with

Arnold than was the case; to hear me you would suppose I had given as good as I got. Seeing the female eyeing me I acted pretty offhand, which was risky, perhaps, with the guv'nor in his present mood. But to my surprise he took it pretty well; he had never liked Arnold, of course.

"Well, I'm damned!" he said, when I had finished, and poured himself another glass. He wasn't grinning, but his brow had cleared. "You young dog! A pretty state of things, indeed. Expelled in disgrace, by gad! Did he flog you? No? I'd have had the hide off your back—perhaps I will, damme!" But he was smiling now, a bit sour, though. "What d'you make of this, Judy?" he said to the woman.

"I take it this is a relative?" she says, letting her fan droop towards me. She had a deep husky voice, and I shivered again.

"Relative? Eh? Oh, dammit, it's my son Harry, girl! Harry, this is Judy. . . . er, Miss Parsons."

She smiled at me now, still with that half-amused look, and I preened myself—I was seventeen, remember—and sized up her points while the father got himself another glass and damned Arnold for a puritan hedge-priest. She was what is called Juno-esque, broad-shouldered and full-breasted, which was less common then than it is now, and it seemed to me she liked the look of Harry Flashman.

"Well," said my father at last, when he had finished fulminating against the folly of putting prigs and scholars in charge of public schools. "Well, what's to be done with you, eh? What'll you do, sir? Now that you've disgraced the home with your beastliness, eh?"

I had been thinking this over on my way home, and said straight out that I fancied the army.

"The army?" he growled. "You mean I'm to buy you colours so that you can live like a king and ruin me with bills at the Guards' Club, I suppose?"

"Not the Guards," I said. "I've a notion for the 11th Light Dragoons."

He stared at this. "You've chosen a regiment already? By gad, here's a cool hand!"

I knew the 11th were at Canterbury, after long service in India, and unlikely for that reason to be posted abroad. I had my own notions of soldiering. But this was too fast for the guv'nor; he went on about the expense of buying in, and the cost of army life, and worked back to my expulsion and my character generally, and so back to the army again. The port was making him quarrelsome, I could see, so I judged it best not to press him. He growled on:

"Dragoons, damme! D'ye know what a cornet's commission costs? Damned nonsense. Never heard the like. Impudence, eh, Judy?"

Miss Judy observed that I might look very well as a dashing dragoon.

"Eh?" said my father, and gave her a queer look. "Aye, like enough he would. We'll see." He looked moodily at me. "In the meantime, you can get to your bed," he said. "We'll talk of this tomorrow. For the moment you're still in disgrace." But as I left them I could hear him blackguarding Arnold again, so I went to bed well pleased, and relieved into the bargain. He was odd fish, all right; you could never tell how he would take anything.

In the morning, though, when I met my father at breakfast, there was no talk of the army. He was too busy damning Brougham—who had, I gathered, made a violent attack on the Queen in the House[1]—and goggling over some scandal about Lady Flora Hastings[2] in the Post, to give me much attention, and left presently for his club. Anyway, I was content to let the matter rest just now; I have always believed in one thing at a time, and the thing that was occupying my mind was Miss Judy Parsons.

Let me say that while there have been hundreds of women in my life, I have never been one of those who are forever boasting about their conquests. I've raked and ridden harder than most, no doubt, and there are probably a number of middle-aged men and women who could answer to the name of Flashman if only they knew it. That's by the way; unless you are the kind who falls in love—which I've never been—you take your tumbles when you've the chance, and the more the better. But Judy has a close bearing on my story.

I was not inexperienced with women; there had been maids at home and a country girl or two, but Judy was a woman of the world, and that I hadn't attempted. Not that I was concerned on that account, for I fancied myself (and rightly) pretty well. I was big and handsome enough for any of them, but being my father's mistress she might think it too risky to frolic with the son. As it turned out, she wasn't frightened of the guv'nor or anyone else.

She lived in the house—the young Queen was newly on the throne then, and people still behaved as they had under the Prince Regent and King Billy; not like later on, when mistresses had to stay out of sight. I went up to her room before noon to spy out the land, and found her still in bed, reading the papers. She was glad to see me, and we talked, and from the way she looked and laughed and let me toy with her hand I knew it was only a question of finding the time. There was an abigail fussing about the room, or I'd have gone for her then and there.

However, it seemed my father would be at the club that night, and playing late, as he often did, so I agreed to come back and play écarte with her in the evening. Both of us knew it wouldn't be cards we would be playing. Sure enough, when I did come back, she was sitting prettying herself before her glass, wearing a bed-gown that would have made me a small handkerchief. I came straight up behind her, took her big breasts out in either hand, stopped her gasp with my mouth, and pushed her on to the bed. She was as eager as I was, and we bounced about in rare style, first one on top and then the other. Which reminds me of something which has stayed in my head, as these things will: when it was over, she was sitting astride me, naked and splendid, tossing the hair out of her eyes—suddenly she laughed, loud and clearly, the way one does at a good joke. I believed then she was laughing with pleasure, and thought myself a hell of a fellow, but I feel sure now she was laughing at me. I was seventeen, you remember, and doubtless she found it amusing to know how pleased with myself I was.

Later we played cards, for form's sake, and she won, and then I had to sneak off because my father came home early. Next day I tried her again, but this time, to my surprise, she slapped my hands and said: "No, no, my boy; once for fun, but not twice. I've a position to keep up here." Meaning my father, and the chance of servants gossiping, I supposed.

I was annoyed at this, and got ugly, but she laughed at me again. I lost my temper, and tried to blackmail her by threatening to let my father find out about the night before, but she just curled her lip.

14

"You wouldn't dare," she said. "And if you did, I wouldn't care."

"Wouldn't you?" I said. "If he threw you out, you slut?"

"My, the brave little man," she mocked me. "I misjudged you. At first sight I thought you were just another noisy brute like your father, but I see you've a strong streak of the cur in you as well. Let me tell you, he's twice the man you are—in bed or out of it."

"I was good enough for you, you bitch," I said.

"Once," she said, and dropped me a mock curtsey, "That was enough. Now get out, and stick to servant girls after this."

I went in a black rage, slamming the door, and spent the next hour striding about the Park, planning what I would do to her if ever I had the chance. After a while my anger passed, and I just put Miss Judy away in a corner of my mind, as one to be paid off when the chance came.

Oddly enough, the affair worked to my advantage. Whether some wind of what had happened on the first night got to my father's ears, or whether he just caught something in the air, I don't know, but I suspect it was the second; he was shrewd, and had my own gift of sniffing the wind. Whatever it was, his manner towards me changed abruptly; from harking back to my expulsion and treating me fairly offhand, he suddenly seemed sulky at me, and I caught him giving me odd looks, which he would hurriedly shift away, as though he were embarrassed.

Anyway, within four days of my coming home, he suddenly announced that he had been thinking about my notion of the army, and had decided to buy me a pair of colours. I was to go over to the Horse Guards to see my Uncle Bindley, my mother's brother, who would arrange matters. Obviously, my father wanted me out of the house, and quickly, so I pinned him then and there, while the iron was hot, on the matter of an allowance. I asked for £500 a year to add to my pay, and to my astonishment he agreed without discussion. I cursed myself for not asking £750, but £500 was twice what I'd expected, and far more than enough, so I was pretty pleased, and set off for Horse Guards in a good humour.

A lot has been said about the purchase of commissions—how the rich and incompetent can buy ahead of better men, how the poor and efficient are passed over—and most of it, in my experience, is rubbish. Even with purchase abolished, the rich rise faster in the Service than the poor, and they're both inefficient anyway, as a rule. I've seen ten men's share of service, through no fault of my own, and can say that most officers are bad, and the higher you go, the worse they get, myself included. We were supposed to be rotten with incompetence in the Crimea, for example, when purchase was at its height, but the bloody mess they made in South Africa recently seems to have been just as bad—and they didn't buy their commissions.

However, at this time I'd no thought beyond being a humble cornet, and living high in a crack regiment, which was one of the reasons I had fixed on the 11th Dragoons. Also, that they were close to town.

I said nothing of this to Uncle Bindley, but acted very keen, as though I was on fire to win my spurs against the Mahrattas or the Sikhs. He sniffed, and looked down his nose, which was very high and thin, and said he had never suspected martial ardour in me.

"However, a fine leg in pantaloons and a penchant for folly seem to be all that is required today," he went on. "And you can ride, as I collect?"

"Anything on legs, uncle," says I.

"That is of little consequence, anyway. What concerns me is that you cannot, by report, hold your liquor. You'll agree that being dragged from a Rugby pothouse, reeling, I believe, is no recommendation to an officers' mess?"

I hastened to tell him that the report was exaggerated.

"I doubt it," he said. "The point is, were you silent in your drunken state, or did you rave? A noisy drunkard is intolerable; a passive one may do at a pinch. At least, if he has money; money will excuse virtually any conduct in the army nowadays, it seems."

This was a favourite sneer of his; I may say that my mother's family, while quality, were not over-rich. However, I took it all meekly.

"Yes," he went on, "I've no doubt that with your allowance you will be able either to kill or ruin yourself in a short space of time. At that, you will be no worse than half the subalterns in the service, if no better. Ah, but wait. It was the 11th Light Dragoons, wasn't it?"

"Oh, yes, uncle."

"And you are determined on that regiment?"

"Why, yes," I said, wondering a little.

"Then you may have a little diversion before you go the way of all flesh," said he, with a knowing smile. "Have you, by any chance, heard of the Earl of Cardigan?"

I said I had not, which shows how little I had taken notice of military affairs.

"Extraordinary. He commands the 11th, you know. He succeeded to the title only a year or so ago, while he was in India with the regiment. A remarkable man. I understand he makes no secret of his intention to turn the 11th into the finest cavalry regiment in the army."

"He sounds like the very man for me," I said, all eagerness.

"Indeed, indeed. Well, we mustn't deny him the service of so ardent a subaltern, must we? Certainly the matter of your colours must be pushed through without delay. I commend your choice, my boy. I'm sure you will find service under Lord Cardigan—ah— both stimulating and interesting. Yes, as I think of it, the combination of his lordship and yourself will be rewarding for you both."

I was too busy fawning on the old fool to pay much heed to what he was saying, otherwise I should have realised that anything that pleased him would probably be bad for me. He prided himself on being above my family, whom he considered boors, with some reason, and had never shown much but distaste for me personally. Helping me to my colours was different, of course; he owed that as a duty to a blood relation, but he paid it without enthusiasm. Still, I had to be civil as butter to him, and pretend respect.

It paid me, for I got my colours in the 11th with surprising speed. I put it down entirely to influence, for I was not to know then that over the past few months there had been a steady departure of officers from the regiment, sold out, transferred, and posted—and all because of Lord Cardigan, whom my uncle had spoken of. If I had been a little older, and moved in the right circles, I should have heard all about him, but in the few weeks of waiting for my commission my father sent me up to Leicestershire, and the little time I had in town I spent either by myself or in the company of such of my relatives as could catch me. My mother had had sisters, and although they disliked me heartily they felt it was their duty to look after the poor motherless boy. So they said; in fact they suspected that if I were left to myself I would take to low company, and they were right.

However, I was to find out about Lord Cardigan soon enough.

In the last few days of buying my uniforms, assembling the huge paraphernalia that an officer needed in those days—far more than now—choosing a couple of horses, and arranging for my allowance, I still found time on my hands, and Mistress Judy in my thoughts. My tumble with her had only whetted my appetite for more of her, I discovered; I tried to get rid of it with a farm girl in Leicestershire and a young whore in Covent Garden, but the one stank and the other picked my pocket afterwards, and neither was any substitute anyway. I wanted Judy, at the same time as I felt spite for her, but she had avoided me since our quarrel and if we met in the house she simply ignored me.

In the end it got too much, and the night before I left I went to her room again, having made sure the guv'nor was out. She was reading, and looking damned desirable in a pale green negligée; I was a little drunk, and the sight of her white shoulders and red mouth sent the old tingle down my spine again.

"What do you want?" she said, very icy, but I was expecting that, and had my speech ready.

"I've come to beg pardon," I said, looking a bit hangdog. "Tomorrow I go away, and before I went I had to apologise for the way I spoke to you. I'm sorry, Judy; I truly am; I acted like a cad and ... and a ruffian, and, well ... I want to make what amends I can. That's all."

She put down her book and turned on her stool to face me, still looking mighty cold, but saying nothing. I shuffled like a sheepish schoolboy—I could see my reflection in the mirror behind her, and judge how the performance was going—and said again that I was sorry.

"Very well, then," she said at last. "You're sorry. You have cause to be."

I kept quiet, not looking at her.

"Well, then," she said, after a pause. "Good night."

"Please, Judy," I said, looking distraught. "You make it very hard. If I behaved like a boor—"

"You did."

"—it was because I was angry and hurt and didn't understand why ... why you wouldn't let me ..." I let it trail off and then burst out that I had never known a woman like her before, and that I had fallen in love with her, and only came to ask her pardon because I couldn't bear the thought of her detesting me, and a good deal more in the same strain—simple enough rubbish, you may think, but I was still learning. At that, the mirror told me I was doing well. I finished by drawing myself up straight, and looking solemn, and saying:

"And that is why I had to see you again ... to tell you. And to ask your pardon."

I gave her a little bow, and turned to the door, rehearsing how I would stop and look back if she didn't stop me. But she took me at face value, for as I put my hand to the latch she said:

"Harry." I turned round, and she was smiling a little, and looking sad. Then she smiled properly, and shook her head and said:

"Very well, Harry, if you want my pardon, for what it's worth you have it. We'll say no. . . ."

"Judy!" I came striding back, smiling like soul's awakening. "Oh, Judy, thank you!" And I held out my hand, frank and manly.

She got up and took it, smiling still, but there was none of the old wanton glint about her eye. She was being stately and forgiving, like an aunt to a naughty nephew. The nephew, had she known it, was intent on incest.

"Judy," I said, still holding her hand, "we're parting friends?"

"If you like," she said, trying to take it away. "Goodbye, Harry, and good luck."

I stepped closer and kissed her hand, and she didn't seem to mind. I decided, like the fool I was, that the game was won.

"Judy," I said again, "you're adorable. I love you, Judy. If only you knew, you're all I want in a woman. Oh, Judy, you're the most beautiful thing, all bum, belly and bust, I love you."

And I grabbed her to me, and she pulled free and got away from me.

"No!" she said, in a voice like steel.

"Why the hell not?" I shouted.

"Go away!" she said, pale and with eyes like daggers. "Goodnight!"

"Goodnight be damned," says I. "I thought you said we were parting friends? This ain't very friendly, is it?"

She stood glaring at me. Her bosom was what the lady novelists call agitated, but if they had seen Judy agitated in a negligée they would think of some other way of describing feminine distress.

"I was a fool to listen to you for a moment," she says. "Leave this room at once!"

"All in good time," says I, and with a quick dart I caught her round the waist. She struck at me, but I ducked it, and we fell on the bed together. I had hold of the softness of her, and it maddened me. I caught her wrist as she struck at me again, like a tigress, and got my mouth on hers, and she bit me on the lip for all she was worth.

I yelped and broke away, holding my mouth, and she, raging and panting, grabbed up some china dish and let fly at me. It missed by a long chalk, but it helped my temper over the edge completely. I lost control of myself altogether.

"You bitch!" I shouted, and hit her across the face as hard as I could. She staggered, and I hit her again, and she went clean over the bed and on to the floor on the other side. I looked round for something to go after her with, a cane or a whip, for I was in a frenzy and would have cut her to bits if I could. But there wasn't one handy, and by the time I had got round the bed to her it had flashed across my mind that the house was full of servants and my full reckoning with Miss Judy had better be postponed to another time.

I stood over her, glaring and swearing, and she pulled herself up by a chair, holding her face. But she was game enough.

"You coward!" was all she would say. "You coward!"

"It's not cowardly to punish an insolent whore!" says I. "D'you want some more?"

She was crying—not sobbing, but with tears on her cheeks. She went over to her chair by the mirror, pretty unsteady, and sat down and looked at herself. I cursed her again, calling her the choicest names I could think of, but she worked at her cheek, which was red and bruised, with a hare's foot, and paid no heed. She did not speak at all.

"Well, be damned to you!" says I, at length, and with that I slammed out of the room. I was shaking with rage, and the pain in my lip, which was bleeding badly, reminded me that she had paid for my blows in advance. But she had got something in return, at all events; she would not forget Harry Flashman in a hurry.

The 11th Light Dragoons at this time were newly back from India, where they had been serving since before I was born. They were a fighting regiment, and—I say it without regimental pride, for I never had any, but as a plain matter of fact—probably the finest mounted troops in England, if not in the world. Yet they had been losing officers, since coming home, hand over fist. The reason was James Brudenell, Earl of Cardigan.

You have heard all about him, no doubt. The regimental scandals, the Charge of the Light Brigade, the vanity, stupidity, and extravagance of the man—these things are history. Like most history, they have a fair basis of fact. But I knew him, probably as few other officers knew him, and in turn I found him amusing, frightening, vindictive, charming, and downright dangerous. He was God's own original fool, there's no doubt of that—although he was not to blame for the fiasco at Balaclava; that was Raglan and Airey between them. And he was arrogant as no other man I've ever met, and as sure of his own unshakeable rightness as any man could be—even when his wrong-headedness was there for all to see. That was his great point, the key to his character: he could never be wrong.

They say that at least he was brave. He was not. He was just stupid, too stupid ever to be afraid. Fear is an emotion, and his emotions were all between his knees and his breast-bone; they never touched his reason, and he had little enough of that.

For all that, he could never be called a bad soldier. Some human faults are military virtues, like stupidity, and arrogance, and narrow-mindedness. Cardigan blended all three with a passion for detail and accuracy; he was a perfectionist, and the manual of cavalry drill was his Bible. Whatever rested between the covers of that book he could perform, or cause to be performed, with marvellous efficiency, and God help anyone who marred that performance. He would have made a first-class drill sergeant—only a man with a mind capable of such depths of folly could have led six regiments into the Valley at Balaclava.

However, I devote some space to him because he played a not unimportant part in the career of Harry Flashman, and since it is my purpose to show how the Flashman of *Tom Brown* became the glorious Flashman with four inches in *Who's Who* and grew markedly worse in the process, I must say that he was a good friend to me. He never understood me, of course, which is not surprising. I took good care not to let him.

When I met him in Canterbury I had already given a good deal of thought to how I should conduct myself in the army. I was bent on as much fun and vicious amusement as I could get—my contemporaries, who praise God on Sundays and sneak off to child-brothels during the week, would denounce it piously as vicious, anyway—but I have always known how to behave to my superiors and shine in their eyes, a trait of mine which Hughes pointed out, bless him. This I had determined on, and since the little I knew of Cardigan told me that he prized smartness and show above all things, I took some pains over my arrival in Canterbury.

I rolled up to regimental headquarters in a coach, resplendent in my new uniform, and with my horses led behind and a wagon-load of gear. Cardigan didn't see me arrive, unfortunately, but word must have been carried to him, for when I was introduced to him in his orderly room he was in good humour.

"Haw-haw," said he, as we shook hands. "It is Mr Fwashman. How-de-do, sir. Welcome to the wegiment. A good turn-out, Jones," he went on to the officer at his elbow. "I delight to see a smart officer. Mr Fwashman, how tall are you?"

"Six feet, sir," I said, which was near enough right.

"Haw-haw. And how heavy do you wide, sir?"

I didn't know, but I guessed at twelve and a half stone.

"Heavy for a light dwagoon," said he, shaking his head. "But there are compensations. You have a pwoper figure, Mr Fwashman, and bear yourself well. Be attentive to your duties and we shall deal very well together. Where have you hunted?"

"In Leicestershire, my lord," I said.

"Couldn't be better," says he. "Eh, Jones? Very good, Mr Fwashman—hope to see more of you. Haw-haw."

Now, no one in my life that I could remember had ever been

so damned civil to me, except toad-eaters like Speedicut, who didn't count. I found myself liking his lordship, and did not realise that I was seeing him at his best. In this mood, he was a charming man enough, and looked well. He was taller than I, straight as a lance, and very slender, even to his hands. Although he was barely forty, he was already bald, with a bush of hair above either ear and magnificent whiskers. His nose was beaky and his eyes blue and prominent and unwinking—they looked out on the world with that serenity which marks the nobleman whose uttermost ancestor was born a nobleman, too. It is the look that your *parvenu* would give half his fortune for, that unrufflable gaze of the spoiled child of fortune who knows with unshakeable certainty that he is right and that the world is exactly ordered for his satisfaction and pleasure. It is the look that makes underlings writhe and causes revolutions. I saw it then, and it remained changeless as long as I knew him, even through the roll-call beneath Causeway Heights when the grim silence as the names were shouted out testified to the loss of five hundred of his command. "It was no fault of mine," he said then, and he didn't just believe it; he knew it.

I was to see him in a different mood before the day was out, but fortunately I was not the object of his wrath; quite the reverse, in fact.

I was shown about the camp by the officer of the day, a fair young captain, named Reynolds,[3] with a brick-red face from service in India. Professionally, he was a good soldier, but quiet and no blood at all. I was fairly offhand with him, and no doubt insolent, but he took it without comment, confining himself to telling me what was what, finding me a servant, and ending at the stables where my mare—whom I had christened Judy, by the way—and charger were being housed.

The grooms had Judy trimmed up with her best leather-work —and it was the best that the smartest saddler in London could show—and Reynolds was admiring her, when who should ride up but my lord in the devil of a temper. He reined in beside us, and pointed with a hand that shook with fury to a troop that had just come in, under their sergeant, to the stable yard.

"Captain Weynolds!" he bawled, and his face was scarlet. "Is this your twoop?"

Reynolds said it was.

"And do you see their sheepskins?" bawled Cardigan. These were the saddle sheepskins. "Do you see them, sir? What colour are they, I should like to know? Will you tell me, sir?"

"White, my lord."

"White, you say? Are you a fool, sir? Are you colour-blind? They are not white, they are yellow—with inattention and slovenliness and neglect! They are filthy, I tell you."

Reynolds stood silent, and Cardigan raged on.

"This was no doubt very well in India, where you learned what you probably call your duty. I will not have it here, do you understand, sir?" His eye rolled round the stable and rested on Judy. "Whose horse is this?" he demanded.

I told him, and he turned in triumph on Reynolds.

"You see, sir, an officer new joined, and he can show you and your other precious fellows from India their duty. Mr Fwashman's sheepskin is white, sir, as yours should be—would be, if you knew anything of discipline and good order. But you don't, sir, I tell you."

"Mr Flashman's sheepskin is new, sir," said Reynolds, which was true enough. "They discolour with age."

"So you make excuses now!" snapped Cardigan. "Haw-haw! I tell you, sir, if you knew your duty they would be cleaned, or if they are too old, wenewed. But you know nothing of this, of course. Your slovenly Indian ways are good enough, I suppose. Well, they will not do, let me tell you! These skins will be cwean tomorrow, d'you hear, sir? Cwean, or I'll hold you wesponsible, Captain Weynolds!"

And with that he rode off, head in the air, and I heard his "Haw-haw" as he greeted someone outside the stable yard.

I felt quite pleased to have been singled out for what was, in effect, praise, and I fancy I said something of this to Reynolds. He looked me up and down, as though seeing me for the first time, and said, in that odd, Welsh-sounding voice that comes with long service in India:

"Yc-cs, I can see you will do very well, Mr Flashman. Lord Haw Haw may not like us Indian officers, but he likes plungers, and I've no doubt you'll plunger very prettily."

I asked him what he meant by plunging.

"Oh," says he, "a plunger is a fellow who makes a great turn-out, don't you know, and leaves cards at the best houses, and is sought by the mamas, and strolls in the Park very languid, and is just a hell of a swell generally. Sometimes they even condescend to soldier a little—when it doesn't interfere with their social life. Good-day, Mr Flashman."

I could see that Reynolds was jealous, and in my conceit I was well pleased. What he had said, though, was true enough: the regiment was fairly divided between Indian officers—those who had not left since returning home—and the plungers, to whom I naturally attached myself. They hailed me among them, even the noblest, and I knew how to make myself pleasant. I was not as quick with my tongue as I was to become later, but they knew me for a sporting fellow before I had been there long—good on a horse, good with the bottle (for I took some care at first), and ready for mischief. I toadied as seemed best—not openly, of course, but effectively just the same; there is a way of toadying which is better than fawning, and it consists of acting bluff and hearty and knowing to an inch how far to go. And I had money, and showed it.

The Indian officers had a bad time. Cardigan hated them. Reynolds and Forrest were his chief butts, and he was forever pestering them to leave the regiment and make way for gentlemen, as he put it. Why he was so down on those who had served in India, I was never entirely sure; some said it was because they were not of the smart set, or well connected, and this was true up to a point. He was the damnedest snob, but I think his hatred of the Indian officers ran deeper. They were, after all, real soldiers with service experience, and Cardigan had never heard a shot outside the shooting range in his twenty years' service.[4]

Whatever the cause, he made their lives miserable, and there were several resignations in my first six months' service. Even for us plungers it was bad enough, for he was a devil for discipline, and not all the plungers were competent officers. I saw how the wind set, and studied harder than ever I had at Rugby, mastering my drill, which wasn't difficult, and perfecting myself in the rules of camp life. I had got an excellent servant, named Basset, a square-headed oaf who knew everything a soldier ought to know and nothing more, and with a genius for boot-polish. I thrashed him early in our acquaintance, and he seemed to think the better of me for it, and treated me as a dog does its master.

Fortunately, I cut a good figure on parade and at exercise, which was where it counted with Cardigan. Probably only the regimental sergeant major and one or two of the troop-sergeants were my equals on horseback, and his lordship congratulated me once or twice on my riding.

"Haw-haw!" he would say. "Fwashman sits well, I tell you. He will make an aide yet."

I agreed with him. Flashman was sitting very well.

In the mess things went well enough. They were a fast crowd, and the money ran pretty free, for apart from parties and the high state which Cardigan demanded we should keep, there was some heavy gaming. All this expense discouraged the Indian men, which delighted Cardigan, who was forever sneering at them that if they could not keep up with gentlemen they had better return to farming or set themselves up in trade—"selling shoes and pots and pans," he would say, and laugh heartily, as though this were the funniest thing imaginable.

Strangely enough, or perhaps not strangely, his Indian prejudice did not extend to the men. They were a tough lot, and excellent soldiers so far as I could see; he was a tyrant to them, and never a week passed without a court-martial for neglect of duty or desertion or drunkenness. The last offence was common, but not seriously regarded, but for the other two he punished hard. There were frequent floggings at the rings in the side of the riding school, when we all had to attend. Some of the older officers —the Indian ones—grumbled a good deal and pretended to be shocked, but I guessed they would not have missed it. Myself, I liked a good flogging, and used to have bets with Bryant, my particular crony, on whether the man would cry out before the tenth stroke, or when he would faint. It was better sport than most, anyway.

Bryant was a queer little creature who attached himself to me early in my career and clung like a leech. He was your open toady, with little money of his own, but a gift of pleasing and being on hand. He was smart enough, and contrived to cut a decent figure, although never splendid, and he had all the gossip, and knew everybody, and was something of a wit. He shone at the parties and mess nights which we gave for the local society in Canterbury, where he was very forward. He was first with all the news, and could recount it in a fashion that amused Cardigan —not that this was too difficult. I found him useful, and tolerated him accordingly, and used him as a court jester when it suited—he was adept in this role, too. As Forrest said, if you kicked Bryant's arse, he always bounced most obligingly.

He had a considerable gift of spite against the Indian officers, which also endeared him to Cardigan—oh, we were a happy little mess, I can tell you—and earned him their hatred. Most of them despised me, too, along with the other plungers, but we despised them for different reasons, so we were square there.

But to only one officer did I take an active dislike, which was prophetic, and I guessed that he returned it from the first. His name was Bernier, a tall, hard hawk of a man with a big nose and black whiskers and dark eyes set very close. He was the best blade and shot in the regiment, and until I came on the scene the best rider as well. He didn't love me for that, I suppose, but our real hatred dated from the night when he made some reference to nabob families of no breeding, and seemed to me to look in my direction.

I was fairly wine-flown, or I'd have kept my mouth shut, for he looked like what the Americans call a "killing gentleman"— indeed, he was very like an American whom I knew later, the celebrated James Hickok, who was also a deadly shot. But being part tipsy, I said I would rather be a nabob Briton, and take my chance on breeding, than be half-caste foreign. Bryant crowed, as he always did at my jokes, and said: "Bravo, Flash! Old England forever!" and there was general laughter, for my usual heartiness and general bluffness had earned me the name of being something of a John Bull. Bernier only half-caught what I said, for I had kept my voice low so that only those nearest heard, but someone must have told him later, for he never gave me anything but an icy stare from then on, and never spoke to me. He was sensitive about his foreign name—actually, he was a French Jew, if you went back far enough, which accounts for it.

But it was a few months after this incident that I really ran foul of Bernier, and began to make my reputation—the reputation which I still enjoy today. I pass over a good deal of what happened in that first year—Cardigan's quarrel with the Morning Post,[5] for example, which had the regiment, and the public generally, in a fine uproar, but in which I had no part—and come to the famous Bernier–Flashman duel, which you will still hear talked about. I think of it only with pride and delight, even now. Only two men ever knew the truth of it, and I was one.

It was a year almost to the day after I left Rugby that I was taking the air in Canterbury, in the Park, and on my way to some mama's house or other to make a call. I was in full fig, and feeling generally pleased with myself, when I spied an officer walking under the trees with a lady, arm in arm. It was Bernier, and I looked to see what heifer he was ploughing with. In fact, she was no heifer, but a wicked-looking little black-haired piece with a turned-up nose and a saucy smile. I studied her, and the great thought formed in my head.

I had had two or three mistresses in Canterbury, off and on, but nothing in particular. Most of the younger officers maintained a paramour in the town or in London, but I had never set up any establishment like that. I guessed that this was Bernier's mare of the moment, and the more I looked at her the more she intrigued me. She looked the kind of plump little puss who would be very knowing in bed, and the fact that she was Bernier's—who fancied himself irresistible to women—would make the tumbling all the sweeter.

I wasted no time, but found out her direction by inquiry, chose my time when Bernier was on duty, and called on the lady. She had a pleasant little retreat, very tastefully furnished, but in no great style: Bernier's purse was less fat then mine, which was an advantage. I pursued it.

She was French herself, it turned out, so I could be more direct than with an English girl. I told her straight out that I had taken a fancy to her, and invited her to consider me as a friend—a close friend. I hinted that I had money—she was only a whore, after all, for all her fashionable airs.

At first she made a show of being shocked, and la-la'd a good deal, but when I made to leave she changed her tune. My money aside, I think she found me to her fancy; she toyed with a fan and looked at me over it with big, almond-shaped eyes, playing the sly minx.

"You have poor opeenion of French girls, then?" says she.

"Not I," says I, charming again. "I've the highest opinion of you, for example. What's your name?"

"Josette." She said it very pretty.

"Well, Josette, let's drink to our future acqaintance—at my expense"—and I dropped my purse on the table, at which her eyes widened. It was not a small purse.

You may think me crude. I was. But I saved time and trouble, and perhaps money, too—the money that fools waste in paying court with presents before the fun begins. She had wine in the house, and we drank to each other and talked a good five minutes before I began to tease her into undressing. She played it very prettily, with much pouting and provocative looks, but when she had stripped she was all fire and wickedness, and I was so impatient I had her without getting out of my chair.

Whether I found her unusually delectable because she was Bernier's mistress or because of her French tricks, I can't say, but I took to visiting her often, and in spite of my respect for Bernier, I was careless. It was within a week, certainly, that we were engaged heavily one evening when there were footsteps on the stair, the door flew open, and there was the man himself. He stood glaring for a moment, while Josette squeaked and dived beneath the covers, and I scrambled to get under the bed in my shirt-tail—the sight of him filled me with panic. But he said nothing; a moment passed, the door slammed, and I came out scrabbling for my breeches. At that moment I wanted only to put as much distance between myself and him as I could, and I dressed in some haste.

Josette began to laugh, and I asked her what the devil amused her.

"It is so fonnee," she giggled. "You ... you half beneath de bed, and Charles glaring so fierce at your derrière." And she shrieked with laughter.

I told her to hold her tongue, and she stopped laughing and tried to coax me back to bed again, saying that Bernier had undoubtedly gone, and sitting up and shaking her tits at me. I hesitated, between lust and fright, until she hopped out and bolted the door, and then I decided I might as well have my sport while I could, and pulled off my clothes again. But I confess it was not the most joyous pleasuring I have taken part in, although Josette was at her most spirited; I suspect she was thrilled by the situation.

I was in two minds whether to go back to the mess afterwards, for I was sure Bernier must call me out. But, to my surprise, when I pulled my courage together and went in to dinner, he paid me not the slightest notice. I couldn't make it out, and when next day and the next he was still silent, I took heart again, and even paid Josette another visit. She had not seen him, so it seemed to me that he intended to do nothing at all. I decided that he was a poor-spirited thing after all, and had resigned his mistress to me—not, I was sure, out of fear of me, but because he could not bear to have a trollop who cheated him. Of course the truth was that he couldn't call me out without exposing the cause, and making himself look ridiculous; and knowing more of regimental custom than I did, he hesitated to provoke an affair of honour over a mistress. But he was holding himself in with difficulty.

Not knowing this, I took to throwing my chest out again, and let Bryant into the secret. The toady was delighted, and soon all the plungers knew. It was then only a matter of time before the explosion came, as I should have known it would.

It was after dinner one night, and we were playing cards, while Bernier and one or two of the Indian men were talking near by. The game was vingt-et-un, and it happened that at that game I had a small joke concerning the Queen of Diamonds, which I maintained was my lucky card. Forrest had the bank, and when he set down my five-card hand with an ace and the Queen of Diamonds, Bryant, the spiteful ass, sang out:

"Hullo! He's got your queen, Flashy! That's the biter bit, bigod!"

"How d'ye mean?" said Forrest, taking up the cards and stakes.

"With Flashy it's t'other way, you know," says Bryant. "He makes off with other chaps' queens."

"Aha," says Forrest, grinning. "But the Queen of Diamonds is a good Englishwoman, ain't she, Flash? Mounting French fillies is your style, I hear."

There was a good deal of laughter, and glances in Bernier's direction. I should have kept them quiet, but I was fool enough to join in.

"Nothing wrong in a French filly," I said, "so long as the

jockey's an English one. A French trainer is well enough, of course, but they don't last in a serious race."

It was feeble enough stuff, no doubt, even allowing for the port we had drunk, but it snapped the straw. The next I knew my chair had been dragged away, and Bernier was standing over me as I sprawled on the floor, his face livid and his mouth working.

"What the devil—" began Forrest, as I scrambled up, and the others jumped up also. I was half on my feet when Bernier struck me, and I lost my balance and went down again.

"For God's sake, Bernier!" shouts Forrest, "are you mad?" and they had to hold him back, or he would have savaged me on the ground, I think. Seeing him held, I came up with an oath, and made to go for him, but Bryant grabbed me, crying "No, no, Flash! Hold off, Flashy!," and they clustered round me as well.

Truth is, I was nearly sick with fear, for the murder was out now. The best shot in the regiment had hit me, but with provocation—fearful or not, I have always been quick and clear enough in my thinking in a crisis—and there couldn't be any way out except a meeting. Unless I took the blow, which meant an end to my career in the army and in society. But to fight him was a quick road to the grave.

It was a horrible dilemma, and in that moment, as they held us apart, I saw I must have time to think, to plan, to find a way out. I shook them off, and without a word stalked out of the mess, like a man who must remove himself before he does someone a mischief.

It took me five minutes of hard thinking, and then I was striding back into the mess again. My heart was hammering, and no doubt I looked pretty furious, and if I shook they thought it was anger.

The chatter died away as I came in; I can feel that silence now, sixty years after, and see the elegant blue figures, and the silver gleaming on the table, and Bernier, alone and very pale, by the fireplace. I went straight up to him. I had my speech ready.

"Captain Bernier," I said, "you have struck me with your hand. That was rash, for I could take you to pieces with mine if I chose." This was blunt, English Flashman, of course. "But I prefer to fight like a gentleman, even if you do not." I swung round on my heel. "Lieutenant Forrest, will you act for me?"

Forrest said yes, like a shot, and Bryant looked piqued. He expected I would have named him, but I had another part for him to play.

"And who acts for you?" I asked Bernier, very cool. He named Tracy, one of the Indian men, and I gave Tracy a bow and then went over to the card table as though nothing had happened.

"Mr Forrest will have the details to attend to," I said to the others. "Shall we cut for the bank?"

They stared at me. "By gad, Flash, you're a cool one!" cries Bryant.

I shrugged, and took up the cards, and we started playing again, the others all very excited—too excited to notice that my thoughts were not on my cards. Luckily, vingt-et-un calls for little concentration.

After a moment Forrest, who had been conferring with Tracy, came over to tell me that, with Lord Cardigan's permission, which he was sure must be forthcoming, we should meet behind the riding school at six in the morning. It was assumed I would choose pistols—as the injured party I had the choice.[6] I nodded, very off-hand, and told Bryant to hurry with the deal. We played a few more hands, and then I said I was for bed, lit my cheroot and strolled out with an airy goodnight to the others, as though the thought of the pistols at dawn troubled me no more than what I should have for breakfast. Whatever happened, I had grown in popular esteem for this night at least.

I stopped under the trees on the way to my quarters, and after a moment, as I had expected, Bryant came hurrying after me, full of excitement and concern. He began to babble about what a devil of a fellow I was, and what a fighting Turk Bernier was, but I cut him off short.

"Tommy," says I. "You're not a rich man."

"Eh?" says he. "What the—"

"Tommy," says I. "Would you like ten thousand pounds?"

"In God's name," says he. "What for?"

"For seeing that Bernier stands up at our meeting tomorrow with an unloaded pistol," says I, straight out. I knew my man.

He goggled at me, and then began to babble again. "Christ, Flash, are you crazy? Unloaded . . . why . . ."

"Yes or no," says I. "Ten thousand pounds."

33

"But it's murder!" he squealed. "We'd swing for it!" No thought of honour, you see, or any of that rot.

"Nobody's going to swing," I told him. "And keep your voice down, d'ye hear? Now, then, Tommy, you're a sharp man with the sleight of hand at parties—I've seen you. You can do it in your sleep. For ten thousand?"

"My God, Flash," says he, "I don't dare." And he began babbling again, but in a whisper this time.

I let him ramble for a moment, for I knew he would come round. He was a greedy little bastard, and the thought of ten thousand was like Aladdin's cave to him. I explained how safe and simple it would be; I had thought it out when first I left the mess.

"Go and borrow Reynolds's duelling pistols, first off. Take 'em to Forrest and Tracy and offer to act as loader—you're always into everything, and they'll be glad to accept, and never think twice."

"Won't they, by God?" cried he. "They know I'm hellish thick with you, Flashy."

"You're an officer and a gentleman," I reminded him. "Now who will imagine for a moment that you would stoop to such a treacherous act, eh? No, no Tommy, it's cut and dried. And in the morning, with the surgeon and seconds standing by, you'll load up—carefully. Don't tell me you can't palm a pistol ball."

"Oh, aye," says he, "like enough. But—"

"Ten thousand pounds," I said, and he licked his lips.

"Jesus," he said at length. "Ten thousand. Phew! On your word of honour, Flash?"

"Word of honour," I said, and lit another cheroot.

"I'll do it!" says he. "My God! You're a devil, Flash! You won't kill him, though? I'll have no part in murder."

"Captain Bernier will be as safe from me as I'll be from him," I told him. "Now, cut along and see Reynolds."

He cut on the word. He was an active little rat, that I'll say for him. Once committed he went in heart and soul.

I went to my quarters, got rid of Basset who was waiting up for me, and lay down on my cot. My throat was dry and my hands were sweating as I thought of what I had done. For all the bluff front I had shown to Bryant, I was in a deathly funk. Suppose something went wrong and Bryant muffed it? It had seemed so easy in that moment of panicky thought outside the mess—fear stimulates thought, perhaps, but it may not be clear thought, because one sees the way out that one *wants* to see, and makes headlong for it. I thought of Bryant fumbling, or being too closely overseen, and Bernier standing up in front of me with a loaded pistol in a hand like a rock, and the muzzle pointing dead at my breast, and felt the ball tearing into me, and myself falling down screaming, and dying on the ground.

I almost shouted out at the horror of it, and lay there blubbering in the dark room; I would have got up and run, but my legs would not let me. So I began to pray, which I had not done, I should say, since I was about eight years old. But I kept thinking of Arnold and hell—which is no doubt significant—and in the end there was nothing for it but brandy, but it might as well have been water.

I did no sleeping that night, but listened to the clock chiming away the quarters, until dawn came, and I heard Basset approaching. I had just sense enough left to see that it wouldn't do for him to find me red-eyed and shivering, so I made believe to sleep, snoring like an organ, and I heard him say:

"If that don't beat! Listen to 'im, sound as a babby. Isn't he the game-cock, though?"

And another voice, another servant's, I suppose, replied:

"Thay's all alike, bloody fools. 'E won't be snorin' tomorrow mornin', after Bernier's done with 'im. 'E'll be sleepin' too sound for that."

Right, my lad, whoever you are, I thought, if I come through this it'll be strange if I can't bring you to the rings at the riding school, and we'll see your backbone when the farrier-sergeant takes the cat to you. We'll hear how loud you can snore yourself. And with that surge of anger I suddenly felt confidence replacing fear —Bryant would see it through, all right—and when they came for me I was at least composed, if not cheerful.

When I am frightened, I go red in the face, not pale, as most men do, so that in me fear can pass for anger, which has been convenient more than once. Bryant tells me that I went out to the riding school that morning wattled like a turkey cock; he said the fellows made sure I was in a fury to kill Bernier. Not that they thought I had a chance, and they were quiet for once as we walked across the parade just as the trumpeter was sounding reveille.

They had told Cardigan of the affair, of course, and some had thought he might intervene to prevent it. But when he had heard of the blow, he had simply said:

"Where do they meet?"

and gone back to sleep again, with instruction to be called at five. He did not approve of duelling—although he duelled himself in famous circumstances—but he saw that in this case the credit of the regiment would only be hurt if the affair were patched up.

Bernier and Tracy were already there, with the surgeon, and the mist was hanging a little under the trees. Our feet thumped on the turf, which was still wet with dew, as we strode across to them, Forrest at my side, and Bryant with the pistol case beneath his arm following on with the others. About fifty yards away, under the trees by the fence, was a little knot of officers, and I saw Cardigan's bald head above his great caped coat. He was smoking a cigar.

Bryant and the surgeon called Bernier and me together, and Bryant asked us if we would not resolve our quarrel. Neither of us said a word; Bernier was pale, and looked fixedly over my shoulder, and in that moment I came as near to turning and running as ever I did in my life. I felt that my bowels would squirt at any moment, and my hands were shuddering beneath my cloak.

"Very good, then," says Bryant, and went with the surgeon to a little table they had set up. He took out the pistols, and from the corner of my eye I saw him spark the flints, pour in the charges, and rummage in the shot-case. I daren't watch him closely, and anyway Forrest came just then and led me back to my place. When I turned round again the surgeon was stooping to pick up a fallen powder flask, and Bryant was ramming home a wad in one of the barkers.

They conferred a moment, and then Bryant paced over to Bernier and presented a pistol to him; then he came to me with the other. There was no one behind me, and as my hand closed on the butt, Bryant winked quickly. My heart came up into my mouth, and I can never hope to describe the relief that flooded through my body, tingling every limb. I was going to live.

"Gentlemen, you are both determined to continue with this meeting?" Bryant looked at each of us in turn. Bernier said: "Yes," hard and clear. I nodded.

Bryant stepped back to be well out of the line of fire; the seconds and the surgeon took post beside him, leaving Bernier and me looking at each other about twenty paces apart. He stood sideways to me, the pistol at his side, staring straight at my face, as though choosing his spot—he could clip the pips from a card at this distance.

"The pistols fire on one pressure," called Bryant. "When I drop my handkerchief you may level your pistols and fire. I shall drop it in a few seconds from now." And he held up the white kerchief in one hand.

I heard the click of Bernier cocking his pistol. His eyes were steady on mine. Sold again, Bernier, I thought; you're all in a stew about nothing. The handkerchief fell.

Bernier's right arm came up like a railway signal, and before I had even cocked my pistol I was looking into his barrel—a split second and it shot smoke at me and the crack of the charge was followed by something rasping across my cheek and grazing it— it was the wad. I fell back a step. Bernier was glaring at me, aghast that I was still on my feet, I suppose, and someone shouted: "Missed, by Jesus!" and another cried angrily for silence.

It was my turn, and for a moment the lust was on me to shoot the swine down where he stood. But Bryant might have lost his head, and it was no part of my design, anyway. I had it in my power now to make a name that would run through the army in a week—good old Flashy, who stole another man's girl and took a blow from him, but was too decent to take advantage of him, even in a duel.

They stood like statues, every eye on Bernier, waiting for me to shoot him down. I cocked my pistol, watching him.

"Come on, damn you!" he shouted suddenly, his face white with rage and fear.

I looked at him for a moment, then brought my pistol up no higher than hip level, but with the barrel pointing well away to the side. I held it negligently almost, just for a moment, so that everyone might see I was firing deliberately wide. I squeezed the trigger.

What happened to that shot is now regimental history; I had meant it for the ground, but it chanced that the surgeon had set his bag and bottle of spirits down on the turf in that direction, maybe thirty yards off, and by sheer good luck the shot whipped the neck off the bottle clean as a whistle.

"Deloped, by God!" roared Forest. "He's deloped!"

They hurried forward, shouting, the surgeon exclaiming in blasphemous amazement over his shattered bottle. Bryant slapped me on the back, Forrest wrung my hand, Tracy stood staring in astonishment—it seemed to him, as it did to everyone, that I had spared Bernier and at the same time given proof of astounding marksmanship. As for Bernier, he looked murder if ever a man did, but I marched straight up to him with my hand held out, and he was forced to take it. He was struggling to keep from dashing his pistol into my face, and when I said:

"No hard feelings, then, old fellow?"

he gave an incoherent snarl, and turning on his heel, strode off.

This was not lost on Cardigan, who was still watching from a distance, and presently I was summoned from a boozy breakfast —for the plungers celebrated the affair in style, and waxed fulsome over the way I had stood up to him, and then deloped. Cardigan had me to his office, and there was the adjutant and Jones, and Bernier looking like thunder.

"I won't have it, I tell you!" Cardigan was saying. "Ha, Fwashman, come here! Haw-haw. Now then, shake hands directly, I say, Captain Bernier, and let me hear that the affair is done and honour satisfied."

I spoke up. "It's done for me, and indeed I'm sorry it ever happened. But the blow was Captain Bernier's, not mine. But here's my hand, again."

Bernier said, in a voice that shook: "Why did you delope? You have made a mock of me. Why didn't you take your shot at me like a man?"

"My good sir," I said. "I didn't presume to tell you where to aim your shot; don't tell me where I should have aimed mine."

That remark, I am told, has found its way since into some dictionary of quotations; it was in *The Times* within the week, and I was told that when the Duke of Wellington heard it, he observed:

"Damned good. And damned right, too."

So that morning's work made a name for Harry Flashman—a

name that enjoyed more immediate celebrity than if I had stormed a battery alone. Such is fame, especially in peacetime. The whole story went the rounds, and for a time I even found myself pointed out in the street, and a clergyman wrote to me from Birmingham, saying that as I had shown mercy, I would surely obtain mercy, and Parkin, the Oxford Street gunmaker, sent me a brace of barkers in silver mountings, with my initials engraved—good for trade, I imagine. There was also a question in the House, on the vicious practice of duelling, and Macaulay replied that since one of the participants in the recent affair had shown such good sense and humanity, the Government, while deploring such meetings, hoped this might prove a good example. ("Hear, hear," and cheers.) My Uncle Bindley was heard to say that his nephew had more to him than he supposed, and even Basset went about throwing a chest at being servant to such a cool blade.

The only person who was critical was my own father, who said in one of his rare letters:

"Don't be such an infernal fool another time. You don't fight duels in order to delope, but to kill your adversary."

So, with Josette mine by right of conquest—and she was in some awe of me, I may say—and a reputation for courage, marksmanship, and downright decency established, I was pretty well satisfied. The only snag was Bryant, but I dealt with that easily.

When he had finished toadying me on the day of the duel, he got round to asking about his ten thousand—he knew I had great funds, or at least that my father did, but I knew perfectly well I could never have pried ten thousand out of my guv'nor. I told Bryant so, and he gaped as though I had kicked him in the stomach.

"But you promised me ten thousand," he began to bleat.

"Silly promise, ain't it?—when you think hard about it," says I. "Ten thousand quid, I mean—who'd pay out that much?"

"You lying swine!" shouts he, almost crying with rage. "You swore you'd pay me!"

"More fool you for believing me," I said.

"Right, by God!" he snarled. "We'll see about this! You won't cheat me, Flashman, I'll—"

"You'll what?" says I. "Tell everyone all about it? Confess

that you sent a man into a duel with an unloaded gun? It'll make an interesting story. You'd be confessing to a capital offence—had you thought of that? Not that anyone'd believe you—but they'd certainly kick you out of the service for conduct unbecoming, wouldn't they?"

He saw then how it lay, and there was nothing he could do about it. He actually stamped and tore his hair, and then he tried pleading with me, but I laughed at him, and he finished up swearing to be even yet.

"You'll live to regret this!" he cried. "By God, I'll get you yet!"

"More chance of that than you have of getting ten thousand, anyway," I told him, and he slunk off.

He didn't worry me; what I'd said was gospel true. He daren't breathe a word, for his own safety's sake. Of course if he had thought at all he would have sniffed something fishy about a ten thousand bribe in the first place. But he was greedy, and I've lived long enough to discover that there isn't any folly a man won't contemplate if there's money or a woman at stake.

However, if I could congratulate myself on how the matter had turned out, and can look back now and say it was one of the most important and helpful incidents of my life, there was trouble in store for me very quickly as a result of it. It came a few weeks afterwards, and it ended in my having to leave the regiment for a while.

It had happened not long before that the regiment had been honoured (as they say) by being chosen to escort to London the Queen's husband-to-be, Albert, when he arrived in this country. He had become Colonel of the Regiment, and among other things we had been given a new-designed uniform and had our name changed to the Eleventh Hussars. That by the way; what mattered was that he took a close interest in us, and the tale of the duel made such a stir that he took special notice of it, and being a prying German busybody, found out the cause of it.

That almost cooked my goose for good. His lovely new regiment, he found, contained officers who consorted with French whores and even fought duels over them. He played the devil about this, and the upshot was that Cardigan had to summon me and tell me that for my own good I would have to go away for a while.

"It has been demanded," said he, "that you weave the wegiment—I take it the official intention is that that should be permanent, but I intend to interpwet it as tempowawy. I have no desire to lose the services of a pwomising officer—not for His Woyal Highness or anyone, let me tell you. You might go on weave, of course, but I think it best you should be detached. I shall have you posted, Fwashman, to another unit, until the fuss has died down."

I didn't much like the idea, and when he announced that the regiment he had chosen to post me to was stationed in Scotland, I almost rebelled. But I realised it would only be for a few months, and I was relieved to find Cardigan still on my side—if it had been Reynolds who had fought the duel it would have been a very different kettle of fish, but I was one of his favourites. And one must say it of old Lord Haw Haw, if you were his favourite he would stand by you, right, reason or none. Old fool.

I have soldiered in too many countries and known too many peoples to fall into the folly of laying down the law about any of them. I tell you what I have seen, and you may draw your own conclusions. I disliked Scotland and the Scots; the place I found wet and the people rude. They had the fine qualities which bore me—thrift and industry and long-faced holiness, and the young women are mostly great genteel boisterous things who are no doubt bedworthy enough if your taste runs that way. (One acquaintance of mine who had a Scotch clergyman's daughter described it as like wrestling with a sergeant of dragoons.) The men I found solemn, hostile, and greedy, and they found me insolent, arrogant, and smart.

This for the most part; there were exceptions, as you shall see. The best things I found, however, were the port and the claret, in which the Scotch have a nice taste, although I never took to whisky.

The place I was posted to was Paisley, which is near Glasgow, and when I heard of the posting I as near as a toucher sold out. But I told myself I should be back with the 11th in a few months, and must take my medicine, even if it meant being away from all decent living for a while. My forebodings were realised, and more, but at least life did not turn out to be boring, which was what I had feared most. Very far from it.

At this time there was a great unrest throughout Britain, in the industrial areas, which meant very little to me, and indeed I've never troubled to read up the particulars of it. The working people were in a state of agitation, and one heard of riots in the mill towns, and of weavers smashing looms, and Chartists[7] being arrested, but we younger fellows paid it no heed. If you were country-bred or lived in London these things were nothing to you, and all I gathered was that the poor folk were mutinous and wanted to do less work for more money, and the factory owners were damned if they'd let them. There may have been more to it than this, but I doubt it, and no one has ever convinced me that it was anything but a war between the two. It always has been, and always will be, as long as one man has what the other has not, and devil take the hindmost.

The devil seemed to be taking the workers, by and large, with government helping him, and we soldiers were the government's sword. Troops were called out to subdue the agitators, and the Riot Act was read, and here and there would be clashes between the two, and a few killed. I am fairly neutral now, with my money in the bank, but at that time everyone I knew was damning the workers up and down, and saying they should be hung and flogged and transported, and I was all for it, as the Duke would say. You have no notion, today, how high feeling ran; the mill-folk were the enemy then, as though they had been Frenchmen or Afghans. They were to be put down whenever they rose up, and we were to do it.

I was hazy enough, as you see, on the causes of it all, but I saw further than most in some ways, and what I saw was this: it's one thing leading British soldiers against foreigners, but would they fight their own folk? For most of the troopers of the 11th, for example, were of the class and kind of the working people, and I couldn't see them fighting their fellows. I said so, but all I was told was that discipline would do the trick. Well, thought I, maybe it will and maybe it won't, but whoever is going to be caught between a mob on one side and a file of red coats on the other, it isn't going to be old Flashy.

Paisley had been quiet enough when I was sent there, but the authorities had a suspicious eye on the whole area, which was regarded as being a hotbed of sedition. They were training up the militia, just in case, and this was the task I was given—an officer from a crack cavalry regiment instructing irregular infantry, which is what you might expect. They turned out to be good material, luckily; many of the older ones were Peninsular men, and the sergeant had been in the 42nd Regiment at Waterloo. So there was little enough for me to do at first.

I was billeted on one of the principal mill-owners of the area, a brass-bound old moneybags with a long nose and a hard eye who lived in some style in a house at Renfrew, and who made me welcome after his fashion when I arrived.

"We've no high opeenion o' the military, sir," said he, "and could well be doing without ye. But since, thanks to slack government and that damnable Reform nonsense, we're in this sorry plight, we must bear with having soldiers aboot us. A scandal! D'ye see these wretches at my mill, sir? I would have the half of them in Australia this meenit, if it was left to me! And let the rest feel their bellies pinched for a week or two—we'd hear less of their caterwaulin' then."

"You need have no fear, sir," I told him. "We shall protect you."

"Fear?" he snorted. "I'm not feart, sir. John Morrison doesnae tremble at the whine o' his ain workers, let me tell you. As for protecting, we'll see." And he gave me a look and a sniff.

I was to live with the family—he could hardly do less, in view of what brought me there—and presently he took me from his study through the gloomy hall of his mansion to the family's sitting-room. The whole house was hellish gloomy and cold and smelled of must and righteousness, but when he threw open the sitting-room door and ushered me in, I forgot my surroundings.

"Mr Flashman," says he, "this is Mistress Morrison and my four daughters." He rapped out their names like a roll-call. "Agnes, Mary, Elspeth, and Grizel."

I snapped my heels and bowed with a great flourish—I was in uniform, and the gold-trimmed blue cape and pink pants of the 11th Hussars were already famous, and looked extremely well on me. Four heads inclined in reply, and one nodded—this was Mistress Morrison, a tall, beaknosed female in whom one could detect all the fading beauty of a vulture. I made a hasty inventory of the daughters: Agnes, buxom and darkly handsome—she would do. Mary, buxom and plain—she would not. Grizel, thin and mousy and still a schoolgirl—no. Elspeth was like none of the others. She was beautiful, fair-haired, blue-eyed, and pink-cheeked, and she alone smiled at me with the open, simple smile of the truly stupid. I marked her down at once, and gave all my attention to Mistress Morrison.

It was grim work, I may tell you, for she was a sour tyrant of a woman and looked on me as she looked on all soldiers, Englishmen, and men under fifty years of age—as frivolous, Godless, feckless, and unworthy. In this, it seemed, her husband supported her, and the daughters said not a word to me all evening. I could have damned the lot of them (except Elspeth), but instead I set myself to be pleasant, modest, and even meek where the old woman was concerned, and when we went into dinner—which was served in great state—she had thawed to the extent of a sour smile or two.

Well, I thought, that is something, and I went up in her estimation by saying "Amen" loudly when Morrison said grace, and struck while the iron was hot by asking presently—it was a Saturday—what time divine service was next morning. Morrison went so far as to be civil once or twice, after this, but I was still glad to escape at last to my room—dark brown tomb though it was.

You may wonder why I took pains to ingratiate myself with these puritan boors, and the answer is that I have always made a point of being civil to anyone who might ever be of use to me. Also, I had half an eye to Miss Elspeth, and there was no hope there without the mother's good opinion.

So I attended family prayers with them, and escorted them to church, and listened to Miss Agnes sing in the evening, and helped Miss Grizel with her lessons, and pretended an interest in Mistress Morrison's conversation—which was spiteful and censorious and limited to the doings of her acquaintances in Paisley—and was entertained by Miss Mary on the subject of her garden flowers, and bore with old Morrison's droning about the state of trade and the incompetence of government. And among these riotous pleasures of a soldier's life I talked occasionally with Miss Elspeth, and found her brainless beyond description. But she was undeniably desirable, and for all the piety and fear of hell-fire that had been drummed into her, I thought there was sometimes a wanton look about her eye and lower lip, and after a week I had her as infatuated with me as any young woman could be. It was not so difficult; dashing young cavalrymen with broad shoulders were rare in Paisley, and I was setting myself to charm.

However, there's many a slip 'twixt the crouch and the leap, as the cavalry used to say, and my difficulty was to get Miss Elspeth in the right place at the right time. I was kept pretty hard at it with the militia during the day, and in the evenings her parents chaperoned her like shadows. It was more for form's sake than anything else, I think, for they seemed to trust me well enough by this time, but it made things damnably awkward, and I was beginning to itch for her considerably. But eventually it was her father himself who brought matters to a successful conclusion—and changed my whole life, and hers. And it was because he, John Morrison, who had boasted of his fearlessness, turned out to be as timid as a mouse.

It was on a Monday, nine days after I had arrived, that a fracas broke out in one of the mills; a young worker had his arm crushed in one of the machines, and his mates made a great outcry, and a meeting of workmen was held in the streets beyond the mill gates. That was all, but some fool of a magistrate lost his head and demanded that the troops be called "to quell the seditious rioters." I sent his messenger about his business, in the first place because there seemed no danger from the meeting—although there was plenty of fist-shaking and threat-shouting, by all accounts—and in the second because I do not make a practice of seeking sorrow.

Sure enough, the meeting dispersed, but not before the magistrate had spread panic and alarm, ordering the shops to close and windows in the town to be shuttered and God knows what other folly. I told him to his face he was a fool, ordered my sergeant to let the militia go home (but to have them ready on recall), and trotted over to Renfrew.

There Morrison was in a state of despair. He peeped at me round the front door, his face ashen, and demanded:

"Are they comin', in Goad's name?" and then "Why are ye not at the head of your troops, sir? Are we tae be murdered for your neglect?"

I told him, pretty sharp, that there was no danger, but that if there had been, his place was surely at his mill, to keep his rascals in order. He whinnied at me—I've seldom seen a man in such fright, and being a true-bred poltroon myself, I speak with authority.

"My place is here," he yelped, "defendin' my hame and bairns!"

"I thought they were in Glasgow today," I said, as I came into the hall.

"My wee Elspeth's here," said he, groaning. "If the mob was tae break in. . . ."

"Oh, for God's sake," says I, for I was well out of sorts, what with the idiot magistrate and now Morrison, "there isn't a mob. They've gone home."

"Will they stay hame?" he bawled. "Oh, they hate me, Mr Flashman, damn them a'! What if they were to come here? O, wae's me—and my poor wee Elspeth!"

Poor wee Elspeth was sitting in the window-seat, admiring her reflection in the panes, and perfectly unconcerned. Catching sight of her, I had an excellent thought.

"If you're nervous for her, why not send her to Glasgow, too?" I asked him, very unconcerned.

"Are ye mad, sir? Alone on the road, a lassie?"

I reassured him: I would escort her safely to her Mama.

"And leave me here?" he cried, so I suggested he come as well. But he wouldn't have that; I realised later he probably had his strongbox in the house.

He hummed and hawed a great deal, but eventually fear for his daughter—which was entirely groundless, as far as mobs were concerned—overcame him, and we were packed off together in the gig, I driving, she humming gaily at the thought of a jaunt, and her devoted parent crying instruction and consternation after us as we rattled off.

"Tak' care o' my poor wee lamb, Mr Flashman," he wailed.

"To be sure I will, sir," I replied. And I did.

The banks of the Clyde in those days were very pretty; not like the grimy slums that cover them now. There was a gentle evening haze, I remember, and a warm sun setting on a glorious day, and after a mile or two I suggested we stop and ramble among the thickets by the waterside. Miss Elspeth was eager, so we left the pony grazing and went into a little copse. I suggested we sit down, and Miss Elspeth was eager again—that glorious vacant smile informed me. I believe I murmured a few pleasantries, played with her hair, and then kissed her. Miss Elspeth was more eager still. Then I got to work in earnest, and Miss Elspeth's eagerness knew no bounds. I had great red claw-marks on my back for a fortnight after.

When we had finished, she lay in the grass, drowsy, like a contented kitten, and after a few pleased sighs she said:

"Was that what the minister means when he talks of fornication?"

Astonished, I said, yes, it was.

"Um-hm," said she. "Why has he such a down on it?"

It seemed to me time to be pressing on towards Glasgow. Ignorant women I have met, and I knew that Miss Elspeth must rank high among them, but I had not supposed until now that she had no earthly idea of elementary human relations. (Yet there were even married women in my time who did not connect their husbands' antics in bed with the conception of children.) She simply did not understand what had taken place between us. She liked it, certainly, but she had no thought of anything beyond the act—no notion of consequences, or guilt, or the need for secrecy. In her, ignorance and stupidity formed a perfect shield against the world: this, I suppose, is innocence.

It startled me, I can tell you. I had a vision of her remarking happily: "Mama, you'll never guess what Mr Flashman and I have been doing this evening. . . ." Not that I minded too much, for when all was said I didn't care a button for the Morrisons' opinion, and if they could not look after their daughter it was their own fault. But the less trouble the better: for her own sake I hoped she might keep her mouth shut.

I took her back to the gig and helped her in, and I thought what a beautiful fool she was. Oddly enough, I felt a sudden affection for her in that moment, such as I hadn't felt for any of my other women—even though some of them had been better tumbles than she. It had nothing to do with rolling her in the grass; looking at the gold hair that had fallen loose on her cheek, and seeing the happy smile in her eyes, I felt a great desire to keep her, not only for bed, but to have her near me. I wanted to watch her face, and the way she pushed her hair into place, and the steady, serene look that she turned on me. Hullo, Flashy, I remember thinking; careful, old son. But it stayed with me, that queer empty feeling in my inside, and of all the recollections of my life there isn't one that is clearer than of that warm evening by the Clyde, with Elspeth smiling at me beneath the trees.

Almost equally distinct, however, but less pleasant, is my memory of Morrison, a few days later, shaking his fist in my face and scarlet with rage as he shouted:

"Ye damned blackguard! Ye thieving, licentious, raping devil!

I'll have ye hanged for this, as Goad's my witness! My ain daughter, in my ain hoose! Jesus Lord! Ye come sneaking here, like the damned viper that ye are...."

And much more of the same, until I thought he would have apoplexy. Miss Elspeth had almost lived up to my expectation—only it had not been Mama she had told, but Agnes. The result was the same, of course, and the house was in uproar. The only calm person was Elspeth herself, which was no help. For of course I denied old Morrison's accusation, but when he dragged her in to confront me with my infamy, as he called it, she said quite matter-of-fact, yes, it had happened by the river on the way to Glasgow. I wondered, was she simple? It is a point on which I have never made up my mind.

At that, I couldn't deny it any longer. So I took the other course and damned Morrison's eyes, asking him what did he expect if he left a handsome daughter within a man's reach? I told him we were not monks in the army, and he fairly screamed with rage and threw an inkstand at me, which fortunately missed. By this time others were on the scene, and his daughters had the vapours —except Elspeth—and Mrs Morrison came at me with such murder in her face that I turned tail and ran for dear life.

I decamped without even having time to collect my effects—which were not sent on to me, by the way—and decided that I had best set up my base in Glasgow. Paisley was likely to be fairly hot, and I resolved to have a word with the local commandant and explain, as between gentlemen, that it might be best if other duties were found for me that would not take me back there. It would be somewhat embarrassing, of course, for he was another of these damned Presbyterians, so I put off seeing him for a day or two. As a result I never called on him at all. Instead I had a caller myself.

He was a stiff-shouldered, brisk-mannered fellow of about fifty; rather dapper in an almost military way, with a brown face and hard grey eyes. He looked as though he might be a sporting sort, but when he came to see me he was all business.

"Mr Flashman, I believe?" says he. "My name is Abercrombie."

"Good luck to you, then," says I. "I'm not buying anything today, so close the door as you leave."

He looked at me sharp, head on one side. "Good," says he.

"This makes it easier. I had thought you might be a smooth one, but I see you're what they call a plunger."

I asked him what the devil he meant.

"Quite simple," says he, taking a seat as cool as you please. "We have a mutual acquaintance. Mrs Morrison of Renfrew is my sister. Elspeth Morrison is my niece."

This was an uneasy piece of news, for I didn't like the look of him. He was too sure of himself by half. But I gave him a stare and told him he had a damned handsome niece.

"I'm relieved that you think so," said he. "I'd be distressed to think that the Hussars were not discriminating."

He sat looking at me, so I took a turn round the room.

"The point is," he said, "that we have to make arrangements for the wedding. You'll not want to lose time."

I had picked up a bottle and glass, but I set them down sharp at this. He had taken my breath away.

"What the hell d'you mean?" says I. Then I laughed. "You don't think I'll marry her, do you? Good God, you must be a lunatic."

"And why?" says he.

"Because I'm not such a fool," I told him. Suddenly I was angry, at this damned little snip, and his tone with me. "If every girl who's ready to play in the hay was to get married, we'd have damned few spinsters left, wouldn't we? And d'you suppose I'd be pushed into a wedding over a trifle like this?"

"My niece's honour."

"Your niece's honour! A mill-owner's daughter's honour! I'm to mend that at the altar, am I? Oh, I see the game! You see an excellent chance of a match, eh? A chance to marry your niece to a gentleman? You smell a fortune, do you? Well, let me tell you—"

"As to the excellence of the match," said he, "I'd sooner see her marry a Barbary ape. I take it, however, that you decline the honour of my niece's hand?"

"Damn your impudence! You take it right. Now, get out!"

"Excellent," says he, very bright-eyed. "It's what I hoped for." And he stood up, straightening his coat.

"What's that meant to mean, curse you?"

He smiled at me. "I'll send a friend to talk to you. He will arrange matters. I don't approve of meetings, myself, but I'll be

delighted, in this case, to put either a bullet or a blade into you."
He clapped his hat on his head. "You know, I don't suppose there
has been a duel in Glasgow these fifty years or more. It will cause
quite a stir."

I gaped at the man, but gathered my wits soon enough. "Lord,"
says I, with a sneer, "you don't suppose I would fight you?"

"No?"

"Gentlemen fight gentlemen," I told him, and ran a scornful
eye over him. "They don't fight shop-keepers."

"Wrong again," says he, cheerily. "I'm a lawyer."

"Then stick to your law. We don't fight lawyers, either."

"Not if you can help it, I imagine. But you'll be hard put to it
to refuse a brother officer, Mr Flashman. You see, although I've
no more than a militia commission now, I was formerly of the
93rd Foot—you have heard of the Sutherlands, I take it?—and
had the honour to hold the rank of captain. I even achieved some
little service in the field." He was smiling almost benignly now.
"If you doubt my bona fides, may I refer you to my former chief,
Colonel Colin Campbell?[8] Good day, Mr Flashman."

He was at the door before I found my voice.

"To hell with you, and him! I'll not fight you!"

He turned. "Then I'll enjoy taking a whip to you in the street.
I really shall. Your own chief—my Lord Cardigan, isn't it?—will
find that happy reading in *The Times*, I don't doubt."

He had me in a cleft stick, as I saw at once. It would mean
professional ruin—and at the hands of a damned provincial
infantryman, and a retired one at that. I stood there, overcome
with rage and panic, damning the day I ever set eyes on his
infernal niece, with my wits working for a way out. I tried
another tack.

"You may not realise who you're dealing with," I told him,
and asked if he had not heard of the Bernier affair: it seemed
to me that it must be known about, even in the wilds of Glasgow,
and I said so.

"I think I recollect a paragraph," says he. "Dear me, Mr Flashman, should I be overcome? Should I quail? I'll just have to try
to hold my pistol steady, won't I?"

"Damn you," I shouted, "wait a moment."

He stood attentive, watching me.

51

"All right, blast you," I said. "How much do you want?"

"I thought it might come to that," he said. "Your kind of rat generally reaches for its purse when cornered. You're wasting time, Flashman. I'll take your promise to marry Elspeth—or your life. I'd prefer the latter. But it's one or the other. Make up your mind."

And from that I could not budge him. I pleaded and swore and promised any kind of reparation short of marriage; I was almost in tears, but I might as well have tried to move a rock. Marry or die—that was what it amounted to, for I'd no doubt he would be damnably efficient with the barkers. There was nothing for it: in the end I had to give in and say I would marry the girl.

"You're sure you wouldn't rather fight?" says he, regretfully. "A great pity. I fear the conventions are going to burden Elspeth with a rotten man, but there." And he passed on to discussion of the wedding arrangements—he had it all pat.

When at last I was rid of him I applied myself to the brandy, and things seemed less bleak. At least I could think of no one I would rather be wedded and bedded with, and if you have money a wife need be no great encumbrance. And presently we should be out of Scotland, so I need not see her damnable family. But it was an infernal nuisance, all the same—what was I to tell my father? I couldn't for the life of me think how he would take it—he wouldn't cut me off, but he might be damned uncivil about it.

I didn't write to him until after the business was over. It took place in the Abbey at Paisley, which was appropriately gloomy, and the sight of the pious long faces of my bride's relations would have turned your stomach. The Morrisons had begun speaking to me again, and were very civil in public—it was represented as being a sudden love-match, of course, between the dashing hussar and the beautiful provincial, so they had to pretend I was their beau ideal of a son-in-law. But the brute Abercrombie was never far away, to see I came up to scratch, and all in all it was an unpleasant business.

When it was done, and the guests had begun to drink themselves blind, as is the Scottish custom, Elspeth and I were seen off in a carriage by her parents. Old Morrison was crying drunk, and made a disgusting spectacle.

"My wee lamb!" he kept snuffling. "My bonny wee lamb!"

His wee lamb, I may say, looked entrancing, and no more moved than if she had just been out choosing a pair of gloves, rather than getting a husband—she had taken the whole thing without a murmur, neither happy nor sorry, apparently, which piqued me a little.

Anyway, her father slobbered over her, but when he turned to me he just let out a great hollow groan, and gave place to his wife. At that I whipped up the horses, and away we went.

For the life of me I cannot remember where the honeymoon was spent—at some rented cottage on the coast, I remember, but the name has gone—and it was lively enough. Elspeth knew nothing, but it seemed that the only thing that brought her out of her usual serene lethargy was a man in bed with her. She was a more than willing playmate, and I taught her a few of Josette's tricks, which she picked up so readily that by the time we came back to Paisley I was worn out.

And there the shock was waiting: it hit me harder, I think, than anything had in my life. When I opened the letter and read it, I couldn't speak at first; I had to read it again and again before it made sense.

> "Lord Cardigan [it read] has learned of the marriage contracted lately by Mr Flashman, of this regiment, and Miss Morrison, of Glasgow. In view of this marriage, his lordship feels that Mr Flashman will not wish to continue to serve with the 11th Hussars (Prince Albert's), but that he will wish either to resign or to transfer to another regiment."

That was all. It was signed "Jones"—Cardigan's toady.

What I said I don't recall, but it brought Elspeth to my side. She slid her arms round my waist and asked what was the matter.

"All hell's the matter," I said. "I must go to London at once."

At this she raised a cry of delight, and babbled with excitement about seeing the great sights, and society, and having a place in town, and meeting my father—God help us—and a great deal more drivel. I was too sick to heed her, and she never seemed to notice me as I sat down among the boxes and trunks that had been brought in from the coach to our bedroom. I remember I damned her at one point for a fool and told her to hold her tongue, which .

silenced her for a minute; but then she started off again, and was debating whether she should have a French maid or an English one.

I was in a furious rage all the way south, and impatient to get to Cardigan. I knew what it was all about—the bloody fool had read of the marriage and decided that Elspeth was not "suitable" for one of his officers. It will sound ridiculous to you, perhaps, but it was so in those days in a regiment like the 11th. Society daughters were all very well, but anything that smacked of trade or the middle classes was anathema to his lofty lordship. Well, I was not going to have his nose turned up at me, as he would find. So I thought, in my youthful folly.

I took Elspeth home first. I had written to my father while we were on honeymoon, and had had a letter back saying: "Who is the unfortunate chit, for God's sake? Does she know what she has got?" So all was well enough in its way on that front. And when we arrived there who should be the first person we met in the hall but Judy, dressed for riding. She gave me a tongue-in-the-cheek smile as soon as she saw Elspeth—the clever bitch probably guessed what lay behind the marriage—but I got some of my own back by my introduction:

"Elspeth," I said, "this is Judy, my father's tart."

That brought the colour into her face, and I left them to get acquainted while I looked for the guv'nor. He was out, as usual, so I went straight off in search of Cardigan, and found him at his town house. At first he wouldn't see me, when I sent up my card, but I pushed his footman out of the way and went up anyway.

It should have been a stormy interview, with high words flying, but it wasn't. Just the sight of him, in his morning coat, looking as though he had just been inspecting God on parade, took the wind out of me. When he had demanded to know, in his coldest way, why I intruded on him, I stuttered out my question: why was he sending me out of the regiment?

"Because of your marriage, Fwashman," says he. "You must have known very well what the consequences would be. It is quite unacceptable, you know. The lady, I have no doubt, is an excellent young woman, but she is—nobody. In these circumstances your resignation is imperative."

"But she is respectable, my lord," I said. "I assure you she is from an excellent family; her father—"

"Owns a factory," he cut in. "Haw-haw. It will not do. My dear sir, did you not think of your position? Of the wegiment? Could I answer, sir, if I were asked: 'And who is Mr Fwashman's wife?' 'Oh, her father is a Gwasgow weaver, don't you know?'"

"But it will ruin me!" I could have wept at the pure, block-headed snobbery of the man. "Where can I go? What regiment will take me if I'm kicked out of the 11th?"

"You are not being kicked out, Fwashman," he said, and he was being positively kindly. "You are wesigning. A very different thing. Haw-haw. You are twansferring. There is no difficulty. I wike you, Fwashman; indeed, I had hopes of you, but you have destwoyed them with your foolishness. Indeed, I should be extwemely angwy. But I shall help in your awwangements: I have infwuence at the Horse Guards, you know."

"Where am I to go?" I demanded miserably.

"I have given thought to it, let me tell you. It would be im-pwoper to twansfer to another wegiment at home; it will be best if you go overseas, I think. To India. Yes—"

"India?" I stared at him in horror.

"Yes, indeed. There are caweers to be made there, don't you know? A few years' service there, and the matter of your wesigning fwom my wegiment will be forgotten. You can come home and be gazetted to some other command."

He was so bland, so sure, that there was nothing to say. I knew what he thought of me now: I had shown myself in his eyes no better than the Indian officers whom he despised. Oh, he was being kind enough, in his way; there were "caweers" in India, all right, for the soldier who could get nothing better—and who survived the fevers and the heat and the plague and the hostile natives. At that moment I was at my lowest; the pale, haughty face and the soft voice seemed to fade away before me; all I was conscious of was a sullen anger, and a deep resolve that wherever I went, it would not be India—not for a thousand Cardigans.

"So you won't, hey?" said my father, when I told him.

"I'm damned if I do," I said.

"You're damned if you don't," chuckled he, very amused. "What else will you do, d'you suppose?"

"Sell out," says I.

"Not a bit of it," says he. "I've bought your colours, and by God, you'll wear 'em."

"You can't make me."

"True enough. But the day you hand them back, on that day the devil a penny you'll get out of me. How will you live, eh? And with a wife to support, bigad? No, no, Harry; you've called the tune, and you can pay the piper."

"You mean I'm to go?"

"Of course you'll go. Look you, my son, and possibly my heir, I'll tell you how it is. You're a wastrel and a bad lot—oh, I daresay it's my fault, among others, but that's by the way. My father was a bad lot, too, but I grew up some kind of man. You might, too, for all I know. But I'm certain sure you won't do it here. You might do it by reaping the consequences of your own lunacy—and that means India. D'you follow me?"

"But Elspeth," I said. "You know it's no country for a woman."

"Then don't take her. Not for the first year, in any event, until you've settled down a bit. Nice chit, she is. And don't make piteous eyes at me, sir; you can do without her a while—by all accounts there are women in India, and you can be as beastly as you please.'

"It's not fair!" I shouted.

"Not fair! Well, well, this is one lesson you're learning. Nothing's fair, you young fool. And don't blubber about not wanting to go and leave her—she'll be safe enough here."

"With you and Judy, I suppose?"

"With me and Judy," says he, very softly. "And I'm not sure that the company of a rake and a harlot won't be better for her than yours."

That was how I came to leave for India; how the foundation was laid of a splendid military career. I felt myself damnably ill-used, and if I had had the courage I would have told my father to go to the devil. But he had me, and he knew it. Even if it hadn't been for the money part of it, I couldn't have stood up to him, as I hadn't been able to stand up to Cardigan. I hated them both, then. I came to think better of Cardigan, later, for in his arrogant, pig-headed, snobbish way he was trying to be decent to me, but my father I never forgave. He was playing the swine, and he knew it, and found it amusing at my expense. But what really poisoned me against him was that he didn't believe I cared a button for Elspeth.

There may be better countries for a soldier to serve in than India, but I haven't seen them. You may hear the greenhorns talk about heat and flies and filth and the natives and the diseases; the first three you must get accustomed to, the fifth you must avoid—which you can do, with a little common sense—and as for the natives, well, where else will you get such a docile, humble set of slaves? I liked them better than the Scots, anyhow; their language was easier to understand.

And if these things were meant to be drawbacks, there was the other side. In India there was power—the power of the white man over the black—and power is a fine thing to have. Then there was ease, and time for any amount of sport, and good company, and none of the restrictions of home. You could live as you pleased, and lord it among the niggers, and if you were well-off and properly connected, as I was, there was the social life among the best folk who clustered round the Governor-General. And there were as many women as you could wish for.

There was money to be had, too, if you were lucky in your campaigns and knew how to look for it. In my whole service I never made half as much in pay as I got from India in loot—but that is another story.

I knew nothing of this when we dropped anchor in the Hooghly, off Calcutta, and I looked at the red river banks and sweated in the boiling sun, and smelt the stink, and wished I was in hell rather than here. It had been a damnable four-months voyage on board the crowded and sweltering Indiaman, with no amusement of any kind, and I was prepared to find India no better.

I was to join one of the Company's native lancer regiments[9] in the Benares District, but I never did. Army inefficiency kept me kicking my heels in Calcutta for several weeks before the appropriate orders came through, and by that time I had taken fortune by the foreskin, in my own way.

In the first place, I messed at the Fort with the artillery officers in the native service, who were a poor lot, and whose messing would have sickened a pig. The food was bad to begin with, and by the time the black cooks had finished with it you would hardly have fed it to a jackal.

I said so at our first dinner, and provoked a storm among these gentlemen, who considered me a Johnny Newcome.

"Not good enough for the plungers, eh?" says one. "Sorry we have no *foie gras* for your lordship, and we must apologise for the absence of silver plate."

"Is it always like this?" I asked. "What is it?"

"What is the dish, your grace?" asked the wit. "Why, it's called curry, don't you know? Kills the taste of old meat."

"If that's all it kills, I'm surprised," says I, disgusted. "No decent human being could stomach this filth."

"We stomach it," said another. "Ain't we human beings?"

"You know best about that," I said. "If you take my advice you'll hang your cook." And with that I stalked out, leaving them growling after me. Yet their mess, I discovered, was no worse than any other in India, and better than some. The men's messes were indescribable, and I wondered how they survived such dreadful food in such a climate. The answer was, of course, that many of·them didn't.

However, it was obvious to me that I would be better shifting for myself, so I called up Basset, whom I had brought with me from England—the little bastard had blubbered at the thought of losing me when I left the 11th, God knows why—gave him a fistful of money, and told him to find a cook, a butler, a groom, and half a dozen other servants. These people were to be hired for virtually nothing. Then I went myself to the guard room, found a native who could speak English passably well, and went out to find a house.[10]

I found one not far from the Fort, a pleasant place with a little garden of shrubs, and a verandah with screens, and my nigger fetched the owner, who was a great fat rogue with a red turban; we haggled in the middle of a crowd of jabbering blacks, and I gave him half what he asked for and settled into the place with my establishment.

First of all I sent for the cook, and told him through my nigger:

"You will cook, and cook cleanly. You'll wash your hands, d'ye see, and buy nothing but the finest meat and vegetables. If you don't, I'll have the cat taken to you until there isn't a strip of hide left on your back."

He jabbered away, nodding and grinning and bowing, so I took him by the neck and threw him down and lashed him with my riding whip until he rolled off the verandah, screaming.

"Tell him he'll get that night and morning if his food's not fit to eat," I told my nigger. "And the rest of them may take notice."

They all howled with fear, but they paid heed, the cook most of all. I took the opportunity to flog one of them every day, for their good and my own amusement, and to these precautions I attribute the fact that in all my service in India I was hardly ever laid low with anything worse than fever, and that you can't avoid. The cook was a good cook, as it turned out, and Basset kept the others at it with his tongue and his boot, so we did very well.

My nigger, whose name was Timbu-something-or-other, was of great use at first, since he spoke English, but after a few weeks I got rid of him. I've said that I have a gift of language, but it was only when I came to India that I realised this. My Latin and Greek had been weak at school, for I paid little attention to them, but a tongue that you hear spoken about you is a different thing. Each language has a rhythm for me, and my ear catches and holds the sounds; I seem to know what a man is saying even when I don't understand the words, and my own tongue slips easily into any new accent. In any event, after a fortnight listening to Timbu and asking him questions, I was speaking Hindustani well enough to be understood, and I paid him off. For one thing, I had found a more interesting teacher.

Her name was Fetnab, and I bought her (not officially, of course, although it amounted to the same thing) from a merchant whose livestock consisted of wenches for the British officers and civilian residents in Calcutta. She cost me 500 rupees, which was about 50 guineas, and she was a thief's bargain. I suppose she was about sixteen, with a handsome enough face and a gold stud fixed in her nostril, and great slanting brown eyes. Like most other Indian dancing girls, she was shaped like an hour-glass, with a waist that

I could span with my two hands, fat breasts like melons, and a wobbling backside.

If anything she was a shade too plump, but she knew the ninety-seven ways of making love that the Hindus are supposed to set much store by—though mind you, it is all nonsense, for the seventy-fourth position turns out to be the same as the seventy-third, but with your fingers crossed. But she taught me them all in time, for she was devoted to her work, and would spend hours oiling herself with perfume all over her body and practising Hindu exercises to keep herself supple for night-time. After my first two days with her I thought less and less about Elspeth, and even Josette paled by comparison.

However, I put her to other good uses. In between bouts we would talk, for she was a great chatterbox, and I learned more of the refinements of Hindi from her than I would have done from any munshi. I give the advice for what it is worth: if you wish to learn a foreign tongue properly, study it in bed with a native girl —I'd have got more of the classics from an hour's wrestling with a Greek wench than I did in four years from Arnold.

So this was how I passed my time in Calcutta—my nights with Fetnab, my evenings in one of the messes, or someone's house, and my days riding or shooting or hunting, or simply wandering about the town itself. I became quite a well-known figure to the niggers, because I could speak to them in their own tongue, unlike the vast majority of officers at that time—even those who had served in India for years were usually too bored to try to learn Hindi, or thought it beneath them.

Another thing I learned, because of the regiment to which I was due to be posted, was how to manage a lance. I had been useful at sword exercise in the Hussars, but a lance is something else again. Any fool can couch it and ride straight, but if you are to be any use at all you must be able to handle all nine feet of it so that you can pick a playing card off the ground with the point, or pink a running rabbit. I was determined to shine among the Company men, so I hired a native rissalder of the Bengal Cavalry to teach me; I had no thought then of anything beyond tilting at dummies or wild pig sticking, and the thought of couching a lance against enemy cavalry was not one that I dwelt on much. But those lessons were to save my life once at least—so that was more well-spent money. They also settled the question of my immediate future, in an odd way.

I was out on the maidan one morning with my rissalder, a big, lean, ugly devil of the Pathan people of the frontier, named Muhammed Iqbal. He was a splendid horseman and managed a lance perfectly, and under his guidance I was learning quickly. That morning he had me tilting at pegs, and I speared so many that he said, grinning, that he must charge me more for my lessons.

We were trotting off the maidan, which was fairly empty that morning, except for a palankeen escorted by a couple of officers, which excited my curiosity a little, when Iqbal suddenly shouted:

"See, huzoor, a better target than little pegs!" and pointed towards a pariah dog which was snuffling about some fifty yards away. Iqbal couched his lance and went for it, but it darted out of his way, so I roared "Tally-ho!" and set off in pursuit. Iqbal was still ahead of me, but I was only a couple of lengths behind when he made another thrust at the pi-dog, which was racing ahead of him, swerving and yelping. He missed again, and yelled a curse, and the pi-dog suddenly turned almost beneath his hooves and leaped up at his foot. I dropped my point and by great good luck spitted the beast through the body.

With a shout of triumph I heaved him, twisting and still yelping, high into the air, and he fell behind me. Iqbal cried: "Shabash!" and I was beginning to crow over him when a voice shouted:

"You there! You, sir! Come here, if you please, this moment."

It came from the palankeen, towards which our run had taken us. The curtains were drawn, and the caller was revealed as a portly, fierce-looking gentleman in a frock coat, with a sun-browned face and a fine bald head. He had taken off his hat, and was waving insistently, so I rode across.

"Good morning," says he, very civil. "May I inquire your name?"

It did not need the presence of the two mounted dandies by the palankeen to tell me that this was a highly senior officer. Wondering, I introduced myself.

"Well, congratulations, Mr Flashman," says he. "Smart a piece of work as I've seen this year: if we had a regiment who could all manage a lance as well as you we'd have no trouble with damned Sikhs and Afghans, eh, Bennet?"

"Indeed not, sir," said one of the exquisite aides, eyeing me. "Mr Flashman; I seem to know the name. Are you not lately of the 11th Hussars, at home?"

"Eh, what's that?" said his chief, giving me a bright grey eye. "Bigod, so he is; see his Cherrypicker pants"—I was still wearing the pink breeches of the Hussars, which strictly I had no right to do, but they set off my figure admirably—"so he is, Bennet. Now, dammit, Flashman, Flashman—of course, the affair last year! You're the deloper! Well I'm damned! What are you doing here, sir, in God's name?"

I explained, cautiously, trying to hint without actually saying so, that my arrival in India had followed directly from my meeting with Bernier (which was almost true, anyway), and my questioner whistled and exclaimed in excitement. I suppose I was enough of a novelty to rouse his interest, and he asked me a good deal about myself, which I answered fairly truthfully; in my turn I learned as he questioned me that he was General Crawford, on the staff of the Governor-General, and as such a commander of influence and importance.

"Bigad, you've had bad luck, Flashman," says he. "Banished from the lofty Cherrypickers, eh? Damned nonsense, but these blasted militia colonels like Cardigan have no sense. Eh, Bennet? And you're bound for Company service, are you? Well, the pay's good, but it's a damned shame. Waste your life teaching the sowars how to perform on galloping field days. Damned dusty work. Well, well, Flashman, I wish you success. Good day to you, sir."

And that would have settled that, no doubt, but for a queer chance. I had been sitting with my lance at rest, the point six feet above my head, and some of the pi-dog's blood dribbled down onto my hand; I gave an exclamation of disgust, and turning to Iqbal, who was sitting silently behind, I said:

"Khabadar, rissaldar! Larnce sarf karo, juldi!" which is to say, "Look out, sergeant-major. Take this lance and get it clean, quickly." And with that I tossed it to him. He caught it, and I turned back to take my leave of Crawford. He had stopped in the act of pulling his palankeen curtains.

"Here, Flashman," says he. "How long have you been in India? What, three weeks, you say? But you speak the lingo, dammit!"

"Only a word or two, sir."

"Don't tell me, sir; I heard several words. Damned sight more than I learned in thirty years. Eh, Bennet? Too many 'ee's' and 'um's' for me. But that's damned extraordinary, young man. How'd you pick it up?"

I did more explaining, about my gift for languages, and he shook his bald head and said he'd never heard the like. "A born linguist and a born lancer, bigod. Rare combination—too dam' good for Company cavalry—all ride like pigs, anyway. Look here, young Flashman, I can't think at this time in the morning. You call on me tonight, d'ye hear? We'll go into this further. Hey, Bennet?"

And presently away he went, but I did call on him that evening, resplendent in my Cherrypicker togs, as he called them, and he looked at me and said:

"By God, Emily Eden mustn't miss this! She'd never forgive me!"

To my surprise, this was his way of indicating that I should go with him to the Governor-General's palace, where he was due for dinner, so of course I went, and had the privilege of drinking lemonade with their excellencies on their great marble verandah, while a splendid company stood about, like a small court, and I saw more quality in three seconds than in my three weeks in Calcutta. Which was very pleasant, but Crawford almost spoiled it by telling Lord Auckland about my duel with Bernier, at which he and Lady Emily, who was his sister, looked rather stiff—they were a stuffy pair, I thought—until I said fairly coolly to Crawford that I would have avoided the whole business if I could, but it had been forced upon me. At this Auckland nodded approval, and when it came out that I had been under Arnold at Rugby, the old bastard became downright civil. Lady Emily was even more so —thank God for Cherrypicker pants—and when she discovered I was only nineteen years old she nodded sadly, and spoke of the fair young shoots on the tree of empire.

She asked about my family, and when she learned I had a wife in England, she said:

"So young to be parted. How *hard* the service is."

Her brother observed, fairly drily, that there was nothing to prevent an officer having his wife in India with him, but I muttered something about winning my spurs, an inspired piece of nonsense which pleased Lady E. Her brother remarked that an astonishing number of young officers somehow survived the absence of a wife's consolation, and Crawford chortled, but Lady E. was on my side by now, and giving them her shoulder, asked where I was to be stationed.

I told her, and since it seemed to me that if I played my cards right I might get a more comfortable posting through her interest —Governor-General's aide was actually in my mind—I indicated that I had no great enthusiasm for Company service.

"Don't blame him, either," said Crawford. "Man's a positive Pole on horseback; shouldn't be wasted, eh, Flashman? Speaks Hindustani, too. Heard him."

"Really?" says Auckland. "That shows a remarkable zeal in study, Mr Flashman. But perhaps Dr Arnold may be to thank for that."

"Why must you take Mr Flashman's credit away from him?" says Lady E. "I think it is *quite* unusual. I think he should be found a post where his talents can be *properly* employed. Do you not agree, General?"

"Own views exactly, ma'am," says Crawford. "Should have heard him. 'Hey, rissaldar', says he, 'um-tiddly-o-karo', and the fellow understood every word."

Now you can imagine that this was heady stuff to me; this morning I had been any old subaltern, and here I was hearing compliments from a Governor-General, and General, and the First Lady of India—foolish old trot though she was. You're made, Flashy, I thought; it's the staff for you, and Auckland's next words seemed to bear out my hopes.

"Why not find something for him, then?" says he to Crawford. "General Elphinstone was saying only yesterday that he would need a few good gallopers."

Well, it wasn't the top of the tree, but galloper to a General was good enough for the time being.

"Bigod," says Crawford, "your excellency's right. What d'you say, Flashman? Care to ride aide to an army commander, hey? Better than Company work at the back of beyond, what?"

I naturally said I would be deeply honoured, and was starting to thank him, but he cut me off.

"You'll be more thankful yet when you know where Elphinstone's service'll take you," says he, grinning. "By gad, I wish I was your age and had the same chance. It's a Company army mostly, of course, and a damned good one, but it took 'em a few years of service—as it would have taken you—to get where they wanted to be."

I looked all eagerness, and Lady E. sighed and smiled together.

"Poor boy," she said. "You must not tease him."

"Well, it will be out by tomorrow, anyway," says Crawford. "You don't know Elphinstone, of course, Flashman—commands the Benares Division, or will do until midnight tonight. And then he takes over the Army of the Indus—what about that, eh?"

It sounded all right, and I made enthusiastic noises.

"Aye, you're a lucky dog," says Crawford, beaming. "How many young blades would give their right leg for the chance of service with him? In the very place for a dashing lancer to win his spurs, bigad!"

A nasty feeling tickled my spine, and I asked where that might be.

"Why, Kabul, of course," says he. "Where else but Afghanistan?"

The old fool actually thought I must be delighted at this news, and of course I had to pretend to be. I suppose any young officer in India would have jumped at the opportunity, and I did my best to look gratified and eager, but I could have knocked the grinning idiot down, I was so angry. I had thought I was doing so well, what with my sudden introduction to the exalted of the land, and all it had won me was a posting to the hottest, hardest, most dangerous place in the world, to judge by all accounts. There was talk of nothing but Afghanistan in Calcutta at that time, and of the Kabul expedition, and most of it touched on the barbarity of the natives, and the unpleasantness of the country. I could have been sensible, I told myself, and had myself quietly posted to Benares—but no, I had had to angle round Lady Emily, and now looked like getting my throat cut for my pains.

Thinking quickly, I kept my eager smile in place but wondered whether General Elphinstone might not have preferences of his own when it came to choosing an aide; there might be others, I thought, who had a better claim. . . .

Nonsense, says Crawford, he would go bail Elphinstone would be delighted to have a man who could talk the language *and* handle a lance like a Cossack, and Lady Emily said she was sure he would find a place for me. So there was no way out; I was going to have to take it and pretend that I liked it.

That night I gave Fetnab the soundest thrashing of her pampered life and broke a pot over the sweeper's head.

I was not even given a decent time to prepare myself. General Elphinstone (or Elphy Bey, as the wags called him) received me next day, and turned out to be an elderly, fussy man with a brown wrinkled face and heavy white whiskers; he was kind enough, in a doddering way, and as unlikely a commander of armies as you could imagine, being nearly sixty, and none too well either.

"It is a great honour to me," says he, speaking of his new command, "but I could wish it had fallen on younger shoulders—indeed, I am sure it should." He shook his head, and looked gloomy, and I thought, well, here's a fine one to take the field with.

However, he welcomed me to his staff, damn him, and said it was most opportune; he could use me at once. Since his present aides were used to his service, he would keep them with him just now, to prepare for the journey; he would send me in advance to Kabul—which meant, I supposed, that I was to herald his coming, and see that his quarters were swept out for his arrival. So I had to gather up my establishment, hire camels and mules for their transport, lay in stores for the journey, and generally go to a deal of expense and bother. My servants kept well out of my way in those days, I can tell you, and Fetnab went about whimpering and rolling her eyes. I told her to shut up or I would give her to the Afghans when we got to Kabul, and she was so terrified that she actually kept quiet.

However, after my first disappointment I realised there was no sense crying over spilt milk, and looked on the bright side. I was, after all, to be aide to a general, which would be helpful in years to come, and gave one great distinction. Afghanistan was at least quiet for the moment, and Elphy Bey's term of command could hardly last long, at his age. I could take Fetnab and my household with me, including Basset, and with Elphy Bey's influence I was allowed to enlist Muhammed Iqbal in my party. He spoke Pushtu, of course, which is the language of the Afghans, and could instruct me as we went. Also, he was an excellent fellow to have beside you, and would be an invaluable companion and guide.

Before we started out, I got hold of as much information as I could about matters in Afghanistan. They seemed to stand damned riskily to me, and there were others in Calcutta—but not Auckland, who was an ass—who shared this view. The reason we had sent an expedition to Kabul, which is in the very heart of some of the worst country in the world, was that we were afraid of Russia. Afghanistan was a buffer, if you like, between India and the Turkestan territory which Russia largely influenced, and the Russians were forever meddling in Afghan affairs, in the hope of expanding southwards and perhaps seizing India itself. So Afghanistan mattered very much to us, and thanks to that conceited Scotch buffoon Burnes the British Government had invaded the country, if you please, and put our puppet king, Shah Sujah, on the throne in Kabul, in place of old Dost Mohammed, who was suspected of Russian sympathies.

I believe, from all I saw and heard, that if he had Russian sympathies it was because we drove him to them by our stupid policy; at any rate, the Kabul expedition succeeded in setting Sujah on the throne, and old Dost was politely locked up in India. So far, so good, but the Afghans didn't like Sujah at all, and we had to leave an army in Kabul to keep him on his throne. This was the army that Elphy Bey was to command. It was a good enough army, part Queen's troops, part Company's, with British regiments as well as native ones, but it was having its work cut out trying to keep the tribes in order, for apart from Dost's supporters there were scores of little petty chiefs and tyrants who lost no opportunity of causing trouble in the unsettled times, and the usual Afghan pastimes of blood-feud, robbery, and murder-for-fun were going ahead full steam. Our army prevented any big rising—for the moment, anyway—but it was forever patrolling and manning little forts, and trying to pacify and buy off the robber chiefs, and people were wondering how long this could go on. The wise ones said there was an explosion coming, and as we started out on our journey from Calcutta my foremost thought was that whoever got blown up, it should not be me. It was just my luck that I was going to end up on top of the bonfire.

Travelling, I think, is the greatest bore in life, so I'll not weary you with an account of the journey from Calcutta to Kabul. It was long and hot and damnably dull; if Basset and I had not taken Muhammed Iqbal's advice and shed our uniforms for native dress, I doubt whether we would have survived. In desert, on scrubby plain, through rocky hills, in the forests, in the little mud villages and camps and towns—the heat was horrible and ceaseless; your skin scorched, your eyes burned, and you felt that your body was turning into a dry bag of bones. But in the loose robes and pyjamy trousers one felt cooler—that is, one fried without burning quite black.

Basset, Iqbal and I rode horses, the servants tramped behind with Fetnab in a litter, but our pace was so slow that after a week we got rid of them all but the cook. The servants we turned off, amid great lamentations, and Fetnab I sold to a major in the artillery, whose camp we passed through. I regretted that, for she had become a habit, but she was peevish on the journey and too tired and mopish at night to be much fun. Still, I can't recall a wench I enjoyed more.

We pushed on faster after that, west and then north-west, over the plains and great rivers of the Punjab, through the Sikh country, and up to Peshawar, which is where India ends. There was nothing to remind you of Calcutta now; here the heat was dry and glaring, and so were the people—lean, ugly, Jewish-looking creatures, armed and ready for mischief by the look of them. But none was uglier or looked readier for mischief than the governor of the place, a great, grey-bearded ox of a man in a dirty old uniform coat, baggy trousers, and gold-tasselled forage cap. He was an Italian, of all things, with the spiky waxed moustache that you see on organ-grinders nowadays, and he spoke English with a dreadful dago American accent. His name was Avitabile,[11] and the Sikhs and Afghans were more scared of him than of the devil himself; he had drifted to India as a soldier of fortune, commanded

Shah Sujah's army, and now had the job of keeping the passes open to our people in Kabul.

He did it admirably, in the only way those brutes understood —by fear and force. There were five dead Afghans swinging in the sunlight from his gateway arch when we rode through, which was both reassuring and unnerving at once. No one minded them more than if they had been swatted flies, least of all Avitabile, who had strung them up.

"Goddam, boy," says he, "how you think I keep the peace if I don' keep killing these bastards? These are Gilzais, you know that? Good Gilzais, now I've 'tended to them. The bad Gilzais are up in the hills, between here and Kabul, watchin' the passes and lickin' their lips and thinkin'—but thinkin's all they do just now, 'cos of Avitabile. Sure, we pay 'em to be quiet; you think that would stop them? No, sir, fear of Avitabile"—and he jerked a huge thumb at his chest—"fear's what stops 'em. But if I stopped hangin' 'em now and then, they'd stop bein' afraid. See?"

He had me to dinner that night, and we ate an excellent stew of chicken and fruit on a terrace looking over the dirty rooftops of Peshawar, with the sounds and smells of the bazaar floating up to us. Avitabile was a good host, and talked all night of Naples and women and drink; he seemed to take a fancy to me, and we got very drunk together. He was one of your noisy, bellowing drunkards, and we sang uproariously, I remember, but at dawn, as we were staggering to our beds, he stopped outside my room, with his great dirty hand on my shoulder, and looked at me with his bright grey eyes, and said in a very sober, quiet voice:

"Boy, I think you are another like me, at heart: a condottieri, a rascal. Maybe with a little honour, a little courage. I don't know. But, see now, you are going beyond the Khyber, and some day soon the Gilzais and others will be afraid no longer. Against that day, get a swift horse and some Afghans you can trust— there are some, like the Kuzzilbashis—and if the day comes, don't wait to die on the field of honour." He said it without a sneer. "Heroes draw no higher wages than the others, boy. Sleep well."

And he nodded and stumped off down the passage, with his gold cap still firmly on his head. In my drunken state I took little heed of what he had said, but it came back to me later.

In the morning we rode north into one of the world's awful

places—the great pass of the Khyber, where the track twists among the sun-scorched cliffs and the peaks seem to crouch in ambush for the traveller. There was some traffic on the road, and we passed a commissary train on its way to Kabul, but most of those we saw were Afghan hillmen, rangy warriors in skull caps or turbans and long coats, with immensely long rifles, called jezzails, at their shoulders, and the Khyber knife (which is like a pointed cleaver) in their belts. Muhammed Iqbal was gay at returning to his own place, and had me airing my halting Pushtu on those we spoke to; they seemed taken aback to find an English officer who had their own tongue, however crudely, and were friendly enough. But I didn't like the look of them; you could see treachery in their dark eyes—besides, there is something odd about men who look like Satan and yet wear ringlets and love-locks hanging out beneath their turbans.

We were three nights on the road beyond the Khyber, and the country got more hellish all the way—it beat me how a British army, with all its thousands of followers and carts and wagons and guns had ever got over those flinty paths. But at last we came to Kabul, and I saw the great fortress of Bala Hissar lowering over the city, and beyond it to the right the neat lines of the cantonment beside the water's edge, where the red tunics showed like tiny dolls in the distance and the sound of a bugle came faintly over the river. It was very pretty in the summer's evening, with the orchards and gardens before us, and the squalor of Kabul Town hidden behind the Bala Hissar. Aye, it was pretty then.

We crossed the Kabul River bridge and when I had reported myself and bathed and changed into my regimentals I was directed to the general commanding, to whom I was to deliver despatches from Elphy Bey. His name was Sir Willoughby Cotton, and he looked it, for he was round and fat and red-faced. When I found him he was being hectored by a tall, fine-looking officer in faded uniform, and I at once learned two things—in the Kabul garrison there was no sense of privacy or restraint, and the most senior officers never thought twice about discussing their affairs before their juniors.

"... the biggest damned fool this side of the Indus," the tall officer was saying when I presented myself. "I tell you, Cotton,

72

this army is like a bear in a trap. If there's a rising, where are you? Stuck helpless in the middle of a people who hate your innards, a week from the nearest friendly garrison, with a bloody fool like McNaghten writing letters to that even bloodier fool Auckland in Calcutta that everything's all right. God help us! And they're relieving you—"

"God be thanked," said Cotton.

"—and sending us Elphy Bey, who'll be under McNaghten's thumb and isn't fit to command an escort anyway. The worst of it is, McNaghten and the other political asses think we are safe as on Salisbury Plain! Burnes is as bad as the rest—not that he thinks of anything but Afghan women—but they're all so sure they're right! That's what upsets me. And who the devil are you?"

This was to me. I bowed and presented my letters to Cotton, who seemed glad of the interruption.

"Glad to see you, sir," says he, dropping the letters on the desk. "Elphy's herald, eh? Well, well. Flashman, did you say? Now that's odd. There was a Flashman with me at Rugby, oh, forty years ago. Any relation?"

"My father, sir."

"Ye don't say? Well, I'm damned. Flashy's boy." And he beamed all over his red face. "Why, it *must* be forty years.... He's well I trust? Excellent, excellent. What'll you have, sir? Glass of wine? Here, bearer. Of course, your father will have spoke of me, eh? I was quite a card at school. Got expelled, d'ye know."

This was too good a chance to miss, so I said: "I was expelled from Rugby, too, sir."

"Good God! You don't say! What for, sir?"

"Drunkenness, sir."

"No! Well, damme! Who'd have believed they would kick you out for that? They'll be expellin' for rape next. Wouldn't have done in my time. I was expelled for mutiny, sir—yes, mutiny! Led the whole school in revolt![12] Splendid! Well, here's your health, sir!"

The officer in the faded coat, who had been looking pretty sour, remarked that expulsion from school was all very well, but what concerned him was expulsion from Afghanistan.

"Pardon me," said Cotton, wiping his lips. "Forgot my manners. Mr Flashman, General Nott. General Nott is up from

Kandahar, where he commands. We were discussing the state of the army in Afghanistan. No, no, Flashman, sit down. This ain't Calcutta. On active service the more you know the better. Pray proceed, Nott."

So I sat, a little bewildered and flattered, for generals don't usually talk before subalterns, while Nott resumed his tirade. It seemed that he had been offended by some communication from McNaghten—Sir William McNaghten, Envoy to Kabul, and head British civilian in the country. Nott was appealing to Cotton to support him in protest, but Cotton didn't seem to care for the idea.

"It is a simple question of policy," said Nott. "The country, whatever McNaghten may think, is hostile, and we have to treat it as such. We do this in three ways—through the influence which Sujah exerts on his unwilling subjects, which is little enough; through the force of our army here, which with respect is not as all-powerful as McNaghten imagines, since you're outnumbered fifty to one by one of the fiercest warrior nations in the world; and thirdly, by buying the good will of important chiefs with money. Am I right?"

"Talking like a book," said Cotton. "Fill your glass, Mr Flashman."

"If one of those three instruments of policy fails—Sujah, our strength, or our money—we're done for. Oh, I know I'm a 'croaker', as McNaghten would say; he thinks we are as secure here as on Horse Guards. He's wrong, you know. We exist on sufferance, and there won't be much of that if he takes up this idea of cutting the subsidy to the Gilzai chiefs."

"It would save money," said Cotton. "Anyway, it's no more than a thought, as I understand."

"It would save money if you didn't buy a bandage when you were bleeding to death," said Nott, at which Cotton guffawed. "Aye, laugh, Sir Willoughby, but this is a serious matter. Cutting the subsidy is no more than a thought, you say. Very good, it may never happen. But if the Gilzais so much as suspect it *might*, how long will they continue to keep the passes open? They sit above the Khyber—your lifeline, remember—and let our convoys come and go, but if they think their subsidy is in danger they'll look for another source of revenue. And that will mean convoys ambushed and looted, and a very pretty business on your hands. That is why McNaghten's a fool even to *think* of cutting the subsidy, let alone *talk* about it."

"What do you want me to do?" says Cotton, frowning.

"Tell him to drop the notion at all costs. He won't listen to me. And send someone to talk to the Gilzais, take a few gifts to old what's-his-name at Mogala—Sher Afzul. He has the other Gilzai khans under his thumb, I'm told."

"You know a lot about this country," said Cotton, wagging his head. "Considering this ain't your territory."

"Someone's got to," said Nott. "Thirty years in the Company's service teaches you a thing or two. I wish I thought McNaghten had learned as much. But he goes his way happily, seeing no farther than the end of his nose. Well, well, Cotton, you're one of the lucky ones. You'll be getting out in time."

Cotton protested at this that he was a 'croaker' after all—I soon discovered that the word was applied to everyone who ventured to criticise McNaghten or express doubts about the safety of the British force in Kabul. They talked on for a while, and Cotton was very civil to me and seemed intent on making me feel at home. We dined in his headquarters, with his staff, and there for the first time I met some of the men, many of them fairly junior officers, whose names were to be household words in England within the next year—"Sekundar" Burnes, with his mincing Scotch voice and pretty little moustache; George Broadfoot, another Scotsman, who sat next to me; Vincent Eyre, "Gentleman Jim" Skinner, Colonel Oliver, and various others. They talked with a freedom that was astonishing, criticising or defending their superiors in the presence of general officers, condemning this policy and praising that, and Cotton and Nott joined in. There was not much good said about McNaghten, and a general gloom about the army's situation; it seemed to me they scared rather easily, and I told Broadfoot so.

"Wait till ye've been here a month or two, and ye'll be as bad as the rest," he said brusquely. "It's a bad place, and a bad people, and if we don't have war on our hands inside a year I'll be surprised. Have you heard of Akbar Khan? No? He's the son of the old king, Dost Mohammed, that we deposed for this clown Sujah, and he's in the hills now, going from this chief to that, gathering support for the day when he'll raise the country against us. McNaghten won't believe it, of course, but he's a gommeril."

"Could we not hold Kabul?" I asked. "Surely with a force of five thousand it should be possible, against undisciplined savages."

"These savages are good men," says he. "Better shots than we are, for one thing. And we're badly placed here, with no proper fortifications for the cantonment—even the stores are outside the perimeter—and an army that's going downhill with soft living and bad discipline. Forbye, we have our families with us, and that's a bad thing when the bullets are flying—who thinks of his duty when he has his wife and weans to care for? And Elphy Bey is to command us when Cotton goes." He shook his head. "You'll know him better than I, but I'd give my next year's pay to hear he wasn't coming and we had Nott instead. I'd sleep at nights, anyway."

This was depressing enough, but in the next few weeks I heard this kind of talk on all hands—there was obviously no confidence in the military or political chiefs, and the Afghans seemed to sense this, for they were an insolent crowd and had no great respect for us. As an aide to Elphy Bey, who was still on his road north, I had time on my hands to look about Kabul, which was a great, filthy sprawling place full of narrow lanes and smelling abominably. But we seldom went there, for the folk hardly made us welcome, and it was pleasant out by the cantonment, where there was little attention to soldiering but a great deal of horse-racing and lounging in the orchards and gossiping on the verandahs over cool drinks. There were even cricket matches, and I played myself—I had been a great bowler at Rugby, and my new friends made more of the wickets I took than of the fact that I was beginning to speak Pushtu better than any of them except Burnes and the politicals.

It was at one of these matches that I first saw Shah Sujah, the king, who had come down as the guest of McNaghten. He was a portly, brown-bearded man who stood gravely contemplating the game, and when McNaghten asked him how he liked it, said:

"Strange and manifold are the ways of God."

As for McNaghten himself, I despised him on sight. He had a clerk's face, with a pointed nose and chin, and peered through his spectacles suspiciously, sniffing at you. He was vain as a pea-cock, though, and would strut about in his tall hat and frock-coat, lording it greatly, with his nose turned up. It was evident, as someone said, that he saw only what he wanted to see. Anyone else would have realised that his army was in a mess, for one thing, but not McNaghten. He even seemed to think that Sujah was popular with the people, and that we were honoured guests in the country; if he had heard the men in the bazaar calling us "kaffirs" he might have realised his mistake. But he was too lofty to hear.

However, I passed the time pleasantly enough. Burnes, the political agent, when he heard about my Pushtu, took some interest in me, and as he kept a splendid table, and was an influ-ential fellow, I kept in with him. He was a pompous fool, of course, but he knew a good deal about the Afghans, and would go about from time to time in native dress, mixing with the crowds in the bazaar, listening to gossip and keeping his nose to the wind generally. He had another reason for this, of course, which was that he was forever in pursuit of some Afghan woman or other, and had to go to the city to find them. I went with him on these expeditions frequently, and very rewarding they were.

Afghan women are handsome rather than pretty, but they have this great advantage to them, that their own men don't care for them overmuch. Afghan men would as soon be perverts as not, and have a great taste for young boys; it would sicken you to see them mooning over these painted youths as though they were girls, and our troops thought it a tremendous joke. However, it meant that the Afghan women were always hungry for men, and you could have your pick of them—tall, graceful creatures they were, with long straight noses and proud mouths, running more to muscle than fat, and very active in bed.

Of course, the Afghans didn't care for this, which was another score against us where they were concerned.

The first weeks passed, as I say, pleasantly, and I was begin-ning to like Kabul, in spite of the pessimists, when I was shaken out of my pleasant rut, thanks to my friend Burnes and the anxieties of General Nott, who had gone back to Kandahar but left his warnings ringing in Sir Willoughby Cotton's ears. They must have rung an alarm, for when he sent for me to his office in the cantonment he was looking pretty glum, with Burnes at his elbow.

"Flashman," says Cotton, "Sir Alexander here tells me you get along famously with the Afghans."

Thinking of the women, I agreed.

"Hm, well. And you talk their frightful lingo?"

"Passably well, sir."

"That means a dam' sight better than most of us. Well, I daresay I shouldn't do it, but on Sir Alexander's suggestion"—here Burnes gave me a smile, which I felt somehow boded no good—"and since you're the son of an old friend, I'm going to give you some work to do—work which'll help your advancement, let me say, if you do it well, d'you see?" He stared at me a moment, and growled to Burnes: "Dammit, Sandy, he's devilish young, y'know."

"No younger than I was," says Burnes.

"Umph. Oh, well, I suppose it's all right. Now, look here, Flashman—you know about the Gilzais, I suppose? They control the passes between here and India, and are devilish tricky fellows. You were with me when Nott was talking about their subsidy, and how there were rumours that the politicals would cut it, dam' fools, with all respect, Sandy. Well, it will be cut—in time—but for the present it's imperative they should be told that all's well, d'you see? Sir William McNaghten has agreed to this—fact is, he's written letters to Sher Afzul, at Mogala, and he's the leader of the pack, so to speak."

This seemed to me a pretty piece of duplicity on McNaghten's part, but it was typical of our dealings with the Afghans, as I was to discover.

"You're going to be our postman, like Mr Rowland Hill's fellows at home. You'll take the messages of good will to Sher Afzul, hand 'em over, say how splendid everything is, be polite to the old devil—he's half-mad, by the way—set his mind at rest if he's still worried about the subsidy, and so forth."

"It will all be in the letters," says Burnes. "You must just give any added reassurance that may be needed."

"All right, Flashman?" says Cotton. "Good experience for you. Diplomatic mission, what?"

"It's very important," says Burnes. "You see, if they thought there was anything wrong, or grew suspicious, it could be bad for us."

It could be a damned sight worse for me, I thought. I didn't like this idea above half—all I knew of the Gilzais was that they were murderous brutes, like all country Afghans, and the thought of walking into their nests, up in the hills, with not the slightest hope of help if there was trouble—well, Kabul might not be Hyde Park, but at least it was safe for the present. And what the Afghan women did to prisoners was enough to start my stomach turning at the thought—I'd heard the stories.

Some of this must have showed in my face, for Cotton asked fairly sharply what was the matter. Didn't I want to go?

"Of course, sir," I lied. "But—well, I'm pretty raw, I know. A more experienced officer. . . ."

"Don't fret yourself," says Burnes, smiling. "You're more at home with these folk than some men with twenty years in the service." He winked. "I've seen you, Flashman, remember. Hah-ha! And you've got what they call 'a fool's face.' No disrespect: it means you look honest. Besides, the fact that you have some Pushtu will win their confidence."

"But as General Elphinstone's aide, should I not be here. . . ."

"Elphy ain't due for a week," snapped Cotton. "Dammit, man, this is an opportunity. Any young feller in your shoes would be bursting to go."

I saw it would be bad to try to make further excuses, so I said I was all eagerness, of course, and had only wanted to be sure I was the right man, and so forth. That settled it: Burnes took me to the great wall map, and showed me where Mogala was—needless to say, it was at the back of nowhere, about fifty miles from Kabul, in hellish hill country south of the Jugdulluk Pass. He pointed out the road we should take, assuring me I should have a good guide, and produced the sealed packet I was to deliver to the half-mad (and doubtless half-human) Sher Afzul.

"Make sure they go into his own hands," he told me. "He's a good friend to us—just now—but I don't trust his nephew, Gul Shah. He was too thick with Akbar Khan in the old days. If there's ever trouble among the Gilzais, it will come from Gul, so watch out for him. And I don't have to tell you to be careful of old Azful—he's sharp when he's sane, which he is most of the time. He's lord of life and death in his own parish, and that includes you. Not that he's likely to offer you harm, but keep on his good side."

I began to wonder if I could manage to fall ill in the next hour or two—jaundice, possibly, or something infectious. Cotton set the final seal on it.

"If there's trouble," says he, "you must just ride for it."

To this fatherly advice he and Burnes added a few words about how I should conduct myself if the matter of subsidy was discussed with me, bidding me be reassuring at all costs—no thought of who should reassure me, I may say—and dismissed me. Burnes said they had high hopes of me, a sentiment I found it difficult to share.

However, there was nothing for it, and next morning found me on the road east, with Iqbal and an Afghan guide on either side and five troopers of the 16th Lancers for escort. It was a tiny enough guard to be useless against anything but a stray robber —and Afghanistan never lacked for those—but it gave me some heart, and what with the fresh morning air, and the thought that all would probably be well and the mission another small stepping stone in the career of Lieutenant Flashman, I felt rather more cheerful.

The sergeant in charge of the Lancers was called Hudson, and he had already shown himself a steady and capable man. Before setting out he had suggested I leave behind my sabre—they were poor weapons, the Army swords, and turned in your grip[18]—and take instead one of the Persian scimitars that some of the Afghans used. They were light and strong, and damned sharp. He had been very business-like about it, and about such matters as rations for the men and fodder for the horses. He was one of those quiet, middle-sized, square-set men who seem to know exactly what they are doing, and it was good to have him and Iqbal at my back.

Our first day's march took us as far as Khoord-Kabul, and on the second we left the track at Tezeen and went south-east into the hills. The going had been rough enough on the path, but now it was frightful—the land was all sun-scorched rock and jagged peaks, with stony defiles that were like ovens, where the ponies stumbled over the loose stones. We hardly saw a living creature for twenty miles after we left Tezeen, and when night came we were camped on a high pass, in the lee of a cliff that might have been the wall of hell. It was bitter cold, and the wind howled up the pass; far away a wolf wailed, and we had barely enough wood to keep our fire going. I lay in my blanket cursing the day I got drunk at Rugby, and wishing I were snug in a warm bed with Elspeth or Fetnab or Josette.

Next day we were picking our way up a long stony slope when Iqbal muttered and pointed, and far ahead on a rocky shoulder I made out a figure which vanished almost as soon as I saw it.

"Gilzai scout," said Iqbal, and in the next hour we saw a dozen more of them; as we rode upwards we were aware of them in the hills on either side, behind boulders or on the ledges, and in the last few miles there were horsemen shadowing us on either side and behind. Then we came out of a defile, and the guide pointed ahead to a height crowned with a great grey fortress, with a round tower behind its outer wall, and a cluster of huts outside its embattled gate. This was Mogala, stronghold of the Gilzai chieftain, Sher Afzul. I seldom saw a place I liked less at first sight.

We went forward at a canter, and the horsemen who had been following us galloped into the open on either side, keeping pace to the fort, but not approaching too close to us. They rode Afghan ponies, carried long jezzails and lances, and were a tough-looking crowd; some wore mail over their robes, and a few had spiked helmets; they looked like warriors from an Eastern fairy tale, with their outlandish clothes and fierce bearded faces—and of course, they were.

Close by the gate was a row of four wooden crosses, and to my horror I realised that the blackened, twisted things nailed to them were human bodies. Sher Afzul obviously had his own notions of discipline. One or two of the troopers muttered at the sight, and there were anxious glances at our shadowers, who had lined up on either side of the gateway. I was feeling a trifle wobbly myself, but I thought, to hell with these blackamoors, we are Englishmen, and so I said, "Come on, lads, ride to attention," and we clattered under the frowning gateway.

I suppose Mogala is about a quarter of a mile from wall to wall, but inside its battlements, in addition to its huge keep, there were barracks and stables for Sher Afzul's warriors, storehouses and armouries, and the house of the Khan himself. In fact, it was more of a little palace than a house, for it stood in a pretty garden under the shadow of the outer wall, shaded by cypress trees, and it was furnished inside like something from Burton's

Arabian Nights. There were tapestries on the walls, carpets on the paved floor, intricately carved wood screens in the archways, and a general air of luxury—he did himself well, I thought, but he took no chances. There were sentries all over the place, big men and well armed.

Sher Afzul turned out to be a man about sixty, with a beard dyed jet black, and a lined, ugly face whose main features were two fierce, burning eyes that looked straight through you. He received me civilly enough in his fine presence chamber, where he sat on a small throne with his court about him, but I couldn't doubt Burnes's assertion that he was half-mad. His hands twitched continuously, and he had a habit of jerking his turbanned head in a most violent fashion as he spoke. But he listened attentively as one of his ministers read aloud McNaghten's letter, and seemed satisfied, and he and his people exclaimed with delight over the present that Cotton had sent—a pair of very handsome pistols by Manton, in a velvet case, with a matching shot pouch and powder flask. Nothing would do but we must go straight into the garden for the Khan to try them out; he was a rotten shot, but at the fourth attempt he managed to blow the head off a very handsome parrot which sat chained on a perch, screeching at the explosions until the lucky shot put an end to it.

There was loud applause, and Sher Afzul wagged his head and seemed well pleased.

"A splendid gift," he told me, and I was pleased to find that my Pushtu was quite good enough for me to follow him. "You are the more welcome, Flashman bahadur, in that your guns are true. By God, it is a soldier's weapon!"

I said I was delighted, and had the happy idea of presenting one of my own pistols on the spot to the Khan's son, a bright, handsome lad of about sixteen, called Ilderim. He shouted with delight, and his eyes shone as he handled the weapon—I was off to a good start.

Then one of the courtiers came forward, and I felt a prickle up my spine as I looked at him. He was a tall man—as tall as I was— with those big shoulders and the slim waist of an athlete. His coat was black and well fitting, he wore long boots, and there was a silk sash round his waist to carry his sabre. On his head he had one of those polished steel casques with vertical prongs, and the face under it was strikingly handsome in the rather pretty Eastern way which I personally don't like. You have seen them—straight nose, very full lips, woman's cheeks and jaw. He had a forked beard and two of the coldest eyes I ever saw. I put him down as a nasty customer, and I was right.

"I can kill parrots with a sling," he said. "Are the feringhee pistols good for anything else?"

Sher Afzul damned his eyes, more or less, for casting doubt on his fine new weapons, and thrusting one into the fellow's hand, told him to try his luck. And to my amazement, the brute turned straight about, drew a bead on one of the slaves working in the garden, and shot him on the spot.

I was shaken, I can tell you. I stared at the twitching body on the grass, and the Khan wagging his head, and at the murderer handing back the pistol with a shrug. Of course, it was only a nigger he had killed, and I knew that among Afghans life is dirt cheap; they think no more of killing a human being than you and I do of shooting a pheasant or catching a fish. But it's a trifle unsettling to a man of my temperament to know that he is in the power—for, guest or no, I was in their power—of blackguards who kill as wantonly and readily as that. That thought, more than the killing itself, rattled me.

Young Ilderim noticed this, and rebuked the black-coated man —not for murder, mark you, but for discourtesy to a guest!

"One does not bite the coin of the honoured stranger, Gul Shah," was what he said, meaning you don't look a gift horse in the mouth. For the moment I was too fascinated at what I had seen to pay much heed, but as the Khan, talking rapidly, escorted me inside again, I remembered that this Gul Shah was the customer Burnes had warned me about—the friend of the archrebel, Akbar Khan. I kept an eye on him as I talked with Sher Afzul, and it seemed to me he kept an eye on me in return.

Sher Afzul talked sanely enough, mostly about hunting and blood-letting of a sterner kind, but you couldn't miss the wild gleam in his eye, or the fact that his evil temper was never far from the surface. He was used to playing the tyrant, and only to young Ilderim, whom he adored, was he more than civil. He snarled at Gul from time to time, but the big man looked him in the eye and didn't seem put out.

That evening we dined in the Khan's presence chamber, sitting about on cushions forking with our fingers into the bowls of stew and rice and fruit, and drinking a pleasant Afghan liquor which had no great body to it. There would be about a dozen there, including Gul Shah, and after we had eaten and belched accordingly, Sher Afzul called for entertainment. This consisted of a good conjurer, and a few weedy youths with native flutes and tom-toms, and three or four dancing girls. I had pretended to be amused by the conjurer and musicians, but one of the dancing girls struck me as being worth more than a polite look: she was a glorious creature, very tall and long-legged, with a sulky, cold face and hair that had been dyed bright red and hung down in a tail to her backside. It was about all the covering she had; for the rest she wore satin trousers clasped low on her hips, and two brass breastplates which she removed at Sher Afzul's insistence.

He beckoned her to dance close in front of him, and the sight of the golden, near-naked body writhing and quivering made me forget where I was for the moment. By the time she had finished her dance, with the tom-toms throbbing and the sweat glistening on her painted face, I must have been eating her alive with my eyes; as she salaamed to Sher Afzul he suddenly grabbed her by the arm and pulled her towards him, and I noticed Gul Shah lean forward suddenly on his cushion.

Sher Afzul saw it too, for he looked one way and the other, grinning wickedly, and with his free hand began to fondle the girl's body. She took it with a face like stone, but Gul was glowering like thunder. Sher Afzul cackled and said to me:

"You like her, Flashman bahadur? Is she the kind of she-cat you delight to scratch with? Here, then, she is yours!"

And he shoved her so hard towards me that she fell headlong into my lap. I caught her, and with an oath Gul Shah was on his feet, his hand dropping to his hilt.

"She is not for any Frank dog," he shouted.

"By God, is she not?" roared Sher Afzul. "Who says so?"

Gul Shah told him who said so, and there was a pretty little exchange which ended with Sher Afzul ordering him from the room—and it seemed to me that the girl's eyes followed him with disappointment as he stamped off. Sher Afzul apologised for the disturbance, and said I must not mind Gul Shah, who was an impudent bastard, and very greedy where women were concerned. Did I like the girl? Her name was Narreeman, and if she did not please me I was not to hesitate to flog her to my heart's content.

All this, I saw, was deliberately aimed at Gul Shah, who presumably lusted after this female himself, thus giving Sher Afzul a chance to torment him. It was a dilemma for me: I had no desire to antagonise Gul Shah, but I could not afford to refuse Sher Afzul's hospitality, so to speak—also the hospitality was very warm and naked, and was lying across my lap, gasping still from the exertion of her dance, and causing me considerable excitement.

So I accepted at once, and waited impatiently while the time wore on with Sher Afzul talking interminably about his horses and his dogs and his falcons. At last it was over, and with Narreeman following I was conducted to the private room that had been allotted me—it was a beautiful, balmy evening with the scents wafting in from the garden, and I was looking forward to a sleepless night. As it turned out, it was a tremendous sell, for she simply lay like a side of beef, staring at the roof as though I weren't there. I coaxed at first, and then threatened, and then taking Sher Afzul's advice I pulled her across my knees and smartened her up with my riding switch. At this she suddenly rounded on me like a panther, snarling and clawing, and narrowly missed raking my eyes. I was so enraged that I laid into her for all I was worth, but she fought like fury, naked as she was, and only when I got home a few good cuts did she try to run for it. I hauled her away from the door, and after a vicious struggle I managed to rape her—the only time in my life I have found it necessary, by the way. It has its points, but I shouldn't care to do it regularly. I prefer willing women.

Afterwards I shoved her out—I'd no wish to get a thumbnail in my eye during the night—and the guards took her away. She had not uttered a word the whole time.

Sher Afzul, seeing my scratched face in the morning, demanded details, and he and his toadies crowed with delight when I told them. Gul Shah was not present, but I had no doubt willing tongues would bear the tale to him.

Not that I cared, and there I made a mistake. Gul was only a nephew of Sher Afzul, and a bastard at that, but he was a power among the Gilzais for his fighting skill, and was itching to topple old Sher Afzul and steal his throne. It would have been a poor look-out for the Kabul garrison if he had succeeded, for the Gilzais were trembling in the balance all the time about us, and Gul would have tipped the scale. He hated the British, and in Afzul's place would have closed the passes, even if it had meant losing the lakhs that were paid from India to keep them open. But Afzul, although ageing, was too tough and clever to be deposed just yet, and Ilderim, though only a boy, was well liked and regarded as certain to succeed him. And both of them were friendly, and could sway the other Gilzai chieftains.

A good deal of this I learned in the next two days, in which I and my party were the honoured guests of Mogala. I kept my eyes and ears open, and the Gilzais were most hospitable, from Afzul down to the villagers whose huts crouched outside the wall. This I will say for the Afghan—he is a treacherous, evil brute when he wants to be, but while he is your friend he is a first-rate fellow. The point is, you must judge to a second when he is going to cease to be friendly. There is seldom any warning.

Looking back, though, I can say that I probably got on better with the Afghans than most Britons do. I imagine Thomas Hughes would have said that in many respects of character I resembled them, and I wouldn't deny it. However it may be, I enjoyed those first two days: we had horse races and other riding competitions, and I earned a good deal of credit by showing them how a Persian pony can be put over the jumps. Then there was hawking, in which Sher Afzul was an adept, and tremendous feasting at nights, and Sher Afzul gave me another dancing girl, with much cackling and advice on how to manage her, which advice proved to be unnecessary.

But while it was pleasant enough, you could never forget that in Afghanistan you are walking a knife-edge the whole time, and that these were cruel and blood-thirsty savages. Four men were executed on the second day, for armed robbery, in front of a delighted crowd in the courtyard, and a fifth, a petty chieftain, was blinded by Sher Afzul's physician. This is a common punishment among the Afghans: if a man is too important to be slaughtered like an ordinary felon, they take away his sight so that he can do no more harm. It was a sickening business, and one of my troopers got into a fight with a Gilzai over it, calling them filthy foreigners, which they could not understand. "A blind man is a dead man," was how they put it, and I had to make excuses to Sher Afzul and instruct Sergeant Hudson to give the trooper a punishment drill.

In all this I had nearly forgotten Gul Shah and the Narreeman affair, which was careless. I had my reminder on the third morning, when I was least expecting it.

Sher Afzul had said we must go boar-hunting, and we had a good hour's sport in the thicketed gullies of the Mogala valley, where the wild pigs bred. There were about twenty of us, including Hudson, Muhammed Iqbal and myself, with Sher Afzul directing operations. It was exciting work, but difficult in that close country, and we were frequently separated. Muhammed Iqbal and I made one sortie which took us well away from the main body, into a narrow defile where the forest ended, and there they were waiting for us—four horsemen, with spears couched, who made not a sound but thundered straight down on us. Instinctively I knew they were Gul's people, bent on murdering me—and no doubt compromising Sher Afzul with the British at the same time.

Iqbal, being a Pathan and loving a fight, gave a yell of delight, "Come on, huzoor!" and went for them. I didn't hesitate; if he wanted to take on odds it was his affair; I wheeled my pony and went hell-for-leather for the forest, with one eye cocked over my shoulder for safety.

Whether he realised I was leaving him alone, I don't know; it wouldn't have made any difference to him. Like me, he had a lance, but in addition he had a sword and pistol in his belt, so he got rid of the lance at once, hurling it into the chest of the leading Gilzai, and driving into the other three with his sabre swinging. He cut one down, but the other two swerved past him—it was me they wanted.

I dug my spurs in as they came tearing after me, with Iqbal wheeling after them in turn. He was bawling at me to turn and fight, the fool, but I had no thought but to get away from those hellish lance-points and the wolf-like bearded faces behind them. I rode like fury—and then the pony stumbled and I went over his head, crashing into the bushes and finishing up on a pile of stones with all the breath knocked out of me.

The bushes saved me, for the Gilzais couldn't come at me easily. They had to swerve round the clump, and I scrambled behind a tree. One of the ponies reared up and nearly knocked the other off balance; the rider yelled and had to drop his lance to save being thrown, and then Iqbal was on them, howling his war-cry. The Gilzai who was clutching his pony's mane was glaring at me and cursing, and suddenly the snarling face was literally split down the middle as Iqbal's sabre came whistling down on his head, shearing through cap and skull as if they had been putty. The other rider, who had been trying to get in a thrust at me round the tree-trunk, wheeled as Iqbal wrenched his sword free, and the pair of them closed as their ponies crashed into each other.

For one cursing, frantic moment they were locked together, Iqbal trying to get his point into the other's side, and the Gilzai with his dagger out, thrusting at Iqbal's body. I heard the thuds as the blows struck, and Iqbal shouting: "Huzoor! huzoor!" and then the ponies parted and the struggling men crashed into the dust.

From behind my tree I suddenly noticed that my lance was lying within a yard of me, where it had dropped in my fall. Why I didn't follow the instinct of a lifetime and simply run for it and leave them to fight it out, I don't know—probably I had some thought of possible disgrace. Anyway, I darted out and grabbed the lance, and as the Gilzai struggled uppermost and raised his bloody knife, I jammed the lance-point squarely into his back. He screamed and dropped the knife, and then lurched into the dust, kicking and clutching, and died.

Iqbal tried to struggle up, but he was done for. His face was grey, and there was a great crimson stain welling through his shirt. He was glaring at me, and as I ran to him he managed to rear up on one elbow.

"Soor kabaj," he gasped. "Ya, huzoor! Soor kabaj!"

Then he groaned and fell back, but as I knelt over him his eyes opened for a moment, and he gave a little moan and spat in my face, as best he could. So he died, calling me "son of a swine" in Hindi, which is the Muslim's crowning insult. I saw his point of view, of course.

So there I was, and there also were five dead men—at least, four were dead and the one whom Iqbal had sabred first was lying a little way up the defile, groaning with the side of his skull split. I was shaken by my fall and the scuffle, but it came to me swiftly that the quicker that one breathed his last, the better, so I hurried up with my lance, took a rather unsteady aim, and drove it into his throat. And I had just jerked it out, and was surveying the shambles, when there was a cry and a clatter of hooves, and Sergeant Hudson came galloping out of the wood.

He took it in at a glance—the corpses, the blood-stained ground, and the gallant Flashy standing in the middle, the sole survivor. But like the competent soldier he was, as soon as he realised that I was all right, he went round the bodies, to make sure no one was playing possum. He whistled sadly over Iqbal, and then said quietly: "Orders, sir?"

I was getting my wind and my senses back, and wondering what to do next. This was Gul's work, I was sure, but what would Sher Afzul do about it? He might argue that here was his credit destroyed with the British anyway, and make the best of a bad job by cutting all our throats. This was a happy thought, but before I had time to digest it there was a crashing and hallooing in the woods, and out came the rest of the hunting party, with Afzul at their head.

Perhaps my fear sharpened my wits—it often does. But I saw in a flash that the best course was to take a damned high hand. So before they had done more than shout their astonishment and call on the name of God and come piling off their ponies, I had strode forward to where Afzul was sitting his horse, and I shook the bloody lance point under his nose.

"Gilzai hospitality!" I roared. "Look on it! My servant murdered, myself escaped by a miracle! Is this Gilzai honour?"

He glared at me like someone demented, his mouth working horribly, and for a minute I thought we were done for. Then he covered his face with his hands, and began bawling about shame and disgrace and the guests who had eaten his salt. He was mad enough at the moment, I think, and probably a good thing too, for he kept wailing on in the same strain, and tearing at his beard, and finally he rolled out of the saddle and began beating at the ground. His creatures hurried round him, lamenting and calling on Allah—all except young Ilderim, who simply gazed at the carnage and said:

"This is Gul Shah's doing, my father!"

This brought old Afzul up short, and he set off on a new tack, raving about how he would tear out Gul's eyes and entrails and hang him on hooks to die by inches, and more excellent ideas. I turned my back on him, and mounted the pony which Hudson had brought, and at this Afzul came hurrying up to me, and grabbed my boot, and swore, with froth on his lips, that this assault on my person and his honour would be most horribly avenged.

"My person is my affair," says I, very British-officer-like, "and your honour is yours. I accept your apology."

He raved some more at this, and then began imploring me to tell him what he could do to put things right. He was in a rare taking for his honour—and no doubt his subsidy—and swore that anything I named should be done: only let him and his be forgiven.

"My life! My son's life! Tribute, treasure, Flashman bahadur! Hostages! I will go to McNaghten huzoor, and humble myself! I will pay!"

He went babbling on, until I cut him short by saying that we did not accept such things as payment for debts of honour. But I saw that I had better go a little easier while his mood lasted, so I ended by saying that, but for the death of my servant, it was a small matter, and we would put it from our minds.

"But you shall have pledges of my honour!" cries he. "Aye, you shall see that the Gilzai pay the debt! In God's name! My son, my son Ilderim, I will give as a hostage to you! Carry him to McNaghten huzoor, as a sign of his father's faith! Let me not be shamed, Flashman huzoor, in my old age!"

Now this business of hostages was a common one with the Afghans, and it seemed to me that it had great advantages in this case. With Ilderim in my keeping, it wasn't likely that this hysterical old lunatic, when his madness took a new turn, would try any mischief. And young Ilderim looked pleased enough at the idea; he was probably thinking of the excitement of going to Kabul, and seeing the great Queen's army, and riding with it, too, as my protégé.

So there and then I took Sher Afzul at his word, and swore that the dishonour would be wiped out, and Ilderim would ride with me until I released him. At this the old Khan grew maudlin, and hauled out his Khyber knife and made Ilderim swear on it that he would be my man, which he did, and there was general rejoicing, and Sher Afzul went round and kicked all the corpses of the Gilzais and called on God to damn them good and proper. After which we rode back to Mogala, and I resisted the old Khan's entreaties to stay longer in proof of friendship: I had orders, I said, and must go back to Kabul. It would not do, I added, for me to linger when I had so important a hostage as the son of the khan of Mogala to take back.

He took this most seriously, and swore that his son would go as befitted a prince (which was stretching it a bit), and gave him a dozen Gilzai riders as escort, to stay with him and me. So there was more oath-swearing, and Sher Afzul finished up in excellent humour, vowing it was an honour to the Gilzais to serve such a splendid warrior as Flashman huzoor, who had accounted for four enemies single-handed (Iqbal being conveniently forgotten), and who would forever be dear to the Gilzais for his courage and magnanimity. As proof of which he would send me Gul Shah's ears, nose, eyes, and other essential organs as soon as he could lay hold of them.

So we left Mogala, and I had collected a personal following of Afghan tribesmen, and a reputation, as a result of the morning's work. The twelve Gilzais and Ilderim were the best things I found in Afghanistan, and the nickname "Bloody Lance," which Sher Afzul conferred, did me no harm either. Incidentally, as a result of all this Sher Afzul was keener than ever to maintain his alliance with the British, so my mission was a success as well. I was pretty pleased with myself as we set off for Kabul.

Of course, I had not forgotten that I had also made an outstanding enemy in Gul Shah. How bitter an enemy I was to find out in time.

Any excitement that the affair at Mogala might have caused in Kabul when we got back and told our tale was overshadowed by the arrival on the same day of the new army commander, General Elphinstone, my chief and sponsor. I was piqued at the time, for I thought I had done pretty well, and was annoyed to find that no one thought my skirmish with the Gilzais and securing of hostages worth more than a cocked eyebrow and an "Oh, really?"

But looking back I can say that, all unwittingly, Kabul and the army were right to regard Elphy's arrival as an incident of the greatest significance. It opened a new chapter: it was a prelude to events that rang round the world. Elphy, ably assisted by Mc-Naghten, was about to reach the peak of his career; he was going to produce the most shameful, ridiculous disaster in British military history.

No doubt Thomas Hughes would find it significant that in such a disaster I would emerge with fame, honour, and distinction—all quite unworthily acquired. But you, having followed my progress so far, won't be surprised at all.

Let me say that when I talk of disasters I speak with authority. I have served at Balaclava, Cawnpore, and Little Big Horn. Name the biggest born fools who wore uniform in the nineteenth century—Cardigan, Sale, Custer, Raglan, Lucan—I knew them all. Think of all the conceivable misfortunes that can arise from combinations of folly, cowardice, and sheer bad luck, and I'll give you chapter and verse. But I still state unhesitatingly, that for pure, vacillating stupidity, for superb incompetence to command, for ignorance combined with bad judgement—in short, for the true talent for catastrophe—Elphy Bey stood alone. Others abide our question, but Elphy outshines them all as the greatest military idiot of our own or any other day.

Only he could have permitted the First Afghan War and let it develop to such a ruinous defeat. It was not easy: he started with a good army, a secure position, some excellent officers, a dis-organised enemy, and repeated opportunities to save the situa-tion. But Elphy, with the touch of true genius, swept aside these obstacles with unerring precision, and out of order wrought complete chaos. We shall not, with luck, look upon his like again.

However, I tell you this not as a preface to a history of the war, but because if you are to judge my career properly, and under-stand how the bully expelled from Rugby became a hero, you have to know how things were in that extraordinary year of 1841. The story of the war and its beginnings is the background of the picture, although dashing Harry Flashman is the main figure in the foreground.

Elphy came to Kabul, then, and was met with great junketings and packed streets. Sujah welcomed him at the Bala Hissar, the army in the cantonment two miles outside the city paraded for him, the ladies of the garrison made much of him, McNaghten breathed a sigh of relief at seeing Willoughby Cotton's back, and there was some satisfaction that we had got such a benevolent and popular commander. Only Burnes, it seemed to me on that first day, when I reported in to him, did not share the gaiety.

"I suppose it is right to rejoice," he told me, stroking in his conceited way at his little black moustache. "But, you know, Elphy's arrival changes nothing. Sujah is no firmer on his throne, and the defences of the cantonment are no better, simply because Elphy turns the light of his countenance on us. Oh, I daresay it will be all right, but it might have been better if Calcutta had sent us a stronger, brisker man."

I suppose I should have resented this patronising view of my chief a little, but when I saw Elphy Bey later in the day there was no doubt that Burnes was right. In the weeks since I had parted from him in Calcutta—and he had not been in the best of health then—he had gone downhill. There was this wasted, shaky look about him, and he preferred not to walk much; his hand trembled as he shook mine, and the feel of it was of a bundle of dry sticks in a bag. However, he was pleased to see me.

"You have been distinguishing yourself among the Gilzais, Flashman," he said. "Sir Alexander Burnes tells me you have won hostages of importance; that is excellent news, especially to our friend the Envoy," and he turned to McNaghten, who was sitting by drinking tea and holding his cup like an old maid.

McNaghten sniffed. "The Gilzais need not concern us very much, I think," says he. "They are great brigands, of course, but only brigands. I would rather have hostages for the good behaviour of Akbar Khan."

"Shall we send Mr Flashman to bring some?" says Elphy, smiling at me to show I shouldn't mind McNaghten's snub. "He seems to have gifts in that direction." And he went on to ask for details of my mission, and told me that I must bring young Ilderim Khan to meet him, and generally behaved very civilly to me.

But it was an effort to remember that this frail old gentleman, with his pleasant small talk, was the commander of the army. He was too polite and vague, even in those few minutes, and deferred too much to McNaughten, to inspire confidence as a military leader.

"How would he do, do you think, if there was any trouble with the Afghans?" says Burnes later. "Well, let's hope we don't have to find out."

In the next few weeks, while I was in fairly constant attendance on Elphy, I found myself sharing his hope. It was not just that Elphy was too old and feeble to be much use as an active leader: he was under McNaghten's thumb from the start, and since McNaghten was determined to believe that all was well, Elphy had to believe it, too. And neither of them got on with Shelton, a rude boor of a man who was Elphy's second-in-command, and this dissension at the top made for uneasiness and mistrust farther down.

If that was not bad enough, the situation of the army made it worse. The cantonment was a poor place for a garrison to be, without proper defences, with its principal stores outside its walls, and some of the principal officers—Burnes himself, for example— quartered two miles away in Kabul City. But if protests were made to McNaghten—and they were, especially by active men like Broadfoot—they were dismissed as "croaking", and it was pointed out sharply that the army was unlikely to be called on to fight anyway. When this kind of talk gets abroad, there is no confidence, and the soldiers get slack. Which is dangerous anywhere, but especially in a strange country where the natives are unpredictable.

Of course, Elphy pottering about the cantonment and Mc-Naghten with his nose deep in correspondence with Calcutta, saw nothing to indicate that the peaceful situation was an uneasy one. Nor did most of the army, who were ignorantly contemptuous of the Afghans, and had treated the Kabul expedition as a holiday from the first. But some of us did.

A few weeks after Elphy's arrival Burnes obtained my detachment from the staff because he wanted to make use of my Pushtu and my interest in the country. "Oh dear," Elphy complained, "Sir Alexander is so busy about everything. He takes my aides away, even, as though I could readily spare them. But there is so much to do, and I am not well enough to be up to it." But I was not sorry to go; being about Elphy was like being an orderly in a medical ward.

Burnes was keen that I should get about and see as much of the country as I could, improve my command of the language, and become known to as many influential Afghans as possible. He gave me a number of little tasks like the Mogala one—it was carrying messages, really, but it was valuable experience—and I travelled to towns and villages about Kabul, meeting Douranis and Kohistanis and Baruzkis and so on, and "getting the feel of the place," as Burnes put it.

"Soldiering's all very well," he told me, "but the men who make or break the army in a foreign country are we politicals. We meet the men who count, and get to know 'em, and sniff the wind; we're the eyes and ears—aye, and the tongues. Without us the military are blind, deaf, and dumb."

So although boors like Shelton sneered at "young pups gadding about the hills playing at niggers," I listened to Burnes and sniffed the wind. I took Ilderim with me a good deal, and sometimes his Gilzais, too, and they taught me some of the lore of the hills, and the ways of the people—who mattered, and what tribes were better to deal with, and why, and how the Kohistanis were more friendly disposed to us than the Abizai were, and which families were at feud with each other, and how the feeling ran about the Persians and the Russians, and where the best horses could be obtained, and how millet was grown and harvested: all the trivial information which is the small change of a country's life. I don't pretend that I became an expert in a few weeks, or that I ever "knew" Afghanistan, but I picked up a little here and there, and began to realise that those who studied the country only from the cantonment at Kabul knew no more about it than you would learn about a strange house if you stayed in one room of it all the time.

But for anyone with eyes to look beyond Kabul the signs were plain to see. There was mischief brewing in the hills, among the wild tribes who didn't want Shah Sujah for their king, and hated the British bayonets that protected him in his isolation in the Bala Hissar fortress. Rumours grew that Akbar Khan, son of old Dost Mohammed whom we had deposed, had come down out of the Hindu Kush at last and was gathering support among the chiefs; he was the darling of the warrior clans, they said, and presently he would sweep down on Kabul with his hordes, fling Sujah from his throne, and either drive the feringhees back to India or slaughter them all in their cantonment.

It was easy, if you were McNaghten, to scoff at such rumours from your pleasantly furnished office in Kabul; it was something else again to be up on the ridges beyond Jugdulluk or down towards Ghuznee and hear of councils called and messengers riding, of armed assemblies harangued by holy men and signal fires lit along the passes. The covert smiles, the ready assurances, the sight of swaggering Ghazis, armed to the teeth and with nothing apparent to do, the growing sense of unease—it used to make the hairs crawl on my neck.

For don't mistake me, I did not like this work. Riding with my Gilzais and young Ilderim, I was made welcome enough, and they were infallible eyes and ears—for having eaten the Queen's salt they were ready to serve her against their own folk if need be—but it was dangerous for all that. Even in native dress, I would meet black looks and veiled threats in some places and hear the British mocked and Akbar's name acclaimed. As a friend of the Gilzais and a slight celebrity—Ilderim lost no opportunity of announcing me as "Bloody Lance"—I was tolerated, but I knew the toleration might snap at any moment. At first I went about in a continual funk, but after a while one became fatalistic; possibly it came from dealing with people who believe that every man's fortune is unchangeably written on his forehead.

So the clouds began to gather on the mountains, and in Kabul the British army played cricket and Elphinstone and McNaghten wrote letters to each other remarking how tranquil everything was. The summer wore on, the sentries drowsed in the stifling heat of the cantonment, Burnes yawned and listened idly to my reports, dined me royally and took me off whoring in the bazaar—and one bright day McNaghten got a letter from Calcutta complaining at the cost of keeping our army in Kabul, and looked about for economies to make.

It was unfortunate that he happened, about this time, to be awaiting his promotion and transfer to the Governorship of Bombay; I think the knowledge that he was leaving may have made him careless. At any rate, seeking means of reducing expenditure, he recalled the idea which had appalled General Nott, and decided to cut the Gilzais' subsidy.

I had just come back to Kabul from a visit to Kandahar garrison, and learned that the Gilzai chiefs had been summoned and told that instead of 8,000 rupees a year for keeping the passes open, they were now to receive 5,000. Ilderim's fine young face fell when he heard it, and he said:

"There will be trouble, Flashman huzoor. He would have been better offering pork to a Ghazi than cheat the Gilzais of their money."

He was right, of course: he knew his own people. The Gilzai chiefs smiled cheerfully when McNaghten delivered his decision, bade him good afternoon, and rode quietly out of Kabul—and three days later the munitions convoy from Peshawar was cut to ribbons in the Khoord–Kabul pass by a force of yelling Gilzais and Ghazis who looted the caravan, butchered the drivers, and made off with a couple of tons of powder and ball.

McNaghten was most irritated, but not concerned. With Bombay beckoning he was not going to alarm Calcutta over a skirmish, as he called it.

"The Gilzais must be given a drubbing for kicking up this kind of row," said he, and hit on another bright idea: he would cut down expense by sending a couple of battalions back to India, and they could take a swipe at the Gilzais on their way home. Two birds with one stone. The only trouble was that his two battalions had to fight damned nearly every inch of the way as far as Gandamack, with the Gilzais potting at them from behind rocks and sweeping down in sudden cavalry charges. This was bad enough, but what made it worse was that our troops fought badly. Even under the command of General Sale—the tall, handsome "Fighting Bob" who used to invite his men to shoot him when they felt mutinous—clearing the passes was a slow, costly process.

I saw some of it, for Burnes sent me on two occasions with messages to Sale from McNaghten, telling him to get on with it.

It was a shocking experience the first time. I set off thinking it was something of a joy-ride, which it was until the last half-mile into Sale's rearguard, which was George Broadfoot's camp beyond Jugdulluk. Everything had been peaceful as you please, and I was just thinking how greatly exaggerated had been the reports arriving in Kabul from Sale, when out of a side-nullah came a mounted party of Ghazis, howling like wolves and brandishing their knives.

I just clapped in my spurs, put my head down, and cut along the track as if all the fiends in hell were behind me—which they were. I tumbled into Broadfoot's camp half-dead with terror, which he fortunately mistook for exhaustion. George had the bad taste to find it all rather funny; he was one of those nerveless clods, and was in the habit of strolling about under the snipers' fire polishing his spectacles, although his red coat and even redder beard made him a marked man.

He seemed to think everyone else was as unconcerned as he was, too, for he sent me back to Kabul that same night with another note, in which he told Burnes flatly that there wasn't a hope of keeping the passes open by force; they would have to negotiate with the Gilzais. I backed this up vehemently to Burnes, for although I had had a clear run back to Kabul, it was obvious to me that the Gilzais meant business, and at all the way stations there had been reports of other tribesmen massing in the hills above the passes.

Burnes gave me some rather odd looks as I made my report; he thought I was scared and probably exaggerating. At any rate, he made no protest when McNaghten said Broadfoot was an ass and Sale an incompetent, and that they had better get a move on if they were to have cleared a way to Jallalabad—which was about two-thirds of the way from Kabul to Peshawar—before winter set in. So Sale's brigade was left to struggle on, and Burnes (who was much preoccupied with the thought of getting McNaghten's job as Envoy when McNaghten went to Bombay) wrote that the country was "in the main very tranquil". Well, he paid for his folly.

A week or two later—it was now well into October—he sent me off again with a letter to Sale. Little progress was being made in clearing the passes, the Gilzais were as active as ever and out-shooting our troops all the time, and there were growing rumours of trouble brewing in Kabul itself. Burnes had sense enough to show a little concern, although McNaghten was still as placidly blind as ever, while Elphy Bey simply looked from one to the other, nodding agreement to whatever was said. But even Burnes showed no real urgency about it all; he just wanted to nag at Sale for not keeping the Gilzais quiet.

This time I went with a good escort of my Gilzais, under young Ilderim, on the theory that while they were technically sworn to fight their own kinsfolk, they would be unlikely in practice to get into any shooting scrapes with them. However, I never put this to the test, for it became evident as we rode east-ward through the passes that the situation was worse than any-one in Kabul had realised, and I decided that I, at any rate, would not try to get through to Sale. The whole country beyond Jugdulluk was up, and the hills were swarming with hostile Afghans, all either on their way to help beat up Sale's force, or else preparing for something bigger—there was talk among the villagers of a great *jehad* or holy war, in which the feringhees would be wiped out; it was on the eve of breaking out, they said. Sale was now hopelessly cut off; there was no chance of relief from Jallalabad, or even from Kabul—oh, Kabul was going to be busy enough looking after itself.

I heard this shivering round a camp-fire on the Soorkab road, and Ilderim shook his head in the shadows and said:

"It is not safe for you to go on, Flashman huzoor. You must return to Kabul. Give me the letter for Sale; although I have eaten the Queen's salt my own people will let me through."

This was such obvious common sense that I gave him the letter without argument and started back for Kabul that same night, with four of the Gilzai hostages for company. At that hour I wanted to get as many miles as possible between me and the gathering Afghan tribes, but if I had known what was waiting for me in Kabul I would have gone on to Sale and thought myself lucky.

Riding hard through the next day, we came to Kabul at nightfall, and I never saw the place so quiet. Bala Hissar loomed over the deserted streets; the few folk who were about were grouped in little knots in doorways and at street corners; there was an air of doom over the whole place. No British soldiers were to be seen in the city itself, and I was glad to get to the Residency, where Burnes lived in the heart of the town, and hear the courtyard gates grind to behind me. The armed men of Burnes's personal guard were standing to in the yard, while others were posted on the Residency walls; the torches shone on belt-plates and bayonets, and the place looked as though it was getting ready to withstand a siege.

But Burnes himself was sitting reading in his study as cool as a minnow, until he saw me. At the sight of my evident haste and disorder—I was in Afghan dress, and pretty filthy after days in the saddle—he started up.

"What the deuce are you doing here?" says he.

I told him, and added that there would probably be an Afghan army coming to support my story.

"My message to Sale," he snapped. "Where is it? Have you not delivered it?"

I told him about Ilderim, and for once the dapper little dandy forgot his carefully cultivated calm.

"Good God!" says he. "You've given it to a *Gilzai* to deliver?"

"A friendly Gilzai," I assured him. "A hostage, you remember."

"Are you mad?" says he, his little moustache all a-quiver. "Don't you know that you can't trust an Afghan, hostage or not?"

"Ilderim is a khan's son and a gentleman in his own way," I told him. "In any event, it was that or nothing. I couldn't have got through."

"And why not? You speak Pushtu; you're in native dress— God knows you're dirty enough to pass. It was your duty to see that message into Sale's own hand—and bring an answer. My God, Flashman, this is a pretty business, when a British officer cannot be trusted . . ."

"Now, look you here, Sekundar," says I, but he came up straight like a little bantam and cut me off.

"Sir Alexander, if you please," says he icily, as though I'd never seen him with his breeches down, chasing after some big Afghan bint. He stared at me and took a pace or two round the table.

"I think I understand," says he. "I have wondered about you lately, Flashman—whether you were to be fully relied on, or . . . Well, it shall be for a court-martial to decide—"

"Court-martial? What the devil!"

"For wilful disobedience of orders," says he. "There may be other charges. In any event, you may consider yourself under arrest, and confined to this house. We are all confined anyway— the Afghans are allowing no one to pass between here and the cantonment."

"Well, in God's name, doesn't that bear out what I've been telling you?" I said. "The country's all up to the eastward, man, and now here in Kabul . . ."

'There is no rising in Kabul," says he. "Merely a little unrest which I propose to deal with in the morning." He stood there, cock-sure little ass, in his carefully pressed linen suit, with a flower in his button-hole, talking as though he was a schoolmaster promising to reprimand some unruly fags. "It may interest you to know—you who turn tail at rumours—that I have twice this evening received direct threats to my life. I shall not be alive by morning, it is said. Well, well, we shall see about that."

"Aye, maybe you will," says I. "And as to your fine talk that I turn tail at rumours, you may see about that, too. Maybe Akbar Khan will come to show you himself."

He smiled at me, not pleasantly. "He is in Kabul; I have even had a message from him. And I am confident that he intends no harm to us. A few dissidents there are, of course, and it may be necessary to read them a lesson. However, I trust myself for that."

There was no arguing with his complacency, but I pitched into him hard on his threat of a court-martial for me. You might have thought that any sensible man would have understood my case, but he simply waved my protests aside, and finished by ordering me to my room. So I went, in a rare rage at the self-sufficient folly of the man, and heartily hoping that he would trip over his own conceit. Always so clever, always so sure—that was Burnes. I would have given a pension to see him at a loss for once.

But I was to see it for nothing.

It came suddenly, just before breakfast-time, when I was rubbing my eyes after a pretty sleepless night which had dragged itself away very slowly, and very silently for Kabul. It was a grey morning, and the cocks were crowing; suddenly I became aware of a distant murmur, growing to a rumble, and hurried to the window. The town lay still, with a little haze over the houses; the guards were still on the wall of the Residency compound, and in the distance, coming closer, the noise was identifiable as the tramping of feet and the growing clamour of a mob.

There was a shouted order in the courtyard, a clatter of feet on the stairs, and Burnes's voice calling for his brother, young Charlie, who lived in the Residency with him. I snatched my robe from its peg and hurried down, winding my puggaree on to my head as I went. As I reached the courtyard there was the crack of a musket shot, and a wild yell from beyond the wall; a volley of blows hammered on the gate, and across the top of the wall I saw the vanguard of a charging horde streaming out from between the nearest houses. Bearded faces, flashing knives, they surged up to the wall and fell back, yelling and cursing, while the guards thrust at them with their musket butts. For a moment I thought they would charge again and sweep irresistibly over the wall, but they hung back, a jostling, shrieking crowd, shaking their fists and weapons, while the guardsmen lining the wall looked anxiously back for orders and kept their thumbs poised on their musket-locks.

Burnes strolled out of the front door and stood in full view at the top of the steps. He was as fresh and calm as a squire taking his first sniff of the morning, but at the sight of him the mob redoubled its clamour and rolled up to the wall, yelling threats and insults while he looked right and left at them, smiling and shaking his head.

"No shooting, havildar," says he to the guard commander. "It will all quieten down in a moment."

"Death to Sekundar!" yelled the mob. "Death to the feringhee pig!"

Jim Broadfoot, who was George's younger brother, and little Charlie Burnes, were at Sekundar's elbow, both looking mighty anxious, but Burnes himself never lost his poise. Suddenly he raised his hand, and the mob beyond the wall fell quiet; he grinned at that, and touched his moustache in that little, confident gesture he had, and then he began to talk to them in Pushtu. His voice was quiet, and must have carried only faintly to them, but they listened for a little as he coolly told them to go home, and stop this folly, and reminded them that he had always been their friend and had done them no harm.

It might have succeeded, for he had the gift of the gab, but show-off that he was, he carried it just too far, and patronised them, and first there were murmurs, and then the clamour swelled up again, more savage than before. Suddenly one Afghan started forward and hurled himself on to the wall, knocking down a sentry; the nearest guard drove at the Afghan with his bayonet, someone in the crowd fired his jezzail, and with one hellish roar the whole mob swept forward, scrambling up the wall.

The havildar yelled an order, there was the ragged crash of a volley, and the courtyard was full of struggling men, crazy Afghans with their knives hacking and the guard falling back, stabbing with their bayonets and going down beneath the rush. There was no holding them; I saw Broadfoot grab Burnes and hustle him inside the house, and a moment later I was inside myself, slamming the side door in the face of a yelling Ghazi with a dozen of his fellows bounding at his heels.

It was a stout door, thank God, like the others in the Residency; otherwise we should all have been butchered within five minutes. Blows shattered on the far side of it as I slipped the bar home, and as I hurried along the passage to the main hallway I could hear above the shrieking and shooting outside the crash and thud of countless fists and hilts on panels and shutters—it was like being inside a box with demented demons pounding on the lid. Suddenly above the din there was the crash of an ordered volley from the courtyard, and then another, and as the yelling subsided momentarily the havildar's voice could be heard urging the remnant of the guard into the house. Little bloody odds it would make, I thought; they had us cornered, and it was a case of having our throats cut now or later.

Burnes and the others were in the hallway, and Sekundar as usual was showing off, affecting carelessness in a tight spot.

"Wake Duncan with thy knocking," he quoted, cocking his head on one side at the pounding of the mob. "How many of the guard are inside, Jim?"

Broadfoot said about a dozen, and Burnes said: "That's splendid. That makes, let's see, twelve, and the servants, and us three—hullo, here's Flashman! Mornin' Flash; sleep well? Apologise for this rude awakening—about twenty-five, I'd say; twenty fighting men, anyway."

"Few enough," says Broadfoot, examining his pistols. "The niggers'll be inside before long—we can't cover every door and window, Sekundar."

A musket ball crashed through a shutter and knocked a cloud of plaster off the opposite wall. Everyone ducked, except Burnes.

"Nonsense!" says he. "Can't cover 'em from down here, I grant you, but we don't have to. Now Jim, take the guard, all of 'em, upstairs, and have 'em shoot down from the balconies. That'll clear these mad fellows away from the sides of the house. There ain't many guns among them, I fancy, so you can get a good sight of them without fear of being hit—much. Up you go, laddie, look sharp!"

Broadfoot clattered away, and a moment later the red-coated jawans were mounting the stairs, with Burnes shouting "Shabash!" to encourage them while he belted his sword over his suit and stuck a pistol in his belt. He seemed positively to be enjoying himself, the bloody ass. He clapped me on the shoulder and asked didn't I just wish I'd galloped on to Sale after all—but never a word of acknowledgement that my warning had proved correct. I reminded him of it, and pointed out that if he had listened then, we shouldn't be going to get our throats cut now, but he just laughed and straightened his button-hole.

"Don't croak so, Flashy," says he. "I could hold this house with two men and a whore's protector." There was a sound of ragged firing over our heads. "You see? Jim's setting about 'em already. Come on, Charlie, let's see the fun!" And he and his brother hurried upstairs, leaving me alone in the hall.

"What about my bloody court-martial?" I shouted after him, but he never heard.

Well, his plan worked, at first. Broadfoot's men did clear away the rascals from round the walls, shooting down from the upper windows and balcony, and when I joined them on the upper floor there were about twenty Ghazi corpses in the courtyard. A few shots came the other way, and one of the jawans was wounded in the thigh, but the main mob had now retreated to the street, and contented themselves with howling curses from the cover of the wall.

"Excellent! Bahut achha!" said Burnes, puffing a cheroot and peering out of the window. "You see, Charlie, they've drawn off, and presently Elphy will be wondering down in the cantonment what all the row's about, and send someone to see."

"Won't he send troops, then?" says little Charlie.

"Of course. A battalion, probably—that's what I'd send. Since it's Elphy, though, he's as likely to send a brigade, eh, Jim?"

Broadfoot, squatting at the other window, peered along his pistol barrel, fired, swore, and said: "So long as he sends someone."

"Don't you fret," says Burnes. "Here, Flashy, have a cheroot. Then you can try your hand at potting off some of these chaps beyond the wall. I'd say Elphy'll be on the move inside two hours, and we'll be out of here in three. Good shot, Jim! That's the style!"

Burnes was wrong, of course. Elphy didn't send troops; indeed, so far as I've been able to learn, he did nothing at all. If even a platoon had arrived in that first hour, I believe the mob would have melted before them; as it was, they began to pluck up courage, and started clambering the wall again, and sneaking round to the rear, where the stables gave them cover. We kept up a good fire from the windows—I shot three myself, including an enormously fat man, at which Burnes said: "Choose the thin ones, Flashy; that chap couldn't have got in the front door anyway." But as two hours passed he joked rather less, and actually made another attempt to talk to our attackers from the balcony, but they drove him inside with a shot or two and a volley of missiles.

Meanwhile, some of the Ghazis had set fire to the stables, and the smoke began to drift into the house. Burnes swore, and we all strained our eyes peering across the rooftops towards the cantonment, but still no sign of help appeared, and I felt the pumping of fear again in my throat. The howling of the mob had risen again, louder than ever, some of the jawans were looking scared, and even Burnes was frowning.

"Blast Elphy Bey," says he. "He's cutting it dooced fine. And I believe these brutes have got muskets from somewhere at last—listen." He was right; there were as many shots coming from outside as from inside the house. They were smacking into the walls and knocking splinters from the shutters, and presently another jawan gave a yelp and staggered back into the room with his shoulder smashed and blood pouring down his shirt.

"Hm," says Burnes, "this is gettin' warm. Like Montrose at the Fair, eh, Charlie?" Charlie gave him the ghost of a smile; he was scared stiff and trying not to show it.

"How many rounds have you got, Flashy?" says Burnes. I had only six left, and Charlie had none; the ten jawans had barely forty among them.

"How about you, Jim?" shouts Burnes to Broadfoot, who was at the far window. Broadfoot shouted something back, but in the din I didn't catch it, and then Broadfoot stood slowly up, and turned towards us, looking down at his shirt-front. I saw a red spot there, and suddenly it grew to a great red stain, and Broadfoot took two steps back and went head first over the window sill. There was a sickening crash as he hit the courtyard, and a tremendous shriek from the mob; the firing seemed to redouble, and from the rear, where the smoke of the burning stables was pouring in on us, came the measured smashing of a ram at the back door.

Burnes fired from his window, and ducked away. He squatted down near me, spun his pistol by the guard, whistled for a second or two through his teeth, and then said: "Charlie, Flashy, I think it's time to go."

"Where the hell to?" says I.

"Out of here," says he. "Charlie, cut along to my room; you'll find native robes in the wardrobe. Bring 'em along. Lively, now." When Charlie had gone, he said to me "It's not much of a chance, but it's all we have, I think. We'll try it at the back door; the smoke looks pretty thick, don't you know, and with all the confusion we might get clear away. Ah, good boy, Charlie. Now send the havildar across to me."

While Burnes and Charlie struggled into their gowns and pug-garees, Burnes talked to the havildar, who agreed that the mob probably wouldn't hurt him and his men, not being feringhees, but would concentrate on looting the place.

"But you, sahib, they will surely kill," he said. "Go while ye can, and God go with you."

"And remain with you and yours," says Burnes, shaking his hand. "Shabash and salaam, havildar. All ready, Flash? Come on, Charlie."

And with Burnes in the lead and myself last, we cut out down the staircase, across the hall, and through the passage towards the kitchen. From the back door, out of sight to our right, there came a crackling of breaking timber; I took a quick glance through a loophole, and saw the garden almost alive with Ghazis.

"Just about in time," says Burnes, as we reached the kitchen door. I knew it led into a little fenced-off pen, where the swill-tubs were kept; once we got into that, and provided we weren't actually seen leaving the house, we stood a fair chance of getting away.

Burnes slipped the bar quietly from the door, and opened it a crack.

"Luck of the devil!" says he. "Come on, juldi!"

We slipped out after him; the pen was empty. It consisted of two high screen walls running from either side of the door; there was no one in sight through the opening at the other end, and the smoke was billowing down in great clouds now, with the mob kicking up the most hellish din on either side of us.

"Pull her to, Flashy!" snapped Burnes, and I shut the door behind us. "That's it—now, try to batter the damned thing down!" And he jumped at the closed door, hammering with his fists. "Open, unbelieving swine!" he bawled. "Feringhee pigs, your hour has come! This way, brothers! Death to the bastard Sekundar!"

Seeing his plan, we hammered along with him, and presently round the end of the pen came a handful of Ghazis to see what was what. All they saw, of course, was three of the Faithful try-ing to break down a door, so they joined in, and after a moment we left off, Burnes cursing like blazes, and went out of the pen, ostensibly to seek another entrance to hammer at.

There were Afghans all over the garden and round the burning stables; most of them, it seemed to me, were just berserk and running about and yelling for no particular reason, waving their knives and spears, and presently there was a tremendous howl and a crash as the back door caved in, and a general move in that direction. The three of us kept going for the stable gate, past the burning building; it was a creepy feeling, hurrying through the confused crowd of our enemies, and I was in dread that little Charlie, who was new to native dress, and not nearly as dark as Burnes and I, would do something to be spotted. But he kept his hood well forward over his face, and we got outside the gate in safety, where the hangers-on were congregated, yelling and laughing as they watched the Residency, hoping no doubt to see the bodies of the hated feringhees launched from the upper windows.

"May dogs defile the grave of the swine Burnes!" roared Sekundar, spitting towards the Residency, and the bystanders gave him a cheer. "So far, so good," he added to me. "Now shall we stroll down to the cantonments and have a word with Elphy? Ready, Charlie? Best foot forward, then, and try to swagger like a regular badmash. Take your cue from Flashy here; ain't he the ugliest-lookin' Bashie-Bazouk you ever saw?"

With Burnes in the lead we pushed out boldly into the street, Sekundar thrusting aside the stragglers who got in the way like any Yusufzai bully; I wanted to tell him to go easy, for it seemed to me he must attract attention, and his face was all too familiar to the Kabulis. But they gave way before him, with a curse or two, and we won clear to the end of the street without being spotted; now, thought I, we're home in a canter. The crowd was still fairly thick, but not so noisy, and every stride was taking us nearer the point where, at worst, we could cut and run for it towards the cantonment.

And then Burnes, the over-confident fool, ruined the whole thing.

We had reached the end of the street, and he must pause to yell another curse against the feringhees, by way of a final brag: I could imagine him showing off later to the garrison wives, telling them how he'd fooled the Afghans by roaring threats against himself. But he overdid it; having called himself the grandson of seventy pariah dogs at the top of his voice, he muttered something in an undertone to Charlie, and laughed at his own witticism.

The trouble is, an Afghan doesn't laugh like an Englishman. He giggles high-pitched, but Burnes guffawed. I saw a head turn to stare at us, and grabbing Burnes by one arm and Charlie by the other I was starting to hurry them down the street when I was pushed aside and a big brute of a Ghazi swung Burnes round by the shoulder and peered at him.

"Jao, hubshi!" snarled Burnes, and hit his hand aside, but the fellow still stared, and then suddenly shouted:

"Mashallah! Brothers, it is Sekundar Burnes!"

There was an instant's quiet, and then an almighty yell. The big Ghazi whipped out his Khyber knife, Burnes locked his arm and snapped it before he could strike, but then about a dozen others were rushing in on us. One jumped at me, and I hit him so hard with my fist that I overbalanced; I jumped up, clawing for my own sword, and saw Burnes throwing off the wounded Ghazi and shouting:

"Run, Charlie, run!"

There was a side-alley into which Charlie, who was nearest, might have escaped, but he hesitated, standing white-faced, while Burnes jumped between him and the charging Afghans. Sekundar had his Khyber knife out now; he parried a blow from the leader, closed with him, and shouted again:

"Get out, Charlie! Cut, man!"

And then, as Charlie still hesitated, petrified, Burnes yelled in an agonised voice:

"Run, baby, please! Run!"

They were the last words he spoke. A Khyber knife swept down on his shoulder and he reeled back, blood spouting; then the mob was on top of him, hacking and striking. He must have taken half a dozen mortal cuts before he even hit the ground. Charlie gave a frenzied cry, and ran towards him; they cut him down before he had gone three steps.

I saw all this, because it happened in seconds; then I had my own hands full. I jumped over the man I had hit and dived for the alley, but a Ghazi was there first, screaming and slashing at me. I had my own sword out, and turned his cut, but the way was blocked and the mob was howling at my heels. I turned, slashing frantically, and they gave back an instant; I got my back to the nearest wall as they surged in again, the knives flashed before my eyes, I thrust at the snarling faces and heard the screams and curses. And then something hit me a dreadful blow in the stomach and I went down before the rush of bodies; a foot stamped on my hip, and even as I thought, oh, sweet Jesus, this is death, I had one fleeting memory of being trampled in the scrimmage in the School-house match. Something smashed against my head, and I waited for the horrible bite of sharp steel. And then I remember nothing more.[14]

When I came to my senses I was lying on a wooden floor, my cheek against the boards. My head seemed to be opening and shutting with pain, and when I tried to raise it I found that my face was stuck to the boards with my own dried blood, so that I cried out with the pain as it pulled free. The first thing I noticed was a pair of boots, of fine yellow leather, on the floor about two yards away; above them were pyjamy trousers and the skirt of a black coat, and then a green sash and two lean hands hooked into it by the thumbs, and above all, a dark, grinning face with pale grey eyes under a spiked helmet. I knew the face, from my visit to Mogala, and even in my confused state I thought: this is bad news. It was my old enemy, Gul Shah.

He sauntered over and kicked me in the ribs. I tried to speak, and the first words that came out, in a hoarse whisper, were: "I'm alive."

"For the moment," said Gul Shah. He squatted down beside me, smiling his wolf's smile. "Tell me, Flashman: what does it feel like to die?"

"What d'ye mean?" I managed to croak.

He jerked his thumb. "Out in the street yonder: you were down, with the knives at your neck, and only my timely intervention saved you from the same fate as Sekundar Burnes. They cut him to pieces, by the way. Eighty-five pieces, to be exact: they have been counted, you see. But you, Flashman, must have known what it was like to die in that moment. Tell me: I am curious."

I guessed there was no good coming from these questions; the evil look of the brute made my skin crawl. But I thought it best to answer.

"It was bloody horrible," says I.

He laughed with his head back, rocking on his heels, and others laughed with him. I realised there were perhaps half a dozen others—Ghazis, mostly—in the room with us. They came crowding round to leer at me, and if anything they looked even nastier than Gul Shah.

When he had finished laughing he leaned over me. "It can be more horrible," says he, and spat in my face. He reeked of garlic.

I tried to struggle up, demanding to know why he had saved me, and he stood up and kicked me again. "Yes, why?" he mocked me. I couldn't fathom it; I didn't want to. But I thought I'd pretend to act as though it were all for the best.

"I'm grateful to you, sir," says I, "for your timely assistance. You shall be rewarded—all of you—and. . . ."

"Indeed we will," says Gul Shah. "Stand him up."

They dragged me to my feet, twisting my arms behind me. I told them loudly that if they took me back to the cantonment they would be handsomely paid, and they roared with laughter.

"Any paying the British do will be in blood," says Gul Shah. "Yours first of all."

"What for, damn you?" I shouted.

"Why do you suppose I stopped the Ghazis from quartering you?" says he. "To preserve your precious skin, perhaps? To hand you as a peace offering to your people?" He stuck his face into mine. "Have you forgotten a dancing girl called Narreeman, you pig's bastard? Just another slut, to the likes of you, to be defiled as you chose, and then forgotten. You are all the same, you feringhee swine; you think you can take our women, our country, and our honour and trample them all under foot. We do not matter, do we? And when all is done, when our women are raped and our treasure stolen, you can laugh and shrug your shoulders, you misbegotten pariah curs!" He was screaming at me, with froth on his lips.

"I meant her no harm," I was beginning, and he struck me across the face. He stood there, glaring at me and panting. He made an effort and mastered himself.

"She is not here," he said at last, "or I would give you to her and she would give you an eternity of suffering before you died. As it is, we shall do our poor best to accommodate you."

"Look," says I. "Whatever I've done, I beg your pardon for it. I didn't know you cared for the wench, I swear. I'll make amends, any way you like. I'm a rich man, a really rich man." I went on to offer him whatever he wanted in ransom and as compensation to the girl, and it seemed to quiet him for a minute.

"Go on," says he, when I paused. "This is good to listen to."

I would have done, but just the cruel sneer told me he was mocking me, and I fell silent.

"So, we are where we began," says he. "Believe me, Flashman, I would make you die a hundred deaths, but time is short. There are other throats besides yours, and we are impatient people. But we shall make your passing as memorable as possible, and you shall tell me again what it is like to die. Bring him along."

They dragged me from the room, along a passage, and I roared for help and called Gul Shah every filthy name I could lay tongue to. He strode on ahead, heedless, and presently threw open a door; they ran me across the threshold and I found I was in a low, vaulted chamber, perhaps twenty yards long. I had half-expected racks and thumbscrews or some such horrors, but the room was entirely bare. The one curious feature of it was that half way it was cut in two by a deep culvert, perhaps ten feet wide and six deep. It was dry, and where it ran into the walls on either side the openings were stopped up with rubble. This had obviously been done only recently, but I could not imagine why.

Gul Shah turned to me. "Are you strong, Flashman?"

"Damn you!" I shouted. "You'll pay for this, you dirty nigger!"

"Are you strong?" he repeated. "Answer, or I'll have your tongue cut out."

One of the ruffians grabbed my jaw in his hairy paw and brought his knife up to my mouth. It was a convincing argument. "Strong enough, damn you."

"I doubt that," smiled Gul Shah. "We have executed two rascals here of late, neither of them weaklings. But we shall see." To one of his crew he said: "Bring Mansur. I should explain this new entertainment of mine," he went on, gloating at me. "It was inspired partly by the unusual shape of this chamber, with its great trench in the middle, and partly by a foolish game which your British soldiers play. Doubtless you have played it yourself, which will add interest for you, and us. Yah, Mansur, come here."

As he spoke, a grotesque figure waddled into the room. For a moment I could not believe it was a man, for he was no more than four feet high. But he was terrific. He was literally as broad as he was long, with huge knotted arms and a chest like an ape's. His enormous torso was carried on massive legs. He had no neck that I could see, and his yellow face was as flat as a plate, with a hideous nose spread across it, a slit of a mouth, and two black button eyes. His body was covered in dark hair, but his skull was as smooth as an egg. He wore only a dirty loincloth, and as he shuffled across to Gul Shah the torchlight in that windowless room gave him the appearance of some hideous Nibelung dragging itself through dark burrows beneath the earth.

"A fine manikin, is he not?" said Gul Shah, regarding the hideous imp. "Your soul must be as handsome, Flashman. Which is fitting, for he is your executioner."

He snapped an order, and the dwarf, with a glance at me and a contortion of his revolting mouth which I took to be a grin, suddenly bounded into the culvert, and with a tremendous spring leaped up the other side, catching the edge and flipping up, like an acrobat. That done he turned and faced us, arms outstretched, a disgusting yellow giant-in-miniature.

The men who held me now dragged my arms in front of me, and bound my wrists tightly with a stout rope. One of them then took the coil and carried it across to the dwarf's side of the culvert; the manikin made a hideous bubbling noise and held his wrists up eagerly, and they were bound as mine had been. So we stood, on opposite edges of the culvert, bound to ends of the same rope, with the slack of it lying in the great trench between us.

There had been no further word of explanation, and in the hellish uncertainty of what was to come, my nerve broke. I tried to run, but they hauled me back, laughing, and the dwarf Mansur capered on his side of the culvert and snapped his fingers in delight at my terror.

"Let me go, you bastards!" I roared, and Gul Shah smiled and clapped his hands.

"You start at shadows," he sneered. "Behold the substance. Yah, Asaf."

One of his ruffians came to the edge of the trench, bearing a leather sack tied at the neck. Cautiously undoing it, and holding it by the bottom, he suddenly up-ended it into the culvert. To my horror, half a dozen slim, silver shapes that glittered evilly in the torchlight, fell writhing into the gap; they plopped gently to the floor of the culvert and then slithered with frightening speed towards the sides. But they could not climb up at us, so they glided about their strange prison in deadly silence. You could sense the vicious anger in them as they slid about beneath us.

"Their bite is death," said Gul Shah. "Is all now plain, Flashman? It is what you call a tug-of-war—you against Mansur. One of you must succeed in tugging the other into the trench, and then—it takes a few moments for the venom to kill. Believe me, the snakes will be kinder than Narreeman would have been."

"Help!" I roared, although God knows I expected none. But the sight of those loathsome things, the thought of their slimy touch, of the stab of their fangs—I thought I should go mad. I raged and pleaded, and that Afghan swine clapped his hands and yelled with laughter. The dwarf Mansur hopped in eagerness to begin, and presently Gul Shah stepped back, snapped an order to him, and said to me:

"Pull for your life, Flashman. And present my salaams to Shaitan."

I had retreated as far as I could go from the culvert's edge, and was standing, half-paralysed, when the dwarf snapped his wrists impatiently at the rope. The jerk brought me to my senses; as I have said before, terror is a wonderful stimulant. I braced my boot-heels on the rough stone floor, and prepared to resist with all my strength.

Grinning, the dwarf scuttled backwards until the rope stretched taut between us; I guessed what his first move would be, and was ready for the sudden jerk when it came. It nearly lifted me off my feet, but I turned with the rope across my shoulder and gave him heave for heave. The rope drummed like a bowstring, and then relaxed; he leered across at me and made a dribbling, piping noise. Then he bunched his enormous shoulder muscles, and leaning back, began to pull steadily.

By God, he was strong. I strained until my shoulders cracked and my arms shuddered, but slowly, inch by inch, my heels slithered across the rough surface towards the edge of the trench. The Ghazis urged him on with cries of delight, Gul Shah came to the brink so that he could watch me as I was drawn inexorably to the limit, I felt one of my heels slip into space, my head seemed to be bursting with the effort and my ears roared—and then the tearing pain in my wrists relaxed, and I was sprawled on the very edge, exhausted, with the dwarf prancing and laughing on the other side and the rope slack between us.

The Ghazis were delighted, and urged him to give me a quick final jerk into the culvert, but he shook his head and backed away again, snapping the rope at me. I glanced down; the snakes seemed almost to know what was afoot, for they had concentrated in a writhing, hissing mass just below me. I scrambled back, wet with fear and rage, and hurled my weight on the rope to try to heave him off balance. But for all the impression I made it might have been anchored to a tree.

He was playing with me; there was no question he was far the stronger of us two, and twice he hauled me to the lip and let me go again. Gul Shah clapped his hands and the Ghazis cheered; then he snapped some order to the dwarf, and I realised with sick horror that they were going to make an end. In despair I rolled back again from the edge and got to my feet; my wrists were torn and bloody and my shoulder joints were on fire, and when the dwarf pulled on the rope I staggered forward and in doing so I nearly got him, for he had expected a stronger resistance, and almost overbalanced. I hauled for dear life, but he recovered in time, glaring and piping angrily at me as he stamped his feet for a hold.

When he had finally settled himself he started to draw again on the rope, but not with his full strength, for he pulled me in only an inch at a time. This, I supposed, was the final hideous refinement; I struggled like a fish on a line, but there was no resisting that steady, dreadful pull. I was perhaps ten feet from the lip when he turned away from me, as a tug-of-war team will when it has its opponents on the run, and I realised that if I was to make any last desperate bid it must be now, while I had a little space to play with. I had almost unbalanced him by an accidental yielding; could I do it deliberately? With the last of my strength I dug my heels in and heaved tremendously; it checked him and he glanced over his shoulder, surprise on the hideous face. Then he grinned and exerted his strength, lunging away on the rope. My feet slipped.

"Go with God, Flashman," said Gul Shah ironically.

I scrabbled for a foothold, found it only six feet from the edge, and then bounded forward. The leap took me to the very lip of the culvert, and the dwarf Mansur plunged forward on his face as the rope slackened. But he was up like a jack-in-the-box, gibbering with rage, in an instant; planting his feet, he gave a savage heave on the rope that almost dislocated my shoulders and flung me face down. Then he began to pull steadily, so that I was dragged forward over the floor, closer and closer to the edge, while the Ghazis cheered and roared and I screamed with horror.

"No! No!" I shrieked. "Stop him! Wait! Anything—I'll do anything! Stop him!"

My hands were over the edge now, and then my elbows; suddenly there was nothing beneath my face, and through my streaming tears I saw the bottom of the culvert with the filthy worms gliding across it. My chest and shoulders were clear, in an instant I should overbalance; I tried to twist my head up to appeal to the dwarf, and saw him standing on the far edge, grinning evilly and coiling the slack rope round his right hand and elbow like a washerwoman with a clothes line. He glanced at Gul Shah, preparing to give the final pull that would launch me over, and then above my own frantic babbling and the roaring in my ears I heard the crash of a door flung open behind me, and a stir among the watchers, and a voice upraised in Pushtu.

The dwarf was standing stock-still, staring beyond me towards the door. What he saw I didn't know, and I didn't care; half-dead with fear and exhaustion as I was, I recognised that his attention was diverted, that the rope was momentarily slack between us, and that he was on the very lip of the trench. It was my last chance.

I had only the purchase of my body and legs on the stone; my arms were stretched out ahead of me. I jerked them suddenly back, sobbing, with all my strength. It was not much of a pull, but it took Mansur completely unawares. He was watching the doorway, his eyes round in his gargoyle face; too late he realised that he had let his attention wander too soon. The jerk, slight as it was, unbalanced him, and one leg slipped over the edge; he shrieked and tried to throw himself clear, but his grotesque body landed on the very edge, and he hung for a moment like a see-saw. Then with a horrible piping squeal he crashed sprawling into the culvert.

He was up again with a bound, and springing for the rim, but by the grace of God he had landed almost on top of one of those hellish snakes, and even as he came upright it struck at his bare leg. He screamed and kicked at it, and the delay gave a second brute the chance to fix itself in his hand. He lashed out blindly, making a most ghastly din, and staggered about with at least two of the things hanging from him. He ran in his dreadful waddling way in a little circle, and fell forward on his face. Again and again the serpents struck at him; he tried feebly to rise, and then collapsed, his misshapen body twitching.

I was dead beat, with exertion and shock; I could only lie heaving like a bellows. Gul Shah strode to the edge of the culvert and screamed curses at his dead creature; then he turned, pointing to me, and shouted:

"Fling that bastard in beside him!"

They grabbed me and ran me to the pit's edge, for I could make no resistance. But I remember I protested that it wasn't fair, that I had won, and deserved to be let go. They held me on the edge, hanging over the pit, and waited for the final word from my enemy. I closed my eyes to blot out the sight of the snarling faces and those dreadful reptiles, and then I was pulled back, and the hands fell away from me. Wondering, I turned wearily; they had all fallen silent, Gul Shah with the rest of them.

A man stood in the doorway. He was slightly under middle height, with the chest and shoulders of a wrestler, and a small, neat head that he turned from side to side, taking in the scene. He was simply dressed in a grey coat, clasped about with a belt of chain mail, and his head was bare. He was plainly an Afghan, with something of the pretty look that was so repulsive in Gul Shah, but here the features were stronger and plumper; he carried an air of command, but very easily, without any of the strutting arrogance that so many of his race affected.

He came forward, nodding to Gul Shah and eyeing me with polite interest. I noticed with astonishment that his eyes, oriental though they were in shape, were of vivid blue. That and the slightly curly dark hair gave him a European look, which suited his bluff, sturdy figure. He sauntered to the edge of the culvert, clicked his tongue ruefully at the dead dwarf, and asked conversationally:

"What has happened here?"

He sounded like a vicar in a drawing-room, he was so mild, but Gul Shah kept mum, so I burst out:

"These swine have been trying to murder me!"

He gave me a brilliant smile. "But without success," cried he. "I felicitate you. Plainly you have been in terrible danger, but have escaped by your skill and bravery. A notable feat, and what a tale for your children's children!"

It was really too much. Twice in hours I had been on the brink of violent death, I was battered, exhausted, and smeared with my own blood, and here I was conversing with a lunatic. I almost broke down in tears, and I certainly groaned: "Oh, Jesus."

The stout man raised an eyebrow. "The Christian prophet? Why, who are you then?"

"I'm a British officer!" I cried. "I have been captured and tortured by these ruffians, and they'd have killed me, too, with their hellish snakes! Whoever you are, you must—"

"In the hundred names of God!" he broke in. "A feringhee officer? Plainly there has almost been a very serious accident. Why did you not tell them who you were?"

I gaped at him, my head spinning. One of us must be mad. "They knew," I croaked. "Gul Shah knew."

"Impossible," says the stout fellow, shaking his head. "It could not be. My friend Gul Shah would be incapable of such a thing; there has been an unfortunate error."

"Look," I said, reaching out towards him, "you must believe me: I am Lieutenant Flashman, on the staff of Lord Elphinstone, and this man has tried to do me to death—not for the first time. Ask him," I shouted, "how I came here! Ask the lying, treacherous bastard!"

"Never try to flatter Gul Shah," said the stout man cheerfully. "He'll believe every word of it. No, there has been a mistake, regrettably, but it has not been irreparable. For which God be thanked—and my timely arrival, to be sure." And he smiled at me again. "But you must not blame Gul Shah, or his people: they did not know you for what you were."

Now, as he said those words, he ceased to be a waggish madman; his voice was as gentle as ever, but there was no mistaking the steel underneath. Suddenly things became real again, and I understood that the kindly smiling man before me was strong in a way that folk like Gul Shah could never be: strong and dangerous. And with a great surge of relief I realised too that with him by I was safe: Gul Shah must have sensed it also, for he roused himself and growled that I was his prisoner, feringhee officer or not, and he would deal with me.

"No, he is my guest," said the stout man reprovingly. "He has met with a mishap on his way here, and needs refreshment and care for his wounds. You have mistaken again, Gul Shah. Now, we shall have his wrists unbound, and I shall take him to such entertainment as befits a guest of his importance."

My bonds were cut off in a moment, and two of the Ghazis— the same evil-smelling brutes that a few moments ago had been preparing to hurl me to the snakes—supported me from that hellish place. I could feel Gul Shah's eyes boring into my back, but he said not a word; it seemed to me that the only explanation was that this must be the stout man's house, and under the strict rules of Musselman hospitality his word was law. But in my exhausted state I couldn't attempt to make sense of it all, and was only glad to stagger after my benefactor.

They took me to a well-furnished apartment, and under the stout man's supervision the crack in my head was bathed, the blood washed from my torn wrists and oiled bandages applied, and then I was given strong mint tea and a dish of bread and fruit. Although my head ached damnably I was famishing, not having eaten all day, and while I ate the stout man talked.

"You must not mind Gul Shah," he said, sitting opposite me and toying with his small beard. "He is a savage—what Gilzai isn't?—and now that I think on your name I connect you with the incident at Mogala some time ago. 'Bloody Lance', is it not?" And he gave me that tooth-flashing smile again. "I imagine you had given him cause for resentment—"

"There was a woman," I said. "I didn't know she was his woman." Which wasn't true, but that was by the way.

"There is so often a woman," he agreed. "But I imagine there was more to it than that. The death of a British officer at Mogala would have been convenient politically for Gul—yes, yes, I see how it may have been. But that is past." He paused, and looked at me reflectively. "And so is the unfortunate incident in the cellar today. It is best, believe me, that it should be so. Not only for you personally, but for all your people here."

"What about Sekundar Burnes and his brother?" said I. "Your soft words won't bring them back."

"A terrible tragedy," he agreed. "I admired Sekundar. Let us hope that the ruffians who slew him will be apprehended, and meet with a deserved judgement."

"Ruffians?" says I. "Good God, man, those were Akbar Khan's warriors, not a gang of robbers. I don't know who you are, or what your influence may be, but you're behind the times where news is concerned. When they murdered Burnes and sacked his Residency, that was the beginning of a war. If the British haven't marched from their cantonment into Kabul yet, they soon will, and you can bet on that!"

"I think you exaggerate," he said mildly. "This talk of Akbar Khan's warriors, for example—"

"Look you," I said, "don't try to tell me. I rode in from the east last night: the tribes are up along the passes from here to Jugdulluk and beyond, thousands of 'em. They're trying to wipe out Sale's force, they'll be here as soon as Akbar has a mind to take Kabul and slit Shah Sujah's throat and seize his throne. And God help the British garrison and loyalists like yourself who help them as you've helped me. I tried to tell Burnes this, and he laughed and wouldn't heed me. Well, there you are." I stopped; all that talk had made me thirsty. When I had taken some tea I added: "Believe it or not as you like."

He sat quiet for a moment, and then remarked that it was an alarming story, but that I must be mistaken. "If it were as you say, the British would have moved by now—either out of Kabul, or into the Bala Hissar fort, where they would be safe. They are not fools, after all."

"You don't know Elphy Bey, that's plain," says I. "Or that ass McNaghten. They don't want to believe it, you see; they want to think all's well. They think Akbar Khan is still skulking away in the Hindu Kush; they refuse to believe the tribes are rallying to him, ready to sweep the British out of Afghanistan."

He sighed. "It may be as you say: such delusions are common. Or they may be right, and the danger smaller than you think." He stood up. "But I am a thoughtless host. Your wound is paining you, and you need rest, Flashman huzoor. I shall weary you no longer. Here you can have peace, and in the morning we can talk again; among other things, of how to return you safely to your people." He smiled, and the blue eyes twinkled. "We want no more 'mistakes' from hotheads like Gul Shah. Now, God be with you."

I struggled up, but I was so weak and weary that he insisted I be seated again. I told him I was deeply grateful for all his kindness, that I would wish to reward him, but he laughed and turned to go. I mumbled some more thanks to him, and it occurred to me that I still didn't know who he was, or how he had the power to save me from Gul Shah. I asked him, and he paused in the curtained doorway.

"As to that," he said, "I am the master of this house. My close friends call me Bakbook, because I incline to talk. Others call me by various names, as they choose." He bowed. "You may call me by my given name, which is Akbar Khan. Good night, Flashman huzoor, and a pleasant rest. There are servants within—call if you need them."

And with that he was gone, leaving me gaping at the doorway, and feeling no end of a fool.

In fact, Akbar Khan did not return next day, or for a week afterwards, so I had plenty of time to speculate. I was kept under close guard in the room, but comfortably enough; they fed me well and allowed me to exercise on a little closed verandah with a couple of armed Barukzis to keep an eye on me. But not a word would anyone say in answer to my questions and demands for release. I couldn't even discover what was going on in Kabul, or what our troops were doing—or what Akbar Khan himself might be up to. Or, most important of all, why he was keeping me prisoner.

Then, on the eighth day, Akbar returned, looking very spruce and satisfied. When he had dismissed the guards he inquired after my wounds, which were almost better, asked if I was well cared for and so forth, and then said that if there was anything I wished to know he would do his best to inform me.

Well, I lost no time in making my wishes known, and he listened smiling and stroking his short black beard. At last he cut me off with a raised hand.

"Stop, stop, Flashman huzoor. I see you are like a thirsty man; we must quench you a little at a time. Sit down now, and drink a little tea, and listen."

I sat, and he paced slowly about the room, a burly, springy figure in his green tunic and pyjamys which were tucked into short riding boots. He was something of a dandy, I noticed; there was gold lace on the tunic, and silver edging to the shirt beneath it. But again I was impressed by the obvious latent strength of the man; you could see it even in his stance, with his broad chest that looked always as though he was holding a deep breath, and his long, powerful hands.

"First," he said, "I keep you here because I need you. How, you shall see later—not today. Second, all is well in Kabul. The British keep to their cantonment, and the Afghans snipe at them from time to time and make loud noises. The King of Afghanistan,

Shah Sujah"—here he curled his lip in amusement—"sits doing nothing among his women in the Bala Hissar, and calls to the British to help him against his unruly people. The mobs rule Kabul itself, each mob under its leader imagining that it alone has frightened the British off. They do a little looting, and a little raping, and a little killing—their own people, mark you—and are content for the moment. There you have the situation, which is most satisfactory. Oh, yes, and the hill tribes, hearing of the death of Sekundar Burnes, and of the rumoured presence in Kabul of one Akbar Khan, son of the true king Dost Mohammed, are converging on the capital. They smell war and plunder. Now, Flashman huzoor, you are answered."

Well, of course, in answering half a dozen questions he had posed a hundred others. But one above all I had to be satisfied about.

"You say the British keep to their cantonment," I cried. "But what about Burnes's murder? D'you mean they've done nothing?"

"In effect, nothing," says he. "They are unwise, for their inaction is taken as cowardice. You and I know they are not cowards, but the Kabuli mobs don't, and I fear this may encourage them to greater excesses than they have committed already. But we shall see. However, all this leads me to my purpose in visiting you today —apart from my desire to inquire into your welfare." And he grinned again, that infectious smile which seemed to mock but which I couldn't dislike. "You understand that if I satisfy your curiosity here and there, I also have questions which I would wish answered."

"Ask away," says I, rather cautious.

"You said, at our first meeting—or at least you implied—that Elfistan Sahib and McLoten Sahib were . . . how shall I put it? . . . sometimes less than intelligent. Was that a considered judgement?"

"Elphinstone Sahib and McNaghten Sahib," says I, "are a pair of born bloody fools, as anyone in the bazaar will tell you."

"The people in the bazaar have not the advantage of serving on Elfistan Sahib's staff," says he drily. "That is why I attach importance to your opinion. Now, are they trustworthy?"

This was a deuced odd question, from an Afghan, I thought, and for a moment I nearly replied that they were English officers, blast his eyes. But you would have been wasting your time talking that way to Akbar Khan.

"Yes, they're trustworthy," I said.

"One more than the other? Which would you trust with your horse, or your wife—I take it you have no children?"

I didn't think long about this. "I'd trust Elphy Bey to do his best like a gentleman," I said. "But it probably wouldn't be much of a best."

"Thank you, Flashman," says he, "that is all I need to know. Now, I regret that I must cut short our most interesting little discussion, but I have many affairs to attend to. I shall come again. and we shall speak further."

"Now, hold on," I began, for I wanted to know how long he intended to keep me locked up, and a good deal more, but he turned me aside most politely, and left. And there I was, for another two weeks, damn him, with no one but the silent Barukzis for company.

I didn't doubt what he had told me about the situation in Kabul was true, but I couldn't understand it. It made no sense—a prominent British official murdered, and nothing done to avenge him. As it proved, this was exactly what had happened. When the mob looted the Residency and Sekundar was hacked to bits, old Elphy and McNaghten had gone into the vapours, but they'd done virtually nothing. They had written notes to each other, wondering whether to march into the city, or move into the Bala Hissar fort, or bring Sale—who was still bogged down by the Gilzais at Gandamack—back to Kabul. In the end they did nothing, and the Kabuli mobs roamed the city, as Akbar said, doing what they pleased, and virtually besieging our people in the cantonment.

Elphy could, of course, have crushed the mobs by firm action, but he didn't; he just wrung his hands and took to his bed, and McNaghten wrote him stiff little suggestions about the provisioning of the cantonment for the winter. Meanwhile the Kabulis, who at first had been scared stiff when they realised what they had done in murdering Burnes, got damned uppish, and started attacking the outposts near the cantonment, and shooting up our quarters at night.

One attempt, and only one, was made to squash them, and that foul-tempered idiot, Brigadier Shelton, bungled it handsomely. He took a strong force out to Beymaroo, and the Kabulis—just a damned drove of shopkeepers and stablehands, mark you, not real Afghan warriors—chased him and his troops back to the cantonment. After that, there was nothing to be done; morale in the cantonment went to rock-bottom, and the countryside Afghans, who had been watching to see what would happen, decided they were on a good thing, and came rampaging into the city. The signs were that if the mobs and the tribesmen really settled down to business, they could swarm over the cantonment whenever they felt like it.

All this I learned later, of course. Colin Mackenzie, who was through it all, said it was pathetic to see how old Elphy shilly-shallied and changed his mind, and McNaghten still refused to believe that disaster was approaching. What had begun as mob violence was rapidly developing into a general uprising, and all that was wanting on the Afghan side was a leader who would take charge of events. And, of course, unknown to Elphy and McNaghten and the rest of them, there was such a leader, watching events from a house in Kabul, biding his time and every now and then asking me questions. For after a fortnight's lapse Akbar Khan came to me again, polite and bland as ever, and talked about it and about, speculating on such various matters as British policy in India and the rate of march of British troops in cold weather. He came ostensibly to gossip, but he pumped me for all he was worth, and I let him pump. There was nothing else I could do.

He began visiting me daily, and I got tired of demanding my release and having my questions deftly ignored. But there was no help for it; I could only be patient and see what this jovial, clever gentleman had in mind for me. Of what he had in mind for himself I was getting a pretty fair idea, and events proved me right.

Finally, more than a month after Burnes's murder, Akbar came and told me I was to be released. I could have kissed him, almost, for I was fed up with being jailed, and not even an Afghan bint to keep me amused. He looked mighty serious, however, and asked me to be seated while he spoke to me "on behalf of the leaders of the Faithful." He had three of his pals with him, and I wondered if he meant them.

One of them, his cousin, Sultan Jan, he had brought before, a leery-looking cove with a fork beard. The others were called Muhammed Din, a fine-looking old lad with a silver beard, and Khan Hamet, a one-eyed thug with the face of a horse-thief. They sat and looked at me, and Akbar talked.

"First, my dear friend Flashman," says he, all charm, "I must tell you that you have been kept here not only for your own good but for your people's. Their situation is now bad. Why, I do not know, but Elfistan Sahib has behaved like a weak old woman. He has allowed the mobs to rage where they will, he has left the deaths of his servants unavenged, he has exposed his soldiers to the worst fate of all—humiliation—by keeping them shut up in cantonments while the Afghan rabble mock at them. Now his own troops are sick at heart; they have no fight in them."

He paused, picking his words.

"The British cannot stay here now," he went on. "They have lost their power, and we Afghans wish to be rid of them. There are those who say we should slaughter them all—needless to say, I do not agree." And he smiled. "For one thing, it might not be so easy—"

"It is never easy," said old Muhammed Din. "These same feringhees took Ghuznee Fort; I saw them, by God."

"—and for another, what would the harvest be?" went on Akbar. "The White Queen avenges her children. No, there must be a peaceful withdrawal to India; this is what I would prefer myself. I am no enemy of the British, but they have been guests in my country too long."

"One of 'em a month too long," says I, and he laughed.

"You are one feringhee, Flashman, who is welcome to stay as long as he chooses," says he. "But for the rest, they have to go."

"They came to put Sujah on the throne," says I. "They won't leave him in the lurch."

"They have already agreed to do so," said Akbar smoothly. "Myself, I have arranged the terms of withdrawal with McLoten Sahib."

"You've seen McNaghten?"

"Indeed. The British have agreed with me and the chiefs to march out to Peshawar as soon as they have gathered provisions for the journey and struck their camp. Sujah, it is agreed, remains on the throne, and the British are guaranteed safe conduct through the passes."

So we were quitting Kabul; I didn't mind, but I wondered how Elphy and McNaghten were going to explain this away to Calcutta. Inglorious retreat, pushed out by niggers, don't look well at all. Of course, the bit about Sujah staying on the throne was all my eye; once we were out of the way they'd blind him quietly and pop him in a fortress and forget about him. And the man who would take his place was sitting watching how I took the news.

"Well," says I at last, "there it is, but what have I to do with it? I mean, I'll just toddle off with the rest, won't I?"

Akbar leaned forward. "I have made it sound too simple, perhaps. There are problems. For example, McLoten has made his treaty to withdraw not only with myself, but with the Douranis, the Gilzais, the Kuzzilbashies, and so on—all as equals. Now, when the British have gone, all these factions will be left behind, and who will be the master?"

"Shah Sujah, according to you."

"He can rule only if he has a united majority of the tribes supporting him. As things stand, that would be difficult, for they eye each other askance. Oh, McLoten Sahib is not the fool you think him; he has been at work to divide us."

"Well, can't you unite them? You're Dost Mohammed's son, ain't you—and all through the passes a month ago I heard nothing but Akbar Khan and what a hell of a fellow he was."

He laughed and clapped his hands. "How gratifying! Oh, I have a following, it is true—"

"You have all Afghanistan," growls Sultan Jan. "As for Sujah—"

"I have what I have," Akbar interrupted him, suddenly chilly. "It is not enough, if I am to support Sujah as he must be supported."

There was a moment of silence, not very comfortable, and Akbar went on:

"The Douranis dislike me, and they are powerful. It would be better if their wings were clipped—theirs and a few others. This cannot be done after the British have left. With British help it can be done in time."

Oho, I thought, now we have it.

"What I propose is this," says Akbar, looking me in the eye. "McLoten must break his treaty so far as the Douranis are concerned; he must assist me in their overthrow. In return for this, I will allow him—for with the Douranis and their allies gone I shall have the power—to stay in Kabul another eight months. In that time I shall become Sujah's Vizier, the power at his elbow. The country will be so quiet then—so quiet, that the cheep of a Kandahar mouse will be heard in Kabul—that the British will be able to withdraw in honour. Is not this fair? The alternative now is a hurried withdrawal, which no one here can guarantee in safety, for none has the power to restrain the wilder tribes. And Afghanistan will be left to warring factions."

I have observed, in the course of a dishonest life, that when a rogue is outlining a treacherous plan, he works harder to convince himself than to move his hearers. Akbar wanted to cook his Afghan enemies' goose, that was all, and perfectly understandable, but he wanted to look like a gentleman still—to himself.

"Will you carry my proposal secretly to McLoten Sahib, Flashman?" he asked.

If he'd asked me to carry his proposal of marriage to Queen Victoria I'd have agreed, so of course I said "Aye" at once.

"You may add that as part of the bargain I shall expect a down payment of twenty lakhs of rupees," he added, "and four thousand a year for life. I think McLoten Sahib will find this reasonable, since I am probably preserving his political career."

And your own, too, thinks I. Sujah's Vizier, indeed. Once the Douranis were out of the way it would be farewell Sujah, and long live King Akbar. Not that I minded; after all, I would be able to say I was on nodding terms with a king—even if he was only a king of Afghanistan.

"Now," went on Akbar, "you must deliver my proposals to McLoten Sahib personally, and in the presence of Muhammed Din and Khan Hamet here, who will accompany you. If it seems" —he flashed his smile—"that I don't trust you, my friend, let me say that I trust no one. The reflection is not personal."

"The wise son," croaked Khan Hamet, opening his mouth for the first time, "mistrusts his mother." Doubtless he knew his own family best.

I pointed out that the plan might appear to McNaghten to be a betrayal of the other chiefs, and his own part in it dishonourable; Akbar nodded, and said gently:

"I have spoken with McLoten Sahib, remember. He is a politician."

He seemed to think that was answer enough, so I let it be. Then Akbar said:

"You will tell McLoten that if he agrees, as I think he will, he must come to meet me at Mohammed's Fort, beyond the cantonment walls, the day after tomorrow. He must have a strong force at hand within the cantonment, ready to emerge at the word and seize the Douranis and their allies, who will be with me. Thereafter we will dispose matters as seems best to us. Is this agreed?" And he looked at his three fellows, who nodded agreement.

"Tell McLoten Sahib," said Sultan Jan, with a nasty grin, "that if he wills he may have the head of Amenoolah Khan, who led the attack on Sekundar Burnes's Residency. Also, that in this whole matter we of the Barukzis have the friendship of the Gilzais."

If both Gilzais and Barukzis were in the plot, it seemed to me that Akbar was on solid ground; McNaghten would think so too. But to me, sitting looking at those four faces, bland Akbar and his trio of villains, the whole thing stank like a dead camel. I would have trusted the parcel of them as much as Gul Shah's snakes.

However, I kept a straight face, and that afternoon the guard at the cantonment's main gate was amazed by the sight of Lieutenant Flashman, clad in the mail of a Barukzi warrior, and accompanied by Muhammed Din and Khan Hamet,[15] riding down in state from Kabul City. They had thought me dead a month ago, chopped to bits with Burnes, but here I was larger than life. The word spread like fire, and when we reached the gates there was a crowd waiting for us, with tall Colin Mackenzie[16] at their head.

"Where the devil have you come from?" he demanded, his blue eyes wide open.

I leaned down so that no one else should hear and said, "Akbar Khan;" he stared at me hard, to see if I was mad or joking, and then said: "Come to the Envoy at once," and cleared a way through the crowd for us. There was a great hubbub and shouting of questions, but Mackenzie shepherded us all three straight to the Envoy's quarters and into McNaghten's presence.

"Can't it wait, Mackenzie?" says he peevishly. "I'm just about to dine." But a dozen words from Mackenzie changed his tune. He stared at me through his spectacles, perched as always on the very tip of his nose. "My God, Flashman! Alive! And from Akbar Khan, you say? And who are these?" And he indicated my companions.

"Once you suggested I should bring you hostages from Akbar, Sir William," says I. "Well, here they are, if you like."

He didn't take it well, but snapped to me to come in directly to dinner with him. The two Afghans, of course, wouldn't eat at an unbeliever's table, so they waited in his office, where food was brought to them. Muhammed Din reminded me that Akbar's message must be delivered only in their presence, so I contented myself by telling McNaghten that I felt as though I was loaded with explosives, but that it must wait till after dinner.

However, as we ate I was able to give him an account of Burnes's murder and my own adventures with Gul Shah; I told it very plain and offhand, but McNaghten kept exclaiming "Good God!" all the way through, and at the tale of my tug-of-war his glasses fell into his curry. Mackenzie sat watching me narrowly, pulling at his fair moustache, and when I was done and McNaghten was spluttering his astonishment, Mackenzie just said: "Good work, Flash." This was praise, from him, for he was a tough, cold ramrod of a man, and reckoned the bravest in the Kabul garrison, except maybe for George Broadfoot. If he told my tale—and he would—Flashy's stock would rise to new heights, which was all to the good.

Over the port McNaghten tried to draw me about Akbar, but I said it must wait until we joined the two Afghans; not that I minded, much, but it made McNaghten sniffy, which was always excuse enough for me. He said sarcastically that I seemed to have gone native altogether, and that I did not need to be so nice, but Mackenzie said shortly that I was right, which put His Excellency into the sulks. He muttered that it was a fine thing when important officials could be bearded by military whipper-snappers, and the sooner we got to business the better it would be.

So we adjourned to his study, and presently Muhammed and Hamet came in, greeted the Envoy courteously, and received his cool nod in reply. He was a conceited prig, sure enough. Then I launched into Akbar's proposal.

I can see them still: McNaghten sitting back in his cane chair, legs crossed, finger-tips together, staring at the ceiling; the two silent Afghans, their eyes fixed on him; and the tall, fair Mackenzie, leaning against the wall, puffing a cheroot, watching the Afghans. No one said a word as I talked, and no one moved. I wondered if McNaghten understood what I was saying; he never twitched a muscle.

When I was finished he waited a full minute, slowly took off his glasses and polished them, and said quietly:

"Most interesting. We must consider what the Sirdar Akbar has said. His message is of the greatest weight and importance. But of course it is not to be answered in haste. Only one thing will I say now: the Queen's Envoy cannot consider the suggestion of bloodshed contained in the offer of the head of Amenoolah Khan. That is repugnant to me." He turned to the two Afghans. "You will be tired, sirs, so we will detain you no longer. Tomorrow we will talk again."

It was still only early evening, so he was talking rot, but the two Afghans seemed to understand diplomatic language; they bowed gravely and withdrew. McNaghten watched the door close on them; then he sprang to his feet.

"Saved at the eleventh hour!" cried he. "Divide and conquer! Mackenzie, I had dreamed of something precisely like this." His pale, worn face was all smiles now. "I knew, I knew, that these people were incapable of keeping faith with one another. Behold me proved right!"

Mackenzie studied his cigar. "You mean you'll accept?"

"Accept? Of course I shall accept. This is a heaven-sent opportunity. Eight months, eh? Much can happen in that time: we may never leave Afghanistan at all, but if we do it will be with credit." He rubbed his hands and set to among the papers on his desk. "This should revive even our friend Elphinstone, eh, Mackenzie?"

"I don't like it," says Mackenzie. "I think it's a plot."

McNaghten stopped to stare at him. "A plot?" Then he laughed, short and sharp. "Oho, a plot! Let me alone for that—trust me for that!"

"I don't like it a bit," says Mackenzie.

"And why not, pray? Tell me why not. Isn't it logical? Akbar must be cock o' the walk, so out must go his enemies, the Douranis. He'll use us, to be sure, but it is to our own advantage."

"There's a hole in it," says Mac. "He'll never serve as Vizier to Sujah. He's lying in that, at least."

"What of it? I tell you, Mackenzie, it doesn't matter one per cent whether he or Sujah rules in Kabul, we shall be secured by this. Let them fight among themselves as they will; it makes us all the stronger."

"Akbar isn't to be trusted," Mac was beginning, but McNaghten pooh-poohed him.

"You don't know one of the first rules of politics: that a man can be trusted to follow his own interest. I see perfectly well that Akbar is after undisputed power among his own people; well, who's to blame him? And I tell you, I believe you wrong Akbar Khan; in our meetings he has impressed me more than any other Afghan I have met. I judge him to be a man of his word."

"The Douranis are probably saying that, too," says I, and had the icy spectacles turned on me for my pains. But Mackenzie took me up fast enough, and asked me what I thought.

"I don't trust Akbar either," says I. "Mind you, I like the chap, but he ain't straight."

"Flashman probably knows him better than we do," says Mac, and McNaghten exploded.

"Now, really, Captain Mackenzie! I believe I can trust my own judgement, do you know? Against even that of such a distinguished diplomatist as Mr Flashman here." He snorted and sat down at his desk. "I should be interested to hear precisely what Akbar Khan has to gain by treachery towards us? What purpose his proposal can have other than that which is apparent? Well, can you tell me?"

Mac just stubbed out his cheroot. "If I could tell you, sir,—if I could see a definite trick in all this—I'd be a happier man. Dealing with Afghans, it's what I don't see and don't understand that worries me."

"Lunatic philosophy!" says McNaghten, and wouldn't listen to another word. He was sold on Akbar's plan, plain enough, and so determined that next morning he had Muhammed and Hamet in and signified his acceptance in writing, which they were to take back to Akbar Khan. I thought that downright foolish, for it was concrete evidence of McNaghten's part in what was, after all, a betrayal. One or two of his advisers tried to dissuade him from putting pen to paper, at least, but he wouldn't budge.

"Trouble is the man's desperate," Mackenzie told me. "Akbar's proposal came at just the right moment, when McNaghten felt the last ray of hope was gone, and he was going to have to skulk out of Kabul with his tail between his legs. He wants to believe Akbar's offer is above board. Well, young Flash, I don't know about you, but when we go out to see Akbar tomorrow I'm taking my guns along."

I was feeling pretty nervous about it myself, and I wasn't cheered by the sight of Elphy Bey, when McNaghten took me along to see him that afternoon. The old fellow was lying on a daybed on his verandah, while one of the garrison ladies—I forget who—was reading the Scriptures to him. He couldn't have been more pleased to see me, and was full of praise for my exploits, but he looked so old and wasted, in his night-cap and gown, that I thought, my God, what chance have we with this to command us?

McNaghten was pretty short with him, for when Elphy heard of Akbar's plan he looked down in the mouth, and asked if McNaghten wasn't afraid of some treachery.

"None at all," says McNaghten. "I wish you to have two regiments and two guns got ready, quickly and quietly, for the capture of Mohammed Khan's fort, where we shall meet Sirdar Akbar tomorrow morning. The rest you can leave to me."

Elphy looked unhappy about this. "It is all very uncertain," says he, fretting. "I fear they are not to be trusted, you know. It is a very strange plot, to be sure."

"Oh, my God!" says McNaghten. "If you think so, then let us march out and fight them, and I am sure we shall beat them."

"I can't, my dear Sir William," says old Elphy, and it was pathetic to hear his quavering voice. "The troops aren't to be counted on, you see."

"Well, then, we must accept the Sirdar's proposals."

Elphy fretted some more, and McNaghten was nearly beside

himself with impatience. Finally he snapped out: "I understand these things better than you!" and turned on his heel, and stamped off the verandah.

Elphy was much distressed, and lamented on about the sad state of affairs, and the lack of agreement. "I suppose he is right, and he does understand better than I. At least I hope so. But you must take care, Flashman; all of you must take care."

Between him and McNaghten I felt pretty down, but evening brought my spirits up, for I went to Lady Sale's house, where there was quite a gathering of the garrison and wives, and found I was something of a lion. Mackenzie had told my story, and they were all over me. Even Lady Sale, a vinegary old dragon with a tongue like a carving knife, was civil.

"Captain Mackenzie has given us a remarkable account of your adventures," says she. "You must be very tired; come and sit here, by me."

I pooh-poohed the adventures, of course, but was told to hold my tongue. "We have little enough to our *credit*," says Lady Sale, "so we must make the most of what we have. You, at least, have behaved with *courage* and common sense, which is more than can be said for some *older* heads among us."

She meant poor old Elphy, of course, and she and the other ladies lost no time in taking his character to pieces. They did not think much of McNaghten, either, and I was surprised at the viciousness of their opinions. It was only later that I understood that they were really frightened women; they had cause to be.

However, everyone seemed to enjoy slanging Elphy and the Envoy, and it was quite a jolly party. I left about midnight; it was snowing, and bright moonlight, and as I walked to my billet I found myself thinking of Christmas-time in England, and the coach-ride back from Rugby when the half ended, and warm brandy-punch in the hall, and the roaring fire in the dining-room grate with Father and his cronies talking and laughing and warming their backsides. I wished I was there, with my young wife, and at the thought of her my innards tightened. By God, I hadn't had a woman in weeks, and there was nothing to be had in the cantonments. That was something I would speedily put right after we had finished our business with Akbar in the morning, and things were back to normal. Perhaps it was reaction from listening to those whining females, but it seemed to me as I went to sleep that McNaghten was probably right, and our plot with Akbar was all for the best.

I was up before dawn, and dressed in my Afghan clothes; it was easier to hide a brace of pistols beneath them than in a uniform. I buckled on my sword, and rode over to the gate where Mc-Naghten and Mackenzie were already waiting, with a few native troopers; McNaghten, in his frock coat and top hat, was sitting a mule and damning the eyes of a Bombay Cavalry cornet; it seemed the escort was not ready, and Brigadier Shelton had not yet assembled the troops who were to overpower the Douranis.

"You may tell the Brigadier there is never anything ready or right where he is concerned!" McNaghten was saying. "It is all of a piece; we are surrounded by military incompetents; well, it won't do. I shall go out to the meeting, and Shelton must have his troops ready to advance within the half hour. Must, I say! Is that understood?"

The cornet scuttled off, and McNaghten blew his nose and swore to Mackenzie he would wait no longer. Mac urged him to hold on at least till there was some sign that Shelton was moving, but McNaghten said:

"Oh, he is probably in his bed still. But I've sent word to Le Geyt; he will see the thing attended to. Ah, here are Trevor and Lawrence; now gentlemen, there has been time enough wasted. Forward!"

I didn't like this. The plan had been that Akbar and the chiefs, including the Douranis, should be assembled near Mohammed's Fort, which was less than a quarter of a mile from the cantonment gates. Once McNaghten and Akbar had greeted each other, Shelton was to emerge from the cantonment at speed, and the Douranis would be surrounded and overcome between our troops and the other chiefs. But Shelton wasn't ready, we didn't even have an escort, and it seemed to me that the five of us and the native troopers—who were only half a dozen or so strong—might have an uncomfortable time before Shelton came on the scene.

Young Lawrence thought so, too, for he asked McNaghten as we trotted through the gate if it would not be better to wait; Mc-Naghten snapped his head off and said we could simply talk to Akbar until Shelton emerged, when the thing would be done.

"Suppose there's treachery?" says Lawrence. "We'd be better to have the troops ready to move at the signal."

"I can't wait any longer!" cries McNaghten, and he was shaking, but whether with fear or cold or excitement I didn't know. And I heard him mutter to Lawrence that he knew there might be treachery, but what could he do? We must just hope Akbar would keep faith with us. Anyway, McNaghten would rather risk his own life than be disgraced by scuttling hangdog out of Kabul.

"Success will save our honour," says he, "and make up for all the rest."

We rode out across the snowy meadow towards the canal. It was a sparkling clear morning, bitterly cold; Kabul City lay straight ahead, grey and silent; to our left Kabul River wound its oily way beneath the low banks, and beyond it the great Bala Hissar fort seemed to crouch like a watchdog over the white fields. We rode in silence now, our hooves crunching the snow; from the four in front of me the white trails of breath rose over their shoulders. Everything was very quiet.

We came to the canal bridge, and just beyond it was the slope running down from Mohammed's Fort beside the river. The slope was dotted with Afghans; in the centre, where a blue Bokhara carpet was spread on the snow, was a knot of chieftains with Akbar in their midst. Their followers waited at a distance, but I reckoned there must be fifty men in view—Barukzis, Gilzais, Douranis, yes, by God, and Ghazis.[17] That was a nasty sight. We're mad, I thought, riding into this; why, even if Shelton advances at the double, we could have our throats cut before he's half way here.

I looked back over my shoulder to the cantonment, but there was no sign of Shelton's soldiers. Mind you, at this stage that was just as well.

We rode to the foot of the slope, and what I was shivering with was not the cold.

Akbar rode down to meet us, on a black charger, and himself very spruce in a steel back-and-breast like a cuirassier, with his spiked helmet wrapped about with a green turban. He was all smiles and called out greetings to McNaghten; Sultan Jan and the chiefs behind were all looking as jovial as Father Christmas, and nodding and bowing towards us.

'This looks damned unhealthy," muttered Mackenzie. The chiefs were advancing straight to us, but the other Afghans, on the slopes on either side, seemed to me to be edging forward. I gulped down my fear, but there was nothing for it but to go on now; Akbar and McNaghten had met, and were shaking hands in the saddle.

One of the native troopers had been leading a lovely little white mare, which he now took forward, and McNaghten presented it to Akbar, who received it with delight. Seeing him so cheerful, I tried to tell myself it was all right—the plot was laid, McNaghten knew what he was doing, I really had nothing to fear. The Afghans were round us now, anyway, but they seemed friendly enough still; only Mackenzie showed, by the cock of his head and his cold eye, that he was ready to drop his hand on his pistol butt at the first sign of a false move.

"Well, well," cries Akbar. "Shall we dismount?"

We did, and Akbar led McNaghten on to the carpet. Lawrence was right at their heels, and looking pretty wary; he must have said something, for Akbar laughed and called out:

"Lawrence Sahib need not be nervous. We're all friends here."

I found myself with old Muhammed Din beside me, bowing and greeting me, and I noticed that Mackenzie and Trevor, too, were being engaged in friendly conversation. It was all so pally that I could have sworn there was something up, but McNaghten seemed to have regained his confidence and was chatting away smoothly to Akbar. Something told me not to stand still, but to keep on the move; I walked towards McNaghten, to hear what was passing between him and Akbar, and the ring of Afghans seemed to draw closer to the carpet.

"You'll observe also that I'm wearing the gift of pistols received from Lawrence Sahib," Akbar was saying. "Ah, there is Flashman. Come up, old friend, and let me see you. McLoten Sahib, let me tell you that Flashman is my favourite guest."

"When he comes from you, prince," says McNaghten, "he is my favourite messenger."

"Ah, yes," says Akbar, flashing his smile. "He is a prince of messengers." Then he turned to look McNaghten in the eye, and said: "I understand that the message he bore found favour in your excellency's sight?"

The buzz of voices around us died away, and it seemed that everyone was suddenly watching McNaghten. He seemed to sense it, but he nodded in reply to Akbar.

"It is agreed, then?" says Akbar.

"It is agreed," says McNaghten, and Akbar stared him full in the face for a few seconds, and then suddenly threw himself forward, clapping his arms round McNaghten's body and pinning his hands to his sides.

"Take them!" he shouted, and I saw Lawrence, who had been just behind McNaghten, seized by two Afghans at his elbows. Mackenzie's cry of surprise sounded beside me, and he started forward towards McNaghten, but one of the Barukzis jumped between, waving a pistol. Trevor ran at Akbar, but they wrestled him down before he had gone a yard.

I take some pride when I think back to that moment; while the others started forward instinctively to aid McNaghten, I alone kept my head. This was no place for Flashman, and I saw only one way out. I had been walking towards Akbar and McNaghten, remember, and as soon as I saw the Sirdar move I bounded ahead, not at him, but past him, and so close that my sleeve brushed his back. Just beyond him, on the edge of the carpet, stood the little white mare which McNaghten had brought as a gift; there was a groom at her head, but I was too fast for him.

I mounted in one flying leap, and the little beast reared in astonishment, sending the groom flying and causing the others to give back from her flashing fore-hooves. She curvetted sideways before I got her under control with a hand in her mane; one wild glance round for a way out was all I had time for, but it showed me the way.

On all sides Afghans were running in towards the group on the carpet; the knives were out and the Ghazis were yelling blue murder. Straight downhill, ahead of me, they seemed thinnest; I jammed my heels into the mare's sides and she leaped forward, striking aside a ruffian in a skull-cap who was snatching at her head. The impact caused her to swerve, and before I could check her she was plunging towards the struggling crowd in the centre of the carpet.

She was one of your pure-bred, mettlesome bitches, all nerves and speed, and all I could do was clamp my knees to her flanks and hang on. One split second I had to survey the scene before she was in the middle of it; McNaghten, with two Afghans holding his arms, was being pushed headlong down the hill, his tall hat falling from his head, his glasses gone, and his mouth open in horror. Mackenzie I saw being thrown like a bolster over the flanks of a horse with a big Barukzi in the saddle, and Lawrence was being served the same way; he was fighting like a mad thing. Trevor I didn't see, but I think I heard him; as my little mare drove into the press like a thunderbolt there was a horrid, bubbling scream, and an exultant yell of Ghazi voices.

I had no time for anything but clinging to the mare, yet even in my terror I noticed Akbar, sabre in hand, thrusting back a Ghazi who was trying to come at Lawrence with a knife. Mackenzie was shouting and another Ghazi thrust at him with a lance, but Akbar, cool as you please, struck the lance aside with his sword and shouted with laughter.

"Lords of my country, are you?" he yelled. "You'll protect me, will you, Mackenzie Sahib?"

Then my mare had bounded past them, I had a few yards to steady her and to move in, and I set her head downhill.

"Seize him!" shouted Akbar. "Take him alive!"

Hands grabbed at the mare's head and at my legs, but we had the speed, thank God, and burst through them. Straight downhill, across the canal bridge, there was the level stretch beside the river, and beyond lay the cantonment. Once over the bridge, on this mare, there wasn't a mounted Afghan who could come near me. Gasping with fear, I clung to the mane and urged her forward.

It must have taken longer to seize my mount, burst through the press, and take flight than I had imagined, for I was suddenly aware that McNaghten and the two Afghans who were carrying him off were twenty yards down the hill, and almost right in my path. As they saw me bearing down on them one of them sprang back, grasping a pistol from his belt. There was no way of avoiding the fellow, and I lugged out my sword with one hand, holding on grimly with the other. But instead of shooting at me, he levelled his piece at the Envoy.

"For God's sake!" McNaghten cried, and then the pistol banged and he staggered back, clutching at his face. I rode full tilt into the man who had shot him, and the mare reared back on her haunches; there was a mob around us now, slashing at McNaghten as he fell, and bounding over the snow at me. I yelled in rage and panic, and swung my sword blindly; it whistled through the empty air, and I nearly overbalanced, but the mare righted me, and I slashed again and this time struck something that crunched and fell away. The air was full of howls and threats; I lunged furiously and managed to shake off a hand that was clutching at my left leg; something cracked into the saddle beside my thigh, and the mare shrieked and bounded forward.

Another leap, another blind slash of my sword and we were clear, with the mob cursing and streaming at our heels. I put my head down and my heels in, and we went like a Derby winner in the last furlong.

We were down the slope and across the bridge when I saw ahead of me a little party of horsemen trotting slowly in our direction. In front I recognised Le Geyt—this was the escort that was to have guarded McNaghten, but of Shelton and his troops there was no sign. Well, they might just be in time to convoy his corpse, if the Ghazis left any of it; I stood up in the stirrups, glancing behind to make sure the pursuit was distanced, and hallooed.

But the only effect was that the cowardly brutes turned straight round and made for the cantonment at full pelt; Le Geyt did make some effort to rally them, but they paid no heed. Well, I am a poltroon myself, but this was ridiculous; it costs nothing to make a show, when all is said. Acting on the thought, I wheeled my mare; sure enough, the nearest Afghans were a hundred yards in my rear, and had given up chasing me. As far again beyond them a crowd was milling round the spot where McNaghten had fallen; even as I watched they began to yell and dance, and I saw a spear upthrust with something grey stuck on the end of it. Just for an instant I thought: "Well, Burnes will get the job now," and then I remembered, Burnes was dead. Say what you like, the political service is a chancy business.

I could make out Akbar in his glittering steel breastplate, surrounded by an excited crowd, but there was no sign of Mackenzie or Lawrence. By God, I thought, I'm the only survivor, and as Le Geyt came spurring up to me I rode forward a few paces, on impulse, and waved my sword over my head. It was impressively bloody from having hit somebody in the scramble.

"Akbar Khan!" I roared, and on the hillside faces began to turn to look down towards me. "Akbar Khan, you forsworn, treacherous dog!" Le Geyt was babbling at my elbow, but I paid no heed.

"Come down, you infidel!" I shouted. "Come down and fight like a man!"

I was confident that he wouldn't, even if he could hear me, which was unlikely. But some of the nearer Afghans could; there was a move in my direction.

"Come away, sir, do!" cries Le Geyt. "See, they are advancing!"

They were still a safe way off. "You dirty dog!" I roared. "Have you no shame, you that call yourself Sirdar? You murder unarmed old men, but will you come and fight with Bloody Lance?" And I waved my sabre again.

"For God's sake!" cries Le Geyt. "You can't fight them all!"

"Haven't I just been doing that?" says I. "By God, I've a good mind—"

He grabbed me by the arm and pointed. The Ghazis were advancing, straggling groups of them were crossing the bridge. I didn't see any guns among them, but they were getting uncomfortably close.

"Sending your jackals, are you?" I bawled. "It's you I want, you Afghan bastard! Well, if you won't, you won't, but there'll be another day!"

With which I wheeled about, and we made off for the cantonment gate, before the Ghazis got within charging distance; they can move fast, when they want to.

At the gate all was chaos; there were troops hastily forming up, and servants and hangers-on scattering everywhere; Shelton was wrestling into his sword-belt and bawling orders. Red in the face, he caught sight of me.

"My God, Flashman! What is this? Where is the Envoy?"

"Dead," says I. "Cut to bits, and Mackenzie with him, for all I know."

He just gaped. "Who—what?—how?"

"Akbar Khan cut 'em up, sir," says I, very cool. And I added: "We had been expecting you and the regiment, but you didn't come."

There was a crowd round us—officers and officials and even a few of the troops who had broken ranks.

"Didn't come?" says Shelton. "In God's name, sir, I was coming this moment. This was the time appointed by the General!"

This astonished me. "Well, he was late," says I. "Damned late."

There was a tremendous hubbub about us, and cries of "Massacre!" "All dead but Flashman!" "My God, look at him!" "The Envoy's murdered!" and so on. Le Geyt pushed his way through them, and we left Shelton roaring to his men to stand fast till he found what the devil was what. He spurred up beside me, demanding to know what had taken place, and when I told him all of it, damning Akbar for a treacherous villain.

"We must see the General at once," says he. "How the devil did you come off alive, Flashman?"

"You may well ask, sir," cries Le Geyt. "Look here!" And he pointed to my saddle. I remembered having felt a blow near my leg in the skirmish, and when I looked, there was a Khyber knife with its point buried in the saddle bag. One of the Ghazis must have thrown it; two inches either way and it would have disabled me or the mare. Just the thought of what that would have meant blew all the brag I had been showing clean away. I felt ill and weak.

Le Geyt steadied me in the saddle, and they helped me down at Elphy's front door, while the crowd buzzed around. I straightened up, and as Shelton and I mounted the steps I heard Le Geyt saying:

"He cut his way through the pack of 'em, and even then he would have ridden back in alone if I hadn't stopped him! He would, I tell you, just to come at Akbar!"

That lifted my spirits a little, and I thought, aye, give a dog a good name and he's everyone's pet. Then Shelton, thrusting everyone aside, had us in Elphy's study, and was pouring out his tale, or rather, my tale.

Elphy listened like a man who cannot believe what he sees and hears. He sat appalled, his sick face grey and his mouth moving, and I thought again, what in God's name have we got for a commander? Oddly enough, it wasn't the helpless look in the man's eyes, the droop of his shoulders, or even his evident illness that affected me—it was the sight of his skinny ankles and feet and bedroom slippers sticking out beneath his gown. They looked so ridiculous in one who was a general of an army.

When we had done, he just stared and said:

"My God, what is to be done? Oh, Sir William, Sir William, what a calamity!" After a few moments he pulled himself together and said we must take counsel what to do; then he looked at me and said:

"Flashman, thank God you at least are safe. You come like Randolph Murray, the single bearer of dreadful news. Tell my orderly to summon the senior officers, if you please, and then have the doctors look at you."

I believe he thought I was wounded; I thought then, and I think now, that he was sick in mind as well as in body. He seemed, as my wife's relatives would have said, to be "wandered."

We had proof of this in the next hour or two. The cantonment, of course, was in a hubbub, and all sorts of rumours were flying. One, believe it or not, was that McNaghten had not been killed at all, but had gone into Kabul to continue discussions with Akbar, and in spite of having heard my story, this was what Elphy came round to believing. The old fool always fixed on what he wanted to believe, rather than what common sense suggested.

However, his daydream didn't last long. Akbar released Lawrence and Mackenzie in the afternoon, and they confirmed my tale. They had been locked up in Mohammed Khan's fort, and had seen McNaghten's severed limbs flourished by the Ghazis. Later the murderers hung what was left of him and Trevor on hooks in the butchers' stalls of the Kabul bazaar.

Looking back, I believe that Akbar would rather have had McNaghten alive than dead. There is still great dispute about this, but it's my belief that Akbar had deliberately lured McNaghten into a plot against the Douranis to test him; when McNaghten accepted Akbar knew he was not to be trusted. He never intended to hold power in Afghanistan in league with us; he wanted the whole show for himself, and McNaghten's bad faith gave him the opportunity to seize it. But he would rather have held McNaghten hostage than kill him.

For one thing, the Envoy's death could have cost Akbar all his hopes, and his life. A more resolute commander than Elphy—anyone, in fact—would have marched out of the cantonment to avenge it, and swept the killers out of Kabul. We could have done it, too; the troops that Elphy had said he couldn't rely on were furious over McNaghten's murder. They were itching for a fight, but of course Elphy wouldn't have it. He must shilly-shally, as usual, so we skulked all day in the cantonment, while the Afghans themselves were actually in a state of fear in case we might attack them. This I learned later; Mackenzie reckoned if we had shown face the whole lot would have cut and run.

Anyway, this is history. At the time I only knew what I had seen and heard, and I didn't like it a bit. It seemed to me that having slaughtered the Envoy the Afghans would now start on the rest of us, and having seen Elphy wringing his hands and croaking I couldn't see what was to stop them. Perhaps it was the shock of my morning escape, but I was in the shivering dumps for the rest of the day. I could feel those Khyber knives and imagine the Ghazis yelling as they cut us to bits; I even wondered if it might not be best to get a fast horse and make off from Kabul as quickly as I could, but that prospect was as dangerous as staying.

But by the next day things didn't look quite so bad. Akbar sent some of the chiefs down to express his regrets for McNaghten's death, and to resume the negotiations—as if nothing had happened. And Elphy, ready to clutch at anything, agreed to talk; he didn't see what else he could do, he said. The long and short of it was that the Afghans told us we must quit Kabul at once, leaving our guns behind, and also certain married officers and their wives as hostages!

It doesn't seem credible now, but Elphy actually accepted. He offered a cash subsidy to any married officer who would go with his family as hostages to Akbar. There was a tremendous uproar over this; men were saying they would shoot their wives sooner than put them at the mercy of the Ghazis. There was a move to get Elphy to take action for once, by marching out and occupying the Bala Hissar, where we could have defied all Afghanistan in arms, but he couldn't make up his mind, and nothing was done.

The day after McNaghten's death there was a council of officers, at which Elphy presided. He was in terribly poor shape; on top of everything else, he had had an accident that morning.

He had decided to be personally armed in view of the emergency, and had sent for his pistols. His servant had dropped one while loading it, and the pistol had gone off, the ball had passed through Elphy's chair, nicking his backside but doing no other damage.

Shelton, who could not abide Elphy, made the most of this.

"The Afghans murder our people, try to make off with our wives, order us out of the country, and what does our commander do? Shoots himself in the arse—doubtless in an attempt to blow his brains out. He can't have missed by much."

Mackenzie, who had no great regard for Elphy either, but even less for Shelton, suggested he might try to be helpful instead of sneering at the old fellow. Shelton rounded on him.

"I will sneer at him, Mackenzie!" says he. "I *like* sneering at him!"

And after this, to show what he thought, he took his blankets into the council and lay on them throughout, puffing at a cheroot and sniffing loudly whenever Elphy said anything unusually foolish; he sniffed a good deal.

I was at the council, in view of my part in the negotiations, I suppose, and for pure folly it matches anything in my military career—and I was with Raglan in the Crimea, remember. It was obvious from the first that Elphy wanted to do anything that the Afghans said he must do; he desired to be convinced that nothing else was possible.

"With poor Sir William gone, we are at a nonplus here," he kept repeating, looking around dolefully for someone to agree with him. "We can serve no purpose that I can see by remaining in Afghanistan."

There were a few spoke out against this, but not many. Pottinger, a smart sort of fellow who had succeeded by default to Burnes's job, was for marching into the Bala Hissar; it was madness, he said, to attempt to retreat through the passes to India in midwinter with the army hampered by hundreds of women and children and camp followers. Anyway, he didn't trust Akbar's safe conduct; he warned Elphy that the Sirdar couldn't stop the Ghazis cutting us up in the passes, even if he wanted to.

It seemed good sense to me: I was all for the Bala Hissar myself, so long as someone else led the way and Flashy was at his post beside Elphy Bey, with the rest of the army surrounding us. But the voices were all against Pottinger; it wasn't that they agreed with Elphy, but they didn't fancy staying in Kabul through the winter under his command. They wanted rid of him, and that meant getting him and the army back to India.

"God knows what he'll do if we stay here," someone muttered. "Make Akbar Political Officer, probably."

"A quick march through the passes," says another. "They'll let us go rather than risk trouble."

They argued on, until at last they were too tired and dispirited to talk any further. Elphy sat glooming round in the silence, but not giving any decision, and finally Shelton got up, ground out his cheroot, and snaps:

"Well, I take it we go? Upon my word, we must have a clear direction. Is it your wish, sir, that I take order for the army to remove to India with all possible speed?"

Elphy sat looking miserable, his fingers twitching together in his lap.

"It will be for the best, perhaps," he said at last. "I could wish it were otherwise, and that you had a commander not incapacitated by disease. Will you be so kind, Brigadier Shelton, as to take what order you think most fitting?"

So with no proper idea of what lay ahead, or how we should go, with the army dispirited and the officers divided, and with a commander announcing hourly that he was not fit to lead us, the decision was taken. We were to quit Kabul.

It took about a week to conclude the agreement with the Afghans, and even longer to gather up the army and all its followers and make it even half-fit for the road. As Elphy's aide I had my hands full, carrying his orders, and then other orders to countermand the first ones, and listening to his bleating and Shelton's snarling. One thing I was determined on, that Flashy at any rate was going to get back to India, whoever else did not. I had my idea about how this should be done, and it did not consist of taking my simple chance with the rest. The whole business of getting the army to pull up its roots, and provisioned and equipped for the journey, proved to be such a mess that I was confident most of them would never see Jallalabad, beyond the passes, where Sale was now holding out and we could count ourselves safe.

So I looked out Sergeant Hudson, who had been with me at Mogala, and was as reliable as he was stupid. I told him I wanted twelve picked lancers formed into a special detail under my command—not my Gilzais, for in the present state of the country I doubted whether they would be prepared to get their throats cut on my behalf. The twelve would make as good an escort as I could hope for, and when the time came for the army to founder, we could cut loose and make Jallalabad on our own. I didn't tell Hudson this, of course, but explained that this troop and I would be employed on the march as a special messenger corps, since orders would be forever passing up and down the column. I told Elphy the same thing, and added that we could also act as mounted scouts and general busybodies. He looked at me like a tired cow.

"This will be dangerous work, Flashman," says he. "I fear it will be a perilous journey, and this will expose you to the brunt of it."

"Never say die, sir," says I, very manful. "We'll come through, and anyway, there ain't an Afghan of the lot of them that's a match for me."

"Oh, my boy," says he, and the silly old bastard began piping his eye. "My boy! So young, so valiant! Oh, England," says he, looking out of the window, "what dost thou not owe to thy freshest plants! So be it, Flashman. God bless you."

I wanted rather more insurance than that, so I made certain that Hudson packed our saddlebags with twice as much hard-tack as we would need; supplies were obviously going to be short, and I believed in getting our blow in first. In addition to the lovely little white mare I had taken from Akbar, I picked out another Afghan pony for my own use; if one mount sank I should have the other.

These were the essentials for the journey, but I had an eye to the luxuries as well. Confined to the cantonments as we were, I had not had a woman for an age, and I was getting peckish. To make it worse, in that Christmas week a messenger had come through from India with mails; among them was a letter from Elspeth. I recognised the handwriting, and my heart gave a skip; when I opened it I got a turn, for it began, "To my most beloved Hector," and I thought, by God, she's cheating on me, and has sent me the wrong letter by mistake. But in the second line was a reference to Achilles, and another to Ajax, so I understood she was just addressing me in terms which she accounted fitting for a martial paladin; she knew no better. It was a common custom at that time, in the more romantic females, to see their soldier husbands and sweethearts as Greek heroes, instead of the whoremongering, drunken clowns most of them were. However, the Greek heroes were probably no better, so it was not so far off the mark.

It was a commonplace enough letter, I suppose, with news that she and my father were well, and that she was Desolate without her True Love, and Counted the Hours till my Triumphant Return from the Cannon's Mouth, and so on. God knows what young women think a soldier does for a living. But there was a good deal about how she longed to clasp me in her arms, and pillow my head on her breast, and so on (Elspeth was always rather forthright, more so than an English girl would have been), and thinking about that same breast and the spirited gallops we had taken together, I began to get feverish. Closing my eyes, I could imagine her soft, white body, and Fetnab's, and Josette's, and what with dreaming to this tune I rapidly reached the point where even Lady Sale would have had to cut and run for it if she had happened to come within reach.

However, I had my eye on younger game, in the excellent shape of Mrs Parker, the merry little wife of a captain in the 5th Light Cavalry. He was a serious, doting fellow, about twenty years older than she, and as fondly in love as only a middle-aged man with a young bride can be. Betty Parker was pretty enough, in a plump way, but she had buck teeth, and if there had been Afghan women to hand I would hardly have looked at her. With Kabul City out of all bounds there was no hope of that, so I went quickly to work in that week after Christmas.

I could see she fancied me, which was not surprising in a woman married to Parker, and I took the opportunity at one of Lady Sale's evenings—for the old dragon kept open house in those days, to show that whoever was dismayed, she was full of spirit—to play loo with Betty and some others, and press knees with her beneath the table. She didn't seem to mind by half, so I tested the ground further later on; I waited till I could find her alone, and gave her tits a squeeze when she least expected it. She jumped, and gasped, but since she didn't swoon I guessed that all was well and would be better.

The trouble was Parker. There was no hope of doing anything while we remained in Kabul, and he was sure to stick close as a mother hen on the march. But chance helped me, as she always does if you keep your wits about you, although she ran it pretty fine and it was not until a couple of days before we were due to depart that I succeeded in removing the inconvenient husband.

It was at one of those endless discussions in Elphy's office, where everything under the sun was talked about and nothing done. In between deciding that our men must not be allowed to wear rags round their legs against the snow as the Afghans did to keep off frost-bite, and giving instructions what fodder should be carried along for his fox-hounds, Elphy Bey suddenly remembered that he must send the latest instructions about our departure to Nott at Kandahar. It would be best, he said, that General Nott should have the fullest intelligence of our movements, and Mackenzie, coming as near to showing impatience as I ever knew him, agreed that it was proper that one half of the British force in Afghanistan should know what the other half was doing.

"Excellent," says Elphy, looking pleased, but not for long. "Who shall we send to Kandahar with the despatches?" he wondered, worrying again.

"Any good galloper will do," says Mac.

"No, no," says Elphy, "he must be a man in whom we can repose the most perfect trust. An officer of experience is required," and he went rambling on about maturity and judgement while Mac drummed his fingernails on his belt.

I saw a chance here; ordinarily I never intruded an opinion, being junior and not caring a damn anyway, but now I asked if I might say a word.

"Captain Parker is a steady officer," says I, "if it ain't out of place for me to say so. And he's as sure in the saddle as I am, sir."

"Didn't know that," says Mac. "But if you say he's a horseman, he must be. Let it be Parker, then," says he to Elphy.

Elphy hummed a bit. "He is married, you know, Mackenzie. His wife would be deprived of his sustaining presence on our journey to India, which I fear may be an arduous one." The old fool was always too considerate by half. "She will be a prey to anxiety for his safety. . . ."

"He'll be as safe on the road to Kandahar as anywhere," says Mac. "And he'll ride all the harder there and back. The fewer loving couples we have on this march the better."

Mac was a bachelor, of course, one of these iron men who are married to the service and have their honeymoon with a manual of infantry drill and a wet towel round their heads; if he thought sending off Parker would cut down the number of loving couples he was going to be mistaken; I reckoned it would increase it.

So Elphy agreed, shaking his head and chuntering, and I rounded off the morning's work later by saying to Mac when we were outside that I was sorry for naming Parker, and that I'd forgotten he was a married man.

"You too?" says Mac. "Has Elphy infected you with his disease of worrying over everything that don't matter and forgetting those that do? Let me tell you, Flash, we shall spend so much time wagging our heads over nonsenses like Parker and Elphy's dogs and Lady McNaghten's chest-of-drawers that we'll be lucky if we ever see Jallalabad." He stepped closer and looked at me with those uncomfortable cold eyes of his. "You know how far it is? Ninety miles. Have you any notion how long it will take, with an army fourteen thousand strong, barely a quarter of 'em fighting troops, and the rest a great rabble of Hindoo porters and servants, to say nothing of women and children? And we'll be marching through a foot of snow on the worst ground on earth, with the temperature at freezing. Why, man, with an army of Highland ghillies I doubt if it could be done in under a week. If we're lucky we might do it in two—if the Afghans let us alone, and the food and firing hold out, and Elphy doesn't shoot himself in the other buttock."

I'd never seen Mackenzie in such a taking before. Usually he was as cool as a trout, but I suppose being a serious professional and having to work with Elphy had worn him thin.

"I wouldn't say this to anybody but you, or George Broadfoot if he were here," says he, "but if we come through it'll be by pure luck, and the efforts of one or two of us, like you and me. Aye, and Shelton. He's a surly devil, but he's a fighting soldier, and if

Elphy will let him alone he might get us to Jallalabad. There, now, I've told you what I think, and it's as near to croaking as I hope I'll ever get." He gave me one of his wintry smiles. "And you're worried about Parker!"

Having heard this, I was worried only about me. I knew Mackenzie; he wasn't a croaker, and if he thought our chances were slim, then slim they were. Of course, I knew from working in Elphy's office that things weren't shaping well; the Afghans were hampering us at every turn in getting supplies together, and there were signs that the Ghazis were moving out of Kabul along the passes—Pottinger was sure they were going to lie in wait for us, and try to cut us up in the really bad defiles, like Khoord-Kabul and Jugulluk. But I had reasoned that an army fourteen thousand strong ought to be safe, even if a few fell by the wayside; Mac had put it in a different light, and I began to feel again that looseness low down in my guts and the sick sensation in my throat. I tried to tell myself that soldiers like Shelton and Mackenzie, yes, and Sergeant Hudson, weren't going to be stopped by a few swarms of Afghans, but it was no good. Burnes and Iqbal had been good soldiers, too, and that hadn't saved them; I could still hear the hideous chunk of those knives into Burnes's body, and think of McNaghten swinging dead on a hook, and Trevor screaming when the Ghazis got him. I came near to vomiting. And half an hour back I had been scheming so that I could tumble Mrs Parker in a tent on the way back to Jallalabad; that reminded me of what Afghan women do to prisoners, and it didn't bear thinking about.

I was hard put to it to keep a good face on things at Lady Sale's last gathering, two nights before we left. Betty was there, and the look she gave me cheered me up a little; her lord and master would be half way to Kandahar by now, and I toyed with the notion of dropping in at her bungalow that night, but with so many servants about the cantonment it would be too risky. Better to wait till we're on the road, thinks I, and nobody knows one tent from another in the dark.

Lady Sale spent the evening as usual, railing about Elphy and the general incompetence of the staff. "There never was such a set of yea-and-nays. The only *certain* thing is that our chiefs have no mind for two minutes on end. They seem to think of *nothing* but contradicting each other, when harmony and *order* are most needed."

She said it with satisfaction, sitting in her last chair while they fed her furniture into the stove to keep the room tolerably warm. Everything had gone except her chest-of-drawers, which was to provide fuel to cook her meals before our departure; we sat round on the luggage which was piled about the walls, or squatted on the floor, while the old harpy sat looking down her beaky nose, her mittened hands folded in front. The strange thing was that no one thought of her as a croaker, although she complained unendingly; she was so obviously confident that *she* would get to Jallalabad in spite of Elphy's bungling that it cheered people up.

"Captain Johnson informs me," says she, sniffing, "that there is food and fodder for ten days at the most, and that the Afghans have no *intention* of providing us with an escort through the passes."

"Better without 'em," says Shelton. "The fewer we see the better I'll like it."

"Indeed? And who, then, is to *guard* us from the badmashes and brigands lurking in the hills?"

"Good God, ma'am," cries Shelton, "aren't we an army? We can protect ourselves, I hope."

"You may hope so, indeed. I am not so sure that some of your *native* troops will not take the first opportunity to make themselves *scarce*. We shall be quite without friends, and food, and *firewood*."

She then went on to tell us cheerfully that the Afghans certainly meant to try to destroy our whole force, in her opinion, that they meant to get all our women into their possession, and that they would leave only one man alive, "who is to have his legs and hands cut off and is to be placed at the entrance of the Khyber pass, to deter all feringhees from entering the country again."

"My best wishes to the Afghan who gets *her*," growled Shelton as we were leaving. "If he's got any sense he'll stick *her* up in the Khyber—that'll keep the feringhees out with a vengeance."

The next day I spent making sure that my picked lancers were all in order, that our saddle-bags were full, and that every man had sufficient rounds and powder for his carbine. And then came the last night, and the chaos of last-minute preparations in the dark, for Shelton was determined to be off before first light so that we might pass Khoord-Kabul in the first day's march, which meant covering fifteen miles.

Possibly there has been a greater shambles in the history of warfare than our withdrawal from Kabul; probably there has not. Even now, after a lifetime of consideration, I am at a loss for words to describe the superhuman stupidity, the truly monumental incompetence, and the bland blindness to reason of Elphy Bey and his advisers. If you had taken the greatest military geniuses of the ages, placed them in command of our army, and asked them to ruin it utterly as speedily as possible, they could not—I mean it seriously—have done it as surely and swiftly as he did. And he believed he was doing his duty. The meanest sweeper in our train would have been a fitter commander.

Shelton was not told that we would march on the morning of the 6th January, until evening on the 5th. He laboured like a madman through the night, loading up the huge baggage train, assembling the troops within the cantonment in their order of march, and issuing orders for the conduct and disposal of the entire force. It is a few words on paper: as I remember it, there was a black night of drifting snow, with storm lanterns flickering, troops tramping unseen in the dark, a constant babble of voices, the neighing and whining of the great herd of baggage animals, the rumble of wagons, messengers dashing to and fro, great heaps of luggage piled high outside the houses, harassed officers demanding to know where such-and-such a regiment was stationed, and where so-and-so had gone, bugle calls ringing in the night wind, feet stamping, children crying, and on the lighted verandah of his office, Shelton, red-faced and dragging at his collar, with his staff scurrying about him while he tried to bring some order out of the inferno.

And as the sun came up from the Seeah Sung hills, it seemed that he had done it. The army of Afghanistan was standing ready to march—everyone was dead tired, of course—strung out through the length of the cantonment, with everything loaded (except sufficient food), and all the troops fallen in and armed (with hardly any powder and ball among them), and Shelton shouting his last orders in a voice gone hoarse, while Elphy Bey finished an unhurried breakfast of devilled ham, omelette, and a little pheasant. (I know because he invited me to join him with the other staff officers.)

And while he was making his final toilet, with his staff and servants fussing round him, and the army waiting in the cold, I rode out to the cantonment gate to see what was happening over towards Kabul. The city was alive, with crowds on the roof-tops and scattered over the snowy ground from Bala Hissar to the river; they were there to watch the feringhees go, but they seemed quiet enough just now. The snow was falling gently; it was damned cold.

In the cantonments the bugles shrilled together, and "Forward!" was the command, and with a great creaking and groaning and shuffling and bellowing the march began.

First out came Mackenzie with his jezzailchis, the wild hill marksmen who were devoted to him; like me, he was wearing poshteen cloak and turban, with his pistols stuck in his belt, and he looked the genuine Afridi chief with his long moustache and his ugly rascals behind him. Then Brigadier Anquetil with the 44th, the only British infantry regiment in the army, very dapper in their shakos and red coats with white crossbelts; they looked fit to sweep away all the hordes of Afghanistan, and my spirits rose at the sight of them. They had a few fifes playing "Yankee Doodle," of all things, and stepped out smartly.

A squadron of Sikh cavalry, escorting the guns and sappers and miners, came next, and then in a little group the English women and families, all on camels or ponies, the children and older ladies travelling in camel howdahs, the younger women riding. And of course Lady Sale was to the fore, wearing an enormous turban and riding a tiny Afghan pony side-saddle. "I was saying to Lady McNaghten that I believe we *wives* would make the best troopers of all," she cries out. "What do you think, Mr Flashman?"

"I'd take your ladyship into my troop any time," says I, at which she simpered horribly—"but the other horses might be jealous," I says to myself quietly, at which the lancers set up a great laugh.

There were about thirty white women and children, from tiny babies to grandmothers, and Betty Parker gave me a knowing smile and a wave as she trotted past. Thinks I, wait till tonight, there'll be one snug blanket-roll on the Jallalabad road anyway.

Then came Shelton, blown and weary but cursing as loud as ever, on his charger, and the three Indian regiments of foot, black faces, red coats and white trousers, their naked feet churning up the slush. And behind them the herd—for that was what it was —of baggage animals, lowing and roaring with their tottering bundles and creaking carts. There were hundreds of camels, and the stench was furious; they and the mules and ponies churned the cantonment road into a sea of liquid chocolate, through which the hordes of camp followers and their families waded up to the knee, babbling and shouting. There were thousands of them, men, women, and children, with no order whatever, their few belongings carried on their backs, and all in great consternation at the thought of the march back to India; no proper provision had been made for feeding them on the way, or quartering them at night. They were apparently just to forage what they could and sleep in the drifts.

This great brown mob surged by, and then came the rearguard of Indian infantry and a few cavalry troops. The great procession was all strung out across the plain to the river, a sprawling, humming mass that stumbled slowly through the snow; steam rose from it like smoke. And then last of all Elphy Bey's entourage came out to canter up the line and take its place with the main body beside Shelton, but Elphy was already beset by doubts, and I heard him debating loudly with Grant whether it might not be better to delay setting off.

Indeed, he actually sent a messenger to stop the vanguard at the river, but Mackenzie deliberately disobeyed and pushed on; Elphy wrung his hands and cried: "He mustn't do it! Tell Mackenzie to stop, I say!" but by that time Mac was over the bridge, so Elphy had to give up and come along with the rest.

We were no sooner out of the compound than the Afghans were in. The crowds that had been watching had moved round slowly, keeping a safe distance from us, but now they rushed into the cantonments, yelling and burning, looting what was left in the houses and even opening fire on the rearguard. There was some rough work at the gates, and a few Indian troopers were knocked from their saddles and butchered before the rest got clear.

One effect of this was to cause a panic among the porters and camp-followers, many of whom flung away their loads and ran for dear life. The snow on either side of the road was soon dotted with bundles and sacks, and it has been reckoned that a good quarter of our stores were lost this way before we had even reached the river.

With the mob hanging on the heels of the column we got across, marched past the Bala Hissar, and turned on to the Jallalabad road. We were travelling at a snail's pace, but already some of the Indian servants were beginning to fall out, plumping down and wailing in the snow, while the bolder spirits among the Afghan spectators came close to jeer and pelt us with stones. There was some scuffling and a shot or two, but in the main the Kabulis just seemed glad to let us go—and so far we were glad enough to be going. If we had even dreamed what lay ahead we would have turned back as one, even if all Afghanistan had been pursuing, but we did not know.

On Elphy's instructions Mackenzie and I and our troops kept up a constant patrol along the flanks of the column, to discourage the Afghans from coming too close and prevent straggling. Some bodies of Afghans were moving along with us, but well out on either side of the road, and we kept a sharp eye on them. One of these groups, drawn up on a little knoll, took my eye; I decided to keep well clear of them, until I heard my name called, and who should be sitting at their head, large as life, but Akbar Khan.

My first instinct was to turn tail for the column, but he rode a little forward from his companions, calling to me, and presently I edged my pony up to within a short pistol shot of him. He was all in his steel back-and-breast, with his spiked helmet and green turban, and smiling all over his face.

"What the devil do you want?" says I, beckoning Sergeant Hudson up beside me.

"To bid you God speed and a good journey, old friend," says he, quite cheerful. "Also to give you a little advice."

"If it's the kind you gave Trevor and McNaghten, I don't need it," says I.

"As God is my judge," says he, "that was no fault of mine. I would have spared him, as I would spare all of you, and be your friend. For this reason, Flashman huzoor, I regret to see you marching off before the escort is ready that I was assembling for your safety."

"We've seen some of your escorts before," says I. "We'll do very well on our own."

He rode closer, shaking his head. "You do not understand. I, and many of us, wish you well, but if you go off to Jallalabad before I have taken proper measures for your protection on the march, why then, it is no fault of mine if you meet disaster. I cannot control the Ghazis, or the Gilzais."

He seemed serious, and quite sincere. To this day I cannot be sure whether Akbar was a complete knave or a fairly honest man caught up in a stream of circumstances which he could not resist. But I wasn't trusting him in a hurry, after what had happened.

"What d'ye want us to do?" says I. "Sit down in the snow and wait for you to round up an escort while we freeze to death?" I wheeled my pony round. "If you have any proposals to make, send them to Elfistan Sahib, but I doubt if he'll listen to 'em. Man alive, your damned Kabulis have been sniping at our rearguard already; how's that for keeping faith?"

I was for riding off, but he suddenly spurred up closer yet. "Flashman," says he, speaking very fast and low. "Don't be a fool. Unless Elfistan Sahib lets me help him, by providing an escort in exchange for hostages, you may none of you reach Jallalabad. You can be one of those hostages; I swear on the grave of my mother you would be safe. If Elfistan Sahib will wait, it shall be arranged. Tell him this, and let him send you out again with a reply."

He was so earnest that I was half-convinced. I imagine now that what he was chiefly interested in was hostages, but it is also possible that he genuinely believed that he could not control his tribesmen, and that we should be massacred in the passes. If that happened, Afghanistan might well see another British army the following year, and it would be shooting as it came. At the time, however, I was more concerned about his interest in me.

"Why should you want to preserve my life?" says I. "What do you owe me?"

"We have been friends," says he, grinning that sudden grin of his. "Also I admired the compliments you paid me as you rode away from Mohammed Khan's fort the other day."

"They weren't meant to flatter you," says I.

"The insults of an enemy are a tribute to the brave," laughs he. "Think on what I have said, Flashman. And tell Elfistan Sahib."

He waved and rode back up the hill, and the last I saw of his troop they were following slowly on our flank, the tips of their spears winking on the snowy hillside.

All that afternoon we toiled on, and we were long short of Khoord-Kabul when night came freezing down. The Afghans hung on our flanks, and when men—aye, and women and children—dropped by the wayside, they were pounced on as soon as the column had passed and murdered. The Afghans saw that our chiefs were not prepared to fight back, so they snapped at our heels, making little sorties on the baggage train, cutting up the native drivers, and scattering into the rocks only when our cavalry approached. Already the column was falling into utter disorder; the main body gave no thought to the thousands of native camp-followers, who were bitterly affected by the cold and want of food; hundreds fell by the way, so that in our wake there was a litter not only of bundles and baggage, but of corpses. And this was within a twenty-minute gallop of Kabul.

I had taken Akbar's message to Elphy when I rejoined the column, and it sent him into a great taking. He dithered and consulted his staff, and eventually they decided to push on.

"It will be for the best," bleated Elphy, "but we should maintain our relations with the Sirdar in the meantime. You shall ride to him tomorrow, Flashman, and convey my warmest good wishes. That is the proper way of it."

The stupid old bastard seemed oblivious of the chaos around him. Already his force was beginning to wither at the edges. When we camped it was a question of the troops simply lying down on the snow, in huddled groups for warmth, while the unfortunate niggers wailed and whimpered in the dark. There were some fires, but no field kitchens or tents for the men; much of the baggage was already lost, the order of march had become confused, some regiments had food and others none, and everyone was frozen to the bone.

The only ones fairly well off were the British women and their children. The dragon Lady Sale saw to it that their servants pitched little tents or shelters; long after dark her sharp, high voice could be heard carping on above the general moan and whimper of the camp-followers. My troopers and I were snug enough in the lee of some rocks, but I had left them at dusk to help with the ladies' tents, and in particular to see where Betty was installed. She seemed quite gay, despite the cold, and after I had made sure that Elphy was down for the night, I returned to the little group of wagons where the women were. It was now quite dark, and starting to snow, but I had marked her little tent, and found it without difficulty.

I scratched on the canvas, and when she called out who was there I asked her to send away her servant, who was in the tent with her for warmth. I wanted to talk to her, I said, keeping my voice down.

The native woman who served her came snuffling out presently, and I helped her into the dark with my boot. I was too cock-a-hoop to care whether she gossiped or not; she was probably too frightened, like the rest of the niggers, to worry about anything except her own skin that night.

I crawled under the low canvas, which was only about two feet high, and heard Betty move in the darkness. There was a pile of blankets covering the floor of the tent, and I felt her body beneath them.

"What is it, Mr Flashman?" says she.

"Just a friendly call," says I. "Sorry I couldn't send in a card."

She giggled in the dark. "You are a great tease," she whispered, "and very wrong to come in like this. But I suppose the conditions are so unusual, and it is kind of you to look after me."

"Capital," says I, and without wasting more time I dived under the blankets and took hold of her. She was still half-dressed against the cold, but gripping that young body sent the fire running through me, and in a moment I was on top of her with my mouth on hers. She gave a gasp, and then a yelp, and before I knew it she was writhing away, striking at me, and squeaking like a startled mouse.

"How dare you!" she squealed. "Oh, how dare you! Get away! Get away from me this instant!" And lunging in the dark she caught me a great crack on the eye.

161

"What the devil!" says I. "What's the matter?"

"Oh, you brute!" she hissed—for she had the sense to keep her voice down—"you filthy, beastly brute! Get out of my tent at once! At once, d'you hear?"

I could make nothing of this, and said so. "What have I done? I was only being friendly. What are you acting so damned missish for?"

"Oh, base!" says she. "You . . . you. . . ."

"Oh, come now," says I. "You're in very high ropes, to be sure. You weren't so proper when I squeezed you the other night."

"Squeezed me?" says she, as though I had uttered some unmentionable word.

"Aye, squeezed. Like this." And I reached over and, with a quick fumble in the dark, caught one of her breasts. To my amazement, she didn't seem to mind.

"Oh, that!" she says. "What an evil creature you are! You know that is nothing; all gentlemen do that, in affection. But you, you monstrous beast, presume on my friendship to try to. . . . Oh, oh, I could die of shame!"

If I had not heard her I shouldn't have believed it. God knows I have learned enough since of the inadequacies of education given to young Englishwomen, but this was incredible.

"Well," says I, "if you're accustomed to gentlemen doing that to you, in affection, you know some damned queer gentlemen."

"You . . . you foul person," says she, in indignation. "It is no more than shaking hands!"

"Good God!" says I. "Where on earth were you brought up?"

At this, by the sound of it, she buried her face in the blankets and began to weep.

"Mrs Parker," says I, "I beg your pardon. I have made a mistake, and I am very sorry for it." The quicker I got out of this, the better, or she might start shouting rape round the camp. I'll say this for her, ignorant and full of amazing misconceptions as she was, she had appeared angry rather than frightened, and had kept her abuse of me down to a whisper. She had her own reputation to think about, of course.

"I shall go," says I, and started crawling for the flap. "But I may tell you," I added, "that in polite society it ain't usual for gentlemen to squeeze ladies' tits, whatever you may have been told. And it ain't usual, either, for ladies to let gentlemen do it; it gives the gentlemen a wrong impression, you know. My apologies, again. Good night."

She gave one last muffled squeak, and then I was out in the snow. I had never heard anything like it in my life, but I didn't know, then, how astonishingly green young women could be, and what odd notions they could get. Anyway, I had been well set down, for certain; by the looks of it I should have to contain my enthusiasm until we reached India again. And that, as I huddled down in my blankets beside my troopers, with the cold getting keener every minute, was no consolation at all.

Looking back on it now, I suppose it is funny enough, but lying shivering there and thinking of the pains I had been at to get Captain Parker out of the way, I could have twisted Mrs Betty's pretty neck for her.

It was a bitter, biting night, and there was little sleep to be had, for if the cold was not bad enough the niggers kept up a great whining and wailing to wake the dead. And by morning not a few of the poor devils *were* dead, for they had no more than a few rags of clothing to cover them. Dawn broke on a scene that was like something from an icy hell; everywhere there were brown corpses lying stiff in the drifts, and the living crackled as they struggled up in their frozen clothes. I saw Mackenzie actually crying over the body of a tiny native child; he was holding her in his arms, and when he saw me he cried out:

"What are we to do? These people are all dying, and those that don't will be slaughtered by those wolves on the hillside yonder. But what can we do?"

"What, indeed?" says I. "Let 'em be; there's no help for it." He was remarkably concerned, it seemed to me, over a nigger. And he was such a ramrod of a man, too.

"If only I could take her with me," says he, laying the small body back in the snow.

"You couldn't take 'em all," says I. "Come on, man, let's get some breakfast." He saw this was sensible advice, and we were lucky enough to get some hot mutton at Elphy's tent.

Getting the column under way was tremendous work; half the sepoys were too frost-bitten to be able to lift their muskets, and the other half had deserted in the night, skulking back to Kabul.

We had to flog them into line, which warmed everyone up, but the camp followers needed no such urging. They were crowding ahead in panic in case they should be left behind, and threw Anquetil's vanguard into tremendous confusion. At this point a great cloud of mounted Ghazis suddenly came yelling out of a nullah in the hillside, and rode into the mob, cutting down everything in their way, soldiers and civilians, and made off with a couple of Anquetil's guns before he could stop them.

He made after them, though, with a handful of cavalry, and there was a warm skirmish; he couldn't get back the guns, but he spiked them, while the 44th stood fast and did nothing. Lady Sale damned them for cowards and hang-backs—the old baggage should have been in command, instead of Elphy—but I didn't blame the 44th myself. I was farther down the column, and in no hurry to get near the action until Anquetil was riding back, when I brought my lancers up at the canter (true to life, Tom Hughes, eh?). The guns were going to be no use to us, anyway.

We blundered along the road for a mile or two, with troops of Afghans hanging on our flanks and every now and then swooping down at a weak part of the column, cutting up a few folk, snatching at the stores, and riding off again. Shelton kept roaring for everyone to hold his place and not be drawn in pursuit, and I took the opportunity to damn his eyes and demand to know what we were soldiers for, if not to fight our enemies when we saw them in front of us.

"Steady on, old Flash," says Lawrence, who was with Shelton just then. "It's no use chasing 'em and getting cut up in the hills; they'll be too many for you."

"It's too bad!" I bawled, slapping my sabre. "Are we just to wait for 'em to chew us up as they please, then? Why, Lawrence, I could clear that hillside with twenty Frenchmen, or old ladies!"

"Bravo!" cries Lady Sale, clapping her hands. "You hear, gentlemen?"

There was a knot of the staff round Elphy's palankeen, with Shelton in the middle of them, and they were none too pleased to hear the old dragon crowing at them. Shelton bristled up, and told me to hold my place and do as I was told.

"At your orders, sir," says I, mighty stiff, and Elphy joined in.

"No, no, Flashman," says he. "The Brigadier is right. We must preserve order." This, in the middle of a column that was a great sprawling mass of troops and people and animals, with no direction at all, and their baggage scattered.

Mackenzie, coming up, told me that my party and his jezzailchis must flank the column closely, watching the likely places, and driving in hard when the Afghans appeared—what the Americans call "riding herd." You can guess what I thought of this, but I agreed heartily with Mac, especially when it came to picking out the most likely spots for attack, so that I could keep well clear of them. It was simple enough, really, for the Afghans would only come where we were not, and at this time they were less interested in killing soldiers than in cutting up the unarmed niggers and pillaging the baggage animals.

They made pretty good practice at this during the morning, running in and slitting a throat and running off again. I did pretty well, halloo-ing to my lancers and thundering along the line of march, mostly near the headquarters section. Only once, when I was down by the rearguard, did I come face to face with a Ghazi; the fool must have mistook me for a nigger, in my poshteen and turban, for he came yelling down on a party of servants close by and cut up an old woman and a couple of brats. There was a troop of Shah's cavalry not far off, so I couldn't hang back; the Ghazi was on foot, so I let out a great roar and charged him, hoping he would sheer off at the sight of a mounted soldier. He did, too, and like an ass I tried to ride him down, thinking it would be safe enough to have a swipe at him. But the brute whipped round and slashed at me with his Khyber knife, and only by the grace of God did I take the cut on my sabre. I drove on past him, and wheeled just in time to see one of my lancers charging in to skewer him beautifully. Still, I had a good hack at him, for luck, and was able to trot up the line presently looking stern, and with my point impressively bloody.

It had been a lesson to me, though, and I took even greater care to be out of distance whenever they made a sortie out of the hills. It was nerve-racking work, and it was all I could do to maintain a bold-looking front as the morning wore on; the brutes were getting braver all the time, and apart from their charges there was an uncomfortable amount of sniping taking place.

165

At last Elphy got fed up, and ordered a halt, which was the worst thing he could have done. Shelton swore and stamped, and said we must push on; it was our only hope to get through Khoord-Kabul before dark. But Elphy insisted we must stop to try and make some sort of peace with the Afghan leaders, and so stop the slow bleeding to death of the army at the hands of the harassing tribesmen. I was for this, and when Pottinger spotted a great mass of Afghans far up the slope, with Akbar at their head, he had no difficulty in persuading Elphy to send out messengers to him.

By God, I was sorry to be on hand when that happened, for of course Elphy's eye lighted on me. There was nothing I could do about it, of course; when he said I must ride to Akbar and demand to know why the safe-conduct was not being observed, I had to listen to his orders as though my guts were not dissolving inside me, and say, "Very good, sir," in a steady voice. It was no easy task, I can tell you, for the thought of riding out to meet those ruffians chilled me to the backbone. What was worse, Pottinger said I should go alone, for the Afghans might mistake a party for an attacking force.

I could have kicked Pottinger's fat backside for him; he was so damned full of self-importance, standing there looking like Jesus Christ, with his lovely brown beard and whiskers. But I just had to nod as though it was all in the day's work; there was a fair crowd round, for the womenfolk and English families naturally clung as close to Elphy's presence as they could—much to Shelton's annoyance—and half the officers in the main body had come up to see what was happening. I noticed Betty Parker, in a camel howdah, looking bewildered and mimmish until she caught my eye, when she looked quickly away.

So I made the best of it. As I wheeled my pony I shouted out to Gentleman Jim Skinner:

"If I don't come back, Jim, settle Akbar Khan for me, will you?"

Then I clapped in the spurs and went at the slope hell-for-leather; the faster I went the less chance I stood of getting picked off, and I had a feeling that the closer I got to Akbar Khan the safer I should be.

Well, it was right enough; no one came near me, and the Ghazi parties on the hill just stared as I swept by; as I came up towards where Akbar sat his horse before his host—for there must have been five or six hundred of them—he waved to me, which was a cheering sight.

"Back again, prince of messengers," he sings out. "What news from Elfistan Sahib?"

I pulled up before him, feeling safer now that I was past the Ghazi outliers. I didn't believe Akbar would let me be harmed, if he could help it.

"No news," says I. "But he demands to know if this is how you keep faith, setting on your men to pillage our goods and murder our people."

"Did you not tell him?" says he, jovial as ever. "He himself broke faith, by leaving Kabul before the escort was ready for him. But here it is—" and he gestured at the ranks behind him "— and he may go forward in peace and safety."

If this was true, it was the best news I had heard in months. And then, glancing past him at the ranks behind, I felt as though I had been kicked in the stomach: immediately in his rear, and glaring at me with his wolf smile, was my old enemy, Gul Shah. Seeing him there was like a dash of cold water in the face; here was one Afghan who did not want to see Flashman, at least, depart in peace and safety.

Akbar saw my look, and laughed. Then he brought his horse up closer to mine, so that we were out of earshot, and said:

"Have no fear of Gul Shah. He no longer makes mistakes, such as the one which was almost so unfortunate for yourself. I assure you, Flashman, you need not mind him. Besides, his little snakes are all back in Kabul."

"You're wrong," says I. "There are a damned lot of them sitting either side of him."

Akbar threw back his head, and laughed again, flashing those white teeth.

"I thought the Gilzais were friends of yours," says he.

"Some of them," says I. "Not Gul Shah's."

"It is a pity," says Akbar, "for you know that Gul is now Khan of Mogala? No? Oh, the old man—died, as old men will. Gul has been very close to me, as you know, and as a reward for faithful service I granted him the lordship."

167

"And Ilderim?" I asked.

"Who is Ilderim? A friend of the British. It is not fashionable, Flashman, greatly though I deplore it, and I need friends myself— strong friends, like Gul Shah."

Well, it didn't matter to me, but I was sorry to see Gul Shah advanced, and sorrier still to see him here, watching me the way a snake watches a mouse.

"But Gul is difficult to please, you know," Akbar went on. "He and many others would gladly see your army destroyed, and it is all I can do to hold them back. Oh, my father is not yet King again in Afghanistan; my power is limited. I can guarantee you safe-conduct from the country only on conditions, and I fear that my chiefs will make those conditions harsher the longer Elfistan Sahib resists them."

"As I understand it," says I, "your word is pledged already."

"My word? Will that heal a cut throat? I talk of what is; I expect Elfistan Sahib to do the same. I can see him safe to Jallalabad if he will deliver up six hostages to me here, and promises me that Sale will leave Jallalabad before your army reaches it."

"He can't promise that," I protested. "Sale isn't under his command now; he'll hold Jallalabad till he is given orders from India to leave."

Akbar shrugged. "These are the terms. Believe me, old friend, Elfistan Sahib must accept them—he must!" And he thumped his fist against my shoulder. "And for you, Flashman; if you are wise you will be one of the six hostages. You will be safer with me than down yonder." He grinned, and reined back his pony. "Now, go with God, and come again soon with a wise answer."

Well, I knew better than to expect any such thing from Elphy Bey, and sure enough, when I carried Akbar's message to him he croaked and dithered in his best style. He must consider, he said, and in the meantime the army was so exhausted and confused that we should march no farther that day. It was only two o'clock.

Shelton flew into a great passion at this, and stormed at Elphy that we must press on. One more good march would take us through Khoord-Kabul Pass and, what was more important, out of the snow, for beyond the pass the ground dropped away. If we spent another night in the freezing cold, said Shelton, the army must die.

So they argued and wrangled, and Elphy had his way. We stayed where we were, thousands of shivering wretches on a snow-swept road, with nearly half our food already gone, no fuel left, and some of the troops even reduced to burning their muskets and equipment to try to keep a tiny flicker of warmth in their numb bodies. The niggers died in droves that night, for the mercury was far below freezing, and the troops kept alive only by huddling together in huge groups, burrowing in among each other like animals.

I had my blankets, and enough dried meat in my saddlebags not to go hungry. The lancers and I slept in a tight ring, as the Afghans do, with our cloaks above; Hudson had seen to it that each man carried a flask of rum, and so we kept out the cold tolerably well.

In the morning we were covered with snow, and when I clambered out and saw the army, thinks I, this is as far as we'll go. Most of them were too frozen to move at first, but when the Afghans were seen gathering on the slopes in the dawn light, the camp-followers flew into a panic and blundered off down the road in a great mob. Shelton managed to heave the main body of troops up in their wake, and so we stumbled on, like a great wounded animal with no brain and no heart, while the crackle of that hellish sniping started afresh, and the first casualties of the day began to totter from the ranks to die in the drifts on either side.

From other accounts of that frightful march that I have read—mostly Mackenzie's and Lawrence's and Lady Sale's[18]—I can fit a few of my recollections into their chronicle, but in the main it is just a terrible, bloody nightmare even now, more than sixty years after. Ice and blood and groans and death and despair, and the shrieks of dying men and women and the howling of the Ghazis and Gilzais. They rushed and struck, and rushed and struck again, mostly at the camp-followers, until it seemed there was a slashed brown body every yard of the way. The only place of safety was in the heart of Shelton's main body, where the sepoys still kept some sort of order; I suggested to Elphy when we set off that I and my lancers should ride guard on the womenfolk, and he agreed at once. It was a wise move on my part, for the attacks on the flanks were now so frequent that the work we had been doing yesterday was become fatally dangerous. Mackenzie's jezzailchis were cut to ribbons stemming the sorties.

As we neared Khoord-Kabul the hills rose up on either side, and the mouth of that awful pass looked like a gateway into hell. Its walls were so stupendous that the rocky bottom was in perpetual twilight; the dragging tread of the army, the bellowing of the beasts, the shouts and groans and the boom of shots echoed and rang from its cliffs. The Afghans were on the ledges, and when Anquetil saw them he halted the vanguard, because it seemed certain death to go on.

There was more consulting and arguing around Elphy, until Akbar and his people were seen among the rocks near the pass mouth. Then I was sent off again, and it was to tell him that at last Elphy had seen reason: we would give up six hostages, on condition that Akbar called off his killers. He agreed, clapping me on the shoulders and swearing that all should now be well; I should come as one of the hostages, he said, and a merry time we would have of it. I was torn two ways about this; the farther away I could keep from Gul Shah, the better; on the other hand, how safe would it be to remain with the army?

It was settled for me, for Elphy himself called on Mackenzie, Lawrence, and Pottinger to give themselves over to Akbar. They were among the best we had, and I suppose he thought Akbar would be the more impressed by them. Anyway, if Akbar kept his word it did not matter much who remained with the army, since it would not have to fight its way to Jallalabad. Lawrence and Pottinger agreed at once; Mac took a little longer. He had been a trifle cool with me—I suppose because my lancers had not shared the fighting that day, and his folk had been so badly mauled. But he said nothing, and when Elphy put it to him he didn't answer, but stood staring out over the snow. He was in a sad pass, with his turban gone and his hair all awry, his poshteen spattered with blood and a drying wound on the back of his hand.

Presently he drew his sword, and dropped it point first into the ground, and walked over without a word to join Pottinger and Lawrence. Watching his tall figure moving away I felt a little chill touch me; being a ruffian, perhaps I know a good man when I see one better than most, and Mac was one of the mainstays of our force. A damned prig, mind you, and given to immense airs, but as good a soldier—for what that's worth—as I've met.

Akbar wanted Shelton as well, but Shelton wouldn't have it. "I trust that black bastard as far as I'd trust a pi-dog," says he. "Anyway, who's to look after the army if I'm gone?"

"I shall be in command still," says Elphy, taken aback.

"Aye," says Shelton, "that's what I mean."

This started another bickering match, of course, which ended with Shelton turning on his heel and stumping off, and Elphy whining about discipline. And then the order to march sounded again, and we turned our faces towards Khoord-Kabul.

At first it was well enough, and we were unmolested. It looked as though Akbar had his folk under control, and then suddenly the jezzails began to crack from the ledges, and men began to fall, and the army staggered blindly in the snow. They were pouring fire into the pass at almost point-blank range, and the niggers began to scream and run, and the troops broke their ranks, with Shelton bawling, and then in a moment everyone was running or riding full tilt through that hellish defile. It was just a great wild rush, and the devil take the hindmost; I saw a camel with two white women and two children shot, and it staggered into the snow and threw them out. An officer ran to help, and went down with a ball in his belly, and then the crowd surged over them all. I saw a Gilzai mounted warrior seize on a little girl of about six and swing her up screaming to his saddlebow and make off; she kept shrieking "Mummy! Mummy!" as he bore her away. Sepoys were throwing down their muskets and running blindly forward, and I saw an officer of the Shah's Cavalry riding in among them, belabouring them with the flat of his sword and yelling his head off. Baggage was being flung recklessly away, the drivers were abandoning their animals, no one had any thought but to rush through the pass as fast as possible, away from that withering fire.

I can't say I wasted much time myself: I put my head down to my pony's neck, dug in my heels and went like billy-be-damned, threading through the pack and praying to God I wasn't hit by a stray ball. The Afghan ponies are as sure-footed as cats, and she never stumbled once. Where my lancers were I had no idea, not that I cared; it was every man (and woman) for himself, and I wasn't too particular who I rode over in my flight. It was nip and tuck like a steeplechase, with the shots crashing and echoing and thousands of voices yelling; only once did I check for an instant, when I saw young Lieutenant Sturt shot out of his saddle; he rolled into a drift and lay there screaming, but it would have done no good to stop. No good to Flashy, anyway, and that was what mattered.

How long it took to make the passage I don't know, but when the way began to widen and the mass of fugitives ahead and around began to slow down I reined in to take stock. The firing had slackened, and Anquetil's vanguard were forming up to cover the flight of those still coming behind. Presently there was a great mob streaming out of the defile, troops and people all mixed together, and when they reached the light of day they just collapsed in the snow, dead beat.

Three thousand people died in Khoord-Kabul, they say, most of them niggers, and we lost all our remaining baggage. When we made camp beyond the eastern limit of the pass we were in the middle of a snow-storm, all order was completely lost; stragglers kept coming in until dark, and I remember one woman who arrived having carried her baby on foot the whole way. Lady Sale had been shot in the arm, and I can see her now holding her hand out to the surgeon and shutting her eyes tight while he cut the ball out; she never flinched, the tough old bitch. There was a major struggling with his hysterical wife, who wanted to go back for her lost child; he was weeping and trying to stop the blows she was aiming wildly at his chest. "No, no, Jenny!" he kept saying. "She's gone! Pray to Jesus to look after her!" Another officer, I forget who, had gone snow-blind, and kept walking about in circles until someone led him away. Then there was a British trooper, reeling drunk on an Afghan pony and singing a barrack-room song; where he had got the liquor, God knows, but there was plenty of it, apparently, for presently he fell into the snow and lay there snoring. He was still there next morning, frozen dead.

Night was hell again, with the darkness full of crying and groaning. There were only a handful of tents left, and the English women and children all crowded into one of them. I wandered about all night, for it was freezing too bitterly to sleep, and anyway I was in a fearful funk. I could see now that the whole army was going to be destroyed, and myself with it; being a hostage with Akbar would be no better, for I had convinced myself by this that when he had finished butchering the army he would kill his prisoners too. There was only one hope that I could see, and that was to wait with the army until we were clear of the snow, and then strike out by night on my own. If the Afghans spotted me I would ride for it.

Next day we hardly advanced at all, partly because the whole force was so frozen and starved as to be incapable of going far, but also because Akbar sent a messenger into camp saying that we should halt so that he could have provisions brought up. Elphy believed him, in spite of Shelton's protests; Shelton almost went on his knees to Elphy, urging that if we could only keep going till we were out of the snow, we might come through yet. But Elphy doubted if we could get even that far.

"Our only hope is that the Sirdar, taking pity on our plight, will succour us at this late hour," says he. "You know, Shelton, he is a gentleman; he will keep his word."

Shelton just walked away in disgust and rage. The supplies never came, of course, but the following day comes another messenger from Akbar, suggesting that since we were determined to march on, the wives and families of the British officers should be left in his care. It was just this suggestion, made back in Kabul, that had provoked such indignation, but now every married man leaped at it. Whatever anyone might say openly, however much Elphy might talk as though he still expected to march to Jallalabad, everyone knew that the force as it stood was doomed. Frost-bitten, starving, cluttered still with camp-followers like brown skeletons who refused to die, with its women and children slowing it down, with the Ghazis and Gilzais sniping and harrying, death stared the army in the face. With Akbar, at least, the women and children would stand a chance.

So Elphy agreed, and we watched the little convoy, on the last of the camels, set off into the snow, the married men going along with their wives. I remember Betty riding bareheaded, looking very pretty with the morning sun shining on her hair, and Lady Sale, her wounded arm in a sling, poking her head out of a camel howdah to rebuke the nigger who was trotting alongside carrying the last of her belongings in a bundle. But I didn't share the general satisfaction that they were leaving us; I was keeping as well out of harm's way as I could by staying next to Elphy, but even that was not going to be safe for long.

I still had dried mutton enough left in my saddle-bags, and Sergeant Hudson seemed to have a secret store of fodder for his horse and those of the lancers who survived—there were about half a dozen left of my original party, I think, but I didn't count. But even clinging to Elphy's palankeen, on the pretext of riding bodyguard, I was in no doubt of what must happen eventually. In the next two days the column was under constant attack; in about ten miles we lost the last of the camp-followers, and in one terrible affray which I heard behind us but took good care not to see, the last of the sepoy units were fairly wiped out. To tell the truth, my memories of that period are hazy; I was too exhausted and afraid to pay much heed. Some things, though, are clear in my mind; images like coloured pictures in a magic lantern that I shall never forget.

Once, for example, Elphy had all the officers of the force line up at the rearguard, to show a "united front,"[19] as he called it, to our pursuers. We stood there for a full half hour, like so many scarecrows, while they jeered at us from a distance, and one or two of us were shot down. I remember Grant, the Adjutant-General, clapping his hands over his face and shouting, "I'm hit! I'm hit!" and falling down in the snow, and the young officer next to me—a boy with yellow side-whiskers covered with frost— saying, "Oh, poor old fellow!"

I saw an Afghan boy, once, chuckling to himself as he stabbed and stabbed again at a wounded sepoy; the boy was not over ten years old. And I remember the glazed look in the eyes of dying horses, and a pair of brown feet marching in front of me that left bloody footprints on the ice. I remember Elphy's grey face, with his jowls wobbling, and the rasping sound of Shelton's voice, and the staring eyes in the dark faces of the few Indians that were left, soldiers and camp-followers—but mostly I remember the fear that cramped my stomach and seemed to turn my legs to jelly as I listened to the crackle of firing before and behind, the screams of stricken men, and the triumphant screeching of the Afghans.

I know now that when we were five days out from Kabul, and

had reached Jugdulluk, the army that had been fourteen thousand strong was just over three thousand, of whom a bare five hundred were fighting troops. The rest, apart from a few hostages in the hands of the enemy, were dead. And it was here that I came to my senses, in a barn at Jugdulluk where Elphy had made his quarters.

It was as though I came out of a dream to hear him arguing with Shelton and some of the staff over a proposal that had come from Akbar that Elphy and Shelton should go to see him under a flag of truce, to negotiate. What they were to negotiate, God knows, but Shelton was dead against it; he stood there, his red cheeks fallen in, but his moustache still bristling, swearing that he would go on for Jallalabad if he had to do it alone. But Elphy was for negotiating; he would go and see Akbar, and Shelton must come, too; he would leave Anquetil to command the army.

Aye, thought I, and somehow my brain was as clear as ice again, this is where Flashman takes independent action. They would never come back from Akbar, of course; he would never let such valuable hostages go. If I, too, let myself fall into Akbar's hands, I would be in imminent danger from his henchman, Gul Shah. If I stayed with the army, on the other hand, I would certainly die with it. One obvious course suggested itself. I left them wrangling, and slipped out in search of Sergeant Hudson.

I found him dressing his horse, which was so thin and jaded now it looked like a run-down London hack.

"Hudson," says I, "you and I are riding out."

He never blinked. "Yes, sir," says he. "Where to, sir?"

"India," says I. "Not a word to anyone; these are special orders from General Elphinstone."

"Very good, sir," says he, and I left him knowing that when I came back he would have our beasts ready, saddle-bags as full as he could manage, and everything prepared. I went back to Elphy's barn, and there he was, preparing to leave to see Akbar. He was fussing as hard as ever, over such important matters as the whereabouts of his fine silver flask, which he intended to take as a gift to the Sirdar—this while the remnants of his army were dying in the snow round Jugdulluk.

"Flashman," says he, gathering his cloak round him and pulling his woollen cap over his head, "I am leaving you for only a little time, but in these desperate days it is not wise to count too far ahead. I trust I find you well enough in a day or two, my boy. God bless you."

And God rot you, you old fool, I thought; you won't find me in a day or two, not unless you ride a damned sight faster than I think you can. He sniffed some more about his flask, and shuffled out, helped by his valet. Shelton wasn't yet ready, apparently, and the last words I heard Elphy say were: "It is really too bad." They should be his epitaph; I raged inwardly at the time when I thought of how he had brought me to this; now, in my maturer years, I have modified my view. Whereas I would have cheerfully shot him then, now I would hang, draw and quarter him for a bungling, useless, selfish old swine. No fate could be bad enough for him.

Hudson and I waited for night, and then we simply saddled up and slipped off into the dark, striking due east. It was so easy I could have laughed; no one challenged us, and when about ten minutes out we met a party of Gilzais in the dark I gave them good night in Pushtu and they left us alone. There was no moon, but light enough for us to pick our way easily enough through the snowy rocks, and after we had ridden a couple of hours I gave the order to halt, and we bedded down for the night in the lee of a little cliff. We had our blankets, and with no one to groan around us I slept the best sleep I had had in a week.

When I woke it was broad day, and Sergeant Hudson had a little fire going and was brewing coffee. It was the first hot drink I had tasted in days; he even had a little sugar for it.

"Where the devil did you come by this, Hudson?" says I, for there had been nothing but dried mutton and a few scraps of biscuit on the last few days of the march.

"Foraged, sir," says he, cool as you please, so I asked no more questions, but sipped contentedly as I lay in my blankets.

"Hold on, though," I said, as he dropped more sticks on his fire. "Suppose some damned Ghazi sees your smoke; we'll have the whole pack of 'em down on us."

"Beg pardon, sir," says he, "but this hardwood don't make no smoke worth mentioning." And neither it did, when I came to look at it.

A moment later he was begging my pardon again, and asking if I intended we should ride on shortly, or perhaps rest for that day where we were. He pointed out that the ponies were used up, what with lack of fodder, but that if they were rested and given a good feed next morning, we should be out of the snow soon and into country where we might expect to come by grazing.

I was in two minds about this, for the more distance we put between ourselves and Akbar's ruffians—and Gul Shah especially

—the better I would like it. On the other hand, both the beasts and ourselves would be the better of rest and in this broken country it didn't seem likely that we would be spotted, except by sheer chance. So I agreed, and found myself considering this Sergeant Hudson for the first time, for beyond noting that he was a steady man I had given him not much notice before. After all, why should one notice one's men very much?

He was about thirty, I suppose, powerfully built, with fair hair that had a habit of falling over one eye, when he would brush it away. He had one of those square tough faces that you see on working men, with grey eyes and a cleft in his chin, and he did everything very deft and smartly. By his accent I would have said he was from somewhere in the west, but he was well spoken enough, and, although he knew his place, was not at all your ordinary trooper, half-yokel, half-guttersnipe. It seemed to me as I watched him tending the fire, and presently rubbing down the ponies, that I had made a lucky choice in him.

Next morning we were up and off before dawn, Hudson having given the beasts the last of the fodder which he confessed he had been hoarding in his bags—"just in case we was going to need one last good day's gallop." Using the sun, I set off south-east, which meant we had the main road from Kabul to India somewhere away to our right; it was my intention to follow this line until we came to the River Soorkab, which we would ford and follow along its southern bank to Jallalabad, about sixty miles away. That should keep us well clear of the road, and of any wandering bands of Afghans.

I was not greatly concerned about what tale we would tell when we got there; God knew how many folk had become separated from the main army, like Hudson and myself, or how many would eventually turn up at Jallalabad. I doubted if the main force would ever get there, and that would give everyone too much to think about to worry about a few strays like us. At need I could say we had become separated in the confusion; Hudson wasn't likely to blab my remark about being despatched on orders from Elphy —and God knew when Elphy would return to India, if he ever did.

So I was in excellent fettle as we threaded our way through the little snowy passes, and well before noon we crossed the Soorkab and made capital speed along its southern shore. It was rocky enough, to be sure, but there were occasional places where we could raise a gallop, and it seemed to me that at this rate we should soon be out of the snows and on to easier, drier going. I pressed on hard, for this was Gilzai country, and Mogala, where Gul Shah lorded it when he was at home, was not far away. The thought of that grim stronghold, with the crucifixes at the gates, cast a shadow over my mind, and at that moment Sergeant Hudson edged his pony up beside mine.

"Sir," says he. "I think we're being followed."

"What d'ye mean?" says I, nastily startled. "Who is it?"

"Dunno," says he, "but I can feel it, if you know what I mean, sir." He looked round us; we were on a fairly clear stretch, with the river rumbling away to our left, and broken hills to our right. "Mebbe this way isn't as lonely as we thought."

I'd been long enough in the hills to know that when a seasoned soldier has that instinct, he is generally right; a less experienced and less nervous officer might have pooh-poohed his fears, but I knew better. At once we turned away from the river and up a narrow gully into the hill country; if there were Afghans behind us we would let them pass on while we took a long loop into the hills. We could still hold our course for Jallalabad, but midway between the Soorkab and the main road.

It was slower going, of course, but after an hour or so Hudson said he felt we were clear of whoever had been behind us. Still I kept well away from the river, and then another interruption came: from far away to our right, very faint on the afternoon air, came the sound of firing. It was ragged, but there was enough of it to suggest that a fair-sized force was involved.

"By God!" says Hudson. "It's the army, sir!"

The same thought struck me; it might be that the army, or what was left of it, would have got this far on the road. I guessed that Gandamack would be somewhere up ahead of us, and as I knew that the Soorkab swings south in that area, we had no choice but to ride towards the firing if we were not to risk running into our mysterious pursuers on the river.

So we pushed on, and always that damned firing came closer. I guessed it couldn't be more than a mile off now, and was just about to call to Sergeant Hudson, who had forged ahead, when he turned in his saddle and waved to me in great excitement. He had come to a place where two great rocks reared up at the mouth of a gully that ran down steeply in the direction of the Kabul road: between them we had a clear view down from the heights, and as I reined in and looked I saw a sight I shall never forget.

Beneath us, and about a mile away, lay a little cluster of huts, with smoke rising from them, that I guessed must be Gandamack village. Close by, where the road swung north again, was a gentle slope, strewn with boulders, rising to a flat summit about a hundred yards across. That whole slope was crawling with Afghans; their yells came clearly up the gully to us. On the summit of the slope was a group of men, maybe a company strong; at first, seeing their blue poshteens, I took them for Afghans, but then I noticed the shakos, and Sergeant Hudson's voice, shaking with excitement, confirmed me:

"That's the 44th! Look at 'em, sir! It's the 44th, poor devils!"

They were in a ragged square, back to back on the hilltop, and even as we watched I saw the glitter of bayonets as they levelled their pieces, and a thin volley crashed out across the valley. The Afghans yelled louder than ever, and gave back, but then they surged in again, the Khyber knives rising and falling as they tried to hack their way into the square. Another volley, and they gave back yet again, and I saw one of the figures on the summit flourishing a sword as though in defiance. He looked for all the world like a toy soldier, and then I noticed a strange thing; he seemed to be wearing a long red, white and blue weskit beneath his poshteen.

I must have said something of this to Hudson, for he shouted out:

"By God, it's the colours! Damn the black bastards, give it to 'em, 44th! Give 'em hot hell!"

"Shut up, you fool!" says I, although I needn't have worried, for we were too far away to be heard. But Hudson stopped shouting, and contented himself with swearing and whispering encouragement to the doomed men on the hilltop.

For they were doomed. Even as we watched the grey and black robed figures came charging up the slope again, from all sides, another volley cracked out, and then the wave had broken over them. It boiled and eddied on the hilltop, the knives and bayonets flashing, and then it rolled slowly back with one great, wailing yell of triumph, and on the hilltop there were no figures standing up. Of the man with the colours round his waist there was no sign; all that remained was a confusion of vague shapes scattered among the rocks, and a haze of powder smoke that presently drifted off into nothing on the frosty air.

Somehow I knew that I had just seen the end of the army of Afghanistan. Of course one would have expected the 44th to be the last remnant, as the only British regiment in the force, but even without that I would have known. This was what Elphy Bey's fine army of more than fourteen thousand had come to, in just a week. There might be a few prisoners; there would be no other survivors. I was wrong, as it turned out; one man, Dr Brydon, cut his way out and brought the news to Jallalabad, but there was no way of knowing this at the time.

There is a painting of the scene at Gandamack,[20] which I saw a few years ago, and it is like enough the real thing as I remember it. No doubt it is very fine and stirs martial thoughts in the glory-blown asses who look at it; my only thought when I saw it was, "You poor bloody fools!" and I said so, to the disgust of other viewers. But I was there, you see, shivering with horror as I watched, unlike the good Londoners, who let the roughnecks and jailbirds keep their empire for them; they are good enough for getting cut up at the Gandamacks which fools like Elphy and McNaghten bring 'em to, and no great loss to anybody.

Sergeant Hudson was staring down, with tears running over his cheeks. I believe, given a chance, he would have gone charging down to join them. All he would say was, "Bastards! Black bastards!" until I gave him the right about, pretty sharp, and we hurried away on our path, letting the rocks shut off the hellish sight behind us.

I was shaken by what we had seen, and to get as far away from Gandamack as we could was the thought that drove me on that day at a dangerous pace. We clattered along the rocky paths, and our ponies scrambled down the screes in such breakneck style that I go cold to look back on it. Only darkness stopped us, and we were well on our way next morning before I would rein in. By this time we had left the snow-line far behind us, and feeling the sun again raised my spirits once more.

It was as certain as anything could be that we were the only survivors of the army of Afghanistan still moving eastward in good order. This was a satisfactory thought. Why shouldn't I be frank about it? Now that the army was finished, there was little chance of meeting hostile tribesmen farther east than the point where it had died. So we were safe, and to come safe out of a disaster is more gratifying than to come safe out of none at all. Of course, it was a pity about the others, but wouldn't they have felt the same gratification in my place? There is great pleasure in catastrophe that doesn't touch you, and anyone who says there isn't is a liar. Haven't you seen it in the face of a bearer of bad news, and heard it in the unctuous phrases at the church gate after a funeral?

So I reflected, and felt mighty cheery, and perhaps this made me careless. At any rate, moralists will say I was well served for my thoughts, as our ponies trotted onwards, for what interrupted them was the sudden discovery that I was looking along the barrel of a jezzail into the face of one of the biggest, ugliest Afridi badmashes I have ever seen. He seemed to grow out of the rocks like a genie, and a dozen other ruffians with him, springing out to seize our bridles and sword-arms before we could say galloping Jesus.

"Khabadar, sahib!" says the big jezzailchi, grinning all over his villainous face, as though I needed telling to be careful. "Get down," he added, and his mates hauled me from the saddle and held me fast.

"What's this?" says I, trying to brave it out. "We are friends, on our way to Jallalabad. What do you want with us?"

"The British are everyone's friends," grins he, "and they are all going to Jallalabad—or were." And his crew cackled with laughter. "You will come with us," and he nodded to my captors, who had a thong round my wrists and tied to my own stirrup in a trice.

There was no chance of putting up a fight, even if all the heart had not gone out of me. For a moment I had hoped they were just broken men of the hills, who might have robbed us and let us go, but they were intent on holding us prisoner. For ransom? That was the best I could hope for. I played a desperate card.

"I am Flashman huzoor," cries I, "the friend of Akbar Khan Sirdar. He'll have the heart and guts of anyone who harms Bloody Lance!"

"Allah protect us!" says the jezzailchi, who was a humorist in his way, like all his lousy kind. "Guard him close, Raisul, or he'll stick you on his little spear, as he did to the Gilzais at Mogala." He hopped into my saddle and grinned down at me. "You can fight, Bloody Lance. Can you walk also?" And he set the pony off at a brisk trot, making me run alongside, and shouting obscene encouragement. They had served Hudson the same way, and we had no choice but to stumble along, jeered at by our ragged conquerors.

It was too much; to have come so far, to have endured so much, to have escaped so often, to be so close to safety—and now this. I wept and swore, called my captor every filthy name I could lay tongue to, in Pushtu, Urdu, English, and Persian, pleaded with him to let us go in return for a promise of great payment, threatened him with the vengeance of Akbar Khan, beseeched him to take us to the Sirdar, struggled like a furious child to break my bonds—and he only roared so hard with laughter that he almost fell from the saddle.

"Say it again!" he cried. "How many lakhs of rupees? Ya'llah, I shall be made for life. What was that? Noseless bastard offspring of a leprous ape and a gutter-descended sow? What a description! Note it, Raisul, my brother, for I have no head for education, and I wish to remember. Continue, Flashman huzoor; share the riches of your spirit with me!"

So he mocked me, but he hardly slackened pace, and soon I could neither swear nor plead or do anything but stumble blindly on. My wrists were burning with pain, and there was a leaden fear in my stomach; I had no idea where we were going, and even after darkness fell the brutes still kept going, until Hudson and I dropped from sheer fatigue. Then we rested a few hours, but at dawn they had us up again, and we staggered on through the hot, hellish day, resting only when we were too exhausted to continue, and then being forced up and dragged onwards at the stirrups.

It was just before dusk when we halted for the last time, at one of those rock forts that are dotted on half the hillsides of Afghanistan. I had a vision of a gateway, with a rickety old gate swung back on rusty hinges, and beyond it an earth courtyard. They did not take us so far, but cut the thongs that held us and shoved us through a narrow door in the gatehouse wall. There were steps leading down, and a most fearsome stink coming up, but they pushed us headlong down and we stumbled on to a floor of mixed straw and filth and God knows what other debris. The door slammed shut, and there we were, too worn out to move.

I suppose we lay there for hours, groaning with pain and exhaustion, before they came back, bringing us a bowl of food and a chatti of water. We were famished, and fell on it like pigs, while the big jezzailchi watched us and made funny remarks. I ignored him, and presently he left us. There was just light enough from a high grating in one wall for us to make out our surroundings, so we took stock of the cellar, or dungeon, whichever it was.

I have been in a great variety of jails in my life, from Mexico (where they are truly abominable) to Australia, America, Russia, and dear old England, and I never saw a good one yet. That little Afghan hole was not too bad, all round, but it seemed dreadful at the time. There were bare walls, pretty high, and a roof lost in shadow, and in the middle of the filthy floor two very broad flat stones, like a platform, that I didn't half like the look of. For above them, swinging down from the ceiling, was a tangle of rusty chains, and at the sight of them a chill stabbed through me, and I thought of hooded black figures, and the Inquisition, and torture chambers that I had gloated over in forbidden books at school. It's very different when you are actually in one.

I told Hudson what I thought of them, and he just grunted and spat and then begged my pardon. I told him not to be such a damned fool, that we were in a frightful fix, and he could stop behaving as though we were on Horse Guards. I've never been one to stand on ceremony anywhere, and here it was just ridiculous. But it took Hudson time to get used to talking to an officer, and at first he just listened to me, nodding and saying, "Yes, sir," and "Very good, sir," until I swore with exasperation.

For I was in a funk, of course, and poured out my fears to him. I didn't know why they were holding us, although ransom seemed most likely. There was a chance Akbar might get to hear of our plight, which was what I hoped—but at the back of my mind was the awful thought that Gul Shah might hear of us just as easily. Hudson, of course, didn't understand why I should be so horrified at this, until I told him the whole story—about Narreeman, and how Akbar had rescued me from Gul's snakes in Kabul.

Heavens, how I must have talked, but when I tell you that we were in the cellar a week together, without ever so much as seeing beyond the door, and myself in a sweat of anxiety about what our fate might be, you will understand that I needed an audience. Your real coward always does, and the worse his fear the more he blabs. I babbled something sickening in that dungeon to Hudson. Of course, I didn't tell him the story as I've told it here—the Bloody Lance incident, for example, I related in a creditable light. But I convinced him at least that we had every reason to fear if Gul Shah got wind that we were in Afghan hands.

It was difficult to tell how he took it. Mostly he just listened, staring at the wall, but from time to time he would look at me very steady, as though he was weighing me up. At first I hardly noticed this, any more than one does notice a common trooper looking at one, but after a while it made me feel uncomfortable, and I told him pretty sharp to leave off. If he was scared at the fix we were in, he didn't show it, and I admit there were one or two occasions when I felt a sneaking regard for him; he didn't complain, and he was very civil in his speech, and would ask me very respectfully to translate what the Afridi guards said when they brought us our food—for he had no Pushtu or Hindustani.

This was little enough, and we had no way of telling how true it was. The big jezzailchi was the most talkative, but mostly he would only recall how badly the British had been cut up on the march from Kabul, so that not a single man had been left alive, and how there would soon be no feringhees left in Afghanistan at all. Akbar Khan was advancing on Jallalabad, he said, and would put the whole garrison to the sword, and then they would sweep down through the Khyber and drive us out of India in a great jehad that would establish the True Faith from Peshawar to the sea. And so on, all bloody wind and water, as I told Hudson, but he considered it very thoughtfully and said he didn't know how long Sale could hold out in Jallalabad if they laid proper siege to it.

I stared at this, an ordinary trooper passing opinion on a general's business.

"What do you know about it?" says I.

"Not much, sir," says he. "But with respect to General Elphinstone, I'm powerful glad it's General Sale that's laying in Jallalabad and not him."

"Is that so, and be damned to you," says I. "And what's your opinion of General Elphinstone, if you please?"

"I'd rather not say, sir," says he. And then he looked at me with those grey eyes. "He wasn't with the 44th at Gandamack, was he, sir? Nor a lot of the officers wasn't. Where were they, sir?"

"How should I know? And what concern is that of yours?"

He sat looking down for a moment. "None at all, sir," says he at last. "Beg pardon for asking."

"I should damned well think so," says I. "Anyway, whatever you think of Elphy Bey, you can rely on General Sale to give Akbar the right about turn if he shows his nose at Jallalabad. And I wish to God we were there, too, and away from this hellish hole, and these stinking Afridis. Whether it's ransom or not, they don't mean us any good, I can tell you." I didn't think much of Hudson's questions about Gandamack and Elphy at the time; if I had done I would have been as much amused as angry, for it was like a foreign language to me then. But I understand it now, although half our modern generals don't. They think their men are a different species still—fortunately a lot of 'em are, but not in the way the generals think.

Well, another week went by in that infernal cell, and both Hudson and I were pretty foul by now and well bearded, for they gave us nothing to wash or shave with. My anxieties diminished a little, as they will when nothing happens, but it was damned boring with nothing to do but talk to Hudson, for we had little in common except horses. He didn't even seem interested in women. We talked occasionally of escape, but there was little chance of that, for there was no way out except through the door, which stood at the top of a narrow flight of steps, and when the Afridis brought our food one of them always stood at the head of them covering us with a huge blunderbuss. I wasn't in any great hurry to risk a peppering from it, and when Hudson talked of trying a rush I ordered him to drop it. Where would we have got to afterwards, anyway? We didn't even know where we were, except that it couldn't be far to the Kabul road. But it wasn't worth the risk, I said—if I had known what was in store for us I'd have chanced that blunderbuss and a hundred like it, but I didn't. God, I'll never forget it. Never.

It was late one afternoon, and we were lying on the straw dozing, when we heard the clatter of hooves at the gate outside, and a jumble of voices approaching the door of the cell. Hudson jumped up, and I came up on my elbow, my heart in my mouth, wondering who it might be. It might be a messenger bringing news of ransom—for I believed the Afridis must be trying that game —and then the bolts scraped back and the door burst open, and a tall man strode in to the head of the steps. I couldn't see his face at first, but then an Afridi bustled past him with a flaring torch which he stuck in a crevice in the wall, and its light fell on the newcomer's face. If it had been the Devil in person I'd have been better pleased, for it was a face I had seen in nightmares, and I couldn't believe it was true, the face of Gul Shah.

His eye lit on me, and he shouted with joy and clapped his hands. I believe I cried out in horror, and scrambled back against the wall.

"Flashman!" he cried, and came half down the steps like a big cat, glaring at me with a hellish grin. "Now, God is very good. When I heard the news I could not believe it, but it is true. And it was just by chance—aye, by the merest chance, that word reached me you were taken." He sucked in his breath, never taking his glittering eyes from me.

I couldn't speak; the man struck me dumb with cold terror. Then he laughed again, and the hairs rose on my neck at the sound of it.

"And here there is no Akbar Khan to be importunate," says he. He signed to the Afridis and pointed at Hudson. "Take that one away above and watch him." And as two of them rushed down on Hudson and dragged him struggling up the steps, Gul Shah came down into the room and with his whip struck the hanging shackles a blow that set them rattling. "Set him"—and he points at me—"here. We have much to talk about."

I cried out as they flung themselves on me, and struggled helplessly, but they got my arms over my head and set a shackle on each wrist, so that I was strung up like a rabbit on a poulterer's stall. Then Gul dismissed them and came to stand in front of me, tapping his boot with his whip and gloating over me.

"The wolf comes once to the trap," says he at last. "But you have come twice. I swear by God you will not wriggle out of it this time. You cheated me once in Kabul, by a miracle, and killed my dwarf by foul play. Not again, Flashman, And I am glad—aye, glad it fell out so, for here I have time to deal with you at my leisure, you filthy dog!" And with a snarl he struck me back-handed across the face.

The blow loosened my tongue, for I cried out:

"Don't, for God's sake! What have I done? Didn't I pay for it with your bloody snakes?"

"Pay?" sneers he. "You haven't begun to pay. Do you want to know how you will pay, Flashman?"

I didn't, so I didn't answer, and he turned and shouted something towards the door. It opened, and someone came in, standing in the shadows.

"It was my great regret, last time, that I must be so hurried in disposing of you," says Gul Shah. "I think I told you then, did I not, that I would have wished the woman you defiled to share in your departure? By great good fortune I was at Mogala when the word of your capture came, so I have been able to repair the omission. Come," says he to the figure at the top of the steps, and the woman Narreeman advanced slowly into the light.

I knew it was she, although she was cloaked from head to foot and had the lower half of her face shrouded in a flimsy veil: I remembered the eyes, like a snake's, that had glared up at me the night I took her in Mogala. They were staring at me again, and I found them more terrifying than all Gul's threats. She didn't make a sound, but glided down the steps to his side.

"You do not greet the lady?" says Gul. "You will, you will. But of course, she is a mere slut of a dancing girl, although she is the wife of a prince of the Gilzai!" He spat the words into my face.

"Wife?" I croaked. "I never knew ... believe me, sir, I never knew. If I. ..."

"It was not so then," says Gul. "It is so now—aye, though she has been fouled by a beast like you. She is my wife and my woman none the less. It only remains to wipe out the dishonour."

"Oh, Christ, please listen to me," says I. "I swear I meant no harm ... how was I to know she was precious to you? I didn't mean to harm her, I swear I didn't! I'll do anything, anything you wish, pay anything you like. ..."

Gul leered at me, nodding, while the woman's basilisk eyes stared at me. "You will pay indeed. No doubt you have heard that our Afghan women are delicately skilled in collecting payment? I see from your face that you have. Narreeman is very eager to test that skill. She has vivid recollections of a night at Mogala; vivid recollections of your pride...." He leaned forward till his face was almost touching mine. "Lest she forget it, she wishes to take certain things from you, very slowly and cunningly, for a remembrance. Is it not just? You had your pleasure from her pain; she will have hers from yours. It will take much longer, and be infinitely more artistic... a woman's touch." He laughed. "That will be for a beginning."

I didn't believe it; it was impossible, outrageous, horrible; it was enough to strike me mad just listening to it.

"You can't!" I shrieked. "No, no, no, you can't! Please, please, don't let her touch me! It was a mistake! I didn't know, I didn't mean to hurt her!" I yelled and pleaded with him, and he crowed with delight and mocked me, while she never moved a muscle, but still stared into my face.

"This will be better than I had hoped," says he. "Afterwards, we may have you flayed, or perhaps roasted over hot embers. Or we may take out your eyes and remove your fingers and toes, and set you to some slave-work in Mogala. Yes, that will be best, for you can pray daily for death and never find it. Is the price too high for your night's pleasure, Flashman?"

I was trying to close my ears to this horror, trying not to believe it, and babbling to him to spare me. He listened, grinning, and then turned to the woman and said:

"But business before pleasure. My dove, we will let him think of the joyous reunion that you two will have—let him wait for—how long? He must wonder about that, I think. In the meantime, there is a more urgent matter." He turned back to me. "It will not abate your suffering in the slightest if you tell me what I wish to know; but I think you will tell me, anyway. Since your pathetic and cowardly army was slaughtered in the passes, the Sirdar's army has advanced towards Jallalabad. But we have no word of Nott and his troops at Kandahar. It is suggested that they have orders—to march on Kabul? On Jallalabad? We require to know. Well?"

It took a moment for me to clear my mind of the hellish pictures he had put there, and understand his question.

"I don't know," I said. "I swear to God I don't know."

"Liar," said Gul Shah. "You were an aide to Elfistan; you must know."

"I don't! I swear I don't!" I shouted. "I can't tell you what I don't know, can I?"

"I am sure you can," says he, and motioning Narreeman aside he flung off his poshteen and stood in his shirt and pyjamy trousers, skull-cap on head and whip in hand. He reached out and wrenched my shirt from my back.

I screamed as he swung the whip, and leaped as it struck me. God, I never knew such pain; it was like a fiery razor. He laughed and swung again and again. It was unbearable, searing bars of burning agony across my shoulders; my head swam and I shrieked and tried to hurl myself away, but the chains held me and the whip seemed to be striking into my very vitals.

"Stop!" I remember shrieking, and over and over again. "Stop!" He stepped back, grinning, but all I could do was mouth and mumble at him that I knew nothing. He lifted the whip again; I couldn't face it.

"No!" I screamed. "Not me! Hudson knows! The sergeant who was with me—I'm sure he knows! He told me he knew!" It was all I could think of to stop that hellish lashing.

"The havildar knows, but not the officer?" says Gul. "No, Flashman, not even in the British army. I think you are lying." And the fiend set about me again, until I must have fainted from the pain, for when I came to my senses, with my back raging like a furnace, he was picking his robe from the floor.

"You have convinced me," says he, sneering. "Such a coward as I know you to be would have told me all he knew at the first stroke. You are not brave, Flashman. But you will be even less brave soon."

He signed to Narreeman, and she followed him up the steps. At the door he paused to mock me again.

"Think on what I have promised you," says he. "I hope you will not go mad too soon after we begin."

The door slammed shut, and I was left sagging in my chains, sobbing and retching. But the pain on my back was as nothing to the terror in my mind. It wasn't possible, I kept saying, they can't do it ... but I knew they would. For some awful reason, which I cannot define even now, a recollection came to me of how I had tortured others—oh, puny, feeble little tortures like roasting fags at school; I babbled aloud how sorry I was for tormenting them, and prayed that I might be spared, and remembered how old Arnold had once said in a sermon: "Call on the Lord Jesus Christ, and thou shalt be saved."

God, how I called; I roared like a bull calf, and got nothing back, not even echoes. I would do it again, too, in the same position, for all that I don't believe in God and never have. But I blubbered like an infant, calling on Christ to save me, swearing to reform and crying gentle Jesus meek and mild over and over again. It's a great thing, prayer. Nobody answers, but at least it stops you from thinking.

Suddenly I was aware of people moving into the cell, and shrieked in fear, closing my eyes, but no one touched me, and when I opened them there was Hudson again, chained up beside me with his arms in the air, staring at me in horror.

"My God, sir," says he, "what have the devils done to you?"

"They're torturing me to death!" I roared. "Oh, dear saviour!" And I must have babbled on, for when I stopped he was praying, too, the Lord's Prayer, I think, very quietly to himself. We were the holiest jail in Afghanistan that night.

There was no question of sleep; even if my mind had not been full of the horrors ahead, I could not have rested with my arms fettered wide above my head. Every time I sagged the rusty manacles tore cruelly at my wrists, and I would have to right myself with my legs aching from standing. My back was smarting, and I moaned a good deal; Hudson did his best to cheer me up with the kind of drivel about not being done yet and keeping one's head up which is supposed to raise the spirits in time of trouble— it has never done a damned thing for mine. All I could think of was that woman's hating eyes coming closer, and Gul smiling savagely behind her, and the knife pricking my skin and then slicing—oh, Jesus, I couldn't bear it, I would go raving mad. I said so, at the top of my voice, and Hudson says:

"Come on, sir, we ain't dead yet."

"You bloody idiot!" I yelled at him. "What do you know, you

clod? They aren't going to cut your bloody pecker off! I tell you I'll have to die first! I must!"

"They haven't done it yet, sir," says he. "Nor they won't. While I was up yonder I see that half them Afridis have gone off —to join up wi' the others at Jallalabad, I reckon—an' there ain't above half a dozen left, besides your friend and the woman. If I can just...."

I didn't heed him; I was too done up to think of anything except what they would do to me—when? The night wore away, and except for one visit at noon next day, when the jezzailchi came to give us some water and food, no one came near us before evening. They left us in our chains, hanging like stuck pigs, and my legs seemed to be on fire one minute and numb the next. I heard Hudson muttering to himself from time to time, as though he was working at something, but I never minded; then, just when the light was beginning to fade, I heard him gasp with pain, and exclaim: "Done it, by God!"

I turned to look, and my heart bounded like a stag. He was standing with only his left arm still up in the shackle; the right one, bloody to the elbow, was hanging at his side.

He shook his head, fiercely, and I was silent. He worked his right hand and arm for a moment, and then reached up to the other shackle; the wrist-pieces were kept apart by a bar, but the fastening of the manacles was just a simple bolt. He worked at it for a moment, and it fell open. He was free.

He came over to me, an ear cocked towards the door.

"If I let you loose, sir, can you stand?"

I didn't know if I could, but I nodded, and two minutes later I was crouched on the floor, groaning with the pain in my shoulders and legs that had been cramped in one position so long. He massaged my joints, and swore softly over the weals that Gul Shah's whip had left.

"Filthy nigger bastard," says he. "Look'ee, sir, we've got to look sharp they don't take us unawares. When they come in we've got to be standing up, with the chains on our wrists, pretendin' we're still trussed up, like."

"What then?" says I.

"Why, sir, they'll think we're helpless, won't they? We can take 'em by surprise."

"Much good that'll do," says I. "You say there's half a dozen apart from Gul Shah."

"They won't all come," says he. "For God's sake, sir, it's our only hope."

I didn't think it was much of one, and said so. Hudson said, well, it was better than being sliced up by that Afghan tart, wasn't it, begging my pardon, sir, and I couldn't disagree. But I guessed we would only get slaughtered for our pains, at best.

"Well," says he, "we can make a bloody good fight of it. We can die like Englishmen, 'stead of like dogs."

"What difference does it make whether you die like an Englishman or like a bloody Eskimo?" says I, and he just stared at me and then went on chafing my arms. Pretty soon I could stand and move as well as ever, but we took care to stay close by the chains, and it was as well we did. Suddenly there was a shuffling at the door, and we barely had time to take our positions, hands up on the shackles, when it was thrown back.

"Leave it to me, sir," whispered Hudson, and then drooped in his fetters. I did the same, letting my head hang but watching the door out of the corner of my eye.

There were three of them, and my heart sank. First came Gul Shah, with the big jezzailchi carrying a torch, and behind was the smaller figure of Narreeman. All my terrors came rushing back as they descended the steps.

"It is time, Flashman," says Gul Shah, sticking his sneering face up to mine. "Wake up, you dog, and prepare for your last love play." And he laughed and struck me across the face. I staggered, but held tight to the chains. Hudson never moved a muscle.

"Now, my precious," says Gul to Narreeman. "He is here, and he is yours." She came forward to his side, and the big jezzailchi, having placed the torch, came on her other side, grinning like a satyr. He stood about a yard in front of Hudson, but his eyes were fixed on me.

The woman Narreeman had no veil now; she was turbanned and cloaked, and her face was like stone. Then she smiled, and it was like a tigress showing its teeth; she hissed something to Gul Shah, and held out her hand towards the dagger at his belt.

Fear had me gripped, or I would have let go the chains and rushed blindly past them. Gul put his hand on his hilt, and slowly, for my benefit, began to slide the blade from its sheath.

Hudson struck. His right hand shot down to the big jezzailchi's waist band, there was a gleam of steel, a gasp, and then a hideous shriek as Hudson drove the man's own dagger to the hilt in his belly. As the fellow dropped Hudson tried to spring at Gul Shah, but he struck against Narreeman and they both went sprawling. Gul leaped back, snatching at his sabre, and I let go my chains and threw myself out of harm's way. Gul swore and aimed a cut at me, but he was wild and hit the swinging chains; in that moment Hudson had scrambled to the dying jezzailchi, grabbed the sabre from his waist, and was bounding up the steps to the door. For a moment I thought he was deserting me, but when he reached the doorway it was to slam the door to and shoot the inside bolt. Then he turned, sabre in hand, and Gul, who had sprung to pursue him, halted at the foot of the steps. For a moment the four of us were stock still, and then Gul bawls out:

"Mahmud! Shadman! Idderao, juldi!"

"Watch the woman!" sings out Hudson, and I saw Narreeman in the act of snatching up the bloody dagger he had dropped. She was still on hands and knees, and with one step I caught her a flying kick in the middle that flung her breathless against the wall. Out of the tail of my eye I saw Hudson spring down the steps, sabre whirling, and then I had thrown myself at Narreeman, catching her a blow on the head as she tried to rise, and grabbing her wrists. As the steel clashed behind me, and the door re-echoed to pounding from outside, I dragged her arms behind her back and held them, twisting for all I was worth.

"You bitch!" I roared at her, and wrenched so that she screamed and went down, pinned beneath me. I held her so, got my knee on the small of her back, and looked round for Hudson.

He and Gul were going at it like Trojans in the middle of the cell. Thank God they teach good swordsmanship in the cavalry,[21] even to lancers, for Gul was as active as a panther, his point and edge whirling everywhere while he shouted oaths and threats and bawled to his rascals to break in. The door was too stout for them, though. Hudson fought coolly, as if he was in the gymnasium, guarding every thrust and sweep, then shuffling in and lunging so that Gul had to leap back to save his skin. I stayed where I was, for I daren't leave that hell-cat for a second, and if I had Gul might have had an instant to take a swipe at me.

Suddenly he rushed Hudson, slashing right and left, and the lancer broke ground; that was what Gul wanted, and he sprang for the steps, intent on getting to the door. Hudson was right on his heels, though, and Gul had to swing round halfway up the steps to avoid being run through from behind. He swerved outside Hudson's thrust, slipped on the steps, and for a moment they were locked, half-lying on the stairway. Gul was up like a rubber ball, swinging up his sabre for a cut at Hudson, who was caught all a-sprawl; the sabre flashed down, ringing on the stone and striking sparks, and the force of the blow made Gul overbalance. For a moment he was crouched over Hudson, and before he could recover I saw a glittering point rise out of the centre of his back; he gave a choked, awful cry, straightened up, his head hanging back, and crashed down the steps to the cell floor. He lay there, writhing, mouth gaping and eyes glaring; then he was still.

Hudson scrambled down the steps, his sabre red to the forte. I let out a yell of triumph.

"Bravo, Hudson! Bravo, shabash!"

He took one look at Gul, dropped his sabre, and to my amazement began to pull the dead man out of the middle of the floor to the shadowy side of the cellar. He laid him flat on his back, then hurried over to me.

"Make her fast, sir," says he, and while I trussed Narreeman's arms with the jezzailchi's belt, Hudson stuffed a gag into her mouth. We dropped her on the straw, and Hudson says:

"Only one chance, sir. Take the sabre—the clean one—and stand guard over that dead bugger. Put your point to his throat, an' when I open the door, tell 'em you'll slaughter their chief unless they do as we say. They won't see he's a corp, in this light, an' the bint's silenced. Now, sir, quick!"

There could be no argument; the door was creaking under the Afridis' hammering. I ran to Gul's side, snatching up his sabre on the way, and stood astride him, the point on his breast. Hudson took one look round, leaped up the steps, whipped back the bolt, and regained the cell floor in a bound. The door swung open, and in surged the lads of the village.

"Halt!" roars I. "Another move, and I'll send Gul Shah to make his peace with Shaitan! Back, you sons of owls and pigs!"

They bore up sharp, five or six of them, hairy brutes, at the head of the steps. When they saw Gul apparently helpless beneath me one lets out an oath and another a wail.

"Not another inch!" I shouted. "Or I'll have his life!"

They stayed where they were, gaping, but for the life of me I didn't know what to do next. Hudson spoke up, urgently.

"Horses, sir. We're right by the gate; tell 'em to bring two—no, three ponies to the door, and then all get back to the other side o' the yard."

I bawled the order at them, sweating in case they didn't do it, but they did. I suppose I looked desperate enough for anything, stripped to the waist, matted and bearded, and glaring like a lunatic. It was fear, not rage, but they weren't to know that. There was a great jabbering among them, and then they scrambled back through the doorway; I heard them yelling and swearing out in the dark, and then a sound that was like music— the clatter of ponies' hooves.

"Tell 'em to keep outside, sir, an' well away," says Hudson, and I roared it out with a will. Hudson ran to Narreeman, swung her up into his arms with an effort, and set her feet on the steps.

"Walk, damn you," says he, and grabbing up his own sabre he pushed her up the steps, the point at her back. He disappeared through the doorway, there was a pause, and then he shouts:

"Right, sir. Come out quick, like, an' bolt the door."

I never obeyed an order more gladly. I left Gul Shah staring up sightlessly, and raced up the steps, pulling the door to behind me. It was only as I looked round the courtyard, at Hudson astride one pony, with Narreeman bound and writhing across the other, at the little group of Afghans across the yard, fingering their knives and muttering—only then did I realise that we had left our hostage. But Hudson was there, as usual.

"Tell 'em I'll spill the bint's guts all over the yard if they stir a finger. Ask 'em how their master'll like that—an' what he'll do to 'em afterwards!" And he dropped his point over Narreeman's body.

It held them, even without my repetition of the threat, and I was able to scramble aboard the third pony. The gate was before us; Hudson grabbed the bridle of Narreeman's mount, we drove in our heels, and in a clatter of hooves we were out and away, under a glittering moon, down the path that wound from the fort's little hill to the open plain.

When we reached the level I glanced back; Hudson was not far behind, although he was having difficulty with Narreeman, for he had to hold her across the saddle of the third beast. Behind, the ugly shape of the fort was outlined against the sky, but there was no sign of pursuit.

When he came up with me he said:

"I reckon down yonder we'll strike the Kabul road, sir. We crossed it on the way in. Think we can chance it, sir?"

I was so trembling with reaction and excitement that I didn't care. Of course we should have stayed off the road, but I was for anything that would get that damned cellar far behind us, so I nodded and we rode on. With luck there would be no one moving on the road at night, and anyway, only on the road could we hope to get our bearings.

We reached it before very long, and the stars showed us the eastern way. We were a good three miles from the fort now, and it seemed, if the Afridis had come out in pursuit, that they had lost us. Hudson asked me what we should do with Narreeman.

At this I came to my senses again; as I thought back to what she had been preparing to do my gorge rose, and all I wanted to do was tear her apart.

"Give her to me," says I, dropping my reins and taking a grip on the sabre hilt.

He had one hand on her, sliding her out of the saddle; she slipped down on to the ground and wriggled up on her knees, her hands tied behind her, the gag across her mouth. She was glaring like a mad thing.

As I moved my pony round, Hudson suddenly reined into my way.

"Hold on, sir," says he. "What are you about?"

"I'm going to cut that bitch to pieces," says I. "Out of my way."

"Here, now, sir," says he. "You can't do that."

"Can't I, by God?"

"Not while I'm here, sir," says he, very quiet.

I didn't credit my ears at first.

"It won't do, sir," says he. "She's a woman. You're not yourself, sir, what wi' the floggin' they gave you, an' all. We'll let her be, sir; cut her hands free an' let her go."

I started to rage at him, for a mutinous dog, but he just sat there, not to be moved, shaking his head. So in the end I gave in —it occurred to me that what he could do to Gul Shah he might easily do to me—and he jumped down and loosed her hands. She flew at him, but he tripped her up and remounted.

"Sorry, miss," says he, "but you don't deserve better, you know."

She lay there, gasping and staring hate at us, a proper handsome hell-cat. It was a pity there wasn't time and leisure, or I'd have served her as I had once before, for I was feeling more my old self again. But to linger would have been madness, so I contented myself with a few slashes at her with my long bridle, and had the satisfaction of catching her a ringing cut over the backside that sent her scurrying for the rocks. Then we turned east and drove on down the road towards India.

It was bitter cold, and I was half-naked, but there was a poshteen over the saddle, and I wrapped up in it. Hudson had another, and covered his tunic and breeches with it; between us we looked a proper pair of Bashi-Bazouks, but for Hudson's fair hair and beard.

We camped before dawn, in a little gully, but not for long, for when the sun came up I recognised that we were in the country just west of Futtehabad, which is a bare twenty miles from Jallalabad itself. I wouldn't feel safe till we had its walls around us, so we pushed on hard, only leaving the road when we saw dust-clouds ahead of us that indicated other travellers.

We took to the hills for the rest of the day, skirting Futtehabad, and lay up by night, for we were both all in. In the morning we pressed on, but kept away from the road, for when we took a peep down at it, there were Afghans thick on it, all travelling east. There was more movement in the hills now, but no one minded a pair of riders, for Hudson shrouded his head in a rag to cover his blond hair, and I always looked like a Khyberi badmash anyway. But as we drew nearer to Jallalabad I got more and more anxious, for by what we had seen on the road, and the camps we saw dotted about in the gullies, I knew we must be moving along with an army. This was Akbar's host, pushing on to Jallalabad, and presently in the distance we heard the rattle of musketry, and knew that the siege must be already under way.

Well, this was a pretty fix; only in Jallalabad was there safety, but there was an Afghan army between us and it. With what we had been through I was desperate; for a moment I thought of by-passing Jallalabad and making for India, but that meant going through the Khyber, and with Hudson looking as much like an Afghan as a Berkshire hog we could never have made it. I cursed myself for having picked a companion with fair hair and Somerset complexion, but how could I have foreseen this? There was nothing for it but to push on and see what the chances were of getting into Jallalabad and of avoiding detection on the way.

It was a damned risky go, for soon we came into proper encampments, with Afghans as thick as fleas everywhere, and Hudson nearly suffocating inside the turban rag which hooded his whole head. Once we were hailed by a party of Pathans, and I answered with my heart in my mouth; they seemed interested in us, and in my panic all I could think to do was start singing—that old Pathan song that goes:

> There's a girl across the river
> With a bottom like a peach—
> And alas, I cannot swim.

They laughed and let us alone, but I thanked God they weren't nearer than twenty yards, or they might have realised that I wasn't as Afghan as I looked at a distance.

It couldn't have lasted long. I was sure that in another minute someone would have seen through our disguise, but then the ground fell away before us, and we were sitting our ponies at the top of a slope running down to the level, and on the far side of it, maybe two miles away, was Jallalabad, with the Kabul river at its back.

It was a scene to remember. On the long ridge on either side of us there were Afghans lining the rocks and singing out to each other, or squatting round their fires; down in the plain there were thousands of them, grouped any old way except near

Jallalabad, where they formed a great half-moon line facing the city. There were troops of cavalry milling about, and I saw guns and wagons among the besiegers. From the front of the half-moon you could see little prickles of fire and hear the pop-pop of musketry, and farther forward, almost up to the defences, there were scores of little sangars dotted about, with white-robed figures lying behind them. It was a real siege, no question, and as I looked at that tremendous host between us and safety my heart sank: we could never get through it.

Mind you, the siege didn't seem to be troubling Jallalabad unduly. Even as we watched the popping increased, and we saw a swarm of figures running hell-for-leather back from before the earthworks—Jallalabad isn't a big place, and had no proper walls, but the sappers had got some good-looking ramparts out before the town. At this the Afghans on the heights on either side of us set up a great jeering yell, as though to say they could have done better than their retreating fellows. From the scatter of figures lying in front of the earthworks it looked as though the besiegers had been taking a pounding.

Much good that was to us, but then Hudson sidled his pony up to mine, and says, "There's our way in, sir." I followed his glance, and saw below and to our right, about a mile from the foot of the slope and maybe as far from the city, a little fort on an eminence, with the Union Jack fluttering over its gate, and flashes of musketry from its walls. Some of the Afghans were paying attention to it, but not many; it was cut off from the main fortifications by Afghan outposts on the plain, but they obviously weren't caring much about it just now. We watched as a little cloud of Afghan horsemen swooped down towards it and then sheered off again from the firing on its walls.

"If we ride down slow, sir," says Hudson, "to where them niggers are lying round sniping, we could make a dash for it."

And get shot from our saddles for our pains, thinks I; no thank 'ee. But I had barely had the thought when someone hails us from the rocks on our left, and without a word we put our ponies down the slope. He bawled after us, but we kept going, and then we hit the level and were riding forward through the Afghans who were lying spread out among the rocks watching the little fort. The horsemen who had been attacking were wheeling about to our left, yelling and cursing, and one or two of the snipers shouted to us as we passed them by, but we kept on, and then there was just the last line of snipers and beyond it the little fort, three-quarters of a mile off, on top of its little hill, with its flag flying.

"Now, sir," snaps Hudson, and we dug in our heels and went like fury, flying past the last sangars. The Afghans there yelled out in surprise, wondering what the devil we were at, and we just put our heads down and made for the fort gate. I heard more shouting behind us, and thundering hooves, and then shots were whistling above us—from the fort, dammit. Oh Jesus, thinks I, they'll shoot us for Afghans, and we can't stop now with the horsemen behind us!

Hudson flung off his poshteen, and yelled, rising in his stirrups. At the sight of the blue lancer tunic and breeches there was a tremendous yelling behind, but the firing from the fort stopped, and now it was just a race between us and the Afghans. Our ponies were about used up, but we put them to the hill at top speed, and as the walls drew near I saw the gate open. I whooped and rode for it, with Hudson at my heels, and then we were through, and I was slipping off the saddle into the arms of a man with enormous ginger whiskers and a sergeant's stripes on his arm.

"Damme!" roars he. "Who the hell are ye?"

"Lieutenant Flashman," says I, "of General Elphinstone's army," and his mouth opened like a cod's. "Where's your commanding officer?"

"Blow me!" says he. "I'm the commanding officer, so far's there is one. Sergeant Wells, Bombay Grenadiers, sir. But we thought you was all dead. . . ."

It took us a little time to convince him, and to learn what was happening. While his sepoys cracked away from the parapet overhead at the disappointed Afghans, he took us into the little tower, sat us on a bench, gave us pancakes and water—which was all they had—and told us how the Afghans had been besieging Jallalabad three days now, in ever-increasing force, and his own little detachment had been cut off in this outlying fort for that time.

"It's a main good place for them to mount guns, d'ye see, sir, if they could run us out," says he. "So Cap'n Little—'e's back o' the tower 'ere, wi' 'is 'ead stove in by a bullet, sir—said as we 'ad to 'old out no matter what. 'To the last man, sergeant,' 'e sez, an' then 'e died—that was yesterday evenin', sir. They'd bin 'ittin' us pretty 'ard, sir, an' 'ave bin since. I dunno as we can last out much longer, 'cos the water's runnin' low, an' they damn near got over the wall last night, sir."

"But can't they relieve you from Jallalabad, for God's sake?" says I.

"I reckon they got their 'ands full, sir," says he, shaking his head. "They can 'old out there long enough; ol' Bob Sale—Gen'l Sale, I should say—ain't worried about that. But makin' a sortie to relieve us 'ud be another matter."

"Oh, Christ," says I, "out of the frying pan into the fire!"

He stared at me, but I was past caring. There seemed no end to it; there was some evil genie pursuing me through Afghanistan, and he meant to get me in the end. To have come so far, yet again, and to be dragged down within sight of safety! There was a palliasse in the corner of the tower, and I just went and threw myself down on it; my back was still burning, I was half-dead with fatigue, I was trapped in this hellish fort—I swore and wept with my face in the straw, careless of what they thought.

I heard them muttering, Hudson and the sergeant, and the latter's voice saying: "Well, strike me, 'e's a rum one!" and they must have gone outside, for I heard them no more. I lay there, and must have fallen asleep out of sheer exhaustion, for when I opened my eyes again it was dark in the room. I could hear the sepoys outside, talking; but I didn't go out; I got a drink from the pannikin on the table and lay down again and slept until morning.

Some of you will hold up your hands in horror that a Queen's officer could behave like this, and before his soldiers, too. To which I would reply that I do not claim, as I've said already, to be anything but a coward and a scoundrel, and I've never play-acted when it seemed pointless. It seemed pointless now. Possibly I was a little delirious in those days, from shock—Afghanistan, you'll admit, hadn't been exactly a Bank Holiday outing for me—but as I lay in that tower, listening to the occasional crackle of firing outside, and the yelling of the besiegers, I ceased to care at all for appearances. Let them think what they would; we were all surely going to be cut up, and what do good opinions matter to a corpse?

However, appearances still mattered to Sergeant Hudson. It was he who woke me after that first night. He looked pouch-eyed and filthy as he leaned over me, his tunic all torn and his hair tumbling into his eyes.

"How are you, sir?" says he.

"Damnable," says I. "My back's on fire. I ain't going to be much use for a while, I fear, Hudson."

"Well, sir," says he, "let's have a look at your back." I turned over, groaning, and he looked at it.

"Not too bad," says he. "Skin's only broke here an' there, and not mortifying. For the rest, it's just welts." He was silent a moment. "Thing is, sir, we need every musket we can raise. The sangars are closer this morning, an' the niggers are massing. Looks like a proper battle, sir."

"Sorry, Hudson," says I, rather weak. "I would if I could, you know. But whatever my back looks like, I can't do much just yet. I think there's something broken inside."

He stood looking down at me. "Yes, sir," says he at length, "I think there is." And then he just turned and walked out.

I felt myself go hot all over as I realised what he meant by that; for a moment I almost jumped off the palliasse and ran after him. But I didn't, for at that moment there was a sudden yelling on the parapets, and the musketry crashed out, and Sergeant Wells was bawling orders; but above all I heard the blood-curdling shrieks of the Ghazis, and I knew they were rushing the wall. It was all too much for me; I lay shuddering on the straw while the sounds of fighting raged outside. It seemed to go on forever, and every moment I expected to hear the Afghan war-cries in the yard, hear the rush of feet, and see the bearded horrors dashing in the door with their Khyber knives. I could only hope to God that they would finish me off quickly.

As I say, I may genuinely have had a shock, or even a fever, at this time, although I doubt it; I believe it was just simple fear that was almost sending me out of my mind. At all events, I have no particular idea of how long that fight lasted, or when it stopped and the next assault began, or even how many days and nights passed by. I don't recall eating and drinking, although I suppose

I must have, or even answering the calls of nature. That, incidentally, is one effect that fear does not have on me; I do not wet or foul myself. It has been a near thing once or twice, I admit. At Balaclava, for example, when I rode with the Light Brigade—you know how George Paget smoked a cigar all the way to the guns? Well, my bowels moved all the way to the guns, but there was nothing inside me but wind, since I hadn't eaten for days.

But in that fort, at the very end of my tether, I seemed to lose my sense of time; *delirium funkens* had me in its grip. I know Hudson came in to me, I know he talked, but I can't remember what he said, except for a few isolated passages, and those I think were mostly towards the end. I do remember him telling me Wells had been killed, and myself replying, "That's bad luck, by God, is he much hurt?" For the rest, my waking moments were less clear than my dreams, and those were vivid enough. I was back in the cell, with Gul Shah and Narreeman, and Gul was laughing at me, and changing into Bernier with his pistol raised, and then into Elphy Bey saying, "We shall have to cut off all your essentials, Flashman, I'm afraid there is no help for it. I shall send a note to Sir William." And Narreeman's eyes grew greater and greater, until I saw them in Elspeth's face—Elspeth smiling and very beautiful, but fading in her turn to become Arnold, who was threatening to flog me for not knowing my construe. "Unhappy boy, I wash my hands of you; you must leave my pit of snakes and dwarves this very day." And he reached out and took me by the shoulder; his eyes were burning like coals and his fingers bit into my shoulder so that I cried out and tried to pull them free, and found myself scrabbling at Hudson's fingers as he knelt beside my couch.

"Sir," says he, "you've got to get up."

"What time is it?" says I. "And what d'ye want? Leave me, can't you, leave me be—I'm ill, damn you."

"It's no go, sir. You can't stay here any longer. You must stand up and come outside with me."

I told him to go to the devil, and he suddenly lunged forward and seized me by the shoulders.

"Get up!" he snarled at me, and I realised his face was far more haggard than I'd ever seen it, drawn and fierce like an animal's. "Get up! You're a Queen's officer, by God, an' you'll behave like one! You're not ill, Mr Precious Flashman, you're plain white-livered! That's all your sickness! But you'll get up an' look like a man, even if you aren't one!" And he started to drag me from the straw.

I struck out at him, calling him a mutinous dog, and telling him I'd have him flogged through the army for his insolence, but he stuck his face into mine and hissed:

"Oh, no, you won't! Not now nor never. Because you an' me ain't going back where there's drum-heads an' floggings or anything, d'ye see? We're stuck here, an' we'll die here, because there's no way out! We're done for, lieutenant; this garrison is finished! We haven't got nothing to do, except die!"

"Damn you, then, what d'ye want me for? Go and die in your own way, and leave me to die in mine." I tried to push him away.

"Oh, no sir. It ain't as easy as that. I'm all that's left to fight this fort, me and a score of broken-down sepoys—and you. And we're going to fight it, Mr Flashman. To the last inch, d'ye hear?"

"You bloody fight it!" I shouted at him. "You're so confounded brave! You're a bloody soldier! All right, I'm not! I'm afraid, damn you, and I can't fight any more—I don't care if the Afghans take the fort and Jallalabad and the whole of India!" The tears were running down my cheeks as I said it. "Now go to hell and let me alone!"

He knelt there, staring at me, and pushed the hair out of his eyes. "I know it," he said. "I half-knew it from the minute we left Kabul, an' I was near sure back in that cellar, the way you carried on. But I was double certain sure when you wanted to kill that poor Afghan bitch—*men* don't do that. But I couldn't ever say so. You're an officer and a gentleman, as they say. But it doesn't matter now, sir, does it? We're both going, so I can speak my mind."

"Well, I hope you enjoy doing it," says I. "You'll kill a lot of Afghans that way."

"Maybe I will, sir," says he. "But I need you to help. And you will help, for I'm going to stick out here as long as I can."

"You poor ninny," says I. "What good'll that do, if they kill you in the end?"

"This much good, that I'll stop those niggers mounting guns on this hill. They'll never take Jallalabad while *we* hold out—and every hour gives General Sale a better chance. That's what I'm going to do, sir."

One meets them, of course. I've known hundreds. Give them a chance to do what they call their duty, let them see a hope of martyrdom—they'll fight their way on to the cross and bawl for the man with the hammer and nails.

"My best wishes," says I. "I'm not stopping you."

"Yes, you will, sir, if I let you. I need you—there's twenty sepoys out there who'll fight all the better if there's an officer to sick 'em on. They don't know what you are—not yet." He stood up. "Anyway, I'm not arguing, sir. You'll get up—now. Or I'll drag you out and I'll cut you to bits with a sabre, a piece at a time." His face was dreadful to see just then, those grey eyes in that drawn, worn skin. He meant it; not a doubt of it. "So just get up, sir, will you?"

I got up, of course. I was well enough in body; my sickness was purely moral. I went outside with him, into a courtyard with half a dozen or so sepoy bodies laid in a row with blankets over them near the gate; the living ones were up on the parapet. They looked round as Hudson and I went up the rickety ladder to the roof, their black faces tired and listless under their shakos, their skinny black hands and feet ridiculous protruding from red uniform jackets and white trousers.

The roof of the tower was no more than ten feet square, and just a little higher than the walls surrounding it; they were no more than twenty yards long—the place was less a fort than a toy castle. From the tower roof I could see Jallalabad, a mile away, apparently unchanged, except that the Afghan lines seemed to be closer. On our own front they were certainly nearer than they had been, and Hudson hustled me quickly under cover before the Afghans could get a bead on us.

We were watching them, a great crowd of horsemen and hillmen on foot, milling about out of musket shot, when Hudson pointed out to me a couple of cannon that had been rolled up on their right flank. They had been there since dawn, he said, and he expected they would start up as soon as powder and shot had been assembled. We were just speculating when this might be— or rather, Hudson was, for I wasn't talking to him—when there was a great roar from the horsemen, and they started to roll forward towards our fort. Hudson thrust me down the ladder, across the yard, and up to the parapet; a musket was shoved into my hands, and I was staring through an embrasure at the whole mob surging at us. I saw then that the ground outside the walls was thick with dead; before the gate they were piled up like fish on a slab.

The sight was sickening, no doubt, but not so sickening as the spectacle of those devils whooping in towards the fort. I reckoned there were about forty of them, with footmen trailing along behind, all waving their knives and yelling. Hudson shouted to hold fire, and the sepoys behaved as though they'd been through this before—as they had. When the chargers were within fifty yards, and not showing any great enthusiasm, it seemed to me, Hudson bawled "Fire!" the volley crashed out, and about four went down, which was good shooting. At this they wavered, but still came on, and the sepoys grabbed up their spare muskets, rolling their eyes at Hudson. He roars "Fire!" again, and another half dozen were toppled, at which the whole lot sheered off.

"There they go!" yells Hudson. "Reload, handily now! By God," says he, "if they had the bottom for one good charge they could bowl us over like ninepins!"

This had occurred to me. There were hundreds of Afghans out yonder, and barely twenty men in the fort; with a determined rush they could have carried the walls, and once inside they would have chewed us up in five minutes. But I gathered that this had been their style all along—half-hearted charges that had been beaten off, and only one or two that had reached the fort itself. They had lost heavily; I believe that they didn't care much about our little place, really, but would rather have been with their friends attacking Jallalabad, where the loot was. Sensible fellows.

But it was not going to last; I could see that. For all that our casualties had not been heavy, the sepoys were about done; there was only a little flour left for food, and barely a pannikin of water a man in the big butt down by the gate; Hudson watched it like a hawk.

There were three more charges that day, or maybe four, and none more successful than the first. We banged away and they cleared out, and my mind began to go dizzy again. I slumped beside my embrasure, with a poshteen draped over me to try to keep off the hellish heat; flies buzzed everywhere, and the sepoy on my right moaning to himself incessantly. By night it was as bad; the cold came, so bitter that I sobbed to myself at the pain of it; there was a huge moon, lighting everything in brilliant silver, but even when it set the dark wasn't sufficient to enable the Afghans to creep up on us, thank God. There were a few alarms and shots, but that was all. Dawn came, and the snipers began to crack away at us; we kept down beneath the parapet, and the shots chipped flakes off the tower behind us.

I must have been dozing, for I was shaken awake by an almighty crash and a thunderous explosion; there was a great cloud of dust swirling about, and as it cleared I saw that a corner of the tower had gone, and a heap of rubble was lying in the courtyard.

"The cannon!" shouts Hudson. "They're using the cannon!"

Out across the plain, there it was, sure enough—one of their big guns, directed at the fort, with a mob of Afghans jostling round it. Five minutes it took them to reload, and then the place shook as if an earthquake had hit it, and there was a gaping hole in the wall beside the gate. The sepoys began to wail, and Hudson roared at them to stand fast; there was another terrific crash, and then another; the air was full of flying dust and stones; a section of the parapet along from me gave way, and a screaming sepoy went down with it. I launched myself for the ladder, slipped, and rolled off into the debris, and something must have struck my head, for the next thing I knew I was standing up, not knowing where I was, looking at a ruined wall beyond which there was an empty plain with figures running towards me.

They were a long way away, and it took me a moment to realise that they were Afghans; they were charging, sure enough, and then I heard a musket crack, and there at the ruined wall was Hudson, fumbling with a ramrod and swearing, the side of his face caked with blood. He saw me, and bawled:

"Come on! Come on! Lend a hand, man!"

I walked towards him, my feet weighing a ton apiece; a red-coated figure was moving in the shadow of the wall, beside the gate; it was one of the sepoys. Curiously, the wall had been shot in on either side, but the gate was still standing, with the flag trailing at its staff on top, and the cords hanging down. As the shrieks of the Ghazis drew nearer, a thought entered my head, and I stumbled over towards the gate and laid hold of the cords.

"Give in," I said, and tugged at the cords. "Give in, and make 'em stop!" I pulled at the cords again, and then there was another appalling crash, the gates opened as though a giant hand had whirled them inwards, the arch above them fell, and the flagstaff with it; the choking dust swirled up, and I blundered through it, my hands out to grab the colours that were now within reach.

I knew quite clearly what I wanted to do; I would gather up the flag and surrender it to the Afghans, and then they would let us alone; Hudson, even in that hellish din and horror, must have guessed somehow what was in my mind, for I saw him crawling towards the colours, too. Or perhaps he was trying to save them, I don't know. But he didn't manage it; another round shot ploughed into the rubble before me, and the dirty, blue-clad figure was suddenly swept away like a rag doll into an engulfing cloud of dust and masonry. I staggered forward over the stones, touched the flagstaff and fell on my knees; the cloth of the flag was within reach, and I caught hold of it and pulled it up from the rubbish. From somewhere there came a volley of musketry, and I thought, well, this is the finish, and not half as bad as I thought it would be, but bad enough for all that, and God, I don't want to die yet.

There was a thunder like a waterfall, and things were falling on me; a horrible pain went through my right leg, and I heard the shriek of a Ghazi almost in my ear. I was lying face down, clutching at the flag, mumbling, "Here, take the bloody thing; I don't want it. Please take it; I give in." The musketry crashed again, the roaring noise grew louder, and then sight and hearing died.

There are a few wakenings in your life that you would wish to last forever, they are so blissful. Too often you wake in a bewilderment, and then remember the bad news you went to sleep on, but now and then you open your eyes in the knowledge that all is well and safe and right, and there is nothing to do but lie there with eyes gently shut, enjoying every delicious moment.

I knew it was all fine when I felt the touch of sheets beneath my chin, and a soft pillow beneath my head. I was in a British bed, somewhere, and the rustling sound above me was a punkah fan. Even when I moved, and a sudden anguish stabbed through my right leg, I wasn't dismayed, for I guessed at once that it was only broken, and there was still a foot to waggle at the end of it.

How I had got there I didn't care. Obviously I had been rescued at the last minute from the fort, wounded but otherwise whole, and brought to safety. Far away I could hear the tiny popping of muskets, but here there was peace, and I lay marvelling at my own luck, revelling in my present situation, and not even bothering to open my eyes, I was so contented.

When I did, it was to find myself in a pleasant, whitewashed room, with the sun slanting through wooden shutters, and a punkah wallah dozing against the wall, automatically twitching the string of his big fan. I turned my head, and found it was heavily bandaged; I was conscious that it throbbed at the back, but even that didn't discourage me. I had got clear away, from pursuing Afghans and relentless enemies and beastly-minded women and idiot commanders—I was snug in bed, and anyone who expected any more from Flashy—well, let him wish he might get it!

I stirred again, and my leg hurt, and I swore, at which the punkah wallah jumps up, squeaking, and ran from the room crying that I was awake. Presently there was a bustling, and in came a little spectacled man with a bald head and a large canvas jacket, followed by two or three Indian attendants.

"Awake at last!" says he. "Well, well, this is gratifying. Don't move, sir. Still, still. You've a broken leg here and a broken head there, let's have peace between 'em, what?" He beamed at me, took my pulse, looked at my tongue, told me his name was Bucket, pulled his nose, and said I was very well, considering. "Fractured femur, sir—thigh bone; nasty, but uncomplicated. Few months and you'll be bounding over the jumps again. But not yet—no; had a nasty time of it, eh? Ugly cuts about your back—ne'er mind, we'll hear about that later. Now Abdul," says he, "run and tell Major Havelock the patient's awake, juldi jao. Pray don't move, sir. What's that?—yes, a little drink. Better? Head still, that's right—nothing to do for the present but lie properly still."

He prattled on, but I wasn't heeding him. Oddly enough, it was the sight of the blue coat beneath the canvas jacket that put me in mind of Hudson—what had become of him? My last recollection was of seeing him hit and probably killed. But was he dead? He had better be, for my sake—for the memory of our latter relations was all too vivid in my mind, and it suddenly rushed in on me that if Hudson was alive, and talked, I was done for. He could swear to my cowardice, if he wanted to—would he dare? Would he be believed? He could prove nothing, but if he was known as a steady man—and I was sure he would be— he might well be listened to. It would mean my ruin, my disgrace —and while I hadn't cared a button for these things when I believed death was closing in on me and everyone else in that fort, well, I cared most damnably for them now that I was safe again.

Oh, God, says I to myself, let him be dead; the sepoys, if any survived, don't know, and wouldn't talk if they did, or be believed. But Hudson—he *must* be dead!

Charitable thoughts, you'll say. Aye, it's a hard world, and while bastards like Hudson have their uses, they can be most inconvenient, too. I wanted him to be dead, then, as much as I ever wanted anything.

My suspense must have been written on my face, for the little doctor began to babble soothingly to me, and then the door opened and in walked Sale, his big, kind, stupid face all beaming as red as his coat, and behind him a tall, flinty-faced, pulpit-looking man; there were others peeping round the lintel as Sale strode forward and plumped down into a chair beside the bed, leaning forward to take my hand in his own. He held it gently in his big paw and gazed at me like a cow in milk.

"My boy!" says he, almost in a whisper. "My brave boy!"

Hullo, thinks I, this don't sound too bad at all. But I had to find out, and quickly.

"Sir," says I—and to my astonishment my voice came out in a hoarse quaver, it had been so long unused, I suppose—"sir, how is Sergeant Hudson?"

Sale gave a grunt as though he had been kicked, bowed his head, and then looked at the doctor and the gravedigger fellow with him. They both looked damned solemn.

"His first words," says the little doctor, hauling out a handkerchief and snorting into it.

Sale shook his head sadly, and looked back at me.

"My boy," says he, "it grieves me deeply to tell you that your comrade—Sergeant Hudson—is dead. He did not survive the last onslaught on Piper's Fort." He paused, staring at me compassionately, and then says: "He died—like a true soldier."

" 'And Nicanor lay dead in his harness' ", says the gravedigger chap, taking a look at the ceiling. "He died in the fullness of his duty, and was not found wanting."

"Thank God," says I. "God help him, I mean—God rest him, that is." Luckily my voice was so weak that they couldn't hear more than a mumble. I looked downcast, and Sale squeezed my hand.

"I think I know," says he, "what his comradeship must have meant to you. We understand, you see, that you must have come together from the ruins of General Elphinstone's army, and we can guess at the hardships—oh, my boy, they are written all too plainly on your body—that you must have endured together. I would have spared you this news until you were stronger. . . ." He made a gesture and brushed his eye.

"No, sir," says I, speaking a little stronger, "I wanted to know now."

"It is what I would have expected of you," says he, wringing my hand. "My boy, what can I say? It is a soldier's lot. We must console ourselves with the thought that we would as gladly sacrifice ourselves for our comrades as they do for us. And we do not forget them."

" 'Non omnis moriar'," says the gravedigger. "Such men do not wholly die."

"Amen," says the little doctor, sniffing. Really, all they needed was an organ and a church choir.

"But we must not disturb you too soon," says Sale. "You need rest." He got up. "Take it in the knowledge that your troubles are over, and that you have done your duty as few men would have done it. Aye, or could have done it. I shall come again as soon as I may; in the meantime, let me say what I came to tell you: that I rejoice from my heart to see you so far recovered, for your delivery is the finest thing that has come to us in all this dark catalogue of disasters. God bless you, my boy. Come, gentlemen."

He stumped out, with the others following; the gravedigger bowed solemnly and the little doctor ducked his head and shooed the nigger attendants before him. And I was left not only relieved but amazed by what Sale had said—oh, the everyday compliments of people like Elphy Bey are one thing, but this was Sale, after all, the renowned Fighting Bob, whose courage was a byword. And *he* had said my deliverance was "the finest thing," and that I had done my duty as few could have done it—why, he had talked as though I was a hero, to be reverenced with that astonishing pussy-footing worship which, for some reason, my century extended to its idols. They treated us (I can say "us") as though we were too delicate to handle normally, like old Chinese pots.

Well, I had thought, when I woke up, that I was safe and in credit, but Sale's visit made me realise that there was more to it than I had imagined. I didn't find out what, though, until the following day, when Sale came back again with the gravedigger at his elbow—he was Major Havelock, by the way, a Bible-moth of the deepest dye, and a great name now.[22] Old Bob was in great spirits, and entertained me with the latest news, which was that Jallalabad was holding out splendidly, that a relief force under Pollock was on its way, and that it didn't matter anyway, because we had the measure of the Afghans and would probably sally out and break the siege whenever we felt like it. Havelock looked a bit sour at all this; I gathered he didn't hold a high opinion of Sale—nobody did, apart from admiring his bravery—

and was none too sure of his capabilities when it came to raising sieges.

"And this," says Bob, beaming with enthusiasm, "this we owe to you. Aye, and to the gallant band who held that little fort against an army. My word, Havelock, did I not say to you at the time that there never was a grander thing? It may not pay for all, to be sure; the catastrophe of Afghanistan will call forth universal horror in England, but at least we have redeemed something. We hold Jallalabad, and we'll drive this rabble of Akbar's from our gates—aye, and be back in Kabul before the year is out. And when we do—" and he swung round on me again "—it will be because a handful of sepoys, led by an English gentleman, defied a great army alone, and to the bitter end."

He was so worked up by his own eloquence that he had to go into the corner and gulp for a little, while Havelock nodded solemnly, regarding me.

"It had the flavour of heroism," says he, "and heaven knows there has been little enough of that to date. They will make much of it at home."

Well, I'm not often at a nonplus (except when there is physical danger, of course), but this left me speechless. Heroism? Well, if they cared to think so, let 'em; I wouldn't contradict them—and it struck me that if I did, if I were idiot enough to let them know the truth, as I am writing it now, they would simply have thought me crazy as a result of my wounds. God alone knew what I was supposed to have done that was so brave, but doubtless I should learn in time. All I could see was that somehow appearances were heavily on my side—and who needs more than that? Give me the shadow every time, and you can keep the substance—it's a principle I've followed all my life, and it works, if you know how to act on it.

What was obvious was that nothing must now happen to spoil Sale's lovely dream for him; it would have been cruel to the old fellow. So I addressed myself to the task at once.

"We did our duty, sir," says I, looking uncomfortable, and Havelock nodded again, while old Bob came back to the bed.

"And I have done mine," says he, fumbling in his pocket. "For I conceived it no less, in sending my latest despatch to Lord Ellenborough—who now commands in Delhi—to include an account of your action. I'll read it," says he, "because it speaks more clearly than I can at present, and will enable you to see how others judged your conduct."

He cleared his throat, and began.

"Humph—let's see—Afghans in strength—demands that I surrender—aye, aye—sharp engagement by Dennie—ah, here we have it. 'I had despatched a strong guard under Captain Little to Piper's Fort, commanding an eminence some way from the city, where I feared the enemy might establish gun positions. When the siege began, Piper's Fort was totally cut off from us, and received the full force of the enemy's assault. In what manner it resisted I cannot say in detail, for of its garrison only five now survive, four of them being sepoys, and the other an English officer who is yet unconscious with his wounds, but will, as I trust, soon recover. How he came in the fort I know not, for he was not of the original garrison, but on the staff of General Elphinstone. His name is Flashman, and it is probable that he and Dr Brydon are the only survivors of the army so cruelly destroyed at Jugdulluk and Gandamack. I can only assume that he escaped the final massacre, and so reached Piper's Fort after the siege began.'"

He looked at me. "You shall correct me, my boy, if I go wrong, but it is right you should know what I have told his excellency."

"You're very kind sir," says I, humbly. Too kind by a damned sight, if you only knew.

" 'The siege continued slowly on our own front, as I have already informed you,' " says Sale, reading on, " 'but the violence of the assaults on Piper's Fort was unabated. Captain Little was slain, with his sergeant, but the garrison fought on with the utmost resolution. Lieutenant Flashman, as I learn from one of the sepoys, was in a case more suited to a hospital than to a battle-field, for he had evidently been prisoner of the Afghans, who had flogged him most shockingly, so that he was unable to stand, and must lie in the fort tower. His companion, Sergeant Hudson, assisted most gallantly in the defence, until Lieutenant Flashman, despite his wounds, returned to the action.

" 'Charge after charge was resisted, and the enemy most bloodily repulsed. To us in Jallalabad, this unexpected check to the Sirdar's advance was an advantage beyond price. It may well have been decisive.' "

Well, Hudson, thinks I, that was what you wanted, and you got it, for all the good it did you. Meanwhile, Sale laid off for a minute, took a wipe at his eye, and started in again, trying not to quaver. I suspect he was enjoying his emotion.

" 'But there was no way in which we could succour Piper's Fort at this time, and, the enemy bringing forward cannon, the walls were breached in several places. I had now resolved on a sortie, to do what could be done for our comrades, and Colonel Dennie advanced to their relief. In a sharp engagement over the very ruins of the fort—for it had been pounded almost to pieces by the guns—the Afghans were entirely routed, and we were able to make good the position and withdraw the survivors of the garrison which had held it so faithfully and well.' "

I thought the old fool was going to weep, but he took a great pull at himself and proceeded:

" 'With what grief do I write that of these there remained only five? The gallant Hudson was slain, and at first it seemed that no European was left alive. Then Lieutenant Flashman was found, wounded and unconscious, by the ruins of the gate, where he had taken his final stand in defence not only of the fort, but of his country's honour. For he was found, in the last extremity, with the colours clutched to his broken body, his face to the foemen, defiant even unto death.' "

Hallelujah and good-night, sweet prince, says I to myself, what a shame I hadn't a broken sword and a ring of my slain around me. But I thought too soon.

" 'The bodies of his enemies lay before him,' " says old Bob, " 'At first it was thought he was dead, but to our great joy it was discovered that the flame of life still flickered. I cannot think that there was ever a nobler deed than this, and I only wish that our countrymen at home might have seen it, and learned with what selfless devotion their honour is protected even at the ends of the earth. It was *heroic!* and I trust that Lieutenant Flashman's name will be remembered in every home in England. Whatever may be said of the disasters that have befallen us here, his valour is testimony that the spirit of our young manhood is no whit less ardent than that of their predecessors who, in Pitt's words, saved Europe by their example.' "

Well, thinks I, if that's how we won the battle of Waterloo, thank God the French don't know or we shall have them at us again. Who ever heard such humbug? But it was glorious to listen to, mind you, and I glowed at the thought of it. This was fame! I didn't understand, then, how the news of Kabul and Gandamack would make England shudder, and how that vastly conceited and indignant public would clutch at any straw that might heal their national pride and enable them to repeat the old and nonsensical lie that one Englishman is worth twenty foreigners. But I could still guess what effect Sale's report would have on a new Governor-General, and through him on the government and country, especially by contrast with the accounts of the inglorious shambles by Elphy and McNaghten that must now be on their way home.

All I must do was be modest and manly and wait for the laurel wreaths.

Sale had shoved his copy of the letter back in his pocket, and was looking at me all moist and admiring. Havelock was stern; I guessed he thought Sale was laying it on a deal too thick, but he couldn't say so. (I gathered later that the defence of Piper's Fort wasn't quite so important to Jallalabad as Fighting Bob imagined; it was his own hesitation that made him hold off so long attacking Akbar, and in fact he might have relieved us sooner.)

It was up to me, so I looked Sale in the eye, man to man.

"You've done us great credit, sir," says I. "Thank'ee. For the garrison, it's no less than they deserve, but for myself, well, you make it sound . . . a bit too much like St George and the Dragon, if you don't mind my saying so. I just . . . well, pitched in with the rest, sir, that was all."

Even Havelock smiled at this plain, manly talk, and Sale nearly burst with pride and said it was the grandest thing, by heaven, and the whole garrison was full of it. Then he sobered down, and asked me to tell him how I had come to Piper's Fort, and what had happened to separate Hudson and me from the army. Elphy was still in Akbar's hands, along with Shelton and Mackenzie and the married folk, but for the rest they had thought them all wiped out except Brydon, who had come galloping in alone with a broken sabre trailing from his wrist.

With Havelock's eye on me I kept it brief and truthful. We had come adrift from the army in the fighting about Jugdulluk, I said, had escaped by inches through the gullies with Ghazis pursuing us, and had tried to rejoin the army at Gandamack, but had only been in time to see it slaughtered. I described the scene accurately, with old Bob groaning and damning and Havelock frowning like a stone idol, and then told how we had been captured and imprisoned by Afridis. They had flogged me to make me give information about the Kandahar force and other matters, but thank God I had told them nothing ("bravo!" says old Bob), and had managed to slip my fetters the same night. I had released Hudson and together we had cut our way past our captors and escaped.

I said nothing of Narreeman—least said soonest mended—but concluded with an account of how we had skulked through the Afghan army, and then ridden into the fort hell-for-leather.

There I left it, and old Bob exclaimed again about courage and endurance, but what reassured me most was that Havelock, without a word, shook my right hand in both of his. I can say that I told it well—off-hand, but not over-modest; just a blunt soldier reporting to his seniors. It calls for nice judgement, this art of bragging; you must be plain, but not too plain, and you must smile only rarely. Letting them guess more than you say is the kernel of it, and looking uncomfortable when they compliment you.

They spread the tale, of course, and in the next few days I don't suppose there was an officer of the garrison who didn't come in to shake hands and congratulate me on coming through safe. George Broadfoot was among the first, all red whiskers and spectacles, beaming and telling me what a devil of a fellow I was —and this from Broadfoot, mind you, whom the Afghans called a brave among braves. To have people like him and Mayne and Fighting Bob making much of me—well, it was first-rate, I can tell you, and my conscience didn't trouble me a bit. Why should it? I didn't ask for their golden opinions; I just didn't contradict 'em. Who would?

It was altogether a splendid few weeks. While I lay nursing my leg, the siege of Jallalabad petered out, and Sale finally made another sortie that scattered the Afghan army to the winds. A few days after that Pollock arrived with the relief force from Peshawar, and the garrison band piped them in amongst universal cheering.

Of course, I was on hand; they carried me out on to the verandah, and I saw Pollock march in. Later that evening Sale brought him to see me, and expounded my gallantries once again, to my great embarrassment, of course. Pollock swore it was tremendous, and vowed to avenge me when he marched on to Kabul; Sale was going with him to clear the passes, brink Akbar to book, if possible, and release the prisoners—who included Lady Sale—should they still be alive.

"You can stay here and take your well-earned repose while your leg mends," says Fighting Bob, at which I decided a scowl and a mutter might be appropriate.

"I'd rather come along," says I. "Damn this infernal leg."

"Why, hold on," laughs Sale, "we'd have to carry you in a palankeen. Haven't you had enough of Afghanistan?"

"Not while Akbar Khan's above ground," says I. "I'd like to take these splints and make him eàt 'em."

They laughed at this, and Broadfoot, who was there, cries out:

"He's an old war-horse already, our Flashy. Ye want tae be in at the death, don't ye, ye great carl? Aye, well, ye can leave Akbar tae us; forbye, I doubt if the action we'll find about Kabul will be lively enough for your taste."

They went off, and I heard Broadfoot telling Pollock what a madman I was when it came to a fight—"when we were fighting in the passes, it was Flashman every time that was sent out as galloper to us with messages; ye would see him fleein' over the sangars like a daft Ghazi, and aye wi' a pack o' hostiles howling at his heels. He minded them no more than flies."

That was what he made out of the one inglorious occasion when I had been chased for my life into his encampment. But you will have noticed, no doubt, that when a man has a reputation good or bad, folk will always delight in adding to it; there wasn't a man in Afghanistan who knew me but who wanted to recall having seen me doing something desperate, and Broadfoot, quite sincerely, was like all the rest.

Pollock and Sale didn't catch Akbar, as it turned out, but they did release the prisoners he had taken, and the army's arrival in Kabul quieted the country. There was no question of serious reprisals; having been once bitten, we were not looking for trouble a second time. The one prisoner they didn't release, though, was old Elphy Bey; he had died in captivity, worn out and despairing, and there was a general grief in which I, for one, didn't share. No doubt he was a kindly old stick, but he was a damned disaster as a commander. He, above all others, murdered the army of Afghanistan, and when I reckon up the odds against my own survival in that mess—well, it wasn't Elphy's fault that I came through.

But while all these stirring things were happening, while the Afghans were skulking back into their hills, and Sale and Pollock and Nott were showing the flag and blowing up Kabul bazaar for spite; while the news of the catalogue of disasters was breaking on a horrified England; while the old Duke of Wellington was damning Auckland's folly for sending an army to occupy "rocks, sands, deserts, ice and snow"; while the general public and Palmerston were crying out for vengeance, and the Prime Minister was retorting that he wasn't going to make another war for the sake of spreading the study of Adam Smith among the Pathans— while all this was happening I was enjoying a triumphal progress back to India. With my leg still splinted, I was being borne south as the hero—or, at least, the most convenient of a few heroes—of the hour.

It is obvious now that the Delhi administration regarded me as something of a godsend. As Greville said later of the Afghan war, there wasn't much cause for triumph in it, but Ellenborough in Delhi was shrewd enough to see that the best way to put a good gloss on the whole horrible nonsense was to play up its few creditable aspects—and I was the first handy one.

So while he was trumpeting in orders of the day about "the illustrious garrison" who had held Jallalabad under the noble Sale, he found room to beat the drum about "gallant Flashman," and India took its cue from him. While they drank my health they could pretend that Gandamack hadn't happened.

I got my first taste of this when I left Jallalabad in a palankeen, to go down the Khyber with a convoy, and the whole garrison turned out to hurrah me off. Then at Peshawar there was old Avitabile, the Italian rascal, who welcomed me with a guard of honour, kissed me on both cheeks, and made me and himself riotously drunk in celebration of my return. That night was memorable for one thing—I had my first woman for months, for

Avitabile had in a couple of lively Afghan wenches, and we made splendid beasts of ourselves. It isn't easy, I may say, handling a woman when your leg is broken, but where there's a will there's a way, and in spite of the fact that Avitabile was almost sick laughing at the spectacle of me getting my wench buckled to, I managed most satisfactorily.

From there it was the same all the way—at every town and camp there were garlands and congratulations and smiling faces and cheering, until I could almost believe I *was* a hero. The men gripped my hand, full of emotion, and the women kissed me and sniffled; colonels had my health drunk in their messes, Company men slapped me on the shoulder, an Irish subaltern and his young wife got me to stand godfather to their new son, who was launched into life with the appalling name of Flashman O'Toole, and the ladies of the Church Guild at Lahore presented me with a silk scarf in red, white, and blue with a scroll embroidered "Steadfast." At Ludhiana a clergyman preached a tremendous sermon on the text, "Greater love hath no man than this that a man lay down his life for his friends"—he admitted, in a round-about way, that I hadn't actually laid down mine, but it hadn't been for want of trying, and had been a damned near thing altogether. Better luck next time was about his view of it, and meanwhile hosannah and hurrah for Flashy, and let us now sing "Who would true valour see."

All this was nothing to Delhi, where they actually had a band playing "Hail the conquering hero comes", and Ellenborough himself helped me out of the palankeen and supported me up the steps. There was a tremendous crowd, all cheering like billy-o, and a guard of honour, and an address read out by a fat chap in a red coat, and a slap-up dinner afterwards at which Ellenborough made a great speech which lasted over an hour. It was dreadful rubbish, about Thermopylae and the Spanish Armada, and how I had clutched the colours to my bleeding breast, gazing proudly with serene and noble brow o'er the engorged barbarian host, like Christian before Apollyon or Roland at Roncesvalles, I forget which, but I believe it was both. He was a fearful orator, full of bombast from Shakespeare and the classics, and I had no difficulty in feeling like a fool long before he was finished. But I sat it out, staring down the long white table with all Delhi society gaping at

me and drinking in Ellenborough's nonsense; I had just sense
enough not to get drunk in public, and by keeping a straight face
and frowning I contrived to look noble; I heard the women say as
much behind their fans, peeping at me and no doubt wondering
what kind of a mount I would make, while their husbands
thumped the table and shouted "bravo!" whenever Ellenborough
said something especially foolish.

Then at the end, damned if he didn't start croaking out "For
he's a jolly good fellow!" at which the whole crowd rose and
roared their heads off, and I sat red-faced and trying not to laugh
as I thought of what Hudson would have said if he could have
seen me. It was too bad, of course, but they would never have
made such a fuss about a sergeant, and even if they had, he
couldn't have carried it off as I did, insisting on hobbling up to
reply, and having Ellenborough say that if I must stand, it should
be his shoulder I should lean on, and by God, he would boast
about it ever after.

At this they roared again, and with his red face puffing claret
beside me I said that this was all too much for one who was only
a simple English gentleman ("amen to that," cries Ellenborough,
"and never was proud title more proudly borne") and that what
I had done was my duty, no more or less, as I hoped became a
soldier. And while I didn't believe there was any great credit to
me in it (cries of "No! No!"), well, if they said there was, it
wasn't due to me but to the country that bore me, and to the old
school where I was brought up as a Christian, I hoped, by my
masters. (What possessed me to say this I shall never understand,
unless it was sheer delight in lying, but they raised the roof.) And
while they were so kind to me they must not forget those others
who had carried the flag, and were carrying it still ("hear! hear!"),
and who would beat the Afghans back to where they came from,
and prove what everyone knew, that Englishmen never would be
slaves (thunderous applause). And, well, what I had done hadn't
been much, but it had been my best, and I hoped I would always
do it. (More cheering, but not quite as loud, I thought, and I
decided to shut up.) So God bless them all, and let them drink with
me to the health of our gallant comrades still in the field.

"Your simple honesty, no less than your manly aspect and
your glorious sentiments, won the admiration and love of all who

heard you," Ellenborough told me afterwards. "Flashman, I salute you. Furthermore," says he, "I intend that England shall salute you also. When he returns from his victorious campaign, Sir Robert Sale will be despatched to England, where I doubt not he will receive those marks of honour which become a hero."[23] (He talked like this most of the time, like a bad actor.[24] Many people did, sixty years ago.) "As is fitting, a worthy herald shall precede him, and share his glory. I mean, of course, yourself. Your work here is done, and nobly done, for the time being. I shall send you to Calcutta with all the speed that your disability allows, there to take ship for England."

I just stared at the man; I had never thought of this. To get out of this hellish country—for if, as I've said, I can now consider that India was kind to me, I was still overjoyed at the thought of leaving it—to see England again, and home, and London, and the clubs and messes and civilised people, to be fêted there as I had been assured I would be, to return in triumph when I had set out under a cloud, to be safe beyond the reach of black savages, and heat, and filth, and disease, and danger, to see white women again, and live soft, and take life easy, and sleep secure at nights, to devour the softness of Elspeth, to stroll in the park and be pointed out as the hero of Piper's Fort, to come back to life again —why, it was like waking from a nightmare. The thought of it all set me shaking.

"There are further reports to be made on affairs in Afghanistan," says Ellenborough, "and I can think of no more fitting messenger."

"Well, sir," says I. "I'm at your orders. If you insist, I'll go."

It took four months to sail home, just as it had taken four months to sail out, but I'm bound to say I didn't mind this time. Then I had been going into exile; now I was coming home a hero. If I'd had any doubts of that the voyage dispelled them. The captain and his officers and the passengers were as civil as butter, and treated me as if I were the Duke himself; when they found I was a cheery sort who liked his bottle and talk we got along famously, for they never seemed to tire of hearing me tell of my engagements with Afghans—male and female—and we got drunk most nights together. One or two of the older chaps were a bit leery of me, and one even hinted that I talked a deal too much, but I didn't care for this, and said so. They were just sour old package-rats, anyway, or jealous civilians.

I wonder, now, looking back, that the defence of Jallalabad made such a stir, for it was a very ordinary business, really. But it did, and since I was the first out of India who had been there, and borne a distinguished part, I got the lion's share of admiration. It was so on the ship, and was to prove so in England.

During the voyage my broken leg recovered almost entirely, but there was not much activity on shipboard anyway, and no women, and, boozing with the boys apart, I had a good deal of time to myself. This, and the absence of females, naturally turned me to thoughts of Elspeth; it was strange and delightful to think of going home to a wife, and I got that queasy feeling deep in my bowels whenever I found myself dreaming about her. It wasn't all lust, either, not more than about nine-tenths—after all, she wasn't going to be the only woman in England—but when I conjured up a picture of that lovely, placid face and blonde hair I got a tightness in my throat and a trembling in my hands that was quite apart from what the clergy call carnal appetites. It was the feeling I had experienced that first night I rattled her beside the Clyde—a kind of hunger for her presence and the sound of her voice and the dreamy stupidity of her blue eyes. I wondered if I was falling in love with her, and decided that I was, and that I didn't care, anyway—which is a sure sign.

So in this moonstruck state I whiled away the long voyage, and by the time we docked among the forest of shipping in London pool I was in a fine sweat, romantic and horny all at once. I made great haste for my father's house, full of excitement at the thought of surprising her—for of course she had no idea that I was coming—and banged the knocker so hard that passers-by turned to stare at the big, brown-faced fellow who was in such a devilish hurry.

Old Oswald opened, just as he always did, and gaped like a sheep as I strode past him, shouting. The hall was empty, and both strange and familiar at once, as things are after a long absence.

"Elspeth!" I roared. "Halloo! Elspeth! I'm home!"

Oswald was gabbling at my elbow that my father was out, and I clapped him on the back and pulled his whiskers.

"Good for him," says I, "I hope they have to carry him home tonight. Where's your mistress? Elspeth! Hallo!"

He just went on clucking at me, between delight and amazement, and then I heard a door open behind me, and looked round, and who should be standing there but Judy. That took me aback a bit; I hadn't thought she would still be here.

"Hallo," says I, not too well pleased, although she was looking as handsome as ever. "Hasn't the guv'nor got a new whore yet?"

She was about to say something, but at that moment there was a step on the staircase, and Elspeth was standing there, staring down at me. God, what a picture she was: corn-gold hair, red lips parted, blue eyes wide, breast heaving—no doubt she was wearing something, but I couldn't for the life of me remember what it was. She looked like a startled nymph, and then the old satyr Flashy was bounding up the stairs, grabbing her, and crying:

"I'm home! I'm home! Elspeth! I'm home!"

"Oh, Harry!" says she, and then her arms were round my neck and her lips were on mine.

If the Brigade of Guards had marched into the hall just then to command me to the Tower I'd not have heard them. I picked her up bodily, tingling at the feel of her, and without a word spoken carried her into the bedroom, and tumbled her there and then. It was superb, for I was half-drunk with excitement and longing, and when it was over I simply lay there, listening to her prattle a thousand questions, clasping her to me, kissing every inch of her, and answering God knows what. How long we spent there I can't imagine, but it was a long, golden afternoon, and ended only when the maid tapped on the door to say that my father was home again, and demanding to see me.

So we must get dressed, and straighten ourselves, giggling like naughty children, and when Elspeth had herself in order the maid came tapping again to say that my father was growing impatient. Just to show that heroes weren't to be hurried, I caught my darling up again, and in spite of her muffled squeals of protest, mounted her once more, without the formality of undressing. *Then* we went down.

It should have been a splendid evening, with the family welcoming the prodigal Achilles, but it wasn't. My father had aged in two years; his face was redder and his belly bigger, and his hair was quite white at the temples. He was civil enough, damned me for a young rascal, and said he was proud of me: the whole town had been talking over the reports from India, and Ellenborough's eulogies of myself and Sale and Havelock were all over the place. But his jollity soon wore off, and he drank a good deal too much at dinner, and fell into a silence at last. I could see then there was something wrong, although I didn't pay him much heed.

Judy dined with us, and I gathered she was now entirely one of the household, which was bad news. I didn't care for her any better now than I had two years before, after our quarrel, and I made it pretty plain. It seemed rather steep of my father to keep his dolly at home with my wife there, and treat them as equals, and I decided to speak to him about it. But Judy was cool and civil, too, and I gathered she was ready to keep the peace if I did.

Not that I minded her or my father much. I was all over Elspeth, revelling in the dreamy way she listened to my talk—I had forgotten what a ninny she was, but it had its compensations. She sat wide-eyed at my adventures, and I don't suppose anyone else got a word in edgeways all through the meal. I just bathed myself in that simple, dazzling smile of hers and persuaded her of what a wonderful husband she had. And later, when we went to bed, I persuaded her more so.

It was then, though, that the first little hint of something odd in her behaviour crossed my mind. She had dropped off to sleep, and I was lying there exhausted, listening to her breathing, and feeling somehow dissatisfied—which was strange, considering. Then it came to me, this little doubt, and I dismissed it, and then it came back.

I had had plenty of experience with women, as you know, and can judge them in bed as well as anyone, I reckon. And it seemed to me, however hard I pushed the thought away, that Elspeth was not as she had been before I went away. I've often said that she only came to life when she was at grips with a man —well, she had been willing enough in the few hours of my homecoming, I couldn't deny, but there hadn't been any of the rapturous passion on her part that I remembered. These are fine things, and difficult to explain—oh, she was active enough at the time, and content enough afterwards, but she was easier about it all, somehow. If it had been Fetnab or Josette, I wouldn't have noticed, I dare say; it was their work as well as their play. But I had a different emotion about Elspeth, and it told me there was something missing. It was just a shadow, and when I woke next morning I had forgotten it.

If I hadn't, the morning's events would have driven it from my mind. I came down late, and cornered my father in his study before he could slip out to his club. He was sitting with his feet along the couch, preparing for the rigours of the day with a glass of brandy, and looking liverish, but I plunged right in, and told him my thoughts about Judy.

"Things have changed," says I, "and we can't have her seen about the place nowadays." You'll gather that two years among the Afghans had changed my attitude to parental discipline; I wasn't so easy to cow as I had been.

"Oh, aye," says he, "and how have things changed?"

"You'll find," I told him, "that I'm known about the town henceforth. What with India and so on. We'll be more in the public eye now, and folk will talk. It won't do for Elspeth, for one thing."

"Elspeth likes her," says he.

"Does she, though? Well, that's no matter. It ain't what Elspeth likes that counts, but what the town likes. And they won't like us if we keep this . . . this pet pussy in the house."

"My, we're grown very nice." He sneered and took a good pull at his brandy. I could see the flush of temper on his face, and wondered why he hadn't lost it yet. "I didn't know India bred such fine sensibilities," he went on. "Quite the reverse, I'd have thought."

"Oh, look, father, it won't do and you know it. Send her up to Leicestershire if you want, or give her a maison of her own—but she can't stay here."

He looked at me a long while. "By God, maybe I've been wrong about you all along. I know you're a wastrel, but I never thought you had the stuff to be brave—in spite of all the tales from India. Perhaps you have, or perhaps it's just insolence. Anyway, you're on the wrong scent, boy. As I said, Elspeth likes her—and if she don't want her away, then she stays."

"In God's name, what does it matter what Elspeth likes? She'll do as I tell her."

"I doubt it," says he.

"What's that?"

He put down his glass, wiped his lips, and said:

"You won't like it, Harry, but here it is. Who pays the piper calls the tune. And your Elspeth and her damned family have been calling the tune this year past. Hold on, now. Let me finish. You'll have plenty to say, no doubt, but it'll wait."

I could only stare at him, not understanding.

"We're in Queer Street, Harry. I hardly know how, myself, but there it is. I suppose I've been running pretty fast, all my life, and not taking much account of how the money went—what are lawyers for, eh? I took some bad tumbles on the turf, never heeded the expenses of this place, or Leicestershire, didn't stint any way at all—but it was the damned railway shares that really did the trick. Oh, there are fortunes being made out of 'em—the right ones. I picked the wrong ones. A year ago I was a ruined man, up to my neck with the Jews, ready to be sold up. I didn't write to you about it—what was the point? This house ain't mine, nor our place in Leicestershire; it's hers—or it will be, when old Morrison goes. God rot and damn him, it can't be too soon."

He jumped up and walked about, finally stopping before the fireplace.

"He met the bill, for his daughter's sake. Oh, you should have seen it! More canting, head-wagging hypocrisy than I've seen in years in Parliament, even! He had the effrontery to stand in my own hall, by God, and tell me it was a judgement on him for letting his daughter marry beneath herself! Beneath herself, d'ye hear? And I had to listen to him, and keep myself from flooring the old swine! What could I do? I was the poor relation; I still am. He's still paying the bills—through the simpering nitwit you married. He lets her have what she wants, and there you are!"

"But if he's settled an allowance on her. . . ."

"He's settled nothing! She asks him, and he provides. Damned if I would if I was him—but, there, perhaps he thinks it worth while. He seems to dote on her, and I'll say this for the chit, she's not stingy. But she's the pay-mistress, Harry, my son, and you'd best not forget it. You're a kept man, d'you see, so it don't become you, or me, to say who'll come and who'll go. And since your Elspeth is astonishingly liberal-minded—why, Miss Judy can stay, and be damned to you!"

I heard him out, flabbergasted at first, but perhaps because I was a more practical man than the guv'nor, or had fewer notions of gentility, through having an aristocratic mother, I took a different view of the matter. While he splashed more brandy into his glass, I asked:

"How much does he let her have?"

"Eh? I told you, whatever she wants. The old bastard seems to be warm enough for ten. But you can't get your hands on it, I tell you."

"Well, I don't mind," says I. "As long as the money's there, it don't signify who draws the orders."

He gaped at me. "Jesus," he said, in a choked voice, "have you no pride?"

"Probably as much as you have," says I, very cool. "You're still here, ain't you?"

He took on the old familiar apoplectic look, so I slid out before he threw a bottle at me, and went upstairs to think. It wasn't good news, of course, but I didn't doubt I could come to a good understanding with Elspeth, which was all that mattered. The truth was, I didn't have his pride; it wasn't as if I should have to sponge off old Morrison, after all. No doubt I should have been upset at the thought of not inheriting my father's fortune—or what had been his fortune—but when old Morrison ceased to trouble the world I'd have Elspeth's share of the will, which would quite probably make up for all that.

In the meantime, I tackled her on the subject at the first opportunity, and found her all brainless agreement, which was highly satisfactory.

"What I have is yours, my love," says she, with that melting look. "You know you have only to ask me for anything—anything at all."

"Much obliged," says I. "But it might be a little inconvenient, sometimes. I was thinking, if there was a regular payment, say, it would save all the tiresome business for you."

"My father would not allow that, I'm afraid. He has been quite clear, you see."

I saw, all right, and worked away at her, but it was no use. A fool she might be, but she did what Papa told her, and the old miser knew better than to leave a loophole for the Flashman family to crawl in and lighten him. It's a wise man that knows his own son-in-law. So it was going to have to be cash on demand—which was better than no cash at all. And she was ready enough with fifty guineas when I made my first application—it was all cut and dried, with a lawyer in Johnson's Court, who advanced her whatever she asked for, in reason.

However, apart from these sordid matters there was quite enough to engage me in those first days at home. No one at the Horse Guards knew quite what to do with me, so I was round the clubs a good deal, and it was surprising how many people knew me all of a sudden. They would hail me in the Park, or shake hands in the street, and there was a steady stream of callers at home; friends of my father's whom he hadn't seen for years popped up to meet me and greet him; invitations were showered on us; letters of congratulation piled up on the hall table and spilled on to the floor; there were paragraphs in the press about "the first of the returned heroes from Cabool and Jellulabad," and the new comic paper *Punch* had a cartoon in its series of "Pencillings"[25] which showed a heroic figure, something like me, wielding an enormous scimitar like a pantomime bandit, with hordes of blackamoors (they looked no more like Afghans than Eskimos) trying to wrest the Union Jack from me in vain. Underneath there was the caption: "A Flash(ing) Blade," which gives you some idea of the standard of humour in that journal.

However, Elspeth was enchanted with it, and bought a dozen copies; she was in a whirl of delight at being the centre of so much attention—for the hero's wife gets as many of the garlands as he does, especially if she's a beauty. There was one night at the theatre when the manager insisted on taking us out of our seats to a box, and the whole audience cheered and stamped and clapped. Elspeth was radiant and stood there squeaking and clasping her hands with not the least trace of embarrassment, while I waved, very good-natured, to the mob.

"Oh, Harry!" says she, sparkling. "I'm so happy I could die! Why, you are *famous*, Harry, and I. . . ."

She didn't finish, but I know she was thinking that she was famous too. At that moment I loved her all the more for thinking it.

The parties in that first week were too many to count, and always we were the centre of attraction. They had a military flavour, for thanks to the news from Afghanistan, and China—where we had also been doing well[26]—the army was in fashion more than usual. The more senior officers and the mamas claimed me, which left Elspeth to the young blades. This delighted her, of course, and pleased me—I wasn't jealous, and indeed took satisfaction in seeing them clustering like flies round a jampot which they could watch but couldn't taste. She knew a good many of them, and I learned that during my absence in India quite a few of the young sparks had squired her in the Park or ridden in the Row with her—which was natural enough, she being an army wife. But I just kept an eye open, all the same, and cold-shouldered one or two when they came too close—there was one in particular, a young Life Guards captain called Watney, who was often at the house, and was her riding partner twice in the week; he was a tall, curly-lipped exquisite with a lazy eye, who made himself very easy at home until I gave him the about-turn.

"I can attend Mrs Flashman very well, thank'ee," says I.

"None better," says he, "I'm sure. I had only hoped that you might relinquish her for a half-hour or so."

"Not for a minute," says I.

"Oh, come now," says he, patronising me, "this is very selfish. I am sure Mrs Flashman wouldn't agree."

"I'm sure she would."

"Would you care to test it?" says he, with an infuriating smile. I could have boxed his ears, but I kept my temper very well.

"Go the the devil, you mincing pimp," I told him, and left him standing in the hall. I went straight to Elspeth's room, told her what had happened, and cautioned her against seeing Watney again.

"Which one is he?" she asked, admiring her hair in the mirror.

"Fellow with a face like a horse and a haw-how voice."

"There are so many like that," says she. "I can't tell one from the other. Harry, darling, would I look well with ringlets, do you think?"

This pleased me, as you can guess, and I forgot the incident at once. I remember it now, for it was that same day that everything happened all at once. There are days like that; a chapter in your life ends and another one begins, and nothing is the same afterwards.

I was to call at the Horse Guards to see my Uncle Bindley, and I told Elspeth I would not be home until the afternoon, when we were to go out to tea at someone-or-others. But when I got to Horse Guards my uncle bundled me straight into a carriage and bore me off to meet—of all people—the Duke of Wellington. I'd never seen him closer than a distance, and it made me fairly nervous to stand in his ante-room after Bindley had been ushered in to him, and hear their voices murmuring behind the closed door. Then it opened, and the Duke came out; he was white-haired and pretty wrinkled at this time, but that damned hooked nose would have marked him anywhere, and his eyes were like gimlets.

"Ah, this is the young man," says he, shaking hands. For all his years he walked with the spring of a jockey, and was very spruce in his grey coat.

"The town is full of you just now," says he, looking me in the eyes. "It is as it should be. It was a damned good bit of work— about the only good thing in the whole business, by God, whatever Ellenborough and Palmerston may say."

Hudson, thinks I, you should see me now; short of the heavens opening, there was nothing to be added.

The Duke asked me a few sharp questions, about Akbar Khan,

and the Afghans generally, and how the troops had behaved on the retreat, which I answered as well as I could. He listened with his head back, and said "Hum," and nodded, and then said briskly:

"It is a thorough shame that it has been so shockingly managed. But it is always the way with these damned politicals; there is no telling them. If I had had someone like McNaghten with me in Spain, Bindley, I'd still be at Lisbon, I dare say. And what is to happen to Mr Flashman? Have you spoken to Hardinge?"

Bindley said they would have to find a regiment for me, and the Duke nodded.

"Yes, he is a regimental man. You were in the 11th Hussars, as I remember? Well, you won't want to go back *there*," and he gave me a shrewd look. "His lordship is no better disposed to Indian officers now than he ever was, the more fool he. I have thought of telling him, more than once, that I'm an Indian officer myself, but he would probably just have given me a setdown. Well, Mr Flashman, I am to take you to Her Majesty this afternoon, so you must be here at one o'clock." And with that he turned back to his room, said a word to Bindley, and shut the door.

Well, you can guess how all this dazzled me; to have the great Duke chatting to me, to learn that I was to be presented to the Queen—all this had me walking on the clouds. I went home in a rosy dream, hugging myself at the way Elspeth would take the news; *this* would make her damned father sit up and take notice, all right, and it would be odd if I couldn't squeeze something out of him in consequence, if I played my cards well.

I hurried upstairs, but she wasn't in her room; I called, and eventually old Oswald appeared and said she had gone out.

"Where away?" says I.

"Well, sir," says he, looking mighty sour, "I don't rightly know."

"With Miss Judy?"

"No, sir," says he, "not with Miss Judy. Miss Judy is downstairs, sir."

There was something damned queer about his manner, but there was nothing more to be got from him, so I went downstairs and found Judy playing with a kitten in the morning room.

"Where's my wife?" says I.

"Out with Captain Watney," says she, cool as you please. "Riding. Here, kitty-kitty. In the Park, I dare say."

For a minute I didn't understand.

"You're wrong," says I. "I sent him packing two hours ago."

"Well, they went riding half an hour ago, so he must have unpacked." She picked up the kitten and began to stroke it.

"What the devil d'you mean?"

"I mean they've gone out together. What else?"

"Dammit," says I, furious. "I told her not to."

She went on stroking, and looked at me with her crooked little smile.

"She can't have understood you, then," says she. "Or she would not have gone, would she?"

I stood staring at her, feeling a chill suddenly settle on my insides.

"What are you hinting, damn you?" I said.

"Nothing at all. It is you who are imagining. Do you know, I believe you're jealous."

"Jealous, by God! And what have I to be jealous about?"

"You should know best, surely."

I stood looking thunder at her, torn between anger and fear of what she seemed to be implying.

"Now, look'ee here," I said, "I want to know what the blazes you're at. If you have anything to say about my wife, by God, you'd best be careful...."

My father came stumping into the hall at that minute, curse him, and calling for Judy. She got up and walked past me, the kitten in her arms. She stopped at the door, gave me a crooked, spiteful smile, and says:

"What were *you* doing in India? Reading? Singing hymns? Or did *you* occasionally go riding in the Park?"

And with that she slammed the door, leaving me shot to bits, with horrible thoughts growing in my mind. Suspicion doesn't come gradually; it springs up suddenly, and grows with every breath it takes. If you have a foul mind, as I have, you think foul thoughts readier than clean ones, so that even as I told myself that Judy was a lying bitch trying to frighten me with implications, and that Elspeth was incapable of being false—at the same time I had a vision of her rolling naked in a bed with her arms

234

round Watney's neck. God, it wasn't possible! Elspeth was an innocent, a completely honest fool, who hadn't even known what "fornication" meant when I first met her. . . . *That* hadn't stopped her bounding into the bushes with me, though, at the first invitation. Oh, but it was still unthinkable! She was my wife, and as amiable and proper as a girl could be; she was utterly different from swine like me, she *had* to be. I couldn't be as wrong in my judgement as that, could I?

I was standing torturing myself with these happy notions, and then common sense came to the rescue. Good God, all she had done was go riding with Watney—why, she hadn't even known who he was when I warned her against him that morning. And she was the most scatterbrained thing in petticoats; besides, she wasn't of the mettle that trollops are made of. Too meek and gentle and submissive by half—she wouldn't have dared. The mere thought of what I'd do would have terrified . . . what would I do? Disown her? Divorce her? Throw her out? By God, I couldn't! I didn't have the means; my father was right!

For a moment I was appalled. If Elspeth *was* making a mistress for Watney, or anyone else, there was nothing I could do about it. I could cut her to ribbons, oh, aye, and what then? Take to the streets? I couldn't stay in the army, or in town, even, without means. . . .

Oh, but to the devil with this. It was pure moonshine, aye, and deliberately put into my mind to make me jealous by that brown-headed slut of my father's. This was her making mischief to get her own back for the hammering I'd given her three years ago. That was it. Why, I didn't have the least reason to think ill of Elspeth; everything about her denied Judy's imputations—and, by God, I'd pay that cow out for her lies and sneers. I'd find a way, all right, and God help her when I did.

With my thoughts back in more genial channels, I remembered the news I'd been coming home to tell Elspeth—well, she would have to wait for it until after I'd been to the Palace. Serve her right for going out with Watney, damn him. In the meantime, I spent the next hour looking out my best clothes, arranging my hair, which was grown pretty long and romantic, and cursing Oswald as he helped me with my cravat—I'd have been happier in uniform, but I didn't have a decent one to my name, having spent my time in mufti since I came home. I was so excited that I didn't bother to lunch, but dandied myself up to the nines, and then hurried off to meet His Nose-ship.

There was a brougham at his door when I arrived, and I didn't have to wait two minutes before he came down, all dressed and damning the secretary and valet who were stalking along behind him.

"There probably isn't a damned warming-pan in the place," he was barking. "And it is necessary that everything should be in the finest order. Find out if Her Majesty takes her own bed-linen when she travels. I imagine she does, but don't for God's sake go inquiring indiscreetly. Ask Arbuthnot; he'll know. You may be sure that something will be amiss, in the end, but it can't be helped. Ah, Flashman," and he ran his eye over me like a drill sergeant. "Come along, then."

There was a little knot of urchins and people to raise a cheer as he came out, and someone shouted: "There's the Flash cove! Hurrah!" by which they meant me. There was a little wait after we got in, because the coachman had some trouble with his reins, and a little crowd gathered while the Duke fretted and swore.

"Dammit, Johnson," growls he, "hurry up or we shall have all London here."

The crowd cheered and we rolled off in the pleasant autumn sunshine, with the guttersnipes running behind whooping and people turning on the pavements to lift their hats as the Great Duke passed by.

"If I knew how news travelled I'd be a wiser man," says he. "Can you imagine it? I'll lay odds they know in Dover by this time that I am taking you to Her Majesty. You've never had any dealings with royalty, I take it?"

"Only in Afghanistan, my lord," says I, and he barked a little short laugh.

"They probably have less ceremonial than we do," he says. "It is a most confounded bore. Let me tell you, sir, never become a field-marshal and commander-in-chief. It is very fine, but it means your sovereign will honour you by coming to stay, and not a bed in the place worth a damn. I have more anxiety over the furnishing of Walmer, Mr Flashman, than I did over the works at Torres Vedras."[27]

"If you are as successful this time as you were then, my lord" says I, buttering him, "you have no cause for alarm."

"Huh!" says he, and gave me a sharp look. But he was silent for a minute or two, and then asked me if I felt nervous.

"There is no need why you should be," says he. "Her Majesty is most gracious, although it is never as easy, of course, as it was with her predecessors. King William was very easy, very kind, and made people entirely at home. It is altogether more formal now, and pretty stiff, but if you stay by me and keep your mouth shut, you'll do."

I ventured to say that I'd felt happier at the prospect of charging into a band of Ghazis than I did at going to the palace, which was rubbish, of course, but I thought was probably the thing to say.

"Damned nonsense," says he, sharply. "You wouldn't rather anything of the sort. But I know that the feeling is much the same, for I've experienced both myself. The important thing is never to show it, as I am never tired of telling young men. Now tell me about these Ghazis, who I understand are the best soldiers the Afghans can show."

He was on my home ground there, and I told him about the Ghazis and Gilzais and Pathans and Douranis, to which he listened very carefully until I realised that we were rolling through the palace gates, and there were the Guards presenting arms, and a flunkey running to hold the door and set the steps, and officers clicking to attention, and a swarm of people about us.

"Come on," says the Duke, and led the way through a small doorway, and I have a hazy recollection of stairs and liveried footmen, and long carpeted corridors, and great chandeliers, and soft-footed officials escorting us—but my chief memory is of the slight, grey-coated figure in front of me, striding along and people getting out of his way.

We brought up outside two great double doors with a flunkey in a wig at either side, and a small fat man in a black tail coat bobbed in front of us, and darted forward muttering to twitch at my collar and smooth my lapel.

"Apologies," he twittered. "A brush here." And he snapped his fingers. A brush appeared and he flicked at my coat, very deftly, and shot a glance in the Duke's direction.

"Take that damned thing away," says the Duke, "and stop fussing. We know how to dress without your assistance."

The little fat man looked reproachful and stood aside, motioning to the flunkeys. They opened the door, and with my heart thumping against my ribs I heard a rich, strong voice announce: "His Grace the Duke of Wellington. Mr Flashman."

It was a large, magnificently furnished drawing room, with a carpet stretching away between mirrored walls and a huge chandelier overhead. There were a few people at the other end, two men standing near the fireplace, a girl sitting on a couch with an older woman standing behind, and I think another man and a couple of women near by. We walked forward towards them, the Duke a little in advance, and he stopped short of the couch and bowed.

"Your Majesty," says he, "may I have the honour to present Mr Flashman."

And only then did I realise who the girl was. We are accustomed to think of her as the old queen, but she was just a child then, rather plump, and pretty enough beneath the neck. Her eyes were large and popped a little, and her teeth stuck out too much, but she smiled and murmured in reply—by this time I was bowing my backside off, naturally.

When I straightened up she was looking at me, and Wellington was reciting briskly about Kabul and Jallalabad—"distinguished defence," "Mr Flashman's notable behaviour" are the only phrases that stay in my mind. When he stopped she inclined her head at him, and then said to me:

"You are the *first* we have seen of those who served so bravely in Afghanistan, Mr Flashman. It is *really* a great joy to see you returned safe and well. We have heard the most *glowing* reports of your gallantry, and it is most *gratifying* to be able to express our thanks and admiration for such *brave* and loyal service."

Well, she couldn't have said fairer than that, I suppose, even if she did recite it like a parrot. I just made a rumbling sound in my throat and ducked my head again. She had a thin, oddly-accented voice, and came down heavy on her words every now and then, nodding as she did so.

"Are you *entirely* recovered from your wounds?" she asked.

"Very well, thank'ee, your majesty," says I.

"You are exceedingly brown," says one of the men, and the heavy German accent startled me. I'd noticed him out of the tail of my eye, leaning against the mantel, with one leg crossed over the other. So this is Prince Albert, I thought; what hellish-looking whiskers.

"You must be as brown as an Aff-ghan," says he, and they laughed politely.

I told him I had passed for one, and he opened his eyes and said did I speak the language, and would I say something in it. So without thinking I said the first words that came into my head: "Hamare ghali ana, achha din," which is what the harlots chant at passers-by, and means "Good day, come into our street." He seemed very interested, but the man beside him stiffened and stared hard at me.

"What does it *mean*, Mr Flashman?" says the Queen.

"It is a Hindu greeting, marm," says the Duke, and my guts turned over as I recalled that he had served in India.

"Why, of course," says she, "we are quite an *Indian* gathering, with Mr Macaulay here." The name meant nothing to me then; he was looking at me damned hard, though, with his pretty little mouth set hard. I later learned that he had spent several years in government out there, so my fat-headed remark had not been lost on him, either.

"Mr Macaulay has been reading us his new poems,"[28] says the Queen. "They are *quite* stirring and fine. I think his Horatius must have been your model, Mr Flashman, for you know he defied great odds in defence of Rome. It is a *splendid* ballad, and very inspiring. Do you know the story, Duke?"

He said he did, which put him one up on me, and added that he didn't believe it, at which she cried out and demanded to know why.

"Three men can't stop an army, marm," says he. "Livy was no soldier, or he would hardly have suggested they could."

"Oh, come now," says Mr Macaulay. "They were on a narrow bridge, and could not be outnumbered."

"You see, Duke?" says the Queen. "How *could* they be overcome?"

"Bows and arrows, marm," says he. "Slings. Shoot 'em down. That's what I'd have done."

At this she said that the Tuscans were more chivalrous than he was, and he agreed that very likely they were.

"Which is perhaps why there are no Tuscan empires today, but an extensive British one," says the Prince quietly. And then he leaned forward and murmured something to the Queen, and she nodded wisely, and stood up—she was very small—and signed to me to come forward in front of her. I went, wondering, and the Duke came to my elbow, and the Prince watched me with his head on one side. The lady who had been behind the couch came forward, and handed something to the Queen, and she looked up at me, from not a foot away.

"Our brave soldiers in Afghanistan are to have *four* medals from the Governor-General," she said. "You will wear them in course of time, but there is also a medal from their *Queen*, and it is fitting that you should wear it first of all."

She pinned it on my coat, and she had to reach up to do it, she was so small. Then she smiled at me, and I felt so overcome I didn't know what to say. Seeing this, she went all soulful about the eyes.

"You are a very gallant gentleman," says she. "God bless you."

Oh, lor', I thought, if only you knew, you romantic little woman, thinking I'm a modern Horatius. (I made a point of studying Macaulay's 'Lays' later, and she wasn't too far off, really; only the chap I resembled was False Sextus, a man after my own heart).

However, I had to say something, so I mumbled about her majesty's service.

"England's service," said she, looking intense.

"The same thing, ma'am," says I, flown with inspiration, and she cast her eyes down wistfully. The Duke gave what sounded like a little groan.

There was a pause, and then she asked if I was married. I told her I was, but that I and my wife had been parted for the past two years.

"What a cruel separation," says she, as one might say "What delicious strawberry jam." But she was sure, she said, that our reunion must be all the sweeter for that parting.

"I know what it means to be a *devoted* wife, with the dearest of husbands," she went on, glancing at Albert, and he looked fond and noble. God, I thought, what a honeymoon that must have been.

Then the Duke chimed in, making his farewells, and I realised that this was my cue. We both bowed, and backed away, and she sat looking dumpy on the couch, and then we were in the corridor again, and the Duke was striding off through the hovering attendants.

"Well," says he, "you've got a medal no one else will ever have. Only a few of 'em struck, you see, and then Ellenborough announced that he was giving four of his own, which did not please her majesty at all. So her medal is to be stopped."[29]

He was right as it turned out; no one else ever received the medal, with its pink and green ribbon (I suspect Albert chose the colours), and I wear it on ceremonial days along with my Victoria Cross, my American Medal of Honour (for which the republic graciously pays me ten dollars a month), my San Serafino Order of Purity and Truth (richly deserved), and all the other assorted tinware which serves to disguise a cowardly scoundrel as a heroic veteran.

We passed through the covey of saluting Guardsmen, bowing officials, and rigid flunkeys to our coach, but there was no getting through the gates at first for the crowd which had collected and was cheering its head off.

"Good old Flashy! Hurrah for Flash Harry! Hip! hip! hooray!"

They clamoured at the railings, waving and throwing up their hats, jostling the sentries, surging in a great press round the gateway, until at last the gates were pushed open and the brougham moved slowly through the struggling mass, all the faces grinning and shouting and the handkerchiefs waving.

"Take off your hat, man," snaps the Duke, so I did, and they roared again, pressing forward against the sides of the coach, reaching in to clasp my hand, beating on the panels, and making a tremendous racket.

"He's got a medal!" roars someone. "God save the Queen!"

At that they woke the echoes, and I thought the coach must overturn. I was laughing and waving to them, but what do you suppose I was thinking? This was real glory! Here was I, the hero of the Afghan war, with the Queen's medal on my coat, the world's greatest soldier at my side, and the people of the world's greatest city cheering me to the echo—me! while the Duke sat poker-faced snapping: "Johnson, can't you get us out of this damned mess?" What was I thinking? About the chance that had sent me to India? About Elphy Bey? About the horror of the passes on the retreat, or the escape at Mogala when Iqbal died? Of the nightmare of Piper's Fort or that dreadful dwarf in the snake-pit? About Sekundar Burnes? Or Bernier? Or the women—Josette, Narreeman, Fetnab and the rest? About Elspeth? About the Queen?

None of these things. Strange, but as the coach won clear and we rattled off down the Mall with the cheers dying behind us, I could hear Arnold's voice saying, "There is good in you, Flashman," and I could imagine how he would have supposed himself vindicated at this moment, and preach on "Courage" in chapel, and pretend to rejoice in the redeemed prodigal—but all the time he would know in his hypocrite heart that I was a rotter still.[30] But neither he nor anyone else would have dared to say so. This myth called bravery, which is half-panic, half-lunacy (in my case, all panic), pays for all; in England you *can't* be a hero *and* bad. There's practically a law against it.

Wellington was muttering sharply about the growing insolence of the mob, but he left off to tell me he would set me down at the Horse Guards. When we arrived and I was getting out and thanking him for his kindness, he looks sharply at me, and says:

"I wish you every good fortune, Flashman. You should go far. I don't imagine you're a second Marlborough, mind, but you appear to be brave and you're certainly damned lucky. With the first quality you may easily gain command of an army or two, and lead 'em both to ruin, but with your luck you'll probably lead 'em back again. You have made a good beginning, at all events, and received today the highest honour you can hope for, which is your monarch's mark of favour. Goodbye to you."

We shook hands, and he drove off. I never spoke to him again. Years later, though, I told the American general, Robert Lee, of the incident, and he said Wellington was right—I *had* received the highest honour any soldier could hope for. But it wasn't the medal; for Lee's money it was Wellington's hand.

Neither, I may point out, had any intrinsic value.

I was the object of general admiration at the Horse Guards, of course, and at the club, and finally I took myself home in excellent fettle. It had been raining cats and dogs, but had stopped, and the sun was shining as I ran up the steps. Oswald informed me that Elspeth was above stairs; oho! thinks I, wait till she hears where I've been and who I've seen. She'll be *rather* more attentive to her lord and master now, perhaps, and less to sprigs of Guardees; I was smiling as I went upstairs, for the events of the afternoon had made my earlier jealousy seem silly, and simply the work of the little bitch Judy.

I walked into the bedroom keeping my left hand over the medal, to surprise her. She was sitting before her glass, as usual, with her maid dressing her hair.

"Harry!" she cries out, "where *have* you been? Have you forgot we are to take tea with Lady Chalmers at four-thirty?"

"The devil with Lady Chalmers, and all Chalmerses," says I. "Let 'em wait."

"Oh, how can you say so?" she laughed at me in the mirror. "But *where* have you been, looking so splendid?"

"Oh, visiting friends, you know. Young couple, Bert and Vicky. You wouldn't know 'em."

"Bert and Vicky!" If Elspeth had developed a fault in my long absence, it was that she had become a complete snob—not uncommon among people of her class. "Whoever are they?"

I stood behind her, looking at her reflection, and exposed the medal. I saw her eyes light on it, and widen, and then she swung round.

"Harry! What . . .?"

"I've been to the palace. With the Duke of Wellington. I had this from the Queen—after we had chatted a little, you know, about poetry and . . ."

"The Queen!" she squeals. "The Duke! The palace!"

And she leaped up, clapping her hands, throwing her arms round my neck, while her maid clucked and fussed and I, laughing, swung her round and kissed her. There was no shutting her up, of course; she rained questions on me, her eyes shining, demanding to know who was there, and what they said, and what the Queen wore, and how the Queen spoke to me, and what I replied, and every mortal thing. Finally I pushed her into a chair, sent the maid packing, and sat down on the bed, reciting the whole thing from start to finish.

243

Elspeth sat, round-eyed and lovely, listening breathlessly, and squealing with excitement every now and then. When I told her the Queen had asked about her, she gasped and turned to look at herself in the mirror, I imagine to see if there was a smut on her nose. Then she demanded that I go through it all again, and I did, but not before I had stripped off her gown and pulled her on top of me on the bed, so that between gasps and sighs the breathtaking tale was re-told. I lost track of it several times, I admit.

Even then she was still marvelling at it all, until I pointed out that it was after four o'clock, and what would Lady Chalmers say? She giggled, and said we had better go, and chattered incessantly while she dressed and I lazily put myself in order.

"Oh, it is the most wonderful thing!" she kept saying. "The Queen! The Duke! Oh, Harry!"

"Aye," says I, "and where were you, eh? Sparking in the Row all afternoon with one of your admirers."

"Oh, he is the greatest bore," says she laughing. "Nothing to talk of but his horses. We spent the *entire* afternoon riding in the Park, and he spoke of nothing else for two *hours* on end!"

"Did he, begad," says I. "Why, you must have been soaked."

She was in a cupboard by now, among her dresses, and didn't hear, and idly I reached out, not thinking, and touched the bottle-green riding coat that lay across the end of the bed. I felt it, and my heart suddenly turned to stone. The coat was bone-dry. I twisted round to look at the boots standing by a chair; they shone glossy, with not a mark or a splash on them.

I sat, feeling sick, listening to my heart thumping, while she chattered away. It had rained steadily from the time I had left Wellington at the Horse Guards until I had left the club more than an hour later and come home. She could not have been riding in the Park in that downpour. Well, where the devil had she and Watney been, then, and what . . . ?

I felt rage mounting inside me, rage and spite, but I held myself in, telling myself I might be wrong. She was patting her face with a rabbit's foot before the glass, never minding me, so I said, very easy like:

"Whereabouts did you go for your ride?"

"Oh, in the Park, as I said. Nowhere at all in particular."

Now that's a lie for certain, thinks I, and yet I couldn't believe it. She looked so damned innocent and open, so feather-headed and full of nonsense as she went on and on about my wonderful, wonderful hour at the palace; why, only ten minutes ago she had been coupling with me on the bed, letting me . . . aye, *letting* me. Suddenly the ugly thought of the first night home came rushing back to me—how I had fancied she was less ardent than I remembered her. Perhaps I had been right; perhaps she had been less passionate. Well she might be, if in my absence she had found some jockey who was more to her fancy over the jumps than I was. By God, if that were true I would . . .

I sat there shaking, my head turned away so that she would not see me in the mirror. Had that slut Judy been hinting at the truth, then? Was Watney cuckolding me—and heaven knew who else besides him? I was fairly boiling with shame and anger at the thought. But it couldn't be true! No, not Elspeth. And yet there was Judy's sneer, and those boots winking their wickedness at me—they hadn't been near the Park this afternoon, by God!

While the maid came back and attended to Elspeth's hair again, and I tried to close my ears to the shrill feminine trilling of her talk, I tried to take hold of myself. Maybe I was wrong—oh, God, I hoped so. It wasn't just that strange yearning that I had about Elspeth, it was my . . . well, my honour, if you like. Oh, I didn't give a damn about what the world calls honour, but the thought of another man, or men, frollicking in the hay with *my* wife, who should have been unable to imagine a more masterful or heroic lover than the great Flashman—the hero whose name was on everyone's lips, God help us—the thought of that! . . .

Pride is a hellish thing; without it there isn't any jealousy or ambition. And I was proud of the figure I cut—in bed and in barracks. And here was I, the lion of the hour, medal and all, the Duke's handshake and the Queen's regard still fresh—and I was gnawing my innards out about a gold-headed filly without a brain to her name. And I must bite my lip and not say a word, for fear of the row there would be if I let slip a breath of my suspicions— right or wrong, the fat would be in the fire, and I couldn't afford that.

"Well, how do I look?" says she, coming to stand in front of me in her gown and bonnet. "Why, Harry, you have gone quite pale! I know, it is the excitement of this day! My poor dear!" And she tilted up my head and kissed me. No, I couldn't believe it, looking into those baby-blue eyes. Aye, and what about those baby-black boots?

"We shall go out to Lady Chalmers's," said she, "and she will be quite over the moon when she hears about this. I expect there will be quite a company there, too. I shall be so proud, Harry—so proud! Now, let me straighten your cravat; bring a brush, Susan— what an excellent coat it is. You must always go to that tailor —which is he again? There now; oh, Harry, how handsome you look! See yourself in the glass!"

I looked, and seeing myself so damned dashing, and her radiant and fair beside me, I fought down the wretchedness and rage. No, it couldn't be true. . . .

"Susan, you have not put away my coat, silly girl. Take it at once, before it creases."

By God, though, I knew it was. Or I thought I knew. To the devil with the consequences, no little ninny in petticoats was going to do this to me.

"Elspeth," says I, turning.

"Hang it carefully, now, when you've brushed it. There. Yes, my love?"

"Elspeth. . . ."

"Oh, Harry, you look so strong and fierce, on my word. I don't think I shall feel easy in my mind when I see all these fancy London ladies making eyes at you." And she pouted very pretty and touched her finger on my lips.

"Elspeth, I—"

"Oh, I had nearly forgot—you had better take some money with you. Susan, bring me my purse. In case of any need that may arise, you know. Twenty guineas, my love."

"Much obliged," says I.

What the devil, you have to make do as best you can; if the tide's there, swim with it and catch on to whatever offers. You only go by once.

"Will twenty be sufficient, do you think?"

"Better make it forty."

(At this point the first packet of The Flashman Papers ends abruptly.)

NOTES

1. Lord Brougham's speech in May, 1839, " lashed the Queen ... with unsparing severity" (Greville) and caused great controversy.

2. Lady Flora Hastings, Maid of Honour to the Duchess of Kent, was believed to be pregnant, until medical examination proved that she was not. She won great popular sympathy, but the young Queen, who had been bitterly hostile towards her, suffered dramatically in public esteem.

3. Captain John Reynolds, a particular butt of Cardigan's, was the centre of the notorious Black Bottle affair, in which his resignation was demanded because he was believed to have ordered a bottle of porter in the mess on guest night.

4. Cardigan had, in fact, served in India, when he went out to take command of the 11th at Cawnpore in 1837, but had spent only a few weeks with the regiment.

5. Cardigan was a favourite target of the newspapers, and especially of the *Morning Chronicle* (not the *Post*, as Flashman says). The quarrel referred to here is probably the one in which Cardigan, in response to a press attack, threatened to assault the editor. For details of this and other incidents, and of Lord Cardigan's military career, see Cecil Woodham-Smith's *The Reason Why*.

6. Choice of weapons. In fact this did not necessarily rest with the injured party, but was normally settled by mutual agreement.

7. Mr Attwood, M.P., presented the Chartists' first petition for political reform to the Commons in July 1839. In that year there were outbreaks of Chartist violence; on November 24 people were killed at Newport.

8. Mr Abercrombie's use of the word "chief" is inexplicable, since Sir Colin Campbell's command of the 93rd came much later. Of course, Abercrombie may have served with him in Spain.

9. Military service with the East India Company's regiments was considered socially inferior to service in the army proper, and Flashman must have been conscious of this, which possibly accounts for his casual reference to it. The Company at this time drew its artillery, engineer, and infantry officers from the Addiscombe training establishment; cavalry officers, however, could be appointed direct by the Company's Directors. Cardigan, who seems to have had a liking for Flashman (his judgement of men, when he condescended to use it, was deplorable) may well have had influence with the Board.

10. The Company did not believe in maintaining houses for transients and visitors; they were expected to find hospitality with British residents or pay their own lodgings.

11. Avitabile. Flashman's description of this extraordinary soldier of fortune is accurate; the Italian was noted as a stern, just administrator and intrepid soldier.

12. Cotton was the ringleader of the great Rugby School mutiny of 1797, in which the door of the headmaster, Dr Ingles, was blown in with gunpowder.

13. Poor army swords. The sabres issued to British cavalry at this time were notorious for their greasy brass hilts, which turned in the hand.

14. Flashman's account of Burnes's murder clears up a point which has troubled historians. Previous versions suggest that the Burnes brothers left the Residency in disguise, accompanied by a mysterious third party who has been described as a Kashmiri Musselman. It has been alleged that this third man actually denounced them to the Ghazis. But Flashman could hardly have betrayed them without considerable risk to himself, so his account is probably the true one.

15. The actual names of these two Afghans remain a mystery. Other accounts call them Muhammed Sadeq and Surwar Khan, but Lady Sale seems to suggest that one of them was Sultan Jan.

16. Lieutenant-General Colin Mackenzie has left one of the most vivid accounts of the First Afghan War in *Storms and Sunshine of a Soldier's Life* (1884).

17. Flashman, like many other European writers, uses the word "Ghazi" as though he referred to it as a tribe, although he certainly knew better. In Arabic "ghazi" is literally a conqueror, but may be accurately translated as hero or champion. Europeans usually render it as "fanatic", in which connection it is interesting to note the parallel between the Moslem Ghazis and the Christian medieval ideal of knighthood. The Ghazi sect were dedicated to the militant expansion of Islam.

18. Flashman's account of the retreat tallies substantially with those of such contemporaries as Mackenzie, Lady Sale, and Lieutenant Eyre. This is also true of his version of affairs in Afghanistan generally. His description of McNaghten's murder, for example, is the fullest and most personal to survive. There are omissions and discrepancies here and there—he does not mention "Gentleman Jim" Skinner's part in the liaison work with Akbar Khan, for instance—but on the whole he can be regarded as highly reliable within his self-centred limits. Readers seeking wider and more authoritative accounts are recommended to the standard works, which include Kaye's *History of the War in Afghanistan*, vol. ii, Fortescue's *History of the British Army*, vol. xii, and Patrick Macrory's admirably clear account, *Signal Catastrophe*.

19. The "united front" of officers took place at Jugdulluk on January 11, 1842.

20. In fact some prisoners were taken by the Afghans at Gandamack, including Captain Souter of the 44th Regiment, one of two men who wrapped the battalion colours round their bodies (the other man was killed). The picture to which Flashman refers is by W. B. Wollen, R.A., hung at the Royal Academy in 1898.

21. Flashman may be excused an overstatement here. Possibly Sergeant Hudson was a fine swordsman, but this was not usual in the British

cavalry; Fortescue in his passage on the Charge of the Heavy Brigade at Balaclava refers to the troopers' habit of using their sabres as bludgeons. It was not uncommon for a man to use his sabre-hilt as a knuckle-duster instead of cutting or thrusting.

22. Major Henry Havelock. Later famous as the hero of Lucknow, the "stern Cromwellian soldier" became one of the great figures of the Indian Empire.

23. Sale was indeed hailed as a celebrity, but returned to India and was killed at Mudki in 1845, fighting the Sikhs. Shelton's adventurous career ended when he fell from his horse on parade at Dublin and was killed. Lawrence and Mackenzie both achieved general rank.

24. Flashman saw Ellenborough at his worst. Arrogant, theatrical, and given to flights of rhetoric, the Governor-General went to extravagant lengths to honour the "heroes of Afghanistan", and was widely ridiculed. But in the main he was an able and energetic administrator.

25. *Punch* began publication in 1841; the "Pencillings" were its first full-page cartoons.

26. The "Opium War" in China had ended with a treaty whereby Hong Kong was ceded to Britain.

27. The Duke's reference to the Queen's impending visit to Walmer Castle fixes the date of Flashman's appearance at Buckingham Palace very closely. Wellington wrote to Sir Robert Peel on October 26, 1842, assuring him that Walmer was at the Queen's disposal, and she visited it in the following month.

28. Macaulay's *Lays of Ancient Rome* was first published on October 28, 1842.

29. The Queen's Medal. That Her Majesty was piqued at Lord Ellenborough's decision to issue medals is evident from her letter to Peel on November 29, 1842.

30. Dr Thomas Arnold, father of Matthew Arnold and headmaster of Rugby School, had died on June 12, 1842, aged 47.

GLOSSARY

badmash a scoundrel
feringhee European, possibly a corruption of "Frankish" or "English"
Ghazi a fanatic
havildar sergeant
hubshi negro (literally "woolly-head")
huzoor lord, master, in the sense of "sir" (Pushtu equivalent of "sahib")
idderao come here (imp.)
jao go, get away (imp.)
jawan soldier
jezzail long rifle of the Afghans
juldi quickly, hurry up
khabadar be careful (imp.)
maidan plain, exercise ground
munshi teacher, usually of language
puggarree turban cloth
rissaldar native officer commanding cavalry troop
sangar small stone breastwork like grouse butt
shabash bravo
sowar trooper

ROYAL FLASH

From The Flashman Papers
1842–1843 & 1847–1848

Explanatory Note

The second packet of the Flashman Papers continues the career of the author, Harry Flashman, from the point where the first instalment ended in the autumn of 1842. It covers two separate periods of several months in 1842–43 and 1847–48. There is an intriguing four-year gap which the author seems to indicate he has covered elsewhere in his memoirs.

The present instalment is of historical importance insofar as it describes Flashman's encounters with several persons of international celebrity—including one most eminent statesman whose character and actions may now be subjected to some reappraisal by historians. It also establishes a point of some literary interest, for there can be no doubt that a link exists between Flashman's German adventure and one of the best-selling novels in the Victorian period.

As with the first packet I have confined myself to correcting the author's occasional lapses in spelling. Where Flashman touches on known history he is remarkably accurate, especially when one considers that he was writing in his eighties; wherever he appears to make a minor slip I have left it uncorrected in the text (as, for example, where he describes the pugilist Nick Ward as "the Champion" in 1842, when in fact Ward had lost his title the previous year), but I have added such notes and comments as seemed appropriate.

Like most memorialists, Flashman is vague about exact dates; where these can be established I have entered them in the notes.

G.M.F.

If I had been the hero everyone thought I was, or even a half-decent soldier, Lee would have won the battle of Gettysburg and probably captured Washington. That is another story, which I shall set down in its proper place if brandy and old age don't carry me off first, but I mention the fact here because it shows how great events are decided by trifles.

Scholars, of course, won't have it so. Policies, they say, and the subtly laid schemes of statesmen, are what influence the destinies of nations; the opinions of intellectuals, the writings of philosophers, settle the fate of mankind. Well, they may do their share, but in my experience the course of history is as often settled by someone's having a belly-ache, or not sleeping well, or a sailor getting drunk, or some aristocratic harlot waggling her backside.

So when I say that my being rude to a certain foreigner altered the course of European history, it is a considered judgement. If I had dreamed for a moment how important that man was going to be, I'd have been as civil as the devil to him, yes-me-lording and stroking his back. But in my youth and ignorance I imagined that he was one of those to whom I could be rude with impunity—servants, tarts, bagmen, shopkeepers, and foreigners—and so I gave my unpleasant tongue free rein. In the long run it nearly cost me my neck, quite apart from changing the map of the world.

It was in '42, when I was barely out of my 'teens, but already famous. I had taken a distinguished part in the fiasco known as the First Afghan War, emerged with a hero's laurels, been decorated by the Queen, and lionised all over London. The fact that I had gone through the campaign in a state of abject terror—lying, deceiving, bluffing, and running for dear life whenever possible—was known to no one but myself. If one or two suspected, they kept quiet. It wouldn't have been fashionable to throw dirt at the valiant Harry Flashman just then.

(If you have read the first packet of my memoirs, you will know all this. I mention it here in case the packets should get separated, so that you will know at once that this is the true story of a dishonest poltroon who takes a perverse pride in having attained to an honoured and admired old age, in spite of his many vices and entire lack of virtue—or possibly because of them.)

So there I was, in '42, big, bluff, handsome Harry, beloved of London society, admired at the Horse Guards (although I was only a captain), possessed of a beautiful wife, apparently affluent, seen in the best company, gushed at by the mamas, respected by the men as the perfect beau sabreur. The world was my oyster, and if it wasn't my sword that had opened it, no one was any the wiser.

They were golden days, those. The ideal time to be a hero is when the battle is over and the other fellows are dead, God rest 'em, and you take the credit.

Even the fact that Elspeth was cheating me made no real difference. You would never have thought, to see her angelic face, golden hair, and expression of idiotic innocence, that she was the biggest trollop that ever wore out a mattress. But I was certain, before I'd been home a month, that she was having it off with at least two others; at first I was furious and plotting revenge, but she had the money, you see, through that damned old Scotch moneybags of a father of hers, and if I had played the outraged husband I'd have been in Queer Street, without even a roof over my head. So I kept quiet, and paid her out by whoring to my heart's content. It was a strange situation; we both knew what was what (at least, I think she did, but she was such a fool you could never tell), but we pretended to be a happily married couple. We still bounced about in bed together from time to time, and enjoyed it.

But the real life was to be had outside; respectable society apart, I was in with the fast set, idling, gaming, drinking, and raking about the town. It was the end of the great days of the bucks and blades; we had a queen on the throne, and her cold white hand and her poker-backed husband's were already setting their grip on the nation's life, smothering the old wild ways in their come-to-Jesus hypocrisy. We were entering into what is now called the Victorian Age, when respectability was the thing; breeches were out and trousers came in; bosoms were being covered and eyes modestly lowered; politics was becoming sober, trade and industry were becoming fashionable, the odour of sanctity was replacing the happy reek of brandy, the age of the Corinthian, the plunger, and the dandy was giving way to that of the prig, the preacher, and the bore.

At least I was in at the death of that wicked era, and did my bit to make it die hard. You could still gamble in the hells about Hanover Square, carouse with the toughs in the Cyder Cellars or Leicester Fields, take your pick of the wenches in Piccadilly, set on the police at Whitehall and pinch their belts and hats, break windows and sing bawdy songs all the way home. Fortunes were still lost at cards and hazard, duels were fought (although I stayed well clear of that; my only duel, from which I emerged by fraud with tremendous credit, had taken place some years before, and I had no intention of risking another). Life could still be openly wild, if you cared for it. It has never been the same since; they tell me that young King Edward does what he can nowadays to lower the moral tone of the nation, but I doubt if he has the style for it. The man looks like a butcher.

One night my chum Speedicut, who had been with me at Rugby, and had come sucking round me since my rise to fame (he was well off) suggested we should go to a new haunt in St James— I think it was the Minor Club, in fact.[1] We could try our luck at the tables first, and then at the wenches upstairs, he said, and afterwards go to the Cremorne and watch the fireworks, topping the night off with devilled ham and a bowl of punch, and perhaps some more girls. It sounded all right, so after collecting some cash from Elspeth, who was going to Store Street to listen to one Mr Wilson sing Scottish songs (my God), I set off with Speed for St James.[2]

It was a frost from the start. On the way to the club Speed was taken with the notion of boarding one of the new buses; he wanted to argue with the cad about the fare and provoke him into swearing: the bus cads were quite famous for their filthy language, and Speed reckoned it would be fun to have him get in a bate and horrify the passengers.[3] But the cad was too clever for Speed; he just turned us off without so much as a damn-your-eyes, and the passengers tittered to see us made asses of, which did nothing for our dignity or good temper.

And the club turned out to be a regular hell—the prices even for arrack and cheroots were ruinous, and the faro table was as crooked as a line of Russian infantry and a damned sight harder to beat. It's always the same; the more genteel the company, the fouler the play. In my time I've played nap in the Australian diggings with gold-dust stakes, held a blackjack bank on a South Sea trader, and been in a poker game in a Dodge City livery stable with the pistols down on the blanket—and I've met less sharping in all of 'em put together than you'd find in one evening in a London club.

We dropped a few guineas, and then Speed says:

"This ain't much fun. I know a better game."

I believed him, so we picked up two of the Cyprians in the gaming-room and took them upstairs to play loo for each others' clothes. I had my eye on the smaller of the two, a pert little red-haired piece with dimples; thinks I, if I can't get this one stripped for action in a dozen hands then I've lost my talent for palming and dealing from the bottom. But whether I'd taken too much drink—for we had punished a fair amount of arrack, dear as it was—or the tarts were cheating too, the upshot was that I was down to my shirt-tail before my little minx had removed more than her shoes and gloves.

She was trilling with laughter, and I was getting impatient, when a most unholy din broke out on the floor below. There was a pounding of feet, and shouting, whistles blowing and dogs barking, and then a voice yelled:

"Cut and run! It's the traps!"

"Christ!" says Speed, grabbing for his breeches. "It's a raid! Let's get out of this, Flash!"

The whores squeaked with panic, and I swore and struggled into my clothes. It's no joke trying to dress when the peelers are after you, but I had sense enough to know that there wasn't a hope of escaping unless we were fully clad—you can't run through St James on a fine evening with your trousers in your hand.

"Come on!" Speed was shouting. "They'll be on us in a moment!"

"What shall we do?" wails the red-haired slut.

"Do what you dam' well please," says I, slipping on my shoes. 'Good-night, ladies." And Speed and I slipped out into the corridor.

The place was in uproar. It sounded like a battle royal down on the gaming-floor, with furniture smashing and the Cyprians screaming, and someone bawling: "In the Queen's name!" On our landing there were frightened whores peeping out of the doorways, and men in every stage of undress hopping about looking for somewhere to run to. One fat old rascal, stark naked, was beating on a door bawling:

"Hide me, Lucy!"

He beat in vain, and the last I saw of him he was trying to burrow under a sofa.

People nowadays don't realise that in the forties the law was devilish hot on gaming-hells. The police were forever trying to raid them, and the hell-owners used to keep guard-dogs and scouts to watch out for them. Most hells also had special hiding places for all gambling equipment, so that cards, dice, and boards could be swept out of sight in a moment, for the police had no right of search, and if they couldn't prove that gaming had been going on they could be sued for wrongful entry and trespass.[4]

Evidently they had caught the Minor St James Club napping with a vengeance, and it would be police court and newspaper scandal for us if we couldn't cut out pretty sharp. A whistle shrilled at the foot of the stairs, the trollops screamed and slammed their doors, and feet came pounding upwards.

"This way," says I to Speed, and we darted up the next flight. It was another empty landing—the top one—and we crouched by the bannisters, waiting to see what happened. They were hammering on the doors below, and presently someone came scampering up. He was a fair, chinless youth in a pink coat.

"Oh, my God!" says he, "what will mother say?" He stared wildly round. "Where can I hide?"

"In there," says I, thinking quickly, and pointed at a closed door.

"God bless you," says he. "But what will you do?"

"We'll hold 'em off," says I. "Get out of it, you fool."

He vanished inside, and I winked at Speed, whipped his handkerchief from his breast, and dropped it outside the closed door. Then we tip-toed to a room on the other side of the landing, and took cover behind its door, which I left wide open. From the lack of activity on this floor, and the dust-sheets in the room, it obviously wasn't in use.

Presently the peelers came crashing up, spotted the kerchief, gave a great view halloo, and dragged out the pink youth. But as I had calculated, they didn't bother with our room, seeing the door open; and naturally supposing that no one could be hiding in it. We stood dead still while they tramped about the landing, shouting orders and telling the pink youth to hold his tongue, and presently they all trooped off below, where by the sound of things they were marshalling their prisoners, and being pretty rough about it. It wasn't often they raided a hell successfully, and had a chance to mistreat their betters.

"By George, Flashy," whispered Speed at last. "You're a foxy one, and no mistake. I thought we were done."

"When you've been chased by bloody Afghans," says I, "you learn all there is to know about lying low." But I was pleased at the way my trick had worked, just the same.

We found a skylight, and as luck had it there was a convenient flat roof close by over what proved to be an empty house. We prised up another skylight, crept down two flights of stairs, and got out of a back window into a lane. So far, excellent, but Speed thought it would be capital to go round the front and watch from a safe distance while the peelers removed their victims. I thought it would be fun, too, so we straightened our clothes and then sauntered round into the end of the street.

Sure enough, there was a crowd outside the Minor Club to see the sport. The bobbies were there in their high hats and belts, clustering round the steps while the prisoners were brought down to the closed carts, the men silent and shame-faced or damning their captors for all they were worth, and the trollops crying for the most part, although some had to be carried out kicking and scratching.

If we had been wise we would have kept well clear, but it was growing dusk, and we thought we'd have a closer look. We strolled up to the fringe of the crowd, and as bad luck had it, who should be brought out last, wailing and white-faced, but the youth in the pink coat. Speed guffawed at the woebegone look of him, and sang out to me:

"I say, Flashy, what will mother say?"

The youth must have heard; he twisted round and saw us, and the spiteful little hound gave a yelp and pointed in our direction.

"They were there, too!" he cries. "Those two, they were hiding as well!"

If we had stood fast we could have brazened it out, I dare say, but my instinct to run is too deep ingrained; I was off like a hare before the bobbies had even started towards us, and seeing us run they gave chase at once. We had a fair start, but not enough to be able to get out of view and duck into a doorway or area; St James is a damned bad district to fly from the police in—streets too broad and no convenient alleyways.

They were perhaps fifty yards behind for the first two streets, but then they began to gain—two of them, with their clubs out, yelling after us to stop. I could feel myself going lame in the leg I had broken earlier in the year at Jallalabad; the muscles were still stiff, and pains shot through my thigh at every stride.

Speed saw what was up and slackened his pace.

"Hallo, Flash," says he, "are you done for?"

"Leg's gone," says I. "I can't keep up any longer."

He glanced over his shoulder. In spite of the bad name Hughes gives him in *Tom Brown's Schooldays*, Speedicut was as game as a terrier and ready for a turn-up any time—not like me at all.[5]

"Oh, well, then," says he, "the deuce with this. Let's stand and have it out with 'em. There's only two—no, wait though, there are more behind, damn 'em. We'll just have to do the best we can old son."

"It's no use," I gasped. "I'm in no state to fight."

"You leave 'em to me," cries he. "I'll hold 'em off while you get out of it. Don't stand there, man; don't you see it won't do for the hero of Afghanistan to be dragged in by the traps? Hellish scandal. Doesn't matter for me, though. Come on, you blue-bellied bastards!"

And he turned in the middle of the road, sparring away and daring them to come on.

I didn't hesitate. Anyone who is ass enough to sacrifice himself for Flashy deserves all he gets. Over my shoulder I saw him stop one trap with a straight left, and close with the other. Then I was round the corner, hobbling away as fast as my game leg would carry me. It took me along that street and into the square beyond, and still no bobbies hove in view. I doubled round the central garden, and then my leg almost folded under me.

I rested, gasping, against the railings. Faintly behind me I could hear Speed still singing defiance, and then the nearer patter of feet. Looking round for somewhere to hide I saw a couple of carriages drawn up outside a house fronting onto the railed garden; they weren't far, and the two drivers were together, talking by the horses in the first one. They hadn't seen me; if I could hobble to the rear coach and crawl in, the peelers would pass me by.

Hopping quietly is difficult, but I got to the coach unseen by the drivers, opened the door and climbed in. I squatted down out of sight, heaving to get my breath back and listening for sounds of pursuit. But for several moments all was still; they must be off the scent, thinks I, and then I heard a new sound. Men and women's voices were coming from the doorway of one of the houses; there was laughter and cries of goodnight, some chattering on the pavement and the sound of footsteps. I held my breath, my heart pounding, and then the carriage door opened, light came in, and I found myself staring into the surprised face of one of the loveliest girls I have ever seen in my life.

No—the loveliest. When I look back and review the beautiful women I have known, blonde and dark, slim and buxom, white and brown, hundreds of the creatures—still, I doubt if there was one to touch her. She was standing with one foot on the step, her hands holding back the skirts of her red satin gown, bending forward to display a splendid white bosom on which sparkled a row of brilliants matching the string in her jet-black hair. Dark blue eyes, very large, stared down at me, and her mouth, which was not wide but very full and red, opened in a little gasp.

"God save me!" exclaims she. "A man! What the devil are you doing, sir?"

It wasn't the kind of greeting you commonly heard from ladies in the young Queen's day, I may tell you. Any other would have screamed and swooned. Thinking quickly, I decided that for once truth would answer best.

"I'm hiding," says I.

"I can see that," says she smartly. She had a most lovely Irish lilt to her voice. "Who from, and why in my carriage, if you please?"

Before I could answer, a man loomed up at her elbow, and at

sight of me he let out a foreign oath and started forward as though to protect her.

"Please, please, I mean no harm," I said urgently. "I'm being pursued . . . the police . . . no, I'm not a criminal, I assure you. I was in a club that was raided."

The man just stared at me, but the woman showed her teeth in a delightful smile and then threw her head back,. chuckling. I smiled as ingratiatingly as I could, but for all the effect my charm had on her companion I might as well have been Quasimodo.

"Step out at once," snaps he, in a cold clipped voice. "At once, do you hear?"

I conceived an instant dislike for him. It was not only his manner and his words, but the look of him. He was big, as big as I was, slim-hipped and broad-shouldered, but he was also damned handsome. He had bright grey eyes and one of those clean-cut faces beneath fair hair that make you think of moral Norse gods, too splendid altogether to be in the company of the beauty beside him.

I started to say something, but he barked at me again, and then the woman came to my aid.

"Oh, let him be, Otto," says she. "Can't you see he's a gentleman?"

I would have thanked her gratefully, but at that moment there were heavy feet on the pavement, and a grave voice inquiring if the gentleman had seen anyone running through the square. The peelers were on the scent again, and this time I was cornered.

But before I could move or speak the lady had seated herself in the coach and hissed:

"Get up off the floor, you booby!"

I obeyed, in spite of my leg, and dropped gasping into the seat beside her. And then her companion, damn his eyes, was saying:

"Here is your man, constable. Arrest him, if you please."

A police sergeant poked his head in at the door, surveyed us, and said to the fair man, doubtfully:

"This gentleman, sir?"

"Of course. Who else?"

"Well. . . ." The bobby was puzzled, seeing me sitting there large as life. "Are you sure, sir?"

The fair man rapped out another foreign oath, and said of course he was sure. He called the sergeant a fool.

"Oh, stop it, Otto," says the lady suddenly. "Really, sergeant, it's too bad of him; he's making game of you. This gentleman is with us."

"Rosanna!" The fair man looked outraged. "What are you thinking of? Sergeant, I—"

"Don't play the fool, Otto," says I, taking my cue, and delighted to have my hand squeezed by the lady. "Come on, man, get in and let's be off home. I'm tired."

He gave me a look of utter fury, and then a fine altercation broke out between him and the sergeant, which the lady Rosanna seemed to find vastly amusing. The coachee and another constable joined in, and then suddenly the sergeant, who had been frowning oddly in my direction while the argument raged, stuck his head into the coach again, and says:

"Wait a minnit. I know you, don't I? You're Cap'n Flashman, bigod!"

I admitted it, and he swore and slapped his fist.

"The 'ero of Julloolabad!" cries he.

I smiled modestly at Miss Rosanna, who was looking at me wide-eyed.

"The defender of Piper's Fort!" cries the sergeant.

"Well, well," says I, "it's all right, sergeant."

"The 'Ector of Afghanistan!" cries the sergeant, who evidently studied the press. "Damme! Well, 'ere's a go!"

He was beaming all over his face, which didn't suit my denouncer at all. Angrily he demanded that I be arrested.

"He is a fugitive," he declared. "He invaded our coach without permission."

"I don't give a dam' if 'e invaded Buckin'am Palace without permission," says the sergeant, turning back to me. "Corporal Webster, sir, Third Guards, under Major Macdonald at 'Ougoumont, sir."

"Honoured to know you, sergeant," says I, shaking his hand.

"Honour's mine, sir, 'deed it is. Now then, you, sir, let's 'ave no more of this. You're not English, are you?"

"I am a Prussian officer," says the man called Otto, "and I demand—"

"Cap'n Flashman is a British officer, so you don't demand nothink," says the sergeant. "Now, then! Let's 'ave no trouble." He touched his hat to us and gave me a broad wink. "Wish you good-night, sir, an' you, ma'am."

I thought the German would have an apoplexy, he looked so wild, and his temper was not helped by the lovely Rosanna's helpless laughter. He stood glaring at her for a moment, biting his lip, and then she controlled herself sufficiently to say:

"Oh, come along, Otto, get into the coach. Oh, dear, oh, dear," and she began laughing again.

"I am happy you are amused," says he. "You make a fool of me: it is of a piece with your conduct of this evening." He looked thoroughly vicious. "Very good, madam, perhaps you will regret it."

"Don't be so pompous, Otto," says she. "It's just a joke; come and—"

"I prefer choicer company," says he. "That of ladies, for example." And clapping on his hat he stepped back from the carriage door.

"Oh, the devil fly away with you then!" cried she, suddenly angry. "Whip up, driver!"

And then I had to open my mouth. Leaning across her, I called to him:

"How dare you talk so to a lady, damn you!" says I. "You're a foul-mouthed foreign dog!"

I believe if I had kept silent he would have forgotten me, for his temper was concentrated on her. But now he turned those cold eyes on me, and they seemed to bore like drills. For a moment I was frightened of the man; he had murder on his face.

"I shall remember you," says he. And then, oddly, I saw a look of curiosity come into his eyes, and he stepped a pace closer. Then it was gone, but he was memorising me, and hating me at the same time.

"I shall remember you," he said a second time, and the coach jerked forward and left him standing by the gutter.

* * *

In spite of the momentary fear he had awakened in me, I didn't give a button for his threats—the danger was past, I had recovered my breath, and I could devote my attention to the important question of the beauty alongside me. I had time to examine the splendour of her profile—the broad brow and raven-black hair, the small ever so slightly curved nose, the pouting red cupid's bow, the firm little chin, and the white round breasts pushing themselves impudently up from the red satin gown.

The scent of her perfume, the sidelong look of her dark blue eyes, and the wanton husky Irish voice, were all invitations. As anyone will tell you, put Harry Flashman next to a woman like that and one of two things is inevitable—there will either be screams and slaps, or the lady will surrender. Sometimes both. In this case, just from the look of her, I knew there would be no screaming and slapping, and I was right. When I kissed her it was only a moment before her mouth opened under mine, and I promptly suggested that since my leg was still painful, a woman's touch on it would soothe the cramp out of my muscles. She complied, very teasingly, and with her free hand was remarkably skilful at fending off my advances until the coach reached her house, which was somewhere in Chelsea.

By this time I was in such a state of excitement that I could barely keep my hands still while she dismissed her maid and conducted me to her salon, talking gaily about anything and acting the cool minx. I soon put a stop to that by popping her breasts out the minute the door was closed, and bearing her down on to the settee. Her reaction was startling; in a moment she was grappling with me, digging her nails into me and twining her limbs round mine. The fury of her love-making was almost frightening —I've known eager women, plenty of them, but Miss Rosanna was like a wild animal.

The second time, later in the night, was even more feverish than the first. We were in bed by then, and I had no clothing to protect me from her biting and raking nails; I protested, but it was like talking to a mad woman. She even began to leather me with something hard and heavy—a hair-brush, I believe—and by the time she had stopped writhing and moaning I felt as though I had been coupling with a roll of barbed wire.[6] I was bruised, scratched, bitten, and stabbed from neck to backside.

In between, she was a different creature, gay, talkative, witty, and of a gentleness to match her voice and looks. I learned that she was Marie Elizabeth Rosanna James, no less, the wife of a fellow-officer who was conveniently out of town on garrison duty. Like myself, she was recently returned from India, where he had been stationed; she found life in London deadly dull; such friends as she knew were stiff and boring; there was hardly any of the bright life she craved; she wished she was back in India, or any-where she might have some fun. That was why my appearance in her carriage had been so welcome; she had spent a preposterously dull evening with her husband's relatives, escorted by the German Otto, whom she found stuffy to a degree.

"Just the sight of a man who looked as though he had some—oh, some spunk in him—was enough for me," says she. "I wouldn't have turned you over to the police, my dear, not if you had been a murderer. And it was a chance to take down that conceited Prussian muff—would you believe that a man who looks so splendid could have ice and vinegar in his veins?"

"Who is he?" I asked.

"Otto? Oh, one of these Germans making the Grand Tour in reverse. Sometimes I think there's a bit of the devil in him, but he keeps it well hid; he behaves so properly because like all foreigners he likes to impress the English. Tonight, just to try and breathe some life into that collection of prigs, I offered to show them a Spanish dance—you would have thought I'd said something in-decent. They didn't even say, 'Oh, my dear!' Just turned their heads to one side, the way these English women do, as though they were going to be sick." She tossed her head enchantingly, kneeling on the bed like a naked nymph. "But I saw the glitter in Otto's eyes, just for an instant. I'll be bound he's not so prim among the German wenches at Schonhausen, or wherever it is."

I thought there was too much of Otto, and said so.

"Oh, yes, are you jealous, then?" says she, sticking out her lip at me. "You've made a bad enemy there, my dear. Or is the famous Captain Flashman careless of enemies?"

"They don't concern me, German, French, or nigger," says I. "I don't think much of your Otto at all."

"Well, you should," says she, teasing. "For he's going to be a great man some day—he told me so. 'I have a destiny', he said. 'What's that?' I asked him. 'To rule', says he. So I told him I had ambitions, too—to live as I please, love as I please, and never grow old. He didn't think much of that, I fancy; he told me I was frivolous, and would be disappointed. Only the strong, he said, could afford ambitions. So I told him I had a *much* better motto than that."

"What was that?" says I, reaching out for her, but she caught my hands and held them apart, looking wicked.

"'Courage—and shuffle the cards'," says she.

"Damned sight better motto than his," says I, pulling her down on top of me. "And I'm a greater man than he is, anyway."

"Prove it—again," said Miss Rosanna, biting at my chin. And, at the cost of more scratches and bruises, I did.

That was the beginning of our affair, and a wild, feverish one it was, but it couldn't last long. For one thing, she was so demanding a mistress that she came near to wearing me out, and if she was a novelty, she was one I didn't altogether enjoy. She was too imperious, and I prefer softer women who understand that it is my pleasure that counts. Not with Miss Rosanna, though; she *used* men. It was like being eaten alive, and God help you if you weren't ready to command. Everything had to be at her whim, and I got sick of it.

It was about a week after our first meeting that I finally lost my temper. We had had a tempestuous night, but when I wanted to go to sleep she had to chatter on—and even a husky Irish voice can get sickening when you've heard too much of it. And seeing me inattentive, she suddenly shouts "On guard!" which was her war-cry before a tumble, and jumped on me again.

"In heaven's name!" says I. "Get off. I'm tired."

"Nobody get's tired of me," she flashed back, and started teasing me into action, but I was pegged out, and told her to let me alone. For a moment she persisted, and then she was sulky, and then in an instant she was in a raging fury, and before I knew it I had given her the back of my hand and she was coming at me like a wildcat, screaming and clawing.

Now, I've dealt with raging women before, but I'd never met anything like her. She was dangerous—a beautiful, naked savage, flinging everything that came within reach, calling me the foulest names, and—I admit it freely—terrorising me to the point where I grabbed my clothes and ran for it. "Bastard and coward!" was the least of it, I remember, and a chamber pot smashing on the door-jamb as I blundered through. I roared threats at her from the corridor, at which she darted out, white with fury, flourishing a bottle, and I didn't stay for more. One way and another, I've probably had more practice in dressing running than most men, but this time I didn't bother until I'd got out of shot at the foot of the stairs.

I was badly shaken, I can tell you, and not my own man again till I was well away from her house and pondering, in my philosophic way, on means of getting my own back on the vicious, bad-tempered slut. It will seem to you to be the usual, sordid conclusion to so many Flashman amours, but I have dwelt on it at some length for good reason. It wasn't only that she was, in her way, as magnificent a creature as I've ever had the good fortune to mount, and comes back to my mind whenever I see a hair-brush. That alone would not be sufficient. No, my excuse is that this was my first encounter with one of the most remarkable women in my life—or in the life of anyone in the nineteenth century, for that matter. Who could have guessed then that Marie Elizabeth Rosanna James would turn a crowned head, rule a great kingdom, and leave a name to compare with Dubarry or Nell Gwynn? Well, she was Flashy's girl for a week, at least, which is something to boast of. But I was glad to be shot of her at the time, and not just because of the way she treated me: I discovered soon after that she hadn't been altogether truthful about herself. She hadn't mentioned, for example, that her soldier husband was in the process of divorcing her, which would have been enough to scare me away to less controversial beds if I'd known it sooner. Apart from the unpleasant social aspects of being cited, I couldn't have afforded it.

But she was important in my life in another way—she had been the means of my meeting the splendid Otto. You could say that it was through her that the mischief was born between him and me, and our enmity shaped his future, and the world's.

Nothing might have come of it, though, had I not run into him again, by pure chance, a month or so later. It was at Tom Perceval's place in Leicestershire, where I joined a party to see Nick Ward[7] fight some local pug, and to do a little hunting in Tom's coverts. Young Conyngham,[8] who was a fool of a gambler, was there, and old Jack Gully, who had once been Champion of

England and was now a rich ironmaster and retired from the House of Commons as well; there were about a dozen others whom I've forgotten, and Speedicut, too—when I'd told him how I'd spent the night of his arrest, he just roared with laughter and cried "Flashy's luck! Well, only the brave deserve the fair!" And he insisted on telling everyone how it had happened, himself lying in a dirty cell full of drunkards while I was bumping a beauty.

Most of the company were at Tom's place when I arrived, and when he met me in the hall he told me:

"They're all old acquaintances but one, a foreigner that I can't get rid of, damn him. Friend of my uncle's, and wants to see something of our rustic ways while he's here. Trouble is, he's full of bounce, and some of the fellows are rather sick of it already."

It meant nothing until I went into the gunroom with him, where the boys were cheering up the cold night with punch and a roaring fire, and who should be there, very formal in long coat and trousers among all the buffs and boots, but Otto. He stiffened at the sight of me, and I brought up short.

The fellows gave a hurrah when I came in, and thrust punch and cheroots at me, while Tom did his duty by the stranger.

"Baron," says he—the brute has a title, thinks I—"permit me to present Captain Flashman. Flash, this is Baron Otto von ... er, dammit ... von Schornhausen, ain't it? Can't get my confounded tongue round it."

"Schonhausen," says Otto, bowing stiffly with his eyes on mine. "But that is, in fact, the name of my estate, if you will pardon my correction. My family name is Bismarck."[9]

It's an old man's fancy, no doubt, but it seemed to me that he said it in a way that told you you would hear it again. It meant nothing to me, of course, at the time, but I was sure that it was going to. And again I felt that prickle of fear up my back; the cold grey eyes, the splendid build and features, the superb arrogance of the man, all combined to awe me. If you're morally as soft as butter, as I am, with a good streak of the toad-eater in you, there's no doing anything with people like Bismarck. You can have all the fame that I had then, and the good looks and the inches and the swagger—and I had those, too—but you know you're dirt to him. If you have to tangle with him, as the Ameri-

cans say, you know you'll have to get drunk first; I was sober, so
I toadied.

"Honoured to make your acquaintance, Baron," says I, giving
him my hand. "Trust you're enjoying your visit."

"We are already acquainted, as I'm sure you remember," says
he, shaking hands. He had a grip like a vice; I guessed he was
stronger than I was, and I was damned strong, in body at least.
"You recollect an evening in London? Mrs James was present."

"By God!" says I, all astounded. "So I do! Well, well! And
here you are, eh? Damme, I never expected . . . well, Baron, I'm
glad to see you. Aye, hum. I trust Mrs James is well?"

"Surely I should ask you?" says he, with a thin smile. "I have
not seen the . . . lady, since that evening."

"No? Well, well. I haven't seen a great deal of her lately myself." I was prepared to be pleasant, and let bygones be bygones,
if he was. He stood, smiling with his mouth, considering me.

"Do you know," says he at length, "I feel sure I have seen you
before, but I cannot think where. That is unusual, for I have an
excellent memory. No, not in England. Have you ever been in
Germany, perhaps?"

I said I hadn't.

"Oh, well, it is of no interest," says he coolly, meaning that I
was of no interest, and turned away from me.

I hadn't liked him before, but from that moment I hated
Bismarck, and decided that if ever the chance came to do him a
dirty turn, I wouldn't let it slip past me.

Tom had said he was full of bounce, and at supper that night
we got a good dose of it. It was very free and easy company, as you
can imagine, with no women present, and we ate and drank and
shouted across the table to our heart's content, getting pretty
drunk and nobody minding his manners much. Bismarck ate like a
horse and drank tremendously, although it didn't seem to show
on him; he didn't say much during the meal, but when the port
went round he began to enter the conversation, and before long
he was dominating it.

I'll say this for him, he wasn't an easy man to ignore. You
would have thought that a foreigner would have kept mum and
watched and listened, but not he. His style was to ask a question,
get an answer, and then deliver judgement—for instance, he says

to Tom, what was the hunting like, and Tom remarking that it was pretty fair, Bismarck said he looked forward to trying it, although he doubted if chasing a fox could hold a candle to the boar-hunting he had done in Germany. Since he was a guest, no one pulled his leg, although there were a few odd looks and laughs, but he sailed on, lecturing us about how splendid German hunting was, and how damned good at it he was, and what a treat we were missing, not having wild pigs in England.

When he had done, and there was one of those silences, Speed broke it by remarking that I had done some boar-hunting in Afghanistan; the fellows seemed to be looking to me to take the talk away from Bismarck, but before I had the chance he demanded:

"In Afghanistan? In what capacity were you there, Captain Flashman?"

Everyone roared with laughter at this, and Tom tried to save his guest embarrassment by explaining that I had been soldiering there, and had pretty well won the war single-handed. He needn't have minded, for Bismarck never turned a hair, but began to discourse on the Prussian Army, of all things, and his own lieutenant's commission, and how he regretted that there were so few chances of active service these days.

"Well," says I, "you can have any that come my way, and welcome." (This is the kind of remark that folk love to hear from a hero, of course.) The fellows roared, but Bismarck frowned.

"You would avoid dangerous service?" says he.

"I should just think I would," says I, winking at Speed. If only they had known how true that was. "Damned unpleasant, dangerous service. Bullets, swords, chaps killing each other—no peace and quiet at all."

When the laughter had died down, Tom explained that I was joking; that I was, in fact, an exceptionally brave man who would miss no chance of battle and glory. Bismarck listened, his cold eye never leaving me, and then, would you believe it, began to lecture us on a soldier's duty, and the nobility of serving one's country. He obviously believed it, too, he rolled it out so solemnly, and it was all some of the younger men could do to keep their faces straight. Poor old Tom was in an anguish in case we offended his guest, and at the same time obviously nearly out of patience with Bismarck.

"I wish to God my uncle had found some other poor devil to bear-lead him," says he later to Speedicut and me. "Was there ever a bigger bore and ass? How am I to deal with the fellow, eh?"

We couldn't help him; in fact I resolved to keep as far out of Bismarck's way as possible. He unsettled me; he was so damned superior. Tom was wrong in one thing: Bismarck wasn't an ass, whatever else he might be. In some ways he was like that outstanding idiot Cardigan, under whom I had served in the 11th Hussars, but only on the surface. He had the same splendid certainty in everything he said and did; he looked on the world as created for him alone; he was right, and that was that. But where Cardigan's arrogant eye had the shallow stare of the born fool, Bismarck's didn't. You could see the brain at work behind it, and those who listened only to his rather monotonous sermonisings and noticed only his lack of humour—of *our* kind of humour, anyway—and put him down as a pompous dullard were well wide of the mark.

I wanted nothing to do with him, anyway, but in that short visit at Tom's place Bismarck still contrived to touch me on the raw twice—and in the only two things that I am any good at, too. Coward and rascal that I've always been, I have had two talents, for foreign tongues and for horses. I can master almost any language in a short time, and ride anything with a mane and tail. Looking back, I can almost believe that Bismarck smelled these two gifts and set out to hip me over them.

I don't remember how the conversation at one breakfast came to touch on foreign speech—usually it was women and drink and horses and pugs, with an occasional high flight on something like the scandalous rate of income tax at 7d in the pound.[10] But it did, and my gift was mentioned. Bismarck, lounging back in his chair, gave a sneering little laugh and said that it was a useful talent in head-waiters.[11]

I was furious, and tried to think of some cutting retort, but couldn't. Later it occurred to me that I might have fixed him with a look and said it was also a useful gift in German pimps, but it was too late then. And you could never be quite sure with his remarks whether he was jibing or simply stating what he thought was a fact, so I just had to ignore him.

The second set-down came on a day's hunting, when we had had poor sport and were riding home. Conyngham, drawing rein on top of a slight rise from which you could see miles of rolling countryside in every direction, points to a church which was just visible in the distance through the late afternoon haze, and cries out:

"Who's for a steeplechase?"

"Oh, too much of a fag," says Tom. "Anyway, it's getting dark and the beasts may go wrong. I vote for home."

"Steeplechase?" says Bismarck. "What is that?"

It was explained to him that the object was to race straight across country for the steeple, and he nodded and said it was an excellent sport.

"Good for you!" cries Conyngham. "Come on, you fellows! You, Flashy, are you game?"

"Too far," says I, for like Tom I didn't fancy taking hedges on wettish country with the light starting to fail.

"Nonsense!" cries Bismarck. "What, gentlemen, are the English backward in their own game? Then you and I, Marquis, shall we have it out together?"

"With you! Tally-ho!" yells Conyngham, and of course the other asses took off after them. I couldn't hang back, so cursing Bismarck I clapped in my heels and gave chase.

Conyngham led the field over the first meadows, with Bismarck close behind, but a couple of hedges checked them, and the rest of us caught up. I hung back a little, for steeplechasing in the style of your old-fashioned bucks, when you just go hell-for-leather at everything, is as quick a road to a broken neck as I know. If you have an eye for ground, and watch how the leaders jump and land, you can reap the benefit of their discoveries without the risk of going first. So I rode a nice easy chase for the first mile or so, and then we came into light woodland, with trees well spaced out, and I touched my hunter and moved up.

There is a moment every jockey knows, when he feels his mount surge forward, and he lies with his head down being brushed by the mane, and sees the gap narrowing ahead of him, and knows he has the legs of the field. I felt it then as I thundered past the ruck, hearing the thud of the hooves and seeing the clods thrown up from the wet turf, feeling the wind in my face as the trees flew past; even now I see the scarlet coats in the fading light, and smell the rain-sodden country, and hear the yelps of the fellows as they cheered each other on and laughed and cursed. God, it was good to be young and English then!

We thundered through the woodland like a charge of dragoons and were out on a long, rising incline. Conyngham held the lead to the crest, but as we came over and down it was the turn of the heavier men; Bismarck went past him, and then I, too; we pounded down to the hedgerow, Bismarck went over like a bird— he could ride, I may say—and I launched my hunter at the same gap and came through on his heels. I stayed with him, over hedges, lanes, ditches, and fences, until I saw the steeple perhaps half a mile away, and now, thinks I, is the time to get my nose in front.

I had the speed in hand; his head came round as I drew level, and he hammered in his heels and plied his crop, but I knew I had the distance of him. He was leading by half a length as we took a rail fence; then we were on pasture with only one hedge between us and the common that ran up to the churchyard. I inched up level and then led by a head, scanning the distant hedge for a good jump. It was a nasty one, high hawthorn with trees at intervals throwing their shade over the hedgerow; there was one place that looked likely, where the hawthorn thinned and only a couple of rails covered the gap. I clapped in my heels and made for it; first over was a certain winner. As we closed in, with me half a length in front, I realised that even at the rails the jump was a good five feet; I didn't half fancy it, for as Hughes pointed out, Flashman was good only at those games which didn't entail any physical risk. But there was nothing for it; I had Bismarck headed and must keep my lead, so I steadied the hunter for the jump, and then out of nowhere came Bismarck's grey at my elbow, challenging for the jump.

"Give way!" I roared. "My jump, damn your eyes!"

By God, he paid not the slightest heed, but came boring in, neck and neck with me for the fence. We were almost knee to knee as we rushed down on it.

"Get out, blast you!" I yelled again, but he was just staring ahead, teeth clenched and whip going, and I knew in an instant that it was a case of pull up or have the most unholy smash as two horses tried to take a jump where there was only space for one.

As it was, I came within an ace of a hellish tumble; I reined back and at the same time tried to swerve from the gap; the hunter checked and swung away and we scraped along the face of the hedge with no more damage than a few scratches, while Master Bismarck cleared the rails with ease.

By the time I had trotted back, cursing most foully, the rest of the chase was thundering up; Bismarck was waiting at the lych-gate looking cool and smug when we arrived.

"Don't you know to give way to the leader?" says I, boiling angry. "We might have broken our necks, thanks to you!"

"Come, come, Captain Flashman," says he, "it would have been thanks to *you* if we had, for you would have been foolishly challenging the stronger rider."

"What?" says I. "And who the devil says you are the stronger rider?"

"I won, did I not?" says he.

It was on the tip of my tongue to say that he had ridden foul, but the way the other chaps were hallooing, and telling him what a damned fine race he had ridden, I thought better of it. He had gone up in their estimation; he was a damned good-plucked 'un, they shouted, and they clapped him on the back. So I contented myself with suggesting that he learn the rules of horsemanship before he rode in England again, at which the others laughed and cried:

"That's right, Flash, damn his eyes for him!" and made a joke out of bluff Flashy's bad temper. They hadn't been close enough to see exactly what had happened, and none of them would have imagined for a minute that neck-or-nothing Flashman would give way in the breach; but Bismarck knew, and it showed in his eyes and the cold smile he gave me.

But I had my own back on him before the week was out, and if my initial rudeness in London was the first spark in the mischief between us, what was now to come really started the fire.

It was on the last day, after we had been to see the fight between Nick Ward the Champion, and the local pug. It was a good afternoon's sport, with the pug getting his nose broken and half his teeth knocked out; Bismarck was greatly interested, and seemed to enjoy watching the loser being battered as much as I did myself.

At supper that night the talk was naturally of the fight, and old Jack Gully, who had refereed, held the floor. He wasn't normally an over-talkative man, despite the fact that he had been an M.P., but on his two loves—the prize ring and horseflesh—he was always worth listening to. Though it was more than thirty years since he had held the belt himself—and since retiring he had become most prosperous and was well received everywhere—he had known and seen all the greatest pugs, and was full of stories of such giants as Cribb and Belcher and the Game Chicken.[12]

Of course, the company would have listened all night—I don't suppose there was a man in England, Peel, Russell, or any of them, who could have commanded such universal attention as this quiet old boxing champion. He must have been close to sixty then, and white-haired, but you could see he was still fit as a flea, and when he talked of the ring he seemed to light up and come alive.

Bismarck, I noticed, didn't pay him much attention, but when Jack paused after a story, our German suddenly says:

"You make very much of this boxing, I see. Now, it is an interesting enough spectacle, two of the lower orders thrashing each other with their fists, but does it not become boring after a while? Once, or even twice, perhaps, one might go to watch, but surely men of education and breeding must despise it."

There was a growl round the table, and Speed says:

"You don't understand it because you're a foreigner. It is our game in England. Why, in Germany, according to what you've said, fellows fight duels without any intent to kill each other, but just to get scars on their heads. Well, we wouldn't think much of that, let me tell you."

"The *schlager* endows a man with honourable scars," says Bismarck. "What honour is there in beating an opponent with your fists? Besides, our duelling is for gentlemen."

"Well, as to that, mynheer," says Gully, smiling, "gentlemen in this country ain't ashamed to use their fists. I know I wish I'd a guinea for every coroneted head I've touched with a straight left hand."

"Mine for one, any time you please, Jack," cries Conyngham.

"But in the use of the *schlager* there is soldierly skill," Bismarck insisted, and rapped his fist on the table. Oho, thinks I, what's this? Has our Prussian friend perhaps got a little more liquor on board than usual? He was a mighty drinker, as I've said, but it occurred to me that he might not be holding it so well tonight.

"If you think there's no skill in prize-fighting, my friend, you're well out of court," says one of the others, a heavy-faced Guardee named Spottswood. "Didn't you see Ward, this afternoon, take the starch out of a chap three stone heavier than himself?"

"Oh, your fellow Ward was swift and strong," says Bismarck. "But speed and strength are common enough. I saw no sign of skill in that butchery."

And he emptied his glass as though that settled the matter.

"Well, sir," says old Jack, smiling, "there was skill a-plenty, and you can take my word for it. You wouldn't see it, 'cos you don't know what to look for, just as I wouldn't know what to look for in your schlag-what-you-call-'ems."

"No," says Bismarck, "likely you would not." And the tone of his voice made Gully look sharp at him, although he said nothing. Then Tom Perceval, sensing that there might be trouble if the subject wasn't changed, started to say something about hunting, but I had seen my chance to set this arrogant Prussian down, and I interrupted him.

"Perhaps you think boxing is easy," says I to Bismarck. "D'ye fancy you could hold your own in a mill?"

He stares at me across the table. "With one of those brawlers?" says he at length. "A gentleman does not come to physical contact with those people, surely?"

"We don't have serfs in England," says I. "There isn't a man round this table wouldn't be glad to put 'em up with Nick Ward —aye, and honoured, too. But in your case—suppose there was a sporting German baron whose touch wouldn't sully you? Would you be ready to try it with him?"

"Hold on, Flash—" says Perceval, but I carried on.

"Or a gentleman from among ourselves, for example? Would you be ready to go a round or two with one of us?"

Those cold eyes of his were damned uncomfortable on me, but I held his gaze, for I knew I'd got him. He considered a moment, and then said:

"Is this a challenge?"

"Good God, no," says I. "Only you think that our good old game is just a brawl, and I'd like to show you different. If I were asked, I'd be ready enough to try my hand at this *schlager* business of yours. Well, what d'ye say?"

"I see you are smarting for revenge after our race the other day," says he, smiling. "Very well, Captain, I shall try a round with you."

I believe he had weighed me up for a coward who wouldn't be much good, in which he was right, and that he also thought—like many another ignoramus—that boxing was pure brute force and nothing more, in which he was wrong. Also, he had seen that a good part of it was body wrestling, of which no doubt he had some experience. And he knew he was pretty well as big and strong as I. But I had a surprise in store for him.

"Not with me," says I. "I'm no Nick Ward. Anyway, my idea is instruction, not revenge, and the best instructor in the whole wide world is sitting within ten feet of you." And I nodded at Gully.

All I intended was to make a fool of Bismarck, which I knew Gully could do with one hand behind his back, and so cut his comb for him. I hadn't any hope that Gully would hurt him, for unfortunately old Jack, like most champions, was a gentle, kindly sort of fool. Indeed, at my proposal, he burst out laughing.

"Lord, Flashy," says he. "D'ye know how much I used to be paid to come up to scratch? And you want to see it free, you dog!"

But Bismarck wasn't laughing. "That is a foolish proposal," says he. "Mr Gully is too old."

Gully's laugh was wiped off his face at once. "Now, wait a moment, mynheer," says he, but I was ahead of him again.

"Oh, is that it?" says I. "You wouldn't be chary about milling with a professional, would you?"

Everyone was talking at once, of course, but Bismarck's voice cut through them.

"I have no interèst in whether he is a professional or not—"

"Or the fact that he was once in jail?" says I.

"—but only in the fact that he is very much older than I. As to his being in prison, what has that to do with anything?"

"You know best about that," says I, sneering.

"Now, dammit, hold on here," says Perceval. "What the devil is all this? Flashy—"

"Ah, I'm sick of his airs," says I, "and his sneers at Jack there. All right, he's your guest, Tom, but he goes a bit far. Let him put up or shut up. I only suggested he should try a round with a real boxer, to show him that his jibes were wide of the mark, and he turns up his nose as though Gully weren't good enough for him. It's the wrong side of enough, I say."

"Not good enough?" roars Jack. "What's this . . . ?"

"No one said anything of the sort," cries Tom. "Flashy, I don't know what you're driving at, but—"

"Captain Flashman's intention is apparently to annoy me," says Bismarck. "He has not succeeded. My only objection to boxing with Mr Gully was on the score of his age."

"That'll do about my age, thank'ee!" says Jack, going red. "I'm not so old I can't deal with anyone who don't know his place!"

They calmed him down, and there was a lot of hubbub and noise and nonsense, and the upshot was that most of them, being slightly fuddled anyway, got the notion that I had suggested, friendly-like, to Bismarck, that he try a round with Gully, and that somehow he had insulted old Jack and looked down on him. It was Spottswood who calmed things over, and said there was no cause for shouting or hard feelings.

"The point is, does the Baron want to try his hand in a friendly spar? That's all. If so, Jack'll oblige, won't you, Jack?"

"No, no," says Jack, who was cooled again. "Why, I haven't stood in a ring for thirty years, man. Besides," he added, with a smile, "I didn't understand that our guest was eager to try me."

That brought him a lofty look from Bismarck, but Spottswood says:

"Tell ye what, Jack; if you'll spar a round or two with him, I'll sell you Running Ribbons."

He knew Jack's weak spot, you see; Running Ribbons was own brother to Running Reins, and a prime goer.[18] Jack hummed and hawed a bit, saying no, no, his fighting days were long done, but the fellows, seeing him waver, and delighted at the thought of watching the famous Gully in action (and no doubt of lowering Bismarck a peg or two) urged him on, cheering him and slapping him on the shoulder.

"Well, well," says Jack at last, for his flash of ill-temper had quite gone now, and he was his placid self, "if you must have it, I'll tell you what I'll do. To convince the Baron here, that there's maybe more in the Noble Art than meets his eye, I'll engage to stand up in front of him, with my hands down, and let him try to plant me a few facers. What d'ye say to that, sir?" he asks Bismarck.

The German, who had been sitting very disdainful, looked interested despite himself.

"You mean you will let me strike you, without defending yourself?"

Jack grins at him. "I mean I'll let you *try*," says he.

"But I *must* strike you—unless you run away."

"I reckon you're not too clever in our lingo yet," says Jack, smiling, but looking keen. "What with 'too old' and 'running away', you know. But don't worry, mynheer—I'll stand my ground."

There was a great commotion while the table was thrust against one wall, and the carpet rolled up, and everyone piled furniture to the sides of the room to leave space for the exhibition. Perceval was the only one who wasn't delighted at the prospect; "'Tain't fair," says he, "not to a guest; I don't like it. Ye'll not hurt him, Jack, d'ye hear?"

"Not a hair of his head," says old Jack.

"But his vanity may be a bit bruised when he discovers it ain't so easy to hit a good milling cove as he imagines," says Speed laughing.

"That's what I don't like either," says Perceval. "It looks as though we're making a fool of him."

"Not us," says I. "He'll be doing it himself."

"And serve the German windbag right," says Spottswood. "Who's he to tell us our faults, damn him?"

"I still don't like it," says Perceval. "Curse you, Flash, this is your doing." And he mooched away, looking glum.

At the other end of the room Conyngham and one of the other chaps were helping Bismarck off with his coat. You could see he was wondering how the devil he had got into this, but he put a good face on it, pretending to be amused and interested when they fastened the gloves on him and Jack, and explained what was expected of him. Spottswood led the two of them to the centre of the floor, where a line had been chalked on the boards, and holding one on either hand, called for silence.

"This ain't a regular mill," says he ("Shame!" cries someone). "No, no," says Spottswood, "this is a friendly exhibition in the interests of good sportsmanship and friendship between nations. ('Hurrah!' 'Rule Britannia!' from the fellows). Our old and honoured friend, Jack Gully, champion of champions—" at this there was a great hurrah, which set old Jack grinning and bobbing—"has generously engaged to let Herr Otto von Bismarck stand up to him and try, if he can, to hit him fair on the head and body. Mr Gully engages further not to hit back, but may, if he wishes, use his hands for guarding and blocking. I shall referee"— cries of 'Shame!' 'Watch out for him, Baron, he's a wrong 'un!'— "and at my word the contestants will begin and leave off. Agreed? Now, Baron, you may hit him anywhere above the waist. Are you ready?"

He stepped back, leaving the two facing each other. It was a strange picture: the big candelabra lit the room as clear as day, shining on the flushed faces of the spectators sitting or squatting on the furniture piled round the panelled walls; on the sporting prints and trophies hung above them; on the wide, empty polished floor; on the jumble of silver and bottles and piled plates on the table with its wine-stained cloths; on the two men toe to toe at the chalk line. There was never a stranger pair of millers in the history of the game.

Bismarck, in his shirt and trousers and pumps, with the big padded mauleys on his fists, may have been awkward and uncertain, but he looked well. Tall, perfectly built and elegant as a rapier, with his fair cropped head glistening under the light, he reminded me again of a nasty Norse god. His lips were tight, his eyes narrow, and he was studying his man carefully before making a move.

Gully, on the other hand—oh, Gully! In my time I've seen Mace and Big Jack Heenan and little Sayers, and I watched Sullivan beat Ryan[14] and took $10 off Oscar Wilde over that fight, too, but I doubt if any of them could have lived with Gully at his best. Not that I ever saw that best, but I saw him face up to Bismarck, nearly sixty years old, and that is enough for me. Like most poltroons, I have a sneaking inward regard for truly fearless, strong men, fools though they may be, and I can have an academic admiration for real skill, so long as I don't suffer by it. Gully was fearless and strong and incredibly skilful.

He stood on the balls of his feet, head sunk between his massive shoulders, hands down, his leathery brown face smiling ever so slightly, his eyes fixed on Bismarck beneath beetling brows. He looked restful, confident, indestructible.

"Time!" cries Spottswood, and Bismarck swung his right fist. Jack swayed a little and it went past his face. Bismarck stumbled, someone laughed, and then he struck again, right and left. The right went past Jack's head, the left he stopped with his palm. Bismarck stepped back, looking at him, and then came boring in, driving at Jack's midriff, but he just turned his body sideways, lazily almost, and the German went blundering by, thumping the air.

Everyone cheered and roared with laughter, and Bismarck wheeled round, white-faced, biting his lip. Jack, who didn't seem to have moved more than a foot, regarded him with interest, and motioned him to come on again. Slowly, Bismarck recovered himself, raised his hands and then shot out his left hand as he must have seen the pugs do that afternoon. Jack rolled his head out of the way and then leaned forward a little to let Bismarck's other hand sail past his head.

"Well done, mynheer," he cried. "That was good. Left and right, that's the way. Try again."

Bismarck tried, and tried again, and for three minutes Jack swayed and ducked and now and then blocked a punch with his open hand. Bismarck flailed away, and never looked like hitting him, and everyone cheered and roared with laughter. Finally Spottswood called, "Time", and the German stood there, chest heaving and face crimson with his efforts, while Jack was as unruffled as when he started.

"Don't mind 'em, mynheer," says he. "There's none of 'em would ha' done better, and most not so well. You're fast, and could be faster, and you move well for a novice."

"Are you convinced now, Baron?" says Spottswood.

Bismarck, having got his breath back, shook his head.

"That there is skill, I admit," says he, at which everyone raised an ironical cheer. "But I should be obliged," he goes on to Jack, "if you would try me again, and this time try to hit me in return."

At this the idiots cheered, and said he was damned game and a sportsman, and Perceval said he wouldn't have it, and demanded that the bout should stop at once. But old Jack, smiling his crooked smile, says:

"No, no, Tom. This fellow's more of a boxing man than any you know. I'd not care to mill with anyone who didn't hit back. I'll spar, gentle-like, and when he goes home he can say he's been in a fight."

So they went to it again, and Jack moved about now, smooth as a dancer for all his years, and tapped his glove on Bismarck's head and chin and body, while the other smashed away at him and hit nothing. I encouraged him by haw-hawing every time he missed, for I wanted him to realise what an ass he looked, and he bore in all the harder, flailing at Jack's head and shoulders while the old champion turned, feinted and slipped away, leaving him floundering.

"That's enough!" shouts someone. "Time out, you fellows, and let's drink to it!" and there were several voices which cried aye, aye, at which Jack dropped his hands and looked to Spottswood. But Bismarck rushed in, and Jack, in fending him off with a left, tapped him a little harder than he meant to, and bloodied his nose.

That stopped the German in his tracks, and Jack, all crestfallen, was stepping in to apologise, when to everyone's amazement Bismarck ran at him, seized him round the waist, swung him off his feet, and hurled him to the floor. He landed with a tremendous crash, his head striking the boards, and in a moment everyone was on his feet, shouting and cheering. Some cried "Foul!" while others applauded the German—they were the drunker ones—and then there was a sudden hush as Jack shook his head and slowly got to his feet.

He looked shaken, and furious, too, but he had himself in hand. "All right, mynheer," says he. "I didn't know we was holding and throwing." I don't suppose anything like it had happened to him in his life before, and his pride was wounded far worse than his body. "My own fault, for not looking out," says he. "Well, well, let it go. You can say you've downed John Gully," and he looked round the room, slowly, as though trying to read what everyone was thinking.

"Best stop now, I think," says he at last.

"You do not wish to continue?" cries Bismarck. He looked fairly blown, but the arrogant note in his voice was there, as ever. Gully stared at him a moment. "Best not," says he.

The room was uncomfortably quiet, until Bismarck laughed his short laugh and shrugged his shoulders.

"Oh, very well," says he, "since you do not wish it."

Two red spots came into Jack's pale cheeks. "I think it's best to stop now," says he, in a hard voice. "If you're wise, mynheer, you'll make the most of that."

"As you please," says Bismarck, and to my delight he added: "It is you who are ending the bout, you know."

Jack's face was a study. Spottswood had a hand on his shoulder, and Perceval was at his side, while the rest were crowding round, chattering excitedly, and Bismarck was looking about him with all his old bounce and side. It was too much for Jack.

"Right," says he, shaking Spottswood off. "Put your hands up."

"No, no," cries Perceval, "this has gone far enough."

"I quit to nobody," says Jack, grim as a hangman. "'End the bout', is it? I'll end it for him, sure enough."

"For God's sake, man," says Perceval. "Remember who you are, and who he is. He's a guest, a stranger—"

"A stranger who threw me foul," says old Jack.

"He don't know the rules."

"It was a mistake."

"It was a fair throw."

"No t'wasn't."

Old Jack stood breathing heavily. "Now, look'ee," says he. "I give it him he threw me not knowing it was an unfair advantage, when I was off guard on account of having tapped his claret. I give it him he was angry and didn't think, 'cos I'd been making a pudding of him. I'll shake hands wi' him on all of that—but I won't have him strutting off and saying I asked to end the fight. Nobody says that to me—no, not Tom Cribb himself, by God."

Everyone began to yammer at once, Perceval trying to push them away and calm Jack down, but most of us well content to see the mischief increase—it wasn't every day one could see Gully box in earnest, which he seemed ready to do. Tom appealed to Bismarck, but the German, smiling his superior smile, just says:

"I am prepared to continue."

After that, try as Tom might, he was over-ruled, and presently they were facing up to each other again. I was delighted, of course; this was more than I had hoped for, although I feared that Gully's good nature would make him let Bismarck off lightly. His pride was hurt, but he was a fair-minded fool, and I guessed he would just rap the German once or twice, smartly, to show him who was master, and let it go at that. Perceval was hoping so, at all events. "Go easy, Jack, for God's sake," he cried, and then they set to.

I don't know what Bismarck hoped for. He wasn't a fool, and Gully had demonstrated already that the German was a child in his hands. I can only suppose that he thought he had a chance of throwing Gully again, and was too damned conceited to escape gratefully. At any rate, he went in swinging both arms, and Jack rapped him over the heart and then cracked him a neat left on the head when he was off balance, which knocked him down.

"Time!" cries Spottswood, but Bismarck didn't understand, and bounding up he rushed at Gully, and with a lucky swing, caught him on the ear. Jack staggered, righted himself, and as if by instinct smacked two blows into Bismarck's belly. He went down, gasping and wheezing, and Perceval ran forward, saying that this was the end, he would have no more of it.

But the German, when he had straightened up, got his breath back and wiped the trickle of blood from his nose, was determined to go on. Gully said no, and Bismarck sneered at him, and the upshot was that they squared away again, and Gully knocked him off his feet.

But still he got up, and now Gully was sickened, and refused to go on, and when he held out his hand Bismarck struck at him, at which Gully hammered him one in the face, which sent him headlong, and on the instant Gully was cursing himself for a bad-tempered fool, and calling for Spottswood to take off his gloves, and Tom was raising Bismarck off the floor, and a splendidly gory face he presented, too. And there was a tremendous hubbub, with drunk chaps crying "Shame!" and "Stop the fight!" and "Hit him again!" and Perceval almost crying with mortification, and Gully stamping off in a corner, swearing he hadn't meant to hurt the fellow, but what could he do? and Bismarck white-faced, being helped into one of the chairs, where they sponged his face and gave him brandy. There were apologies, and protestations, and Gully and Bismarck finally shook hands, and Jack said he was ashamed of himself, as an Englishman, and would Bismarck forgive him? Bismarck, with his mouth puffed and split where Jack's last blow had caught him, and his fine aristocratic nose crusted with his own blood—I'd have given twenty guineas to see it properly smashed—said it was nothing, and he was obliged to Mr Gully for the instruction. He then added that he was capable of continuing, and that the fight had not been stopped at his request, at which old Jack took a big breath but said nothing, and the others cheered and Conyngham cried:

"Good for the Prussian! A dam' game bird he is! Hurrah!"

This was the signal for the drinking to start again, in earnest, while two of the company, flown with pugilistic ardour, put on the mauleys and began to spar away drunkenly, and losing their tempers, finished up savaging each other on the floor. Perceval stayed by Bismarck, muttering apologies while the German waved them away and sipped brandy through his battered mouth. Gully simply went over to the sideboard and poured drink into himself until he was completely foxed; no one had ever seen him so shaken and unhappy before, or known him drink more than the most modest amount. But I knew why he was doing it; he was ashamed. It is a terrible thing to have ideals and a conscience, to say nothing of professional pride. He told me later he would have been better to suffer being thrown; beating Bismarck had been the most shameful thing he ever did, he said.

I'd have been delighted to do it, personally, if I'd had his skill; I'd have left that German upstart without a tooth in his head. As it was, when the boozing was at its height, and the uproar was deafening, I chanced by where Bismarck was still sitting, sipping delicately at his glass. He turned and caught my eye, frowned, and said:

"Still I cannot place you, Captain. It is most intriguing; but it will come back, no doubt. However, I trust you were not disappointed with your evening's entertainment."

"It might have been better," says I, grinning at him.

"Even so, you contrived very well. I have you to thank for

these," and he touched his lips and reddened nose. "One day I shall hold you to your promise, and show you the *schlager* play. I look forward to that; we shall see how much credit you obtain from *my* country's sport."

"More than you've got from mine, I hope," says I, laughing.

"Let us hope so," says he. "But I doubt it."

"Go to the devil," says I.

He turned away, chuckling to himself. "After you, I think."

One of the difficulties of writing your memoirs is that they don't run smooth, like a novel or play, from one act to the next. I've described how I met Rosanna James and Otto, but beyond a paragraph in *The Times* announcing her divorce from Captain James towards the end of the year, I didn't hear of her again for months. As for Bismarck, it was a few years before I ran into him again, and then it was too soon.

So in the first place I must skip over a few months to my second meeting with Rosanna, which was brought about because I have a long memory and a great zeal in paying off old scores. She had put herself on the debit side of Flashy's ledger, and when the chance came to pay her out I seized on it.

It was the following summer, while I was still in London, officially waiting for Uncle Bindley at the Horse Guards to find me an appointment, and in fact just lounging about the town and leading the gay life. It wasn't quite so gay as it had been, for while I was still something of an idol in military circles, my gloss was beginning to wear a bit thin with the public. Yesterday's hero is soon forgotten, and while Elspeth and I had no lack of invitations during the season, it seemed to me that I wasn't quite so warmly fêted as I had been. I wasn't invariably the centre of attraction any longer; some chaps even seemed to get testy if I mentioned Afghanistan, and at one assembly I heard a fellow say that he personally knew every damned stone of Piper's Fort by now, and could have conducted sightseers over the ruins.

That's by the way, but it was one of the reasons that I began to find life boring me in the months that followed, and I was all the readier for mischief when the chance came.

I forgot exactly what took me to one of the Haymarket theatres on an afternoon in May—there was an actress, or an acrobat she may have been, whom I was pushing about just then, so it may have been her. In any event, I was standing in the wings with some of the Gents and Mooners,[15] during a rehearsal, when I noticed a female practising dance-steps on the other side of the stage. It was her shape that caught my eye, for she was in the tight fleshings that ballet-dancers wear, and I was admiring her legs when she turned in profile and to my astonishment I recognised Rosanna.

She was wearing her hair a new way, parted in the centre, and held behind her head in a kerchief, but there was no mistaking the face or the figure.

"Splendid piece, ain't she?" says one of the Mooners. "They say Lumley"—he was the manager—"pays her a fortune. 'Pon my soul, I would myself, what?"

Oho, I thought to myself, what's this? I asked the Mooner, offhand, who she might be.

"Why, she's his new danseuse, don't you know," says he. "It seems that opera hasn't been bringing in the tin lately, so Lumley imported her specially to dance between the acts. Thinks she'll make a great hit, and with those legs I'll be bound she will. See here." And he pushed a printed bill into my hand. It read:

HER MAJESTY'S THEATRE

Special Attraction

Mr Benjamin Lumley begs to announce that between the acts of the Opera, Donna Lola Montez, of the Teatro Real, Seville, will have the honour to make her first appearance in England in the Original Spanish dance, El Oleano.

"Ain't she a delight, though?" says the Mooner. "Gad, look at 'em bouncing when she struts!"

"That's Donna Lola Montez, is it?" says I. "When does she perform, d'ye know?"

"Opens next week," says he. "There'll be a crowd and a half, shouldn't wonder. Oh, Lovely Lola!"

Well, I'd never heard of Lola Montez, but I saw there was something here that needed going into. I made a few discreet inquiries, and it seemed that half the town was talking about her already, for Lumley was making a great to-do about his beautiful new attraction. The critics were slavering in advance about "the belle Andalusian", and predicting a tremendous success, but nobody had any notion that she wasn't a genuine Spanish artiste at all. But I was in no doubt about her; I'd been close enough to Rosanna James to be sure.

At first I was just amused, but then it occurred to me that here was a heaven-sent opportunity to have my own back on her. If she was exposed, denounced for what she really was, that would put paid to her making a hit. It would also teach her not to throw piss-pots at me. But how to do it best? I pondered, and in five minutes I had it pat.

I remembered, from the conversations we had had during our passionate week, her mention of Lord Ranelagh, who was one of the leading boys about town just then. She was forever chattering about her admirers, and he was one she had turned down; snubbed him dead, in fact. I knew him only to see, for he was a very top-flight Corinthian, and didn't take much heed even of heroes if they weren't out of the top drawer (and I wasn't). But all I'd heard suggested that he was a first-class swine, and just the man for me.

I hunted him out at his club, slid inside when the porter wasn't looking, and found him in the smoke-room. He was lying on a couch, puffing a cigar with his hat over his brows; I spoke right out.

"Lord Ranelagh," says I. "How are you? I'm Flashman."

He cocked an eye lazily under the brim of his hat, damned haughty.

"I'm certain I haven't had the honour," says he. "Good day to you."

"No, no, you remember me," says I. "Harry Flashman, you know."

He pushed his hat right back, and looked at me as if I was a toad.

"Oh," says he at length, with a sneer, "The Afghan warrior. Well, what is it?"

"I took the liberty of calling on your lordship," says I, "because I chanced to come across a mutual acquaintance."

"I cannot conceive that we have any," drawls he, "unless you happen to be related to one of my grooms."

I laughed merrily at this, although I felt like kicking his noble backside for him. But I needed him, you see, so I had to toad-eat him.

"Not bad, not bad," says I. "But this happens to be a lady. I'm sure she would be of interest to you."

"Are you a pimp, by any chance? If so—"

"No, my lord, I'm not," says I. "But I thought you might be diverted to hear of Mrs James—Mrs Elizabeth Rosanna James."

He frowned, and blew ash off his ridiculous beard, which covered half his shirt-front.

"What of her, and what the devil has she to do with you?"

"Why, nothing, my lord," says I. "But she happens to be taking the stage at Her Majesty's next week, masquerading as a famous Spanish dancer. Donna Lola Montez, she calls herself, and pretends to be from Seville. An impudent imposture."

He digested this, while I watched his nasty mind working.

"How d'ye know this?" says he.

"I've seen her at rehearsal," says I, "and there's no doubt about it—she's Rosanna James."

"And why should this be of interest to me?"

I shrugged at this, and he asked what *my* purpose was in telling him.

"Oh, I was sure you would wish to be at her first performance —to pay your respects to an old friend," says I. "And if so, I would solicit a place for myself in your party. I entertain the same affection for her that I'm sure your lordship does."

He considered me. "You're a singularly unpleasant creature," says he. "Why don't you expose her yourself, since that's obviously what you want?"

"Your lordship, I'm sure, has a style in these things. And you are well known, while I. . . ." I didn't want to be the centre of any scandal, although I wanted to have a front seat to see the fun.

"I can do your dirty work, eh? Well, well."

"You'll go?"

"That is no concern of yours," says he. "Good day."

"May I come?"

"My dear sir, I cannot prevent you going where you choose. But I forbid you absolutely to address me in public."

And he turned over on his side, away from me. But I was satisfied; no doubt he would go, and denounce "Donna Lola". He had his own score to pay off, and was just the sort of mean hound who would do it, too.

* * *

Sure enough, when the fashionable crowd was arriving at Her Majesty's the following Monday, up rolls Lord Ranelagh with a party of bloods, in two coaches. I was on hand, and tailed on to them at the door; he noticed me, but didn't say anything, and I was allowed to follow into the omnibus-box which he had engaged directly beside the stage. One or two of his friends gave me haughty stares, and I took my seat very meek, at the back of the box, while his lordship showed off at the front, and his friends and he talked and laughed loudly, to show what first-rate bucks they were.

It was a splendid house—quite out of proportion to the opera, which was "The Barber of Seville". In fact, I was astonished at the gathering: there was the Queen Dowager in the Royal Box, with a couple of foreign princelings; old Wellington, wrinkled and lynx-eyed, with his Duchess; Brougham, the minister, the Baroness de Rothschild, Count Esterhazy, the Belgian ambassador, and many others. All the most eminent elderly lechers of the day, in fact, and I hadn't a doubt that it wasn't the music they had come for. Lola Montez was the attraction of the night, and the talk through the pit was of nothing else. Rumour had it that at certain select gatherings for the highest grandees in Spain, she had been known to dance nude; it was also being said that she had once been the leading light of a Turkish harem. Oh, they were in a fine state of excitement by the time the curtain went up.

My own idea of theatrical entertainment, I admit, is the music-hall; strapping wenches and low comedians are my line, and your fine drama and music bore me to death. So I found "The Barber of Seville" a complete fag: fat Italians screeching, and not a word to be understood. I read the programme for a bit, and found more entertainment in the advertisements than there was on the stage —"Mrs Rodd's anatomical ladies stays, which ensure the wearer a figure of astonishing symmetry"; I remember thinking that the leading lady in "The Barber" could have profited by Mrs Rodd's acquaintance. Also highly spoken of were Jackson's patent enema machines, as patronised by the nobility when travelling. I wasn't alone, I noticed, in finding the opera tedious; there were yawns in the pit, and Wellington (who was near our box) began to snore until his Duchess dug him in the ribs. Then the first act ended, and when the applause died away everyone sat up, expectant; there was a flourish of Spanish music from the orchestra, and Lola (or Rosanna) shot dramatically on to the stage.

I'm no authority on the dance; the performer, not the perform-ance, is what I pay to see. But it seemed to me that she was damned good. Her striking beauty brought the pit up with a gasp: she was in a black bodice, cut so low that her breasts seemed to be in continual danger of popping out, and her tiny pink skirt showed off her legs to tremendous advantage. The slim white neck and shoulders, the coal-black hair, the gleaming eyes, the scarlet lips curled almost in contempt—the whole effect was startling and exotic. You know these throbbing, Spanish rhythms; well, she swayed and shook and stamped her way through them in splendid passion, and the audience sat spellbound. She was at once inviting and challenging; I doubt if there was any gesture or movement in the whole dance that a magistrate could have taken exception to, and yet the whole effect of it was sensual. It seemed to say "Bed me—if you dare", and every man in the place was taking her clothes off as he watched. What the women thought I can't imagine, but I guess they admired her almost as much as they disliked her.[16]

When she finished abruptly, with a final smash of her foot and clash of cymbals from the orchestra, the theatre went wild. They cheered and stamped, and she stood for a moment still as a statue, staring proudly down at them, and then swept straight off the stage. The applause was deafening, but she didn't come back, and there were sighs and a few groans when the curtain went up again on the next act of the opera, and those damned Macaronis began yelping again.

Through all this Ranelagh had sat forward in his chair, staring at her, but never said a word. He didn't pay the least attention to the opera, but when Lola came on for her second dance, which was even more tempestuous than the first, he made a great show of examining her through his glasses. Everyone else was doing the same, of course, in the hope that her bodice would burst, which it seemed likely to do at any moment, but when the applause broke out, wilder than ever, he kept his glasses glued to his eyes, and when she had gone he was seen to be frowning in a very puzzled way. This was all leading up to the denoument, of course, and when she bounced on, snapping her fan, for the third time, I heard him mutter to his nearest neighbour:

"You chaps keep your eyes on me. I'll give the word, mind, and then we'll see some fun."

She swirled through the dance, showing splendid amounts of her thighs, and gliding about sinuously while peeping over her fan, and at the finish there was a perfect torrent of clapping and shouting, with bouquets plopping down on to the stage and chaps standing up and clapping wildly. She smiled now, for the first time, bowing and blowing kisses before the curtain, and then suddenly, from our box there was a great hissing in unison, at which the applause faltered and died away. She turned to stare furiously in our direction, and as the hissing rose louder than ever there were angry shouts and cries from the rest of the theatre. People craned to see what the row was about, and then Ranelagh climbs to his feet, an imposing figure with his black beard and elegant togs, and cries out, very distinctly:

"Why, this is a proper swindle, ladies and gentlemen! That woman isn't Lola Montez. She's an Irish girl, Betsy James!"

There was a second's silence, and then a tremendous hullabaloo. The hissing started again, with cries of "Fraud!" and "Impostor!", the applause began and sputtered out, and angry cat-calls and boos sounded from the gallery. In a moment the whole mood of the theatre had changed; taking their cut from Ranelagh and his toadies, they began to howl her down; a few coins clattered on the stage; the conductor, gaping at the audience with his mouth open, suddenly flung down his baton and stamped out; and then the whole place was in a frenzy, stamping and calling for their money back, and shouting to her angrily to get back to the bogs of Donegal.

She was standing blazing with fury, and when she moved towards our box some of the chaps scrambled back to get out of harm's way. She stood a moment, her bosom heaving, her eyes sweeping the box—oh, yes, she recognised *me* all right, and when she began to curse at us I think it was me as much as Ranelagh she was getting at. Unfortunately, she swore in English, and the mob caught it and yelled louder than ever. Then she dashed down the bouquet she was holding, stamped on it, kicked it into the orchestra, and with one last damnation in our direction, ran from the stage as the curtain fell.[17]

I must say I was delighted; I hadn't thought it could go off so well. As we crowded out of the place—"The Barber", of course, was entirely forgotten in the sensation—I came up to Ranelagh's elbow and congratulated him; I couldn't have paid her out so splendidly myself, and I told him so. He gave me a cold nod and sailed off, the snobbish bastard, but I wasn't in a mood to mind too much; that was me quits with Mistress Lola for her brickbats and insults, and I went home in high good humour.

She was finished on the London stage, of course. Lumley dismissed her, and although one or two attempts were made to present her at other theatres, the damage was done. All sorts of people now seemed to remember her as Mrs James, and although she wrote a letter of denial to the press, no one believed it. A few weeks later she had disappeared and that, thought I, was the end of Lola Montez so far as I was concerned, and good riddance. A brilliant bed-mate, I don't deny, in her way, and even now the picture of her kneeling naked among the bed-clothes can set me itching—but I'd never liked her particularly, and was glad to see her sent packing.

But it wasn't the end of her, by any means. Although it was some years before I saw her again—in circumstances that I couldn't have dreamed of—one heard of her from time to time through the papers. And always it was sensational news; she seemed to have a genius for thrusting herself into high places and creating scandal. First there was a report of her horse-whipping a policeman in Berlin; next she was dancing on the tables during a civic banquet in Bonn, to the outrage of Prince Albert and our Queen, who were on a State visit at the time. Then she was performing in Paris, and when the audience didn't take to her she stripped off her garters and drawers and flung them at the gallery; she started a riot in the streets of Warsaw, and when they tried to arrest her she held the peelers off with pistols. And of course there were scores of lovers, most of them highly-placed: the Viceroy of Poland, the Tsar of Russia (although I doubt if that's true), and

Liszt the musician.[18] She took up with him two or three times, and once to get rid of her he locked her in a hotel room and sneaked out by the back door.

I met him, later on, by the way, and we discussed the lovely Lola and found ourselves much in agreement. Like me, he admired her as a tumble, but found her all too overpowering. "She is a consuming fire," he told me, shaking his white head ruefully, "and I've been scorched—oh, so often." I sympathised; she had urged me on in love-making with a hair-brush, but with him it had been a dog-whip, and he was a frail sort of fellow, you know.

At all events, these scraps of gossip reached me from time to time over the next few years. In that time I was out of England a good deal—as will be set down in another packet of my memoirs, if I'm spared to write them. My doings in the middle 'forties of the century don't fit in with my present tale, though, so I pass them over for the moment and come to the events to which my meeting with Lola and Otto Bismarck was the prelude.

I can see, now, that if I hadn't deserted Speedicut that night, hadn't been rude to Bismarck, hadn't set Jack Gully on to give him a beating, and finally, hadn't taken my spite out on Lola by peaching on her to Ranelagh—without all these "if's" I would have been spared one of the most frightening and incredible experiences of my life. Another glorious chapter in the heroic career of Harry Flashman would not have been written, and neither would a famous novel.

However, I've seen too much of life to fret over if's and but's. There's nothing you can do about them, and if you find yourself at the end of the day an octogenarian with money in the bank and drink in the house—well, you'd be a fool to wish that things had fallen out differently.

Anyway, I was home again in London in '47, with cash in my pocket for once—my own cash, too, dishonestly got, but no dirtier than the funds which old Morrison, my father-in-law, doled out as charity to keep us respectable "for my wee daughter's sake." His wee daughter, my Elspeth, was as pleased to see me as she ever was; we still suited very well between the sheets, however much she was playing loose with her admirers. I had ceased worrying about that, too.

However, when I arrived home, hoping for a few months' rest to recover from the effects of a pistol-ball which had been dug out of the small of my back, there was a nasty shock awaiting me. My dear parents-in-law, Mr and Mrs Morrison of Paisley, were now in permanent residence in London; I hadn't seen much of them, thank God, since I had married their beautiful, empty-headed trollop of a daughter several years before, when I was a young subaltern in Cardigan's Hussars. We had detested each other then, they and I, and time hadn't softened the emotion, on either side.

To make matters worse, my father was away from home. In the past year or two the old fellow had been hitting the bottle pretty hard—and pretty hard for him meant soaking up liquor in every waking moment. Once or twice they had had to put him away in a place in the country where the booze was sweated out of him and the pink mice which nibbled at his fingers and toes were shoo'ed away—that was what *he* said, anyway—but it seemed that they kept coming back, and he was off getting another "cure".

"A fine thing," sniffed old Morrison—we were at dinner on my first evening home, and I had hoped to have it in bed with Elspeth, but of course we had to do "the polite" by her parents—"a fine thing, indeed. He'll drink himsel' intae the grave, I suppose."

"Probably," says I. "His father and grand-father did, so I don't see why he shouldn't."

Mrs Morrison, who in defiance of probability had grown with the years even more like a vulture, gave a gasp of disgust at this, and old Morrison said he didn't doubt that the son of the house would follow in his ancestors' besotted footsteps.

"Shouldn't wonder," says I, helping myself to claret. "I've got a better excuse than they had."

"And whit does that mean, sir?" bridled old Morrison. I didn't bother to tell him, so he started off on a great rant about ingratitude and perversity, and the dissolute habits of myself and my family, and finished up with his age-old lamentation about his daughter having married a wastrel and a ruffian, who hadn't even the decency to stay at home with his wife like a Christian, but must be forever wandering like Ishmael. . . .

"Hold on," says I, for I was sick of this. "Since I married your daughter I have been twice abroad, on my country's service, and on the first occasion at least I came home with a good deal of credit. I'll wager you weren't slow to boast about your distinguished son-in-law when I came back from India in '42."

"And what have ye made of it?" sneers he. "What are ye? A captain still, and like to remain one."

"You're never tired of reminding Elspeth in your letters that you keep this family, this house, and the rest of it. Buy me a majority, if military rank means so much to you."

"Damn yer impudence!" says he. "Is it no' enough that I keep you and yer drunken father oot o' the poor's-hoose, where ye belong?"

"I'd have thought so," says I, "but if you want me to shoot up the military tree as well—why, it costs money, you know."

"Aye, weel, deil's the penny ye'll get from me," snaps he.

"Enough is bein' spent on wanton folly as it is," and it seemed to me he darted a look at his vinegary spouse, who sniffed and coloured a bit. What's this, I wondered: surely she hasn't been asking him to buy *her* a pair of colours? Horse Guards wouldn't have taken her, anyway, not for a commission: farrier-sergeant, perhaps, but no higher.

No more was said at dinner, which ended in a merry atmosphere of poisonous ill-will, but I got the explanation from Elspeth when we had retired for the night. It seemed that her mother had been growing increasingly concerned at her inability to get Elspeth's two virgin sisters married off: the oldest girl, Mary, had been settled on some commercial creature in Glasgow, and was breeding at a rare rate, but Agnes and Grizel were still single. I said surely there were enough fortune-hunters in Scotland ready to take a shot at her father's money, but she said no, her mother had discouraged them. She was flying higher, reasoning that if Elspeth had been able to get me, who had titled relatives and was at least half-way into the great world of fashionable society, Agnes and Grizel could do even better.

"She's mad," says I. "If they had your looks it might be a half-chance, but one sight of your dear parents is going to scare any eligible sprig a mile off. Sorry, m'dear, but they ain't acceptable, you know."

"My parents certainly lack the advantages," says Elspeth seriously. Marrying me had turned her into a most wonderful snob. "That I admit. But father is extremely rich, as you are aware—"

"To hear him, it's no fault of ours if he is."

"—and you know, Harry, that quite a few of our titled acquaintances are not too nice to look above a fine dowry. I think, with the right introductions, that Mama might find very suitable husbands for them. Agnes is plain, certainly, but little Grizel is really pretty, and their education has been quite as careful as my own."

It isn't easy for a beautiful woman with blue eyes, a milky complexion, and corn-gold hair to look pompous, especially when she is wearing only a French corset decorated with pink ribbons, but Elspeth managed it. At that moment I was overcome again with that yearning affection for her that I sometimes felt, in spite of her infidelities; I can't explain it, beyond saying that she must have had some magic quality, something to do with the child-like, thoughtful look she wore, and the pure, helpless stupidity in her eyes. It is very difficult not to like a lovely idiot.

"Since you're so well-educated," says I, pulling her down beside me, "let's see how much you remember." And I put her through a most searching test which, being Elspeth, she interrupted from time to time with her serious observations on Mrs Morrison's chances of marrying off the two chits.

"Well," says I, when we were exhausted, "so long as I ain't expected to help launch 'em in society, I don't mind. Good luck to it, I say, and I hope they get a Duke apiece."

But of course, I had to be dragged into it: Elspeth was quite determined to use my celebrity for what it was still worth, on her sisters' behalf, and I knew that when she was insistent there was no way of resisting her. She controlled the purse-strings, you see, and the cash I had brought home wouldn't last long at my rate of spending, I knew. So it was a fairly bleak prospect I had come back to: the guv'nor away in the grip of the quacks and demon drink, old Morrison in the house carping and snuffling, Elspeth and Mrs Morrison planning their campaign to inflict her sisters on unsuspecting London, and myself likely to be roped in—which meant being exposed in public alongside my charming Scotch relations. I should have to take old Morrison to my club, and stand behind Mrs Morrison's chair at parties—no doubt listening to her teaching some refined mama the recipe for haggis—and have people saying: "Seen Flashy's in-laws? They eat peat, don't you know, and speak nothing but Gaelic. Well, it wasn't English, surely?"

Oh, I knew what to expect, and determined to keep out of it. I thought of going to see my Uncle Bindley at the Horse Guards, and beseeching him to arrange an appointment for me to some regiment out of town—I was off the active list just then, and was not relishing the idea of half-pay anyway. And while I was hesitating, in those first few days at home, the letter came that helped to solve my difficulties for me and incidentally changed the map of Europe.

It came like the answer to a pagan's prayer, along with a dun from some tailor or other, an anti-popish tract, a demand for my club subscription, and an invitation to buy railway shares—all the usual trash. Why I should remember the others, I don't know; I must have a perverse memory, for the contents of the big white envelope should have been enough to drive them out of my head.

It was a fine, imposing cover—best quality paper, with a coat-of-arms on the back, which I have before me now. There was a shield, quartered red, blue, blue, and white, and in the quarters were a sword, a crowned lion, what looked like a fat whale, and a pink rose. Plainly it was either from someone of tremendous rank or the manufacturers of a new brand of treacle.[19]

Inside there was a letter, and stamped at the top in flowery letters, surrounded by foliage full of pink-bottomed cupids, were the words "Gräfin de Landsfeld". And who the deuce, I wondered, might she be, and what did she want with me.

The letter I reproduce exactly as it now lies in my hand, very worn and creased after sixty years, but still perfectly legible. It is, I think, quite the most remarkable communication I have ever received—even including the letter of thanks I got from Jefferson Davis and the reprieve I was given in Mexico. It said:

> Most Honoured Sir,
>   I write to you on instruction of Her Grace, the Countess de Landsfeld, of whom you had the honour to be acquainted in Londres some years ago. Her Grace commands me to inform you that she holds the warmest recollection of your friendship, and wishes to convey her strongest greetings on this occasion.

I made nothing of this. While I couldn't have recited the names of all the women I had known, I was pretty clear that there weren't any foreign countesses that had slipped my mind. It went on:

> Sir, while Her Grace doubts not that your duties are of the most important and exacting nature, she trusts that you will have opportunity to consider the matter which, on her command, I am now to lay before you. She is confident that the ties of your former friendship, no less than the chivalrous nature of which she has such pleasing memory, will prevail upon you to assist her in a matter of the most extreme delicate.

303

Now he's certainly mad, this fellow, thinks I, or else he's got the wrong chap. I don't suppose there are three women in the world who ever thought me chivalrous, even on short acquaintance.

Her Grace therefore directs me to request that you will, with all speed after receiving this letter, make haste to present yourself to her in München, and there receive, from her own lips, particulars of the service which it is her dearest wish you will be obliged to render to her. She hastens to assure you that it will be of no least expense or hardship to you, but is of such particular nature that she feels that you, of all her many dear friends, are most suitable to its performing. She believes that such is the warmth of your heart that you will at once agree with her, and that the recollection of her friendship will bring you at once as an English gentleman is fitting.

Honoured Sir, in confidence that you will wish to assist Her Grace, I advise you that you should call on William Greig & Sons, attorneys, at their office in Wine Office Court, Londres, to receive instruction for your journey. They will pay £500 in gold for your travelling, etc. Further payments will be received as necessary.

Sir, Her Grace commands me to conclude with the assurance of her deepest friendship, and her anticipation of the satisfaction of seeing you once again.

Accept, dear Sir, etc.,
R. Lauengram,
Chamberlain.

My first thought was that it was a joke, perpetrated by someone not quite right in the head. It made no sense; I had no idea who the Gräfin de Landsfeld might be, or where "München" was. But going over it again several times, it occurred to me that if it had been a fake, whoever had written it would have made his English a good deal worse than it was, and taken care not to write several of the sentences without howlers.

But if it was genuine, what the devil did it mean? What was the service (without expense or hardship, mark you) for which some foreign titled female was willing to slap £500 into my palm —and that only a first instalment, by the looks of it?

I sat staring at the thing for a good twenty minutes, and the more I studied it the less I liked it. If I've learned one thing in this wicked life, it is that no one, however rich, lays out cash for nothing, and the more they spend the rummer the business is likely to be. Someone, I decided, wanted old Flashy pretty badly, but I couldn't for the life of me think why. I had no qualification that I knew of that suited me for a matter of the most "extreme delicate": all I was good at was foreign languages and riding. And it couldn't be some desperate risk in which my supposed heroism would be valuable—they'd as good as said so. No, it beat me altogether.

I have always kept by me as many books and pamphlets on foreign tongues as I can collect, this being my occasional hobby, and since I guessed that the writer of the letter was pretty obviously German I turned up an index and discovered that "München" was Munich, in Bavaria. I certainly knew no one there at all, let alone a Gräfin, or Countess; for that matter I hardly knew any Germans, had never been in Germany, and had no acquaintance with the language beyond a few idle hours with a grammar some years before.

However, there was an obvious way of solving the mystery, so I took myself off to Wine Office Court and looked up William Greig & Sons. I half expected they would send me about my business, but no; there was as much bowing and scraping and "Pray to step this way, sir" as if I had been a royal duke, which deepened my mystification. A young Mr Greig smoothed me into a chair in his office; he was an oily, rather sporty-looking bargee with a very smart blue cutaway and a large lick of black hair— not at all the City lawyer type. When I presented my letter and demanded to know what it was all about, he gave me a knowing grin.

"Why, all in order, my dear sir," says he. "A draft for £500 to be issued to you, on receipt, with proof of identity—well, we need not fret on that score, hey? Captain Flashman is well enough known, I think, ha-ha. We all remember your famous exploits in China—"

"Afghanistan," says I.

"To be sure it was. The draft negotiable with the Bank of England. Yes, all in perfect order, sir."

"But who the devil is she?"

"Who is who, my dear sir?"

"This Gräfin what's-her-name—Landsfeld?"

His smile vanished in bewilderment.

"I don't follow," says he, scratching a black whisker. "You cannot mean that you don't have the lady's aquaintance? Why, her man writes to you here...."

"I've never heard of her," says I, "to my knowledge."

"Well," says he, giving me an odd look. "This is dam— most odd, you know. My dear sir, are you sure? Quite apart from this letter, which seems to suggest a most, ah ... cordial regard, well, I had not thought there was a man in England who had not heard of the beauteous Countess of Landsfeld."

"Well, you're looking at one now," says I.

"I can't believe it," cries he. "What, never heard of the Queen of Hearts? La Belle Espagnole? The monarch, in all but name, of the Kingdom of Bavaria? My dear sir, all the world knows Donna Maria de—what is it again?" and he rummaged among some papers—"aye, here it is 'Donna Maria de Dolores de los Montez, Countess of Landsfeld'. Come, come, sir, surely now...."

At first the name meant nothing, and then it broke on me.

"De los Montez? You don't mean Lola Montez?"

"But who else, sir? The close friend—indeed, some say more than friend—of King Ludwig. Why, the press is never without some fresh sensation about her, some new scandal ..." and he went on, chattering and smirking, but I never heeded him. My head was in a spin. Lola Montez, my Rosanna—a Countess, a monarch in all but name, a royal mistress by the sound of it. And she was writing to me, offering me hard cash—plainly I needed more information.

"Forgive me, sir," says I, breaking in on his raptures. "The title misled me, for I'd never heard it before. When I knew Lola Montez she was plain Mrs James."

"Oh, dear me, my dear sir," says he, very whimsical. "Those days are far behind us now! Our firm, in fact, represented a *Mrs James* some years ago, but we never talk of her! Oh, no, I daresay not! But the Countess of Landsfeld is another matter—a lady of quite a different colour, ha-ha!"

"When did she come by the title?"

"Why, some months ago. How you should not. . . ."

"I've been abroad," says I. "Until this week I hadn't seen an English newspaper in almost a year. I've heard of Lola Montez's doings, of course, any time over the past three years, but nothing of this."

"Oh, and such doings, hey?" says he, beaming lewdly. "Well, my dear sir, your friend at court—ha-ha—is a very great lady indeed. She has the kingdom under her thumb, makes and breaks ministers, dictates policies—and sets all Europe by the ears, upon my word! Some of the stories—why, there was an article in one of the sheets calling her 'The Modern Messalina'"—he dropped his voice and pushed his greasy face towards me—"and describing her picked bodyguard of splendid young men—what, sir, hey? She goes abroad with a guard of cuirassiers riding behind her coach, sets her dogs on whoever dares to cross her path—why, there was some unfortunate who didn't doff his cap, sir—flogged almost to death! True, sir. And none dare say her nay. The King dotes on her, his courtiers and ministers hate her but go in fear and trembling, the students worship her. For luxury and extravagance there has been nothing like her since La Pompadour, they say. Why, sir, she is the nine-day wonder!"

"Well, well," says I. "Little Mrs James."

"Pray, sir!" He pretended distress. "Not that name, I beg you. It is the Countess of Landsfeld who is your friend, if I may be so bold as to remind you."

"Aye, so it is," says I. "Will you tell me what she wants of me, then?"

"My dear sir," says he, smirking. "A matter of 'the most delicate', is it not? What that may be—surely you are in a better position than I to say, eh? Ha-ha. But you will be going to Bavaria, I take it, to hear the particulars 'from her own lips'?"

That was what I was asking myself. It was unbelievable, of course: Lola a queen, to all intents—that was wild enough. But Lola seeking my help—when our last encounter had been distinguished by the screaming of abuse and the crashing of chamberpots—to say nothing of the furore at the theatre when she had seen me among her betrayers . . . well, I know women are fickle, but I doubted if she remembered *me* with any affection. And yet the letter was practically fawning, and she must have dictated the sense of it, if not the words. It might be she had decided to let bygones be bygones—she was a generous creature in her way, as so many whores are. But why? What could she want me for—all she knew of me was my prowess in bed. Did the maîtresse en titre want to instal me as her lover? My mind, which is at its liveliest in amorous imagination, opened on a riotous vision of Flashy, Pride of the Hareem . . . but no. I have my share of conceit, but I could not believe that with the pick of all the young stallions of a palace guard, she was yearning for my bonny black whiskers.

And yet here was a lawyer, authorised on her behalf, ready to advance me £500 to go to Munich—ten times more than was necessary for the journey. It made no sort of sense—unless she *was* in love with me. But that was out of court; I'd been a good enough mount for a week or so, no doubt, but there had been nothing deeper than that, I was certain. What service, then, could I perform that was so obviously of importance?

I have a nose for risk; the uneasy feeling that had come over me on first reading her letter was returning. If I had any sense, I knew, I would bid the greasy Mr Greig good-day and tell him to tear his draft up. But even the biggest coward doesn't run until some hint of danger appears, and there was none here at all—just my uneasy instinct. Against which there was the prospect of getting away from my damned relations—oh, God, and the horrors of accompanying the Morrisons into Society—and the certainty of an immediate tidy sum, with more to follow, and sheer curiosity, too. If I did go to Bavaria, and the signs were less pleasant than appeared at present—well, I could cut stick if I wanted. And the thought of renewing acquaintance with Lola—a 'warm' and 'friendly' Lola—tickled my darker fancies: from Greig's reports, even if they were only half true, it sounded as though there was plenty of sport at the Court of Good King Ludwig. Palace orgies of Roman proportions suggested themselves, with old Flashy waited on like a Sultan, and Lola mooning over me while slaves plied me with pearls dissolved in wine, and black eunuchs stood by armed with enormous gold-mounted hair-brushes. And while cold reason told me there was a catch in it somewhere —well, I couldn't *see* the catch, yet. Time enough when I did.

"Mr Greig," says I, "where can I cash this draft?"

Getting away from London was no great bother. Elspeth pouted a little, but when I had given her a glimpse—a most fleeting one—of Lauengram's signature and of the letter's cover, and used expressions like "special military detachment to Bavaria" and "foreign court service", she was quite happily resigned. The idea that I would be moving in high places appealed to her vacant mind; she felt vaguely honoured by the association.

The Morrisons didn't half like it, of course, and the old curmudgeon flew off about godless gallivanting, and likened me to Cartaphilus, who it seemed had left a shirt and breeches in every town in the ancient world. I was haunted by a demon, he said, who would never let me rest, and it was an evil day that he had let his daughter mate with a footloose scoundrel who had no sense of a husband's responsibilities.

"Since that's the case," says I, "the farther away from her I am, the better you should be pleased."

He was aghast at such cynicism, but I think the notion cheered him up for all that. He speculated a little on the bad end that I would certainly come to, called me a generation of vipers, and left me to my packing.

Not that there was much of that. Campaigning teaches you to travel light, and a couple of valises did my turn. I took my old Cherrypicker uniform—the smartest turnout any soldier ever had anywhere—because I felt it would be useful to cut a dash, but for the rest I stuck to necessaries. Among these, after some deliberation, I included the duelling pistols that a gunsmith had presented to me after the Bernier affair. They were beautiful weapons, accurate enough for the most fastidious marksman, and in those days when revolving pistols were still crude experimental toys, the last word in hand guns.

But I pondered about taking them. The truth was, I didn't want to believe that I might need them. When you are young and raw and on the brink of adventure, you set great store by having your side-arms just right, because you are full of romantic notions of how you will use them. Even I felt a thrill when I first handled a sabre at practice with the 11th Light Dragoons, and imagined myself pinking and mowing down hordes of ferocious but obligingly futile enemies. But when you've seen a sabre cut to the bone, and limbs mangled by bullets, you come out of your daydream pretty sharp. I knew, as I hesitated with those pistols in my hands, that if I took them I should be admitting the possibility of my own sudden death or maiming in whatever lay ahead. This was, you see, another stage in my development as a poltroon. But I'd certainly feel happier with 'em, uncomfortable reminders though they were, so in they went. And while I was at it, I packed along a neat little seaman's knife. It isn't an Englishman's weapon, of course, but it's devillish handy sometimes, for all sorts of purposes. And experience has taught me that, as with all weapons, while you may not often need it, when you do you need it badly.

So, with a word to Uncle Bindley at Horse Guards—who said acidly that the British Army *might* survive my absence a while longer—and with half of my £500 in my money belt (the other half was safe in the bank), I was ready for the road. Only one thing remained to do. I spent a day searching out a German waiter in the town, and when I had found a likely fellow I offered him his fare home and a handsome bonus, just to travel along with me; I had no German at all, but with my gift for languages I knew that if I applied myself on the journey to Munich I should have at least a smattering by the time I arrived there. I've often said that the ideal way to learn a language is in bed with a wench, but failing that an alert, intelligent travelling companion is as good a teacher as any. And learning a new tongue is no hardship to me; I enjoy it.

The fellow I picked on was a Bavarian, as luck had it, and jumped at the chance of getting home. His name, I think, was Helmuth, but at any rate he was a first-rate choice. Like all Germans, he had a passion for taking pains, and when he saw what I wanted he was all enthusiasm. Hour after hour, in boat, train, and coach, he talked away to me, repeating words and phrases, correcting my own pronunciation, explaining grammatical rules, but

above all giving me that most important thing of all—the rhythm
of the language. This is something which only a few people seem
to have, and I am lucky to be one. Let me catch the rhythm, and
I seem to know what a man is saying even if I haven't learned all
the words he uses. I won't pretend that I learned German in a
fortnight, but at the end of that time I could pass my own elementary test, which is to say to a native: "Tell me, speaking
slowly and carefully, what were your father's views on strong
drink," or religion, or horses, or whatever came to mind—and
understand his reply fairly well. Helmuth was astonished at my
progress.

We did not hurry on the journey, which was by way of Paris,
a city I had often wanted to visit, having heard that debauchery
there was a fine art. I was disappointed: whores are whores the
world over, and the Parisian ones are no different from any other.
And French men make me sick; always have done. I'm degenerate,
but they are dirty with it. Not only in the physical sense, either;
they have greasy minds. Other foreigners may have garlic on their
breaths, but the Frogs have it on their thoughts as well.

The Germans are different altogether. If I wasn't an Englishman, I would want to be a German. They say what they think,
which isn't much as a rule, and they are admirably well ordered.
Everyone in Germany knows his place and stays in it, and grovels
to those above him, which makes it an excellent country for
gentlemen and bullies. In England, even in my young day, if you
took liberties with a working man you would be as likely as not
to get a fist in your face, but the lower-class Germans were as
docile as niggers with white skins. The whole country is splendidly
disciplined and organised, and with all their docility the inhabitants are still among the finest soldiers and workers on earth—as
my old friend Bismarck has shown. The basis of all this, of course,
is stupidity, which you must have in people before you can make
them fight or work successfully. Well, the Germans will trouble
the world yet, but since they are closer to us than anyone else, we
may live to profit by it.

However, all this I was yet to discover, although I had an
inkling of it from studying Helmuth on our journey. I don't bore
you with details of our travels, by the way; nothing happened out
of the ordinary, and what I chiefly remember is a brief anxiety

that I had caught the pox in Paris; fortunately, I hadn't, but the scare I got prejudiced me still further against the French, if that were possible.

Munich, when we reached it, I liked the look of very well. It was clean and orderly on the surface, prices were far below our own (beer a halfpenny a pint, and a servant could be hired at two shillings a week), the folk were either civil or servile, and the guide-book which I had bought in London described it as "a very dissolute capital". The very place for old Flash, thinks I, and looked forward to my stay. I should have known better; my eagerness to see Lola again, and my curiosity about what she wanted, had quite driven away those momentary doubts I had felt back in London. More fool I; if I had known what was waiting round the corner I would have run all the way home and felt myself lucky to be able to run.

We arrived in Munich on a Sunday, and having dismissed Helmuth and found a hotel in the Theresienstrasse, I sat down to consider my first move. It was easy enough to discover that Lola was installed in a personal palace which the besotted Ludwig had built specially for her in the Barerstrasse; presumably I might stroll round and announce my arrival. But it pays to scout whenever you can, so I decided to put in an hour or two mooning round the streets and restaurants to see what news I could pick up first. I might even gain some hint of a clue to why she wanted me.

I strolled about the pleasant streets for a while, seeing the Hofgarten and the fine Residenz Palace where King Ludwig lived, and drank the excellent German beer in one of their open-air beer-gardens while I watched the folk and tried out my ear on their conversation. It could hardly have been more peaceful and placid; even in late autumn it was sunny, and the stout contented burghers with their pleasant-faced wives were either sitting and drinking and puffing at their massive pipes, or sauntering ponderously on the pavements. No one hurried, except the waiters; here and there a group of young fellows in long cloaks and gaudy caps, whom I took to be students, stirred things a little with their laughter, but for the rest it was a drowsy, easy afternoon, as though Munich was blinking contentedly in the fine weather, and wasn't going to be bustled by anybody.

However, one way and another, by finding a French newspaper and getting into talk with people who spoke either French or English, I picked up some gossip. I soon found that one did not need to ask about Lola; the good Muncheners talked about her as Britons do about the weather, and with much the same feeling—in other words, they thought she was bad and would get worse, but that nothing could be done about her anyway.

She was, it seemed, the supreme power in Bavaria. Ludwig was right under her thumb, she had swept out the hostile Ultramontane cabinet and had it replaced largely with creatures of her own, and despite the fact that she was a staunch Protestant, the Catholic hierarchy were powerless against her. The professors, who count for much more there than do ours in England, were solidly against her, but the students were violently split. Some detested her, and had rioted before her windows, but others, calling themselves the Allemania, constituted themselves her champions and even her bodyguard, and were forever clashing with her opponents. Some of these Allemania were pointed out to me, in their bright scarlet caps; they were a tough-looking crew, tight-mouthed and cold-eyed and given to strutting and barking, and people got out of their way pretty sharp.

However, with Ludwig infatuated by her, Lola was firmly in the saddle, and according to one outspoken French journalist whose story I read, her supremacy was causing alarm far outside Bavaria. There were rumours that she was an agent of Palmerston, set on to foment revolution in Germany; to the other powers, striving to hold down a growing popular discontent that was spreading throughout Europe, she appeared to be a dangerous threat to the old regime. At least one attempt had been made to assassinate her; Metternich, the arch-reactionary master of Austria, had tried to bribe her to leave Germany for good. The truth was that in those days the world was on the edge of general revolution; we were coming out of the old age and into the new, and anything that was a focus of disorder or instability was viewed with consternation by the authorities. So Lola was not popular; the papers fumed against her, clergymen damned her in their sermons as a Jezebel and a Sempronia, and the ordinary folk were taught to regard her as a fiend in human shape—all the worse because the shape was beautiful.

Here ends Professor Flashman's historical lecture, much of it cribbed from a history book, but some of it at least learned that first day in the Munich beer-gardens.

One thing I was pretty sure of, and it flies in the face of history: whatever may be said, Lola was secretly admired by the common people. They might shake their heads and look solemn whenever her cavalry escort drove a way for her through a crowd of protesting students; they might look shocked when they heard of the orgies in the Barerstrasse palace; they might exclaim in horror when her Allemania horse-whipped an editor and smashed his presses—but the men inwardly loved her for the gorgeous hoyden she was, and the women hid their satisfaction that one of their own sex was setting Europe by the ears. Whenever the insolent, tempestuous Montez provoked some new scandal, there was no lack of those who thought, "Good for you," and quite a few who said it openly.

And what the devil did she want with me? Well, I had come to Munich to find out, so I scribbled a note that Sunday evening, addressed to the Chamberlain Lauengram, saying that I had arrived and was at his disposal. Then I wandered over to the Residenz Palace, and looked at Lola's portrait in the public gallery —that "Gallery of Beauties" in which Ludwig had assembled pictures of the loveliest women of his day. There were princesses, countesses, actresses, and the daughter of the Munich town-crier, among others, and Lola looking unusually nun-like in a black dress and wearing a come-to-Jesus expression.[20] Underneath it was inscribed a verse written by the king, who was given to poetry, which finished up:

> Oh, soft and beauteous as a deer
> Art thou, of Andalusian race!

Well, he was probably in a position to know about that. And to think that only a few years ago she had been a penniless dancer being hooted off a London stage.

I had hoped, considering the urgency of Lauengram's original letter to me, to be bidden to Lola's palace on the Monday, but that day and the next went by, and still no word. But I was patient, and kept to my hotel, and on the Wednesday morning I was rewarded. I was finishing breakfast in my room, still in my dressing-gown, when there was a great flurry in the passage, and a lackey came to announce the arrival of the Freiherr von Starnberg, whoever he might be. There was much clashing and stamping, two cuirassiers in full fig appeared behind the lackey and stationed themselves like statues on either side of my doorway, and then in between them strolled the man himself, a gay young spark who greeted me with a flashing smile and outstretched hand.

"Herr Rittmeister Flashman?" says he. "My privilege to welcome you to Bavaria. Starnberg, very much at your service." And he clicked his heels, bowing. "You'll forgive my French, but it's better than my English."

"Better than my German, at any rate," says I, taking stock of him. He was about twenty, of middle height and very slender, with a clean-cut, handsome face, brown curls, and the wisp of a moustache on his upper lip. A very cool, jaunty gentleman, clad in the tight tunic and breeches of what I took to be a hussar regiment, for he had a dolman over his shoulder and a light sabre trailing at his hip. He was sizing me up at the same time.

"Dragoon?" says he.

"No, hussar."

"English light cavalry mounts must be infernally strong, then," says he, coolly. "Well, no matter. Forgive my professional interest. Have I interrupted your breakfast?"

I assured him he had not.

"Splendid. Then if you'll oblige me by getting dressed, we'll lose no more time. Lola can't abide to be kept waiting." And he lit a cheroot and began to survey the room. "Damnable places, these hotels. Couldn't stay in one myself."

I pointed out that I had been kept kicking my heels in one for the past three days, and he laughed.

"Well, girls will be girls, you know," says he. "We can't expect 'em to hurry for mere men, however much they expect us to jump to it. Lola's no different from the rest—in that respect."

"You seem to know her very well," says I.

"Well enough," says he negligently, sitting himself on the edge of a table and swinging a polished boot.

"For a messenger, I mean," says I, to take some of the starch out of him. But he only grinned.

"Oh, anything to oblige a lady, you know. I fulfil other functions, when I'm so inclined." And he regarded me with an insolent blue eye. "I don't wish to hurry you, old fellow, but we are wasting time. Not that I mind, but she certainly will."

"And we mustn't have that."

"No, indeed. I imagine you have some experience of the lady's fine Latin temper. By God, I'd tame it out of her if she was mine. But she's not, thank heaven. I don't have to humour her tantrums."

"You don't, eh?"

"Not hers, nor anyone else's," says Master von Starnberg, and took a turn round the room, whistling.

Cocksure men irritate me as a rule, but it was difficult to take offence at this affable young sprig, and I had a feeling that it wouldn't do me much good if I did, so while he lounged in my sitting-room I retired to the bed-chamber to dress. I decided to wear my Cherrypicker rig, with all the trimmings of gold-laced blue tunic and tight pants, and when I emerged Starnberg cocked an eye and whistled appreciatively.

"Saucy regimentals," says he. "Very pretty indeed. Lola may not mind too much having been kept waiting, after all."

"Tell me," I said, "since you seem to know so much: why do you suppose she sent for me?—I'm assuming you know that she did."

"Oh, aye," says he. "Well, now, knowing Lola, I suggest you look in your mirror. Doesn't that suggest an answer?"

"Come now," says I, "I know Lola, too, and I flatter as easily as the next man. But she would hardly bring me all the way from England, just to. . . ."

"Why not?" says he. "She brought me all the way from Hungary. Shall we go?"

He led the way down to the street, the two cuirassiers marching at our heels, and showed me into a coach that was waiting at the door. As he swung himself in beside me, with his hand on the window-frame, his sleeve was slightly pulled back, and I saw the star-shaped white scar of a bullet-wound on his wrist. It occurred to me that this von Starnberg was a tougher handful than he looked at first sight; I had noticed the genuine cavalry swing, toes pointing, as he walked, and for all his boyishness there was a compact sureness about him that would have sat on a much older man. This is one to keep an eye on, thinks I.

Lola's house was in the best part of Munich, by the Karolinen Platz. I say "house", but it was in fact a little palace, designed by King Ludwig's own architect, regardless of expense. It was the sight of it, shining new, like a little fairy-tale castle from Italy, with its uniformed sentries at the gate, its grilled windows (a precaution against hostile crowds), its magnificent gardens, and the flag fluttering from its roof, that brought it home to me just how high this woman had flown. This magnificence didn't signify only money, but power—unlimited power. So why could she want me? She couldn't *need* me. Was she indulging some whim—perhaps going to repay me for being in Ranelagh's box the night she was hissed off the stage? She seemed to be capable of anything. In a moment, after clapping eyes on her palace, I was cursing myself for having come—fear springs eternal in the coward's breast, especially when he has a bad conscience. After all, if she was so all-powerful, and happened to be vindictive, it might be damned unpleasant. . . .

"Here we are," says Starnberg, "Aladdin's cave."

It almost justified the description. There were flunkeys to hand us out, and more uniformed sentries in the hall, all steel and colour, and the splendour of the interior was enough to take your breath away. The marble floor shone like glass, costly tapestries hung on the walls, great mirrors reflected alcoves stuffed with white statuary and choice furniture, above the staircase hung a chandelier which appeared to be of solid silver, and all of it was in a state of perfection and brilliance that suggested an army of skivvies and footmen working full steam.

"Aye, it's a roof over her head, I suppose," says Starnberg, as we gave our busbies to a lackey. "Ah, Lauengram, here is Rittmeister Flashman; is the Gräfin receiving?"

Lauengram was a dapper little gentleman in court-dress, with a thin, impassive face and a bird-like eye. He greeted me in French—which I learned later was spoken a good deal out of deference to Lola's bad German—and led us upstairs past more lackeys and sentries to an anteroom full of pictures and people. I have a soldier's eye for such things, and I would say the loot value of that chamber would have kept a regiment for life, with a farm for the farrier-sergeant thrown in. The walls appeared to be made of striped silk, and there was enough gold on the frames to start a mint.

The folk, too, were a prosperous-looking crew, courtly civilians and military in all the colours of the rainbow; some damned handsome women among them. They stopped their chattering as we entered, and I took advantage of my extra three inches on Starnberg to make a chest, touch my moustache, and give them all the cool look-over.

He had barely started to introduce me to those nearest when a door at the far end of the room opened, and a little chap came out backwards, stumbling over his feet, and protesting violently.

"It is no use, madame!" cries he, to someone in the far room. "I have not the power! The Vicar-General will not permit! Ach, no, lieber Herr Gott!" He cowered back as some piece of crockery sailed past him and shattered on the marble floor, and then Lola herself appeared in the doorway, and my heart took a bound at the sight of her.

She was beautiful in her royal rage, just as I remembered, although now she had clothes on. And although her aim seemed as vague as ever, she appeared to have her wrath under better control these days. At all events, she didn't scream.

"You may tell Dr Windischmann," says she, her rich husky voice charged with contempt, "that if the king's best friend desires a private chapel and confessor, she shall have one, and he shall provide it if he values his office. Does he think he can defy me?"

"Oh, madame, please," cries the little chap. "Only be reasonable! There is not a priest in Germany could accept such a confession. After all, your highness is a Lutheran, and—"

"Lutheran, fiddlesticks! I'm a royal favourite, you mean! That's why your master has the impertinence to flout me. Let him be careful, and you, too, little man. Lutheran or not, favourite or not, if I choose to have a chapel of my own I shall have it. Do you hear? And the Vicar-General himself shall hear my confession, if I think fit."

"Please, madame, oh, please!" The little fellow was on the verge of tears. "Why do you abuse me so? It is not my fault. Dr

Windischmann objects only to the suggestion of a private chapel and confessor. He says. . . ."

"Well, what does he say?"

The little man hesitated. "He says," he gulped, "he says that there is a public confessional at Notre-Dame, and you can always go there when you want to accuse yourself of any of the innumerable sins you have committed." His voice went up to a squeal. "His words, madame! Not mine! Oh, God have mercy!"

As she took one furious step forward he turned and ran for his life past us, his hands over his ears, and we heard his feet clatter on the stairs. Lola stamped her foot, and shouted after him, "Damned papist hypocrite!", and at this the sycophantic crowd in the ante-chamber broke out in a chorus of sympathy and reproach.

"Jesuit impertinence!"

"Intolerable affront!"

"Scandalous insolence!"

"Silly old bastard." (This was Starnberg's contribution.)

"Impossible arrogance of these prelates," says a stout, florid man near me.

"I'm Church of England myself," says I.

This had the effect of turning attention on me. Lola saw me for the first time, and the anger died out of her eyes. She surveyed me a moment, and then slowly she smiled.

"Harry Flashman," says she, and held out a hand towards me— but as a monarch does, palm down and pointing to the ground between us. I took my cue, stepping forward and taking her fingers to kiss. If she wanted to play Good Queen Bess, who was I to object?

She held my hand for a moment afterwards, looking up at me with her glowing smile.

"I believe you're even handsomer than you were," says she.

"I would say the same to you, Rosanna," says I, cavalier as be-damned, "but handsome is too poor a word for it."

Mind you, it was true enough. I've said she was the most beautiful girl I ever met, and she was still all of that. If anything, her figure was more gorgeous than I remembered, and since she was clad in a loose gown of red silk, with apparently nothing beneath it, I could study the subject without difficulty. The effect of her at close quarters was dazzling: the magnificent blue eyes, the perfect mouth and teeth, the white throat and shoulders, and the lustrous black hair coiled up on her head—yes, she was worth her place in Ludwig's gallery. But if she had ripened wonderfully in the few years since I had last seen her, she had changed too. There was a composure, a stateliness that was new; you would always have caught your breath at her beauty, but now you would feel a little awe as well as lust.

I was leering fondly down at her when Starnberg chimes in.

"'Rosanna'?" says he. "What's this, Lola? A pet name?"

"Don't be jealous, Rudi," says she. "Captain Flashman is an old, very dear friend. He knew me long before—all this," and she gestured about her. "He befriended me when I was a poor little nobody, in London." And she took my arm in both of hers, reached up, and kissed me, smiling with her old mischief. Well, if that was how she chose to remember our old acquaintance, so much the better.

"Listen, all of you," she called out, and you could have heard a pin drop. "The Rittmeister Flashman is not only the closest to my heart of all my English friends—and those, you remember, include the noblest in the land—but the bravest soldier in the British Army. You see his decorations"—she leaned across me to touch my medals, and the presence of two almost naked, beautifully rounded breasts just beneath my face was delightfully diverting. Lola was always vain of her bosom,[21] and wore it all but outside her gown; I wished I had had a pinch of snuff to offer her. "Who ever saw a young captain with five medals?" she continued, and there was a chorus of murmured admiration. "So you see, he is to be honoured for more reasons than that he is my guest. There is no soldier in Germany with a higher reputation as a Christian champion."

I had sense enough to look quizzical and indulgent at this, for I knew that the most popular heroes are those who take themselves lightly. I had heard this kind of rot time without count in the past few years, and knew how to receive it, but it amused me to see that the audience, as usual, took it perfectly seriously, the men looking noble and the women frankly admiring.

Having delivered her little lecture, Lola took me on a tour of introduction, presenting Baron this and Countess that, and everyone was all smirks and bows and polite as pie. I could sense that they were all scared stiff of her, for although she was her old gay self, laughing and chattering as she took me from group to group, she was still the grande dame under the happy surface, with a damned imperious eye. Oh, she had them disciplined all right.

Only when she had taken me apart, to a couch where a flunkey served us Tokay while the others stood at a respectful distance, did she let the mask drop a little, and the Irish began to creep back into her voice.

"Let me look at you comfortably now," says she, leaning back and surveying me over her glass. "I like the moustaches, Harry, they become you splendidly. And the careless curl; oh, it's the bonny boy still."

"And you are still the most beautiful girl in the world," says I, not to be outdone.

"So they say," says she, "but I like to hear it from you. After all, when you hear it from Germans it's no compliment—not when you consider the dumpy cows they're comparing you with."

"Some of 'em ain't too bad," says I carelessly.

"Ain't they, though? I can see I shall have to keep an eye on you, my lad. I saw Baroness Pechman wolfing you up a moment ago when she was presented."

"Which one was she?"

"Come, that's better. The last one you met—over there, with the yellow hair."

"She's fat. Overblown."

"Ye-es, poor soul, but some men like it, I'm told."

"Not I, Rosanna."

"Rosanna," she repeated, smiling. "I like that. You know that no one ever calls me by that name now. It reminds me of England —you've no notion how famous it is to hear English again. In conversation, I mean, like this."

"Was that why you sent for me—for my conversation?"

"That—and other things."

"What other things?" says I, seeing a chance to get down to business. "What's this very delicate matter that your chamberlain talked about?"

"Oh, that." She put on a coy look. "That can wait a little. You must know I have a new motto since I came to Bavaria: 'pleasure before business'." She gave me a sleepy look from beneath those glorious black lashes that made by heart skip a little. "You wouldn't be so ungallant as to hurry me, would you, Harry?"

"Not where business is concerned," says I, leering again. "Pleasure's another matter."

"Wicked," she says, smiling lazily, like a sleek black cat. "Wicked, wicked, wicked."

It is remarkable what fatuities you can exchange with a beautiful woman. I can think shame when I consider the way I sat babbling with Lola on that couch; I would ask you only to remember that she was as practised a seductress as ever wore out bed linen, and just to be beside her, even in a room full of people, was in itself intoxicating. She was overpowering, like some rich tropical flower, and she could draw a man like a magnet. The same Dr Windischmann, Vicar-General, whose name she had been taking in vain so recently, once said that there was not even a priest in his charge who could have been trusted with her. Liszt put it more bluntly and accurately when he observed to me: "As soon as you meet Lola, your mind leaps into bed."

Anyway, I mention this to explain how it was that after a few moments with her I had forgotten entirely my earlier misgivings about her possible recollection of our parting in London, and my fears that she might harbour a grudge against me for the Ranelagh affair. She had charmed me, and I use the word exactly. Laughing and talking with her over the Tokay, only one thought was in my mind: to get her bedded as swiftly as might be, and the devil with anything else.

While we were chatting so amiably and I, poor ass, was succumbing to her spell, more people were arriving in the ante-room, and presently she had them called up, with Lauengram playing the major-domo, and talked to them in turn. These levées of hers were quite famous in Munich, apparently, and it was her habit to hold court to all sorts of folk: not just distinguished visitors and such odds and ends as artists and poets, but even statesmen and ambassadors. I don't recall who was there that morning, for between Lola and the Tokay I was not paying much heed, but I know they scraped and fawned to her no end.

Presently she announced that we would all go to see her cuirassiers at exercise, and there was a delay while she went off to change; when she returned it was in full Hussar rig, which showed off her curves admirably and would have caused the police to be called in London. The sycophants "Ooh-ed and Aah-ed" and cried "Wunderschön!", and we all trooped after her to the stables and rode out to a nearby park where a couple of squadrons of cavalry were going through their paces.

Lola, who was riding a little white mare, took great pleasure in the spectacle, pointing with her whip and exclaiming authoritatively on the manoeuvres. Her courtiers echoed her applause faithfully, all except Rudi Starnberg, who I noticed was watching with a critical eye, like myself. I ought to know something about cavalry, and certainly Lola's cuirassiers were a smart lot on parade, and looked very well as they thundered past at the charge. Starnberg asked me what I thought of them; very fine, I said.

"Better than the British?" says he, with his cocky grin.

"I'll tell you that when I've seen 'em fight," says I, bluntly.

"You won't deny they're disciplined to perfection," cries he.

"On parade," says I. "No doubt they'd charge well in a body, too. But let's see 'em in a mêlée, every man for himself; that's where good cavalry prove themselves."

This is true; of course, no one would run faster from a mêlée than I, but Starnberg wasn't to know that. For the first time he looked at me almost with respect, nodding thoughtfully, and admitted I was probably right.

Lola got bored after half an hour or so, and we returned to her palace, but then we had to turn out again because she wanted to exercise her dogs in the garden. It seemed that whatever she did, everyone else was expected to tag after her, and by God, her amusements were trivial. After the dogs, there was music indoors, with a fat bastard of a tenor sobbing his soul out, and then Lola sang herself—she had a fine contralto, as it happens—and the mob raised the roof. Then there was a reading of poetry, which was damnable, but would probably have been even more painful if I had been able to understand it fully, and then more conversation in the ante-room. The centre of it was a long-jawed, tough-looking fellow whose name meant nothing to me at the time; he talked interminably, about music and liberal politics, and everyone lionised him sickeningly, even Lola. When we went into an adjoining room for a buffet—"erfrischung" as the Germans call it—

she introduced him to me as Herr Wagner, but the only conversation we had was when I passed him the ginger and he said "danke". (I've dined out on that incident since, by the way, which shows how ridiculous people can be where celebrities are concerned. Of course, I usually expand the story, and let on that I told him that "Drink, puppy, drink" and "The British Grenadiers" were better music than any damned opera, but only because that is the sort of exaggeration that goes well at dinner parties, and suits my popular character.)[22]

But my memories of that afternoon are necessarily vague, in view of what the night was to bring forth. Briefly, I stayed at the palace all day, being unconscionably bored, and impatient to get Lola by herself, which looked like being damned difficult, there was such a crowd always in attendance on her. From time to time we had a word or two, but always with others present, and when we dined I was halfway down the table, with the fat Baroness Pechman one one side of me, and an American whose name I've forgotten on the other.[23] I was pretty piqued with Lola for this; quite apart from the fact that I thought I deserved a place near her at the table top, the Yankee was the damnedest bore you ever met, and the giggling blonde butterball on my other side was infuriating in her shrieks of amusement at my halting German. She also had a tendency to let her hand stray on to my thigh beneath the table—not that I minded the compliment, and she would have been pretty enough in a baby-faced way if she had weighed about six stones less, but my mind was on the lovely Lola, and she was a long way off.

Being bored, I was careless, and didn't keep too close an eye on my glass. It was a magnificent dinner, and the wines followed each other in brilliant succession. Everyone else punished them tremendously, as the Germans always do, and I simply followed suit. It was understandable, but foolish; I learned in later years that the only safe place to get drunk is among friends in your own home, but that evening I made a thorough pig of myself, and the long and short of it was that "Flashy got beastly drunk", to quote my old friend Tom Hughes.

Not that I was alone; the talk got steadily louder, faces got redder, jokes got coarser—the fact that half those present were women made no difference—and eventually they were roaring and singing around the table, or staggering out to be sick, no doubt, and what conversation there was consisted of shouting at full pitch. I remember there was an orchestra playing incessantly at one end of the hall, and at one point my American companion got up unsteadily on to his chair, amid the cheers of the multitude, and conducted them with a knife and fork. Presently he tumbled down, and rolled under the table. This is an orgy, thinks I, but not a proper orgy. I got it into my head—quite understandably—that such bacchanalia should be concluded in bed, and naturally looked round for Lola. She had left the table, and was standing off in an alcove at one side, talking to some people; I got up and weaved my way through such of the guests as were standing about—those who were fit to stand, that is—until I fetched up in front of her.

I must have been heroically drunk, for I can remember her face swimming in and out of focus; she had a diamond circlet in her dark hair, and the lights from the chandelier made it glitter dazzlingly. She said something, I don't recall what, and I mumbled:

"Let's go to bed, Lola. You an' me."

"You should lie down, Harry," says she. "You're very tired."

"Not too tired," says I. "But I'm damned hot. Come on, Lola, Rosanna, let's go to bed."

"Very well. Come along, then." I'm sure she said that, and then she turned away, and I followed her out of the din and stuffiness of the banqueting chamber into a corridor; I was weaving pretty recklessly, for I walked into the wall once, but she waited for me, and guided me to a doorway, which she opened.

"In here," she said.

I stumbled past her, and caught the musky sweetness of her perfume; I grabbed at her, and dragged her to me in the darkness. She was soft and thrilling against me, and for a moment her open mouth was under mine; then she slipped away, and I lost my balance and half-fell on to a couch. I called out to her to come back, and heard her say, "A moment; just in a moment," and then the door shut softly.

I half lay on the couch, my head swimming with drink and my mind full of lustful thoughts, and I believe I must have passed into a brief stupor, for suddenly I was aware of dim light in the room, and a soft hand was stroking my cheek.

"Lola," says I, like a moon-calf, and then there were arms round my neck and a soft voice murmuring in my ear, but it was not Lola. I blinked at the face before me, and my hands came in contact with bare, plump flesh—any amount of it. My visitor was Baroness Pechman, and she was stark naked.

I tried to shove her off, but she was too heavy; she clung to me like a leech, murmuring endearments in German, and pushing me back on the couch.

"Go away, you fat slut," says I, heaving at her. "Gehen Sie weg, dammit. Don't want you; want Lola."

I might as well have tried to move St Paul's; she was all over me, trying to kiss me, and succeeding, her fat face against mine. I cursed and struggled, and she giggled idiotically and began clawing at my breeches.

"No, you don't," says I, seizing her wrist, but I was too tipsy to be able to defend myself properly, or else she was strong for all her blubber. She pinned me down, calling me her duckling, of all things, and her chicken, and then before I knew it she had suddenly hauled me upright and had my fine Cherrypicker pants round my knees, and was squirming her fat backside against me.

"Oh, eine hammelkeule!" she squeaked. "Kolossal!"

No woman does that to me twice; I'm too susceptible. I seized handfuls of her and began thrusting away. She was not Lola, perhaps, but she was there, and I was still too foxed and too randy to be choosy. I buried my face in the blonde curls at the nape of her neck, and she squealed and plunged in excitement. And I was just settling to work in earnest when there was a rattle at the door handle, the door opened, and suddenly there were men in the room.

There were three of them; Rudi Starnberg and two civilians in black. Rudi was grinning in delight at the sight of me, caught flagrante seducto, as we classical scholars say, but I knew this was no joke. Drunk as I was, I sensed that here was danger, dreadful danger when I had least expected it. It was in the grim faces of the two with him, hard, tight-lipped fellows who moved like fighters.

I shoved my fat baroness quickly away, and she went down sprawling flabbily on her stomach. I jumped back, trying to pull up my breeches, but cavalry pants fit like a skin, and the two

326

were on me before I could adjust myself. Each grabbed an arm, and one of them growled in execrable French:

"Hold still, criminal! You are under arrest!"

"What the devil for?" I shouted. "Take your hands off me, damn you! What does this mean, Starnberg?"

"You're arrested," says he. "These are police officers."

"Police? But, my God, what am I supposed to have done?"

Starnberg, arms akimbo, glanced at the woman who had climbed to her feet, and was hastening to cover herself with a robe. To my amazement, she was giggling behind her hand; I wondered was she mad or drunk.

"I don't know what you call it in English," says he coolly, "but we have several impolite names for it here. Off you go, Gretchen," and he jerked a thumb towards the door.

"In God's name, that's not a crime!" I shouted, but seeing him silent and smiling grimly, I struggled for all I was worth. I was sober enough now, and horribly frightened.

"Let me go!" I yelled. "You must be mad! I demand to see the Gräfin Landsfeld! I demand to see the British Ambassador!"

"Not without your trousers, surely," says Rudi.

"Help!" I roared. "Help! Let me loose! You scoundrels, I'll make you pay for this!" And I tried in frenzy to break from the grip of the policemen.

"Ein starker mann," observed Rudi. "Quiet him."

One of my captors shifted quickly behind me, I tried to turn, and a splitting pain shot through the back of my head. The room swam round me, and I felt my knees strike the floor before my senses left me.

* * *

I wonder sometimes if any man on earth has come to in a cell more often than I have. It has been happening to me all my life; perhaps I could claim a record. But if I did some American would be sure to beat it at once.

This awakening was no different from most of the others: two damnable pains, one inside and one outside my skull, a stomachful of nausea, and a dread of what lay ahead. The last was quickly settled, at any rate; just as grey light was beginning to steal through the bars of my window—which I guessed was in a police station, for the cell was decent—a uniformed guard brought me a mug of coffee, and then conducted me along a corridor to a plain, panelled room containing a most official-looking desk, behind which sat a most official-looking man. He was about fifty, with iron grey hair and a curling moustache, and cold eyes flanking a beaky nose. With him, standing at a writing pulpit beside the desk, was a clerk. The guard ushered me in, bleary, unshaven, blood-stained, and in the fiend's own temper.

"I demand to be allowed to communicate with my ambassador this instant," I began, "to protest at the outrageous manner in which—"

"Be quiet," says the official. "Sit down." And he indicated a stool before the desk.

I wasn't having this. "Don't dare to order me about, you cabbage-eating bastard," says I. "I am a British officer, and unless you wish to have a most serious international incident to answer for, you will—"

"I will certainly have you whipped and returned to your cell if you do not curb your foul tongue," says he coldly. "Sit."

I was staring, flabbergasted at this, when a cheerful voice behind me said:

"Better sit down, old fellow; he can do it, you know," and I wheeled round to find Rudi Starnberg lolling against a table by the door, which had hidden him from me when I came in. He was fresh and jaunty, with his undress cap tilted forward rakishly over one eye, smoking a cheroot in a holder.

"You!" cried I, and got no further. He shushed me with a gesture and pointed to the stool; at the same time the official rapped smartly on his table, so I decided to sit. My head was aching so much I doubt if I could have stood much longer anyway.

"This is Doctor Karjuss," says Rudi. "He is a magistrate and legal authority; he has something to say to you."

"Then he can start by telling me the meaning of this dastardly ill-treatment," cries I. "I've been set upon, my skull cracked, thrown into a filthy cell, denied the right to see my ambassador, and God knows what else. Yes, by the lord, I've been threatened with flogging, too!"

"You were placed under arrest last night," says Karjuss, who spoke tolerable French. "You resisted the officers. They restrained you; that is all."

"Restrained me? They bloody well half-killed me! And what is this damned nonsense about arrest? What's the charge, hey?"

"As yet, none has been laid," says Karjuss. "I repeat, as yet. But I can indicate what they may be." He sat very prim and precise, his cold eyes regarding me with distaste. "First, obscene and indecent conduct; second, corruption of public morals; third, disorderly behaviour; fourth, resisting the police; fifth—'

"You're mad!" I shouted. "This is ridiculous! D'you imagine any court in the world would convict me of any of this, on the strength of what happened last night? Good God, there is such a thing as justice in Bavaria, I suppose—"

"There is indeed," snaps he. "And I can tell you, sir, that I do not merely imagine that a court could convict you—I *know* it could. And it will."

My head was reeling with all this. "Oh, to the devil! I'll not listen to this! I want to see my ambassador. I know my rights, and—"

"Your ambassador would be of no help to you. I have not yet mentioned the most serious complaint. It is possible that a charge of criminal assault on a female may be brought against you."

At this I staggered to my feet in horror. "That's a lie! A damned lie! My God, she practically raped *me*. Why, she—"

"That would not be the evidence she would give before a judge and jury." His voice was stone cold. "Baroness Pechman is known as a lady of irreproachable character. Her husband is a former Commissioner of Police for Munich. I can hardly imagine a more respectable witness."

"But . . . but. . . ." I was at a loss for words, but a horrible thought was forming in my brain. "This is a plot! That's it! It's a deliberate attempt to discredit me!" I wheeled on Starnberg, who was negligently regarding his nails. "You're in this, you rascal! You've given false witness!"

"Don't be an ass," says he. "Listen to the magistrate, can't you?"

Stunned and terrified, I sank on to the stool. Karjuss leaned forward, a thin hand tapping the table before him. I had the impression he was enjoying himself.

"You begin to see the seriousness of your position, sir. I have indicated the charges which could be brought—and without doubt, proved—against you. I speak not as an examining magistrate, but as a legal adviser, if you like. These are certainties. No doubt you would persist in denial; against you there would be at least four witnesses of high character—the two police officers who apprehended you, Baroness Pechman, and the Freiherr von Starnberg here. Your word—the word of a known duellist over women, a man who was expelled for drunken behaviour from his school in England—"

"How the devil did you know that?"

"Our gathering of information is thorough. Is it not so? You can guess what your word would count for in the circumstances."

"I don't care!" I cried. "You can't hope to do this! I'm a friend of the Gräfin Landsfeld! She'll speak for me! By God, when she hears of this, the boot will be on the other foot. . . ."

I went no further. Another horrid thought had struck me. Why hadn't the all-powerful Lola, whose lightest word was law in Bavaria, intervened by now? She must know all about it; why, the ghastly affair had happened in her own palace! She had been with me not five minutes before. . . . And then, in spite of my aching, reeling head, the full truth of it was plain. Lola knew all about it, yes; hadn't she lured me to Munich in the first place? And here I was, within twenty-four hours of meeting her again, trapped in what was obviously a damnable, deliberate plot against me. God! Was this her way of punishing me for what had happened years before, when I had laughed at her humiliation in London? Could any woman be so fiendishly cruel, hating so long and bitterly that she would go to such lengths? I couldn't believe it.

And then Karjuss spoke to confirm my worst fears.

"You can hope for no assistance whatever from the Gräfin Landsfeld," says he. "She has already disclaimed you."

I took my aching head in my hands. This was a nightmare; I couldn't believe it was happening.

"But I've done nothing!" I burst out, almost sobbing. "Oh, I galloped that fat trot, yes, but where's the crime in that? Don't Germans do it, for Christ's sake? By God, I'll fight this! My ambassador—"

"A moment." Karjuss was impatient. "It seems I have talked to no purpose. Can I not convince you that, legally, you are without hope? And, on conviction, I assure you, you could be imprisoned for life. Even on the minor charges, it would be possible to ensure a maximum sentence of some years. Is that clear? This, inevitably, is what will happen if, by insisting on seeing your ambassador, and enlisting his interest, you cause the whole scandal to become public. At the moment, I would remind you, no charges have been formulated."

"And they needn't be," says Rudi from behind me. "Unless you insist, of course."

This was too much for me; it made no sense whatever.

"No one wants to be unpleasant," says Rudi, all silky. "But we have to show you where you stand, don't you see? To let you see what *might* happen—if you were obstinate."

"You're blackmailing me, then!" I stared from the thin-lipped Karjuss to the debonair stripling. "In God's name, why? What have I done? What d'ye want me to do?"

"Ah!" says he. "That's better." He tapped me twice smartly on the shoulder with his riding-switch. "Much better. Do you know, Doctor," he went on, turning to Karjuss, "I believe there is no need to trouble you any longer. I'm sure the Rittmeister Flashman has at least realised the—er, gravity of his situation, and will be as eager as we all are to find a mutually satisfactory way out of it. I'm deeply obliged to you, Doctor."

Even in my scared and bewildered state, I noticed that Karjuss took his dismissal as a lackey does from a master. He stood up, bowed to Starnberg, and with his clerk at his heels, strode out of the room.

"That's better too," said young Rudi. "I can't endure these damned scriveners, can you? I wouldn't have troubled you with him, really, but there's no doubt he explains legal technicalities well. Cigar? No?"

"He's explained nothing, except that I'm the object of a damned conspiracy! God, why do you do this to me? Is it that damned bitch Lola? Is this how she takes her revenge on me?"

"Tut-tut," says Rudi. "Be calm." He seated himself on the edge of Karjuss's desk, swung his legs a moment, and looked at me thoughtfully. Then he gave a slow chuckle.

"It's too bad, really. I don't blame you for being annoyed. The truth is, we haven't been quite honest with you. You're sure you won't have a cigar? Oh, well, here's how it is."

He lit himself another weed, and held forth.

"I think Karjuss has convinced you that you're in a most devilish mess. If we choose, we can shut you up for ever, and your own ambassador, and your government, would be the first to say 'Amen'. Considering the charges, I mean."

"Trumped-up lies!" I shouted. "False blasted witnesses!"

"But of course. As you yourself said, a dastardly plot. But the point is—you're caught in it, with no choice but to do as you're told. If you refuse—the charges are brought, you're convicted, and good-night."

And the insolent young hound grinned pleasantly at me and blew a smoke-ring.

"You devil!" cries I. "You—you dirty German dog!"

"Austrian, actually. Anyway, you appreciate your position?"

Oh, I appreciated it, no question of that. I didn't understand how, or why, they had done this to me, but I was in no doubt of what the consequences would be if I didn't play their infernal game for them—whatever it was. Blustering hadn't helped me, and a look at Rudi's mocking face told me that whining wouldn't either. Robbed of the two cards which I normally play in a crisis, I was momentarily lost.

"Will you tell me why you've done this—why to me? What can you want of me, in heaven's name?"

"There is a service—a very important service—which only you can perform," says he. "More than that I can't say, at the moment. But that is why you were brought to Munich—oh, it was all most carefully planned. Lola's letter—dictated by me, incidentally—was not altogether inaccurate. 'Most delicate' really sums it up."

"But what service could there possibly be that only I—"

"You'll have to wait and see, and for heaven's sake stop expostulating like the victim in a melodrama. Take my word for it, we didn't go to so much trouble for nothing. Now, you're a sensible man, I'm sure. Will you bow to the inevitable, like a good chap?"

"That bitch Lola!" I growled. "She's up to the neck in this—this villainy, I suppose."

"Up to a point, not up to the neck. She was the means of getting you to Germany, but it wasn't her idea. We employed her assistance—"

"'We'? Who the devil's 'we'?"

"My friends and I. But you shouldn't be too hard on her, you know. I doubt if she bears you any ill-will—in fact, I think she's rather sorry for you—but she knows which side her bread is buttered. And powerful as she is, there are those in Germany whom even she finds it wise to oblige. Now, no more silly questions: are you going to be a good boy or aren't you?"

"It seems I've no choice."

"Excellent. Now, we'll have that crack in your head seen to, get you a bath and some clean linen, and then—"

"What then?"

"You and I will make a little journey, my dear Flashman. Or, may I call you Harry? You must address me as Rudi, you know; 'dirty dog' and 'devil' and 'swine' and so on are all very well between comparative strangers, but I feel that you and I may be on the brink of a really fruitful and profitable friendship. You don't agree? Well, I'm sorry, but we'll see. Now, if you'll come along, I have a closed carriage waiting which will take us to a little place of mine where we'll have you repaired and made all klim-bim, as the Prussians say. Devilish places, these jails, aren't they; no proper facilities for a gentleman at all. . . ."

Well, what could I do, but trot along at his heels with a mouthful of apprehension? Whatever 'they' were up to, I was in for it, and in the meantime there was nothing to do but go with the tide. With my sure instinct, I knew that the "service" I was being blackmailed into was sure to be unpleasant, and quite likely damned dangerous, but my queasy guts didn't interfere with my logical process. I'm a realist, and it was already in my mind that in whatever lay ahead—a journey, initially, according to Rudi—some opportunity of escape must surely present itself. Unless you are actually locked up, escapes are not as difficult as many folk think; you simply bolt, seize the first available horse, and go like hell for safety—in this case probably the Austrian frontier. Or would Switzerland be better? It was farther, but Rudi and his sinister friends probably had influence in Austria. And they would not reckon on me trying a forced ride to the Swiss border. . . .

"Oh, by the way," says Rudi, as we left the police office and he handed me into a carriage, "to a man of action like yourself it may seem that an opportunity will arise of giving me the slip. Don't try it. I would kill you before you'd gone five yards." And he smiled genially as he settled himself opposite me.

"You're mighty sure of yourself," growls I.

"With cause," says he. "Look here." He gave his right arm a shake, and there was a pocket pistol in his right hand. "I'm a dead shot, too."

"Naturally," says I, but I decided it was probably true. Anyone who keeps a pistol in his sleeve can usually use it.

"And, in all modesty, I'm probably your master with the sabre as well—or with a knife," says Master Rudi, putting his pistol away. "So you see, it wouldn't pay you to run for it."

I said nothing, but my spirits sank a few notches lower. He was going to be an efficient watch-dog, rot him, the more so since he believed me to be "a man of action". He knew enough of my reputation, no doubt, to put me down as a desperate, dangerous fellow who didn't give a damn for risks. If he'd known me for the poltroon I was he might have been less alert.

So in the meantime, I was at the mercy of Freiherr Rudolf von Starnberg, and if I'd known him then as I knew him later I'd have been even more nervous than I was. For this gay, devil-may-care youngster, with his curly head and winning smile, was one of the hardest cases I've ever encountered—a thoroughly bad, unscrupulous and fatally dangerous ruffian—and, as you can imagine, I have known a few. Not many of them, scoundrels that they were, delighted in wickedness for its own sake, but Rudi did. He enjoyed killing, for example, and would kill laughing; he was without shame where women were concerned, and without pity, too. I dare say there may have been crimes he didn't commit, but it can only have been for want of opportunity. He was an evil, vicious, cruel rascal.

We got on very well, really, I suppose, all things considered. This was not just because I shared most of his vices, but because he believed erroneously that I shared his only virtue, which was courage. He was too young to know what fear was, and he imagined that I was as big a daredevil as he was himself—my Afghan reputation was pretty glorious, after all. But in addition I must admit that he could be a good companion when he chose— he had a great fund of amiable conversation and a filthy mind, and loved the good things of life—so it was not difficult to get along with him.

He was all consideration that first day. At the house he took me to there was a most competent French valet who dressed and bathed my head, provided me with a bath and a suit of my own clothes—for they had brought my baggage from my hotel—and later cooked us both a most splendid omelette before we set off for the station. Rudi was in haste to catch the train: we were bound for Berlin, he told me, but beyond that I could get nothing out of him.

"Wait and see," says he. "And while you're waiting, I'd be obliged if you would stop talking French and practise your German—you're going to need it."

With that mysterious instruction I had to be content—and I had to be obedient, too, for devil a word of French would he say or listen to from then on. However, with a bottle of hock inside me, the unknown future looked a little less bleak, and when we boarded the evening train I was at least momentarily resigned to my situation. Time enough to start fretting again when we reached Berlin.

*   *   *

The journey took us three days, although nowadays you would do it in a matter of hours. But those were the early years of railways, and the line between Munich and Berlin was not complete. I know we did part of the trip by coach, but I can't recall where; one night we spent in Leipzig, certainly, but I was paying no great heed to my surroundings. As the miles went by my apprehension was growing again—what the devil did "they" want me for? I tried several times to pump Rudi, but without success.

"You'll find out in good time," was all he would say, with a knowing grin. "I'll tell you this much—I'd do the job in a moment if I had the chance. I envy you, indeed. But you're the only man for it—and don't fret: it's well within your powers."

That should have cheered me up, but it didn't. After all, my powers, so far as he and the world knew them, were all concerned with war, slaughter, and heroism, and I wanted none of that if I could help it. But I had sense enough not to let him get a glimpse of my lily liver; no doubt, if my worst fears were realised, he'd see all he wanted of it, in time.

We spent much of our time in the train playing picquet and ecarté, and recognised each other as fairish sharps, but neither of us was able to take much interest in the game. I was too inwardly nervous, and he was too busy keeping an eye on me—he was one of these extraordinary folk who can be on the hair trigger of action for days and nights on end, and not once in that journey was there a decent chance to take him unawares. Not that I'd have dared to try if there had been; I had got a healthy respect for young Rudi by now, and didn't doubt that he would shoot me without the slightest hesitation, and take his chance on the consequences.

So we came to Berlin, on a night of bitter snow and wind, and there was another coach at the station to whirl us away through the busy lamp-lit streets. Even with our fur-collared coats, and rugs and hot bricks, it was damnably chilly in that coach after the warmth of the train, and I wasn't cheered by the fact that our journey was obviously not going to be a short one—that much was clear from the fact that we had a couple of hampers of food with us and a basket of bottles as well.

It lasted another three days, what with snow-choked roads and the coach shedding a wheel, and damned uncomfortable it was. I guessed we were travelling west, at about twenty miles a day, but beyond that there was nothing to be learned from the dreary German landscape. The snow stuck to the windows, and the coach was like an ice-house; I cursed and grumbled a good deal, but Starnberg sat patiently in his corner, huddled in his great-coat, whistling softly through his teeth—his observations were either insolently cheerful or caustic, and I couldn't decide which I disliked more.

It was towards evening on the third day that I awoke from a doze to find Rudi with the window down, peering out into the dusk. The snow had stopped for the moment, but there was a keen wind whistling into the coach, and I was about to tell him brusquely to shut the window before we froze, when he pulled his head in and said:

"Journey's end, thank God. Now for some decent food at last and a proper bed."

I leaned forward to look out, and I've seen cheerier prospects. We were rolling slowly up a long avenue of trees towards a huge, bleak house, half mansion, half castle; in the fading light, with the wintry sky behind it, it looked in silhouette like the setting for some Gothic novel, all towers and spires and rugged stonework. There were lights in some of the windows, and a great lantern shone yellow above the pointed archway of its main door, but they served only to exaggerate the ancient gloom of the place. Childe Flashy to the Dark Tower came, thinks I, and tried not to imagine what lay within.

It proved to be a match for the exterior. We were shown into an immense, stone-flagged hall, hung round with faded tapestries and a few old trophies of arms and the chase; there were archways without doors leading out of it, and in keeping with a general air of medieval ghastliness, there were even torches burning in brackets on the walls. The place felt like a tomb, and the ancient butler who received us would have made an excellent gravedigger.

But what daunted me most of all was the presence in the hall of a strapping trio of fellows, all of military cut, who welcomed Rudi and weighed me up with cold, professional eyes. One was a massive, close-cropped, typical Prussian, whose fleshy face was wealed with a great sabre cut from brow to chin; the second was a tall, supple, sinister gentleman with sleek black hair and a vulpine smile; the third was stocky and stout, balding and ugly. All were in undress uniforms, and as tough-looking a set of customers as you could wish for; my spirits sank even farther as I realised that with this crew on hand my chances of escape had dwindled out of sight.

Rudi performed introductions. "My friends Kraftstein"—the big Prussian clicked his heels—"de Gautet"—a bow from the sinister Scaramouche—"and Bersonin"—the bald ugly one barely nodded. "Like you and me, they are military men, as you see. You'll find they are devoted to your welfare and er . . . safekeeping," says Master Rudi pleasantly, "and any one of them is almost as tough as I am, nicht wahr?"

337

"Ich glaube es," says the sleek dè Gautet, showing his teeth. Another confident bastard, and decidedly unpleasant.

While he and Kraftstein stayed talking with Rudi, I was conveyed to a room on the second floor by Bersonin, and while he kept a bleak eye on me I was graciously permitted to change, wash, and eat a meal which the ancient butler brought. It was tolerable food, with an excellent Rhenish, and I invited the taciturn Bersonin to join me in a glass, but he shook his head. I tried my German on him, but getting nothing but grunts for my pains I turned my back on him and devoted myself to my meal. If he wanted to play the jailer, he could be treated like one.

Presently back comes Master Rudi, very debonair in a clean shirt, freshly-pressed breeches and polished boots, with the Brothers Grimm, Kraftstein and de Gautet, at his heels.

"All fed and watered?" says he. "Capital. I can see you two have been getting along famously. I trust our good Bersonin hasn't overwhelmed you with his inconsequential chatter. No?" He grinned impudently at Bersonin, who shrugged and scowled. "My, what a madcap he is," went on Rudi, who had evidently dined, too, and was back at the top of his most amiable form. "Well, come along with me, and we'll see what other entertainment this charming establishment can offer."

"All the entertainment I want is to find out what the devil I'm doing here," says I.

"Oh, you haven't long to wait now," says he, and he conducted me down the corridor, up another stairway, and into a long gallery. Just as we set foot in it, there sounded from somewhere ahead of us the unmistakable crack of a pistol-shot; I jumped, but Rudi only grinned over his shoulder.

"Rats," says he. "The place is thick with 'em. We've tried poison and dogs, but our host believes in more direct methods. There he goes again," he added, as another shot sounded. "They must be out in force tonight."

He paused in front of a stout, metal-studded door. "Here we are," cries he, throwing it wide, and waving me in. "Your patience is rewarded."

It was a fine, spacious room, far better appointed than anything I had seen so far, with carpet on the flags, a bright fire in the huge grate, solid-looking leather furniture, several shelves of books round the panelled walls, and a long, narrow polished table running down the centre under a brilliant candelabra. At the far end of the table sat a man, his feet cocked up on the board, reloading a long pistol, and at the sight of him I stopped as though I had walked into a wall. It was Otto von Bismarck.

In a lifetime that has included far too many unpleasant surprises, I can think of few nastier shocks than that moment. Strange as it seems, from the very start of this German affair, Bismarck had never even crossed my mind—probably because I didn't want to remember him. Having done the dirty on him in England with John Gully, I'd had no wish ever to meet him again—especially at such a disadvantage as now. Well, when you've caused a man to be cut up by a prize pug, and made him look an idiot into the bargain, you bar renewing his acquaintance in a lonely castle with four of his hired thugs ushering you into his presence.

Equally alarming was the discovery that he was at the bottom of the plot that had snared me: if it had looked sticky before, it looked a lot worse now.

"Welcome to Schönhausen, Mr Flashman," says he, with the vaguest curl of a smile at the corner of his mouth. "Pray be seated."[24]

Bersonin set a chair for me at the table end opposite Bismarck, and then took station by the door. The other three stood by the fireplace, Rudi leaning against the overmantel. Bismarck studied me along the table's length: he looked as nasty as ever, with those pale blue eyes and his arrogant stare. His face had roughened up a bit, though, since I first knew him, and he was sporting a heavy moustache; booze and guzzling had added a good deal of flesh to him, especially about the neck.

My heart was thumping like a hammer, and as always when I am scared half out of my wits my face was going red. Bismarck misread the signs.

"You don't appear pleased to see me," says he, laying aside his pistol. "But then, why should you? There is a score to settle on my side; I still miss a tooth, thanks to your pugilist friend." He paused, while I quaked. "However, don't imagine that I contrived your coming all the way here from England just to settle a personal difference. It happens, amazing though it may seem, that I need you. What do you think of that?"

"My God," says I, "if that's so, why the devil didn't you ask me, like a civilised human being, instead of going through that damned charade in Munich? Of all the ridiculous, dangerous—yes, and damned bad-mannered—"

"Don't be a fool. We will not pretend that if I had asked you, you would have come. It was necessary to use guile and force, in turn, to ensure your presence here. And to further ensure that you would be—pliable. For you have been left in no doubt what will happen to you if you do not do exactly what I require."

"I've been left in no doubt that I've been bloody well kidnapped! And assaulted and falsely accused! I've been left in no doubt that you're a damned villain. And—"

"Shall we leave these vapourings?" he broke in harshly. "You know something of what I am, and I know exactly what you are—a brutal, lecherous ruffian. Yes, but with certain abilities, which you will use as I direct."

"What the devil is it you want, curse you? What use can I possibly be to you?"

"That is better. Give him a brandy, Kraftstein, and a cigar. Now then, Mr Flashman, you will listen to me, and what I tell you will never be repeated—never, as you love your life."

As I think back on it now, it is still difficult to believe that it happened—that I really sat in that long room, with a glass and a cigar, while that cold, masterful man who was to be the greatest statesman of his age, outlined to me the amazing plan which was to be the first, small stepping-stone in his great career. It was mad, incredible nonsense, but it is true. Bismarck then was nothing—in the political sense, anyway. But he had dreamed his dreams (as Lola had told me years before) and now he was setting about in that cold, German certainty, to make them realities. Strange, isn't it, that without me he could not have begun as he did? He needed the lecherous, brutal ruffian (an incomplete description, but Bismarck always was a great one for half-truths).

"Let me begin by asking you a question," says he. "What do you know of Schleswig and Holstein?"

"Never even met 'em," says I. Rudi laughed aloud, and de Gautet gave his sidelong smile.

Bismarck didn't show any amusement. "They are states," he said, "not persons. I shall tell you about them."

And he began to explain what historians call "the Schleswig-Holstein question." I won't bore you with it here, because even diplomats agree that it is the most infernally complex affair that ever bedevilled European politics. Nobody has ever got to the bottom of it—indeed, Palmerston once said that only three people understood it: one was Pam himself, and he had forgotten it, another was a famous statesman, and he was dead, and the third was a German professor, and he had gone mad thinking about it. So there. But the nub was that the two states, which lay directly between Denmark and the German Confederacy, were nominally ruled by the King of Denmark, although most of the inhabitants were Germans. Both Germany and Denmark claimed Schleswig and Holstein, and the people living there were forever arguing about who they should belong to.

That, then, was the famous question[25]—and of course, Bismarck knew the answer.

"It is beyond dispute," says he, "that these two states are German by right. It has become of the first import that they should be German in fact."

I couldn't see what the devil this had to do with me, and said so.

"Be silent, and listen," he snarled. "You will see very soon. Now, answer me: in the intervals between your drinking and whoring and hunting, do you take any interest in politics?"

"Well, I'm a Tory, I suppose. Haven't ever bothered to vote, mind you. Why?"

"Gerrechter Herr Gott," says he. "This, gentlemen"—he glanced at the others—"is a specimen of the ruling caste of the most powerful country on earth—for the present. Incredible, is it not?" His eyes scornful, he turned back to me. "You know, in effect, nothing of affairs of state—your own, or any others. Very good. But even you, Mr Flashman, must be aware that of late, all over Europe, there have been storm clouds gathering. There is a dangerous sentiment of liberalism, fostered by so-called progressive groups of intellectuals, which is infecting the populaces of states. Discontent and disaffection have been created; everywhere there are movements for reform"—he spat the word out—"reform,

342

that slogan of the shiftless by which they mean destruction of stability in the hope that they will find some pickings among the ruins. Reform! Yes, your own country has given in to it, as probably even you have heard--"

"Should think I have. My guv-nor lost his seat in the House."

"—and with what result? Concession has bred anarchy, as it always does. Are your masses satisfied? Of course not: they never are."

"Not that he ever spent much time there, of course. . . ."

"But as yet England has not reaped the full consequence of her statesmen's stupidity. It will come in time, just as it is coming all over Europe. We have been wasted and enfeebled by peace these thirty years past, until there is hardly a man in Europe—I except Metternich—with the vision to see beyond the borders of his own state, to look past the petty trivialities of his own domestic politics, at the dark picture of the Continent. They blind themselves to what is happening all about them; they consider only how to safeguard their own miserable little countries, with no thought for the whole. They cannot see, it seems, that unless those who lead and rule Europe stand together for the preservation of order and government, they will be swept away piecemeal on a rising tide of revolution."

He had worked himself into a mild passion by this time; his eyes were bright and he was crouched forward in his chair, hurling his words down the table at me.

"Well," says I, "I grant you things are a bit slack, here and there, and my wife has remarked that good servants are getting damned hard to find. But if you think England's in for revolution, you're well off the mark. We leave that sort of thing to Frogs and niggers."

"I am not interested in your imbecile observations. I tell you what is, in Europe, and what its consequences must be unless measures are taken to prevent it. Here, in Germany, we have the cancer in a malignant form: the liberal movements are afoot throughout the confederacy. As a member of the Prussian Diet I see them at work openly in Berlin; as a rural landowner I am aware of them even in the countryside. I see them sapping the strength of the German people. If such insidious doctrines have their way, in a loose, undisciplined confederacy such as ours, the result will be chaotic. Germany, and especially German unity, for which far-sighted men have laboured for generations, will receive a mortal blow, from which it might take a century to recover. That she cannot afford. The world is on the move: the great nations are already jockeying for position in the race for power which is sure to move with incredible swiftness, now that science and industry are providing the impetus. If Germany is to take her place among the leaders, she must have unity, she must have strength, she must have discipline"—his great fist smacked the table with each phrase—"she must submit herself to the guidance and government of a supreme authority, who will do for her what Napoleon did for France, what Washington did for America. These were not liberals, Mr Flashman; these were not progressive intellectuals. Germany must have her Napoleon, if she is to have her—"

"Waterloo?" I was sick of all his bombast. Mind you, the moment I'd said it, I wished I hadn't, for he stopped dead and stared at me in silence with those blazing blue eyes. Then he sat back in his chair, and spoke quietly.

"There will be no Waterloo. However, this is academic, and certainly wasted on a mind such as yours. I have said enough, I think, to explain to you the necessity for ensuring that the spread of liberal thought must be checked before it breeds revolution proper. For this, there must be measures, wherever possible, to buttress existing government, and to preserve order. Stability must be maintained wherever seditious influences are at work. And nowhere are they more in evidence than in Schleswig and Holstein."

"I wondered when we should get back to them," says I, and glanced at the others to see how they had taken Bismarck's tirade. Young Rudi was blowing smoke rings at the ceiling, but de Gautet was all ears, and as for Kraftstein, he was pointing like a damned retriever, as though ready to bark in admiration. It occurred to me that if he found Bismarck's claptrap absorbing, there was probably no lack of other idiots in Germany who would do so too.

"If you care to study the map of Europe above that bookcase," Bismarck continued, "you will see that at the eastern limit of Holstein, where it adjoins Mecklenburg, there is a small duchy called Strackenz. It, like Schleswig and Holstein, has ties both with Germany and Denmark; like them, also, it is riven internally by contending parties. Being a rural, backward province, it is of less apparent importance than its larger neighbours, but this is an illusion. In fact, it is the spark on the tinder; if the dissension between the contending parties in Strackenz were to erupt into disorder, this would undoubtedly be used by revolutionary elements as an excuse to foment unrest in the neighbouring provinces; Denmark and Germany could become involved—believe me, great wars have begun over smaller matters than Strackenz.

"Is it plain to you that the peace must be kept in this little province? If it is, then given time, German diplomacy will ensure the incorporation of Schleswig and Holstein into the German confederacy, and the process of our national unification will have begun. But if in the immediate future anything should occur to plunge Strackenz into unrest, if the rival factions there should be given any crisis to exploit—then, my work will be ruined before it has been commenced."

I can't say I gave a tuppenny damn about his work, or the building of a united German state, and I couldn't for the life of me see what all this had to do with me. Still, I could only listen. Bismarck was leaning forward again, staring at me and tapping the table.

"Such a crisis is at hand. Here are the facts. Strackenz is ruled by a Duchess Irma, who has recently reached marriageable age. She is exceedingly popular with her subjects, being young and personable and therefore supremely fitted to rule, in the eyes of superstitious peasants. It has been arranged that she should marry a prince of the Danish royal family, a nephew, in fact, of King Christian himself, one Prince Carl Gustaf. This informs you of the importance that Denmark attaches to even such a tiny province as Strackenz. The point is that the marriage will be hailed by the Danish faction in Strackenz, who are an unusually troublesome group—possibly because they are so far away from Denmark itself. And if *they* are contented, Strackenz will continue in peace. Its German population will know how to wait," he added with confidence.

I confess I stifled a yawn, but he ignored it.

"Politically, then, the match is not only desirable, but essential. Its stabilising influence apart, I am not without hopes of Carl Gustaf, with whom I am acquainted. He would make a popular consort and ruler in Strackenz."

He hesitated, his eyes unwinking on mine, and I stirred impatiently.

"Well, then," says I, "good luck to the happy couple, and God bless 'em all and Tiny Tim. Will you come to the point as far as I'm concerned—if I am at all, which I'm beginning to doubt."

"Oh, you are," says he, nodding grimly. "I said there was a crisis in Strackenz. It is this: as things stand, the wedding, which is to be solemnised in six weeks' time, cannot take place."

"Can't it, now? Why not?"

"Prince Carl Gustaf, who is in many ways an admirable young man, has nevertheless his share of young men's folly." Bismarck paused. "He has contracted a social disease, which makes it impossible that he marry, at least for the time being."

"A what?"

"A social disease."

"You mean he's got a dose of clap?" I let loose a guffaw. "Well, that's damned inconsiderate of him. Bad luck on Countess what's-her-name, too. Still, boys will be boys, eh? But that makes things awkward, I agree. What are you going to do about it?"

Bismarck didn't reply for a moment. There was a dead silence in the room, an expectant silence that made me uneasy.

"Well," says I at length. "What next?"

Bismarck stood up abruptly, went over to a desk against the wall, and took a small object from it. He weighed it in his hand as he paced slowly back to the table.

"If the wedding does not take place, Strackenz will explode. The Danish party will see to it; liberal agitators will whip up anti-German feeling with tales of a plot. But it is obviously impossible for Prince Carl to marry for several months, when his . . . condition has responded to treatment."

He seemed to expect a comment, so I suggested the wedding be postponed.

"On what pretext? If the real reason were known, the marriage could never take place at all, obviously. And the Strackenz pot would boil over. At the moment, no one knows of Carl Gustaf's malady except his own physician, and two highly-placed Danish ministers. The rest of Denmark, like Germany and Strackenz, suspects nothing amiss, and expects the wedding to go forward."

"You say only three people know that this Prince has Cupid's measles? Then how do you. . . ."

"I have my own sources. The three I mentioned, the Prince, and ourselves are the only people who know. Rest assured." He juggled the object in his hand. "The wedding must take place."

"Well, he'll just have to marry her, clap and all, won't he? What else. . . ."

"Out of the question," says de Gautet, speaking for the first time. "Humanitarian reasons apart, it would surely be discovered afterwards, and the ensuing scandal would have as disastrous an effect as a postponement of the marriage."

"Well, then, talk sense," says I. "If the Prince *can't* marry her in six weeks, the wedding's off, ain't it? You'll have to think of something else."

"We have," says Bismarck. "And the wedding will take place."

"You're talking bloody nonsense," says I. "Anyway, what the hell do I care? What has all this to do with me?"

Bismarck tossed down on the table the thing he had been holding. It slithered along the length of the wood and stopped in front of me. I saw it was a gold case, oval, and about four inches long.

"Open it," says Bismarck.

I touched the catch, and the thing sprang open. In it was a miniature, in very fine colour, showing a man in uniform, youngish, but with a completely bald head which gave him an unnatural look. He wasn't bad-looking, though, and it seemed to me I knew him . . . and then the case dropped from my fingers, and the room seemed to swim about me. For I did know him; saving the bald head, the face in the miniature was my own. It was all too familiar from my own mirror: the likeness was uncanny, exact.

"Prince Carl Gustaf of Denmark," says Bismarck, and his voice seemed to be coming through a fog.

I'm not often at a loss for words, but at that moment I sat stricken dumb. The enormity of the idea—for it was as plain as a pikestaff in an instant—was beyond reasonable comment. I just sat and gaped from them to the miniature and back, and Rudi's jovial laugh rang out.

"Magnificent!" cries he. "I'd not have missed that moment for a dukedom! I wish you could have seen your face—your *own* face, I mean."

"You will remember," says Bismarck, "that when we first met in London I was puzzled to remember where I had seen you before. I had not, of course—but I *had* seen the young Prince Carl when he visited Berlin. I realised then that you were *doppelgängers*, identical bodies, and regarded it as an interesting fact; no more. Three months ago, when I first learned of the Prince's indisposition, and that his response to treatment was too slow to make it possible that he be married on the required date, I remembered the fact again. I perceived that here lay a way out. At first, as you may appreciate, I rejected the notion as absurd. Then I applied myself to study it minutely, and saw that it was possible. Incredible, perhaps, but still possible. I planned it step by step, and saw that with proper care and preparation it was more than that—it was virtually certain of success. My decision taken, I set in motion the events that have brought you here to Schönhausen."

At last I found my tongue. "You're mad!" I shouted, "You're a raving lunatic! You'd substitute *me* . . . for *him* . . . to . . . to . . . pose . . . to attempt the maddest, most ridiculous. . . ."

"Silence!" he shouted, and came round the table, his face working with passion. "Do you suppose I have entered on this matter lightly? That I have not examined it, time and time again, before I determined on it? Do you imagine I designed the plan that has brought you here, and spent the time and money I have used, without being certain that I could complete the whole business?" He bent down, his face close to mine, and spoke rapidly and quietly. "Consider, if you have the intelligence, the minute thoroughness of the stratagem that has brought you this far. Planned, my English numbskull, with a care and precision that your slow wits cannot conceive."

"Genius," says Kraftstein, jerking his head like a doll.

"Only one thing was a matter of chance—your presence in England. It was the prerequisite, and by good fortune it was there. The rest—organisation." Bismarck took a breath and straightened up. "And as we have begun, so we will proceed."

Well, I saw one thing: he *was* mad; they all were. And, by God, if they thought they were dragging me into their lunacy, they had got the wrong man.

"I won't touch it," says I, "and that's flat. D'you think I'm as big a fool as you are? Good God, man, the thing's impossible; I wouldn't last five minutes as . . . a substitute for this poxed-up Danish fellow. And what then, eh?"

Bismarck considered me a moment. Then:

"Fill his glass, Kraftstein." He walked back to his seat, and stretched his legs.

"It is, perhaps, unreasonable to expect you to accept the scheme without being convinced of its soundness. Tell me, why do you suppose it might fail?"

There were about seven hundred answers to that, and I burst out with the first one that came to mind.

"I couldn't get away with it! How could I pretend to be a Danish prince?"

"Take my word for it that you could. The likeness, believe me, is astounding. No one would suspect the imposture for a moment."

"But I don't speak Danish, dammit!"

"But you have a gift for languages, remember? In the few weeks available, you can be given a smattering. No more than that will be necessary, for His Highness speaks German indifferently well, as you will before you take his place. You have a tolerable fluency as it is."

"But . . . but . . . well, how the devil do you propose that I should take his place? Go to Denmark, I suppose, and present suitable references! Balderdash!"

"You need not go to Denmark. I have been in constant communication with Prince Carl Gustaf. Naturally, he does not know of our plan, but he does have great faith in me. One of the ministers I mentioned is in my employ. Through him, all has been arranged. The Prince will set out from Denmark when the time comes with his retinue; he has been led to believe that I have found a way out of his difficulties. He is rather a simple fellow, although amiable, and supposes that I can arrange matters. In that belief he will come to Holstein, en route to Strackenz, and in Holstein the substitution will take place. The mechanics you may leave to me."

It was like listening to some grotesque fairy-tale. The cool, precise way in which he told it was staggering.

"But . . . but this retinue—his people, I mean. . . ."

"The minister who is my agent will accompany the Prince. His name is Detchard. With him at your side, you need have no fears. And *no one will suspect you*: why should they?"

"Because I'll give myself away in a hundred things, man! My voice, my actions—God knows what!"

"That is not so," said Bismarck. "I tell you, I know the Prince, his voice, his mannerisms—all of it. And I tell you that if you shave your head and upper lip, your own mothers would not know you apart."

"It's true," says Rudi, from the fireplace. "You aren't just alike: you're the same man. If you learn a few of his habits—gestures, that sort of thing—it can't fail."

"But I'm not an actor! How can I—"

"You wandered in Afghanistan disguised as a native, did you not?" says Bismarck. "I know as much about you as you do yourself, you see. If you can do that, you can easily do this." He leaned forward again. "All this has been thought of. If you were not a man of action, of proved resource and courage, of *geist und geschicklichkeit*, wit and aptitude, I would not have entertained this scheme for a moment. It is because you *have* all these things, and have proved them, that you are here now."

Well, that was all *he* knew. God help him, he believed the newspapers, and my huge, overblown reputation—he thought I was the daredevil Flash Harry of popular report, the Hero of Jallalabad, and all that tommy-rot. And there was no hope that I could persuade him otherwise.

"But my God!" says I, appalled. "What you are proposing is that I should go to Strackenz and *marry* this damned woman! I mean—I'm married already!"

"You are a Protestant. This will be a Roman ceremony. It will be in no way binding on you, morally or in fact."

"Who cares about that? What I mean is—I'd have to *live* with her, as King of Strackenz, or whatever it is. How could I? What about the real Prince Carl?"

"He will be kept close under lock and key, in a convenient place in Mecklenburg. He will there recover from his illness. And in due course I will explain matters to him—the full truth. I will point out to him that he has no choice but to continue with the remainder of my plan."

"And what's that, in God's name?"

"When he has recovered—in perhaps a month or two after your marriage—you will go hunting from a certain lodge. You will become separated from your companions. They will find you, eventually, or rather they will find the real Prince. He will have fallen from his horse, and taken a slight graze on the head. It will necessitate some day's rest and recovery. Thereafter he will return to Strackenz City and his bride. If she notices any difference in him, it will be attributed to the effect of his head wound. But it will hardly cause her to suspect that he is not the man she married. I expect that they will live and rule long and happily together."

"And what the hell happens to me?"

"You, my dear sir, will by then be far over the frontiers of Germany—with ten thousand pounds sterling in your pocket." Bismarck permitted himself a smile. "We do not ask you to work for nothing, you see. Your silence will be assured—for if you decided to tell your incredible tale, who would believe it? But why should you? You will have come out of the affair most profitably."

Aye, profitably for you, thinks I, with a bullet in the back of my head or a knife between my ribs. It was as clear as day that at the end of the affair I'd be a heap safer dead than alive, from their point of view. I looked from Bismarck to the cheerfully smiling Rudi, who had perched himself on the table edge; to Kraftstein, frowning at me from his massive height; to de Gautet, with his snake's eyes—I even glanced round at Bersonin, glowering in silence by the door. By gum, I've seen some pretty sets of villains in my time, but I believe that if I were ever asked to recruit a band of cut-throats for some nefarious enterprise, Bismarck's beauties would head my list.

"I see what is in your mind," says Bismarck. He rose, taking out his cigar case, and presented me with a weed, which he lit for me from a candle. "You do not trust me. You believe that afterwards I should have you destroyed, nicht wahr? That I would break my promise."

"Oh, well," says I, "the thought hadn't occurred, but now that you mention it. . . ."

"My dear Mr Flashman," says he, "credit me with some intelligence. I have only to put myself in your shoes—as I'm sure you have just been putting yourself in mine. I should be highly suspicious, if I were you. I should require to be convinced that all was—above board, is it not?"

I said nothing, and he took a turn round the table.

"Ask yourself," says he, "what I have to gain by playing you false. Security? Hardly so, since you will be in no case, living, to do harm to us. As I've said, no one would believe your story, which indeed would incriminate you if you were foolish enough to tell it. What else? Killing you would present . . . problems. You are not a child, and disposing of you might well cause some unforeseen complication in my plans."

"We're honest with you, you see," says Rudi, and Kraftstein nodded vigorously. De Gautet tried to smile reassuringly, like a contrite wolf.

"And ten thousand pounds, you may believe me, is neither here nor there," went on Bismarck. "It is a cheap price to pay for laying the foundation of the new Germany—and that is what is at stake here. You may think we are day-dreaming, that we are foolish visionaries—you may even think us villains. I do not care. It does not matter. It is a great thing that we are going to do, and you are only a tiny pawn in it—but, like all tiny pawns, vital. I need you, and I am willing to pay for what I need." He drew himself up, virile, commanding, and full of mastery. "You seek guarantees of my good faith. I have tried to show you that it is in my interest, and Germany's, to keep faith. To this I add my word as a *junker*, a soldier, and a gentleman: I swear on my honour that what I have promised I shall fulfil, and that when you have concluded your part in this scheme you shall have safe-conduct out of Germany, with your reward, and that no harm shall come to you."

He swung about on his heel and went back to his chair; the others sat dead still. And then, after just the right interval had elapsed, he added:

"If you wish, I can swear it on the Bible. For my own part, I believe that a man who will tell a lie will swear one also. I do neither. But I am at your disposal."

It was very prettily said. For a moment he almost had me believing him. But I'd moved in just as seedy company as friend Bismarck, and was up to all the dodges.

"I don't care about Bible oaths," says I. "And, anyway, I'm not sure that I like your little plot. I'm no pauper, you know—"

which was a damned lie, but there—"and I'm not sweatin' to earn your ten thousand. It's dishonest, it's deceitful, and it's downright dangerous. If there was a slip, it would cost me my head—"

"And ours, remember," says de Gautet. "You would be in a position to betray us, if you were taken."

"Thanks very much," says I. "That would be a great consolation. But, d'you know, I don't think I care for the whole thing. I'm all for a quiet life, and—"

"Even in a Bavarian prison," says young Rudi sweetly, "serving ten years as a ravisher?"

"That cock won't fight," says I. "Even suppose you took me back to Munich now, how would you explain my absence between the supposed crime and my arrest? It might not be so easy."

That made them think, and then Bismarck chimed in.

"This is to waste time. Whatever pressures were used on you initially, the point is that you are here, now, and I need hardly tell you what will happen if you refuse my offer. We are very lonely here. None saw you come; none would ever see you go. Am I plain? You have no choice, in fact, but to do as I require, and collect the fee which, I promise, will be paid."

So there we were; the good old naked threat. They could slit my throat as neat as ninepence if they chose, and none the wiser. I was in a most hellish fix, and my innards were churning horribly. But there was no way out—and they *might* be honest at the end of the day. By God, I could use ten thou. But I couldn't believe they would come up to scratch (I wouldn't have, in Bismarck's place, once I'd got what I wanted). I didn't even dare think of the risks of their hare-brained impersonation scheme, but on the other hand I couldn't contemplate the alternative if I refused. On the one side, a lunatic adventure fraught with frightful danger, and possibly a handsome reward; on the other side—death, no doubt at the bare hands of Herr Kraftstein.

"Tell you what, Bismarck," says I. "Make it fifteen thousand."

He stared at me coldly. "That is too much. The reward is ten thousand, and cannot be increased."

I tried to look glum, but this had cheered me up. If he was intending to play me false in the end, he wouldn't have hesitated to raise the stakes; the fact that he didn't suggested he might be going to level after all.

"You're no pauper, you know," chuckled Rudi, damn him.

I sat like a man undecided, and then I cried:

"I'll do it, then."

"Good man!" cries Rudi, and clapped me on the back. "I swear you're one after my own heart!"

De Gautet shook my hand, and announced that they were damned lucky to have such a resolute, resourceful, cool hand in the business with them; Kraftstein brought me another glass of brandy and pledged me; even Bersonin deserted his post at the door and joined in the toast. Bismarck, however, said no more than "Very good. We will begin our further preparations to-morrow," and then took himself off, leaving me with the four jacks in the pack. They were all affability now; we were comrades in fortune, and jolly good fellows, and they did their best to get me gloriously fuddled. I didn't resist; I was shaking with the strain and in need of all the fortifying liquor I could get. But through all their noisy bonhomie and back-slapping one thought kept pounding in my brain; oh, Jesus, in the soup again; how in God's name shall I get out this time?

*   *   *

You can guess how much sleep I had that first night at Schönhausen. Well liquored as I was when Bersonin and Kraftstein helped me to bed and pulled my boots off, my mind was all too clear; I lay there, fully clothed, listening to the wind whining round the turrets, and watching the candle shadows flickering on the high ceiling, and my heart was pumping as though I had run a race. The room was dank as a tomb, but the sweat fairly ran off me. How the devil had it all happened? And what the devil was I to do? I actually wept as I damned the folly that had ever made me come to Germany. I could have been safe at home, pleasuring myself groggy with Elspeth and sponging off her skinflint father, facing nothing worse than the prospect of bear-leading her family in Society, and here I was imprisoned in a lonely castle with five dangerous lunatics bent on dragooning me into a hare-brained adventure that was certain to put my head in a noose. And if I resisted, or tried to escape, they would wipe me out of existence as readily as they would swat a fly.

However, as usual, once I had cursed and blubbered myself

empty, my mind started searching for some ray of comfort—anything to cling to, for if you are coward enough your vainest hopes can be magnified beyond all reason. Six weeks, Bismarck had said, before this impossible wedding—say five weeks or a month at least before my substitution for Carl Gustaf had to take place. Surely much could happen in that time. Clever and wary as they were, Bismarck's gang couldn't watch me all the time—in four weeks there must be a moment when such a practised absconder as myself could cut and run for it. A horse, that was all I needed, and a look at the sun or the stars, and I was confident that my terror could outstrip Bismarck's vengeance. God knew how far away the frontier was, but I was willing to wager my neck that I could reach it faster than any rider living. My neck, of course, was exactly what I would be wagering.

With these jolly musings I passed the night, imagining a score of madcap means of escape—and as many nightmares in which Bismarck caught me in the act. It was all a waste of time, of course; within me I knew that anyone who could plot as subtly as he had done wasn't going to give me the ghost of a hope of escaping. And I had a shrewd suspicion that if a chance did arise, I'd be too funky to take it. These fellows would stop at nothing.

They proved it, too, on my first morning at Schönhausen.

The great oaf Kraftstein summoned me at dawn, and I was pulling on my boots when Rudi strode in, very fresh and whistling cheerfully, rot him.

"And did your highness sleep well?" says he. "I trust your highness is sufficiently rested after your journey."

I told him sourly that I wasn't in a mood for his comedy.

"Oh, no comedy at all," says he. "High drama, and unless you want it to develop into tragedy you'll act as you've never acted before. From this moment you are His Highness Prince Carl Gustaf, blood royal and Lord's anointed. Do you follow me? You speak German, and nothing else—your Danish we'll take care of presently—and you will comport yourself as a member of the Danish ruling house."

"Talk sense," I growled. "I don't know how."

"No, but we're going to teach you—your highness," says he, and for once his eyes had no laughter in them. "So. The first thing is to make you look the part. All right, Kraftstein."

And then and there, despite my protests, Kraftstein sat me in a chair and set to work, first cropping my hair and whiskers, and then soaping and shaving my skull. It was a long and unpleasant process, and when it was done and I looked in the glass I could have burst into tears. The ghastly creature with his great, gleaming dome of a skull was a horrid parody of me—my face, surmounted by a naked convict head.

"Damn you!" I burst out. "Damn you! You've ruined me!"

I expected them to mock me, of course, but neither twitched so much as a muscle.

"Your highness will be under the necessity of shaving your head daily," murmured Rudi. "Kraftstein will instruct you. Now, may I suggest that your highness wears uniform today?"

They had that, too; rather a trim rig, I had to admit, in bottle green, which fitted me perfectly and would have given me a fine dashing air if it hadn't been for that bald monstrosity above the collar.

"Admirable," says Rudi, standing back from me. "May I compliment your highness on your appearance?"

"Drop that, blast you!" I snarled at him. "If I have to play your damned game, you'll spare me your infernal nonsense until it starts, at least. I'm your prisoner, ain't I? Isn't that enough for you?"

He waited a moment, and then says, in exactly the same tone:

"May I compliment your highness on your appearance?"

I stood glaring at him, on the point of swinging my fist into his impassive face, but he just stared me down, and I found myself saying:

"All right. If you must—all right."

"Very good, your highness," says he gravely. "May I respectfully suggest that we go down to breakfast. I find that Schönhausen gives one a rare appetite—the country air, of course. Will you lead on, Kraftstein?"

I wasn't hungry, but Rudi attacked his food in good spirits, and chattered away throughout the meal. He treated me with a nice blend of familiarity and respect, and you would never have guessed if you had seen us that it was all a sham. He was a splendid actor, and although it would have made me feel a complete fool if I hadn't been too miserable to mind, I began to realise even then that there was method in what he was doing. Kraftstein just put his head down and gorged, but on the one occasion he addressed me, he too called me "highness".

Bismarck came in just as we were finishing, and he for one wasn't playing charades. He stopped dead on the threshold, though, at sight of me, and then came into the room slowly, studying my face, walking round me, and examining me carefully for a minute or more. Finally he says:

"The likeness is astounding. In effect, he is Carl Gustaf."

"So your friends have been trying to convince me," I muttered.

"Excellent. It is not quite perfect, though. Two small details remain."

"What's that?" says Rudi.

"The scars. One either side, the left immediately above the ear, the one on the right an inch lower and running slightly downward—so." And he drew his finger across my shaven skin; the touch sent mice scampering down my spine.

"By heaven, you're right," says Rudi. "I'd forgotten. How do we give him those?"

My innards turned to water as Bismarck surveyed me with his icy smile.

"Surgery? It is possible. I've no doubt Kraftstein here could employ his razor most artistically...."

"You're not cutting my bloody head, you bastard!" I shouted, and tried to struggle out of my chair, but Kraftstein seized me with his enormous hands and thrust me back. I yelled and struggled, and he clamped his paw across my jaws and squeezed until the pain made me subside, terrified.

"But there is a better way," says Bismarck. "They can be administered in the proper form—with the schlager. De Gautet can do it without difficulty." He added, with a nasty look at me: "And it will satisfy a small debt that I owe to our friend here."

"Aye," says Rudi doubtfully, "but can he do it exactly—they must be in precisely the right places, mustn't they? No use giving him a wound where Carl Gustaf doesn't have one.".

"I have every confidence in de Gautet," says Bismarck. "With a sabre he can split a fly on the wing."

I was listening to them appalled; these two monsters calmly discussing the best means of giving me a slashed head. If there is one thing I can't endure, it is pain, and the thought of cold steel slicing into my skull nearly made me swoon. As soon as Kraftstein took his hand away I was yammering at them; Bismarck listened scornfully for a few seconds, and then says:

"Silence him, Kraftstein."

The giant seized the nape of my neck, and a fearful pain shot down my back and across my shoulders. He must have fixed on some nerve, and I screamed and writhed in his grasp.

"He can go on doing that until you die," says Bismarck. "Now get up, and stop behaving like an old woman. It won't kill you to have a couple of cuts from a *schlager*. Every German youth is proud to take them; a little drink from the 'soup-plate of honour' will do you good."

"For God's sake!" I burst out. "Look, I've agreed to do what you want, but this is abominable! I won't—"

"You will," says Bismarck. "Prince Carl Gustaf has two duelling scars, received while he was a student at Heidelberg. There is no question of your impersonating him without them. I am sure," he went on, smiling unpleasantly, "that de Gautet will administer them as painlessly as possible. And if they cause you some trifling smart, you may console yourself that they have been paid for in advance, by your amiable friend Mr Gully. You recall the occasion?"

I recalled it all right, and it was no consolation at all. So now the swine was going to get his own back, and if I resisted I'd have Kraftstein pulling pieces out of me with his bare hands for my pains. There was nothing for it but to submit, and so I allowed myself to be led down to a big bare room off the courtyard where there were fencing masks and foils hung on the walls, and chalk lines on the floor, like a fencing school.

"Our gymnasium," says Bismarck. "You will spend some time here during your preparation—you are heavier than Carl Gustaf by a pound or two, I should judge. Perhaps we can relieve you of some of it this morning."

Coming from a man with sausages of fat beginning to bulge over his collar, this was pretty cool, but I was too busy gulping down my fear to mind. Presently de Gautet arrived, looking even more snake-like than he had the previous night, and when Bismarck explained what was to do, you could see the rascal's mouth start to water.

"You must be exact to the inch," says Bismarck. "Look here." He stood in front of me, drawing from his pocket the little miniature he had shown me last night, glancing at it and then at me and frowning. "You see how they run—so and so. Now, the crayon." And to my horror he took a fat black pencil which Kraftstein held out, and with great care began to mark on the skin of my head the places where the cuts were to go.

It was the final obscene touch that brought the bile up into my mouth, so that I almost spewed at him. He stood there, his face close to mine, hissing gently through his teeth and sketching away on my crawling flesh as though it had been a blackboard. I shuddered away, and he growled at me to be still. I was paralysed—I don't think that of all the beastly things that man ever did, or all the terror he caused me, that there was anything as loathsome as that casual marking of my skin for de Gautet to cut at. There is only one word for it—it was German. And if you don't understand what I mean, thank God for it.

At last he was done, and Kraftstein could arm us for the *schlager* play. It seemed horrible to me at the time, but looking back from the safety of old age I can see that it is more childish than anything else. For all their pride in taking scars to impress everyone with how manly they are, the Germans are damned careful not to cause themselves any serious damage. Kraftstein fitted big metal caps onto the crowns of our heads; they were equipped with spectacles of iron in front to protect the eyes and nose, and there were heavy padded stocks to go round our necks. Then there was a quilted body armour to buckle round our middles, with flaps to cover the thighs, and a padded bandage to wrap round the right arm from wrist to shoulder. By the time we were fully equipped I felt like Pantaloon with dropsy; it was so ridiculous that I almost forgot to be afraid.

Even when the *schlager* was put into my hand it looked such a ludicrous weapon that I couldn't take it seriously. It was more than a yard long, with a triangular blade, and had a huge metal bowl at the hilt to protect the hand: it must have been about a foot across.[20]

"The soup-plate of honour," says Bismarck. "You have used a sabre, I suppose?"

"Ask your man about that when we've finished," says I, blustering with a confidence I didn't feel: de Gautet was swishing his *schlager* in a frighteningly professional way.

"Very good," says Bismarck. "You will observe that your opponent's head is covered, as is yours, at all points except for the cheeks and lower temples. These are your targets—and his. I may tell you that, with de Gautet, you are as likely to hit those targets as I was to strike Mr Gully. You may cut, but not thrust. Do you understand? I shall call you to begin and to desist."

He stepped back, and I found myself facing de Gautet across the chalked floor; Rudi and Kraftstein had taken their places along the walls, but Bismarck stayed within a couple of yards of us. armed with a *schlager* to strike up our blades if need be.

De Gautet advanced, saluting with a flourish; in his padding he looked like some kind of sausage-doll, but his eyes were bright and nasty through the spectacles. I didn't salute, but came on guard sabre-fashion, right hand up above my head and blade slanting down before my face.

"Salute!" snaps Bismarck.

"Pish to you!" says I, guessing that it would offend his fine Teutonic spirit to ignore the formalities. I was getting cocky, you see, because all this paraphernalia had convinced me that the business wasn't really serious at all. I'm not a sabre expert—a strong swordsman, rather than a good one, was how the master-at-arms in the 11th Hussars had described me— and if I have to use one I'd rather it wasn't in single combat, but in a mêlée, where you can hang about on the outskirts, roaring your heart out and waiting for an opponent with his back turned. However, it seemed to me now that I ought to be able to guard the unprotected areas that de Gautet would be cutting at.

He came on guard, the blades grated between us, and then he twitched his wrist, quick as light, right and left, aiming deft little cuts at the sides of my head. But Flashy's nobody's fool; I turned my wrist with his, and caught the cuts on my own blade. He cut again, and the blade rang on my cap, but I broke ground and let go a regular roundhouse slash at him, like a dragoon full of drink. With the *schlager*, I learned later, you are supposed to employ only wrist cuts, but I was just an ignorant foreigner. My sweep, if it had landed, would have loosed Mr de Gautet's guts all over the floor, but he was quick and turned it with the forte of his blade.

He came in again, on guard, his narrow eyes on mine, and the blades rasped together. He feinted and cut hard, but I was there again, and as we strained against each other I sneered at him over the crossed blades and exerted all my strength to bear down his guard. I felt his blade giving before mine, and then it whirled like lightning and it was as though a red-hot iron had been laid against my right temple. The pain and shock of it sent me staggering back, I dropped my *schlager* and grabbed at my face, and as Bismarck jumped between us I saw the most unpleasant sight I know, which is my own blood; it coursed down my cheek and on to my hand, and I howled and dabbed at the wound to try to staunch it.

"Halt!" cries Bismarck, and strode over to inspect my wound— not because he gave a tuppenny damn about me, but to see if it was in the right place. He seized my head and peered. "To an inch!" he exclaimed, and tipped his hand triumphantly to de Gautet, who smirked and bowed.

"Fahren sie fort!" cries Bismarck, stepping back, and signing to me to pick up my *schlager*. Shaking with pain and rage, and with the blood feeling as though it were streaming out of me, I told him what he could do with it; I wasn't going to stand up to be cut to bits for his amusement.

He went red with fury. "Pick it up," he rasped, "or I'll have Kraftstein hold you down and we'll set the other scar on you with a rusty saw!"

"It's not fair!" I shouted. "I think my skull's fractured!"

He damned me for a coward, snatched up the *schlager*, and thrust it into my hand. And in case worse should happen, I squared up to de Gautet again, resolving to take the other cut as quickly as possible, and then to settle the account in my own way, if I could.

He shuffled in, full of bounce, cutting smartly right and left. I parried them, tried a quick cut of my own, and then flicked up my point to leave my left side unguarded. Instinctively he slashed at the gap, and I took it with my eyes shut and teeth gritted against the pain. My God, but it hurt, and I couldn't repress a shriek; I reeled, but kept a tight grip on my *schlager*, and as de Gautet stepped back, satisfied with his butchery, and glanced towards Bismarck, I forced myself into a sudden lunge that sent my point through his lousy body.

The next thing I knew I had been hurled to the floor, and as I lay there, blinded with my own blood, all hell broke loose. Someone fetched me a tremendous kick in the ribs, I heard Rudi shouting and de Gautet groaning—delightful sound—and then I must have fainted, for when I opened my eyes I was sprawled on one of the benches, with Kraftstein sponging the blood from my face.

My first thought was: they'll settle my hash now, for certain, and then I realised that Bismarck and de Gautet had vanished, and only young Rudi was left, grinning down at me.

"I couldn't have done better myself," says he. "Not much, anyhow. Our friend de Gautet won't be quite so cock-a-hoop another time. Not that you've damaged him much—you barely nicked his side—but he'll ache for a day or two. So will you, of course. Let's have a look at your honourable scars."

My head was aching abominably, but when he and Kraftstein had examined it, they pronounced it satisfactory—from their point of view. De Gautet had laid his cuts exactly, and provided the wounds were left open they would quickly heal into excellent scars, Kraftstein assured me.

"Give you a most distinguished appearance," says Rudi. "All the little Prussian girls will be fluttering for you."

I was too sick and shocked even to curse at him. The pain seemed to be searing into my brain, and I was half-swooning as Kraftstein bandaged my skull and the pair of them supported me upstairs and laid me down on my bed. The last thing I heard before I slipped into unconsciousness was Rudi saying that it would be best if my highness rested for a while, and I remember thinking it odd that he had slipped out of his play-actor's role for a while and then back into it.

That was my only experience of *schlager*-play, and it was one too many. But it taught me something, and that was a fearful respect for Otto Bismarck and his ruffians. If they were capable of that kind of cold-blooded mutilation then there was nothing they wouldn't do; from that moment I put all thought of trying to escape from Schönhausen out of my mind. I hadn't the game for it.

As to the scars, they healed quickly under Kraftstein's care. I'll carry them to my grave, one close to my right ear, the other slightly higher, but just visible now that my hair is thinner. Neither is disfiguring, fortunately; indeed, as Rudi observed, there is something quite dashing-romantic about them. They've been worth a couple of campaigns, I often think, in giving people the wrong impression of my character.

They hurt most damnably for a couple of days, though, during which I kept to my room. That was all the convalescence they would allow me, for they were in a great sweat to begin what Rudi was pleased to call my "princely education".

This consisted of some of the hardest brain work I've ever had in my life. For a solid month, every waking hour, I lived, talked, walked, ate and drank Prince Carl Gustaf until I could have screamed at the thought of him—and sometimes did. At its worst it amounted to gruelling mental torture, but in recalling it now I have to admit that it was brilliantly done. I wouldn't have believed it possible, but the three of them—Rudi, Kraftstein, and Bersonin—came as close as one humanly could to turning me into another person.

They did it, subtly and persistently, by pretending from the first that I was Carl Gustaf, and spending hour after hour reminding me about myself. I suppose to approach the thing in any other way would have been useless, for it would have been constant admission of the imposture, and what an idiot, hare-brained scheme it was. They took me through that Danish bastard's life a hundred times, from the cradle upwards, until I swear I must have known more about him than he did himself. His childhood ailments, his relatives, his ancestors, his tutors, his homes, his playmates, his education, his likes, his dislikes, his habits—there wasn't a call of nature that he had answered in twenty years that I wasn't letter-perfect in by the time they had done. Hour after hour, day after day, they had me sitting at that long table while they poured fact after fact into me—what food he liked, what pets he had had, what he read, what colour his sister's eyes were, what nursery name his governess had called him (Tutti, of all things), how long he had lived at Heidelberg, what his musical tastes were

("Fra Diavolo", by one Auber, had apparently impressed him, and he was forever whistling an air from it; it says something for their teaching that I've whistled it off and on for fifty years now.) Where they had got all their information, God only knows, but they had two huge folders of papers and drawings which seemed to contain everything that he had ever done and all that was known about him. I couldn't tell you my own grandmother's Christian name, but God help me I know that Carl Gustaf's great-uncle's mastiff was called Ragnar, and he lived to be twenty-three.

"And what was your highness's favourite game when you were little?" Rudi would ask.

"Playing at sailors," I would reply.

"What was the English ship you boasted to your mother you had captured at Copenhagen?"

"The *Agamemnon*."

"How did you come to capture it?"

"How the blazes do I know? I was only three, wasn't I? I can't remember."

"You have been told. It was stuck in a mudbank. In your infant re-enactment you covered yourself in mud in a garden pond, don't you remember?"

That was the kind of thing I had to know, and when I protested that no one was ever likely to ask me what games I had played when I was little, they wouldn't argue, but would pass patiently on—to remind me of the fever I had had when I was fourteen, or the time I broke my arm falling from an apple tree.

All our talk was conducted in German, at which I made capital progress—indeed, Rudi's one fear was that I might be too proficient, for Carl Gustaf apparently didn't speak it too well, for all his Heidelberg education. Bersonin, who despite his taciturnity was a patient teacher, instructed me in Danish, but possibly because he himself only spoke it at second hand, I didn't take to it easily. I never learned to think in it, which is unusual for me, and I found it ugly and dull, with its long vowels that make you sound as though you had wind.

But the real curse of my days was being instructed in the actual impersonation. We had the tremendous advantage, as I was to see for myself later, that Carl Gustaf and I were real *doppelgängers*, as like as two tits. Even our voices were the same, but he had mannerisms and tricks of speech that I had to learn, and the only way was for me to try attitudes and phrases over and over, in different styles, until Rudi would snap his fingers and exclaim: "Er ist es selbst! Now say it again, and yet again."

For example, it seemed that if you asked Carl Gustaf a question to which the normal answer would have been "yes" or "of course", he, instead of contenting himself with "ja", would often say "sicher", which means "positively, certainly", and he would say it with a jaunty air, and a little stab of his right fore-finger. Again, in listening to people, he would look past them, giving tiny occasional nods of his head and making almost inaudible grunts of agreement. Lots of people do this, but I don't happen to be one of them, so I had to practise until I found myself doing it almost without thinking.

And he had a quick, brisk laugh, showing his teeth—I worked at that until my throat smarted and my jaws ached. But this was easy compared with the contortions I went through in trying to mimic his trick of raising one eyebrow by itself; I came near to setting up a permanent twitch in one cheek, and eventually they decided to let it be, and hope that no one noticed that my eyebrows perversely worked together.

Fortunately, Carl Gustaf was a cheerful, easy-going chap, much as I am myself, but I had to work hard to try to correct the sulky look I get when I'm out of sorts, and my habit of glowering and sticking out my lower lip. This ray of Danish sunshine didn't glower, apparently; when he was in the dumps he showed it with an angry frown, so of course I had to knit my brows until they ached.

How well I learned my lessons you may judge when I tell you that to this day I have his trick of rubbing one hand across the back of the other (when thinking deeply), and that I entirely lost my own habit of scratching my backside (when puzzled). Royalty —I have Bersonin's solemn word for it—never claw at their arses to assist thought.

Now the result of all this, day after day, and of the unbroken pretence that my captors kept up, was remarkable and sometimes even frightening. I suppose I'm a good actor, to begin with—after all, when you've been shamming all your life, as I have, it must come pretty natural—but there were times when I forgot that I was acting at all, and began to half-believe that I was Carl Gustaf. I might be practising before the long cheval glass, with Rudi and Bersonin watching and criticising, and I would see this bald-headed young fellow in the green hussar rig flashing his smile and stabbing his forefinger, and think to myself, "Aye, that's me" —and then my mind would try to recapture the picture of the dark, damn-you-me-lad-looking fellow with the curly hair and whiskers—and I would discover that I couldn't do it. That was when I found it frightening—when I had forgotten what my old self looked like.

Mind you, my character didn't change; these flashes were only momentary. But I certainly began to believe that we would carry off the imposture, and the terror that I had originally felt about it subsided to a mere craven apprehension of what the end of it all might be—when payday came and the real Carl Gustaf had come back into his own.

However, that was in the future, and in the meantime I was floating with the tide, as is my habit, and letting my puppet-handlers think that butter wouldn't melt in my mouth. For their part, they seemed to be delighted with my progress, and one day, about three weeks after I had come to Schönhausen, on an evening when Bismarck joined the rest of us at supper, I did something which convinced Rudi and Bersonin that the first round was won at least.

We were sitting down to table, myself at the head, as usual, and Bismarck plumped down in his chair before I did. Now I was so used by this time to being seated first that I simply stared at him, more in curiosity, I imagine, than anything else; and he, catching my glance, actually began to get to his feet. Rudi, who missed nothing, couldn't repress a chuckle and a delighted slap of his thigh.

"Right royal, Otto," says he to Bismarck. "He had you feeling like a bad-mannered little schoolboy there, I'll swear. Bravo, your highness, you'll do."

This was rather more familiarity with me than Rudi had allowed himself since my duel with de Gautet. It didn't matter to me, of course, but Bersonin was shocked, and muttered that Rudi was forgetting himself. It occurred to me then that I was not the only one who was beginning to believe in my own royalty. Anyway, I played up by remarking to Bersonin casually that the Freiherr was still at an age when impudence took precedence before dignity, and was this hock that we were to drink again tonight?

Bismarck observed all this impassively, but I felt sure he was secretly impressed by the naturalness of my princely behaviour, and even more by his own momentary reaction to it.

I should say in passing that Bismarck's appearance that night was a rare one. For days at a time I never saw him, but from casual conversation among the others I gathered that he was frequently in Berlin—he was a member of their Parliament, apparently, when he wasn't kidnapping useful Englishmen and plotting lèse majesté. I also learned that he had a wife in the capital, which surprised me; somehow I had come to think of him as brooding malevolently in his lonely castle, wishing he was Emperor of Germany. I remembered that Lola had thought he was a cold fish where women were concerned, but it seemed that this was only a pose; before his marriage, apparently, he had been saddling up with all the wenches on his estate and breeding bastards like a buck rabbit. They called him the Schönhausen Ogre in those days, but of late he had been devoting himself to politics and his new wife, Bersonin said, and taking a serious interest in his farm property. A likely tale, thinks I; his only interest in politics was to get personal power, no matter how, and to gorge himself with food, drink, and women along the way. Nasty brute.

However, as I say, we didn't see much of him, or of anyone else for that matter. They kept me pretty well confined to one wing of the house, and although there must have been servants I never saw one except the old butler. There wasn't a woman in the place, which was a dead bore, and when I suggested to Rudi that he might whistle up a wench or two to pass the evenings he just shook his head and said it was out of the question.

"Your highness must contain yourself in patience," says he. "May I respectfully remind you that your wedding is not far off?"

"Thanks very much," says I. "And may I respectfully remind you that I'm feeling randified now, and in no mood to hold myself in until my wedding to some young German cow who probably looks like a boatswain's mate."

"Your highness need have no fears on that score," says he, and he showed me a portrait of Duchess Irma of Strackenz which I must say cheered me up considerably. She looked very young, and she had one of those cold, narrow disdainful faces that you find on girls who have always had their own way, but she was a beauty, no question. Her hair was long and blonde, and her features very fine and regular; she made me think of a story I remembered from my childhood about a snow princess who had a heart of ice. Well, I could warm this one up, always assuming our enterprise got that far.

"In the meantime," says I, "what say you to some nice, hearty country girl? She could teach me some more German, you know, and I could teach her anatomy."

But he wouldn't hear of it.

So the weeks ran by, and I suppose that gradually the nightmare impossibility of my position must have begun to seem less incredible than it looks now, half a century after; whatever happens to you, however far-fetched, you get used to eventually, I've found, and when the time came to leave Schönhausen I was ready for it. I was in a fair funk, of course, but so heartily thankful to be getting out of that draughty mausoleum that even the ordeal ahead seemed endurable.

*   *   *

It must have been a week or so after the meeting with Bismarck that I've just described that I was summoned late one evening to his library. They were all there, Rudi, Bismarck, and the Three Wise Men, and I knew at once that something was up. Bismarck was still in his greatcoat, with the last snowflakes melting on its shoulders, and a little pool of water forming round each boot as he stood before the fire. He looked me over bleakly, hands behind his back, and then says:

"The scars are still too livid. Any fool can see they are recent."

This seemed an excellent reason to me for calling off the whole thing, but Kraftstein said in his ponderous way that he could attend to them; he had a salve which could disguise their pinkness and make them look like old wounds. This seemed to satisfy Bismarck, for he grunted and turned to Rudi.

"Otherwise he is ready? He can play the part? Your head depends on this, remember."

"His highness is ready to resume his duties," says Rudi.

Bismarck snorted. "His highness! He is an actor, hired to play a part. Better he should remember that, and the consequences of missing a cue—he'll be less liable to bungle it. Oh, yes, Bersonin, I know all about your theories; I prefer realities. And the reality of this, Mr Flashman, is that tomorrow you leave for Strackenz. You know what is to do, the reward of success—and the price of failure." His cold eyes played over me. "Are you dismayed?"

"Oh, no," says I. "When it's all over I intend to go back to England and take the place of Prince Albert, don't you know."

Rudi laughed, but I saw Kraftstein shake his head—no doubt he was thinking that I didn't look enough like Prince Albert to get away with it.

"Sit down," says Bismarck. "Give him a brandy, de Gautet." He came to stand at the table head, looking down at me. "Listen to me carefully. When you leave here tomorrow you will be accompanied by Freiherr von Starnberg and de Gautet. They will take you by coach to the rendezvous we have appointed—you need to know nothing more than that it is a country mansion owned by a nobleman who is to play host to Prince Carl Gustaf for one night during his journey to Strackenz. The journey to the house will take two days, but we are allowing three, for safety.

"On the appointed day Carl Gustaf and his retinue will arrive at the mansion in the afternoon. It stands in wooded country, but is easily accessible; you will be waiting for evening, and when it comes von Starnberg and de Gautet will take you into the grounds under cover of darkness. You will be admitted by a man who is one of the only three in the world, outside this room, who is in our plot. His name is Detchard, a Danish minister entirely faithful to me. He will conduct you secretly to the Prince's apartment; in the meantime von Starnberg will be effecting the . . . removal of the real Prince. Have I made myself clear so far?"

By God he had, and as I listened all my old fears came galloping back with a vengeance. The thing was obvious lunacy, and this outrageous creature, standing so straight and immaculate in his greatcoat, was a dangerous maniac.

"But . . . but, look here," I began, "suppose something goes wrong—I mean, suppose somebody comes. . . ."

He banged his fist on the table and glared at me. "Nothing will go wrong! No one will come! Righteous Lord God! Do you suppose I know nothing? Do you imagine I have not planned every detail? De Gautet! Tell him—what is the name of the serving-maid whose duty it will be to change the Prince's bed linen while he is at the house?"

"Heidi Gelber," says de Gautet.

"Starnberg—how do you reach the Prince's dressing-room from the door where Detchard will admit you?"

"Twelve paces along a passage, up the stairway to the right, left at the first landing, then ten paces along to a passage on the right. The Prince's dressing-room is the first door on the left."

"From door to door—fifty seconds," says Bismarck. "If you wish, I can tell you the precise nature of the furnishings in the Prince's chamber, and their positions in the room. For example, there is a statuette of a kneeling cupid on the overmantel. Now—are you convinced that my organisation is sound, and my information complete?"

"How do you know that some drunk footman won't come blundering along in the middle of everything?" I cried.

I thought he would hit me, but he restrained himself.

"It will not happen," he said. "Everything will fall out exactly as I have said."

There was no point in arguing, of course; I sat in despair while he went on.

"Once inside that room, you will be Prince Carl Gustaf. That is the fact of paramount importance. From that moment Flashman no longer exists—you understand? With you will be Detchard and the Prince's physician, Orsted, who is also privy to our plans. If at any moment you are in doubt, they will guide you. And when you set out next morning on your royal progress across the border into Strackenz, you will find that among the dignitaries who will greet you will be both de Gautet and Starnberg—it has been arranged that they will join your train as gentlemen of honour. So you will not lack for friends," he added grimly. "Now drink your brandy."

I gulped it down; I needed it. At the back of my mind I suppose there had still been some futile hope that I would be able to slip out of this at the last moment, but Bismarck had squashed it flat. I was going to have to go through with it, with Rudi and de Gautet hovering alongside ready, at the first false move, to put a bullet into me, I didn't doubt. Why the hell, I asked myself for the thousandth time, had I ever come to this bloody country?

"The wedding will take place on the day after your arrival in the city of Strackenz," Bismarck went on, for all the world as though he had been telling me the time of day. "You have already received some instruction in the details of the ceremony, of course. And then—all plain sailing, as your people say."

He sat down, and poured himself a glass of brandy from the decanter. He sipped at it, while I sat mute, staring at my glass. "Well, Mr Flashman; what have you to say?"

"What the hell does it matter what I say?" I burst out. "I've no choice, damn you!"

To my amazement, he actually chuckled. He stretched his legs and twirled the stem of his glass between his fingers.

"None at all," says he, grinning. "Flashman, you should be glad. You will be making history—aye, great history. Do you realise, I wonder, the magnitude of what we are doing? We are nailing a little hinge to a door, a great door which will open to reveal the destiny of a greater Germany! And you—a half-pay officer of no account, a pawn even in your own country's affairs—you are going to make it possible! Can you imagine what it means?" The man was positively beaming now, with a kind of fierce joy in his eyes. "For we are going to win! We six here, we are staking ourselves, our lives, everything—and we are going to succeed! I look at you, and I know we cannot fail. God has sent you to Germany, and I send you now to Strackenz." There was a nice little comparison there, all right. "And in Strackenz you will play such a game as has never been played before in the history of the world. And you will not fail—I know it! What a destiny! To be one of the architects of the new Fatherland!" He lifted his glass. "I salute you, and drink to our enterprise!"

Believe it or not, he actually raised my spirits a little with that. Of course, it was all humbug, designed to put some backbone into me—that was all he knew—but the man was so supremely confident it was infectious: if he really believed we could bring it off—

well, perhaps we could. The others cheered and we all drank, and Bismarck sighed and refilled his glass. I'd never seen him anything like this before; for the moment he was almost jovial, showing an entirely new side of his nature—all carefully calculated for my benefit, I imagine.

"How will we look back on this?" he mused. "When we are old, and in our country places, and the bold lads of a new day are elbowing for power in the chancelleries? I wonder." He shook his head. "I think I will wear leather breeches and allow myself to be laughed at in Stettin wool market, and sell two thalers cheaper to anyone who calls me 'baron'.[27] And you, Flashman—you will sit in your club in St James, and grow fat on port and your memories. But we will have lived, by God! We will have fought! We will have won! Is it not something to have moved great affairs, and shaped the course of time?"

No doubt I should have shared his enthusiasm, like Kraftstein, who was hanging on every word, and looking like a ruptured bullock. But all I could think to myself was, God, I wish John Gully had really set to work on you. What I said aloud was:

"Herr Bismarck, I am much moved. And now, with your permission, I intend to get as drunk as possible. Afterwards, tomorrow, I shall be at your service, since I can't do anything else. But if I'm to shape the destiny of Europe, I'll need a good skinful of liquor inside me to set me off. So will you kindly oblige me with the bottle, and a cigar, and as many dirty drinking songs as you and your friends can remember? And if this seems to you a coarse and pagan spirit in which to approach our glorious adventure for the Fatherland, well—you've made your preparations; let me now make mine."

As a result of the night's excesses, which Bismarck didn't discourage, I had a raging headache and a heaving stomach on the morning of my departure from Schönhausen. So I remember very little of it, which is no loss. For that matter my recollections of the journey north to Strackenz are hazy, too; I've travelled too far in my time to be anything but bored by it, and there was nothing to see that I recall except flat snowy fields, the occasional village, and bleak woodlands of bare black trees.

Rudi was full of spirits as usual, and de Gautet was his smooth, civil self, but I knew he wouldn't forget or forgive that *schlager*-thrust in the guts. I hadn't forgotten the two cuts I owed him, either, so we were even there. He never referred to our encounter, but now and then in the coach I would catch his dark eyes on me, and then they would slide away, looking anywhere but at me. He was one who wouldn't be sorry of the excuse to draw a bead on my back if I tried to run for it.

Following Bismarck's lead, both of them had dropped the pretence of calling me "highness"—Bersonin's "theory", as Bismarck had called it, being well enough in my training period, I suppose, but now considered unnecessary. But they lost no chance of lecturing me on such subjects as the geography of Strackenz, the ceremonial forms of its court, and the details of the wedding ceremony. I suppose I took it all in, for there was nothing else to do, but it has all gone now.

We were three days on the road, and the last afternoon of the journey took us deep into forest-country, all ghostly and silent under the snow. It was very beautiful and solemn, with never a soul to be seen along the rough track winding among the trees, until about four in the afternoon we stopped in a little clearing where a small hut stood, with thin smoke wreathing up from its chimney into the steely sky.

There were two or three brisk-looking fellows in peasant clothes to rub down the horses and usher us into the cottage—not that I took them for peasants, for I heard two of them in talk with Rudi. They were gentlemen, by German standards, but tough, active customers for all that—the kind who'll cut your throat and send back the wine at dinner afterwards.

We had a meal, Rudi and I, while de Gautet paced up and down and peered out at the darkening sky and consulted his watch and fidgeted generally until Rudi told him to leave off, and made him sit down and have a glass of wine with us. I was getting fairly twitchy myself as the hours passed, and Rudi gave me a stiff brandy to steady me.

"Three hours from now," says he, "and you'll be tucked up in a silk night-gown with C.G. embroidered on it. God! I wish I was in your shoes. How many commoners have the chance to be royalty!"

"I'll show you one who's ready to resign his crown any time," says I. The shivers were beginning to run up my spine.

"Nonsense. Give you two days, and you'll be behaving as though you'd been born to the purple. Issuing royal decrees against virginity, probably. What time is it, de Gautet?"

"We should be moving." I heard the strain in his voice.

"Heigh-ho," says Rudi, stretching; he was as cool as though he was off for an evening stroll. "Come along, then."

There was a slight altercation just before setting out when de Gautet, officiously helping me into my cloak, discovered my pistols in the pockets. I'd had them concealed in a pair of boots in my baggage at Schönhausen, and was determined that they were going with me. Rudi shook his head.

"Royalty don't carry side-arms, except for ceremony."

"I do," says I. "Either they go with me, or I don't go at all."

"What good d'you suppose they'll be, man?"

"None, I hope. But if the worst happens they'll perhaps buy me a little elbow-room."

De Gautet was in a sweat to be off, so in the end Rudi cursed and grinned and let me keep them. He knew I wouldn't be fool enough to make a bolt for it now.

With de Gautet leading, Rudi and I behind, and two of the others in the rear, we struck out through the trees, plodding ankle-deep through the snow. It was still as death all round, and hellish dark, but de Gautet led on unerringly for perhaps quarter of an hour, when we came to a high stone wall running across our front. There was a wicket, and then we were skirting past a thicket of high bushes which, by their regular spacing, must be in the garden of some great estate. Even in the darkness I could make out the level sweep of lawn under the snow, and then ahead of us were the blazing lights of a huge mansion, surrounded by terraces, and hedged about by avenues of clipped bushes.

De Gautet strode noiselessly up one of these, with us hard on his heels. There were stone steps rising to a wing of the house that seemed to be in darkness, and then we were clustered round a small doorway under a great stone lintel, and Rudi was softly whistling (of all things) "Marlbrough s'en va-t'en guerre". For a few seconds we waited, breathing hoarsely like schoolboys who have robbed an orchard, and then the door opened.

"Detchard?"

De Gautet went in, and we followed. There was a man in a frock-coat in the dimly-lit passage; he closed the door quickly behind us—the other two were still outside somewhere—and motioned us to silence. He was a tall, distinguished old file with a beaky nose and heavy lower lip; he had grey hair and a beard like a muffler round his jaw-line. He glanced keenly at me, muttered "Donner!", and turned to Rudi.

"A complication. His highness has retired early. He is already in his apartments."

Aha, thinks I, clever little Bismarck's bandobast[28] didn't allow for this; oh, Jesus, we're done for. . . .

"No matter," says Rudi easily. "He has three rooms; he can't be in all of them at once."

This was gibberish to me, but it seemed to reassure Detchard. Without another word he led us along the passage, up a stair, into a well-lighted and carpeted corridor, and round a corner to a large double-door. He paused, listening, cautiously turned the handle, and peered in. A moment later we were all inside.

Detchard stood for a moment, and I could hear my heart thumping like a paddle-wheel. The sound of voices came softly through an adjoining door from the next room.

"His highness is in his bed-chamber," whispers Detchard.

Rudi nodded. "Strip," says he to me, and de Gautet bundled up my gear as I tore it off. He knotted it all in my cloak—I had just sense enough to remember my pistols, and thrust them hurriedly under a cushion—and then I was standing there, mother-naked, while Detchard listened with his ear to the panels of the communicating door.

"Lucky little Duchess Irma," murmurs Rudi, and I saw him grinning at me. "Let's hope the real prince is as royally endowed." He tipped me a mock salute, very debonair. "Bonne chance, your highness. Ready, de Gautet?"

Together they went to the communicating door, Rudi nodded, and in a moment they had opened it and slipped through, with Detchard behind them. There was a second in which the murmur of voices sounded louder, and then the door closed, and I was left, stark in a royal dressing-room in a German mansion, all alone and palpitating. For a moment there wasn't a sound, and then something tumbled next door. Minutes passed, a door was shut somewhere, there was a muttering of voices in the corridor that sent me scampering behind the curtains, and then silence. Several minutes passed, and my teeth began to chatter with cold and apprehension. At last I peeped out, to see if there wasn't a gown or something to wrap up in: there was plenty of furniture in the room, the main article being an enormous decorated commode—it struck me as my usual luck that whereas most royal successions lead to a throne, mine had got me nothing so far but a thunderbox—but devil a rag of clothing beyond a couple of towels. So I wrapped up in the curtain as well as I could, and waited fearfully.

Then the door opened, and Detchard's voice said softly:

"Wo sind sie?"

I poked my head out. He was carrying a big silk dressing-gown, thank God, and I grabbed at it, shuddering.

"His highness has left the house," says he. "Everything is in train. Is all well with you?"

"Oh, splendid—except that I'm almost frozen to death. Isn't there a fire, in God's name?"

"There is a stove in the bedroom," says he, and ushered me through to a splendid apartment, thickly-carpeted, with a huge four-poster bed richly-curtained, and a fine stove with its doors thrown wide to warm the room. While I thawed out Detchard stood with his grey head cocked, considering me and toying with his seals.

"It is truly amazing," says he, at last. "I did not believe it—but you are the same man. Wonderful!"

"Well, I hope the other one's warmer than I am. Haven't you any brandy?"

He poured me a glass, very carefully, and watched me gulp it down.

"You are nervous," says he. "Naturally. However, you will have the night to accustom yourself to the—ah, novelty of your situation. His highness retired early, with a slight headache no doubt brought on by the fatigue of his journey, so you will be undisturbed. Your host, Count von Tarlenheim, has given particular instructions. You will meet him briefly tomorrow, by the way, before we set out for the border. An amiable dotard. His highness —or I should say, your highness—has been quite formal with him so far, so there will be no questions asked if you are no more forthcoming tomorrow than politeness demands."

"Thank God for that," says I. I wanted time to play myself in, so to speak, and the thought of chattering to a breakfast table was out of court altogether.

"The only people who have been close to you on the journey, apart from myself, are Dr Ostred, your physician, and young Josef, your valet. He has been in your service only a day, your old valet, Einar, having become indisposed shortly after we set out."

"Convenient," says I. "Will he live?"

"Of course. You are much concerned about him." He turned, and I leaped violently as the door opened, and a little anxious-looking chap came in.

"Ah, Ostred," says Detchard, and the little chap blinked, looked at me, at Detchard, and back at me again.

"I thought . . ." he stammered. "That is—your pardon, highness. I supposed . . . you had retired . . . that you would be in bed." He looked helplessly to Detchard, and I thought, by heaven, he thinks I'm the real man. He couldn't make out what had gone wrong. So here was a first-rate chance to put the thing to the test; if I could fool my own doctor I could fool anyone.

"I have a headache," says I, quite gently. "That doesn't mean that I have to take to my bed."

"No, no . . . of course not, highness." He licked his lips.

"Perhaps you might take his highness's pulse, doctor," says Detchard, and the little fellow came over and took my wrist as though it was made of porcelain. There were beads of sweat on his brow.

"A little swift," he muttered, and glanced at my face. He was scared and puzzled, and then he literally leaped back as though he had seen a ghost.

"He...he..." he exclaimed, pointing.

"No, Ostred," says Detchard. "He is not the prince."

"But—" the little doctor gargled speechlessly, and I couldn't help laughing. "But he is—identical! Dear Jesus! I could not believe it! I was sure, when I saw him, that something had gone amiss—that it was still the prince. My God!"

"What gave him away?" asks Detchard.

"The scars. They are new, and pink."

Detchard snapped his teeth in annoyance. "The scars, of course. I had forgotten. That might have cost us dear. However, we have the means to put it right." And he took out a flask, which I suppose Rudi had given him, and daubed at my wounds until he and the doctor were satisfied.

"There," says Detchard. "When did you last shave your head?"

"Last night."

"It will do for the moment. Ostred will attend to it again to-morrow." He pulled out his watch. "Now, it may be best if you and I, doctor, return to our hosts." For my benefit he rattled off a few more details about Tarlenheim and the arrangements for the morning. "Your valet will look in shortly, to see you to bed," he concluded. "You may sleep easily, believe me. Now that I have seen you, my doubts are at rest. I seriously question if your own father would detect the imposture. Ha! You see—I said 'your' own father." He smiled grimly. "I half believe in you myself. And so, your highness, I have the honour to bid you good-night."

They withdrew, bowing, and left me trembling—but for once it wasn't funk. I was elated—I had fooled Ostred. By God, it was going to work. I took a turn round the room, grinning to myself, drank another glass of brandy, and another, and stood beaming at myself in the mirror. Well, Prince Harry, thinks I, if only Elspeth could see you now. And old moneybags Morrison. And Lord

Godalmighty Cardigan. He'd be glad enough to have royalty back in his flea-bitten 11th Hussars. For I *was* royal, for the moment—a full-blown prince of the blood, no less, until—aye, until Bismarck's little game was played out. And then—oh, the blazes with him. I had another glass of brandy and took stock of my royal surroundings.

Sumptuous wasn't the word for them—silk sheets, lace pillow, solid silver cup and plate by the bed—with breast of chicken under a napkin, bigod, in case I felt peckish. I resisted a temptation to slip the plate into a pocket—plenty of time for lifting the lumber later. This was only a staging-post on the journey, after all; the pick of the loot would be in the palace of Strackenz. But I felt I could rough it here for the night—excellent liquor, a warm fire, cigars in a tooled leather box, even the pot under the bed was of the best china, with little fat-arsed cherubs running round it. I plumped back on the bed—it was like floating on a cloud. Well, thinks I, they may talk about cares of state, and uneasy lies the head and all that tommy-rot, but this is the life for old Flashy. You may take my word for it, next time you hear about the burdens of monarchy, that royalty do themselves damned proud. I've been one; I know.

My eye fell on an ornament on the mantel; a carved kneeling figure. A little prickle ran through me as I realised that this was the cupid Bismarck had mentioned—by jove, he knew his business, that one. Down to the last detail. I rolled off the bed and looked at it, and felt a slight glow of pleasure as I realised it wasn't a cupid after all—it was a nymph. The great Otto wasn't infallible then, after all. It was most obviously a nymph, and contemplating it I realised there was one thing missing from my princely paradise. Bronze nymphs don't compare to real ones: I hadn't had a woman since the blubbery Baroness Pechman had been so rudely plucked from my embrace—and I hadn't really been able to get to proper grips with her before Rudi had interrupted us. Fat and all as she was, the thought of her was making me feverish, and at that moment there was a soft tap at the door and a slim, very sober-looking fellow slipped in. This was obviously Josef, my valet.

I was on guard again in a moment.

"Is there anything your highness requires?" says he.

"I don't think so, Josef," says I, and gave a yawn. "Just going to bed." And then a splendid idea occurred to me. "You may send up a chambermaid to turn down the covers."

He looked surprised. "I can do that, sir."

Now, Flashy would have growled: "Damn your eyes, do as you're bloody well told." But Prince Carl Gustaf merely said: "No, send the chambermaid."

He hesitated a second, his face expressionless. Then: "Very good, your highness." He bowed and went to the door. "Goodnight, highness."

Of course, it was a dam-fool thing to do, but what with the brandy and my randy thoughts, I didn't care. Anyway, wasn't I a prince? And the real Carl Gustaf was no monk, by all accounts —and damned careless about it, too. So I waited in lustful anticipation, until there was another knock, and a girl peeped in when I called out to enter.

She was a pretty, plump little thing, curly-haired and as broad as she was long, but just the thing for me with my thoughts running on Baroness Pechman. She had a bright eye, and it occurred to me that Josef was perhaps no fool. She curtsied and tripped across to the bed, and when I sauntered over—slipping the doorbolt on the way—and stood beside her, she giggled and made a great show of smoothing out my pillow.

"All work and no play isn't good for little girls," says I, and sitting on the bed I pulled her on to my knee. She hardly resisted, only trying to blush and look demure, and when I pulled down her bodice and kissed her breasts she cooed and wriggled her body against mine. In no time we were thrashing about in first-rate style, and I was making up for weeks of enforced abstinence. She was an eager little bundle, all right, and by the time she had slipped away, leaving me to seek a well-earned rest, I was most happily played out.

I've sometimes wondered what the result of that encounter was, and if there is some sturdy peasant somewhere in Holstein called Carl who puts on airs in the belief that he can claim royal descent. If there is, he can truly be called an ignorant bastard.

*　　　*　　　*

There are ways of being drunk that have nothing to do with

alcohol. For the next few days, apart from occasional moments of panic-stricken clarity, I was thoroughly intoxicated. To be a king —well, a prince—is magnificent; to be fawned at, and deferred to, and cheered, and adulated; to have every wish granted—no, not granted, but attended to immediately by people who obviously wish they had anticipated it; to be the centre of attention, with everyone bending their backs and craning their necks and loving you to ecstasy—it is the most wonderful thing. Perhaps I'd had less of it than even ordinary folk, especially when I was younger, and so appreciated it more; anyway, while it lasted I fairly wallowed in it.

Of course, I'd had plenty of admiration when I came home from Afghanistan, but that was very different. Then they'd said: "There's the heroic Flashman, the bluff young lionheart who slaughters niggers and upholds old England's honour. Gad, look at those whiskers!" Which was splendid, but didn't suggest that I was more than human. But when you're royalty they treat you as though you're God; you begin to feel that you're of entirely different stuff from the rest of mankind; you don't walk, you float, above it all, with the mob beneath, toadying like fury.

I had my first taste of it the morning I left Tarlenheim, when I breakfasted with the Count and about forty of his crowd—goggling gentry and gushing females—before setting out. I was in excellent shape after bumping the chambermaid and having a good night's rest, and was fairly gracious to one and all—even to old Tarlenheim, who could have bored with the best of them in the St James clubs. He remarked that I looked much healthier this morning—the solicitous inquiries after my headache would have put a Royal Commission on the plague to shame—and encouraged, I suppose, by my geniality, began to tell me about what a hell of a bad harvest they'd had that year. German potatoes were in a damnable condition, it seemed.[29] However, I put up with him, and presently, after much hand-kissing and bowing, and clanking of guardsmen about the driveway, I took my royal leave of them, and we bowled off by coach for the Strackenz border.

It was a fine, bright day, with snow and frost all over the place, but warm enough for all that. My coach was a splendid machine upholstered in grey silk, excellently sprung, and with the Danish Royal arms on the panels. (I remembered that the coach Wellington had once taken me in looked like a public cab, and rattled like a wheelbarrow.) There were cuirassiers bumping along in escort— smart enough—and a great train of other coaches bringing up the rear. I lounged and had a cheroot, while Detchard assured me how well things had gone, and would continue to go—he needn't have bothered, for I was in an exalted state of confidence—and then presently we rolled through our first village, and the cheering began.

All along the road, even at isolated houses, there were smiling faces and fluttering handkerchiefs; squires and peasants, farm-girls and ploughmen, infants waving the red and white Danish colours and the curious thistle-like emblem which is the badge of Holstein,[80] labourers in their smocks staring, mounted officials saluting—the whole countryside seemed to have converged on the Strackenz road to see my royal highness pass by. I beamed and waved as we rushed past, and they hallooed and waved back all the harder. It was a glorious dream, and I was enjoying it to the full, and then Detchard reminded me drily that these were only Holsteiners, and I might save some of my royal energy for the Strackenzians.

It was at the border, of course, that the real circus began. There was a great crowd waiting, the toffs to the fore and the mob craning and hurrahing at a more respectful distance. I stepped out of the coach, at Detchard's instruction, and the cheers broke out louder than ever—the crashing three-fold bark that is the German notion of hip-hip-hip-hooray. An elderly cove with snow-white hair, thin and hobbling stiffly, came forward bowing and hand-kissing, to bid me welcome in a creaking voice.

"Marshal von Saldern, Constable of Strackenz," whispered Detchard, and I grasped the old buffer's hand while he gushed over me and insisted that this was the greatest day in Strackenz's history, and welcome, thrice welcome, highness.

In turn I assured him that no visitor to Strackenz had ever arrived more joyfully than I, and that if their welcome was any foretaste of what was to come then I was a hell of a fortunate fellow, or words to that effect. They roared and clapped at this, and then there were presentations, and I inspected a guard of honour of the Strackenz Grenadiers, and off we went again, with von Saldern in my coach, to point out to me objects of interest, like fields and trees and things—the old fellow was as jumpy as a cricket, I realised, and babbled like anything, which I accepted with royal amiability. And then he had to leave off so that I could devote myself to waving to the people who were now lining the road all the way, and in the distance there was the sound of a great throng and a tremendous bustle; far away guns began to boom in salute, and we were rolling through the suburbs of the city of Strackenz itself.

The crowds were everywhere now, massed on the pavements, waving from the windows, crouching precariously on railings, and all yelling to beat the band. There were flags and bunting and the thumping of martial music, and then a great archway loomed ahead, and the coach rolled slowly to a halt.

The hubbub died away a little, and I saw a small procession of worthies in robes and flat caps approaching the coach. Ahead was a stalwart lad carrying a cushion with something on it.

"The keys to the city," quavered von Saldern. "For your highness's gracious acceptance."

Without a thought, I opened the door and jumped down, which I gather was unexpected, but was a happy act, as it turned out. The crowds roared at the sight of me, the band began booming away, and the little burgomaster took the keys—huge heavy things on an enormous collar—and begged me to accept them as an earnest of the loyalty and love of the city.

"Your city, highness," he squeaked. "And your home!"

I knew enough to say that I was deeply sensible of the great honour done me, and to give him the keys back again. And being somewhat exalted, I felt it appropriate to slip my sword-belt over my head, present the weapon to him, and say that it would be ever-ready in the defence of Strackenzian honour and independence, or some such stuff.

I didn't know it, but that brief speech had an enormous political implication, the Danish-Strackenzians being in a great sweat about the German threat to their liberty, and the German-Strackenzians bursting to get away from Danish sovereignty. Anyway, the yell of applause that greeted it was startling, the little burgomaster went red with emotion, and taking the sword he pressed it back on me, tears in his eyes, and calling me the champion of Strackenzian freedom. I don't know which side *he* was on, but it didn't seem to matter; I believe if I'd shouted "Chairs to mend!" they'd have cheered just as loud.

I was then invited to enter the city, and it seemed a good notion to me to ride in on horseback rather than go in the coach. There was delight and confusion at this; orders were shouted, officers scampered to and fro, and then a cavalryman led forward a lovely black gelding, speed written in every line of him, and I mounted amid scenes of enthusiasm. I must have looked pretty fine, if I say it myself; they had dressed me that morning all in pale blue, with the blue sash of the Order of the Elephant over my shoulder (I've worn it in the last few years, by the way, at London functions, to the surprise and scandal of the Danish Embassy, who wondered where the deuce I'd got it. I referred them to former Chancellor Bismarck). The uniform set off my excellent stature famously, and since my disgusting bald head was covered by a plumed helmet, à la Tin-bellies, I've no doubt I looked sufficiently dashing.[81]

The band played, the cheering re-echoed, and I rode through the gateway into the city of Strackenz. Flowers were showered from the balconies, girls blew kisses, the troops lining the street struggled to hold back the press, and I waved and inclined my princely head, left and right, and smiled on my loyal subjects-to-be.

"Well, he can ride," someone called out, and a wit in the crowd shouted back: "Aye, Duchess Irma will find out all about that," at which there was some commotion. I was aware that for all the adulation and hurrahing, there were those in the crowd who stood silent, and even some who looked positively hostile. These would be the Germans, no doubt, who didn't want to see the state bound any closer to Denmark. However, they were a small minority, in the city at all events, and for the most part it was flowers and laughter all the way, with Prince Charming flashing his smile to the prettiest girls and feeling no end of a fellow.

Probably because I was enjoying myself so much, it was no time at all to the town hall. I should say that Strackenz isn't much of a city, being no greater than one of our market towns, although it has a cathedral and a ducal palace of some pretension. For that matter the whole duchy isn't more than a dozen miles across by about thirty in length, having been whittled down over the centuries from a fair-sized province. But it was a perfect hotbed of

nationalist emotions, German and Danish, and fiercely proud of
its traditions, including its ducal house. The Danish faction were
overjoyed at the impending marriage, hence their tumultuous
welcome of me.

At the town hall there were more dignitaries, and bowing and
scraping, and I was presented with an ornamental casket bearing
the city's arms, and invited to sign an order for a jail clearance—
it being the custom here, as elsewhere, to celebrate joyous occasions by letting all the hooligans and harlots out of the local clink.
How this is supposed to add to the general jollity I've never understood—furthermore, although I've been in half the lock-ups between Libby Prison[32] and Botany Bay myself, no one has ever held
a clearance that benefited me. I'm against 'em, on principle, but I
saw nothing for it here but to sign, until the moment I actually
took the pen in my hand and realised, with a fearful qualm, that
one thing my instructors hadn't taught me was how to forge Carl
Gustaf's signature. I didn't even know what his writing looked
like. Probably I could have signed my own fist and no one would
ever have spotted a difference, but at the time I didn't dare to risk
it.

For what seemed a year I hesitated, at the great burgomaster's
table, with the long roll of parchment stretched out in front of me,
and my pen poised, while the crowd goggled expectantly and the
little burgomaster stood waiting to pounce on my signature with
the sand-caster. And then my mother-wit came back to me, and I
laid down the pen and said, very quietly and seriously, that before
signing such a delivery—which I reminded them was a grave
matter indeed—I would wish to hear a report from the justices
assuring me that no malefactor who might prove a danger to the
commonweal would be enlarged by the amnesty. It could wait, I
said firmly, for a day or two, and added that I would find other
and better ways of marking this happy occasion of my arrival.

That pious old hypocrite, Arnold, my headmaster, would have
loved every word of it, but there was a general air of disappointment round the table, although one or two of the toadies muttered
about a prudent prince and wagged their heads approvingly. The
little burgomaster looked ready to cry, but agreed that my wishes
would be met to the letter.

They all cheered up, though, at the next act of the comedy,

when a small child was led in to present me with a peach that they had been preparing for me in the hothouse of the local orphanage. I say led in, because the child was so lame he had to go on little crutches, and there were sighings and affected cooings from the females present. I'm no hand with children at all, and have found them usually to be detestable, noisy, greedy little brats, but it seemed best to be monstrously pleasant to this one. So instead of just accepting the gift I racked my brains quickly for a touching gesture, and was inspired to pick him up—he was no size at all—and sit him on the table, and talk to him, and insisted that we eat the peach between us, then and there. He laughed and cried together, and when I patted his head according to form, he fastened on to my hand, and kissed it. The females were all snivelling foully by this time, and the men were looking pitying and noble. I felt ashamed, and still do. It is the only time in my life I have felt ashamed, which is why I put it on record here, and I still don't know why.

Anyway, I left the town hall in a thoroughly ill temper, and when they told me that next on the programme was a visit to the local academy, I as near as not told them I'd had enough of their damned infants for one day. But I didn't, of course, and presently I was being conducted through the school by the professor, who made an oration in my honour in Greek and then put up his best boys to construe for my entertainment. The things these honest asses imagine will delight royalty!

Of course the selected pupils were the usual mealy wretches who are put up in all schools everywhere on such occasions. Pious, manly little villains of the type I used to oppress myself in happier days—Tom Brown could have made a football side out of 'em, I don't doubt, and had them crying "Play up!" and telling the truth fit to sicken you. So I decided on a bit of mischief, and looked to the back of the school for the local Flashman—aye, there he was, a big, surly lout biting his nails and sneering to himself.

"There's a likely lad, professor," says I. "Let's hear him construe."

So, willy-nilly, they had to put the brute up, and he was paper-colour at the shock of it. Of course he floundered and grunted and glared round for inspiration, and the goody-goodies giggled and nudged each other, and the professor's frown grew blacker every minute.

"Stand down, sir," says he grimly, and to me: "He shall be corrected, highness, I assure you."

"That's your sort, professor," says I. "Lay on with a will." And I left in excellent humour. There would be a raw backside in that school by night, or I was mistaken—mind you, I'd sooner it had happened to the clever little sneaks, but no doubt my counterpart would pass his smarts on to them in turn.

The crowds still filled the streets for my final progress to the palace, which was a fine imposing pile on the outskirts of town, with pillars and balconies, and the running lion flag of Strackenz floating from its roof with the Danish colours alongside. The people were jammed up to the railings, and the sweep of the drive beyond was lined with the yellow-jacketed infantry of the Duchess's guard, all in glittering back-and-breasts, with drawn swords. Trumpeters blew a fanfare, the crowd surged and shouted, and I cantered up the gravel to the broad palace steps. There I turned and waved, for the last time, and wondered why people will make such a fuss over royalty. It's the same with us; we have our tubby little Teddy, whom everyone pretends is the first gentleman of Europe, with all the virtues, when they know quite well he's just a vicious old rake—rather like me, but lacking my talent for being agreeable to order. Anyway, I was aboard Lily Langtry long before he was.

That by the way; all such lofty philosophical thoughts were driven from my mind when I entered the palace, for there I met the Duchess I was to marry next day in the old Cathedral of Strackenz, and it is a tribute to her that while I have only the haziest memories of the brilliant throng that crowded the marble staircase and great ballroom, my first glimpse of her remains fresh in my mind to this day. I can still see her, standing slim and straight on the dais at the far end of the room, with the ducal throne framed in crimson behind her, watching me as I approached, with the spectators suddenly hushed, and only the sound of my marching feet echoing through the silence.

This was one of the moments when it struck me: this is all a fraud, it isn't real. Here was I, not Prince Carl Gustaf of the ancient royal house of Oldenbourg, but rascally old Flashy of the vulgar and lately-arrived house of Flashman, striding ahead to claim my noble bride. God, I remember thinking, the things people get me into, and that thought probably prevented me from wearing the devil-may-care leer that I normally assume in the presence of beautiful women.

She was beautiful, too—far more so than her portrait had made her out. She couldn't have been more than twenty, but already she had the hard, cold loveliness that you find only among Northern women, with their fine, long features looking as though they had been carved from marble. Her figure, in an ivory dress with a train that spread out behind her, was perhaps a trifle on the slim side, with a hint of boyishness about it, but everything was there and in good parade order. She was crowned with a little silver diadem sparking with stones, and her shining fair hair was pulled back and rolled into some kind of jewelled net behind her head. The effect of it all—so pale and pure and perfect—was rather awe-inspiring; I felt almost afraid of her.

The way she looked at me didn't help matters—the grey eyes were cold and proud, and I thought: this is a spoiled, arrogant madame if ever I saw one. Whatever her feelings might be about a duty marriage, she didn't seem to care for me at first glance; I knew she was looking at my glistening bald head, and I thought angrily what a damned shame it was I hadn't my natural adornments of curly mane and whiskers. The hand she held out for me to kiss was as pale and chilly as mist in a cemetery, and just about as welcoming. I took it, murmuring about pleasure and honour and deeply heartfelt felicitous gratification, and felt it quiver ever so slightly before it was withdrawn.

So there we stood together on the dais, with me wondering what to say next, and then someone in the watching multitude began to clap, and in a moment they were crowding forward to get a closer look, I suppose, at the pair of us, and everyone was pleased and happy and clapping away like mad. I found myself grinning and nodding at them, but her grace stood there quite serene, with never a smile, as though this was her due, and rather a bore.

Well, thinks I, this is going to be a chilly wooing, and then an old cove in a frock coat with orders on his breast came bowing up beside us, and turned to the throng with his hand raised for silence. This turned out to be the Chief Minister, one Schwerin; he made a neat little speech in which he managed to wrap up a nice complimentary welcome for me, a note of homage for the duchess (who couldn't get too much of it, as I discovered), a patriotic boost for Strackenz, coupled with the state of Denmark, and a hint to the mob to keep their distance and stay out of the buffet next door until her grace and I saw fit to lead the way.

That was about the size of it, and the good folk—who were a very well-trained court—chattered respectfully among themselves while Schwerin brought forward the more distinguished to be presented to me. These included the various emissaries to Strackenz, the British one among them, and I found myself thanking God that I'd never moved in diplomatic circles at home, or he might have remembered me. As it was, he and the others made their bows, and when they had withdrawn the Duchess indicated to me that we should sit down. We did so, both rather stiff, and while the noble assembly pretended not to notice, we began to get acquainted. It was formality carried to nonsense, of course, and if I didn't have a clear memory of our opening exchanges I wouldn't believe them.

Duchess Irma: I trust your highness's journey has not been tedious.

Flashy: Indeed, no, although I confess I have counted every moment in my impatience to be here.

Duchess: Your highness is very gracious. We of Strackenz can only hope that you are not too disappointed in us—we are very small and provincial here.

Flashy (very gallant): No one could be disappointed who was welcomed by so beautiful and noble a hostess.

Duchess: Oh. (Pause). Was the weather cold on your journey?

Flashy: At times. Occasionally it was quite warm. Nowhere so warm, however, as I find it here. (This with a flashing smile.)

Duchess: You are too hot? I shall order the windows opened.

Flashy: Christ, no. That is . . . I mean, the warmth of your welcome . . . and the people in the streets, cheering. . . .

Duchess: Ah, the people. They are rather noisy.

Well, I don't give up easy, but I confess I was fairly stumped here. Usually, with young women, I get along all too well. Formal chit-chat isn't my style—a little gallantry, a few jocularities to see if she will or she won't, a pinch on the buttocks, and off we go. Either that, or off I go. But I couldn't make anything of the

Duchess Irma; she kept her head tilted high and looked past me, so composed and regal that I began to wonder, was she perhaps terrified out of her wits? But before I could take soundings on that, she rose, and I found myself escorting her into the ante-chamber, where great tables were laid out with silver plate and crystal, and a most scrumptious spread was served by flunkies while a little orchestra struck up in the gallery overhead. I was sharp-set, and while one of the Duchess's ladies looked after her, I laid into the ham and cold fowls, and chatted affably to the nobs and their ladies, who were making the most of the grub them-selves, as the Germans always do.

This kind of function normally bores me out of mind, and beyond the fact that the food was unusually excellent, and that the Duchess seemed intent on not being left alone with me for more than a moment at a time, I haven't any sharp recollection of it. I remember turning once, in that gay company with its buzz of well-bred conversation, and catching her eyes fixed on me; she looked quickly away, and I thought, my God, I'm *marrying* that woman tomorrow. My heart took a skip at the thought; she was unutterably lovely. And then it took a lurch as I remembered the appalling risk that I ràn every moment I was in Strackenz, and wondered what the penalty might be for marrying the heir to the throne under false pretences. Death, certainly. I tried to smile politely at the eager, sycophantic faces around me, and to listen to their incredible inanities of small-talk, while my mind raced away looking for a way out, even although I knew it didn't exist.

I probably drank a little more than I should have done—although I was pretty careful—but at any rate the desperate feel-ing passed. The good will of the Strackenzians towards me was so evident, and so fulsomely expressed, that I suppose it overcame me and banished my fears. I found I could even talk to the Duchess without embarrassment, although it was obvious to me, if not to anyone else, that she didn't like me; she remained haughty and distant—but then, she seemed to be the same to everyone, and they swallowed it and sucked up to her.

Afterwards old Schwerin and a couple of his ministerial col-leagues—I forget their names—took me aside and discussed the next day's ceremony. They were fairly vague, as I remember, and gassed a good deal about the political advantage of the match, and the popular satisfaction, and how it would have a good and stabilising effect.

"Her grace is very young, of course," says old Schwerin. "Very young." He gave me rather a sad smile. "Your highness is not so very much older, but your education, at a great court, and your upbringing have perhaps prepared you better for what lies before you both." (You little know, old son, thinks I.) "It is a great responsibility for you, but you will bear it honourably."

I murmured noble nothings, and he went on:

"It is much to ask of two young folk—I often feel that such marriages of state would be the better of—ah—longer preparation. Perhaps I am a sentimentalist," says he, with a senile smirk, "but it has always seemed to me that a courtship would not be out of place, even between royal personages. Love, after all, does not come in a day."

It depends what you mean by love, thinks I, and one of the others says to Schwerin:

"You have a great heart, Adolf."

"I hope I have. I hope so. And your highness, I know, has a great heart also. It will know how to understand our—our little Irma. She is very much like a daughter to us, you see"—he was going pink about the eyes by this time—"and although she seems so serene and proud beyond her years, she is still very much a child."

Well, I could agree with him that she was an unusually arrogant little bitch for her age, but I kept a princely silence. He looked almost pleading.

"Your highness," he said at last, "will be kind to our treasure."

Strange, my own father-in-law had struck something of the same note before I married Elspeth; it's a polite way of suggesting that you don't make too much of a beast of yourself on the honeymoon. I assumed a look of manly understanding.

"Sirs," says I. "What can I say, except that I trust I shall always bear myself to your duchess as I would to the daughter of my oldest and dearest friend."

That cheered them up no end, and presently the reception began to draw to a close, and the noble guests imperceptibly melted away; Schwerin beamed paternally on the Duchess and myself, and hinted that as the next day was going to be an exhausting

391

one, we should take all the rest we could beforehand. It was still only early afternoon, but I was dog-tired with the novelty and excitement of the morning, and so we said our formal goodbyes to each other. I made mine as pleasant as I could, and the Duchess Irma received it with an inclination of her head and gave me her hand to kiss. It was like talking to a walking statue.

Then Detchard, who had been hovering off my port quarter for several hours, closed in and with attendant flunkies escorted me to the suite reserved for me in the west wing of the palace. They would have made a great fuss of me, but he shooed them away, and what I thought rather odd, he also dismissed Josef, who was waiting to unbutton me and remove my boots. However, I realised he wished us to be private, and when we passed through into my main salon I understood why, for Rudi Starnberg and de Gautet were waiting for us.

The sight of them damped my spirits; it was a reminder of what I was here for, with my custodians dogging me all the time. From being the prince I was become play-actor Flashy again.

Rudi sauntered across and without so much as by-your-leave took hold of my wrist and felt my pulse.

"You're a cool hand," says he. "I watched you down below, and on my oath, you looked a most condescending tyrant. How does it feel to play the prince?"

I hadn't been used to this kind of talk in the past few hours, and found myself resenting it. I damned his impudence and asked where the blazes he had been all day—for he and de Gautet had been supposed to meet me with the others at the frontier.

He cocked an eyebrow at me. "Regal airs, eh? Well, highness, we've been busy about affairs of state if you please. Your affairs, your state. You might show a little appreciation to your loyal servants." He grinned insolently. "But of course, the gratitude of princes is proverbial."

"Then don't presume on it—even with temporary royalty," I growled. "You can both go to the devil. I want to rest."

De Gautet considered me. "A little drunk perhaps?"

"Damn you, get out!"

"I do believe the infection has really taken," chuckled Rudi. "He'll be calling the guard in a moment. Now, seriously, friend Flashman"—and here he tapped me on the chest—"you can put away your ill-temper, for it won't answer. It ain't our fault if the Duchess hasn't languished at you. No, you needn't damn my eyes, but listen. Certain things have happened which may—I say may only—affect our plans."

My stomach seemed to turn to ice. "What d'ye mean?"

"By ill chance, one of the Danish Embassy at Berlin—a fellow Hansen, a senior official—arrived today in Strackenz. He was on his way home, and broke his journey here to attend the wedding. There was no convenient way to get rid of him, so he will be there tomorrow."

"Well, what about it?" says I. "There will be plenty of Danes in the Cathedral, won't there? What's one more or less?"

Detchard spoke from behind me. "Hansen has been a friend of Carl Gustaf's from childhood. Indeed, the most intimate of all his companions."

"Your resemblance to Carl Gustaf is uncanny," put in de Gautet. "But will it deceive his oldest playmate?"

"Jesus!" I sat stricken. "No, no, by God, it won't! It can't! He'll know me!" I jumped up. "I knew it! I knew it! We're done for! He'll denounce me! You ... you bloody idiots, see what you've done, with your lunatic schemes! We're dead men, and...."

"Lower your voice," says Rudi, "and take a grip on your nerves." He pushed me firmly back into my chair. "Your mind's disordered—which is not surprising. Bersonin warned us that even a strong man may show signs of hysteria in the kind of position you're in...."

"He's no fool, that one, is he?" cried I. "What the hell can I do? He'll give me away, this Hansen, and...."

"He will not," says Rudi firmly. "Take my word for it. I can see this thing clearly, which you can't, being the principal actor, and I tell you there is not the slightest risk—provided you keep your head. He'll meet you for a moment at the reception after the wedding, shake your hand, wish you well, and whist!—that is all. He's not looking for an impostor, remember. Why should he?"

"We would not have told you," said Detchard, "if it could have been avoided. But if we had not you might unwittingly have made some fatal blunder."

"That's it exactly," says Rudi. "You had to be ready for him.

Now, we have decided what you shall say when he approaches you in the reception line. Detchard here will be at your elbow, and will whisper 'Hansen' when he reaches you. At the sight of him you'll start, look as delighted as you know how, seize his right hand in both of yours, shake it hard, and exclaim: 'Erik, old friend, where did you spring from?' Then, whatever he says in reply, you'll give your merriest laugh and say: 'This is the happiest surprise of this happy day. God bless you for coming to wish me joy.' And that will be all. I'll see to it that he doesn't get near you before you leave for the lodge at Strelhow, where your honeymoon is being spent."

"And suppose he sees through me, what then?" This news had left me sick with fright. "Suppose he isn't to be put off with this nonsense about happy surprises, and I have to talk to him longer?" I had a dreadful vision. "Suppose he shouts, 'That's not the prince?' What'll you do then?"

"I'll have done it long before he shouts anything," says Rudi quietly. "You may rely on that."

I wasn't so easily reassured. My cowardly instincts were in full cry, and it took all Rudi's and Detchard's arts of persuasion to convince me that the risk wasn't so terrible—indeed, that if I played my part properly, it was barely a risk at all.

"Conduct yourself as you were doing an hour ago," says Rudi, "and the thing's as safe as sleep. Courage, man. The worst's past. You've pulled the wool over all the eyes in Strackenz this day, and right royally, too." I thought there was even a hint of envy in his voice. "All that's to do now is stand up in church with the delightful Duchess, say your vows, and then off for a blissful idyll in your forest love-nest. Aye, let your mind run on the pleasures of putting that dainty little pullet to bed." He nudged me and winked lewdly. "I'll wager the next Duke of Strackenz has fine curly whiskers, for all that his father won't have a hair on his face to bless himself with."

Of course, as so often turns out, there wasn't time to be frightened. Ostred gave me a sleeping draught that night, and in the morning it was all mad bustle and hurry, with never fewer than a dozen folk round me from the moment I rose, dressing me, pushing me, instructing me, reminding me—I felt like a prize beast in the ring as I was conducted down the great marble staircase to the waiting coach that was to carry me to the Cathedral. As we paused on the steps, the sound thundered up from the waiting thousands beyond the palace railings, the cannon boomed in the park, and a great cheer rolled across the steep roofs of Strackenz City.

"God save Prince Carl!"

"Wherever he may be," muttered Rudi. "Forward, your highness!"

It should have been a day to remember, I suppose, but how much of detail does one recall of one's own wedding?—and it was my second, as you know. It seems now like a strange dream, driving through the packed streets in the sunshine, with the roar of the people buffeting my ears, the blare of the trumpets, the clatter of hooves, and the coloured bunting fluttering bravely in the morning breeze—but what sticks in my mind is the red birthmark on the back of the coachman's head, which under his hat was as bald as my own.

And then there was the sudden dimness and hush of the great Cathedral, the pungent smell of the church, the soaring stained glass and the carpeted stone flags underfoot. There was the rustle as hundreds of people rose to their feet, the solemn booming of a great organ, and the hollow thud of my own footsteps on the stones. And there was the shrill sweetness of the choristers, and people softly moving to and fro about me, and the splendid figure of the Bishop of Strackenz, bearded to the eyes, and for all the world like Willie Grace, the great cricket champion nowadays.

I remember standing very lonely and afraid, wondering if perhaps there was such a place as Hell after all—a question which had occupied me a good deal as a small boy, especially when Arnold had been terrifying us with sermons about Kibroth-Hattaavah,[33] where I gathered all kinds of fornication and fun took place. Well, what I was doing in that Cathedral would have ensured me a single ticket to damnation, no doubt of that, but I consoled myself with the thought that the hereafter was the last thing to worry about just then.

And I remember, too, the Duchess suddenly at my side, pale and wondrously lovely in her white gown, with her golden hair crowned with a fillet of brilliant stones. And her tiny hand slipping into mine, her clear voice answering the Bishop, and then my own, husky and nervous. They pressed a ring into my hand, and I fumbled it on to her tiny finger, my palms sweating, and kissed her on the cheek when the old Bishop gave the word. She stood like a wax dummy, and I thought, poor old Carl Gustaf, having to live with this cold fish all his life, and the choir let go a great blast of sound as they placed the ducal coronets on our heads, and the Duchess took the gold staff of her sovereignty and the Sword of State was buckled round my waist.

Then the whole congregation rose and sang a hymn of rejoicing, and various minor clergy decked us out in the remaining Crown Jewels. I must say that for a small state Strackenz was remarkably well off in this respect; apart from the coronets and staff, there were rings for my fingers and a magnificent solid gold chain set with emeralds which they hung round my unworthy neck; it had a star of diamonds pendent from it that must have weighed half a pound.

The Duchess did rather better, she being the reigning prince while poor old Flash was just her consort. (It struck me then, and it strikes me now, that the Salic Law was a damned sound idea.) She had a collar of solid gems, and her rings would have knocked mine all to pieces. Soldierly instinct dies hard, and as the hymn drew to a close I was mentally computing the worth of all this jewelled splendour, and how it could best be stowed: emerald chain in one side pocket, collar in t'other, rings and similar trifles in the fobs—the coronets would be bulky, but they could probably be bent flat for convenience. And the staff was slender enough to stick down your boot.

Of course, I'd probably never have the chance to lay my itchy fingers on this magnificent collection of loot again, but it does no harm to take stock in advance: you never know what opportunities may arise. The Crown Jewels of the Duchy of Strackenz would have kept me and a dozen like me in tremendous style for life, and they looked eminently portable. I decided to keep them in mind.

There was a final hallelujah and amen, and then we were out in the sunlight again with the crowd deafening us and the great bells of the Cathedral pealing overhead. There was an open State coach in which we rode side by side, with the Duchess's brides-maids facing us, and I played up to the mob and waved and beamed, while my bride stirred a languid hand in their direction. She did manage a smile or two, though, and even condescended to exchange a few civilities with me, which was a great advance. Never mind, thinks I, it'll soon be ho for the hunting lodge and beddy-byes, and then we'll bring the roses back to those pearly cheeks.

We drove slowly, so that the populace could get a good look at us, and their enthusiasm was so tremendous that the infantry lining the road had to link arms to hold them back. There were children waving flags and screaming, girls fluttering their handkerchiefs, fellows throwing their hats in the air, and old women sobbing and mopping at themselves. At one point the troops gave way, and the crowd clamoured right up to the coach, stretching over to touch us as though we were holy relics: if only they'd known they'd have scampered off far enough in case they caught Flashy's Evil. The Duchess wasn't too pleased at being adored so closely, and looked ahead pretty stiff, but I shook hands like a good 'un and they cheered me hoarse.

At this point there was an odd incident. Above the cheering I was aware of a voice shouting from the back of the crowd—no, not shouting, but declaiming. It was a strong, harsh trumpet of a voice, although its words were lost in the tumult, and its owner was a most odd-looking fellow who had scrambled up onto some kind of hand-cart and was haranguing the mob full blast. There were soldiers struggling through the press to get at him, and a knot of sturdy, sober-looking chaps round the cart as though to shield the orator, so I gathered he must be denouncing us, or threatening a breach of the peace.

He wasn't a big chap, in height, but he was built like a bull across the shoulders, with a huge, shaggy head and a beard like a sweep's broom. Even at that distance I could see the flashing eyes as he thundered out his message, thumping the air with his fist and laying it off like a Mississippi camp-meeting preacher full of virtue and forty-rod whisky. The people nearest him and his group were shouting threats at him, but he kept bawling away, and it looked to me as though an excellent brawl was in prospect; unfortunately, just as the soldiers reached him and were trying to haul him down, the coach moved out of vision, so I didn't see how it came out.[34]

The Duchess had seen it, too, and we were no sooner at the palace than she summoned Schwerin to the ante-room where we were resting and pitched straight into him.

"Who was that agitator? How dared he raise his voice against me, and whose neglect allowed it to happen?" Her voice was perfectly level, but she was obviously in a furious bait, and the old minister fairly cowered before the slip of a girl. "Have he and his rabble been arrested?"

Schwerin wrung his hands. "Highness, that this should have happened! It is deplorable. I do not know who the man was, but I will ascertain. I believe he was one of the socialist orators—"

"Orator?" says the Duchess, in a tone that would have frozen brandy. "Revolutionary upstart! And on my wedding day!" She turned to me. "It is my shame, and my country's, that this affront should have taken place in your highness's presence, on this sacred occasion."

Well, I didn't mind. I was more interested in her cold rage at what she conceived an affront to her noble dignity; she had a fine, spoiled conceit of herself to be sure. I suggested that the man was probably drunk, and that he had done no harm anyway.

"Denmark must be fortunate in its security against such dangerous criminals," says she. "In Strackenz we find it prudent to take sterner measures against these . . . these orators! Schwerin, I hold you responsible; let me hear presently that they have been arrested and punished."

It would have sounded pompous from a bench of bishops; from a nineteen-year-old girl it was ridiculous, but I kept a straight face. I was learning fast about my little Irma; an imperious young piece. I found myself hoping that she would be thwarted of her vengeance on my big-headed revolutionary; whoever he was, he had looked the kind of likely lad who would sooner spar with the peelers than eat his dinner, and keep things lively all round.

When she had sent Schwerin packing, and her ladies had adjusted invisible flaws in her appearance, we proceeded with tremendous ceremony to the great ballroom, where the brilliant throng had already assembled for the reception. This is a bigger "do" than old Morrison gave for Elspeth and me in Paisley, thinks I, but I'll wager they can't drink more than those Scotch rascals did. The place was a blaze of splendid uniforms and gowns;

orders, medals, and jewellery twinkled everywhere; aristocratic backs bent and a hundred skirts rustled in curtsies as we took our place on the dais for the guests to file by with their respectful congratulations. You never saw such a pack of noble toadies in your life, smirking their way past. They all fawned over the Duchess, of course, the square-heads clicking their heels and bowing stiffly, the dagoes bending double—for we had a fine selection from half the countries in Europe. After all, Duchess Irma was the cousin of our own Britannic Majesty—which made me a sort-of-cousin-in-law to her and Albert, I suppose—and everyone wanted to have a grovel to us. I was delighted to see, though, that the British Ambassador confined himself to a jerky little bow and a "Felicitations, ma'am, and much happiness to both your highnesses." That's the style, thinks I; good old England and damn all foreigners.

I just stood there, nodding my head up and down until my neck creaked, smiling and murmuring my thanks to each passing face—fat, thin, sweating, straining, smiling, adoring, they came in all sizes and expressions. And then Detchard's voice behind me whispered "Hansen," and I glanced sharply to see a fair-haired, long-jawed young fellow just straightening up from his bow to the Duchess. He turned to me, smiling expectantly, and in my sudden nervousness I took a step forward, grinning like a death's head, I shouldn't wonder, grabbed him by the hand, and cried:

"Erik, old friend, this is the most springing surprise of my happy day!" or something equally garbled; I know that I bungled the words hopelessly, but he just laughed and pumped my hand.

"Dear Carl—highness—I had to come to wish you joy." He had that manly, sentimental look, misty-eyed yet smiling, which I personally can only manage in drink. "God bless you both!"

"God bless you, too, old friend," says I, wringing hard at him, and then his smile faded, a puzzled look came into his eyes, and he stepped back.

God knows I've had my bad moments, but seldom such a qualm of sickening dread as I experienced then. I kept my aching grin, because I was so paralysed with panic that I couldn't move a muscle, waiting for the denunciation which I was certain was on his lips.

For a second he stared, and then he made a sudden, nervous gesture of apology and smiled again.

"Pardon," he said. "Your pardon, highness . . . Carl." He moved quickly aside to let in the next guest, bowed again, and then moved off towards the buffets, where the other guests were assembling. There I saw him turn, staring back at me, and presently he rubbed his brow with his fingers, gave his head a quick shake as a man will who is putting some trifle out of his mind, and gave his attention to a waiter who was proffering champagne.

I knew I was crimson with the shock, and one knee was trembling violently, but I forced myself to smile steadily as the guest before me bobbed in a deep curtsey, and her escort swept me a bow. I saw the concern in their faces—when I turn red I'm a daunting sight—so I forced a laugh.

"Forgive me," I told them. "I'm out of breath with saying 'thank you' to several hundred people." They were delighted at being so familiarly addressed by royalty, and then the crisis was past and I had time to steady myself.

But it had been a horrible moment, and I must have gone through the rest of that reception like a man in a dream, for I can remember nothing more until I was back in my own room, alone with Detchard, Rudi and de Gautet, drinking brandy from a glass that rattled against my teeth.

"It was a bad moment," was Rudi's verdict. "For a second I thought we were gone. I had him covered from my pocket, and I swear if he had taken an instant longer to smile I'd have shot him down and claimed he was preparing to assassinate you. And God knows what might have come of that. Phew!"

"But he saw I wasn't the Prince!" I beat on the arm of my chair. "He saw through me! Didn't he? You saw him, de Gautet —didn't he?"

"I doubt it," says he. "For a moment he *thought* there was something strange about you—and then he told himself it was his own imagination. You saw him shake his head—he had tried to puzzle it out, but couldn't—and now he no more doubts you than he doubts himself."

"By God, I hope so." I attacked the brandy again. "Suppose he thinks better of it, though—becomes suspicious?"

"He's being watched every moment he is in Strackenz," says Rudi. "We have other reasons for keeping a sharp eye on Master Hansen."

"What's that?"

"Oh, his journey here wasn't only to dance at your wedding. We know that for months now he and other members of the Danish government have been in correspondence with the more militant Danish faction in Strackenz—people like the Eider Danes[35] over the border, only rather more dangerous. They watch everything German like hawks, hold secret meetings, that sort of thing. There's talk of a clandestine organisation, the 'Sons of the Volsungs', dedicated to fly to arms in the event of any threat from Berlin to Strackenzian independence." Rudi grinned pleasantly. "We'll settle with those gentlemen when the time comes. For the present, neither they nor friend Hansen need trouble you. The game's all but won, my boy"—and he slapped me on the shoulder. "With the wedding behind us there's nothing to do but sit out the weeks until Otto gives the word that our good Carl Gustaf is ready to resume the role in which you are proving such a distinguished understudy. Then back to merry England for you—and let's hope the delectable Irma isn't too disappointed in the change, shall we?"

This was all very well, but I was by no means sure that the worst was past. I'd had some nasty turns in my brief life as Prince Carl Gustaf, and it seemed odds on there being a few more before they'd sweated the clap out of him and he could succeed me on the consort's throne. And even then, would Bismarck keep faith? I didn't want to think about that just yet, but it was always at the back of my mind. Sufficient unto the day is the evil thereof, but you have to watch your step at night, too.

I was still shaking with the Hansen business, and for that matter I was probably suffering from the strain of two days' imposture —at any rate, I punished a half bottle of brandy there and then without noticeable effect, which is always a sign that the funks have got me good and proper. Rudi, although he watched me closely, whistling through his teeth, didn't say me nay; there was no further official business that day, only the drive to the hunting lodge at Strelhow, ten miles from the city, and I didn't have to be stone-cold sober for that.

We were to set out in mid-afternoon, and presently Josef and various minions were admitted to begin my preparations for the road. There was a great bustle as trunks and boxes were taken below stairs, and I was divested of my ceremonial uniform and kitted out in cutaway and topper, as befitted a gentleman bent on his honeymoon. I was sufficiently recovered from my nervous condition—or else the booze was beginning to work—to be able to discuss with Rudi the merits of checked or striped trousers, which had been the great debate among the London nobs that year.[36] I was a check-er myself, having the height and leg for it, but Rudi thought they looked bumpkinish, which only shows what damned queer taste they had in Austria in those days. Of course, if you'll put up with Metternich you'll put up with anything.

While we were talking, an officer of the palace guard put in an appearance, with an escort carrying drawn sabres, to collect the crown jewellery which Josef had removed with my uniform. They had taken my coronet and State sword on our return from the cathedral, but my chain and rings remained, and these were now carefully stowed in velvet-lined cases and given to the guard to carry away.

"Pretty things," says Rudi, cocking his cheroot thoughtfully between his teeth. "Where are you taking them, fähnrich?"

"To the clock-room, herr baron," says the young officer, clicking his heels.

"Aye, that's a strange place, surely. Wouldn't a dungeon be safer?"

"If you please, herr baron, the clock-room is in the top of the main tower of the palace. The tower has one stair, which is under constant guard." The youth hesitated. "I believe they are kept there because in the old Duke's time it was his grace's delight to visit the clock-room every day and examine the state treasure."

I was taking this in, for what it was worth, and noting that Rudi von Starnberg was showing an uncommon interest in it, too. Dishonest young pup; I knew what he was thinking.

We left the palace on the stroke of three, to be cheered out of town by the loyal Strackenzians, who had been making the most of the free buffets and unlimited wine being dispensed in all the public buildings. The whole population seemed to be half-shot, and the applause as we drove through the streets was abandoned and hilarious. I sat with the Duchess in an open landau, accompanied by Rudi and a strikingly pretty red-haired lady-in-waiting whose foot he kept stroking with his boot during the journey. Otherwise he was on his best behaviour, which meant that his conduct stopped just short of open insolence.

However, Irma was in no frame of mind to notice; she was in something of a pet, chiefly, I gathered, because Schwerin had not been able to report the apprehension of the agitator who had been abusing us on our drive from the cathedral. And there had been difficulties with her trousseau, the people who were waving us goodbye were over-familiar in their expressions, the open carriage was not suitable for such a cold day—and so on, every damned thing seemed to be wrong, for no obvious reason. To me it seemed that, whatever the rest of her trousseau was like, her blue travelling gown and fur hat, à la hussar, became her admirably. I said so, and she condescended to acknowledge the compliment, but very formally. We were still as distant as dowagers in church, and it struck me again that for all her prim composure, she was probably quaking underneath. I found this gratifying, and resolved to let her stew in it for a while; I wasn't over-solicitous, and for most of the journey we rode in silence.

It was a sunny afternoon, and warm in spite of Irma's complaint. The road from Strackenz runs through some splendid forest country, which encloses an unusual feature for that part of the world in a short range of little crags and cliffs called the Jotun Gipfel. They are very pretty, very wild, as our late Queen would say, and rather like the English lake hills in miniature. Apart from a few shepherds' huts they are fairly empty, most of the inhabitants of Strackenz province living down in the flat lands near the city, but they contain one or two beautiful mountain tarns, in one of which stands the old castle of Jotunberg, which was the stronghold of the Dukes of Strackenz in the bad old days. It was kept now by the Bülow family, a Strackenzian branch of the great German house of that name.

The hunting lodge of Strelhow stands some miles from the Jotun Gipfel, tucked away in the woods a little distance off the main road. It has been the country seat of the ruling house for generations, and is an excellent little box, all rough timber and fur rugs, with fine open fires, leaded windows, comfortable appointments, and plenty of room—altogether a bang-up place. We were travelling fairly informally; there were two Strackenzian aides for me, apart from de Gautet and Rudi, and the Duchess had three ladies and about five maids—God knows why she needed all those. Detchard had come, too, but elected to stay in the village, and of course I had Josef with me. There were other servants, and various grooms and attendants, and it looked like being quite a lively country party. And it was—lively and deathly.

We arrived at the lodge just before dusk. My bride was nervous and irritable, and had the servants who came out to greet us scurrying in all directions. There was a meal prepared in the panelled dining-room, with a cheery blaze in the grate, and all looking mighty snug and inviting, but she excused herself and went off above-stairs with her lady-in-waiting and a cloud of lackeys hovering in her wake. However, we men-folk were sharp-set, and fell on supper with a will, and after that the port and brandy, and before long we were making a good roaring evening of it. What with sensing that her haughty highness was out of sorts, and the food and wine, I was in excellent trim, and although de Gautet was his usual saturnine self—I was growing to loathe that sleek, silent smile—Rudi and the two Strackenzians took their cue from me and caroused like cricketers.

For all their other faults, I must own that Germans are excellent fellows at a gorging-and-drinking party. Rudi was in fine fettle, with his tunic undone and his curly hair a-tumble, leading the singing in a capital baritone (but his eyes were still bright and clear; I doubt if he was ever the worse for drink in his life, that one). I was ladling the liquor down at a fair rate, and had just reached that state where I begin to search for mischief, when a footman brought down word that her grace the duchess was about to retire, and requested that the disturbance of the evening should cease.

At this the others fell silent. Rudi sat back in his chair and smiled into his glass; the Strackenzians glanced uneasily at each other. I got to my feet, staggering a little and upsetting my chair, and said that if her grace was retiring, so was I. I bade them good-night, and walked—rather unsteadily, I imagine—to the door.

One of the Strackenzian aides jumps up, and asked, could he help my highness?

"No, thank'ee, my son," says I. "I'm of age, you know."

At which he fell back, blushing, and as I strode out I heard Rudi laughing and calling out:

"Gentlemen, a toast! The Prince Carl Gustaf, coupled, if you follow me, with her grace the Duchess of Strackenz."

I blundered upstairs, shed my clothes in my dressing-room, thrust Josef out, threw on a gown, and strode through into the bedroom. I was full of booze and lewdness, and the sight of Irma, caught unawares, standing there in a white nightgown, did nothing to sober me. Her cold, proud beauty brought out the worst in me, I threw off the gown, and she shrieked and covered her eyes.

"Cheer up, little wife," says I, "there won't be any more singing downstairs," and I stooped and whipped the nightdress clean off, over her head. She gave a little cry, and since I maintain that the best way to deal with nervous females is to treat 'em hearty, I lifted her up bodily, popped her on, and stumped round the room singing:

"This is the way the ladies ride, trit-trot, trit-trot, trit-trot."

As near as I can remember I sang it in English, but I doubt if she noticed. At all events I know we finished the business on the bed, with me laughing weakly and babbling about "hobble-dee, hobble-dee, and down in a ditch" and assuring her that she was a damned fine duchess and a credit to her country.[37]

I suppose I dozed off, but I woke up and had at her again, and being slightly more sober by this time I was aware that she lay as still as a corpse, and didn't enter into the fun of the thing at all. If it had been any other woman I'd have smartened her up with a few cuts across the rump, but with a duchess one ought to practise patience, I felt.

And I was right, you see, because after that I went to sleep, leaving her lying there, with her eyes closed, like a beautiful ghost in the candlelight, and what should awaken me—I don't know how many hours later—but a tiny hand creeping across my thigh, and long hair snuggling up to my face, and I thought, well, damme, royal or not, they're all alike under the skin. I was beat, I can tell you, but one must act like a gentleman, so I went to work again, and this time she clung like a leech. Just like Elspeth, I remember thinking—all chaste purity to look at, maidenly beauty personified, and randy as a monkey.

I've known too many women, far too many, to claim to understand 'em. Their minds work in ways too mysterious for me to fathom; anyway, my studies have generally been confined to their bodies, which perhaps accounts for it. But I know that Duchess Irma of Strackenz was a different woman after that night—to me, at any rate. She had been a proud, autocratic, thoroughly spoiled little brat the day before; nervous as a mouse and as cold as a whale's backside. And I'd not have been surprised if after the way I'd handled her, she'd been put off men for good. But next morning she was positively meek, in a thoughtful but apparently contented way, and very attentive to me; she seemed to be in a state of wonder, almost, and yet she was ready to talk to me, and what was even more remarkable, listen to me, too—not that I'm a great hand at conversation in the mornings.

I don't mention this in a boastful way, or to suggest that with a chap like me it's just a matter of catch 'em young, treat 'em rough, roger 'em hard, and they eat out of my hand. Far from it; I've used women that way, and had them try to repay me with cold steel, or run a mile next time I looked at them. But with Irma, for some reason, it had quite the opposite effect; I can say that from that night on, as long as I knew her, she treated me with something near to worship. Which shows you how stupid a love-struck young woman can be.

All this, of course, made for a most happy sojourn at Strelhow. There was plenty to do during the day, what with picnic parties—for although some snow still lay, it was pleasantly warm for the season—and shooting in the woods, and riding (on horses) in the afternoon, and in the evening we had musical entertainment from the ladies, or played billiards, and the food and drink were of the best. I began to feel like royalty again, with people waiting on me hand and foot, and jumping to my slightest wish, and it is mighty pleasant to have a beautiful young duchess hanging on your arm, adoring you, even if she does keep you from getting much sleep at nights. It was the life, all right—lazing, feasting, shooting, tickling the pills in the billiard room and sweating it out in bed with Irma—all the trivial amusements that are simply nuts to chaps like me.

Rudi and de Gautet were the only flies in the ointment, for their very presence was a constant jog to my memory of the business in hand. But strangely enough, I became a little closer to de Gautet, for I discovered that he shared one of my chief interests, which is horseflesh. He was an authority, of the true kind who never pretends more than he knows, and in the saddle he was nearly as good as I was myself, which is to say he would have been top-notch among any horsemen in the world—even the Cheyennes of the American plains, who are the best I know. We rode together a good deal, but I made sure we always had one of the Strackenzians or a couple of grooms along—I'm nervous about going into the woods alone with fellows whom I've cut open with a *schlager*, and who I'm pretty sure haven't forgotten it.

De Gautet, at any rate, was a silent, unassertive fellow, which was more than could be said of the bold Rudi. Now that he was confident I could play my role in perfect safety, he was treating me exactly as he would have used the real Prince Carl, which is to say with his customary impertinence. Of course, he cared for no one, and even let his bright eye play over Irma, while he would address her with that half-mocking deference which he seemed to reserve for his social superiors. She was woman enough to be taken by his good looks and easy charm, but she sensed, I think, that here was a real wrong 'un, and confessed to me on one occasion that she was sure he was not a gentleman. I promised to replace him with a new aide when we returned to the city—and took some malicious pleasure in telling him about it later, so that he should realise that one woman, at least, had read him correctly. But he was only amused.

"I knew the chit had no taste," says he. "Why, she's taken to you. But don't imagine you can get rid of me so easily, your highness—I'm your loyal, obedient, and ever-present servant until the time comes to end our little comedy." He blew a smoke-ring and eyed me, tongue in cheek. "I think you'll be sorry when it's over, won't you? Princely life suits you, or I'm mistaken."

In fact, he *was* mistaken. Oh, it was very idyllic there in Strelhow, and I was idler than even royalty usually are, but already I had a notion that the future that faced Carl Gustaf wasn't going to be all roses and wine. It may seem rare to be a crowned head, and no doubt if you're an absolute monarch with unlimited power, it's right enough—but a prince consort, which is more or less what I was, isn't quite the same thing. He can't trim the heads off those he don't like, or order up any good-looking skirt who takes his fancy. He's always one step behind his adoring spouse, and even if she dotes on him—and who knows how long that will last?—he still has to get his own way, if he wants it, through her good leave. Even in those blissful early days with Irma, I could see how it would be, and I didn't much like it. God knows how our late lamented Albert stuck it out, poor devil. If I'd been him, six months would have seen me on the boat back to Saxe-Coburg or wherever it was. But perhaps he didn't mind playing second fiddle —he wasn't English.

However, I consoled myself that I was having the best of both worlds—my luxurious enslavement was both enjoyable and temporary. Now and then I fretted a little over what the outcome of the comedy would be, but there was nothing to be done about it. Either Bismarck would keep his bargain or he wouldn't—and I forced myself to put the latter possibility out of my mind. This is the real coward's way, of course—I wanted to believe he would play fair, and so I did, even though common sense should have warned me that he wouldn't. And as so often happens, I almost fell a prey to my own comfortable, lily-livered hopes.

We had been about ten days at Strelhow, I suppose, when one evening we were in the billiard room, and the talk turned to horses. Someone—Rudi, I think—mentioned the fine stable kept by a gentleman over beyond the Jotun Gipfel; I expressed interest, and it was suggested that next day we should ride over and call on him. It was all very easy and casual, like any of the other expeditions and picnics we had enjoyed, and I gave it no thought at all.

So next morning de Gautet and one of the Strackenzian aides and I set off. The quickest way was through the Jotun Gipfel on horseback, and Irma came with us by carriage as far as the road allowed. Thereafter we turned off towards the crags, she fluttering her handkerchief lovingly after her departing lord, and presently we were climbing into the hills by one of the bridle-paths that are the only tracks through that wild and picturesque little region.

It was a splendid day for such a jaunt, clear and sunny, and the scenery was pleasant—any of our Victorian artists would have sketched it in a moment, with its nice little crags and trees and occasional waterfalls, and would have thrown in a couple of romantic shepherds with whiskers and fat calves for good measure. But we saw no one as we moved up towards the summit, and I was enjoying the ride and musing on last night's sporting with Irma, when the Strackenzian aide's horse went lame.

I've often wondered how they arranged that, for the horse was certainly lame, and I doubt if the aide—his name was Steubel, just a boy—had anything to do with it. I cursed a bit, and de Gautet suggested we turn and go back. The boy wouldn't hear of it; he would walk his horse slowly down to Strelhow, he said, and we should go on. De Gautet looked doubtful—he was a clever actor, that one—but I was fool enough to agree. I can't think, now, how I was so green, but there it was. I never thought of foul play —I, who normally throw myself behind cover if someone breaks wind unexpectedly, was completely off guard. I had my pistols, to be sure, and even my knife, for I'd got into the wise habit of going armed whenever I left the lodge; but de Gautet's manner must have disarmed me completely.

We went on together, and about twenty minutes after parting from Steubel we had reached the summit, a pleasant little tree-fringed plateau, split by a deep gorge through which a river rushed, throwing up clouds of mist against the rocky sides. The whole table-top was hemmed in by trees, but there was a clear patch of turf near the edge of the gorge, and here we dismounted to have a look down into the bottom, a hundred feet below. I don't care for heights, but the scene was so pleasant and peaceful that I never felt a moment's unease, until de Gautet spoke.

"The Jotunschlucht," says he, meaning the gorge, and something in his voice sounded the alarm in my brain. It may have been the flatness of his tone, or the fact that he was closer behind me than I felt he should have been, but with the instinct of pure panic I threw myself sideways on the turf, turning as I fell to try to face him.

If his pistol hadn't misfired he would have got me; I heard the click even as I moved, and realised that he had been aiming point-blank at my back. As I tried to scramble up he dropped it with an oath, drew its mate from beneath his tunic, and levelled it at me. I screamed, "No! No!" as he thumbed back the lock, and he hesitated a split second, to see if I should leap again, and to make sure of his aim.

In a novel, of course, or a play, murders are not committed so; the villain leers and gloats, and the victim pleads. In my practical experience, however, killing gentlemen like de Gautet are far too practised for such nonsense; they shoot suddenly and cleanly, and the job's done. I knew I had perhaps a heart-beat between me and damnation, and in sheer terror I snatched the seaman's knife from the top of my boot and hurled it at him with all my force, sprawling down again as I did so.

If I've had more than my share of bad luck in my life, I've had some good to make up for it. I had some now; the knife only hit him butt first, on the leg, but it caused him to take a quick step back, his heel caught on a stone or tuft, he overbalanced, the pistol cracked, the ball went somewhere above my head, and then I was on top of him, smashing blindly with my fists, knees, and anything else, trying to beat him into the ground.

He was tall and active, but nothing like my weight, and Flashy in the grip of mortal fear, with nowhere to run to and no choice but to fight, is probably a dreadful opponent. I was roaring at the top of my voice and clawing at him for dear life; he managed to shove me off once, but he made the error of lunging for the fallen knife, and I was able to get one solid, full-blown boot against the side of his head. He groaned and fell back, his eyes rolling up in his head, and collapsed limply on the turf.

For a moment I thought I'd killed him, but I didn't wait about to see. The training of years asserted itself, and I turned and bolted headlong down the path, with no thought but to put as much distance as I could between me and the scene of possible danger. Before I'd gone far I had to stop to be sick—no doubt from the shock of my narrow escape—and during the pause I had time to consider what I was doing. Where could I run to? Not back to Strelhow, for certain; the Bismarck gang had shown their hand now, and my life wouldn't be worth a china orange if I went anywhere they could come at me. And why had they tried to kill me now? What purpose was there in having me dead *before* the real Carl Gustaf was ready to take my place? Maybe he was ready—although if he'd been rotten with pox they had tidied him up mighty quick. Or had Bismarck's whole tale been pure moonshine? Maybe Carl Gustaf was dead, maybe—oh, maybe a thousand things. I had no way of knowing.

As I think I've said before, while fear usually takes control of my limbs, particularly my running equipment, it seldom prevents me from thinking clearly. Even as I stood there spewing I knew what had to be done. It was essential that I make tracks out of Strackenz at once. But reason told me that to do that in safety I must have a clear notion of what my enemies were up to, and the only man who could tell me that was de Gautet, if he was still alive. The longer I hesitated, the longer he had to revive; my pistols were in my saddle holsters at the summit, so back up the track I went at full speed, pausing only near the top to have a stealthy skulk and see how the land lay.

The horses had gone, scared no doubt by the pistol shot, but de Gautet was still where I had left him. Was he shamming? It would have been like the foxy bastard, so I lay low and watched him. He didn't stir, so I tossed a stone at him. It hit him, but he didn't move. Reassured, I broke cover, snatched up the knife, and crouched panting beside him. He was dead to the world, but breathing, with a fine red lump on his skull; in a moment I had his belt off and trussed his elbows with it; then I pulled off his boots, secured his ankles with my own belt, and felt comfortably safer. Several excellent ideas were already forming in my mind about how to deal with Master de Gautet when he came to, and I waited with a pleasant sense of anticipation. He had a hole in one sock, I noticed; there would be holes in more than that before I'd finished with the murderous swine.

Presently he groaned and opened his eyes, and I had the pleasure of watching his expression show bewilderment, rage, and fear all in turn.

"Well, de Gautet," says I. "What have you got to say, you back-shooting rat, you?"

He stayed mum, glaring at me, so I tickled him up with the knife and he gasped and cursed.

"That's it," says I, "get some practice. And see here: I'm not going to waste time with you. I'm going to ask questions, and you'll answer 'em, smartly, d'you see? Because if you don't—well, I'll show you the advantages of an English public school education, that's all. Now, first, why did you try to kill me? What are you and our good friend Otto Bismarck up to?"

He struggled, but saw it was no go and lay still.

"You will learn nothing from me," says he.

"Your error," says I. "See here."

By good luck I had a piece of string with me, which I looped over two of his toes, placing a nice sharp pebble in between them. I put a stick through the loop and twisted it a little. It always used to liven the Rugby fags up, although of course one couldn't go too far with them, and de Gautet's response was gratifying. He squealed and writhed, but I held his legs down easily.

"You see, my boy," says I, "you'd better open your potato trap or it'll be the worse for you."

"You villain!" cries he, sweating with fear. "Is this how you treat a gentleman?"

"No," says I, enjoying myself. "It's how I treat a dirty, coward-ly, murdering ruffian." And I twisted the stick, hard. He screamed, but I kept on twisting, and his yells were such that I had to stuff my glove in his mouth to quiet him. I'd no real fear of interrup-tion, for he had been at such pains to get me alone that I doubted if any of his precious friends were in the district, but it seemed best to keep him as mum as possible.

"Nod your head when you've had enough, de Gautet," says I cheerfully. "When I've broken all your toes I'll show you how the Afghan ladies treat their husbands' prisoners."

And I went back to work on him. I confess that I thoroughly enjoyed it, as only a true coward can, for only your coward and bully really understand how terrible pain can be. De Gautet wasn't much braver than I am; a few more twists and he was jerking his head up and down like Punch, and for some reason this put me into a great fury. I gave him a few more twists for luck, until the string broke. Then I pulled the gag out.

He was groaning and calling me filthy names, so I taught him manners with the point of the knife in his leg.

"Now, you bastard, why did you try to kill me?"

"It was the Baron's order. Ah, dear God!"

"Never mind God. What for? What about my ten thousand pounds, damn you?"

"It . . . it was never intended that you would be paid."

"You mean I was to be murdered from the start, is that it?"

He rolled over, moaning and licking his lips, looking at me with terror in his eyes.

"If I tell you . . . all . . . oh, my feet! If I tell you . . . do you swear, on your honour as a gentleman, to let me go?"

"Why should I? You'll tell me anyway. Oh, all right then, on my honour as a gentleman. Now, then."

But he insisted that I swear on my mother's memory, too—what he thought all that swearing was worth I can't imagine, but he wasn't feeling himself, I dare say, and foreigners tend to take an Englishman's word when he gives it. That's all they know.

So I swore his oaths, and it all came tumbling out. The Prince Carl Gustaf hadn't had pox at all; he was clean as an old bone. But Bismarck had plotted with Detchard to spirit him away and put me in his place—as they had indeed done. The pox story had simply been an excuse for my benefit, and if it seems ludicrously thin now I can only assert that it seemed damned convincing coming from Bismarck in his lonely stronghold with Kraftstein waiting to fillet me if I didn't believe it. Anyway, their little plan was that after a few days, when Strackenz was convinced it had got a genuine consort for its Duchess, I was to be murdered, in the Jotun Gipfel, and de Gautet was to vanish over the German border. There would be a hue and cry, and my body would be found and carried back to Strackenz amid general consternation.

And then, wonder of wonders, papers would be found in my clothing to suggest that I wasn't Prince Carl at all, but a daring English impostor called Flashman, an agent of Lord Palmerston, if you please, and up to God-knows-what mischief against the security and well-being of the Duchy of Strackenz. There would be chaos and confusion, and a diplomatic upheaval of unprecedented proportions.

I couldn't take it in at first. "You bloody liar! D'ye expect me to believe this cock-and-bull? For that matter, who in the world would credit it?"

"Everyone." His face was working with pain. "You are not the Prince—you would be identified for what you really are—even if it took time, witnesses who knew you could be brought. Who would doubt it?—it is true."

My brain was reeling. "But, in God's name, what for? What could Bismarck gain from all this?"

"The discredit of England—your Lord Palmerston. Utter bewilderment and rage, in Strackenz. Dane and German are on a knife-edge here—there would be bloodshed and disorder. That is what the Baron wants—ah, Herr Gott, my feet are on fire!"

"Damn your feet! Why the hell does he want bloodshed and disorder?"

"As a—pretext. You know that Strackenz and Schleswig and Holstein are bitterly divided between Dane and German. Disorder in one would spread to the others—the old rivalry between Berlin and Copenhagen would be fanned into flame—for the sake of German interest, Berlin would march into Strackenz, then into the other two. Who could stop her? It is only the—excuse—that is lacking."

"And how would my murder be explained, in God's name?"

"It would not need—explaining. That you were an English agent—that would be enough."

Well, that seemed the silliest bit of all, to me, and I said so—who was going to buy me as an agent?

"Feel the lining of your tunic—on the right side." For all his pain, he couldn't keep a grin of triumph off his face. "It is there—feel."

By God, it was. I ripped out the lining with my knife, and there was a paper, covered in tiny cryptograms—God knows what they meant, but knowing Bismarck I'll wager it was good, sound, incriminating stuff. I sat gazing at it, trying to understand what de Gautet had been telling me.

"It has all been exactly planned," says he. "It could not fail. Confusion and riot must follow on your death—and Germany would seize the opportunity to march."

I was trying vainly to make sense of the whole, incredible scheme—and to find a flaw in it.

"Aha, hold on," says I. "This is all very fine—but just because Bismarck has fine ideas about marching into Strackenz don't mean a thing. There's a government in Berlin, I believe—suppose they don't share his martial ardour—what then?"

"But it is planned, I tell you," cries he. "He has friends—men of power—in high places. It is concerted—and when the chance comes in Strackenz, they will act as he says. He can force the thing—he has the vision—*das genie*."

Aye, perhaps he had the genius. Now, of course, I know that he could have done it—I doubt if there was any diplomatic coup that

that brilliant, warped intelligence couldn't have brought off; for all that he was the most dreadful bastard who ever sat in a chancellery, he was the greatest statesman of our time. Yes, he could have done it—he did, didn't he, in the end, and where is Strackenz now? Like Schleswig and Holstein, it is buried in the German empire that Otto Bismarck built.

It was just my bad luck that I had been cast—through the sheer chance of an uncanny resemblance—to be the first foundation-stone of his great dream. This was to be his initial step to power, the opening move in his great game to unify Germany and make it first of the world's states. Squatting there, on the damp turf of the Jotun Gipfel, I saw that the crazy scheme in which he had involved me had a flawless logic of its own—all he needed was something to strike a spark in Strackenz, and I was the tinder. Thereafter, with him gently guiding from the wings, the tragic farce could run its course.

De Gautet groaned, and brought me back to earth. He was lying there, this foul brute who would have put a bullet in my back—aye, and had already planted his sabre cuts in my skull. In a rage I kicked him—this was the pass that he and his damned friends had brought me to, I shouted, stranded in the middle of their blasted country, incriminated, helpless, certain to be either murdered by Bismarck's crew or hanged by the authorities. He roared and pleaded with me to stop.

"Aye, you can howl now," says I. "You were ready enough an hour ago to show me no mercy, curse you!" A thought struck me. "I don't suppose you showed any to that poor Danish sod, either. Where's Carl Gustaf, then? Lying somewhere with his throat cut and a letter in his pocket saying: 'A present from Flashy and Lord Palmerston'?"

"No, no—he is alive—I swear it! He is being kept—safe."

"What for? What use is he to bloody Bismarck?"

"He was not to be—nothing was to befall him—until—until...."

"Until I'd had my weasand slit? That's it, isn't it? You dirty dogs, you! Where is he then, if he's still alive?"

At first he wouldn't say, but when I flourished the knife at him he changed his mind.

"In Jotunberg—the old castle of the Duke. Yonder, over the

crags—in the Jotunsee. I swear it is true. He is under guard there —he knows nothing. The Baron leaves nothing to chance—if aught had gone wrong, he might have been needed—alive."

"You callous hound! And otherwise—he would have got a bullet, too, eh?"

I had to give him some more toe-leather before he would answer, but when he did it was in some detail. To ensure that no mischance should lead to his being rescued, Carl Gustaf was in a dungeon in the castle, with a handy shaft in its floor that came out somewhere under the Jotunsee. His body would never be found once they popped him down there—which they would certainly do once they heard that my corpse had been delivered back to Strackenz, and the uproar over my identity was going nicely. Well, it looked bad for Carl Gustaf in any event—not that it was any concern of mine, but it helped to fan my righteous indignation, which was powerful enough on my own behalf, I can tell you.

"De Gautet," says I. "You're a foul creature—you don't deserve to live another minute—"

"You swore!" He babbled, struggling in his bonds. "You gave me your solemn promise!"

"So I did," says I. "To let you go, wasn't it? Well, I will. Come along, let's have you up."

I dragged him to his feet, and took my belt from round his ankles. He could hardly stand with the pain of his toes, and I had to support him.

"Now, de Gautet," says I. "I'm going to let you go—but where, eh? That's the point, ain't it?"

"What do you mean?" His eyes were staring with fear. "You promised!"

"So did Bismarck—so did you. You're a dirty creature, de Gautet; I think you need a wash." I propelled him to the edge of the precipice, and held him for a second. "I'll let you go, all right, you murderous cur—down there."

He let out a shriek you could have heard in Munich, and tried to wrench free, but I held him fast and let him look, just to let him know he was really going to die. Then I said: "Gehen sie weg, de Gautet," and gave him a push.

For an instant he tottered on the brink, trying to keep his

balance, and screaming hoarsely; then he fell out and down, and I watched him turn slowly over in the air, crash onto the jutting rocks half-way down the cliff, and spin outwards, like a rag doll with his legs waving, before he vanished into the spray at the precipice foot.

It was an interesting sight. I'd killed before, of course, although never in what you might call cold blood, but I've never felt anything but satisfaction over the end of de Gautet. He deserved to die, if anyone ever did. He was a heartless, cruel rascal, and I'd have been lucky to come off as easily if things had been the other way round. I'm not justifying myself, either for torturing him or killing him, for I don't need to. Both had to be done—but I'm honest enough to admit I enjoyed doing them. He was a good horseman, though.

However, his death, though first-rate in its way, solved nothing so far as my immediate comfort and safety were concerned. I was still in the very devil of a pickle, I realised, as I gazed round the empty clearing and tried to decide what to do next. It was certain that de Gautet had arranged some means of getting word quickly to Rudi and Co. to say that Flashy was a goner and all was well. How long would it be before they realised something had gone wrong? An hour or two? A day? I must assume it would be sooner rather than later—and then the hunt would be up with a vengeance, with me as the poor little fox. I had to get out of Strackenz at once—but where to?

These thoughts put me into a blue funk, of course, and I paced up and down that summit muttering "Where? where? Oh, Jesus, how can I get out of this?" Then I steadied up, telling myself that when you've been hounded by Afghans and come safe home, you need hardly take the vapours over a pack of Germans. Which is just rubbish, of course, as I assured myself a second later; one's as beastly dangerous as the other. Still, this was a comparatively civilised country, I spoke the language tolerably, and I'd had enough experience of skulking, surely, to get me out of it. I hadn't a horse, and only a knife for protection—de Gautet's empty pistols were useless—but the first thing was to get down from the Jotun Gipfel, and plot my course as I went.

Before starting out, I burned the incriminating papers they had sewn in, my tunic. Then I took to the woods at right angles from the path we had been following, scrambling down over mossy rocks and through thick brushwood; it wasn't easy going, but I was too busy with my thoughts to notice much. One point stuck clear in my mind, and it was the advice given by the late lamented Sergeant Hudson when he and I were on the run from the Afridis on the Jallalabad road: "When the bastards are after you, go in the direction where they'll never think o' looking for you—even it it's right back in their faces."

Well, I wasn't going to Strelhow, that was flat. But if I was Bismarck or Rudi, where would I expect Flashy to run? North, for certain, towards the coast, less than a hundred miles away. So that was out of court. Of the other directions, which was the *least* likely for a fugitive? All were hazardous, since they would take me long journeys through Germany, but south seemed the most dangerous of all. By God, the last place they would expect me to make for was Munich, at the far end of the country, where all the bother had begun.

My legs trembled at the thought, but the more I considered it the better it seemed. They'd never believe I'd risk it, so they wouldn't look thereaway. It was horribly chancy, but I was certain that if Hudson had been with me that was the way he'd have pointed. Let me get a horse—no matter how—and I could be over the Strackenz border by nightfall and galloping south. I'd have to beg, hire, borrow, or steal, changes on the way—well, it wouldn't be the first time. I might even use the railway, if it seemed safe to do so. At any rate I was free, for the moment, and if they could catch old Flashy with the wind up him—well, they were smarter fellows than I thought they were.

I hurried on down the hillside, and found myself after half an hour or so on more level land, where the trees thinned out. There was a wisp of smoke coming from behind a copse, and I stole forward cautiously to have a look-see. There was a little farm-building with great trees behind it, but no one about except a few cows in the field to one side and an old dog drowsing in the yard. It didn't look like the kind of place where the new ducal consort of Strackenz would be known, which suited me—the fewer folk who got a glimpse of me, the less chance Bismarck's bullies had of getting on my track.

I was wondering whether to go forward boldly, or scout round for a horse to pinch, when the farm door opened and an old man in gaiters and a sugar-loaf hat came out. He was a peasant, with a face like a walnut, and when he saw me he brought up short and stood glowering at me, the way country folk do at everyone who hasn't got dung on his boots. I gave him a civil good day, and told him my horse had thrown me while I was riding in the Jotun Gipfel; could he oblige me with a remount, for which I would pay generously? And I showed him a handful of crowns.

He mumbled a bit, watching me with the wary, hostile eyes of the old, and then said that his daughter was in the house. She turned out to be a big, strapping creature, plain enough in the face, but just about my weight, so I gave her my best bow and repeated my request with a charming smile. The long and short of it was that they sat me down in the kitchen with some excellent beer and bread and cheese while the old man went off round the house, and presently came back to say that Franz had gone to find Willi, who would be able to borrow Wolf's horse, no doubt, and if the gentleman would be pleased to rest and eat, it would be along in a little while.

I was happy enough with this, for neither of them seemed to have any notion of who I was—or rather, who I was supposed to be—and it gave me the chance to get something under my belt. They were both a little in awe, though, at having such a fine gentleman in their humble home, and seemed too tongue-tied to say much. If the dotard hadn't been there I dare say I could have had the buxom piece dancing the mattress quadrille within the hour, but as it was I had to confine my refreshment to the victuals and beer.

After an hour had passed, though, I began to get restless. I'd no wish to linger here, with Rudi possibly combing the Jotun Gipfel for me already, and when a second hour passed, and then a third, I became feverish. The old clod kept assuring me, in answer to my impatient demands, that Wolf or Franz or Willi would soon be along, with the horse. An excellent horse, he added. And there seemed to be nothing to do but wait, chewing my nails, while the old man sat silent, and the woman went very soft-footed about her work.

It was four hours before they came, and they didn't have a horse. What they did have, though, was weapons. There were four of them, hefty lads in peasant clothes, but with a purposeful look about them that suggested they didn't give all their time to ploughing. Two had muskets, another had a pistol in his belt, and the leader, who was a blond giant at least a head taller than I, had a broadsword, no less, hanging at his side. I was on my feet, quaking, at the sight of them, but the big fellow held up a hand and made me a jerky bow.

"Highness," says he, and the others bobbed their heads behind him. My bald head was evidently better known than I'd realised. Uneasily, I tried to put on a bold front.

"Well, my lads," says I cheerfully, "have you a horse for me?"

"No highness," says the big one. "But if you will please to come with us, my master will attend to all your needs."

I didn't like the sound of this, somehow.

"Who is your master, then?"

"If you please, highness, I am to ask you only to come with us. Please, highness."

He was civil enough, but I didn't like it.

"I want a horse, my good fellow, not to see your master. You know who I am, it seems. Well, bring me a horse directly."

"Please, highness," he repeated stolidly. "You will come with us. My master commands."

At this I became very princely and peremptory, but it didn't do a straw's worth of good. He just stood there insisting, and my bowels went more chilly every moment. I hectored and stormed and threatened, but in the end there was nothing for it. I went with them, leaving the farm couple round-eyed behind us.

To my consternation they led me straight back towards the Jotun Gipfel, but although I protested they held their course, the big fellow turning every now and then to mutter apologies, while his pals kept their muskets handy and their eyes carefully on me. I was beside myself with fright and anger; who the devil were they, I demanded, and where was I being taken? But not a word of sense was to be had from them, and the only consolation I could take was a vague feeling that whoever they were, they weren't Rudi's creatures, and didn't seem to mean me any harm—as yet.

How far we tramped I don't know, but it must have taken fully two hours. I wouldn't have believed the Jotun Gipfel was so extensive, or so dense, but we seemed to be moving into deeper forest all the time, along the foot of the crags. The sun was westering, so far as I could judge, when I saw people ahead, and then we were in a little clearing with perhaps a dozen fellows waiting for us; stalwart peasants like my four guards, and all of them armed.

There was a little cabin half-hidden among the bushes at the foot of a small cliff that ran up into the overhanging forest, and before the cabin stood two men. One was a tall, slender, serious-looking chap dressed like a quality lawyer, and grotesquely out of place here; the other was burly and short, in a corduroy suit and leggings, the picture of a country squire or retired military man. He had grizzled, close-cropped hair, a bulldog face, and a black patch over one eye. He was smoking a pipe.

They stood staring at me, and then the tall one turned and said urgently to his companion: "He is wrong. I am sure he is wrong."

The other knocked out his pipe on his hand. "Perhaps," says he. "Perhaps not." He took a step towards me. "May I ask you, sir, what is your name?"

There was only one answer to that. I took a deep breath, looked down my nose, and said:

"I think you know it very well. I am Prince Carl Gustaf. And I think I may be entitled to ask, gentlemen, who you may be, and what is the explanation of this outrage?"

For a man with his heart in his mouth, I think I played it well. At any rate, the tall one said excitedly:

"You see! It could not be otherwise. Highness, may I. . . ."

"Save your apologies, doctor," says the short one. "They may be in order, or they may not." To me he went on: "Sir, we find ourselves in a quandary. I hear you say who you are; well, my name is Sapten, and this is Dr Per Grundvig, of Strackenz. Now, may I ask what brings you to Jotun Gipfel, with your coat muddied and your breeches torn?"

"You ask a good deal, sir!" says I hotly. "Must I remind you who I am, and that your questions are an impertinence? I shall. . . ."

"Aye, it sounds like the real thing," says Sapten, smiling a grim little smile. "Well, we'll see." He turned his head. "Hansen! Step this way, if you please!"

And out of the hut, before my horrified gaze, stepped the young man who had greeted me at the wedding reception—Erik Hansen, Carl Gustaf's boyhood friend. I felt my senses start to swim with sick terror; he had sensed something wrong then—he couldn't fail to unmask me now. I watched him through a haze as he walked steadily up to me and gazed intently at my face.

"Prince Carl?" he said at last. "Carl? Is it you? Is it really you?"

I forced myself to try to smile. "Erik!" God, what a croak it was. "Why, Erik, what brings you here?"

He stepped back, his face white, his hands trembling. He looked from Sapten to the doctor, shaking his head. "Gentlemen, I don't know . . . it's he . . . and yet . . . I don't know. . . ."

"Try him in Danish," says Sapten, his single grey eye fixed on me.

I knew then I was done for. Bersonin's efforts had been insufficient to give me more than the crudest grasp of one of the hardest tongues in Europe. It must have shown in my face as Erik turned back to me, for the damned old villain Sapten added:

"Ask him something difficult."

Erik thought a moment, and then, with an almost pleading look in his eyes, spoke in the soft, slipshod mutter that had baffled my ear at Schönhausen. I caught the words "Hvor boede" and hardly anything else. Christ, he wanted to know where somebody lived, God knows who. Desperately I said:

"Jeg forstar ikke" to show that I didn't understand, and it sounded so hellish flat I could have burst into tears. Slowly an ugly look came over his fair young face.

"Ny," he said slowly. "De forstar my ikke." He turned to them, and said in a voice that shook: "He may be the devil himself. It is the Prince's face and body. But it is not Carl Gustaf— my life on it!"

There wasn't a sound in the clearing, except for my own croaking breaths. Then Sapten put his pipe in his pocket.

"So," says he. "Right, my lad, into that hut with you, and if you make a wrong move, you're with your Maker. Jacob," he shouted. "Sling a noose over the branch yonder."

Cowards, as Shakespeare has wisely observed, die many times before their deaths, but not many of them can have expired in spirit more often than I. And I've seldom had better reason than when Sapten threw that order to his followers; there was an air of grim purpose about the man that told you he would do exactly what he promised, and that offhand instruction was more terrible than any mere threat could have been. I stumbled into the hut and collapsed on a bench, and the three followed me and closed the door.

"Now," says Sapten, folding his arms, "who are you?"

There was no question of brazening it out, any more than there was hope of making a run for it. My only chance lay in talking my way out of the noose—not that the three grim faces offered any encouragement. But anyway, here goes, thought I, reminding myself that there's no lie ever invented that's as convincing as half-truth.

"Gentlemen," I began, "believe me, I can explain this whole fearful business. You're quite right; I am not Prince Carl Gustaf. But I most solemnly assure you that these past few days I have had no choice but to pretend that I was that man. No choice— and I believe when you have heard me out you will agree that the true victim of this abominable hoax is my unhappy self."

"Like enough," says Sapten, "since you'll certainly hang for it."

"No, no!" I protested. "You must hear me out. I can prove what I say. I was forced to it—dreadfully forced, but you must believe me innocent."

"Where is the Prince?" burst out Hansen. "Tell us that, you liar!"

I ignored this, for a good reason. "My name is Arnold—Captain Thomas Arnold. I'm a British Army officer"—and my idiot tongue nearly added "of no fixed abode"—"and I have been. kidnapped and tricked into this by enemies of Strackenz."

That threw them into a talking; both Grundvig and Hansen started volleying questions at me, but Sapten cut them off.

"British Army, eh?" says he. "How many regiments of foot guards have you?—quick, now."

"Why, three."

"Humph," says he. "Go on."

"Well," says I. "It's an incredible tale . . . you won't believe it. . . ."

"Probably not," says Sapten, whom I was liking less and less. "Get to the point."

So I told it them, from the beginning, sticking as close as I could to the truth. My brain was working desperately as I talked, for the tale wouldn't do entirely as it stood. I left Lola Montez out of it, and invented a wife and child for myself who had accompanied me to Germany—I was going to need them. I described my abduction in Munich, without reference to Baroness Pechman, and related the Schönhausen episode exactly as it had happened.

"Otto Bismarck, eh?" says Sapten. "I've heard of him. And young Starnberg—aye, we know of that one."

"This is unbelievable," exclaims Grundvig. "The man is plainly lying in everything he says. Why, who could. . . ."

"Easy, doctor," says Sapten. "Unbelievable—yes." He pointed at me. "He's unbelievable, too—but he's sitting here in front of us." He nodded to me. "Continue."

Thank God there was at least one cool head among them. I went on, relating how I came to Strackenz, how I had gone through the farce in the Cathedral, how de Gautet had tried to murder me, and how I had killed him in fair fight at the top of the Jotun Gipfel that morning. Sapten's icy eye never left my face, but Grundvig kept giving exclamations of incredulity and horror, and finally Hansen could contain himself no longer.

"Why did you do it? My God, you villain, why? Have you no shame, no honour? How could you live, and commit such a monstrous crime?"

I looked him full in the face, like a man struggling with tremendous emotion. (I was, and it was funk, but I tried to look as though I was bursting with wrought-up indignation and distress.)

"Why, sir?" says I. "You ask 'why'. Do you suppose I would have consented to this infamy—have played this awful masquer-

424

ade—unless they had compelled me with a weapon that no man, however honourable, could resist?" I gave a mighty gulp. "They held my wife and child, sir. Do you realise what that means?" I shouted the question at him, and decided that this was the time to break down. "My God, my God!" I exclaimed. "My precious jewels! My little golden-headed Amelia! Shall I ever see thee again?"

It would have had them thumping on the seat-backs in any theatre in London, I'll swear, but when I raised my head from my hands there was no sign of frantic applause from this audience. Hansen looked bewildered and Grundvig's long face was working with rage; Sapten was filling his pipe.

"And Prince Carl Gustaf—where's he?" he asked.

I had thought, at the beginning, that eventually I might bargain with them—my life for the information—but now instinct told me that it wouldn't answer. Sapten would have hanged me on the spot, I'm sure—anyway, it wouldn't have suited the character I was trying desperately to establish. In that, I saw, lay my only hope—to make them believe that I had been a helpless victim of a dastardly plot. And God help me, wasn't it true?

So I told them about Jotunberg, and the plans for disposing of Carl Gustaf. Grundvig clasped his temples, Hansen exclaimed in horror, Sapten lit his pipe and puffed in silence.

"Aye," says he, "and then what? This fellow tried to murder you—you killed him, you say. What did you propose to do next?"

"Why—why—I hardly knew. I was distraught—my wife and child—the fate of the prince—I was half-mad with anxiety."

"To be sure," says he, and puffed some more. "And this was all played out, you tell us, so that this Otto Bismarck could start to build a German Empire? Well, well."

"You've heard what I've told you, sir," says I. "I warned you it was incredible, but it's true—every word of it."

Grundvig, who had been pacing up and down, spun on his heel.

"I for one cannot believe it! It is impossible! Major, Erik! Would anyone but a madman credit such a story? It is not to be imagined!" He glared at me. "This man—this scoundrel—can you believe anyone as infamous as he has confessed himself to be?"

"Not I, for one," says Hansen.

Sapten scratched his grizzled head. "Just so," says he, and my heart sank. "But I suggest, doctor, and you too, Erik, that there's a question to be asked. Can either of you—" and his bright eye went from one to the other—"looking at this fellow here, a man who we know has successfully imposed himself for two weeks on a whole nation—can either of you, in the face of the fact, suggest a better story than he's told us?"

They stared at him. He nodded at me.

"There he is. Account for him." He knocked out his pipe. "If he has lied—then what's the true explanation?"

They babbled a good deal at this, but of course there was no answering him. My story was enough to defy imagination, Sapten agreed—but any alternative must be equally incredible.

"If we can accept that a *doppelgänger* of the Prince's can take his place for two weeks—and we know that has happened—then I for one can accept anything," says he.

"You mean you believe him?" cries Grundvig.

"For want of evidence to disprove his story—yes." My heart fluttered up like a maiden's prayer, "You see," says Sapten grimly, "it fits. Haven't we been starting at every German shadow this twenty years back? You know that, Grundvig. Isn't fear for the security of our duchy the reason we're here? What are we Sons of the Volsungs for?" He shook his head. "Show me a hole in this fellow's tale, for I can't see one."

At this they went into a frantic discussion, which of course got them nowhere. Baffled, they turned back on me.

"What are we to do with him?" says Grundvig.

"Hang him," snaps Hansen. "The swine deserves it."

"For the crime he has committed against our duchess," says Grundvig, glowering at me, "he deserves no less."

They were all looking like Scotch elders in a brothel, but I saw that here was my cue again. I looked bewildered, and then let outraged indignation take its place.

"What do you mean by that?" I cried.

"You were married to her for more than a week," says Sapten significantly.

I made hoarse noises of fury. "You infamous old man!" I shouted. "D'you dare to suggest? . . . My God, sir, have you forgotten that I am a British officer? Have you the effrontery to imply that I would. . . ."

I choked as with great rage, but I doubt if Sapten was much impressed. The other two looked doubtful, though.

"I am not so dead to honour," says I, trying to look noble and angry together, "that I would stoop to carry my imposture as far as that. There are some things that no gentleman. . . ." And I broke off as though it was too much for me.

"It must have been thought strange," mutters Grundvig. Palpitating, I maintained a stiff silence.

They were quiet for a moment, contemplating their duchess's virginity, I suppose. Then Grundvig said:

"Do you swear . . . that . . . that. . . ."

"My word of honour," says I, "as a British officer."

"Oh, well, that settles it," says Sapten, and I'll swear his mouth twitched under his moustache. "And at the risk of seeming disloyal, gentlemen, I'd suggest that the fate of Prince Carl Gustaf is perhaps as important as what may or mayn't have happened to . . . well, let it be." He swung round on me. "You'll stay here. If you move outside this hut you're a dead man—which you may be, anyway, before we're done. I suggest we continue our deliberations elsewhere, doctor. If what we have learned today is true, we haven't much time to prevent our duchess becoming a widow before she's been a bride. To say nothing of saving her duchy for her. Come."

The door slammed behind them, and I was left alone with my thoughts. Not pleasant ones, but they could have been worse. They seemed to have accepted my story, and I was pretty sure that the fictitious parts of it would defy their efforts to pick holes —they weren't important lies, anyway, but merely colour to enhance my character of innocent-in-the-grip-of-cruel-fate. Best of all, I was reasonably sure they weren't going to hang me. Sapten was the strong mind among them, and while I read him as one who wouldn't think twice about taking human life if he had to, there didn't seem any good reason why they should do away with me. He was a realist, and not swayed by emotion like Grundvig and Hansen. But Grundvig, too, I believed would stop short of murder—he seemed a decent, sensitive sort of fool. Hansen was the one I offended most, probably because he was the Prince's close friend. He would have slaughtered me for old time's sake, so to speak, but I fancied he would be out-voted.

So there I was, with nothing to do but wait and think. At least I was safe from Bismarck's bravos, which was something. If these were the Sons of the Volsungs—the clandestine Danish sympathisers whom Rudi had spoken of with contempt—I couldn't be in better hands, from that point of view. Rudi, it seemed to me, had under-estimated them; I had no idea what they could do about rescuing their precious prince from Jotunberg, and didn't care either, but they looked a lively and workmanlike lot. It was pleasant to think that they might put a spoke in bloody Otto's little wheel, after all—Sapten was just the man for that, if I knew anything. He was steady, and saw quickly to the heart of things, and seemed to be full of all the best virtues, like resolution and courage and what-not, without being over-hampered by scruple. Given him on the retreat from Kabul our army would have got home safe enough, and probably brought all the loot of the Bala Hissar into the bargain.

Anyway, I wasn't too displeased with my own situation, and passed the time wondering when they would let me go. God knows why I was so optimistic—reaction, possibly, after having escaped unpleasant death twice in one day—but I ought to have known better. If I had been thinking clearly I'd have realised that from their point of view, the safest place for me was six feet under, where I couldn't cause any scandal. As it was, what they got me into was very nearly as bad, and caused me to die several more of Shakespeare's deaths.

I was left alone for several hours, during which time the only soul I saw was the big peasant, who brought me some food and beer (still addressing me as "highness", but in a rather puzzled way). It was night before my three inquisitors returned, and I noticed that both Sapten and Hansen were splashed with mud about the legs, as though they'd ridden hard. Sapten set down a lamp on the table, threw aside his cloak, and eyed me grimly.

"Captain Arnold," says he, "if that is your name, you puzzle me. I don't like being puzzled. As these gentlemen here have pointed out, no sane man would believe your story for a moment. Well, maybe I'm not sane, but I've decided to believe it—most of it anyway. I don't know whether you're the biggest knave or the unluckiest wretch who ever drew breath—I incline to the first view, personally, having a nice nose for knavery—no, don't bother to protest, we've heard all that. But I can't be sure, you see, and it suits me to assume that you're honest—up to a point. So there."

I kept quiet, fearful and hopeful together. He produced his pipe and began to rub tobacco.

"Fortunately, we can test you and serve our own ends at the same time," he went on. "Now then,"—he fixed me with that cold eye—"here's the point. Victim or scoundrel, whichever you may be, you've committed a monstrous wrong. Are you prepared to help to set it right?"

With those three grim faces on me in the lamplight, I was in no doubt about the right answer here—no doubt at all.

"Gentlemen," says I, "God bless you. Whatever I can do"— and I couldn't think, thank God, that there was much—"that I shall do, with all the power at my command. I have been thinking, as I sat here, of the terrible—"

"Aye, we know," Sapten cut in. "You needn't tell us." He lit his pipe, pup-pup-pup, and blew smoke. "All we want is yes or no, and I take it the answer's yes."

"With all my heart," I cried earnestly.

"I doubt it," says Sapten, "but never mind. You're a soldier, you say. Tell me—have you seen much service?"

Well, I could answer truthfully to that—I had seen plenty, and I didn't see any need to tell him that I'd been sweating with panic all through it. Like a fool, I implied that I'd been in some pretty sharp stuff, and come out with (in all manly modesty) some distinction. The words were out before I realised that I might be talking myself into more trouble.

"So," says he, "well enough—you've the look of a man of your hands. We may have cause to be glad of that. Now then, here's the position. You tell us that Prince Carl Gustaf is in Jotunberg under guard of Bismarck's men, and that they can do away with him— and leave no evidence—at the first sign of alarm. They'll weight his body, shove it down this hell-hole of theirs—and good-bye." I noticed Grundvig shudder. "So if we were to storm the place— and it wouldn't be easy—all that we would find would be a party of gentlemen who no doubt would have an innocent tale of being the guests of Adolf Bülow, the owner—he's tactfully out of the country, by the way. And we'd have lost Prince Carl. The Jotunsee is deep, and we'd never even find his body."

Hansen gave a little gasp, and I saw there were absolute tears on his cheek.

"So that won't do," says Sapten, puffing away. "Now—suppose we leave Jotunberg alone. Suppose we return you to Strelhow, and wait and see what our German friends in the castle do then. It would gain us time."

By God, I didn't like this. De Gautet might have failed with me, but some one else would surely succeed—the last place I wanted to be was anywhere on public view in Strackenz.

"They would hardly murder the prince," says Grundvig, "while you were on the consort's throne. At least, they have not done it yet."

"It offers us time," repeated Sapten slowly, "but what could we do with it, eh?"

I tried to think of something—anything.

"Perhaps if I were to abdicate," I suggested hurriedly. "I mean ... if it would help...."

"Waiting increases the risks, though," went on Sapten, as though I hadn't spoken. "Of your discovery; of the Prince's murder."

"We cannot leave him there, with those villains!" burst out Hansen.

"No, so we've rejected that," says Sapten. "And we come back to the only course—a desperate and dangerous one, for it may cost his life in the end. But nothing else remains."

He paused, and I felt my spine dissolve. Oh, Jesus, here it was again—whenever I hear the words "desperate and dangerous" I know that I'm for it. I could only wait to hear the worst.

"To storm Jotunberg is impossible," says Sapten. "It stands in the lake of the Jotunsee, and only at one point is it accessible from the shore, where a causeway runs out towards it. There were two guards on the causeway tonight, at the outer end, where the gap between causeway and castle is spanned by a drawbridge. That bridge is raised, which is a sign that those within know that their plans have gone astray. Doubtless when the man you killed this morning failed to return to his friends, they took alarm. Two of them, at any rate, rode into the castle tonight—Hansen and I saw them; a youngster, a gay spark, for all he looked little more than a boy, and a big ruffian along with him—"

"Starnberg and Kraftstein," says I. "Major Sapten, they are a devilish pair—they'll stop at nothing!"

"Well, how many more were already in the castle, we don't know. Probably no more than a handful. But we could never hope to surprise them. So we must find another way, and quickly." He sat back. "Erik; it is your scheme. Let him hear it."

One look at Hansen's face—his eyes were glittering like a fanatic's—prepared me for the worst.

"Where a storming party must fail, we may prevail by stealth. Two brave men could cross the Jotunsee at night from the opposite bank, by boat as close as they dared, and then by swimming. Part of the fortress is in ruin; they could land in the darkness, enter the castle silently, and discover where the prince is hidden. Then, while one guarded him, the other would hasten to the drawbridge and lower it so that our people, hidden on the shore, could storm across the causeway. They could easily owerpower its garrison—but somehow the prince's life would have to be preserved while the fighting lasted. Whether this could be done—" he shrugged. "At least the two who had entered first could die trying."

And the very fact that they were telling me this informed me who one of those two was going to be. Of all the lunatic, no-hope schemes I ever heard, this seemed to be the primest yet. If they thought they were going to get me swimming into that place in the dark, with the likes of Rudi and Kraftstein waiting for me, they didn't know their man. The mere thought was enough to set my guts rumbling with fright. I'd see them damned first. I'd sooner be—swinging at the end of Sapten's rope? That was what would happen, of course, if I refused.

While I was gulping down these happy thoughts, Grundvig—whom I'd known from the first was a clever chap—sensibly suggested that where two men could swim, so could a dozen, but Hansen shook his fat head with determination.

"No. Two may pass unobserved, but not more. It is out of the question." He turned to look at me, his face set, his eyes expressionless. "I shall be one of the two—Carl Gustaf is my friend, and if he is to die I shall count myself happy to die with him. You do not know him—yet without you, he would not be where he is. Of all people, you at least owe him a life. Will you come with me?"

Whatever I may be, I'm not slow-witted. If ever there was a situation made for frantic pleading in the name of common sense, I was in it now—I could have suggested that they try to bargain with Rudi, or send a messenger to Bismarck (wherever he was) and tell him that they were on to his games; I could have gone into a faint, or told them that I couldn't swim, or that I got hay fever if I went out after dark—I could simply have roared for mercy. But I knew it wouldn't do; they were deadly serious, frightened men—frightened for that Danish idiot, instead of for themselves, as any sane man would have been—and if I hesitated, or argued, or did anything but accept at once they would rule me out immediately for a coward and a hypocrite and a backslider. And then it would be the Newgate hornpipe for Flashy, with the whole damned crew of Sons of the Volsungs hauling on the rope. I knew all this in the few seconds that I sat there with my bowels melting, and I heard a voice say in a deadly croak:

"Yes, I'll come."

Hansen nodded slowly. "I do not pretend that I take you from choice; I would sooner take the meanest peasant in our band. But you are a soldier, you are skilled in arms and in this kind of work." (Dear lad, I thought, how little you know.) "You are a man of resource, or you could never have done the infamous thing that has brought you here. Perhaps there is a queer fate at work in that. At all events, you are the man for this."

I could have discussed that with some eloquence, but I knew better. I said nothing, and Hansen said: "It will be for tomorrow night, then," and he and Grundvig got up and went without another word.

Sapten lingered, putting on his cloak, watching me. At last he spoke.

"It is one of the lessons a man learns as he grows old," says he, "to put away desires and emotions—aye, and even honour—and to do what must be done with the tools to hand, whatever they may be. So I let you go with Hansen tomorrow. Succeed in what is to do, for as God's my witness, if you don't I'll kill you without pity." He turned to the door. "Perhaps I misjudge you; I don't know. In case I am guilty of that, I promise that whatever befalls, I shall not rest until I have ensured the safety of that wife and daughter who so concerned you earlier today, but whom you seem to have forgotten tonight. Take comfort from the knowledge that little golden-haired Amelia is in my thoughts." He opened the door. "Goodnight, Englishman."

And he went out, no doubt very pleased with himself.

I spent the next hour frantically trying to dig under the wall of the cabin with my bare hands, but it was no go. The earth was too hard, and full of roots and stones; I made a pitifully small scrape, and then hurriedly filled it in again and stamped it down in case they saw what I'd been up to. Anyway, even if I had succeeded in breaking out, they'd have run me to earth in the forest; they were trained woodsmen and I'd no idea where I was.

Once my initial panic had passed, I could only sit in miserable contemplation. There was a slim chance that before tomorrow evening something might happen to change Hansen's lunatic plan —or I might receive a heaven-sent opportunity to escape, although I doubted that. Failing these things, I should certainly be launched —literally, too—into the most dangerous adventure of my life, and with precious little prospect of coming through it. So I would end here, in a god-forsaken miserable German ruin, trying to rescue a man I'd never met—I, who wouldn't stir a finger to rescue my own grandmother. It was all too much, and I had a good self-pitying blubber to myself, and then I cursed and prayed a bit, invoking the God in whom I believe only in moments of real despair to intervene on my behalf.

I tried to console myself that I'd come out of desperate straits before—aye, but wasn't my luck about due to run out, then? No, no, Jesus would see the repentant sinner right, and I would never swear or fornicate or steal or lie again—I strove to remember the seven deadly sins, to make sure I missed none of them, and then cudgelled my brains for the Ten Commandments, so that I could promise never to break them again—although, mind you, I'd never set up a graven image in my life.

I should have felt purified and at peace after all this, but I found I was just as terrified as ever, so I ended by damning the whole system. I knew it would make no difference, anyway.

That next day was interminable; my heart was in my mouth every time footsteps approached the cabin door, and it was almost a relief when Sapten and his two companions came for me in the evening. They brought a good deal of gear with them, explaining

433

that we should make all our preparations here before setting out, and just the activity of getting ready took my mind momentarily off the horrors ahead.

First Hansen and I stripped right down, so that we could be rubbed all over with grease as a protection against the cold when we took to the water. Sapten whistled softly when he saw my scars—the place where a pistol ball had burrowed from my side towards my spine, the whip-marks left by the swine Gul Shah, and the white weal on my thigh where my leg was broken at Piper's Fort. It was an impressive collection—and even if most of them were in the rear, they weren't the kind of decorations you normally see on a coward.

"You've been lucky," says he. "So far."

When we had been thoroughly greased, we put on rough woollen underclothes—a most disgusting process—and then heavy woollen shirts and smocks, tucked into our breeches. We wore stockings and light shoes, and Sapten bound bandages round our wrists and ankles to keep our clothing gathered in place.

"Now, then," says he, "to arms," and produced a couple of heavy broadswords and an assortment of hunting knives. "If you want fire-arms you'll have to persuade our friends in Jotunberg to give you some," he added. "Useless to try to take them with you."

Hansen took a sword and a long dagger, but I shook my head.

"Haven't you a sabre?"

Sapten looked doubtful, but a search among his band of brigands outside produced the required article—it was old but a good piece of steel, and I shuddered inwardly at the sight of it. But I took it— if I have to fight, God forbid, I'll do it with a weapon I understand, and if I was no Angelo[38] with a sabre, at least I'd been trained in its use. For the rest, they gave me back my seaman's knife, and each of us was provided with a flask of spirits.

We carried the swords on our backs, looped securely at shoulder and waist, and Hansen bound a length of cord round his middle. There was some debate as to whether we should take flint and steel, but there seemed no point to it. Finally, we each had an oilskin packet containing some meat and bread and cheese, in case, as Sapten cheerfully remarked, we had time to stop for a snack.

"You may feel the need of something when you get out of the water," he added. "Eat and drink if chance serves. Now, then,

"this is no *kindergarten* you are venturing into, my lad. These are very practical men, as you may discover." I was eager to take some of the bounce out of him.

"That'll do," growls Sapten. "All ready, then? Lassen sie uns gehen."

There were horses outside, and men moving about us in the gloom; we rode in silent cavalcade through the woods, along a path that wound upwards into the Jotun Gipfel, and then down through dense thickets of bush and bracken. There was no chance of escape, even if I had dared; two men rode at my stirrups all the way. We halted frequently—while scouts went ahead, I suppose—and I took the opportunity to sample the contents of my flask. It held brandy, about half a pint, and it was empty by the time the journey was half done. Not that it made much odds, except to warm me; I could have drunk a gallon without showing it just then.

At last we halted and dismounted; shadowy hands took my bridle, and I was pushed forward through the bushes until I found myself on the banks of a tiny creek, with water lapping at my feet. Hansen was beside me, and there was much whispering in the dark; I could see the vague outline of a boat and its rowers, and then the moon came out from behind the clouds, and through the tangled branches at the creek's mouth I saw the choppy grey water of the lake, and rising out of it, not three furlongs off, the stark outline of Jotunberg.

It was a sight to freeze your blood and make you think of monsters and vampires and bats squeaking in gloomy vaults—a Gothic horror of dark battlements and towers with cloud-wrack behind it, silent and menacing in the moonlight. My imagination peopled it with phantom shapes waiting at its windows—and they wouldn't have been any worse than Rudi and Kraftstein. Given another moment I believe I would have sunk down helpless on the shore, but before I knew it I was in the boat, with Hansen beside me.

"Wait for the moon to die." Sapten's hoarse whisper came out of the dark behind, and presently the light was blotted out, and Jotunberg was only a more solid shadow in the dark. But it was still there, and all the more horrid in my mind's eye. I had to grip my chin to stop my teeth chattering.

Sapten muttered again in the gloom, the boat stirred as the dim forms of the rowers moved, and we were sliding out of the creek onto the face of the Jotunsee. The breeze nipped as we broke cover, and then the bank had vanished behind us.

It was as black as the earl of hell's weskit, and deadly silent except for the chuckle of water under our bow and the soft rustle as the oarsmen heaved. The boat rocked gently, but we were moving quite quickly, with the dim shape of the castle growing bigger and uglier every moment. It seemed to me that we were rowing dangerously close to it; I could see the faint glare of a light at one of the lower windows, and then Hansen softly said "Halt", and the oarsmen stopped rowing.

Hansen touched my shoulder. "Ready?" I was trying to suppress the bile of panic that was welling up into my throat, so I didn't answer. "Folgen sie mir ganz nahe," says he, and then he had slipped over the side like an otter, with hardly a sound.

For the life of me I couldn't bring myself to follow; my limbs were like jelly; I couldn't move. But petrified though I was, I knew I daren't stay either; let me refuse now, and Sapten would make cold meat of me very shortly afterwards. I leaned over the side of the boat, clumsily trying to copy Hansen, and then I had overbalanced, and with an awful, ponderous roll I came off the gunwale and plunged into the Jotunsee.

The cold was hideous, cutting into my body like a knife, and I came up spluttering with the sheer pain of it. As I gasped for breath Hansen's face came out of the darkness, hissing at me to be quiet, his hand searching for me underwater.

"Geben sie acht, idiot! Stop splashing!"

"This is bloody madness!" I croaked at him. "Christ, it's midwinter, man! We'll freeze to death!"

He grabbed my shoulder while we trod water, snarling at me to be quiet. Then, turning from the boat, he began to strike out slowly for the castle, expecting me to follow. For a second I considered the possibility, even at this late hour, of making for the shore and taking my chance in the woods, but I realised I could never swim the distance—not at this temperature, and with the sabre strapped to my back and my sodden clothes dragging at me. I had to stay with Hansen, so I struck out after him, as quietly as I could, sobbing with fear and frustration.

437

God, I remember thinking, this is too bad. What the hell had I done to deserve this? Left alone I'm a harmless enough fellow, asking nothing but meat and drink and a whore or two, and not offending anyone much—why must I be punished in this hellish fashion? The cold seemed to be numbing my very guts; I knew I couldn't go much longer, and then a blinding pain shot through my left leg, and I was under water, my mouth filling as I tried to yell. Flailing with my good leg I came up, bleating for Hansen.

"Cramp!" I whimpered. "Christ, I'll drown!" Even then, I had sense enough to keep my voice down, but it was loud enough to reach him, for next time I went under he hauled me up again, swearing fiercely at me to be quiet, and to stop thrashing about.

"My leg! my leg!" I moaned. "Jesus, I'm done for. Save me, you selfish bastard! Oh, God, the cold!" My leg was one blinding pain, but with Hansen gripping me and holding my face above water I was able to rest until gradually it subsided to a dull ache; I stretched it cautiously, and it seemed to be working again.

When he was sure I could swim on, he whispered that we must hurry, or the cold would get us for certain. I was almost past caring, and told him so; he and his bloody prince and Sapten and the rest of them could rot in hell for me, I said, and he struck me across the face and threatened to drown me if I didn't keep quiet.

"It's your life, too, fool!" he hissed. "Now be silent, or we're lost."

I called him the filthiest names I knew (in a whisper), and then he swam on, with me behind him, striking out feebly enough, but it wasn't far now; another couple of freezing minutes and we were under the lee of the castle wall, where it seemed to rise sheer out of the water, and there wasn't a sight or sound to suggest we had been heard.

Hansen trod water in front of me, and when I came up with him he pointed ahead, and I saw what seemed to be a shadowy opening at the foot of the wall.

"There," says he. "Silence."

"I can't take much more of this," I whispered feebly. "I'll freeze, I tell you—I'm dying—I know I am. God damn you, you scabby-headed Danish swine, you . . . wait for me!"

He was swimming slowly into the gap in the wall; and at that moment the moon chose to come out again, striking its cold light on the rearing battlement above us, and showing that the gap was in fact a tiny harbour, cut out of the rock of the Jotunberg itself. To the left and ahead it was enclosed by the castle wall; to the right the wall seemed to be ruined, and there were dark areas of shadow where the moonlight didn't penetrate.

I felt a chill that was not from the water as I paddled slowly towards it; exhausted and shocked as I was, I could smell danger from the place. When you burgle a house, you don't go in by the open front door. But Hansen was already out of sight in the shadow; I swam after him round an angle of the rock, and saw him treading water with his hand up on the stone ledge that bordered the harbour. When he saw me he turned face on to the stone, put up his other hand, and heaved himself out of the water.

For a second he hung there, poised, straining to pull his body onto the ledge; the moonlight was full on him, and suddenly something glittered flying above the water and smacked between his shoulder blades; his head shot up and his body heaved convulsively; for a second he hung, motionless, and then with a dreadful, bubbling sigh he flopped face down on the stone and slid slowly back into the water. As he slipped under I could distinctly see the knife-hilt standing out of his back; then he was floating, half-submerged, and I was scrabbling frantically away from him, choking back the shriek of terror in my throat.

There was a low, cheerful laugh out of the shadows above me, and then someone whistled a line or two of "Marlbrough s'en va-t'en guerre".

"Swim this way, Flashman, Prince of Denmark," said Rudi's voice. "I have you beaded, and you won't float long if I put lead ballast into you. Come along, there's a good chap; you don't want to catch cold, do you?"

* * *

He watched me as I clambered miserably out, shaking with fright and cold, and stood hand on hip, smiling easily at me.

"This is a not entirely unexpected pleasure," says he. "I had a feeling you would turn up, somehow. Eccentric way you have of arriving, though." He nodded towards the water. "Who's our dead friend?"

I told him.

"Hansen, eh? Well, serve him right for a meddling fool. I did him rather proud, I think—twenty-five feet, an uncertain light, and a rather clumsy hunting-knife—but I put it right between his shoulders. Rather pretty work, wouldn't you say? But you're trembling, man!"

"I'm cold," I chattered.

"Not as cold as he is," chuckled this hellish ruffian. "Well, come along. Ah, but first, the formalities." He snapped his fingers, and two men came out of the shadows behind him. "Michael, take the gentleman's sabre, and that most un-English knife in his belt. Excellent. This way."

They took me through a ruined archway, across a paved yard, through a postern-like door in what seemed to be the main keep, and into a vast vaulted hall with a great stone stairway winding round its wall. To my left was a lofty arch through which I could see dimly the outline of massive chains and a great wheel: I supposed this would be the drawbridge mechanism—not that it mattered now.

Rudi, humming merrily, led the way upstairs and into a chamber off the first landing. By contrast with the gloomy medieval stonework through which we had come, it was pleasantly furnished in an untidy bachelor way, with clothes, papers, dog-whips, bottles, and so on scattered everywhere; there was a fire going and I made straight for it.

"Here," says he, pushing a glass of spirits into my hand. "Michael will get you some dry clothes." And while I choked over the drink, and then stripped off my soaking weeds, he lounged in an armchair.

"So," says he, once I had pulled on the rough clothes they brought, and we were alone, "de Gautet bungled it, eh? I told them they should have let me do the business—if I'd been there you would never even have twitched. Tell me what happened."

Possibly I was light-headed with the brandy and the shock of what I had been through, or my fear had reached that stage of desperation where nothing seems to matter; anyway, I told him how I had disposed of his colleague, and he chuckled appreciatively.

"You know, I begin to like you better and better; I knew from the first that we'd get along splendidly. And then what? Our Dansker friends got hold of you, didn't they?" Seeing me hesitate, he leaned forward in his chair. "Come along, now; I know much more than you may think, and can probably guess the rest. And if you hold back, or lie to me—well, Mr Play-actor, you'll find yourself going for a swim with friend Hansen, I promise you. Who sent you here? It was the Danish faction, wasn't it—Sapten's precious bandits?"

"The Sons of the Volsungs," I admitted. I daren't try to deceive him—and what would have been the point?

"Sons of the Volsungs! Sons of the Nibelungs would be more appropriate. And you and Hansen were to try to rescue Carl Gustaf? I wonder," he mused, "how they found out about him. No matter. What did you expect to accomplish, in heaven's name? Two of you couldn't hope . . . ah, but wait a moment! You were the mine under the walls, weren't you? To open the way for the good Major Sapten's patriotic horde." He gave a ringing laugh. "Don't look so surprised, man! D'ye think we're blind in here? We've been watching them scuttle about the shore all day. Why, with a night-glass in the tower we watched your boat set out an hour ago! Of all the bungling, ill-judged, badly-managed affairs! But what would one expect from that pack of yokels?" He roared with laughter again. "And how did they coerce you into this folly? A knife at your back, no doubt. Well, well, I wonder what they'll think of next?"

Now, I was beginning to get some of my senses back, what with the warmth and the rest of sitting down. I was out of the frying-pan into the fire, no question, but I couldn't for the life of me see why he had killed Hansen and taken me prisoner—unless it was for information. And when he had got all that he wanted, what was he going to do with me? I could guess.

"Yes, what will they think of next?" He sauntered in front of the fireplace, slim and elegant in his tight-fitting black tunic and breeches, and turned to flash his teeth at me. "Suppose you tell me?"

"I don't know," says I. "It was . . . as you've guessed. We were to try to release him and let down the bridge."

"And if that failed?"

"They didn't say."

"Mm. Do they know our garrison?"

"They think ... only a few."

"Well guessed—or well spied out. Not that it'll help them. If they try to storm the place their dear Prince will be feeding the fishes in the Jotunsee before they're over the causeway—do they know that, I wonder?"

I nodded. "They know all about it."

He grinned happily. "Well, then, we needn't fret about them, need we? It gives us time to consider. How many men have they over yonder, by the way? And be very, very careful how you answer."

"I heard them say fifty."

"Wise Flashman. I knew, you see." Suddenly he clapped me on the shoulder. "Would you like to meet your royal twin? I've been longing to bring the pair of you face to face, you know—and you can see, at the same time, the excellent arrangements we have for his . . . shall we say, security?—in the event of burglars. Come along." He flung open the door. "Oh, and Flashman." he added, carelessly smiling. "You will bear in mind that I'm *not* de Gautet, won't you? You'll do nothing foolish, I mean? You see, it would be a great waste, because I think . . . I think we may be able to try out a little scheme of mine together, you and I. We'll see." He bowed and waved me through. "After you, your highness."

We went down to the great hall, and there Rudi turned into a side-passage, and down a steep flight of stone steps which spiralled into the depths of the castle. There were oil lamps at intervals, glistening on the nitre which crusted the bare stone, and in places the steps were slippery with moss. We came out into a flagged cloister, with mighty, squat columns supporting the low ceiling; the place was in shadow, but ahead of us light shone from an archway, and passing through we were in a broad stone chamber where two men sat over cards at a rough table. They looked up at our approach, one with his hand on a pistol; they were burly, tall fellows in what looked like cavalry overalls, and their sabres hung at their elbows, but I wasn't concerned with them. Beyond them was a great iron grille, stretching from floor to ceiling, and before it stood Kraftstein, his huge hands on his hips, like an ogre in the flickering lamplight.

"Here he is, Kraftstein," says Rudi lightly. "Our old drinking-companion from Schönhausen. Aren't you pleased, now, that I didn't let you shoot him in the water? Kraftstein's got no manners, you know," he added over his shoulder to me. "And how is our royal guest this evening?"

Kraftstein said nothing, but having glowered at me he turned and drew a bolt in the grille. Rudi waved me through the gate as it groaned back on its hinges, and with the hair prickling on my neck, but spurred by curiosity, I passed through.

The grille, I saw, cut off the end of the vault, and we were in an enclosure perhaps forty feet deep and half as wide. At the end, opposite me, a man lay on a low couch set against the wall; there was a table with a lamp beside him, and at the sound of the creaking hinge he sat up, shading his eyes and peering towards us.

For some reason I felt a nervousness that had nothing to do with the danger of my situation; I felt I was about to see something uncanny—and this although I knew what it was going to be.

"Guten abend, highness," says Rudi, as we went forward. "Here's a visitor for you."

The man took his hand from his face, and I couldn't help letting out an exclamation. For there I sat, looking at me—my own face, puzzled, wary, and then in an instant, blank with amazement, the mouth open and eyes staring. He shrank back, and then suddenly he was on his feet.

"What is this?" His voice was strained and hoarse. "Who is this man?"

As he moved, there was a heavy, clanking noise, and with a thrill of horror I saw that there was a heavy chain on his left ankle, fettering him to a great stone weight beside the bed.

"May I have the honour to present an old acquaintance, highness?" says Rudi. "I'm sure you remember him, from your mirror?"

It was a weird experience, looking at that face, and hearing that voice when he spoke again—perhaps a trifle deeper than my own, I fancied, and now that I looked at him, he was a shade slimmer than I, and less tall by a fraction. But it was an amazing resemblance, none the less.

"What does it mean?" he demanded. "In God's name, who are you?"

"Until recently, he was Prince Carl Gustaf of Denmark," says Rudi, obviously enjoying himself. "But you'd regard him as a most presumptive heir to the title, I'm sure. In fact, he's an Englishman, your highness, who has been kind enough to deputise for you during your holiday here."

He took it well, I'll say that for him. After all, I'd known for weeks that my spitten image was walking about somewhere, but it was all new to him. He stared at me for a long moment, and I stared back, tongue-tied, and then he said slowly:

"You're trying to drive me mad. Why, I don't know. It is some filthy plot. In God's name, tell me, if you have any spark of pity or decency, what it means. If it is money you want, or ransom, I have told you—say so! If it is my life—well, damn you! take it!" He tried to stride forward, but the chain wrenched at his ankle and almost upset him. "Damn you!" he roared again, shaking his fist at us. "You vile, cowardly villains! Let me loose, I say, and I'll send that creature with my face straight to hell—and you, too, you grinning mountebank!" He was a fearsome sight, wrestling at his chain, and cursing like a Smithfield porter.

Rudi clicked his tongue. "Royal rage," says he. "Gently, your highness, gently. Don't promise what you couldn't perform."

For a moment I thought Carl Gustaf would burst himself with rage; his face was purple. And then his temper subsided, he strove to compose himself, and he jerked back his lips in that gesture that I had spent so many weary hours trying to copy.

"I forget myself, I think," he said, breathing hard. "To what end? Who you are, fellow, I don't know—or what this means. I'll not entertain you by inquiring any further. When you choose to tell me—if you choose to tell me—well! But understand," and he dropped his voice in a way which I knew so well, because I do it myself, "that you had better kill me and have done, because if you do not, by God's help I'll take such a revenge on you all. . . ."

He left it there, nodding at us, and I had to admit that whatever our resemblance in looks, he was as different from me in spirit as day from night. You wouldn't have got me talking as big as that, chained up in a dungeon—well, I've been in that very situation, and I blubbered for mercy till I was hoarse. I know what's fitting. But he didn't, and much good his defiance was doing him.

"Oh, never fear, highness," says Rudi. "We'll certainly kill you when the time is ripe. Remember the royal progress we have prepared for you."

And he pointed off to the side of the great cell; I looked, and my heart gave a lurch at what I saw.

To that side the flags sloped down in a depression, perhaps a dozen feet across and about four feet deep. The sloping stones looked smooth and slippery, and at the bottom of the shallow funnel which they formed there was a gaping hole, circular and more than a yard wide. Carl Gustaf's face went pale as he, too, looked, and his mouth twitched, but he said nothing. My skin crawled at the thought of what lay beyond the mouth of that shaft.

"Merry lads, the old lords of Jotunberg," says Rudi. "When they tired of you, down you went, suitably weighted—as our royal guest is here—and hey, splash! It's not a trip I'd care to take myself—but your highness may not mind so much when I tell you that one of your friends is waiting for you in the Jotunsee. Hansen, his name was."

"Hansen? Erik Hansen?" The prince's hand shook. "What have you done to him, you devil?"

"He went swimming at the wrong time of year," says Rudi cheerily. "So rash—but there. Young blood. Now, your highness, with your gracious permission, we'll withdraw." He made a mocking bow, and waved me ahead of him towards the grille.

As we reached it, Carl Gustaf suddenly shouted:

"You—you with my face! Haven't you a tongue in your head? Why don't you speak, damn you?"

I blundered out; that hellish place was too much for me; I could imagine all too clearly slithering down into that shaft—ugh! And these murdering monsters would do it to me as soon as to him, if it suited them.

Young Rudi's laughter rang after me as I stumbled through the vault; he strode up beside me, clapping his hand round my shoulders and asking eagerly what I had thought of meeting my double face to face—had it made me wonder who I was? Had I noticed the amazement of Carl Gustaf, and what did I suppose *he* was making of it all?

"I'll swear I hadn't realised how alike you were till I saw you together," says he, as we reached his room again. "It's supernatural. Do you know . . . it makes me wonder if Otto Bismarck didn't miss the true possibility of his scheme. By God!" He stopped dead, rubbing his chin. Then:

"You remember a few moments ago I spoke of a plan that you and I might try together? I'll be frank; it occurred to me the moment I saw you swimming in the lake, and realised that I had both the court cards in my hand, with no one but the worthy Kraftstein to interfere—and he doesn't count. The two court cards," he repeated, grinning, "and one of them a knave. Have a drink, play-actor. And listen."

You'll have noticed that since my arrival in Jotunberg I had said very little—and, of course, the situation was really beyond comment. Events in the past forty-eight hours had brought me to the point where intelligent thought, let alone speech, was well-nigh impossible. The only conscious desire I felt was to get out of this nightmare as fast as possible, by any means. And yet, the hectoring way in which this cocksure young upstart shoved me into a chair and commanded me to listen, stirred a resentment beneath my miserable fear. I was heartily sick of having people tell me to listen, and ordering me about, and manipulating me like a damned puppet. Much good it had done me to take it all meekly—it had been one horror after another, and only by the luck of the devil was I still in one piece. And here, unless I mistook the look in Starnberg's eye, was going to be another brilliant proposal to put me through the mill. Open defiance wasn't to be thought of, naturally, but in that moment I felt that if I did manage to muster my craven spirits to do *something* on my own behalf, it probably couldn't be any worse than whatever he had in mind for me.

"Look here," says he, "how many of these damned Danes know that you are really an impostor?"

I could think of Grundvig and Sapten for certain; their peasant followers I wasn't sure of, but Rudi brushed them aside as unimportant.

"Two who matter," says he. "And on my side—Bismarck, Bersonin and Kraftstein—we can forget Detchard and that squirt of a doctor. Now—suppose our captive Prince goes down that excellent pipe tonight, and we let down the bridge to encourage your friends to attack? It would be possible to arrange a warm

446

reception for them—warm enough to ensure that Grundvig and Sapten never got off that causeway alive, anyhow. Kraftstein could easily meet with a fatal accident during the fight—somehow I'm sure he would—and by the time the Sons of the Volsungs had fought their way in and cut up the survivors, you and I could be on our way to the shore, by boat. Then, back to Strackenz and the acclaim of everyone who has been wondering where their beloved prince has been. Oh, we could invent some tale—and who would there be to give you away? Detchard and the doctor daren't. Your Danish friends couldn't, being dead. And by this time Bismarck and Bersonin are far too busy, I'll be bound, to worry about Strackenz."

Seeing my bewildered look, he explained.

"You haven't heard the news, of course. Berlin is alive with alarms, it seems. The revolution's coming, my boy; the student rabble and the rest will have the King of Prussia off his throne in a week or two. So dear Otto has other fish to fry for the moment. Oh, it's not only in Germany, either; I hear that France is up in arms, and Louis-Phillipe's deposed, they say. It's spreading like wildfire."[39] He laughed joyously. "Don't you see, man? It's a heaven-sent chance. We could count on weeks—nay, months—before anyone gave a thought to this cosy little duchy—or to the identity of the duchess's consort."

"And what use would that be to us?"

"God, you're brainless! To hold the reins of power—real power —in a European state, even a little one like Strackenz? If we couldn't squeeze some profit out of that—enough to set us up for life—before we took leave of 'em, then we aren't the men I think we are. D'you know what the revenues of a duchy amount to?"

"You're mad," I said. "Raving mad. D'you think I'd put my neck into that again?"

"Why not? Who's to stop you?"

"We wouldn't last a week—why, half the bloody peasants in Strackenz probably know that there are two Carl Gustafs loose about the place! They'll talk, won't they?"

"Bah, where's your spirit, play-actor?" he jeered. "Who would listen to them? And it's only for a few weeks—you've done it once already, man! And think of the fun it would be!"

They are rare, but they do exist, and you can only call them adventurers. Rudi was one; it was the excitement, the mischief, that he lived for, more than the reward; the game, not the prize. Mad as hatters, mark you, and dangerous as sharks—they are not to be judged by the standards of yellow-bellies like me. Flashy don't want anything to do with 'em, but he knows how their minds work. Because of this, I was wondering furiously how to deal with him.

"You can go back to your pretty duchess, too," says he.

"Don't want her," says I. "I've had her, anyway."

"But there's a fortune in it, man!"

"I'd rather be alive and poor, thank'ee."

He stood considering. "You don't trust me, is that it?"

"Well," says I, "now that you mention it. . . ."

"But that's the point!" He clapped his hands. "We are the ideal partners—neither of us trusts the other an inch, but we need each other. It's the only guarantee in any business. You're as big a rascal as I am; we would sell each other tomorrow, but there isn't the need."

Our financiers know all this, of course, but I've often thought that our diplomatists and politicians could have gone to school to Professor Starnberg. I can see him still, arms akimbo, flashing eyes, curly head, brilliant smile, and ready to set fire to an orphan asylum to light his cheroot. I'm a dirty scoundrel, but it has come to me naturally; Rudi made a profession out of it.

"Come on, man, what d'you say?"

I caught the note of impatience in his voice; careful, now, I thought, or he'll turn vicious. His scheme was unthinkable, but I daren't tell him so. What was the way out, then? I must pretend to go along with him for the moment; would a chance of escape offer? It was growing on me that the only safe way out—or the least risky—was to find some way of doing what Sapten had wanted. How could I get the drawbridge down; would I survive the assault that would follow? Aye, but for the moment, pretend.

"Could we make certain of Sapten and Grundvig?" I asked doubtfully.

"Be sure of that," says he. "There are two little cannon below stairs—ornamental things, but they'll work. Load 'em with chain, and we'll sweep that causeway from end to end when the rescuers come charging home."

"There are fifty of them, remember; have you enough here to man the guns and hold the place until we can get away?"

"Two of us, the three you saw in the cellar, and another three in the tower," says he. "Then there are two on the causeway, but they'll go in the first rush. They needn't concern us." Oh, he was a born leader, all right. But now I knew how many men he had, and where they were. The vital fact was that there was no one, apparently, guarding the drawbridge mechanism on the inside.

"So," he cried, "you're with me?"

"Well," says I, doubtfully, "if we can be sure of holding those damned Volsungs on the bridge long enough. . . ."

"We'll concentrate all our force by the guns at the drawbridge arch," says he. "Why, we can have all ready in half an hour. Then, down with the bridge, and let the flies come streaming towards our parlour." His eyes were shining with excitement, and he put out his hand. "And then, my friend, we embark on our profitable partnership."

Suddenly it struck me that it was now or never; he would move fast, and somehow I had to forestall him while his small forces were still scattered about the castle and all unsuspecting. I fought down my rising fear of what was to do, steeling myself for a desperate effort. My hand was sweating in his grasp.

"Let's drink to it!" cries he exultantly, and turned to the table, where the bottles stood.

Oh, Jesus, good luck to me, I thought. I moved up to his side, and as he splashed brandy into the glasses I made a swift examination of the other bottles standing by. A sturdy flask caught my eye, and I made a careless show of examining it, turning it by the neck to see the label. He was so confident in his youth and strength and arrogance that he never thought of being caught off-guard— why should he worry, in a castle held by his men, with only the feeble-spirited Flashman to be watched?

"Here," says he, turning with a glass, and I breathed a silent prayer, shifted my hand on the bottle neck, and swung it with all my force at his head. He saw the movement, but had no time to duck; the flask shattered on his temple with an explosion like a pistol-shot, and he staggered back, wine drenching his hair and tunic, and hurtled full length to the floor.

I was beside him in a flash, but he was dead to the world, with a great ugly gash welling blood among his curls. For a few seconds I waited, listening, but there was no sound from without. I rose, my heart pounding, and strode quickly across the room, pausing only to take up a sabre from a rack in the corner. I'd done it now, and was in a state of active funk, but there was nothing for it but to hurry ahead and hope.

The door creaked abominably as I pulled it gently open and peeped out. All was still; the stair-lamps shone dimly on the great empty hall. There was no sound of footsteps. I closed the door softly and tiptoed to the top of the stairs, keeping close to the wall. Through the great arch across the hall I could see the wheel and chains of the drawbridge; they looked gigantic, and I wondered uneasily could I lower the bridge single-handed, and would I have the time to do it before someone came into the hall?

I cursed myself for not finishing Starnberg off while I had the chance; suppose he came to? Should I go back and settle him? But I baulked at that, and every second I lingered now increased the chance of discovery. Gulping down my fear I sped down the steps and across the hall, taking cover in the shadows of the archway, holding my breath and trying to listen above the thumping of my heart. Still no sound, and the lighted entrance to the passage leading to the dungeons, which I could see from my hiding-place, remained empty. I stole across to the great wheel, gently laid my sabre on the flags, and tried to make out how the mechanism worked.

There was a big handle on the wheel, with room for at least two men; that was how they wound it up. But there must be a brake on the wheel to hold it; I fumbled in the dark, chittering with fright, and could find nothing that seemed to answer the case. The chains were taut with strain, and when I went farther into the arch I found that its outer end was closed by the raised wooden bridge itself; it was at least ten feet broad and might be three times that in length, for its upper end was lost in the dark above my head; faint streaks of moonlight came through at either side.

Well, at least there were no doors or portcullis to worry about; once the bridge was down the way was open—if I could get it down, and if it survived the fall. The bloody thing looked as though it weighed a ton; when it crashed down across the gap to the causeway there would be no need of any further signal to Sapten and his boarding-party—they would hear the row in Strackenz City. Aye, that would wake the castle, all right, and young Flash would have to light out full tilt for cover before the shooting started.

But I had to get the damned thing down first, by God; how long was it since I had left Rudi? Suppose he was stirring? In a panic I scurried back to the wheel, kicked my sabre in the dark, and sent it clattering across the flags, making a most hellish din. I grabbed at it, whispering curses, and at that moment came the blood-chilling sound of footsteps from the passage-way across the hall. I actually clapped my hand across my own mouth, and dived for the shelter of the wheel, burrowing in close at its foot and trying not to breathe while the steps tramped out into the hall.

There were two of them, Kraftstein and another. They stopped in the middle of the hall, and Kraftstein glanced upwards towards the room where I had left Rudi. Oh my God, I thought, please don't let them go up; let the lousy bastards go away.

"Was machen sie?" said the second one, and Kraftstein grunted something in reply which I didn't catch. The other one shrugged and said he was fed up with sitting in the cellar with Carl Gustaf for company, and Kraftstein remarked that at least he was better off than the guards out on the causeway. They laughed at that, and both looked towards the arch where I was hiding; I lay still as a corpse, my nerves almost snapping, watching them through the spokes of the wheel. And then I saw something that brought the icy sweat starting out of me: the hall light, casting its shaft into the mouth of my archway, was glittering on the point of the sabre that lay where I had knocked it, half in and half out of the shadow.

Oh Christ, they couldn't help but see it—it was shining like a blasted lighthouse. They were standing there, staring straight in my direction, not a dozen paces away; another few seconds and I believe I'd have come bolting out like a rabbit, and then the second one yawned enormously and said:

"Gott, Ich bin müde; wie viel uhr glauben sie dass es sei?"

Kraftstein shook his head. "'Ist spät. Gehen sie zu bette."

I was willing them feebly both to go to bed, and at last the other one mooched off on his own; Kraftstein took a turn round

451

the hall while my pulse increased to a sickening gallop, and then he went back into the passage leading below.

I waited, trembling, until his footsteps had died away, and then stole out and retrieved my sabre. To my disordered imagination it seemed incredible that there was still no sound from Rudi's room —though in fact it probably wasn't five minutes since I had left him. I came back to the wheel, forcing myself to inspect it calmly; it must be held at some point. I felt it all over, both sides, feeling sicker every moment—and then I saw it. Where its rims almost touched the ground there was a bolt thrust through one of the spokes into the housing of the windlass; if it was withdrawn, I guessed, the wheel would be released, but it wasn't going to be a simple business of pulling it out. It was going to have to be driven out with force.

Well, in God's name, there had to be something handy to knock it clear; I fumbled about in the shadows, ears pricked and whimpering nonsensical instructions to myself, but the best thing I could find was a heavy billet of wood among some rubbish in the corner. I could only hope that it would do; I was desperate by now, anyway, and I fairly sped round the other side of the windlass, praying audibly as I went, and bashed at the protruding end of the bolt with all my strength.

The thumping was fit to wake the dead; oh, Jesus, it wasn't moving! I belaboured the bolt frantically, swearing at it, and it moved in a fraction. I hammered away, and suddenly it shot out of sight, there was an ear-splitting clang, the wheel whirred round like some huge animal springing to life, and the handle shot by within an inch of braining me.

I flung myself out of the way, my ears filled with the shrieking and clanking of the chains as they rasped over their rollers; it sounded like a thousand iron demons banging on anvils in hell. But the bridge was falling; I saw it yawn away from the outer arch, and moonlight flooded in, and then with an appalling crash the great mass of wood fell outwards, smashing against the stonework of the causeway, leaping as if it were alive, and settling— oh, thank God!—across the gap.

The clap of the explosion was in my ears as I grabbed my sabre and took cover at the side of the archway. My first thought was to rush out across the bridge—anywhere out of that damned castle—

but an outcry from the causeway stopped me. The guards! I couldn't see them, but they were there, all right, and then I saw a pin-point of light from the far end of the causeway, and the crack of a shot hard behind it. Sapten's merry men must be getting into action; there was a ragged volley from the shore and a scream, and I hesitated no longer. Anything emerging across that bridge was going to be a prime target; this was no place for Harry Flashman, and I fled back into the hall, looking for a safe corner to hide in until the forthcoming passage of arms was over. By God, I had done my share, and no mistake; not for me to try to steal all the glory which the Sons of the Volsungs so richly deserved.

Someone was running and yelling in the passage from the dungeons; another voice was bellowing from up aloft. The hall was going to be fairly busy in a moment or two, so I scampered towards a doorway hitherto unnoticed, midway between the main gate and the dungeon passage. It was locked; I battered on it for a futile moment, and then swung round to look for another bolt-hole. But it was too late; Kraftstein was leaping across the hall, sword drawn, bawling to everyone to come and lend a hand; two more were emerging from beyond the stairs. I shrank back in the doorway—fortunately it was fairly deep, and they hadn't seen me, being intent on their yawning front door.

"Pistols!" roared Kraftstein. "Quickly, they're coming across! Heinrich! Back this way, man! Come on!" He vanished into the archway, with the other two close behind him; I heard them start shooting, and congratulated myself on having left them a clear field in that direction. Sapten wasn't going to have things all his own way, by the sound of things, and presently two more of the garrison came racing out of the dungeon arch, and another from the stairs; unless I had miscounted, the whole of the Jotunberg friendly society was now gathered in the main entrance—all except Rudi, who was presumably still stretched out above stairs, and bleeding to death, with any luck.

I wondered if the last man up from below had cut Carl Gustaf's throat and sent him down the pipe; not that I cared much, but the besiegers would probably feel better disposed towards me if they found him alive. However, he could take his chance; in the meantime, it seemed reasonable that I should seek out another refuge elsewhere; if I made a quick bolt for it there seemed little chance that the defenders would notice me—they were warmly engaged by the sound of yelling and banging from the direction of the drawbridge.

I peeped cautiously out; the dungeon passage seemed a good place, for I recollected openings off it where I ought to be able to lurk in comparative safety. The hall was empty; I made sure there was no one in sight at the main arch, and was flitting stealthily out when a voice from the stairway stopped me dead in my tracks, yelping as I did so.

"Hold on, play-actor! The comedy's not finished yet!"

Rudi was standing on the bottom step, leaning against the stone balustrade. He was grinning, but his face was ghastly pale, except down the right side, where the blood had dried in a dark streak. He had a sabre in his free hand, and he lifted the point in my direction.

"Bad form to sneak away without saying goodbye to your host," says he. "Damned bad form. Didn't they teach you manners at that English school of yours?"

I made a dart towards the dungeon passage, but with a speed that astonished me, considering the wound on his head, he bounded off the step and was there before me, slashing at me so close that I had to leap back out of harm's way. He laughed savagely and feinted to lunge, tossing the curls out of his eyes.

"Not quick enough, were we? It isn't de Gautet this time, you know."

I circled away from him, and he followed me with his eyes, smiling grimly and making his point play about in front of me. I heard a movement behind me, towards the arch, but before I could turn, he sang out:

"No, no, don't shoot! You attend to the rats outside! I'll settle the one in here!"

He advanced slowly, his eyes flashing as the light caught them.

"It isn't played out yet, you know," says he. "Perhaps your friends will find Jotunberg a tougher nut to crack than they imagined. And if they do—well, they'll find twin corpses to cheer 'em up!" He flicked out his point, and I parried it and sprang away. He laughed at that. "Don't like cold steel, do we? We'll like it even less in a minute. Come on guard, curse you!"

I couldn't fly; he'd have had his point through my back in a twinkling. So I had to fight. Not many foemen have seen old Flashy's face in battle, but Rudi was destined to be one of them, and I couldn't have had a more deadly opponent. I knew he would be as practised with a sword as he was with a knife or a pistol, which put him well above my touch, but there was nothing for it but to grip my hilt with a sweating hand and defend myself as long as I could. I could see only one faint hope; if he was so greedy for my blood that he wasn't going to let his pals intervene, there was just a chance that I might hold him off long enough for Sapten to overcome the defenders—if I wasn't a swordsman of his brilliance, I was at least as good as the master-at-arms of the 11th Hussars could make me, and I was strong enough, while Rudi must be weakened by the smash on the head I had given him.

Perhaps the thought showed in my face, for he laughed again and took a cut at me.

"You can have your choice of how you die," jeers he. "A nice thrust? Or a good backhand cut—it can take a head off very pretty, as I'm sure you know!"

And with that he came in, foot and hand, and had me fighting for my life as I fell back across the hall. His blade was everywhere, now darting at my face, now at my chest; now slashing at my left flank, now at my head—how I parried those thrusts and sweeps is beyond me, for he was faster than any man I'd ever met, and his wrist was like a steel spring. He drove me back to the foot of the stairs and then dropped his point, laughing, while he glanced towards the main gate, where the pistols were cracking away, and the smoke was drifting back like mist into the hall.

"Stand to 'em, Kraftstein!" he shouted. "What, they're only a pack of ploughmen! Fire away, boys! Sweep 'em into the lake!"

He waved his sabre in encouragement, and I seized the chance to take a wild slash at his head. By God, I nearly had him, too, but his point was up in the nick of time, and then he was driving in at me again, snarling and thrusting with such speed that I had to duck under his blade and run for it.

"Stand and fight, damn you!" cries he, coming after me. "Are you all white-livered, you damned British? Stand and fight!"

"What for?" I shouted. "So that you can show off your sabre-work, you foreign mountebank? Come and get me if you're so bloody clever! Come on!"

455

It was the last thing I'd have thought of saying to anybody, normally, but I knew what I was doing. I'd noticed, as he turned to follow me, that he had staggered a little, and as he stood now, poised to lunge, he was swaying unsteadily from side to side. He was groggy from his wound, and tiring, too; for all his speed and skill he wasn't as strong a man as I. If I could lure him away from the hall, away from the chance to call in his men, I might be able to exhaust him sufficiently to disable or kill him; at least I might hold him in play until Sapten and his damned dilatory Danes came on the scene. So I fell back towards the dungeon doorway, calling him an Austrian pimp, a bedroom bravo, a Heidelberg whoremaster, and anything else that came to mind.

Possibly he didn't need this kind of encouragement; it only seemed to amuse him, but he came after me hard enough, stamp-stamp-stamp, with arm and sabre straight as a lance when he lunged. I retreated along the passage nimbly, keeping him at full stretch, and got my footing on the steps. After that it was easier, for whoever had built the steps had known his business; they spiralled down to the right, so that I could fight with the wall to cover my open flank, while his was exposed.

"You can't run forever," cries he, cutting back-handed.

"So they told Wellington," says I, taking it on my hilt. "Why didn't you learn to fence properly, you opera-house buffoon?"

"Sticks and stones," laughs he. "We'll have room enough in a moment, and see how well you can fence without a wall to burrow under."

He came down the stairs at a run, thrusting close to the wall, and I had to jump away and scramble downwards for dear life. He was at my back on the instant, but I won clear with a couple of swinging cuts and went headlong down the steps, stumbling at the bottom and only regaining my balance just in time as he followed me into the open.

"Close thing that time, play-actor," says he, pausing to brush the hair out of his eyes. He was breathing heavy, but so was I; if he didn't tire soon I was done for. He came at me slowly, circling his point warily, and then sprang, clash-clash, and I fell back before him. We were in the low cloister now, with plenty of pillars for me to dodge round, but try as I might I found him forcing me back towards the lighted arch leading to the guard-room and Carl Gustaf's cell. He was fighting at full pitch, his point leaping at me like quicksilver, and it was all I could do to keep my skin intact as he drove me through into the lighted area.

"Not much farther to run now," says he. "D'ye know any prayers, you English coward?"

I was labouring too hard to answer him with a taunt of my own; the sweat was coming off me like water, and my right wrist was aching damnably. But he was almost spent, too; as he cut at me and missed he staggered, and in desperation I tried the old Flashman triple pass—a sudden thrust at the face, a tremendous kick at his essentials, and a full-blooded downward cut. But where I had been to school, Rudi had graduated with honours; he side-stepped thrust and kick, and if I hadn't postponed my intended cut in favour of an original parry—a blind sideways sweep accompanied by a squeal of alarm—he would have had me. As it was his point raked my left forearm before I could get out of range. He paused, panting, to jeer at me.

"So that's the way gentlemen fight in England, is it?" says he. "No wonder you win your wars."

"You should talk, you back-stabbing guttersnipe." I was scared sick at the narrowness of my escape, and glad of the respite. "When did you last fight fair?"

"Let's see, now," says he, falling on guard again and trying another thrust. "It would be '45, I think, or '46—I was young then. But I was never as crude as you—see now."

And making a play at my head he suddenly spat straight at me, and as I hesitated in astonishment he tried to run me through, but his tiredness betrayed him, and his point went wide.

"Now who's a gentleman?" I shouted, but his only answer was a laugh and a sudden rush that drove me back almost to the grille of Carl Gustaf's cell. One backward glance I had to take— God, the grille door was open, and I went through it like a jack rabbit, slamming it as he came rushing after. He got a foot in, and we heaved and cursed at each other. My weight must have told, but suddenly there was a shout behind me, and something crashed against the bars close to my head. It was a pewter pot—that damned Carl Gustaf was not only still alive but hurling his furniture at me. I must have relaxed instinctively, for Rudi forced the door back, and I went reeling into the middle of the chamber just as the royal idiot behind me let fly with a stool, which fortunately missed.

"I'm on your side, you crazy bastard!" I shouted. "Throw them at him!"

But he had nothing left now but his lamp, and he didn't apparently fancy leaving us in the dark; he stood staring while Rudi rushed me, slashing for all he was worth. I hewed desperately back; the sabres clanged hilt to hilt, and we grappled, kicking and tearing at each other until he broke free. I caught him a cut on the left shoulder, and he swore foully and sprang into the attack again.

"You'll go together, then!" he shouted, and drove me back across the cell. His face and shoulder were bleeding, he was all in, but he laughed in my face as he closed in for the kill.

"This way! This way!" bawls Carl Gustaf. "To me, man!"

I couldn't have done it, not for a kingdom; I could feel my arm failing before Starnberg's cuts. One I stopped a bare inch from my face, and lurched back; his arm straightened for the thrust—and then in a moment he stopped dead, his head turning towards the grille, as a shot sounded from the stairs.

"Help!" yelled Carl Gustaf. "Quickly! This way!"

Rudi swore and sprang back to the grille door; there was the sound of shouting and feet clattering on the steps. He waited only an instant, and glanced back at me.

"Another time, damn you," he cried. "Au revoir, your highnesses!", and he swung his sabre once and let it fly at me, whirling end over end. It sailed over my head, ringing on the stones, but I had started back instinctively, my feet slipped out from under me, and I came crashing down on the flags. Christ! they weren't level! I was sliding backwards, and in a moment of paralysing horror I remembered the funnel and that ghastly pit at its base. I heard Carl Gustaf's cry of warning too late and Rudi's exultant yell of laughter; they seemed to slide upwards out of my sight as I clawed frantically at the slippery stone. I couldn't stop myself; my foot caught for an instant and I slewed round sprawling, helpless as a cod on a fishmonger's slab. Now I was sliding head first; I had an instant's glimpse of that hellish black hole as I slithered towards it, then my head was over the void, my arms were flailing empty air, and I shot over the lip, screaming, into the depths. Jesus, down the drain, went through my mind as I hurtled headlong towards certain death.

The pipe ran at an angle; my shoulders, hips and knees crashed against its sides as I rushed into the inky blackness. For sheer horror I have known nothing to come near it, for this without doubt was the end—the frightful, unspeakable finish; I was being shot into the bowels of hell beyond all hope, into eternal dark. Down I went, the ghastly wail of my own screams in my ears, and ever down, down, and then with shattering force I was plunged into icy water, plummeting through it like a stone until it gradually drew me to a halt, and I felt myself rising.

For a moment I thought I must have shot out into the Jotunsee, a moment of frantic hope, but before I had risen a foot my back bumped against the pipe. Christ! I was trapped like a rat, for the shaft was too narrow to turn; I was head down with nothing to do but drown!

That I didn't go mad in that moment is still a wonder to me. I honestly believe that a brave man would have lost his reason, for he would have known he was beyond hope; only one of my senseless, unreasoning cowardice would have struggled still, stretching down with frantic fingers and clawing at the pipe beneath me. I had had no time to take breath before hitting the water; my mouth and nose were filling as my hands clawed at the pipe and found a ledge. I hauled with the strength of despair, and slid a little farther down the pipe; my fingers found another ledge and hauled again, but then my strength went and I found myself turning on my back. I was gulping water; the stifling agony in my throat was spreading to my chest; I beat feebly at the roof of the pipe, thinking Christ, Christ, don't let me die, don't let me die, but I am dying, I am— and as I felt my senses going I was dimly aware that my face was not against the pipe, but only my chest and body.

I can't remember thinking clearly what this meant, but I know that my hands came up beside my face, which had in fact come out of the pipe's end, and pushed punily at the stone that was imprisoning me. I must have thrust outwards, for I felt my body rasp slowly along the pipe as I tilted upwards. There was a dreadful roaring in my ears, and nothing but crimson before my eyes, but I could feel myself rising, rising, and I know a vague thought of floating up to heaven went through what remained of my consciousness. And then there was air on my face—cold, biting air—only for a second before the water enveloped me again. But half-dead as I was, my limbs must have answered to the knowledge, for my head came into the air again, and this time I thrashed feebly and kept it above the surface. My sight cleared, and there was a starry sky above me, with a huge, white cold moon, and I was spewing and retching on the surface of the Jotunsee.

Somehow I kept afloat while the agony in my chest subsided and my senses came back enough for me to realise that the water was freezing cold, and threatening to suck me down once more. Sobbing and belching water, I paddled feebly with my hands, and looked about me; to my right the lake stretched away forever, but there on my left, looming upwards, was the great rock of Jotunberg with its beautiful, welcoming, splendid castle. It was a bare twenty yards away; I struggled with all my strength, kicking out against the water, and by the grace of God the rock when I reached it was shelving. I got my head and shoulders on to it and clawed my way out, and then I lay, helpless as a baby, with my face on that blessed cold wet stone, and went into a dead faint.

I think I must have lain there only a few minutes; perhaps the mental shock of the ghastly experience I had endured was greater than the physical one, for the next thing I remember is stumbling slowly over the rocks by the waterside, without knowing where or who I was. I sat down, and gradually it all came back, like a terrible nightmare; it took some moments before I could assure myself that I was alive again.

Looking back, of course, I realise that from the moment I slipped into the funnel in the dungeon until I clambered ashore again on the Jotunberg, can hardly have been more than two minutes. My initial plunge must have taken me to within a foot or two of the pipe's outlet; I had scrambled out by sheer panicky good luck, and floated to the surface. It was a miracle, no doubt, but a truly horrifying one. If I'm a coward, haven't I cause to be? Only those who know what it is to die can really fear death, I think, and by God I knew. It haunts me still; any time I have a bellyful of cheese or lobster I try to stay awake all night, for if I drop off, sure as fate, there I am again in that hellish sewer beneath Jotunberg, drowning upside down.

However, at the time, when I realised that I wasn't dead yet, but that I would be if I sat there much longer, of cold and exhaustion, I took stock of the situation. At the point where I had left the scene of the action so abruptly, it had sounded as though help had arrived. Presumably Kraftstein and his cronies had been overcome, and with any luck Rudi had met a well-deserved end into the bargain. Happy thought! maybe they had slung him down the pipe after me. I couldn't think of anyone I would rather have had it happen to. Anyway, they were probably getting Carl Gustaf out of his fetters by now, and all would be jollity. How would they respond to my reappearance? It would be a bit of a blow to them, after I had appeared to die so conveniently—would they be tempted to do the job properly this time? No, surely not—not after all I'd done for them, much against my will though it had been.

Anyway, it was settled for me. If I stayed there any longer I would certainly freeze to death. I must just go into the castle and take my chance.

*   *   *

From where I stood I could see the causeway, about a hundred yards ahead, and as I stumbled round the base of the island the drawbridge came into view. There were figures in the castle gateway, and they looked like Volsungs; sure enough, as I came closer, I saw that they were, so I hallooed and scrambled up the little rocky path that ended at the bridge's foot.

Three gaping, sturdy peasants, they helped me up and led me through the debris-strewn archway into the hall. God, what a mess it was. Kraftstein lay beside the wheel, with his skull split and his great hands crooked like talons; I remembered their grip and shuddered. Nearby were half a dozen other bodies—Sapten had kept his word, then; there would be no survivors of the Jotunberg garrison. There was a pool of blood in the very centre of the hall, and lying in it was the fellow who had complained to Kraftstein of boredom; well, ennui wouldn't trouble him any longer. The smell of powder was harsh in my nostrils, and a faint cloud of it still hung in the shadows overhead.

The peasants pushed me down on to a bench, and while one helped me strip my sodden clothes—the second time that night—

another washed the stinging gash in my arm and bandaged it round. The third, practical fellow, realising that I had to be clad in something, was pulling the garments off one of the corpses—he chose one who had been neatly shot in the head, and had been considerate enough not to bleed much—and I can't say that I felt any revulsion at all about wearing dead men's weeds. In fact, they fitted uncommon well.

Then they presented me with a flask of schnapps, and I sent half of it down my throat at once, and felt the fiery warmth running back along my limbs. I poured a little into my palm and rubbed it on my face and neck—a trick Mackenzie taught me in Afghanistan; nothing like it for the cold, if you can spare the liquor.

I sipped the rest slowly, looking round. There were several Volsungs in the hall, staring curiously about them, and I could hear the voices of others in the upper rooms; they seemed to have everything in hand. Of Sapten and Grundvig there was no sign.

Well, this was fine, so far as it went. I was beginning to feel excellent, now that the shock—no, the series of hellish frights—of the evening were wearing off, and I was savouring the blissful knowledge that here I was, hale and whole, with drink in me, warm clothes, and nothing more to fear. With every moment, as I realised what I had endured and escaped, my spirits rose; I could contemplate the future, for the first time in months, without feeling my bowels drooping down into my legs.

"Where's Major Sapten, then?" says I, and they told me he was down in the dungeon still; on no account, they said, was anyone to intrude. Well, I knew the prohibition wouldn't include me, so I brushed aside their protests with a show of princely authority—remarkable how habits stick, once learned—and marched across to the passage. I checked at the archway, though, and asked if they were sure all the defenders were dead, and they beamed and chorused "Jah, jah." I took a sabre along anyway—not for protection—but because I knew it would look well, and went down the staircase and into the cloister. Through the far archway I heard the murmur of voices, and as I came closer Sapten was saying:

"—Hansen's body in the moat. I wish we had laid Starnberg by the heels, though; that's one overdue in hell."

That was bad news; I took a hurried look round, and then cursed my nervousness. Wherever Rudi was, it wouldn't be here.

"It all passes belief," said another voice, and I recognised it as Carl Gustaf's. "Can it be true? A man who could take my place ... an English impostor ... and yet he came here, alone with Hansen, to try to save me."

"He didn't have much choice," growls Sapten. "It was that or a rope." Well, damn him; there was gratitude.

"Nay, nay, you wrong him." It was Grundvig now, excellent chap. "He tried to make amends, Sapten; no man could have done more. Without him. . . ."

"Do I not know it?" says Carl Gustaf. "I saw him fight; he saved me from that scoundrel. My God! what a death!"

There was a pause, and then Sapten says:

"Aye, well, give him the benefit of the doubt. But, I have to say it, in dying he performed you a service, highness, for alive he might have been a confounded embarrassment."

Well, I wasn't standing for this—besides, I know a cut when I hear one. I stepped softly through the archway.

"Sorry to be inconvenient, major," says I, "but embarrassment or not, I am still here to serve his highness."

It produced a most satisfactory effect; Sapten spun round on his heel, his pipe clattering on the floor; Grundvig sprang up, staring in amazement; the Prince, who had been seated at the table, swore in astonishment; there were two others there, behind the Prince's chair, and doubtless they were suitably stricken, too.

Well, there was a fine babble and cries of wonder and inquiry, I can tell you; they were certainly surprised to see me, even if they weren't exactly overjoyed. Of course, it was a difficult situation for them; heroes are so much less of a nuisance when they're dead. There was even a hint of resentment, I thought, in the questions they poured at me—how had I escaped, where had I come from; I'll swear Sapten was on the brink of demanding what the devil I meant by it.

I answered fairly offhand, describing the plumbing system of Jotunberg briefly, and how I had escaped from the lake. Grundvig and the Prince agreed it was a marvel; Sapten recovered his pipe and stuffed it with tobacco.

"And so," says I, in conclusion, "I came back to offer my further services—if they are needed." And I laid my sabre gently on the table and stood back. This chap Irving has nothing on me.

There was an awkward, very long silence. Sapten puffed—he wasn't going to break it; Grundvig fidgeted, and then the Prince, who had been frowning at the table, looked up. God, he was like me.

"Sir," says he slowly, "these gentlemen have been telling me . . . what has happened in Strackenz of late. It—it defies understanding . . . mine at least. It seems you have been party to the most dastardly deception, the strangest plot, I ever heard of. Yet it seems it was against your will—is this not so?" He looked at the others, and Grundvig nodded and looked bewildered. "Perhaps I am not clear in my mind," the Prince went on, "after all this—" and he gestured about him, like a man in a fog, "—but at least I have the evidence of my eyes. Whoever you are, whatever the reasons for what you did . . ." he broke off, at a loss, and then pulled himself together. "You saved my life tonight, sir. That much I know. If there has been wrong on your side—well, that is for your soul. But it has been cancelled out, for me at least." He looked at the others, Grundvig still nodding, Sapten puffing grimly and staring at his boots. Then Carl Gustaf stood up, and held out his hand.

I took it, very manly, and we shook and looked each other in the eye. It was not canny, that resemblance, and I know he felt the same eeriness as I did, for his hand fell away.

"Indeed, I think I am in your debt," says he, a little shaky. "If there is anything I can do . . . I don't know."

Well, to tell the truth, I hadn't been thinking of rewards, but he seemed to be hinting at something. However, I knew the best policy was to shut up, so I simply waited, and another uncomfortable silence fell. But this time it was Sapten who broke it.

"There's no question of debt," says he, deliberately. "Mr Arnold may be said to have made amends. He's lucky to go off with his life."

But at this Grundvig and the Prince cried out.

"At lease we owe him civility," says the Prince. "Mr Arnold, you have had my thanks; understand it is the thanks of Strackenz and Denmark also."

"Aye, very fine," sneers Sapten. "But with your highness's leave, a clear passage to our frontier is the most, I think, that Mr Arnold will expect." He was pretty angry, all right; I began to understand that if Carl Gustaf hadn't survived it would have been waltzing matilda for Flashy if Sapten had had his way. I didn't think it politic to mention his promise on behalf of little golden-headed Amelia; the less said about her the better.

"At least he must be allowed to rest first," says the Prince, "and then conveyed in safety to the border. We owe him that."

"He can't stay here," croaked Sapten. "In God's name, look at his face! We'll have difficulty preventing a scandal as it is. If there are two men with the prince's figurehead in the state, we'll never keep it quiet."

The Prince bit his lip, and I saw it was time for a diplomatic intervention.

"If your highness pleases," says I, "Major Sapten is right. Every moment I continue in Strackenz is dangerous, for both of us, but especially for you. I must go, and quickly. Believe me, it is for the best. And as the major has remarked, there is no debt."

Wasn't there, though! I kept my face smooth, but underneath I was beginning to smart with hurt and anger. I hadn't asked to be embroiled in the politics of their tin-pot little duchy, but I had been bloody near killed more times than I could count, cut and wounded and half-drowned, scared out of my wits—and all I was getting at the end of it was the sneers of Sapten and the hand-shake of his blasted highness. Ten minutes before I had been thankful to come out with a whole skin, but suddenly now I felt full of spite and anger towards them.

There was a bit of mumbling and grumbling, but it was all hypocrisy; indeed, I don't doubt that if Carl Gustaf had been given an hour or two longer to recover from the scare he had had, and his consequent gratitude to me, he would have been ready to listen to a suggestion from Sapten that I should be slipped back down the pipe for a second time—with my hands tied this time. After all, his face was like mine, so his character might be, too.

For the moment, though, he had the grace to look troubled; he probably thought he owed it to his princely dignity to do something for me. But he managed to fight it down—they usually do— and the upshot of it was that they agreed that I should ride out as quickly as possible. They would stay where they were for the night, so that his highness could rest and take counsel, and there was a broad hint that I had better be over the frontier by morning. Grundvig seemed the only one who was unhappy about my sudden dismissal; he was an odd one, that, and I gathered from what he said that he alone had come round to the view that I was more sinned against than sinning. He actually seemed rather sorry for me, and he was the one who eventually escorted me up from that dungeon, and ordered a horse to be found, and stood with me in the castle gateway while they went to the mainland for it.

"I am a father, too, you see," says he, pacing up and down. "I understand what it must mean to a man, when his loved ones are torn from him, and used as hostages against him. Who knows? I, too, might have acted as you did. I trust I should have behaved as bravely when the time came."

Silly bastard, I thought, that's all you know. I asked him what had happened to Rudi, and he said he didn't know. They had seen him vanish through a side door in the outer cell, and had given chase, but had lost him in the castle. Presumably he knew its bolt-holes, and had got away. I didn't care for the sound of this, but it was long odds I wouldn't run into him again, anyway. I wasn't planning on lingering—just long enough for the notion that was beginning to form in my mind.

Then one of the peasants returned with a horse, and a cloak for me. I asked a few directions of Grundvig, accepted a flask and a pouch of bread and cheese, and swung into the saddle. Just the feel of the horse moving under me was heartening; I could hardly wait to be away from that beastly place and everything in it.

Grundvig didn't shake hands, but he waved solemnly, and then I turned the horse's head, touched her with my heel, and clattered away across the bridge, out of the lives of Carl Gustaf, the Sons of the Volsungs, Old Uncle Tom Cobley, and all. I took the Strackenz City road, and never looked back at the cold pile of Jotunberg. I hope they all caught pneumonia.

You would think, no doubt, that after what I had gone through, I would have no thought but to get out of Strackenz and Germany as fast as a clean pair of heels could take me. Looking back, I wonder that I had any other notion, but the truth is that I did. It's a queer thing; while I'm the sorriest coward in moments of danger, there is no doubt that escape produces an exhilaration in me. Perhaps it is simple reaction; perhaps I become light-headed; perhaps it is that in my many aftermaths I have usually had the opportunity of some strong drink—as I had now—and that all three combine to produce a spirit of folly. God knows it isn't courage, but I wish I had a guinea for every time I've come through some hellish crisis, babbling thankfully to be still alive—and then committed some idiocy which I wouldn't dare to contemplate in a rational moment.

And in this case I was angry, too. To be harried and bullied and exposed to awful danger—and then just cut adrift with hardly a thank-you-damn-your-eyes from a man who, but for me, would have been feeding the fishes—God, I found myself hating that shilly-shally Carl Gustaf, and that sour-faced old turd Sapten—aye, and that mealy Grundvig, with his pious maundering. I'd pay them out, by gum, would I. And it would be poetic justice, too, in a way—Bismarck had promised me a grand reward; well, I'd come out of Strackenz with something for my pains.

And, of course, it was really safe enough. There was hardly any risk at all, for I had a certain start of several hours, and I'd know how to cover my tracks. By God, I'd show them; they'd learn that a little gratitude would have been starvation cheap. I could do their dirty work for them, and then I could just piss off, could I? They'd learn to think a little more of Harry Flashman than that, the mean bastards.

So I reasoned, in my logical way. But the main thing was, I was sure there was no danger in what I intended. And what is there,

I ask you, that a man will not dare, so long as he has a fast horse and a clear road out of town?

The night sky was just beginning to lighten when I came to Strackenz City, with the dawn wind rustling the trees along the landstrasse. The suburbs were quiet as I cantered through, my hooves ringing on the cobbles; I skirted the old city to come to the ducal palace, where two sleepy sentries stared open-mouthed at me through the railings.

"Oeffnen!" says I, and while one tried to present arms and dropped his musket, the other made haste to swing open the gates. I clattered through, leaving them to marvel at the sight of their new prince, whose absence must have been the talk of the duchy, arriving unkempt and unshaven at this hour of the day.

There were more guards at the door, to whom I gave sharp orders to have a strong horse saddled and ready for me within ten minutes. I issued further instructions that no one was on any account to be allowed to leave the palace, nor was anyone to be admitted without reference to me. They saluted and stamped and fell over themselves in their hurry to obey; one flung open the doors for me, and I strode masterfully into the hall—this was going to be easy, thinks I.

A sleepy major-domo or night porter came starting out of the chair where he had been dozing; he cried out at the sight of me, and would have roused the palace, but I hushed him with a word.

"Send someone to the kitchens," says I. "Get them to put together such cold foods as will go into a saddle-bag, and bring it here. Also some wine and a flask of spirits. Oh, and some money—bring a purse. Now, go."

"Your highness is riding out again?" quavers he.

"Yes," I snapped. "Beeilen sie sich."

"But, highness . . . I have instructions . . . her highness the duchess must be informed."

"The duchess? She's here? Not at Strelhow?"

"No, indeed, sir. She returned last night, after . . . after you were not to be found." His eyes were round with fright. "There has been terrible concern, highness. Orders have been issued that if word came about you, her highness was to know at once."

I hadn't counted on this; she ought to have been at Strelhow still, damn her. It complicated matters—or did it? I stood thinking quickly, while the major-domo hopped from one foot to the other, and made up my mind.

"Well, I'll tell her myself," says I. "Now, my good fellow, do exactly as I have told you—and the less said about my return the better—understand?"

I left him chattering obedience, and went up the great staircase four at a time, and strode along to the duchess's apartments. There were the usual yellow-jacketed sentries at her door, stiffening to attention at the sight of me, and rolling their eyes in astonishment —wouldn't have done for the 11th Hussars, I'll tell you. I thumped on the panels, and after a moment a feminine voice called out sleepily: "Wer klopft?"

"Carl Gustaf," says I, and to the sentries: "Let no one pass."

There was a feminine squeaking from within, and the door opened on the pert little red-haired lady-in-waiting whom Rudi had fancied; she was staring astonishment with one eye and rubbing the sleep out of the other—a very pretty picture of disarray, with one tit peeping out of her night-dress. It's as well I'm leaving Strackenz, thinks I, for I wouldn't have been a faithful husband for long.

"Where's your mistress?" says I, and at that moment the inner door opened, and Irma appeared, a gown pulled hastily round her shoulders.

"What is it, Helga? Who was knock—", and then at the sight of me she gave a little scream, swayed for a moment, and then flung herself forward into my arms. "Carl! Oh, Carl! Carl!"

Oh, well, I might have been faithful for a while, anyway; the feel of that warm young body against mine was like an electric shock, and it was no pretence when I hugged her to me and returned the kisses that she rained on my lips and cheeks.

"Oh, Carl!" She stared up at me, tears on her lovely face. "Oh, my dear, what has happened to your head?"

For a moment I didn't understand; then I remembered. My fine bald poll hadn't had the razor over it for two or three days now, and I was sporting a fine black bristle, like an old brush. Trust a woman to hit on the least important thing!

"Nothing, my dear darling," says I, and smothered her lovingly. "All's well, now that I have you again."

"But what has happened? Where have you been? I was mad

with anxiety—" She gave a little scream. "You are wounded! Your arm—"

"There, there, sweeting," says I, giving her another squeeze for luck. "Set your fears at rest. It's a scratch, nothing more." I turned her round, murmuring endearments, and led her into her own bedchamber, away from the delighted and curious gaze of young Helga. I shut the door, and at once her questions broke out afresh. I hushed her and sat down on the edge of the bed—it would have been splendid to curl up with her, but there wasn't time.

"There has been a rebellion—a plot, rather, against the duchy. Your throne, our lives, were threatened." I cut short her cry of dismay. "It is all over—nearly over, at any rate. There is a little still to do, but thanks to the loyalty of certain of your subjects— our subjects—the worst is passed, and there is no more to fear."

"But . . . but I don't understand," she began, and then that beautiful face hardened. "Who was it? Those agitators—those creatures of the gutter! I knew it!"

"Now, now," says I soothingly, "calm yourself. It is all past; Strackenz is safe—and most of all, you are safe, my sweet." And I wrapped her up again, most enjoyably.

She began to tremble, and then to sob. "Oh, Carl, oh, thank God! You have really come back! Oh, my dear, I have been ready to die! I thought . . . I thought you were . . ."

"Ah, well, you see, I wasn't. There, there. Now dry your eyes, my darling, and listen." She blinked at me, dabbing at her eye-lashes—God, she was a beauty, in her flimsy night-rail—they seemed to be wearing them very low in Strackenz that winter, and I was beginning to come all over of a heat, what with her nearness and the scent of her hair, and the troubled adoration in her lovely eyes.

"It is quite crushed, this—this plot," says I. "No, hear me out —I shall explain everything in time, but for the moment you must trust me, and do precisely as I say. It is done—finished—safe, all but for a few details, which require my attention. . . ."

"Details? What details?"

"There's no time now. I must be away again." She cried out at this. "It is only for a moment, darling—a few hours, and I shall be with you, and we'll never be parted again—never."

She started to weep again, clinging to me, refusing to let me go, protesting that I would be going into danger, and all the rest of it. I tried to comfort her, and then the baggage opened her mouth on mine, and pushed her hand between my thighs, murmuring to me to stay.

By gum, it agitated me; I wondered if I had time? No, by God, I daren't—I had lost precious minutes already. She was stroking away, and my head was swimming with her, but I just put lust second to common sense for once, and forced her gently away.

"You must stay here," says I firmly. "With a strong guard on the palace and on your room itself. Oh, darling, believe me, it is vital! I would not go, but I must—and you must remember that you are a duchess, and the protector of your people—and, and all that. Now will you trust me, and believe me that I do this for the safety of Strackenz and my own darling?"

These royal wenches are made of stern stuff, of course; tell 'em it's for their country's sake and they become all proudly dutiful and think they're Joan of Arc. I gave her some more patriotism mixed with loving slush, and at last she agreed to do what she was told. I swore I'd be back in an hour or two, and hinted that we would stay in bed for a week, and at this she flung herself on me again.

"Oh, my darling!" says she, wriggling against me. "How can I let you go?"

"Just for a bit," says I. "And then—ah, but I can't stop now." She was getting me into a fever. "No, I promise I shall take care. I won't get hurt—and if I do, there'll be another chap along shortly—that is, no . . . I mean . . . I shall return, my darling." I gave her one last tremendous hug, and left her stretching out her arms to me. It was quite touching, really—she loved me, you know, and if I hadn't been in such a damned hurry I'd have been quite sorry to leave her.

Next door Mistress Helga had restored herself to decency, but from the flush on her cheeks I suspected she'd been listening at the door. I instructed her sternly to look after her mistress and to see that she kept to her room; then I stepped out into the passage. The sentries were stiff as ramrods; I repeated my orders that no one was to pass, either way, and set off for the clock tower.

It wasn't difficult to find; up another flight of the main stairs—

there were two more sentries at the top, whom I sent to join Irma's guard—and then up a spiral stairway and along a short passage to a wrought-iron gateway. Just before the gate there was a little guard-room, where I found an ensign and two sentries; the men were playing cards and the ensign was lounging in a chair, but at sight of me they were on their feet in an instant, goggling and fumbling with buttons. I lost no time.

"Fahnrich," says I, "there has been an attempt at a coup d'état. The duchess's life has been threatened."

They stared at me aghast.

"No time to tell you more," I went on briskly. "The situation is in hand, but I have to leave the palace at once in order to take charge at the scene of the outbreak. You understand? Now, then, what's your name?"

"W-w-wessel, please your highness," he stammered.

"Very good, Fahnrich Wessel. Now, attend to me. For the safety of the duchess, I have already mounted a guard on her apartments. You, with your men here, will proceed there at once, and you will take command. You will permit no one—no one, you understand—to pass into her highness's apartment until I return. Is that clear?"

"Why—why, yes, your highness. But our post here—the crown jewels...."

"There is a jewel, infinitely more precious to us all, to be guarded," says I portentously. "Now, take your men and go quickly."

"Of course, highness . . . on the instant." He hesitated. "But, pardon, highness—it is the first order of the palace guard that never shall the jewels be left unwatched. These are explicit instructions...."

"Fahnrich Wessel," says I, "do you wish to be a lieutenant some day? Or would you prefer to be a private? I know the sacred value of the regalia as well as you, but there are times when even jewels are unimportant." (I couldn't think of one, offhand, but it sounded well.) "So, off with you. I take full responsibility. Indeed, I'll do better. Give me the keys, and I shall carry them myself."

That settled it. He clicked his heels, squeaked at his men, and sent them off at the double. He took the keys from his own belt, and passed them to me as though they were red-hot; then he gathered up his sabre and cap and was off, but I called him back.

"Wessel," says I, in a softer voice. "You are not married?"

"No, highness."

"But you are perhaps a lover?"

He went pink. "Highness, I. . . ."

"You understand, I think." I frowned and forced a smile together—one of those grimaces of the strong man moved—and laid a hand on his shoulder. "Take care of her for me, won't you?"

He was one of those very young, intense creatures of the kind you see addressing heaven in the background of pictures showing Napoleon crossing the Alps in dancing pumps; he went red with emotion.[40]

"With my life, highness," says he, gulping, and he snatched my hand, kissed it, and sped away.

Well, that was Ensign Wessel taken care of. He'd cut the whole bloody German army to bits before he let anyone near Irma. Likewise, and more important, he didn't doubt his prince for a minute. Ah, the ideals of youth, I thought, as I sorted out the keys.

There were three of them; one to the ironwork gate, a second to the door beyond it, and a third to the little cage, shrouded in velvet, which stood on a table in the centre of the small jewel-room. It was so easy I could have cheered. There was a valise in the guard-room, and I laid it open beside the table and went to work.

God, what a haul it was! There were the rings, the staff of sovereignty, the diamond-and-emerald gold chain, the duchess's collar, and the two crowns—they didn't have to be bent, after all. The Sword of State I left behind, as too unwieldy, but there were a couple of necklaces I hadn't seen before and a jewelled casket, so in they went.

I was sweating, not with exertion but excitement, as I shut the valise and strapped it up; it weighed about a ton, and suddenly I was asking myself: where was I going to fence this collection? Oh, well, time to worry about that when I was safe over the border, and back in England or France. Thank God the only name Sapten and Co. knew me by was Thomas Arnold—they were welcome to call at *his* tombstone if they felt like it, and ask for their money back. They had no way of tracing me, even if they dared—for if they ever did ferret me out, what could they do that wouldn't cause an unholy international scandal? But they'd never even know where to look in England—I was safe as houses.

Aye—once I'd got away: time was flying. It was full dawn outside by now. I locked the cage, arranged its velvet cover, locked the door and the gate, and set off down the stairs, lugging my bag with me. I emerged cautiously at the head of the grand staircase—thanks to my sending the sentries away there wasn't a soul in sight. I stole down, and was tip-toeing towards the head of the last flight when I heard footsteps along the passage. Quickly I thrust the valise behind the base of a statue; I was just in time. Old Schwerin, the Chief Minister, still with his nightcap on and a robe-de-chambre flapping round his ankles, was hobbling along towards me, with a little knot of attendants fussing in his wake.

He was in a tremendous taking, of course; I thought the old ass would have a seizure. Forcing myself not to panic at the delay, I stilled his questions with the same recital of tommy-rot that I'd served up to Irma and the ensign—well, I say I stilled them, but he babbled on, demanding details and explanations, and eventually I only shut him up by taking a strong line, insisting on the need for haste on my part—I had to get back to the scene of the action at once, I told him.

"Oh, God!" groans he, and sank down on a sofa. "Oh, the unhappy country! What shall we do?"

"Nonsense, sir," says I, stifling a sudden desire to run for it, "I have told you the alarm is over—all but over, anyway. What remains to do is to see that no disorders follow—to quiet our contending factions, Danish and German, in the city itself. This shall be your first concern." And for some reason I asked: "Which side are you on, by the way?"

He stopped moaning and gazed up at me like a dying retriever. "I am for Strackenz, highness,'" says he. He was no fool, this one, for all he was an old woman.

"Excellent!" I cried. "Then summon the ministers at once—you'd better get dressed first—and send these people"—I indicated his followers—"to wait upon the duchess."

It was going to be like a galloping field day at her apartments, but the more of them were out of the way the better.

"Above all," says I, "try to communicate as little disquiet as possible. Now set about it, if you please."

He gathered himself up, and shooed away the crowd.

"And yourself, highness?" he quavered. "You are going into danger? But you will take a strong escort with you?"

"No," says I, "the fewer who see me go, the better." That was God's truth, too. "Not another word, sir. For the duchess's sake, do as I have bidden you."

"You will have a care, highness?" he pleaded. "I beg of you. For her sake—and for our country's. Oh, but must you go?"

I was almost bursting with anxiety, but I had to humour the senile bastard.

"Sir," says I, "have no fear. Briefly as I have been in Strackenz, I owe a debt to this duchy already, and I intend to pay it in full."

He drew himself upright and straightened his night-cap. "God bless you, highness," says he, all moist and trembling. "You are in the true mould of the Oldenbourgs."

Well, from what I've seen of European royalty, he may well have been right. I gave him my manliest smile, pressed his hand, and watched him totter away to guard the destiny of the duchy, God help it. He was going to have his work cut out.

As soon as he was round the corner I heaved out my valise, adjusted it over my shoulder by a strap, and pulled my riding-cloak over that side. The swag had a tendency to clank as I walked, so I paced slowly down the broad staircase and across the hall; the little major-domo was waiting, hopping in anxiety. There was a horse at the door, he pointed out, and its saddle-bags were packed. I thanked him and walked out into the morning.

There were guardsmen there, of course, and a couple of officers all agog at the rumours that must have been flying about. I instructed them to post their men at the palace railings, and to let no one pass without my orders—with any luck they might blow Sapten's grizzled head off when he arrived. Then I mounted, very carefully, which is damned difficult to do when you have a stone or two of loot swinging under your cloak, took the reins in my free hand, and addressed the officers again:

"I ride to Jotunberg!"

I cantered off down the great carriage-sweep, and they opened the gates at my approach. I stopped at the sentry and quietly inquired which was the western road to Lauenburg, and he told me—that would reach Sapten's ears, for certain, and should set him on the wrong track. Five minutes later I was clattering out of Strackenz City, making south-east towards Brandenburg.

I've noticed that in novels, when the hero has to move any distance at all, he leaps on to a mettlesome steed which carries him at breakneck speed over incredible distances—without ever casting a shoe, or going lame, or simply running out of wind and strength. On my flight from Strackenz, admittedly, my beast bore up remarkably well, despite the fact that I rode him hard until we were over the border and into Prussia. After that I went easier, for I'd no wish to have him founder under me before I'd put some distance between myself and possible pursuit. But thirty miles, with my weight to carry, is asking a lot of any animal, and by afternoon I was looking for a place to lie up until he was fit for the road again.

We found one, in an old barn miles from anywhere, and I rubbed him down and got him some fodder, before using up some of my store of cold food for myself. I took a tack to the south next day, for it seemed to me on reflection that the wider I could pass from Berlin, the better. I know my luck—I was going to have to go closer to Schönhausen than was comfortable, and it would have been just like it if I'd run into dear Otto on the way. (As it happened, I needn't have worried; there was plenty to occupy him in Berlin just then.) But I had planned out my line of march: acting on the assumption that the safest route was through the heart of Germany to Munich, where I could choose whether to go on to Switzerland, Italy, or even France, I had decided to make first of all for Magdeburg, where I could take to the railway. After that it should be plain sailing to Munich, but in the meantime I would ride by easy stages, keeping to the country and out of sight so far as possible—my baggage wouldn't stand examination, if I ran across any of the great tribe of officials who are always swarming in Germany, looking for other folk's business to meddle in.

In fact, I was being more cautious than was necessary. There was no telegraph in those days to overtake the fugitive,[41] and even if there had been, and the Strackenzians had been silly enough to use it, no one in Germany would have had much time for me. While I was sneaking from one Prussian hedge to another with my bag of loot, Europe was beginning to erupt in the greatest convulsion she had known since Napoleon died. The great revolts, of which I had heard a murmur from Rudi, were about to burst on an astonished world: they had begun in Italy, where the excitable spaghettis were in a ferment; soon Metternich would be scuttling from Vienna; the French had proclaimed yet another republic; Berlin would see the barricades up within a month, and Lola's old leaping-partner, Ludwig, would shortly be bound for the knacker's yard. I knew nothing of all these things, of course, and I take some pride in the fact that while thrones were toppling and governments melting away overnight, I was heading for home with a set of crown jewels. There's a moral there, I think, if I could only work out what it was.

Possibly it doesn't apply only to me, either. You will recall that while the Continent was falling apart, old England went her way without revolutions or disturbances beyond a few workers' agitations. We like to think we are above that sort of thing, of course; the Englishman, however miserably off he is, supposes that he's a free man, poor fool, and pities the unhappy foreigners raging against their rulers. And his rulers, of course, trade on that feeling, and keep him underfoot while assuring him that Britons never shall be slaves. Mark you, our populace may be wiser than it knows, for so far as I can see revolutions never benefited the ordinary folk one bit; they have to work just as hard and starve just as thin as ever. All the good they may get from rebellion is perhaps a bit of loot and rape at the time—and our English peasantry doesn't seem to go in for that sort of thing at home, possibly because they're mostly married men with responsibilities.

Anyway, the point I'm making is that I've no doubt the revolts of '48 did England a bit of good—by keeping out of them and making money. And that, as you've gathered, was the intention of H. Flashman, Esq., also.

However, things never go as you intend, even in European revolutions. My third night on the road I came down with a raging fever—fiery throat, belly pumping, and my head throbbing like a steam engine. I suppose it was sure to happen, after being immersed in icy water twice in one night, taking a wound, and being three parts drowned—to say nothing of the nervous damage I had suffered into the bargain. I had just enough strength to stumble out of the copse where I'd been lying up, and by sheer good luck came on a hut not far away. I pounded on the door, and the old folk let me in, and all I remember is their scared faces and myself staggering to a truckle bed, kicking my precious valise underneath, and then collapsing. I was there for the best part of a week, so near as I know, and if they were brave enough to peep into my bag while I was unconscious—which I doubt—they were too frightened to do anything about it.

They were simple, decent peasants, and as I discovered when I was well enough to sit up, went in some awe of me. Of course they could guess from my cut that I wasn't any common hobble-dehoy; they hovered round me, and I suppose the old woman did a fair job of nursing me, and all told I counted myself lucky to have come upon them. They fed me as well as they could, which was damned badly, but the old chap managed to look after my horse, so that eventually I was able to take the road again in some sort of order, though still a trifle shaky.

I gave them a nicely-calculated payment for their trouble—too little or too much might have had them gossiping—and set out southward again. I was within a day's ride of Magdeburg, but having lost so much time by my sickness I was in a nervous sweat in case a hue and cry should have run ahead of me. However, no one paid me any heed on the road, and I came to Magdeburg safely, abandoned my horse (if I knew anything it would soon find an owner, but I didn't dare try to sell it), and took a train southward.

There was a shock for me at the station, though. Magdeburg had been one of the earliest cities in Germany to have the railway, but even so the sum of thalers they took for my fare left me barely enough to keep myself in food during the journey. I cursed myself for not trying to realise something on my horse, but it was too late now, so I was carried south with a fortune in jewels in my valise and hardly the price of a shave in my pocket.

Needless to say, this shortage of blunt worried me a good deal. I could get to Munich, but how the devil was I to travel on from there? Every moment I was in Germany increased the chances of my coming adrift somehow. I wasn't worried about being in Bavaria, for I was persuaded that Rudi's threats of criminal charges in Munich had been all trumped-up stuff to frighten me, and there was no danger on that score. And I was a long way from Strackenz, in the last place that Sapten—or Bismarck—would have looked for me. But that damned valise full of booty was an infernal anxiety; if anyone got a whiff of its contents I was scuppered.

So I gnawed my nails the whole way—God knows I was hungry enough—and finally reached Munich in a rare state of jumps, my belly as hollow as a coffin, and my problem still unsolved.

As soon as I stepped from the station, clutching my bag and huddling in my cloak, I felt the hairs rising on my neck. There was something in the air, and I've sensed it too often to be mistaken. I had felt it in Kabul, the night before the Residency fell; I was to know it again at Lucknow, and half a dozen other places —the hushed quiet that hangs over a place that is waiting for a blow to fall. You sense it in a siege, or before the approach of a conquering army; folk hurry by with soft footsteps, and talk in low voices, and there is an emptiness about the streets. The life and bustle die, and the whole world seems to be listening, but no one knows what for. Munich was expectant and fearful, waiting for the whirlwind that was to rise within itself.

It was a dim, chilly evening, with only a little wind, but shops and houses were shuttered as against an impending storm. I found a little beer shop, and spent the last of my coppers on a stein and a piece of sausage. As I munched and drank I glanced over a newspaper that someone had left on the table; there had been student rioting, apparently over the closure of the university, and troops had been called out. There had been some sharp clashes, several people had been wounded, property had been destroyed, and the houses of prominent people had been virtually besieged.

The paper, as I recall, didn't think much of all this, but it seemed to be on the students' side, which was odd. There were a few hints of criticism of King Ludwig, which was odder still, journalists being what they are, and knowing which side their bread is buttered—at all events, they didn't see a quick end to the general discontent, unless the authorities "heeded the voice of popular alarm and purged the state of those poisons which had for all too long eaten into the very heart of the nation"—whatever that meant.

All in all, it looked as though Munich was going to be a warm town, and no place for me, and I was just finishing my sausage and speculating on how the devil to get away, when a tremendous commotion broke out down the street, there was a crash of breaking glass, and the voice of popular alarm was raised with a vengeance. Everyone in the shop jumped to his feet, and the little landlord began roaring for his assistants to get the shutters up and bar the door; there was a rising chorus of cheering out in the dark, the thunder of a rushing crowd, the shop window was shattered, and almost before I had time to get under the table with my bag there was a battle royal in progress in the street.

Amidst the din of shouts and cheers and cracking timber, to say nothing of the babble in the shop itself, I grabbed my bag and was making for the back entrance, but a stout old chap with grey whiskers seized hold of me, bellowing to make himself heard.

"Don't go out!" he roared. "Here we are safe! They will cut you to pieces out there!"

Well, he knew what he was talking about, as I realised when the sound of the struggle had passed by, and we took a cautious peep out. The street looked as though a storm had swept through it; there wasn't a whole window or shutter left, half a dozen bodies, dead or unconscious, were lying on the road, and the pavement was a litter of brickbats, clubs, and broken glass. A hundred yards down the street a handcart was being thrown on to an improvised bonfire; there were perhaps a score of fellows dancing round it, and then suddenly there were cries of alarm and they broke and ran. Round the corner behind came a solid mob of youths, rushing in pursuit with their vanguard carrying a banner and howling their heads off; some carried torches and I had a glimpse of red caps as they bore down, chanting "Allemania! Allemania!"

More than that I didn't see, for we all ducked back inside again, and then they had stormed past like a charge of heavy cavalry, the sound of their chanting dying into the distance, and the occasional smashing of glass and crash of missiles grew fainter and fainter.

The old chap with whiskers was swearing fearfully beside me.

"Allemania! Scum! Young hounds of hell! Why don't the soldiers sabre them down? Why are they not crushed without mercy?"

I remarked that crushing them was probably easier said than done, from what I'd seen, and asked who they were. He turned pop-eyes on me.

"Where have you been, sir? The Allemania? I thought everyone knew they were the hired mob of that she-devil Montez, who is sent to trouble the world, and Munich in particular!" And he called her several unpleasant names.

"Ah, she won't trouble it much longer, though," says another one, a thin cove in a stove-pipe hat and mittens. "Her time is almost run."

"God be thanked for it!" cries the old chap. "The air of Munich will be sweeter without her and her filthy bordello perfumes." And he and the thin cove fell to miscalling her with a will.

Now, as you can guess, I pricked up my ears at this, for it sounded like excellent news. If the good Muncheners were kicking Lola out at last, they would get three cheers and a tiger from me. She had been in my mind, of course, ever since I'd decided to make for Munich, although I'd determined to keep well clear of her and the Barerstrasse. But if she had fallen from favour I was agog to hear all about it; I couldn't think of anything I'd rather listen to. I pressed the stout old fellow for details, and he supplied them.

"The king has given way at last," says he. "He has thrown her out—the one good thing to come out of all this civil unrest that is sweeping the country. Herr Gott! the times we live in!" He looked me up and down. "But you, then, are a stranger to Munich, sir?"

I said I was, and he advised me to continue to be one. "This is no place for honest folk these days," says he. "Continue your journey, I say, and thank God that wherever you come from has not been ruined by the rule of a dotard and his slut."

"Unless," says the thin chap, grinning, "you care to linger for an hour or two- and watch Munich exorcising its demon. They stoned her house last night, and the night before; I hear the crowds are in the Barerstrasse this evening again; perhaps they'll sack the place."

Well, this was splendid altogether. Lola, who had dragged me into the horror of Schönhausen and Jotunberg at Bismarck's prompting, was being hounded out of Munich by the mob, while I, the poor dupe and puppet, would be strolling out with my pockets lined with tin. She was losing everything—and I was gaining a fortune. It isn't often justice is so poetic.

True, I still had to solve my immediate problem of getting out of Munich without funds. I daren't try to pop any of my swag, and short of waylaying someone in an alley—and I hadn't the game for that—I could see no immediate way of raising the wind. But it was a great consolation to know that Lola's troubles were infinitely more pressing—by the sound of it she'd be lucky to get through the night alive. Would they sack her palace? The thought of being on hand to gloat from a safe distance was a famous one— if it *was* safe, of course.

"What about her Allemania?" I asked. "Won't they defend her?"

"Not they," says the thin man, sneering. "You'll find few of them near the Barerstrasse tonight—they riot down here, where they conceive themselves safe, but they'll risk no encounter with the folk who are crying 'Pereat Lola' at her gates. No," says he, rubbing his mittens, "our Queen of Harlots will find she has few friends left when the mob flush her out."

Well, that settled it; I wasn't going to miss the chance of seeing the deceitful trollop ridden out of town on a rail—supposing the Germans had picked up that fine old Yankee custom. I could spare and hour or two for that, so off we set, the thin chap and I, for the Barerstrasse.

A mob is a frightening thing, even when it is a fairly orderly German one, and you happen to be part of it. As we came to the Barerstrasse, across the Karolinen Platz, we found ourselves part of a general movement; in ones and twos, and in bigger groups, folk were moving towards the street where Lola's bijou palace stood; long before we reached it we heard the rising murmur of thousands of voices, swelling into a sullen roar as we came close to the fringes of the mob itself. The Barerstrasse was packed by an enormous crowd, the front ranks pressing up against the railings. I lost the thin chap somewhere in the press, but being tall, and finding a step on the opposite side to stand on, I could look out across the sea of heads to the line of cuirassiers drawn up inside the palace railings—she still had her guard, apparently—and see the lighted windows towards which the crowd were directing a steady stream of catcalls and their favourite chant of "Pereat Lola! Pereat Lola!" Splendid stuff; I wondered if she was quite such a proud and haughty madame now, with this pack baying for her blood.

There wasn't much sign that they would do anything but chant, however; I didn't know, then, that they were mostly there in the expectation of seeing her go, for apparently the word had gone round that she was leaving Munich that night. I was to be privileged to see that remarkable sight—and to share in it; I would have been better crawling out of Munich on my hands and knees, and all the way to the frontier, but I wasn't to know that, either.

I had been there about half an hour, I suppose, and was getting weary of it, and starting to worry again about my valise, which I was gripping tightly under my coat. It didn't look as though they were going to break in and drag her out, anyway, which was what I'd have liked, and I was wondering where to go next, when a great roar went up, and everyone began craning to see what was happening. A carriage had come from the back of the palace, and was drawn up at the front door; you could feel the excitement rising up from the mob like steam as they jostled for a better look.

I could see over their heads beyond the line of guardsmen to the front door; there were figures moving round the coach, and then a tremendous yell went up as the door opened. A few figures emerged, and then one alone; even at that distance it was obviously a woman, and the crowd began to hoot and roar all the louder.

"Pereat Lola! Pereat Lola!"

It was her, all right; as she came forward into the light that shone from the big lanterns on either side of the doorway I could recognise her quite easily. She was dressed as for travelling, with a fur beaver perched on her head, and her hands in a muff before her. She stood looking out, and the jeers and abuse swelled up to a continuous tumult; the line of guardsmen gave back ever so slightly as the folk in front shook their fists and menaced her through the railings.

There was a moment's pause, and some consultation among the group round her on the steps; then there were cries of surprise from the street as the coach whipped up and wheeled down towards the gates, for Lola was still standing in the doorway.

"She's not going!" someone sang out, and there was consternation as the gates opened and the coach rolled slowly forward. The
crowd gave back before it, and it was able to move through the
lane they made; the coachee was looking pretty scared, and keeping his whip to himself, but the mob weren't interested in him.
He drove a little way, and then stopped not twenty yards from
where I· was; the crowd, murmuring in bewilderment, couldn't
make out what it was all about. There was a man in the coach,
but no one seemed to know who he was.

Lola was still standing on the steps of the house, but now she
came down them and began to walk towards the gate, and in that
moment the roar of the mob died away. There was a mutter of
astonishment, and then that died, too, and in an almost eery
silence she was walking steadily past the line of cuirassiers, towards the crowd waiting in the street.

For a minute I wondered if she was mad; she was making
straight for the crowd who had been roaring threats and curses at
her only a moment before. They'll kill her, I thought, and felt the
hairs prickling on the nape of my neck; there was something
awful in the sight of that small, graceful figure, the hat perched
jauntily on her black hair, the muff swinging in one hand, walking quite alone down to the open gates.

There she stopped, and looked slowly along the ranks of the
mob, from side to side. They were still silent; there was a cough, a
stifled laugh, an isolated voice here and there, but the mass of
them made never a sound, watching her and wondering. She
stood there a full half-minute, and then walked straight into the
front rank.

They opened up before her, people jostling and treading on
each other and cursing to move out of her way. She never faltered,
but made straight ahead, and the lane to her coach opened up
again, the people falling back on both sides to let her through. As
she drew closer I could see her lovely face under the fur hat; she
was smiling a little, but not looking to either side, as unconcerned
as though she had been the hostess at a vicarage garden party
moving among her guests. And for all their hostile eyes and grim
faces, not one man-jack made a move against her, or breathed a
word, as she went by.

Years later I heard a man who had been in that crowd—an

embassy chap, I think he was—describing the scene to some others in a London club.

"It was the bravest thing, by gad, I ever saw in my life. There she was, this slip of a girl, walking like a queen—my stars, what a beauty she was, too! Straight into that mob she went, that had been howling for her life and would have torn her limb from limb if one of them had given the lead. She hardly noticed them, dammit; just smiled serenely, with her head high. She was quite unguarded, too, but on she walked, quite the thing, while those cabbage-eating swabs growled and glared—and did nothing. Oh, she had the measure of those fellows, all right. But to see her, so small and defenceless and brave! I tell you, I never was so proud to be an Englishman as in that moment; I wanted to rush forward to her side, to show her there was a countryman to walk with her through that damned, muttering pack of foreigners. Yes, by gad, I would have been happy—proud and happy—to come to her assistance, to be at her side."

"Why didn't you, then?" I asked him.

"Why not, sir? Because the crowd was too thick, damme. How could I have done?"

No doubt he was damned glad of the excuse, too; I wouldn't have been at her side for twice the contents of my valise. The risk she ran was appalling, for it would probably have taken only one spark to set them rushing in on her—the way they had been baying for her only a few minutes before would have frozen any ordinary person's blood. But not Lola; there was no cowing her; she was showing them, deliberately putting herself at their mercy, daring them to attack her—and she knew them better than they knew themselves, and they let her pass without a murmur.

It was pure idiot pride on her part, of course; typically Montez —and of a piece with what she had done, I heard, in the previous night's disturbance, when they were throwing brickbats at her windows, and the crazy bitch came out on her balcony, dressed in her finest ball gown and littered with gems, and toasted them in champagne. The plain truth about her was that she didn't care a damn—and they went in awe of her for it.[42]

She reached the coach and the chap inside hopped out and handed her in, but the coachee couldn't whip up until the crowd began to disperse. They went quietly, almost hang-dog; it was the queerest thing you ever saw. And then the coach began to go forward, at a walk, and the coachee still didn't whip up, even when the way was quite clear.

I tagged along a little way in the rear, marvelling at all this and not a little piqued to see her get off scot-free. Why, the brutes hadn't even given her a rotten egg to remember them by, but that is like the Germans. Let anyone stand up to 'em and they shuffle and look at each other and touch their forelocks to him. An English crowd, now—they'd either have murdered her or carried her shoulder-high, cheering, but these square-heads didn't have the bottom to do either.

The coach went slowly across the Karolinen Platz, where there was hardly any crowd at all, and into the street at the far side. I was still following on, to see if something was going to happen, but nothing did; no one seemed to be paying any attention to it now, as it rolled slowly up the street—and in that moment I was suddenly struck by a wonderful idea.

I had to get out of Munich—suppose I caught up with the coach and begged her to take me with her? She couldn't still be holding a grudge against me, surely—not after what I'd suffered through her contrivance? She'd paid off any score she owed me over Lord Ranelagh, a dozen times over—if she didn't know that, I could damned soon tell her. And she was no longer in any position to have me arrested, or locked up; dammit, anyway, we had been lovers, once; surely she wouldn't cast me adrift?

If I'd had a moment to think, I dare say I wouldn't have done it, but it was decision taken on the edge of an instant. Here was a chance to get out of Munich, and Germany too, probably, before the traps got after me—and in a moment I was running after the coach, gripping my valise, and calling out to it to stop. Possibly it was just my natural instinct: when in danger, get behind a woman's skirts.

The coachee heard me, and of course at once whipped up, thinking, I suppose, that some particularly bloodthirsty hooligan in the mob had changed his mind, and was bent on mischief. The coach rumbled forward, and I ran roaring in its wake, cursing at the driver to rein in, and trying to make him understand.

"Halt, dammit!" I shouted. "Lola! It's me—Harry Flashman! Hold on, can't you?"

487

But he just went faster than ever, and I had to run like billy-o, splashing through the puddles and bellowing. Luckily he couldn't go too fast over the cobbles, and I hove alongside, just about blown, and swung myself onto the side step.

"Lola!" I roared, "Look—it's me!" and she called out to the coachee to pull up. I opened the door and tumbled in.

The chap with her, her little servant, was ready to leap at me, but I pushed him off. She was staring at me as though I were a ghost.

"In heaven's name!" she exclaimed. "You!—what are you doing here? And what the devil have you done to your head?"

"Oh, my God, Lola!" says I, "I've had the very deuce of a time! Lola, you must help me! I've no money, d'you see, and that damned Otto Bismarck is after me! Look—you ask about my head? He and his ruffians tried to murder me! They did—several times! Look here." And I showed her the bandage sticking out of my left cuff.

"Where have you been?" she demanded, and I looked in vain for that womanly concern in her splendid eyes. "Where have you come from?"

"Up in the north," says I. "Strackenz—my God, I've had a terrible time. I'm desperate, Lola—no money, not a damned farthing, and I must get out of Germany, you see? It's life or death for me. I've been at my wit's end, and I was coming to you because I knew you'd help—"

"You were, were you?" says she.

"—and I saw you back there, with those villains menacing you —my God! you were magnificent, my darling! I've never seen such splendid spirit, and I've been in some tight spots, as you know. Lola—please, dear Lola, I've been through hell—and it was partly because of you. You won't fail me now, will you? Oh, my darling, say you won't."

I must say it was pretty good, on the spur of the moment; the distraught, pleading line seemed the best to follow, and I must have looked pretty wild—and yet harmless. She looked at me, stony-faced, and my spirits sank.

"Get out of my coach," says she, very cold. "Why should I help you?"

"Why—after what I've suffered? Look, they slashed me with

sabres, those damned friends of yours—Bismarck and that swine Rudi! I've escaped by a miracle, and they're still after me—they'll kill me if they find me, don't you understand?"

"You're raving," says she, sitting there cold and beautiful. "I don't know what you're talking about; it has nothing to do with me."

"You can't be so heartless," says I. "Please, Lola, all I ask is to be allowed to leave Munich with you—or if you'll lend me some money, I'll go alone. But you can't refuse me now—I'm punished for whatever you had against me, aren't I? Good God, I wouldn't cast you adrift—you know that! We're both English, my darling, after all...."

I have an idea that I went down on my knees—it's all the harder to tip a grovelling creature out of a coach, after all, and she bit her lip and swore and looked both ways in distraction. Her little servant settled it for the time being.

"Let him stay, madame; it is not wise to linger here. We should hurry on to Herr Laibinger's house without delay."

She still hesitated, but he was insistent, and I raised the roof with my entreaties, so eventually she snapped to the coachee to drive on. I was loud in my gratitude, and would have described the events leading up to my present situation at some length, but she shut me up pretty sharp.

"I have some concerns of my own to occupy me," says she. "Where you have been or what devilment you've been doing you may keep to yourself."

"But Lola—if I could only explain—"

"The devil take your explanation!" snaps she, and her Irish was as thick as Paddy's head. "I've no wish to hear it."

So I sat back meekly, with my valise between my feet, and she sat there opposite me, thoughtful and angry. I recognised the mood—it was one step short of her piss-pot flinging tantrum—perhaps that mad walk through the crowd had shaken her, after all, or she was simply fretting about tomorrow. I tried one placatory remark:

"I'm most awfully sorry, Lola—about what has happened, I mean. They seem to have treated you shamefully—"

But she paid no attention, though, so I shut up. It came back to me, all of a sudden, how it was in a coach I had first met her, years ago—and I had been a fugitive then, and she had rescued me. If necessary I might remind her of it, but not now. But thinking of it, I made comparisons; yes, even in my present desperation, I could appreciate that she was as lovely now as she had been then—if I made up to her, carefully, who knew but she might relent her present coldness (that Ranelagh business must have bitten deep). She might even let me accompany her all the way out of Germany—the prospect of another tumble or two presented themselves to my ever-ready imagination, and very delightful thoughts they were.

"Stop leering like that!" she shot at me suddenly.

"I beg your pardon, Lola, I—"

"If I help you—and I say 'if'—you'll behave yourself with suitable humility." She considered me. "Where do you want to go?"

"Anywhere, darling, out of Munich—out of Germany, if possible. Oh, Lola, darling—"

"I'll take you out of Munich, then, tomorrow. After that you can fend for yourself—and it's more than you deserve."

Well, that was something. I'm still, even now, at a loss to know why she was so hard on me that night—I do believe it was not so much dislike of me as that she was distraught at falling from power and having to leave Bavaria in disgrace. And yet, it may have been that she had still not forgiven me for having her hooted off the London stage. At any rate, it seemed that her kindness to me when I first came to Munich had been all a sham to lull me into easy prey for Rudi. Oh, well, let her dislike me as long as she gave me a lift. It was better here than tramping round Munich, starting at every shadow.

We stayed that night at a house in the suburbs, and I was graciously permitted to share a garret with her servant, Papon, who snored like a horse and had fleas. At least, I got fleas, so they must have been his. In the morning word came that the station was closed, as a result of the recent disorders, and we had to wait a day, while Lola fretted and I sat in my attic and nursed my valise. Next day the trains were still uncertain, and Lola vowed she wouldn't stay another night in Munich, which pleased me considerably. The sooner we were off, the better. So she decided that we should drive out of town a day's journey and catch a train at some village station or other—I've forgotten the name now. All these arrangements, of course, were made without any reference to me; Lola determined everything with the people of the house, while poor old Flashy lurked humbly in the background, out of sight, and expecting to be asked to clean the master's boots at any minute.

However, in the wasted day that we spent waiting, Lola did speak to me, and was even civil. She didn't inquire about what had happened to me in the time since she had helped to have me shanghaied out of Munich by Rudi, and when I took advantage of the thaw in her manner to try to tell her, she wouldn't have it. "There is no profit in harking back," says she. "Whatever has happened, we shall let bygones by bygones." I was quite bucked up at this, and tried to tell her how grateful I was, and how deeply I realised how unworthy I was of her kindness, etc., and she did give me a rather quizzical smile, and said we would not talk about it, but we got no warmer than that. However, when it came to set out on the day after, I found she had gone to the trouble of getting me a clean shirt from the master of the house, and she was quite charming as we got into the coach, and even called me Harry.

Come, thinks I, this is better and better; at this rate I'll be mounting her again in no time. So I set myself to be as pleasant as I know, and we talked away quite the thing (but not about the past few months). It got better still during the morning; she began to laugh again, and even to rally me in her old Irish style—and when Lola did that, turning on you the full glory of those brilliant eyes—well, unless you were blind or made of wood you were curling round her little finger in no time at all.

I must say I was a little puzzled by this change of mood towards me at first—but, after all, I said to myself, she was always an unpredictable piece—melting one minute, raging the next, cold and proud, or gay and captivating, a queen and a little girl all in one. I must also say again that she had uncanny powers of charming men, far beyond the simple spell of her beauty, and by afternoon we were back on our old best terms again, and her big eyes were taking on that wanton, languorous look that had used to set me twitching and thinking lewdly of beds and sofas.

Altogether, by afternoon it was understood that she would not part company with me as she had intended; we would catch the train together, with Papon, of course, and travel on south. She had still not decided where to go, but she talked gaily of plans for what she might do in Italy, or France, or whatever place might take her fancy. Wherever it was, she would rebuild her fortune, and perhaps even find another kingdom to play with.

"Who cares a snap for Germany?" says she. "Why, we have the whole world before us—the courts, the cities, the theatres, the fun!" She was infectious in her gaiety, and Papon and I grinned like idiots. "I want to live before I die!" She said that more than once; another of her mottoes, I suppose.

So we talked and joked as the coach rattled along, and she sang little Spanish songs—gay, catchy ditties—and coaxed me to sing, too. I gave them "Garryowen", which she liked, being Irish, and "The British Grenadiers", at which she and Papon laughed immoderately. I was in good spirits; it was gradually dawning on me at last that I was going to get away high, wide, and handsome, jewels and all, and I was warm at the thought that all the time the brilliant, lovely Lola never suspected what she was helping me to escape with.

*   *   *

At our village we discovered there was a train south next day, so we put up at the local inn, a decent little place called Der Senfbusch—the Mustard-Pot—I remember Lola laughing over the name. We had a capital dinner, and I must have drunk a fair quantity, for I have only vague memories of the evening, and of going to bed with Lola in a great creaking four-poster which swayed and squealed when we got down to business—she giggled so much at the row we made that I was almost put off my stroke. Then we had a night-cap, and my last memory of her before she blew out the candle is of those great eyes and smiling red lips and the black hair tumbling down over my face as she kissed me.

"Your poor head," says she, stroking my bristling skull. "I do hope it grows curly again—and those lovely whiskers, too. You'll wear them again for me, won't you, Harry?"

Then we went to sleep, and when I woke I was alone in the bed, with the sun streaming bright in at the window, and a most devilish headache to keep me company. I ploughed out, but there was no sign of her; I called for Papon, but no reply. The landlord must have heard me, for he came up the stairs to see what I wanted.

"Madame—where is she?" says I, rubbing my eyes.

"Madame?" He seemed puzzled. "Why—she has gone, sir. With her servant. They went to the station above three hours ago."

I gaped at him, dumbfounded.

"What the devil d'ye mean—gone? We were travelling together, man—she can't have gone without me?"

"I assure you, sir, she has gone." He fumbled beneath his apron. "She left this for your excellency, to be given to you when you woke." And the lout held out a letter, smirking.

I took it from him; sure enough, there was Lola's hand on the cover. And then an awful thought struck me—I sped back into my room, blundering over a chair, and tearing open the cupboard door with a mounting fear in my throat. Sure enough—my valise was gone.

I couldn't believe it for a moment. I hunted under the bed, behind the curtains, everywhere in the room, but of course it was not to be seen. I was shaking with rage, mouthing filthy curses to myself, and then I flung down on the bed, beating at it with my fists. The thieving slut had robbed me—God, and after what I had been through for that swag! I called her every foul name I could think of, futile, helpless curses—for it didn't take an instant's thought to see that there was nothing I could do. I couldn't lay an accusation of theft for stuff I had lifted myself; I couldn't pursue, because I hadn't the means. I had lost it—everything, to a lovely, loving, tender harlot who had charmed me into carelessness—aye, and drugged me, too, by the state of my tongue and stomach—and left me stranded while she went off with my fortune.

I sat there raging, and then I remembered the letter, crumpled in my fist, and tore it open. God! It even had her coat-of-arms on the sheet. I cleared my eyes and read:

> My dear Harry,
>
> My need is greater than thine. I cannot begin to guess where you came by such a treasure trove, but I know it must have been dishonestly, so I do not shrink from

removing it. After all, you have a rich wife and family to keep you, and I am alone in the world.

You will find a little money in your coat pocket; it should get you out of Germany if you are careful.

Try not to think too hardly of me; after all, *you* would have played *me* false when it suited you. I trust we shall not meet again—and yet I say it with some regret, dear worthless, handsome Harry. You may not believe it, but there will always be a place for you in the heart of

Rosanna.

P.S. Courage! And shuffle the cards.

I sat there, speechless, goggling at it. So help me God, if I could have come at her in that moment, I would have snapped her neck in cold blood, for a lying, canting, thieving, seducing, hypocritical, smooth-tongued, two-faced slut. To think that only yesterday I had been laughing up my sleeve about how she was helping me on my way home with a fortune unsuspected, while she was going to have to go back to regular whoring to earn a living! And now she was away, beyond hope of recovery, and my britches arse was hanging out again, and she would live in the lap of luxury somewhere on my hard-gotten booty. When I thought of the torture and risk I had gone through for that priceless haul, I raved aloud.

Well, it was no wonder I was put out then. Now, after so many years, it doesn't seem to matter much. I have that letter still; it is old and worn and yellow—like me. She never became like that; she died as lovely as she had always been, far away in America—having lived before she died. I suppose I'm maudlin, but I don't think particularly hard of her now—she was in the game for the same things as the rest of us—she got more of them, that's all. I'd rather think of her as the finest romp that ever pressed a pillow—the most beautiful I ever knew, anyway. And I still wear my whiskers. One doesn't forget Lola Montez, ever. Conniving bitch.

Of course, when you're old and fairly well pickled in drink you can forgive most things past, and reserve your spite for the neighbours who keep you awake at night and children who get under your feet. In youth it's different, and my fury that morning was frightful. I rampaged about that room, and hurled the furniture about, and when the landlord came to protest I knocked him down and kicked him. There was a tremendous outcry then, the constable was summoned, and it was a damned near thing that I wasn't hauled before a magistrate and jailed.

In the end, there was nothing for it but to pack up what little I had and make back for Munich. I had a little cash now, thanks to Lola—God, that was the crowning insult—so that at long last I was able to make for home, weary and angry and full of venom. I left Germany poorer than I came in—although of course there was still £250 of Lola's (or Bismarck's) money in the bank at home. I had two sabre cuts and a gash on my arm, a decent grasp of the German language, and several white hairs, I imagine, after what I'd been through. Oh, that was another thing, of course—I had a scalp that looked like a hog's back for bristles, although it grew right in time. And to make my temper even worse, by the time I reached the Channel I heard news that Lola was in Switzerland, fornicating with Viscount Peel, the old prime minister's son—no doubt he was well peeled, too, by the time she had finished with him.

I've only once been back to Germany. Indeed, I don't include it even among the garrulous reminiscences that have made me the curse of half the clubs in London—those that'll have me. Only once did I tell the tale, and that was privately some years ago, to young Hawkins, the lawyer—I must have been well foxed, or he was damned persuasive—and he has used it for the stuff of one of his romances, which sells very well, I'm told.

He made it into a heroic tale, of course, but whether he believed it or not when I told it, I've no idea; probably not. It's a good deal stranger than fiction, and yet not so strange, because such resemblances as mine and Carl Gustaf's do happen. Why, I can think of another case, connected with this very story, and I saw it when the Duchess Irma came to London in the old Queen's diamond year—they were related, as I've said. It's the only time I've seen Irma since—I kept well in the background, of course, but I had a good look at her, and even at seventy she was a damned handsome piece, and set me itching back over the years. She was a widow then, Carl Gustaf having died of a chill on the lungs back in the '60's, but she had her son with her; he was a chap in his forties, I should say, and the point is that he was the living spit of Rudi von Starnberg—well, that can only have been coincidence, of course. It gave me quite a turn, though, and for a moment I was glancing nervously round for a quick retreat.

Rudi I last heard of with the Germans when they marched on Paris; there was a rumour of his death, so he's probably been stoking Lucifer's fires these thirty years and good luck to him. Unlike Mr Rassendyll I did *not* exercise myself daily in arms in expectation of trying another round with him: one was enough to convince me that with fellows like young Rudi the best weapon you can have is a long pair of legs and a good start.

Bismarck—well, all the world knows about him. I suppose he was one of the greatest statesmen of the age, a shaper of destiny and all the rest of it. He got to his feet for me, though, when I looked down my nose at him—I like to think back on that. And it is queer to consider that but for me, the course of history in Europe might have been very different—though who's to know? Bismarck, Lola, Rudi, Irma, and I—the threads come together, and then run very wide, and are all gathered together again, and go into the dark in the end. You see, I can be philosophical—I'*m* still here.[45]

I wasn't feeling so philosophical, though, when I journeyed back from Munich to London, and arrived home at last, soaked and shivering with weariness and our damned March weather. I seem to have come home to that front door so many times—covered with glory once or twice, and other times limping along with my boots letting in. This was one of the unhappier homecomings, and it wasn't improved by the fact that when I was let into the hall, my dear father-in-law, old Morrison, was just coming downstairs. That was almost the last straw—my bloody Scotch relatives were still on the premises when I had hoped that they might have gone back to their gloomy sewer in Renfrew. The only bright spot I had been able to see was that I would be able to celebrate my return in bed with Elspeth, and here was this curmudgeon welcoming me in true Celtic style.

"Huh!" says he. "It's you. You're hame." And he muttered something about another mouth to feed.

I gripped my temper as I gave my coat to Oswald, bade him good afternoon, and asked if Elspeth was at home.

"Oh, aye," says he, looking me over sourly. "She'll be glad tae see ye, nae doot. Ye're thinner," he added, with some satisfaction.

"I take it Germany didnae agree wi' ye—if that's where ye've been."

"Yes, it's where I've been," says I. "Where's Elspeth?"

"Oh, in the drawin'-room—takin' tea wi' her friends, I suppose. We have all the fashionable habits in this hoose—includin' your ain faither's intemperance."

"He's well again?" I asked, and Oswald informed me that he was upstairs, lying down.

"His accustomed position," says old Morrison. "Weel, ye'd better go up, sir, and be reunited wi' the wife ye'll have been yearning for. If ye make haste ye'll be in time for tea, from her fine new silver service—aye, a' the luxuries o' the Saltmarket." And to the sound of his whining I ran upstairs and into the drawing-room, feeling that tightness in my chest that I always felt when I was coming back again to Elspeth.

She gave a little cry at the sight of me, and rose, smiling, from behind the tray from which she had been dispensing tea to the females who were sitting about, all bonnets and gentility. She looked radiantly stupid, as ever, with her blonde hair done a different way, in ringlets that framed her cheeks.

"Oh, Harry!" She came forward, and stopped. "Why—Harry! Whatever have you done to your head?"

I should have expected that, of course, and kept my hat on, or worn a wig, or anything to prevent the repetition of that dam-fool question. Oh, well, I was home again, and in one piece, and Elspeth was holding out her hands and smiling and asking:

"What did you bring me from Germany, Harry?"

(The end of the second packet of The Flashman Papers)

APPENDIX I: THE PRISONER OF ZENDA

Whether Flashman's real-life experiences in Germany provided Anthony Hope with the basis of his famous romance, *The Prisoner of Zenda*, is a matter which readers must decide for themselves. Flashman is quite definite in the text in two places—especially where he refers to "Hawkins", which was Hope's real name. There is certainly some similarity in events, and names like Lauengram, Kraftstein, Detchard, de Gautet, Bersonin, and Tarlenheim are common to both stories; Flashman's "Major Sapten" is literary twin brother to Hope's "Colonel Sapt", and no amateur of romantic fiction will fail to identify Rudi von Starnberg with the Count of Hentzau.

APPENDIX II: LOLA MONTEZ

Although several of the notes following this appendix refer to Lola Montez, she deserves fuller mention than can be conveniently included there. She was, after all, one of the most remarkable adventuresses in history, with an intellect and personality to match her looks; for these gifts, rather than her capacity for scandalous behaviour, she is worth remembering.

Her real name was Marie Dolores Eliza Rosanna Gilbert, and she was born in Limerick in 1818, the daughter of a British Army officer. He was probably Scottish; her mother was part-Spanish, and Lola was brought up in India, in Scotland, and on the Continent. When she was 18 she ran off with a Captain James, and after living in India, returned to England in 1841. She seems to have begun on her long succession of lovers while still in her 'teens, and James divorced her in 1842. Her career as a Spanish dancer followed, and after a series of Continental appearances, lovers, and scandals, she became the mistress of Ludwig of Bavaria. It has been suggested that his interest in her was purely intellectual; that is a matter of opinion. What is not to be doubted is that she was the ruler of Bavaria—and there have been worse governors of nations—until the revolution of 1848 forced her to leave the country. She later went to America, where she lectured on such subjects as beauty and fashion, and died in New York in 1861, when she was only 43.

Apart from Captain James she had two other husbands, a young officer named Heald, who died, and a San Francisco editor, Patrick Hall, who divorced her.

This is the briefest outline of her short life; there is no room to include all the lovers, real and reputed (apart from those mentioned by Flashman, gossip included even Lord Palmerston), or the endless catalogue of scandals, scenes, escapes, and triumphs. These can be found in her biographies, of which *The Magnificent*

Montez, by Horace Wyndham, is particularly recommended.

Flashman's account of Lola's behaviour, and his assessment of her character, seem both authentic and fair. His enthusiasm for her looks and personality were generally shared (even by his old Indian acquaintance, the Hon. Emily Eden); there is ample evidence of her promiscuity, her optimistic cheerfulness, her sudden furious rages, and her tendency to physical violence—the men she horse-whipped included a Berlin policeman, the boots of a Munich hotel, and the editor of the *Ballarat Times*, Australia. But none of her contemporaries has left such an intimate portrait of her as Flashman has, or come closer to explaining the magnetism she exerted. And in spite of his conduct towards her, he obviously respected her deeply.

NOTES

1. The Minor St James Club may have been new to Flashman in 1842, but it was notorious to fashionable London. Its proprietor, a Mr Bond, was successfully sued in that year by a disgruntled punter who received £3500 in respect of his losses. (See L. J. Ludovici's *The Itch for Play*.)

2. Mr Wilson's performances were a great success all over England, especially with exiled Scots like Mrs Flashman. His repertoire included "A Nicht wi' Burns", and a lecture on the '45 Rebellion, as well as popular songs. He died during a tour of the United States.

3. Horse-drawn omnibuses had been running in London since Flashman was a small boy; possibly he is referring to a new service. Their conductors, or "cads", had a reputation for violence and obscenity which lingers in the word to this day.

4. Raiding of gambling-hells was common after the Police Act of 1839, which permitted forced entry. Flashman's observations on the proprietors' precautions and their right to sue the police are accurate. (See Ludovici.)

5. Hughes' passing reference to Speedicut certainly brackets him with Flashman, and can therefore be taken to be highly uncomplimentary. Flashman shows him in a new light, which prompts the thought that Speedicut may have been one (or both) of the anonymous companions in "Tom Brown" who spared the fags in the blanket-tossing episode and was later in favour of only partially roasting Tom before the fire.

6. The "barbed wire" comparison must have occurred to Flashman at some later date; it was not in common use before the 1870's.

7. Nick Ward claimed the championship of England after beating Deaf James Burke in September, 1840, and Ben Caunt in February, 1841. He lost a return bout with Caunt three months later.

8. The second Marquis of Conyngham was among the victims fleeced at Mr Bond's Minor Club; he lost at least £500 on two occasions in 1842.

9. Flashman's description of Bismarck evokes a different picture from the popular impression of the Iron Chancellor, but it tallies with those details of his early life which biographers seldom dwell on at length. Bismarck's taste for playful violence, his boorish conduct in public places, his whoring, carousing, and riotous behaviour (the habit of firing a pistol into the ceiling to announce his arrival to friends, for example), and his 25 duels in his first term at Göttingen, all testify to a nature not invariably statesmanlike. He appears, in fact, to have been an unpleasant young man, brilliant beyond his years but given to cynicism and arrogance. He was as tall, strong, and handsome as Flashman remembers him, with blond-red hair and an aristocratic bearing.

As to his presence in London in 1842, he did indeed travel extensively in Britain that year, and was rebuked for whistling in the streets of Leith on a Sunday. He is said to have liked the British; his affection encompassed at least one beautiful English girl, Laura Russell, with whom he had been infatuated some years earlier, but who had broken their engagement to marry an older man. Possibly this prejudiced him in later life.

10. Peel's introduction in 1842 of an income tax of 7d in the pound on all incomes above £150 was regarded as iniquitous. Lord Brougham argued (with what effect we all know) that "such a tax ought on no account to form a part of the ordinary revenue . . . but should cease with the necessity which alone could justify its imposition".

11. Bismarck was accounted something of a wit, and like most wits he seems to have had a habit of repeating himself. His remark that a gift for languages was a fine talent for a head-waiter is also recorded in Prince von Bülow's "Memoirs", where it is suggested that Bismarck was in the habit of using it on linguistically-gifted young diplomats.

12. John Gully, M.P. (1783–1863) was one of the most popular and respected champions of the bare-knuckle ring. The son of a Bath butcher, he conducted his father's business so unsuccessfully that he was imprisoned for debt, but while in the King's Bench in 1805 he was visited by an acquaintance, Henry "Game Chicken" Pearce, then champion of England. In a friendly spar with the champion in the jail, Gully was so impressive that sporting patrons paid his debts, and he met Pearce for the title at Hailsham, Sussex, a fortnight before Trafalgar. Before a huge crowd which included Beau Brummel and the Duke of Clarence (later William IV), Pearce narrowly beat Gully over 64 rounds; it has since been suggested that Gully out-fought the champion, but was reluctant to knock out his benefactor. This seems unlikely. However, Gully won the title two years later with decisive victories over Bob Gregson, "the Lancashire Giant", and then retired, aged only 24. He made a fortune on the turf, where he owned several Classic winners, and by investments in coal and land. He was M.P. for Pontefract from 1832 to 1837, was twice married, and had 24 children.

   Flashman's portrait of Gully accords with other contemporary accounts of the gentle, quiet six-footer who, when roused, was one of the most savage and scientific fighters of boxing's golden age. "At heart," says Nat Fleischer, "his ambition was to belong to the gentry. He had little use for the professional ring and its shady followers." Fleischer is probably right when he suggests that, but for chance, Gully would never have become a pugilist at all.

13. Flashman's reference to a horse called "Running Reins" is most interesting. In May, 1844, a year and a half after the party at Perceval's place, the Derby was won by a horse entered as "Running Rein"; it proved, upon inquiry, to be a four-year-old named Maccabeus, and was disqualified, but not before the scandal had developed into a court case (Wood v. Peel) and become the talk of the sporting world. The principal villain in the case, Abraham Levi Goodman, fled the country; the horse Maccabeus disappeared. But there certainly was a genuine Running Rein, whose performances in the 1843 season had given rise to suspicion. Flashman's mention seems to suggest that Running Rein (his rendering of the name as Reins is obviously a slip) had a reputation still earlier, although not an unsavoury one. Turf records of the day contain no mention of Running Ribbons, however, so Spottswood was probably doing Gully no great favour in offering to sell him.

14. John L. Sullivan won the first recognised world heavy-weight title when he knocked out Paddy Ryan in nine rounds at Mississippi City,

on Feb. 7, 1882. It is reported that the spectators included Henry Ward Beecher, the Rev. T. De Witt Talmage, and Jesse James.

15. Gents and Mooners. In the 1840's the term Gent was most particularly applied to the young middle-class idler who aped his superiors and dressed extravagantly; the Mooner was rather older and spent his time "mooning" at shop windows and ambling gently about the town. Flashman would consider both species to be well beneath him.

16. Despite Flashman's enthusiastic notice, it seems probable that Lola Montez was not a particularly good artiste, although the historian Veit Valentin observes that she had "the tigerish vivacity that inspires the Andalusian dance".

17. The account of Lola's disastrous appearance at Her Majesty's Theatre (June 3, 1843) is splendidly accurate, not only in its description of Lord Ranelagh's denunciation, but even in such details as the composition of the audience and the programme notes. (See Wyndham's *Magnificent Montez*.) This is a good, verifiable example of Flashman's ability as a straight reporter, and encourages confidence in those other parts of his story where corroboration is lacking and checking of the facts is impossible.

18. Lola had a passionate affair with Liszt in the year following her departure from London; after their first rapture she appears to have had much the same effect on the famous pianist as she did on Flashman. He tired of her, and did indeed abandon her in a hotel, whereupon she spent several hours smashing the furniture. Typically, Lola bore no grudge; in her high days in Munich she wrote to Liszt offering him Bavarian honours.

19. The coat-of-arms of the Countess of Landsfeld is accurately described; the "fat whale" was a silver dolphin.

20. Stieler's portrait of Lola in Ludwig's gallery is a model of Victorian respectability. A more characteristic Montez is to be seen in Dartiguenave's lithograph; he has caught not only her striking beauty, but her imperious spirit. [See Mr Barbosa's rendering of Stieler's portrait of Lola on the left side of the front cover of this edition.]

21. "Lola was always vain of her bosom". She was indeed, if the story of her first meeting with Ludwig is to be believed. He is supposed to have expressed doubts about the reality of her figure: her indignant reply was to tear open the top of her dress.

22. There is no supporting evidence that Wagner visited Lola in Munich at this time, but it is not impossible. They met for the first time in 1844, when Liszt took her to a special performance of "Rienzi" at Dresden, and Wagner's impression was of "a painted and jewelled woman with bold, bad eyes". He also described her as "demonic and heartless". Curiously, the great composer gained as much favour from Ludwig II as Lola had done from Ludwig I—so much so that the wits nicknamed him "Lolotte".

23. The American may have been C. G. Leland, a student at Munich University and a friend of Lola's. He claimed that he was the only one of her intimates at whom she had never thrown "a plate or a book, or attacked with a dagger, poker, broom, or other deadly weapon".

24. Schönhausen. Flashman's view of the castle's "medieval ghastliness" was echoed by Bismarck himself; he described it to a friend as an "old haunted castle, with pointed arches and walls four feet thick, (and) thirty rooms of which two are furnished." He also complained about its rats and the wind in the chimneys.

25. Flashman's summary of the Schleswig-Holstein Question is accurate so far as it goes; enthusiasts in diplomatic history who wish greater detail are referred to Dr David Thomson's *Europe Since Napoleon*, pp. 242–3 and 309–11. German and Danish versions of the problem should not be read in isolation.

26. The *schlager* play of the German students, whereby they could receive superficial head and face wounds which left permanent scars for public admiration, was a unique form of the duel. The equipment is as Flashman describes it; the *schlager* itself was three-and-a-half feet long, with an unusually large guard ("the soup-plate of honour"). The practice of leaving the wounds open to form the largest possible scar is curiously paralleled by the custom of certain primitive African tribes. In the duel itself, thrusting was strictly forbidden, except at the University of Jena, where there were many theological students. These young men would have found facial scars an embarrassment in their careers, so instead of cutting at the head, Jena students were allowed to run each other through the body, thus satisfying honour without causing visible disfigurement.

27. Bismarck liked to picture himself eventually becoming a rustic landowner; his remark about Stettin wool market occurs again in his recorded conversation, when he spoke of his ambition to "raise a family, and ruin the morals of my peasants with brandy".

28. Bandobast: organisation (Hindustani).

29. In 1847 Germany suffered its second successive failure of the potato crop. In the northern areas wheat had doubled its price in a few years.

30. The emblem of Holstein was, in fact, a nettle-leaf shape.

31. "a plumed helmet, à la Tin-bellies". Flashman is here almost certainly referring to the New Regulation Helmet which had been announced for the British Heavy Dragoons in the previous autumn. Its ridiculously extravagant plumage—popularly supposed to be an inspiration of Prince Albert's—had been the talk of fashionable London in the weeks shortly before Flashman's departure for Munich.

32. Libby Prison, in Richmond, Va., was notorious in the U.S. Civil War. Federal officers were confined there by the Confederates, often in conditions of dreadful overcrowding; it was the scene of a mass escape by tunnel in 1864, and two subsequent Federal cavalry raids to rescue prisoners. Flashman's reference seems to suggest that he was confined there himself; no doubt examination of those packets of his papers as yet unopened will confirm this.

33. Kibroth-Hattaavah—"there they buried the people that lusted" (Numbers 11: 34, 35)—seems to have been a popular subject for sermons at public schools. Dr Rowlands preached on this text in *Eric, or Little by Little*, by Dean Farrar.

34. It is just possible that the orator was Karl Marx. The Strackenzian coronation must have taken place before his recorded return to Germany from Brussels, where he had conceived the *Communist Manifesto*, but it is not inconceivable that he visited Strackenz beforehand. The coronation certainly offered a tempting target at a time when European politics generally were in a precarious state. Against the fact that there is no evidence of his ever having visited the duchy, must be balanced Flashman's description of the orator, which is Marx to the life.

35. Eider Danes, a faction who wished to make Schleswig Danish as far as the River Eider. Von Starnberg's concern about pro-Danish militant

organisations in Strackenz is understandable, as is his anxiety over Hansen's unexpected appearance at the wedding. What struck the editor as curious was that none of Bismarck's conspirators seem ever to have been alarmed at the prospect of Danish royalty attending the ceremony; that surely would have led to Flashman's exposure. But obviously none did attend, and this can only be explained by the fact that King Christian of Denmark died on January 20, 1848—shortly before the wedding took place—and that this kept the Danish Court at home, in mourning. A rare stroke of luck for the conspiracy; one does not like to think it was anything else.

36. "Punch" stayed neutral in the checked-or-striped trousers controversy. One of its cartoons suggested that "checks are uncommon superior, but stripes is most nobby". But it was a middle- rather than an upper-class debate.

37. Flashman believes he sang the old nursery rhyme in English, yet it is interesting to note (see Opie's *Oxford Dictionary of Nursery Rhymes*) that it appeared in German, apparently for the first time in that language, in 1848 ("So reiten die herren auf ihren stolzen Pferden, tripp trapp, tripp trapp, tripp trapp") the year in which he and the Duchess Irma were married. Possibly she had noticed after all.

38. Domenico Angelo Tremamondo (1717–1804), known as Angelo, founded a dynasty of fencing-masters who conducted an academy of arms in London in the eighteenth and nineteenth centuries.

39. Revolution swept across Europe in those early months of 1848. Within the space of a few weeks revolts took place in Sicily, France, Austria, Italy, Germany, and Poland; new constitutions and reforms were adopted in Naples, Tuscany, Piedmont, Rome, Budapest, and Berlin, and the *Communist Manifesto* appeared. In Britain a Chartist petition was unsuccessful, and John Stuart Mill produced the *Principles of Political Economy*.

40. Presumably Flashman is referring to David's highly romantic painting of Napoleon in the Alps, and confusing it with other works by the same artist in which the Emperor is shown with retinues of suitably respectful subordinates.

41. In fact the telegraph had been in existence for some years, but its use was not sufficiently widespread to have caused Flashman concern.

42. There is some confusion about Lola Montez's movements during her final weeks in Munich; more than once she changed her mind about leaving, and made efforts to re-establish her hold over Ludwig. As to her walk through the hostile crowd, it is mentioned by at least one authority, and there is no doubt that the incident of her appearance on the balcony, splendidly dressed and toasting a raging crowd in champagne, is authentic. Her indifference to physical danger was remarkable.

43. And in the end Bismarck got his way; by waging war on Denmark in 1864 he achieved the occupation of Schleswig by Prussia and Holstein by Austria, thus helping to provoke the Austro-Prussian war of 1866. With Austria defeated as a rival, Bismarck by the Franco-Prussian war of 1870 united Germany minus Austria, and Schleswig and Holstein became part of the German Empire.

FLASH
FOR FREEDOM!

From The Flashman Papers
1848–1849

Explanatory Note

When the first two packets of the Flashman Papers were first published, there was some controversy over their authenticity. It was asked whether the papers were, in fact, the true personal memoirs of Harry Flashman, the notorious bully of *Tom Brown's Schooldays* and later an eminent British soldier, or were simply an impudent fake.

This was not a controversy in which either Mr Paget Morrison, the owner of the papers, or I, his editor, thought fit to join. The matter was thoroughly discussed in various journals, and also on television, and if any doubters remain they are recommended to study the authoritative article which appeared in the *New York Times* of July 29, 1969, and which surely settles the question once and for all.

The third packet continues his story in the year 1848 and the early months of 1849. It is remarkable as a first-hand account of an important social phenomenon of the early Victorian years—the Afro-American slave trade—and in its illumination of the characters of two of the most eminent statesmen of the century, one a future British Prime Minister and the other a future American President. Flashman's recollections cast interesting light on what may be called their formative years.

When the Flashman Papers were brought to light at Ashby, Leicestershire, in 1965, it was noted that while the great volume of manuscript had obviously been examined and re-arranged round about 1915, no alteration or amendment had been made to the text as set down by Flashman himself in 1903–1905. Closer examination of the third packet reveals, however, that an editorial hand has been lightly at work. I suspect that it belonged to Grizel de Rothschild, the youngest of Flashman's sisters-in-law, who with a fine Victorian delicacy has modified those blasphemies and improprieties with which the old soldier occasionally emphasised his narrative. She was by no means consistent in this, for while she paid close attention to oaths, she left untouched those passages in which Flashman retails his amorous adventures; possibly she did not understand what he was talking about. In any event, she gave up the task approximately half-way through the manuscript, but I have left her earlier editing as it stands, since it adds a certain period charm to the narrative.

For the rest, I have as usual inserted occasional explanatory notes.

G.M.F.

Mr Thomas Arnold, attend to me. From here we ride to the Jotun-see, which will take us the best part of three hours. There the boat is waiting, with two stout men at the oars; they will take you as close to the castle as seems advisable—there is a moon, but we can't help that. The clouds are thick, so you should get close in unobserved. Then you swim for it—and remember, they will be watching and listening in yonder."

He let me digest this, his head cocked and his hands thrust deep in his pockets—strange how these pictures stay with one—and then went on:

"Once inside the castle, Hansen is in command, you understand? He will decide how to proceed—who is to guard the prince, who to lower the bridge. So far as we know, it is wound up and down by a windlass. Knock out the pin and the bridge will fall. That will be our signal to storm the causeway—fifty men, led by myself and Grundvig here." He paused, pulling out his pouch. "It is not our intention to leave any survivors of the garrison."

"They must all die," says Grundvig solemnly.

"To the last man," says Hansen.

It seemed to call for something from me, so I said: "Hear, hear."

"Serve us well in this," added Sapten, "and the past will be forgotten. Try to play us false—" He left it unspoken. "Now, is all clear?"

It was clear, right enough, all too clear; I did my best not to think of it. I didn't want to know any more dreadful details—indeed, the only question in my mind was a completely unimportant one, and had nothing to do with what lay ahead. But I was curious, so I asked it.

"Tell me," I said to Hansen. "Back in Strackenz City—what made you think I wasn't Carl Gustaf?"

He stared at me in surprise. "You ask now? Very well—I was not sure. The likeness is amazing, and yet . . . there was something wrong. Then I knew, in an instant, what it was. Your scars are in the wrong places—the left one is too low. But there was more than that, too. I don't know—you just were not Carl Gustaf."

"Thank'ee," says I. Poor old Bismarck—wrong again.

"How did you come by these scars?" asked Sapten.

"They cut them in my head with a *schlager*," says I, offhand, and Grundvig drew in his breath. "Oh, yes," I added to Hansen,

I believe it was that sight of that old fool Gladstone, standing in the pouring rain holding his special constable's truncheon as though it were a bunch of lilies, and looking even more like an unemployed undertaker's mute than usual, that made me think seriously about going into politics. God knows I'm no Tory, and I never set eyes on a Whig yet without feeling the need of a bath, but I remember thinking as I looked at Gladstone that day: "Well, if *that's* one of the bright particular stars of English public life, Flashy my boy, you ought to be at Westminster yourself."

You wouldn't blame me; you must have thought the same, often. After all, they're a contemptible lot, and you'll agree that I had my full share of the qualities of character necessary in political life. I could lie and dissemble with the best, give short change with a hearty clap on the shoulder, slip out from under long before the blow fell, talk, toady, and turn tail as fast as a Yankee fakir selling patent pills. Mark you, I've never been given to interfering in other folks' affairs if I could help it, so I suppose that would have disqualified me. But for a little while I did think hard about bribing my way to a seat—and the result of it was that I came within an ace of being publicly disgraced, shanghaied, sold as a slave, and God knows what besides. I've never seriously considered politics since.

It was when I came home from Germany in the spring of '48, after my skirmish with Otto Bismarck and Lola Montez. I was in d - - - - d bad shape, with a shaven skull, a couple of wounds, and the guts scared half out of me, and all I wanted was to go to ground in London until I was my own man once more. One thing I was sure of: nothing was going to drag me out of England again—which was ironic, when you consider that I've spent more than half of the last fifty years at the ends of the earth, in uniform as often as not, and doing most of my walking backwards.

Anyway, I came home across the Channel one jump ahead of half the monarchs and statesmen in Europe. The popular rebellion I'd seen in Munich was only one of a dozen that broke out that spring, and all the fellows who'd lost their thrones and chancellorships seemed to have decided, like me, that old England was the safest place. So it proved, but the joke was that for a few weeks after I came home it looked touch and go whether England didn't have a revolution of her own, which would have sold the fleeing monarchs properly, and serve 'em right.

Mind you, I thought it was all gammon myself; I'd just seen a real rebellion, with mobs chanting and smashing and looting, and I couldn't imagine it happening in St James's. But that crabbed old Scotch miser, Morrison, my abominable father-in-law, thought different, and poured out his fears to me on my first evening at home.

"It's thae bluidy Chartists," cries he, with his head in his hands. "The d - - - - d mob is loose aboot the toon, or soon will be. It's no' enough, their Ten Hoors Bill, they want tae slake their vengeance on honest fowk as well. Burn them a', the wicked rascals! And whit does the Government do, will ye tell me? Naethin'! Wi' rebellion in oor midst, an' the French chappin' at oor doors!"

"The French have too much on hand with their own rebels to mind about us," says I. "As to the Chartists, I recall you expressing the same fears, years ago, in Paisley, and nothing came of it. If you remember—"

"Naethin' came o't, d'ye say?" cries he, with his chops quivering. "I ken whit came o't! You, that should hae been at your post, were loupin' intae the bushes wi' my Elspeth. Oh, Goad," says he, groaning, "as if we hadnae tribulation enough. Wee Elspeth, in her . . . her condeetion."

That was another thing, of course. My beautiful Elspeth, after eight years of wedded bliss, had now conceived at last, and to hear her father, mother, and sisters you would have thought it was Judgement Day. Myself, I believe she'd done it just to be topsides with the Queen, who had recently produced yet another of her innumerable litter. But what concerned me most was the identity of the father; I knew my darling feather-head, you see, for the trollop she was—you would never have thought it, to look at her beguiling innocence, but it had long been an unspoken bargain between us that we let each other's private lives alone, and I could guess she had been in the woodshed with half a dozen during my absence. Mind you, I might have pupped her myself before I went to Germany, but who could tell? And if she gave birth to something with red hair and a pug nose there was liable to be talk, and God knows what might come of that.

You see, we were an odd family. Old Morrison was as rich as an Amsterdam Jew, and when my guv'nor went smash over railway stock, Morrison had paid the bills for Elspeth's sake. He had been paying ever since, keeping me and my guv'nor on a pittance while he used our house, and got what credit he could out of being related to the Flashman family. Not that that was much, in my opinion, but since we were half-way into Society, and Morrison had daughters to marry off, he was prepared to tolerate us. He *had* to tolerate *me*, anyway, since I was married to his daughter. But it was a d - - - - d tricky business, all round, for he could kick me out if he chose, and would do like a shot the moment Elspeth decided she'd had enough of me. As it was, we dealt well enough with each other, but with a child on the way things might, I suspected, be different. I'd no wish to be out in the street trying to scrape by on a captain's half pay.

So what with Elspeth pregnant and old Morrison expecting the Communist rabble at the door at any moment, it was a fairly cheerless homecoming. Elspeth seemed pleased enough to see me, all right, but when I tried to bundle her into bed she would have none of it, in case the child was harmed. So instead of bouncing her about that evening I had to listen fondly to her drivelling about what name we should give our Little Hero—for she was sure it must be a boy.

"He shall be Harry Albert Victor," says she, holding my hand and gazing at me with those imbecile blue eyes which never lost their power, somehow, to make my heart squeeze up inside me, God knows why. "After you, *my* dearest love, and our dear, dear Queen and *her* dearest love. Would you approve, my darling?"

"Capital choice," says I. "Couldn't be better." Not unless, I thought to myself, you called him Tom, or Dick, or William, or whatever the fellow's name was who was in the hay with you. (After all, we'd been married a long while and made the springs creak time without number, and devil a sign of our seed multiplying. It seemed odd, now. Still, there it was.)

"You make me so happy, Harry," says she, and do you know, I believed it. She was like that, you see; as immoral as I was, but without my intelligence. No conscience whatever, and a blissful habit of forgetting her own transgressions—or probably she never thought she had any to forget.

She leaned up and kissed me, and the smell and feel of her blonde plumpness set me off, and I made a grab at her tits, but she pushed me away again.

"We must be patient, my own," says she, composing herself. "We must think only of dear Harry Albert Victor."

(That, by the way, is what he is called. The bastard's a bishop, too. I can't believe he's mine.)

She cooed and maundered a little longer, and then said she must rest, so I left her sipping her white-wine whey and spent the rest of the evening listening to old Morrison groaning and snarling. It was the same old tune, more or less, that I'd grown used to on the rare occasions when we had shared each other's company over the past eight years—the villainy of the workers, the weakness of government, the rising cost of everything, my own folly and extravagance (although heaven knows he never gave me enough to be extravagant with), the vanity of his wife and daughters, and all the rest of it. It was pathetic, and monstrous, too, when you considered how much the old skinflint had raked together by sweating his mill-workers and cheating his associates. But I observed that the richer he got, the more he whined and raged, and if there was one thing I'll say for him, he got richer quicker than the only sober man in a poker game.

The truth was that, coward and skinflint though he was, he had a shrewd business head, no error. From being a prosperous Scotch mill owner when I married his daughter he had blossomed since coming south, and had his finger in a score of pies—all d - - - - d dirty ones, no doubt. He had become known in the City, and in Tory circles too, for if he was a provincial nobody he had the golden passport, and it was getting fatter all the time. He was already angling for his title, although he didn't get it until some little time later, when Russell sold it to him—a Whig minister ennobling a Tory miser, which just goes to show. But with all these glittering prizes in front of him, the little swine was getting greedier by the hour, and the thought of it all dissolving in revolution had him nearly puking with fear.

"It's time tae tak' a stand," says he, goggling at me. "We have to defend our rights and our property"—and I almost burst out laughing as I remembered the time in Paisley when his mill-workers got out of hand, and he cringed behind his door, bawling for me to lead my troops against them. But this time he was really frightened; I gathered from his vapourings that there had been recent riots in Glasgow, and even in Trafalgar Square, and that in a few days there was to be a great rally of Chartists—"spawn of Beelzebub" he called them—on Kennington Common, and that it was feared they would invade London itself.

To my astonishment, when I went out next day to take my bearings, I discovered there was something in it. At Horse Guards there were rumours that regiments were being brought secretly to town, the homes of Ministers were to be guarded, and supplies of cutlasses and firearms were being got ready. Special constables were being recruited to oppose the mob, and the Royal Family were leaving town. It all sounded d - - - - d serious, but my Uncle Bindley, who was on the staff, told me that the Duke was confident nothing would come of it.

"So you'll win no more medals this time," says he, sniffing. "I take it, now that you have consented to honour us with your presence again, that you are looking to your family" (he meant the Pagets, my mother's tribe) "to find you employment again."

"I'm in no hurry, thank'ee," says I. "I'm sure you'd agree that in a time of civil peril a gentleman's place is in his home, defending his dear ones."

"If you mean the Morrisons," says he, "I cannot agree with you. Their rightful place is with the mob, from which they came."

"Careful, uncle," says I. "You never know—you might be in need of a Scotch pension yourself some day." And with that I left him, and sauntered home.

The place was in a ferment. Old Morrison, carried away by

terror for his strong-boxes, had actually plucked up courage to go
to Marlborough Street and 'test as a special constable, and when
I came home he was standing in the drawing-room looking at his
truncheon as though it was a snake. Mrs Morrison, my Medusa-
in-law, was lying on the sofa, with a maid dabbing her temples
with eau-de-cologne, Elspeth's two sisters were weeping in a
corner, and Elspeth herself was sitting, cool as you please, with a
shawl round her shoulders, eating chocolates and looking beautiful. As always, she was the one member of the family who was
quite unruffled.

Old Morrison looked at me and groaned, and looked at the
truncheon again.

"It's a terrible thing to tak' human life," says he.

"Don't take it, then," says I. "Strike only to wound. Get your
back against a brick wall and smash 'em across the knees and
elbows."

The females set up a great howl at this, and old Morrison looked
ready to faint.

"D'ye think . . . it'll come tae . . . tae bloodshed?"

"Shouldn't wonder," says I, very cool.

"Ye'll come with me," he yammered. "You're a soldier—a man
of action—aye, ye've the Queen's Medal an' a'. Ye've seen service
—aye—against the country's enemies! Ye're the very man tae
stand up to this . . . this trash. Ye'll come wi' me—or maybe tak'
my place!"

Solemnly I informed him that the Duke had given it out that on
no account were the military to be involved in any disturbance
that might take place when the Chartists assembled. I was too well
known; I should be recognised.

"I'm afraid it is for you civilians to do your duty," says I. "But
I shall be here, at home, so you need have no fear. And if the worst
befalls, you may be sure that my comrades and I shall take stern
vengeance."

I left that drawing-room sounding like the Wailing Wall, but
it was nothing to the scenes which ensued on the morning of the
great Chartist meeting at Kennington. Old Morrison set off,
amidst the lamentations of the womenfolk, truncheon in hand,
to join the other specials, but was back in ten minutes having

sprained his ankle, he said, and had to be helped to bed. I was sorry, because I'd been hoping he might get his head stove in, but it wouldn't have happened anyway. The Chartists did assemble, and the specials were mustered in force to guard the bridges—it was then that I saw Gladstone with the other specials, with his nose dripping, preparing to sell his life dearly for the sake of constitutional liberty and his own investments. But it poured down, everyone was soaked, the foreign agitators who were on hand got nowhere, and all the inflamed mob did was to send a monstrous petition across to the House of Commons. It had five million signatures, they said; I know it had four of mine, one in the name of Obadiah Snooks, and three others in the shape of X's beside which I wrote, "John Morrison, Arthur Wellesley, Henry John Temple Palmerston, their marks".

But the whole thing was a frost, and when one of the Frog agitators in Trafalgar Square got up and d - - - - d the whole lot of the Chartists for English cowards, a butcher's boy tore off his coat, squared up to the Frenchy, and gave the snail-chewing scoundrel the finest thrashing you could wish for. Then, of course, the whole crowd carried the butcher's boy shoulder high, and finished up singing "God Save the Queen" with tremendous gusto. A thoroughly English revolution, I dare say.[1]

You may wonder what all this had to do with my thinking about entering politics. Well, as I've said, it had lowered my opinion of asses like Gladstone still further, and caused me to speculate that if I were an M.P. I couldn't be any worse than that sorry pack of fellows, but this was just an idle thought. However, if my chief feeling about the demonstration was disappointment that so little mischief had been done, it had a great effect on my father-in-law, crouched at home with the bed-clothes over his head, waiting to be guillotined.

You'd hardly credit it, but in a way he'd had much the same thought as myself, although I don't claim to know by what amazing distortions of logic he arrived at it. But the upshot of his panic-stricken meditations on that day and the following night, when he was still expecting the mob to reassemble and run him out of town on a rail, was the amazing notion that I ought to go into Parliament.

"It's your duty," cries he, sitting there in his night-cap with his ankle all bandaged up, while the family chittered round him, offering gruel. He waved his spoon at me. "Ye should hiv a seat i' the Hoose."

I'm well aware that when a man has been terrified out of his wits, the most lunatic notions occur to him as sane and reasonable, but I couldn't follow this.

"Me, in Parliament?" I loosed a huge guffaw. "What the devil would I do there? D'ye think that would keep the Chartists at bay?"

At this he let loose a great tirade about the parlous state of the country, and the impending dissolution of constitutional government, and how it was everyone's duty to rally to the flag. Oddly enough, it reminded me of the kind of claptrap I'd heard from Bismarck—strong government, and lashing the workers—but I couldn't see how Flashy, M.P., was going to bring that about.

"If yesterday's nonsense has convinced you that we need a change at Westminster," says I, "—and I'd not disagree with you there—why don't you stand yourself?"

He glowered at me over his gruel-bowl. "I'm no' the Hero of Kabul," says he. "Forbye, I've business enough to attend to. But you—ye've nothing to hinder ye. Ye're never tired o' tellin' us whit a favourite ye are wi' the public. Here's your chance to make somethin' o't."

"You're out of your senses," says I. "Who would elect me?"

"Anybody," snaps he. "A pug ape frae the zoological gardens could win a seat in this country, if it was managed right." Buttering me up, I could see.

"But I'm not a politician," says I. "I know nothing about it, and care even less."

"Then ye're the very man, and ye'll find plenty o' kindred spirits at Westminster," says he, and when I hooted at him he flew into a tremendous passion that drove the females weeping from the room. I left him raging.

But when I came to think about it, do you know, it didn't seem quite so foolish after all. He was a sharp man, old Morrison, and he could see it would do no harm to have a Member in the family, what with his business interests and so on. Not that I'd be much use to him that I could see—I didn't know, then, that he had been maturing some notion of buying as many as a dozen seats. I'd no idea, you see, of just how wealthy the old rascal was, and how he was scheming to use that wealth for political ends. You won't find much in the history books about John Morrison, Lord Paisley, but you can take my word for it that it was men like him who pulled the strings in the old Queen's time, while the political puppets danced. They still do, and always will.

And from my side of the field, it didn't look a half bad idea. Flashy, M.P. Sir Harry Flashman, M.P., perhaps. Lord Flash of Lightning, Paymaster of the Forces, with a seat in the Cabinet, d - - n your eyes. God knows I could do *that* job as well as Thomas Babbling Macaulay. Even in my day dreaming I stopped short of Flashy, Prime Minister, but for the rest, the more I thought of it the better I liked it. Light work, plenty of spare time for as much depraved diversion as I could manage in safety, and the chance to ram my opinions down the public's throat whenever I felt inclined. I need never go out of London if I didn't want to—I would resign from the army, of course, and rest on my considerable if ill-gotten laurels—and old Morrison would be happy to foot the bills, no doubt, in return for slight services rendered.

The main thing was, it would be a quiet life. As you know, in spite of the published catalogue of my career—Victoria Cross, general rank, eleven campaigns, and all that mummery—I've always been an arrant coward and a peaceable soul. Bullying underlings and whipping trollops always excepted, I'm a gentle fellow—which means I'll never do harm to anyone if there's a chance he may harm me in return. The trouble is, no one would believe it to look at me; I've always been big and hearty and looked the kind of chap who'd go three rounds with the town tough if he so much as stepped on my shadow, and from what Tom Hughes has written of me you might imagine I was always ready for devilment. Aye, but as I've grown older I've learned that devilment usually has to be paid for. God knows I've done my share of paying, and even in '48, at the ripe old age of twenty-six, I'd seen enough sorrow, from the Khyber to German dungeons by way of the Borneo jungles and the torture-pits of Madagascar, to convince me that I must never go looking for trouble again.² Who'd have thought that old Morrison's plans to seat me at Westminster could have led to . . . well, ne'er mind. All in good time.

As to getting a suitable seat, that would be easy enough, with Morrison's gelt greasing the way. Which prompted the thought that I ought to have a word with him about issues of political importance.

"Two thousand a year at least," says I.

"Five hundred and no' a penny more," says he.

"Dammit, I've appearances to keep up," says I. "Elspeth's notions ain't cheap."

"I'll attend to that," says he. "As I always have done." The cunning old bastard wouldn't even let me have the administration of my own wife's household; he knew better.

"A thousand, then. Good God, my clothes'll cost that."

"Elspeth can see tae your wardrobe," says he, smirking. "Five hundred, my buckie; it's mair than your worth."

"I'll not do it, then," says I. "And that's flat."

"Aye, weel," says he, "that's a peety. I'll just have to get one that will. Ye'll find it a wee bit lean on your army half-pay, I'm thinkin'."

"Damn you," says I. "Seven-fifty."

And eventually I got it, but only because Elspeth told her father I should have it. She, of course, was delighted at the thought of my having a political career. "We shall have soirées, attended by Lord John and the Marquis of Lansdowne,"³ she exclaimed. "People with *titles*, and their ladies, and—"

"They're Whigs," says I. "I've an idea your papa will expect me to be a Tory."

"It doesn't signify in the least," says she. "The Tories are a better class of people altogether, I believe. Why, the Duke is a Tory, is he not?"

"So the rumour runs," says I. "But political secrets of that kind must be kept quiet, you know."

"Oh, it is all quite wonderful," says she, paying me no heed at all. "You will be famous again, Harry—you are so clever, you are sure to be a success, and I—I will need at least four page boys with buttons, and footmen in proper uniform." She clapped her hands, her eyes sparkling, and pirouetted. "Why, Harry! We shall need a new house! I must have clothes—oh, but papa will see to it, he is so kind!"

It occurred to me that papa might decide he had bitten off more than he could chew, listening to her, although personally I thought her ideas were excellent. She was in tremendous spirits, and I took the opportunity to make another assault on her; she was so excited that I had her half out of her dress before she realised what I was about, and then the wicked little b - - - h teased me along until I was thoroughly randified, only to stop me in the very act of boarding her, because of her concern for dear little Harry Albert Victor, blast his impudence.

"To think," says she, "that he will have a great statesman for a father!" She had me in the Cabinet already, you see. "Oh, Harry, how proud we shall be!"

Which was small consolation to me just then, having to button myself up and restrain my carnal appetites. To be sure I eased them considerably in the next week or two, for I looked out some of the Haymarket tarts of my acquaintance, and although they were a poor substitute for Elspeth they helped me to settle in again to London life and regular whoring. So I was soon enjoying myself, speculating pleasantly about the future, taking my ease with the boys about the town, forgetting the recent horrors of Jotunberg and Rudi Starnberg's gang of assassins, and waiting for old Morrison to start the wheels of my political career turning.

He was helped, of course, by my own celebrity and the fact that my father—who was now happily settled down with his delirium tremens at a place in the country—had been an M.P. in his time, and a damned fine hand at the hustings; he had got in on a popular majority after horse-whipping his opponent on the eve of the poll and offering to fight bare-knuckle with any man the Whigs could put up, from Brougham down. He had a good deal more bottom than I, but they did for him at Reform, and if I didn't have his ardour I was certain I had a greater talent for survival, political and otherwise.

Anyway, it was some weeks before Morrison announced that I was to meet some "men in the know" as he called them, and that we were to go down to Wiltshire for a few days, to the house of a local big-wig, where some politicos would be among the guests. It sounded damned dull, and no doubt would have been, had it not been for my own lechery and vanity and the shockingest turn of ill luck. Apart from anything else, I missed the Derby.

We left Elspeth at home, working contentedly at her Berlins,[4] and took the train for Bristol, Morrison and I. He was the damndest travelling companion you ever saw, for apart from being a thundering bore he carped at everything, from the literature at the station book stalls, which he pronounced trash, to the new practice of having to pay a bob "attendance money" to railway servants.[5] I was glad to get to Devizes, I can tell you, whence we drove to Seend, a pretty little place where our host lived in a fairish establishment called Cleeve House.

He was the kind of friend you'd expect Morrison to have—a middle-aged moneybags of a banker called Locke, with reach-me-down whiskers and a face like a three-day corpse. He was warm enough, evidently, but as soon as I saw the females sitting about in chairs on the gravel with their bonnets on, reading improving books, I could see this was the kind of house-party that wasn't Flashy's style at all. I was used to hunting weeks where you dined any old how, with lots of brandy and singing, and chaps p - - - - g in the corner and keeping all hours, and no females except the local bareback riders, as old Jack Mitton used to call them. But by '48 they were going out, you see, and it was as much as you dare do, at some of the houses, to produce the cards before midnight after the ladies had retired. I remember Speed telling me, round about this time, of one place he'd been to where they got him up at eight for morning prayers, and gave him a book of sermons to read after luncheon.

Cleeve House wasn't quite as raw as that, but it would have been damned dreary going if one of the girls present hadn't been quite out of the ordinary run. I fixed on her from the start—a willowy blonde piece with a swinging hip and a knowing eye. Strange, I met her at Cleeve, and didn't see her again till I came on her cooking breakfast for a picket of Campbell's Highlanders outside Balaclava six years later, the very morning of Cardigan's charge. Fanny Locke her name was;[6] she was the young sister of our host, a damned handsome eighteen with the shape of a well-developed matron. Like so many young girls whose body out-grows their years, she didn't know what to do with it—well, I could give her guidance there. As soon as I saw her swaying down the staircase at Cleeve, ho-ho, thinks I, hark forrard. You may be sure I was soon in attendance, and when I found she was a friendly little thing, and a keen horsewoman, I laid my plans accordingly, and engaged to go riding with her next day, when she would show me the local country—it was the long grass I had in mind, of course.

In the meantime, the first evening at Cleeve was quite as much fun as a Methodist service. Of course, all Tory gatherings are the same, and Locke had assembled as choice a collection of know-all prigs as you could look for. Bentinck I didn't mind, because he had some game in him and knew more about the turf than anyone I ever met, but he had in tow the cocky little sheeny D'Israeli, whom I never could stomach. He was pathetic, really, trying to behave like the Young Idea when he was well into greasy middle age, with his lovelock and fancy vest, like a Punjabi whoremaster. They were saying then that he had spent longer "arriving" at Westminster than a one-legged Irish peer with the gout; well, he "arrived" in the end, as we know, and if I'd been able to read the future I might have toadied him a good deal more, I dare say.[7]

Locke, our host, introduced us as we were going in to dinner, and I made political small talk, as old Morrison had told me I should.

"Bad work for your lot in the Lords, hey?" says I, and he lowered his lids at me in that smart-affected way he had. "You know," says I, "the Jewish Bill getting thrown out. Bellows to mend in Whitechapel, what? Bad luck all round," I went on, "what with Shylock running second at Epsom, too. I had twenty quid on him myself."[8]

I heard Locke mutter "Good God", but friend Codlingsby just put back his head and looked at me thoughtfully. "Indeed," says he. "How remarkable. And you aspire to politics, Mr Flashman?"

"That's my ticket," says I.

"Truly remarkable," says he. "Do you know, I shall watch your career with bated breath." And then Locke mumbled him away, and I pounced on Miss Fanny and took her in to dinner.

Of course, it was all politics at table, but I was too engaged with Fanny to pay much heed. When the ladies had gone and we'd all moved up, I heard more, but it didn't stick. I remember they were berating Russell's idleness, and the government's extravagance, on which D'Israeli made one of those sallies which you could see had been well polished beforehand.

"Lord John must not be underestimated," says he. "He understands the first principle, that the great strength of the British Constitution lies in the money it costs us. Make government cheap and you make it contemptible."

Everyone laughed except old Morrison, who glared over his glass. "That'll look well in one o' your nov-elles, sir, I don't doubt. But let me tell you, running a country is like running a mill, and waste'll ruin the baith o' them."

D'Israeli, being smart, affected to misunderstand. "I know nothing of running *mills*," says he. "Pugilism is not among my interests," which of course turned the laugh against old Morrison.

You may judge from this the kind of rare wit to be found at political gatherings; I was out of all patience after an hour of it, and by the time we joined the ladies Miss Fanny, to my disgust, had gone to bed.

Next day, however, she and I were off on our expedition soon after breakfast, with sandwiches and a bottle in my saddlebag, for we intended to ride as far as Roundway Down, a place which she was sure must interest me, since there had been a battle fought there long ago. On the way she showed me the house where she had once lived, and then we cantered on across the excellent riding country that lies north of Salisbury Plain. It was the jolliest day, with a blue sky, fleecy clouds, and a gentle breeze, and Fanny was in excellent trim. She looked mighty fetching in a plum-coloured habit with a tricorne hat and feather, and little black boots, and I never saw a female better in the saddle. She could keep up with *me* at a gallop, her fair hair flying and her pretty little lips parted as she scudded along, so to impress her I had to show her some of the riding tricks I'd picked up in Afghanistan, like running alongside my beast full tilt, with a hand on the mane, and swinging over the rump to land and run on t'other side. D----d showy stuff, and she clapped her hands and cried bravo, while the bumpkins we passed along the way hallooed and waved their hats.

All this put me in capital form, of course, and by the time we got to Roundway I was nicely primed to lure Miss Fanny into a thicket and get down to business. She was such a jolly little thing, with such easy chatter and a saucy glint in her blue eye, that I anticipated no difficulty. We dismounted near the hill, and we led our beasts while she told me about the battle, in which it seemed the Cavaliers had thoroughly chased the Roundheads.

"The people hereabouts call it Runaway Down," says she, laughing, "because the Roundheads fled so fast."

It was the best thing I'd ever heard about Cromwell's fellows; gave me a fellow-feeling for 'em, and I made some light remark to this effect.

"Oh, you may say so," says she. "You who have never run away." She gave me an odd little look. "Sometimes I wish I were a man, with the strength to be brave, like you."

Flashy knows a cue when he hears it. "I'm not always brave, Fanny," says I, pretty solemn, and stepping close. "Sometimes —I'm the veriest coward." By G-d, I never spoke a truer word.

"I can't believe—" says she, and got no further, for I kissed her hard on the lips; for a moment she bore it, and then to my delight she began teasing me with her tongue, but before I could press home my advantage she suddenly slipped away, laughing.

"No, no," cries she, very merry, "this is Runaway Down, remember," and like a fool I didn't pursue on the instant. If I had done, I don't doubt she'd have yielded, but I was content to play her game for the moment, and so we walked on, chatting and laughing.

You may think this trivial; the point is that if I'd mounted Miss Fanny that day I daresay I'd have lost interest in her—at all events I'd have been less concerned to please her later, and would have avoided a great deal of sorrow, and being chased and bullyragged halfway round the world.

As it was, it was the most d - - - ably bothersome day I remember. Half a dozen times I got to grips with her —over the luncheon sandwiches, during our walk down from the hill, even in the saddle on the way home—and each time she kissed like a novice

French whore and then broke off, teasing. And either because we met people on the way, or because she was as nimble as a fly-weight, I never had a chance to go to work properly. Of course, I'd known chits like this before, and experience told me it would come all right on the night, as the theatricals say, but by the time we were cantering up to Cleeve again I was as horny as the town bull, and not liking it overmuch.

And there was a nasty shock waiting, in the shape of two chaps who came out of the front door, both in Hussar rig, the first one hallo-ing and waving to Fanny and helping her down from her mare. She made him known to me, with a mischievous twinkle, as her fiancé, one Duberly, which would have been bad news at any other time, but all my attention was taken by his companion, who stood back eyeing me with a cool smile, very knowing: my heart checked for a second at the sight of him. It was Bryant.

If you know my memoirs, you know him. He and I had been subalterns in Cardigan's regiment, nine years before; on the occasion when I fought a memorable duel, he had agreed, for a consideration, to ensure that my opponent's pistol was loaded only with blank, so that I had survived the meeting with credit. I had cheated him out of his payment, to be sure, and there had been nothing he could do except make empty threats of vengeance. After that our ways had parted, and I'd forgotten him; and now here he was, like a corpse at a christening. Of course, he still couldn't harm me, but it was a nasty turn to see him, just the same.

"Hollo, Flash," says he, sauntering up. "Still campaigning, I see." And he made his bow to Miss Fanny, while Duberly presented him.

"Most honoured to know you, sir," says this Duberly, shaking my hand as I dismounted. He was a fattish, whiskered creature, with muff written all over him. "Heard so much—distinguished officer—delighted to see you here, eh, Fan?" And she, cool piece that she was, having sensed in an instant that Bryant and I were at odds, chattered gaily about what a jolly picnic we had made, while Duberly humphed and grinned and was all over her. Presently he led her indoors, leaving Bryant and me by the horses.

"Spoiled the chase for you has he, Flash?" says he, with his spiteful little grin. "D - - - lish nuisance, these fiancés; sometimes as inconvenient as husbands, I dare say."

"I can't imagine you'd know about that," says I, looking him up and down. "When did Cardigan kick you out, then?" For he wasn't wearing Cherrypicker rig. He flushed at that, and I could see I'd touched him on the raw.

"I transferred to the Eighth Irish," says he. "We don't all leave regiments as you do, with our tails between our legs."

"My, my, it still rankles, Tommy, don't it?" says I, grinning at him. "Feeling the pinch, were we? I always thought the Eleventh was too expensive for you; well, if you can't come up to snuff in the Eighth you can always take up pimping again, you know."

That made his mouth work, all right; in the old days in Canterbury, when he was toadying me, I'd thrown a few guineas his way in return for his services as whoremonger and general creature. He fell back a step.

"D - - n you, Flashman," says he, "I'll bring you down yet!"

"Not to your own level, if you please," says I, and left him swearing under his breath.

Now, if I'd been as wise then as I am now, I'd have remembered that even as slimy a snake as Bryant still has fangs, but he was such a contemptible squirt, and I'd handled him so easily in the past, that I put him out of my mind. I was more concerned with the inconvenience of this fat fool Duberly, whose presence would make it all the more difficult for me to cock a leg athwart Miss Fanny—I was sure she was game for it, after that day's sparring, but of course Duberly quite cut me out now that he was here, squiring her at tea, and fetching her fan, clucking round her in the drawing-room, and taking her arm in to dinner. Locke and the rest of her family were all for him, I could see, so I couldn't put him down as I'd have done anywhere else. It was d - - - - d vexing, but where's the fun if it's all too easy, I told myself, and set to scheme how I might bring the lady to the sticking point, as we Shakespeare scholars say.

I was much distracted from these fine thoughts by old Morrison, who berated me privately for what he called "godless gallivanting after yon hussy"; it seemed I should have spent the day hanging on the lips of Bentinck and D'Israeli and Locke, who had been deep in affairs. I soothed him with a promise that I'd attend them after dinner, which I did, and steep work it was. Ireland was very much exciting them, I recall, and the sentencing and transportation of some rebel called Mitchel; old Morrison was positive he should have been hanged, and got into a great passion because when they shipped him off to the Indies they didn't send him in chains with a bread-and-water diet.[9]

"If the d - - - d rascal had sailed on any vessel o' mine, it would hae been sawdust he got tae eat, and d - - - - d little o' that," says dear kind papa, and the rest of them cried "hear, hear," and agreed that it was this kind of soft treatment that encouraged sedition; they expected the Paddies to rise at any time, and there was talk of Dublin being besieged. All humbug, of course; you can't mount a rebellion on rotten potatoes.

After that there was fierce debate over whether the working class wanted reform, and one Hume was damned for a scoundrel, and D'Israeli discoursed on the folly of some measure to exclude M.P.s who couldn't pay their debts—no doubt he had a personal interest there—and I sat and listened, bored to death, until Bentinck suggested we join the ladies. Not that there was much sport there either, for Mrs Locke was reading aloud from the great new novel, *Jane Eyre*, and from the expression on the faces of Fanny and the other young misses, I guessed they'd have been happier with *Varney the Vampire* or *Sweeney Todd*.[10] In another corner the older folk were looking at picture books—German churches, probably—another pack of females were sewing and mumbling to each other, and in an adjoining salon some hysterical bitch was singing "Who will o'er the downs with me?" with a governess thrashing away at the pianoforte. A couple of wild old rakes were playing backgammon, and Duberly was explaining to whoever would listen that he would have been glad to serve in India, but his health wouldn't allow, don't ye know. I asked myself how long I could bear it.

I believe it was Bentinck who suggested cards—Locke looked like the kind who wouldn't have permitted such devices of the devil under his roof, but Bentinck was the lion, you see, and couldn't be gainsaid; besides, there was still a little leeway in those days which you'd never have got in the sixties or seventies. I wasn't in at the beginning of the game, having been ambushed by an old dragon in a lace cap who told me how her niece Priscilla had written to her with an envelope, instead of waxing her letter, and what did I think of that? I despaired of getting away, until who should appear but Fanny herself, sparkling and full of nonsense, to insist that I should come and show her how to make her wagers.

"I am quite at sea," says she, "and Henry"—this was Duberly —"vows that counting makes his head ache.[11] You will assist me, Captain Flashman, won't you, and Aunt Selina will not mind, will you, auntie dear?"

I should have told her to go straight to h--l, and clung to Aunt Selina like a shipwrecked lascar—but you can't read the future. Ain't it odd to think, if I'd declined her invitation, I might have been in the Lords today—and a certain American might never have become President? Mind you, even now, if a fresh piece like Fanny Locke stooped in front of me, with those saucy eyes and silken hair, and pushed those pouting lips and white shoulders at me—ah, dry your whiskers, old Flash—you could keep your coronet for me, and I'd take her hand and hobble off to my ruin, whatever it was.

Aunt Selina sniffed, and told her she must not wager more than a pair of gloves—"and not your Houbigants, mind, you foolish little girl. Indeed, I don't know what the world is coming to, or Henry Duberly thinking of, to permit you wagering at cards. No doubt he will be one of these husbands who will allow you to waltz, and drink porter in company. It would not have done in my day. What are the stakes?"

"Oh, ever so little, aunt," says Fanny, tugging at my sleeve. "Farthings and sweets—and Lord George has the bank, and is ever such fun!"

"Is he, indeed?" says Aunt Selina, gathering up her reticule. "Then I shall come myself, to see you are not excessively silly."

There was quite a crowd round the table in the salon, where Bentinck was presiding over vingt-et-un, amid great merriment. He was playing the chef to perfection, calling the stakes and whipping round the pasteboards like a riverboat dude. Even Locke and Morrison were present, watching and being not too sour about it; Mrs Abigail Locke was among the players, with Bryant advising, toady-like, at her elbow; D'Israeli was making a great show of playing indulgently, like a great man who don't mind stooping to trivialities if it will amuse lesser minds, and half a dozen others, old and young, were putting up their counters and laughing with delight at Bentinck's sallies.

As Fanny and Aunt Selina took their seats, an old fellow with white whiskers leans across to me. "I must warn you," says he, "that Lord George has us playing very deep—plunging recklessly, you know." He held up some counters. "The green ones are—a farthing; the blue—a ha'penny; and the yellow—you must take care—are *a penny*! It is desperate work, you see!"

"I'm coming for you, Sir Michael!" cries Bentinck, slapping the pack. "Now, ladies, are you ready? Then, one for all, and all for the lucky winner!" And he flicked the cards round to the players.

It was silly, harmless stuff, you see, all good nature and playfulness—and as desperate a card game as I ever sat in on in my life. Not that you'd have guessed it at first, with Bentinck making everyone merry, and one of the players—a sulky-looking youth of about fourteen, of the kind whose arse I delighted to kick in happier days—protesting that he was cleaned out, and Bentinck solemnly offering to take his note of hand for two-pence. Fanny was all excitement, holding her card up close for me to see and asking how much she should go, which gave me the opportunity to huddle in and stroke her bare shoulder as I whispered in her ear. Next to her, old Aunt Selina was buying cards like a St James's shark, very precise and slow; she took four and paused at 17; Bentinck was watching her, his handsome face very intent, his thumb poised on the next card; she took it, and it was a trey, which meant that she had a five-card hand, at which there was great applause, and Bentinck laughed and cried "Well done, ma'am," as he paid her counters over.

"I never buy beyond 16, you know," Aunt Selina confided to Fanny, "unless it is for a five-card hand. I find it a very good rule."

So the game went round, and I found myself thinking that it doesn't take high stakes to show up who the real gamesters are.

You could sense the rapport there was between Bentinck and Aunt Selina—two folk with not a jot in common, mark you. He was one of the sportsmen of the day, used to playing for thousands, a grandee of the turf and the tables who could watch a fortune slip away in five seconds at Epsom and never bat an eyelid, and here he was, watching like a hawk as some dowager hesitated over a farthing stake, or frowning as the sullen Master Jerry lost his two-penny I.O.U. and promptly demanded further credit. Wasn't it Greville who said that the money Lord George Bentinck won was just so many paper counters to him—it was the game that mattered? And Aunt Selina was another of the same; she duelled with him like a good 'un, and won as often as not, and he liked her for it.

And then the bank passed round to Fanny, and I had to deal the cards for her. Bryant, who had raised a great laugh by coming round to touch Aunt Selina's mittened hand for luck, said we should have a fair deal at last, since I had been notoriously the worst vingt-et-un player in the whole Light Cavalry—there was more polite mirth at this, and I gave him a hard look as he went back to Mrs Locke, and wondered to myself just what he had meant by that. Then Fanny, all twittering as she handled the stakes, claimed my attention, and I dealt the cards.

If you know vingt-et-un—or poor man's baccarat, or blackjack, or pontoon, whichever you like to call it—you know that the object is not to go above 21 with the cards dealt to you. It's a gambler's game, in which you must decide whether to stay pat at 16 or 17, or risk another card which may break you or, if it's a small one, may give you a winning score of 20 or 21. I've played it from Sydney to Sacramento, and learned to stick at 17, like Aunt Selina. The odds are with the bank, since when the scores are level the banker takes the stakes.

Fanny and I had a good bank. I dealt her 19 the first round, which sank everyone except D'Israeli, who had two court cards for 20. The next time I gave Fanny an ace and a knave for vingt-et-un, which swamped the whole board, and she clapped her hands and squealed with delight. Then we ran two five-card hands in succession, and the punters groaned aloud and protested at our luck, and Bentinck jestingly asked Aunt Selina if she would stand good for him, and she cried "With you, Lord George!" and made great play of changing his silver for her coppers.

I was interested in the game by this time—it's a fact, Greville was right, it don't matter a d--n how small the stakes are—and Fanny was full of excitement and admiration for my luck. She shot me an adoring look over her shoulder, and I glanced down at her quivering bosoms and thought to myself, you'll be in rare trim for another kind of game later. Get 'em excited—a fight is best, with the claret flowing, but any kind of sport will do, if there's a hint of savagery in it—and they'll couple like monkeys. And then, as I pulled my eyes away and dealt the first cards of another hand, looking to see that all the stakes were placed, I saw that on Mrs Locke's card there was a pile of yellow counters —about two bob's worth. That meant they had an ace, for certain. And they had, but it did 'em no good; they drew a seven with it, bought a five, and then went broke with a king. But next time round they staked an even bigger pile of yellows, lost again, and came back with a still larger wager for the following hand.

I paused in the act of dealing the second cards. "You're playing double or quits, ma'am," says I to Mrs Locke. "Road to ruin."

But before she could speak, Bryant cut in: "Stakes too high for you, are they? Why, if you can't afford . . ."

"Not a bit," says I. "If my principal's content," and I looked down at Fanny, who was sitting with a splendid pile of counters before her.

"Oh, do go on, please!" cries she. "It is the greatest fun!" So I put round the second cards; if Bryant thought he was going to rattle *me* over a few shillings' worth of stake he was a bigger fool than I thought. But I knew he wasn't a fool, and that he was a d---d sharp hand at card tricks, so I kept my eye on Mrs Locke's place.

They lost again, and next time Mrs Locke would only put up a single yellow, on which they won. There was a good deal of heavy jesting at this, and I saw Bryant whispering busily in her ear. When I dealt the first card he pounced on it, they consulted together, and then they put their whole pile—yellows, blues, everything, on top of the card, and Bryant gave me a nasty grin and stood back waiting.

I couldn't follow this; it couldn't be better than an ace, and it was just a kindergarten game, anyway. Did he think he could score off me by breaking Miss Fanny's bank? I noticed Bentinck was smiling, in a half-puzzled way, and D'Israeli was fingering his card thoughtfully and shifting his lidded glance from Bryant to me. They were wondering, too, and suddenly I felt that cold touch at the nape of my neck that is the warning signal of danger.

It was ridiculous, of course; a ha'penny game in a country house, but I could sense Bryant was as worked up as if there'd been a thousand guineas riding on his partner's card. It wasn't healthy, and I wanted to be out of that game then and there, but I'd have looked a fool, and Aunt Selina was tapping for a second card and looking at me severely.

I put them round, and perhaps because I had that tiny unease I fumbled Master Jerry's second card, so that it fell face up. I should have taken it back, by rights, but it was an ace, and the little scoundrel, who should have been in his bed long before, insisted on keeping it. Bryant snapped up Mrs Locke's second card and showed it to her with a grin; D'Israeli displayed vingt-et-un by laying his second card, a queen, face up across the first one. The rest bought a third or stood pat.

I faced our cards—a knave and a three, which was bad. I faced a third, an ace, which gave us 14; nothing for it but to go on, and I turned up a four. We were at 18, and at least three players were sitting pat on three cards, which meant probably they had 18 or 19 or better. I whispered to Fanny, did she want to try for a five-card trick, which would beat everyone except Codlingsby's vingt-et-un.

"Oh, yes, please!" cries she. "We are in luck, I feel sure of it!"

I put my thumb on the top card, and stopped. Something was d---d far wrong, somewhere, and I knew it. Bentinck knew it, too, and Aunt Selina, who was staring over her spectacles at the pack in my hand. Others in the room sensed something; Locke and Morrison had broken off their conversation to watch. Bryant was smirking across at me.

I flicked over the top card. It was a deuce, giving us 20 and victory, Bentinck cried "Ha!", Aunt Selina muttered something under her breath, and Fanny gave an ecstatic squeal and began to rake in the stakes. I gathered in the cards while everyone chattered and laughed—Mrs Locke had an ace and a nine, I noticed, and I commiserated her on her bad luck. Bryant pipes up at once:

"Very bad luck indeed, I should say."

But I ignored him, and told Fanny we must now pass the bank to D'Israeli, since he had scored vingt-et-un.

"Oh, must we?" cries she, pouting. "And we were doing so well! What a shame it is!"

Aunt Selina exclaimed at her greed, there was more laughter, and D'Israeli took out his eye-glass and bowed to Fanny.

"I would not dream," says he, "of claiming the cards from such a *fair* banker," a pun which was greeted with polite applause.

"Oh, I daresay her partner is quite happy to pass the cards," cries Bryant. "The killing's made, eh, Flashy?"

Now, I daresay we must have won thirty shillings on that bank, most of it from Mrs Locke, and you could take what he'd said as a joke, but the jarring note in his voice, and the grin on his flushed face told me it wasn't. I stared at him, and Bentinck's head whipped round, and suddenly there was a silence, broken only by Miss Fanny's tinkling laughter as she exclaimed to Aunt Selina about her own good luck.

"I think it is your bank, Dizzy," says Bentinck quietly, at last, his eyes on Bryant. "Unless the ladies feel we have played enough."

The ladies protested against this, and then Bryant cut in again:

"I've played quite enough, thank'ee, and I daresay my partner has, too." Mrs Locke looked startled, and Bryant went on:

"I never thought to see—ah, but let it go!"

And he turned from the table, like a man trying to control himself.

There was a second's silence, and then they were babbling, "What did he say?" "What did he mean?" and Bentinck was flushed with anger and demanding to know what Bryant was implying. At this Bryant pointed to me, and says:

"It is really too bad! In a pleasant game, for the ladies, this fellow . . . I beg your pardon, Lord George, but it is too much! Ask him," cries he, "to turn out his pockets—his coat pockets!"

It hit me like a dash of icy water. In the shocked hush, I found my hand going to my left-hand coat pocket, while everyone gaped at me, Bentinck took a pace towards me saying, "No, stop. Not before the ladies..." and then my hand came out, and there were three playing cards in it. I was too horrified and bewildered to speak, there was a shriek from one of the females, and a general gasp, and someone muttered: "Cheat... oh!" I could only stare from the cards to Bentinck's horrified face, to Bryant's, flushed and exultant, and to Dizzy's, white with disbelief. Miss Fanny jumped up with a shriek, starting away from me, and then someone was shepherding the females from the room in a terrible silence, leaving me with the stern, disgusted faces and the exclamations of incredulity and amazement. They crowded forward while I stood there, gazing at the cards in my hand —I can see them yet: the king of clubs, the deuce of hearts, and the ace of diamonds.

Bentinck was speaking, and I forced myself to look round at him, with Bryant, D'Israeli, old Morrison, Locke and the others crowding at his back.

"Gentlemen," my voice was hoarse. "I... I can't imagine. I swear to God..."

"I thought I hadn't seen the ace of diamonds," says someone.

"I saw his hand go to his pocket, at the last deal." This was Bryant.

"Oh, my Goad, the shame o't... Ye wicked, deceitful..."

"The fellow's a damned sharp!"

"A cheat! In this house..."

"Remarkable," says D'Israeli, with an odd note in his voice. "For a few pence? You know, George, it's d----d unlikely."

"The amount never matters," says Bentinck, with a voice like steel. "It's winning. Now, sir, what have you to say?"

I was gathering my wits before this monstrous thing, trying to understand it. God knew I hadn't cheated—when I cheat, it's for something that matters, not sweets and ha'pence. And suddenly it hit me like a lightning flash—Bryant coming round to touch Aunt Selina's hand, standing shoulder to shoulder with me. So this was how he was taking his revenge!

Put me in that situation today, and I'd reason my way out of it, talking calmly. But I was twenty-six then, and panicked—

535

d − − n it, if I *had* been cheating I'd have been ready for them, with my story cut and dried, but for once I was innocent, and couldn't think what to say. I dashed the cards down and faced them.

"It's a b - - - - y lie!" I shouted. "I didn't cheat, I swear it! My God, why should I? Lord George, can you believe it? Mr D'Israeli, I appeal to you! Would I cheat for a few coppers?"

"How came the cards in your pocket, then?" demands Bentinck.

"That little viper!" I shouted, pointing at Bryant. "The jealous little b - - - - - d placed them there, to disgrace me!"

That set up a tremendous uproar, and Bryant, blast his eyes, played it like a master. He took a step back, gritted his teeth, bowed to the company, and says:

"Lord George, I leave it to you to determine the worth of a foul slander from a proven cheat."

And then he turned, and strode from the room. I could only stand raging, and then as I saw how he had foxed me—my God, ruined me, and before the best in the land, I lost control altogether. I sprang for the door, bawling after him, someone caught my sleeve, but I threw him off, and then I had the door open and was plunging through in pursuit.

There was a hubbub behind me, and a sudden squeal of alarm ahead, for there were ladies at the head of the stairs, their white faces turned towards me. Bryant made off at the sight of me, and in blind passion I hurled myself after him. I had only one thought: to catch the undersized little squirt and pound him to death—sense, decency and the rest were forgotten. I got my hand on his collar at the top of the stairs, while the females screamed and shrank back; I wrenched him round, his face grey with fear, and shook him like a rat.

"You foul vermin!" I roared. "Try to dishonour me, would you, you scum of . . . of the Eighth Hussars!" And as I swung him left-handed before me, I drew back my right fist and with all my strength, smashed it into his face.

Nowadays, when I'm day-dreaming over the better moments of my misspent life—galloping Lola Montez and Elspeth and Queen Ranavalona and little Renee the Creole and the fat dancing-wench I bought in India whose name escapes me, and having old Colin

Campbell pinning the V.C. to my unworthy breast, and receiving my knighthood from Queen Victoria (and she in tears, maudlin little woman), and breaking into the Ranee's treasure-cellar and seeing all that splendid loot laid out for the taking—when I think back on these fine things, the recollection of hitting Tommy Bryant invariably comes back to me. God knows it was a nightmare at the time, but in retrospect I can't think of inflicting a hurt that I enjoyed more. My fist caught him full on the mouth and nose so hard that his collar was jerked clean out of my hand, and he went hurtling head foremost down that staircase like an arrow, bouncing once before crashing to rest in the hall, his limbs all a-sprawl.

There were shrieks of hysterical females in my ears, and hands seizing my coat, and men scampering down to lift him up, but all I remember is seeing Fanny's face turned towards me in terror, and Bentinck's voice drifting up the staircase:

"My God, I believe he's killed him!"

As it turned out, Bentinck was wrong, thank God; the little louse didn't die, but it was a near-run thing. Apart from a broken nose, his skull was fractured in the fall, and for a couple of days he hung on the edge, with a Bristol horse-leech working like fury to save him from going over. Once he regained consciousness, and had the impertinence to say, "Tell Flashman I forgive him with all my heart," which cheered me up, because it indicated he was going to live, and wanted to appear a forgiving Christian; if he'd thought he was dying he'd have d - - - - d me to hell and beyond.

But after that he lost consciousness again, and I went through the tortures of the pit. They had confined me to my room—Locke was a justice of the peace—and kept me there with the muff Duberly sitting outside the door like a blasted water-bailiff. I was in a fearful sweat, for if Bryant kicked the bucket it would be a hanging matter, no error, and at the thought of it I could only lie on my bed and quake. I'd seen men swing, and thought it excellent fun, but the thought of the rope rasping on my neck, and the blind being pulled over my brows, and the fearful plunge and sickening snap and blackness—my God, it had me vomiting in the corner. Well, I've had the noose under my chin since then, and waited blubbering for them to launch me off, and even the real thing seems no worse, looking back, than those few days of waiting in that bedroom, with the yellow primroses on the wall-paper, and the blue and red carpet on the floor with little green tigers woven into it, and the print of Harlaxton Manor, near Grantham, Lincolnshire, the seat of one John Longden, Esq., which hung above the bed—I can still recite the whole caption.

With the thought of the gallows driving everything else from my mind, it was small consolation to learn from Duberly—who seemed to be in a mortal funk himself over the whole business—that there was by no means complete agreement that I had been

538

caught cheating. D'Israeli—he was clever, I'll say that for him—had sensibly pointed out that a detected cheat wouldn't have hauled the evidence out of his pocket publicly as soon as he was challenged. He maintained I would have protested, and refused to be searched—he was quite right, of course, but most of the other pious hypocrites disagreed with him, and the general feeling was that I was a fraud and a dangerous maniac who would be well served if I finished up in the prison lime-pit. Whatever happened, it was a hideous scandal; the house had emptied as if by magic next day, Mrs Locke was in a decline, and her husband was apparently only waiting to see how Bryant fared before turning me over to the police.

I don't know, even now, what was determined, or who determined it, in those few days, except that old Morrison was obviously up to the neck in it. Whatever happened to Bryant, my political career was obviously over before it had begun; at best I was probably disgraced as a cheat, and liable to sentence for assault—that was if Bryant lived. In any event, I was a liability to Morrison henceforth, and whether he decided to try to get rid of me permanently, or planned simply to get me out of harm's way for a time, is something on which I've never made up my mind. In fact, I don't suppose he cared above half whether I lived or died, so long as his own interests weren't harmed.

He came to see me on the fifth day, and told me that Bryant was out of danger, and I was so relieved that I was almost happy as I listened to him denouncing me for a wastrel, a fornicator, a cheat, a liar, a brute, and all the rest of it—I couldn't fault a word of it, anyway. When he was done, he plumped down, breathing like a bellows, and says:

"My certie, but ye're easier oot o' this than ye deserve. It's no' your fault the mark o' Cain isnae on yer broo this day—a beast, that's whit ye are, Flashman, a ragin', evil beast!" And he mopped his face. "Weel, Locke isnae goin' tae press charges—ye have me tae thank for that—and this fellow Bryant'll keep mum. Huh! A few hundred'll tak' care of him—he's anither 'officer and gentleman' like yersel'. I could buy the lot o' ye! Jist trash." He snarled away under his breath, and shot me a look. "But we'll no' hush up the scandal, for a' that. Ye cannae come home—ye're aware o' that, I suppose?"

I didn't argue; I couldn't, but I was ill-advised enough to mutter something about Elspeth, and for a moment I thought he would strike me. His face went purple, and his teeth chattered.

"Mention her name tae me again—jist once again, and as Goad's my witness I'll see ye transported for this week's work! Ye'll rue the day ye ever set eyes on her—aye, as I have done, most bitterly. Goad alone knows what I and mine have done tae be punished by . . . *you!*"

Well, at least he didn't pray over me, like Arnold; he was a different kind of hypocrite, was Morrison, and as a man of business he didn't waste overmuch holy vituperation before getting down to cases.

"Ye'll be best oot o' England for a spell, until this d - - - able business has blown by—if it ever does. Your fine relatives can mak' your peace wi' the Horse Guards—this kind o' scandal'll be naethin' new there, I dare say. For the rest, I've been at work tae arrange matters—and whether ye like it or not, my buckie, ye'll jump as I whistle, D'ye see?"

"I suppose I've no choice," says I, and then, deciding it would be politic to grovel to the old b - - - - - d, I added: "Believe me, sir, I feel nothing but gratitude for what you are doing, and—"

"Hold your tongue," says he. "Ye're a liar. There's no more tae be said. Now, ye'll pack yer valise, and go at once tae Poole, and there take a room at the 'Admiral' and wait until ye hear from me. Not a word to a soul, and never stir out—or ye'll find my protection and Locke's is withdrawn, and that'll be a felon's cell for ye, and beggary tae follow. There's money," says he, and dropping a purse on the table he turned on his heel and stamped out.

I made no protest; he had me by the neck, and I didn't waste time reflecting on the eagerness with which my relatives and friends have always striven to banish me from England whenever opportunity offered—my own father, Lord Cardigan, and now old Morrison. They could never get shot of me fast enough. And, as on previous occasions, there was no room for argument; I would just have to go, and see what the Lord and John Morrison provided.

I slipped away from the house at noon, and was in Poole by nightfall. And there I waited a whole week, fretting at first, but gradually getting my spirits back. At least I was free, when I might have been going to the condemned hold; whatever lay in front of me, I'd come back to England eventually—it might be no more than a year, and by that time the trouble would be half-forgotten. Curiously enough, the assault on Bryant would be far less to live down than the business over the cards, but the more I thought about that, the more it seemed that no sensible men would take Bryant's word against mine—he was known for a toady and a dirty little hound, whereas I, quite aside from my popular fame, was bluff, honest Harry to everyone who thought they knew me. Indeed, I even toyed with the notion of going back to town and brazening the thing then and there, but I hadn't the gall for that. It was all too fresh, and Morrison would have thrown me into the gutter for certain. No, I would just have to take my medicine, whatever it was; I've learned that there's no sense in kicking against the prick—a phrase which fits old Morrison like a glove. I would just have to make the best of whatever he had in store for me.

What that was I discovered on the eighth day, when a man called to see me just as I was finishing breakfast. In fact, I had finished, and was just chivvying after the servant lass who had come to clear away the dishes from my room; I had chased her into a corner, and she was bleating that she was a good girl, which I'll swear she wasn't, when the knock sounded; she took advantage of it to escape, admitting the visitor while she straightened her cap and snapped her indignation at me.

"Sauce!" says she. "I never—"

"Get out," says the newcomer, and she took.one look at him and fled.

He kicked the door to with his heel and stood looking at me, and there was something in that look that made me bite back the d - - n-your-eyes I'd been going to give him for issuing orders in my room. At first glance he was ordinary looking enough; square built, middle height, plain trousers and tight-buttoned jacket with his hands thrust into the pockets, low-crowned round hat which he didn't trouble to remove, and stiff-trimmed beard and moustache which gave him a powerful, businesslike air. But it wasn't that that stopped me: it was the man's eyes. They were as pale as water in a china dish, bright and yet empty, and as cold as an ice floe. They were wide set in his brown, hook-nosed face, and they looked at you with a blind fathomless stare that told you here was a terrible man. Above them, on his brow, there was a puckered scar that ran from side and side and sometimes jerked as he talked; when he was enraged, as he often was, it turned red. Hollo, thinks I, here's another in my gallery of happy acquaintances.

"Mr Flashman?" says he. He had an odd, husky voice with what sounded like a trace of North Country. "My name is John Charity Spring."

It seemed d----d inappropriate to me, but he was evidently well enough pleased with it, for he sat himself down in a chair and nodded me to another. "We'll waste no time, if you please," says he. "I'm under instructions from my owner to take you aboard my vessel as supercargo. You don't know what that means, I daresay, and it's not necessary that you should. I know why you're shipping with me; you'll perform such duties as I suppose to be within your power. Am I clear?"

"Well," says I, "I don't know about that. I don't think I care for your tone, Mr Spring, and—"

"Captain Spring," says he, and sat forward. "Now see here, Mr Flashman, I don't beat about. You're nothing to me; I gather you've half-killed someone and that you're a short leap ahead of the law. I'm to give you passage out, on the instructions of Mr Morrison." Suddenly his voice rose to a shout, and he crashed his hand on the table. "Well, I don't give a d--n! You can stay or run, d'ye see? It's all one to me! But you don't waste my time!" The scar on his head was crimson, and then it faded and his voice dropped. "Well?"

I didn't like the look of this one, I can tell you. But what could I do?

"Well," says I, "you say Mr Morrison is your ship's owner —I didn't know he had ships."

"Part owner," says he. "One of my directors."

"I see. And where is your ship bound, Captain Spring, and

where are you to take me?"

The pale eyes flickered. "We're going foreign," says he. "America, and home again. The voyage may last six months, so by Christmas you'll be back in England. As supercargo you take a share of profit—a small share—so your voyage won't be wasted."

"What's the cargo?" says I, interested, because I remembered hearing that these short-haul traders on the Atlantic run did quite well.

"General stuffs on the way out—Brummagem, cloths, some machinery. Cotton, sugar, molasses and so forth on the trip home." He snapped the words out. "You ask too d - - - - d many questions, Mr Flashman, for a runner."

"I'm not all that much of a runner," says I. It didn't sound too bad a way of putting by the time till the Bryant business was past. "Well, in that case, I suppose—"

"Good," says he. "Now then: I know you're an Army officer, and it's in deference to that I'm making you supercargo, which means you mess aft. You've been in India, for what that's worth —what d'you know of the sea?"

"Little enough," says I. "I've voyaged out and home, but I sailed in Borneo waters with Rajah Brooke, and can handle a small boat."

"Did you now?" The pale eyes gleamed. "That means you've been part-pirate, I daresay. You look like it—hold your tongue, sir, it doesn't matter to me! I'll only tell you this: on my ship there is no free-and-easy sky-larking! I saw that slut in here just now—well, henceforth you'll fornicate when I give you leave! By God, I'll not have it otherwise!" He was shouting again; this fellow's half-mad, thinks I. Then he was quiet. "You have languages, I understand?"

"Why, yes. French and German, Hindoostani, Pushtu—which is a tongue . . ."

". . . of Northern India," says he impatiently. "I know. Get on."

"Well, a little Malay, a little Danish. I learn languages easily."

"Aye. You were educated at Rugby—you have the classics?"

"Well," says I, "I've forgotten a good deal . . ."

"Hah! *Hiatus maxime deflendus,** says this amazing fellow.

* A want greatly to be deplored.

543

"Or if you prefer it, *Hiatus valde deflendus.*" He glared at me. "Well?"

I gaped at the man. "You mean?—oh, let's see. Great—er, letting down? Great—"

"Christ's salvation!" says he. "No wonder Arnold died young. The priceless gift of education, thrown away on brute minds! You speak living languages without difficulty, it seems—had you not the grace to pay heed, d - - n your skin, to the only languages that matter?" He jumped up and strode about.

I was getting tired of Mr Charity Spring. "They may matter to you," says I, "but in my experience it's precious little good quoting Virgil to a head-hunter. And what the d - - - l has this to do with anything?"

He stood lowering at me, and then sneered: "There's your educated Englishman, right enough. Gentlemen! Bah! Why do I waste breath on you? *Quidquid praecipies, esto brevis,** by God! Well, if you'll pack your precious traps, Mr Flashman, we'll be off. There's a tide to catch." And he was away, bawling for my account at the stairhead.

It was obvious to me that I had fallen in with a lunatic, and possibly a dangerous one, but since in my experience a great many seamen are wanting in the head I wasn't over-concerned. He paid not the slightest heed to anything I said as we made our way down to the jetty with my valise behind on a hand-cart, but occasionally he would bark a question at me, and it was this that eventually prodded me into recollecting one of the few Latin tags which has stuck in my mind—mainly because it was flogged into me at school as a punishment for talking in class. He had been demanding information about my Indian service, mighty offensively, too, so I snapped at him:

"*Percunctatorem fugitus nam garrulus idem est*",† which I thought was pretty fair, and he stopped dead in his tracks.

"Horace, by G - d!" he shouted. "We'll make something of you yet. But it is *fugito*, d'ye see, not *fugitus*. Come on, man, make haste."

He got little opportunity to catechise me after this, for the first

* When you moralise, keep it short.
† Avoid the inquisitive man, for he is a talker.

544

stage of our journey was in a cockly little fishing boat that took us out into the Channel, and since it was h - - lish rough I was in no condition for conversation. I'm an experienced sailor, which is to say I've heaved my guts over the rail into all the Seven Seas, and before we were ten minutes out I was sprawled in the scuppers wishing to God I'd gone back to London and faced the music. This spewing empty misery continued, as it always does, for hours, and I was still green and wobbly-kneed when at evening we came into a bay on the French coast, and sighted Mr Spring's vessel riding at anchor. Gazing blearily at it as we approached, I was astonished at its size; it was long and lean and black, with three masts, not unlike the clippers of later years. As we came under her counter, I saw the lettering on her side: it read *Balliol College*.

"Ah," says I to Spring, who was by me just then. "You were at Balliol, were you?"

"No," says he, mighty short. "I am an Oriel man myself."

"Then why is your ship called *Balliol College*?"

I saw his teeth clench and his scar darkened up. "Because I hate the b - - - - y place!" he cried in passion. He took a turn about and came back to me. "My father and brothers were Balliol men, d'you see? Does that answer you, Mr Flashman?"

Well, it didn't, but at that moment my belly revolted again, and when we came aboard I had to be helped up the ladder, retching and groaning and falling a-sprawl on the deck. I heard a voice say, "Christ, it's Nelson", and then I was half-carried away, and dropped on a bunk somewhere, alone in my misery while in the distance I heard the hateful voice of John Charity Spring bawling orders. I vowed then, as I've vowed fifty times since, that this was the last time I'd ever permit myself to be lured aboard a ship, but my mind must still have been working a little, because as I dropped off to sleep I remember wondering: why does a British ship have to sail from the French coast? But I was too tired and ill to worry just then.

Sometime later someone brought me broth, and having spewed it on to the floor I felt well enough to get up and stagger on deck. It was half-dark, but the stars were out, and to port there were lights twinkling on the French coast. I looked north, towards

England, but there was nothing to be seen but grey sea, and suddenly I thought, my G - d, what am I doing here? Where the deuce am I going? Who is this man Spring? Here I was, who only a couple of weeks before had been rolling down to Wiltshire like a lord, with the intention of going into politics, and now I was shivering with sea-sickness on an ocean-going barque commanded by some kind of mad Oxford don—it was too much, and I found I was babbling to myself by the rail.

It's always the way, of course. You're coasting along, and then the current grips you, and you're swept into events and places that you couldn't even have dreamed about. It seemed to have happened so quickly, but as I looked miserably back over the past fortnight there wasn't, that I could see, anything I could have done that would have prevented what was now happening to me. I couldn't have resisted Morrison, or refused Spring—I'd had to do what I was told, and here I was. I found myself blubbering as I gazed over the rail at the empty waste of sea—if only I hadn't got lusty after that little b - - - h Fanny, and played cards with her, and hit that swine Bryant—ah, but what was the use? It was done, and I was going God knew where, and leaving Elspeth and my life of ease and drinking and guzzling and mounting women behind. But it was too bad, and I was full of self-pity and rage as I watched the water slipping past.

Of course, if I'd been like Jack Merry or Dick Champion, or any of the other plucky little prigs that Tom Brown and his cronies used to read about, setting off to seek my fortune on the bounding wave, I'd have brushed aside a manly tear and faced the future with the stout heart of youth, while old Bosun McHearty clapped me on the shoulder and held me enthralled with tales of the South Seas, and I would have gone to bed at last thinking of my mother and resolving to prove worthy of my resolute and Christian commander, Captain Freeman. (God knows how many young idiots have gone to sea after being fed that kind of lying pap in their nursery books.) Perhaps at twenty-six I was too old and hard-used, for instead of a manly tear I did another manly vomit, and in place of Bosun McHearty there came a rush of seamen tailing on a rope across the deck, hurling me aside with a cry of "Stand from under, you - - - - farmer!", while from the dark above me my

Christian commander bellowed at me to get below and not hinder work. So I went, and fell asleep thinking not of my mother, or of the credit I'd bring my family, but of the chance I'd missed in not rogering Fanny Locke that afternoon at Roundway Down. Aye, the vain regrets of youth.

You will judge from this that I wasn't cut out for the life on the ocean wave. I can't deny it; if Captain Marryat had had to write about me he'd have burned his pen, signed on a Cardiff tramp, and been buried at sea. For one thing, in my first few days aboard I did not thrash the ship's bully, make friends with the nigger cook, or learn how to gammon a bosprit from a leathery old salt who called me a likely lad. No, I spent those days in my bunk, feeling d - - - - d ill, and only crawling on deck occasionally to take the air and quickly scurry below again to my berth. I was a sea-green and corruptible Flashy in those days.

Nor did I make friends, for I saw only four people and disliked all of them. The first was the ship's doctor, a big-bellied lout of an Irishman who looked as though he'd be more at home with a bottle than a lancet, and had cold, clammy hands. He gave me a draught for my sea-sickness which made it worse, and then staggered away to be ill himself. He was followed by a queer, old-young creature with wispy hair who shuffled in carrying a bowl from which he slopped some evil-looking muck; when I asked him who the d - - - l he was he jerked his head in a nervous tic and stammered:

"Please, sir, I'm Sammy."

"Sammy what?"

"Nossir, please sir, Sammy Snivels, cap'n calls me. But they calls me Looney, mostly."

"And what's that?"

"Please sir, it's gruel. The doctor sez for you to eat it, please, sir," and he lumbered forward and spilled half of it over my cot.

"D - - n you!" cries I, and weak and all as I was I caught him a back-handed swipe on the face that sent him half across the cabin. "Take your filth and get out!"

He mowed at me, and tried to scrape some of the stuff off the floor back into the bowl. "Doctor'll thump me if you don't take it, please, sir," says he, pushing it at me again. "Please, sir, it's nice tack, an' all—please, sir," and then he squealed as I lunged out at him, dropped the bowl, and fairly ran for it. I was too weak to do more than curse after him, but I promised myself that when I was better I would put myself in a better frame of mind by giving the blundering half-wit a thumping on my own account, to keep the doctor's company.

Next man in was no half-wit, but a nimble little ferret of a ship's boy with a loose lip and a cast in one eye. He gave me a shifty grin and sniffed at the spilled gruel.

"Looney didn't 'ave no luck, did 'e?" says he. "I told 'im gruel wouldn't go down, no'ow."

I told him to go to blazes and leave me alone.

"Feelin' groggy, eh?" says he, moving towards the bunk. "Grub's no good ter you, mate. Tell yer wot; I'll get in bed wiv yer for a shillin'."

"Get out, you dirty little b - - - - - d," says I, for I knew his kind; Rugby had been crawling with 'em. "I'd sooner have your great-grandmother."

"Snooks!" says he, putting out his tongue. "You'll sing a different tune after three months at sea an' not a wench in sight. It'll be two bob then!"

I flung a pot at him, but missed, and he let fly a stream of the richest filth I've ever listened to. "I'll get Mister Comber ter you, yer big black swine!" he finished up. "'E'll give you what for! Ta-ta!" And with that he slipped out, thumbing his nose.

Mr Comber was the fourth of my new acquaintances. He was third mate, and shared the cabin with me, and I couldn't make him out. He was civil, although he said little enough, but the odd thing was, he was a gentleman, and had obviously been to a good school. What a playing-field beauty like this was doing on a merchantman I couldn't see, but I held my tongue and watched him. He was about my age, tall and fair haired, and too sure of himself for me to get on the wrong side of. I guessed he was as puzzled about me as I was about him, but I was feeling too poorly at first to give much heed to him. He didn't champion the cabin boy, by the way, so that worthy's threat had obviously been bluff.

It was four or five days before I got my sea legs, and by then I was heartily sick of the *Balliol College*. Nowadays you have no

about four feet above the deck on which we stood, there was a kind of half-deck, perhaps seven feet deep, like a gigantic shelf, and above that yet another shelf of the same size. The space down the centre of the deck, between the shelves, was piled high with cargo in a great mound—it must have been a good seventy feet long by twelve high.

"I'll send my clerk to you with the manifest," says Spring, "and a couple of hands to help shift and stow." I became aware that the pale eyes were watching me closely. "Well?"

"Is this the hold?" says I. "It's an odd-looking place for cargo."

"Aye," says he. "Ain't it, though?"

Something in his voice, and in the dank feel of that great, half empty deck, set the worms stirring inside me. I moved forward with the great heap of cargo, bales and boxes, on one side of me, and the starboard shelves on the other. It was all clean and holy-stoned, but there was a strange, heavy smell about it that I couldn't place. Looking about, I noticed something in the shadows at the back of the lower shelf—I reached in, and drew out a long length of light chain, garnished here and there with large brace-lets. I stood staring at them, and then dropped them with a clatter as the truth rushed in on me. Now I saw why the *Balliol College* had sailed from France, why her deck was this strange shape, why she was only half-full of cargo.

"My G - d!" cries I. "You're a slaver!"

"Good for you, Mr Flashman!" says Spring. "And what then?"

"What then?" says I. "Well, you can turn your b - - - - - d boat about, this minute, and let me ashore from her! By G - d, if I'd guessed what you were, I'd have seen you d - - - - d, and old Morrison with you, before I set foot on your lousy packet!"

"Dear me," says he softly. "You're not an abolitionist, surely?"

"D - - n abolition, and you too!" cries I. "I know that slaving's piracy, and for that they stretch your neck below high-water mark! You—you tricked me into this—you and that old swine! But I won't have it, d'ye hear? You'll set me ashore, and—"

I was striding past him towards the ladder, as he stood with his hands thrust deep in his pockets, eyeing me under the brim of his hat. Suddenly he shot out a hand, and with surprising strength swung me round in front of him. The pale eyes gazed into mine, and then his fist drove into my belly, doubling me up with pain; I reeled back, and he came after me, smashing me left and right to the head and sending me sprawling against the cargo.

"D - - n you!" I shouted, and tried to crawl away, but he pinned me with his foot, glaring down at me.

"Now, see here, *Mister* Flashman," says he. "I didn't want you, but I've got you, and you'll understand, here and now, that while you're on this ship, you're mine, d'ye see? You're not going ashore until this voyage is finished—Middle Passage, Indies, homeward run and all. If you don't like slaving—well, that's too bad, isn't it? You shouldn't have signed aboard, should you?"

"I didn't sign! I never—"

"Your signature will be on the articles that are in my cabin this minute," says he. "Oh, it'll be there, sure enough—you'll put it there."

"You're kidnapping me!" I yelled. "My G - d, you can't do it! Captain Spring, I beg you—set me ashore, let me get off—I'll pay you—I'll—"

"What, and lose my new supercargo?" says this devil, grinning at me. "No, no. John Charity Spring obeys his owner's orders—and mine are crystal clear, *Mister* Flashman. And he sees to it that those aboard his ship obey *his* orders, too, ye hear me?" He stirred me with his foot. "Now, get up. You're wasting my time again. You're here; you'll do your duty. I won't tell you twice." And those terrible pale eyes looked into mine again. "D'ye understand me?"

"I understand you," I muttered.

"Sir," says he.

"Sir."

"Come," says he, "that's better. Now, cheer up, man; I won't have sulks, by G - d. This is a happy ship, d'ye hear? It should be, the wages we pay. There's a thought for you, Flashman—you'll be a d - - - - d sight richer by the end of this voyage than you would be on a merchantman. What d'ye say to that?"

My mind was in a maze over all this, and real terror at what the consequences might be. Again I pleaded with him to be set ashore, and he slapped me across the mouth.

"Shut your trap," says he. "You're like an old woman. Scared are you? What of?"

"It's a capital crime," I whimpered.

"Don't be a fool," says he. "Britain doesn't hang slavers, nor do the Yankees, for all their laws say. Look about you—this ship's built for slaving, ain't she? Slavers who run the risk of getting caught aren't built so, with chains in view and slave decks and all. No, indeed, *qui male agit odit lucem**—they pose as honest merchantmen, so if the patrols nab 'em they won't be impounded under the equipment regulations. The *Balliol College* needs no disguises—for the simple reason we're too fast and handy for any d - - - - d patrol ship, English or American. What I'm telling you, *Mister* Flashman, is that *we* don't get caught, so you won't either. Does that set your mind at rest?"

It didn't, of course, but I knew better than to protest again. All I could think of was how the h - - l I was going to get out of this. He took my silence for assent.

"Well enough," growls he. "You'll begin on this lot, then"— and he jerked a thumb at the cargo. "And for Christ's sake, liven up, man! I'll not have you glooming up this ship with a long face, d'ye see? At eight bells you'll leave off and come to my cabin— Mrs Spring will be serving tea for the officers, and will wish to meet you."

I didn't believe my ears. "Mrs Spring?"

"My wife," he snapped, and seeing my bewilderment: "Who the d - - - l else would Mrs Spring be? You don't think I'd ship my mother aboard a slaver, do you?"

And with that he strode off, leaving me in a fine sweat. Thanks to an instant's folly, and the evil of that rotten little toad, my father-in-law, I was a member of the crew of a pirate ship, and nothing to be done about it. It took some digesting, but there it was; I suppose that after all the shocks I'd had in my young life this should have been nothing out of the way, but I found myself shuddering at the thought. Not that I'd any qualms about slaving, mark you, from the holy-holy point of view; they could have transported every nigger in Africa to the moon in chains for all I cared, but I knew it was a d - - - - d chancy business—aye, and old Morrison had known that, too. So the old swine had his fin-

* The evil-doer hates the light.

gers in the blackbird pie—and I'll lay my life *that* was a well concealed ledger in his countinghouse—and had taken advantage of the Bryant affair to shanghai me into this. He had wanted me out of the way, and here was a golden chance of making sure that I would be away for good; no doubt Spring was right, and the *Balliol College* would come through her voyage safe, as most slavers did, but there was always the chance of being caught, and rotting your life away in jail, even if they didn't top you. And there was the risk of getting killed by niggers on the Slave Coast, or catching yellow jack or some foul native disease, as so many slaving crews did—oh, it was the perfect ocean cruise for an unwanted son-in-law. And Elspeth would be a widow, I would never see her, or England, again, for even if I survived the trip, word of it might get home, and I'd be an outlaw, a felon . . .

I sat down on the cargo with my head in my hands, and wept, and raged inwardly against that little Scotch scoundrel. G - d, if ever I had the chance to pay him back—but what was the use of thinking that way in my present plight? In the end, as usual, one thought came uppermost in my mind—survive, Flashy, and let the rest wait. But I resolved to keep my spite warm in the meantime.

In the circumstances it was as well that I had work to do; going through that cargo, as I did when a couple of hands and the ship's clerk came down presently, at least occupied part of my thoughts, and kept me from working myself into a terror about the future. After all, thinks I, men like these didn't sign on in the expectation of dying; they seemed handy, sober fellows who knew their business—very different from the usual tarry-john. One of them, an oldish man named Kirk, had been a slaver all his days, and had served on the notorious *Black Joke;*[12] he wouldn't have shipped on any other kind of vessel.

"What," says he, "at £15 a month? I'd be a fool. D'ye know, I've four thousand quid put by, in Liverpool and Charleston banks—how many sailormen have the tenth of that? Risk? I've been impounded once, on the *Joke*, shipwrecked once, and seen two cargoes of black ivory slung overside—which meant a dead loss for the owners, but I drew me pay, didn't I? Oh, aye, I've been chased a score o' times, and been yard-arm to yard-arm in running fights wi' Limey an' Yankee patter-rollers, but no harm done. An' for sickness, ye've more chance of that from some poxed-up yellow tart in Havana than on the coast these days. You've been east—well, you know to keep yourself clean an' boil your water, then."

He made it sound not half bad, apart from the stuff about fighting the patrols, but I understood that this was a rare event— the *Balliol College* had never been touched in five trips that he knew of, although she had been sighted and chased times without number.

"She's built light, see, like all the Baltimore brigs an' clippers," says Kirk. "Save a patch o' calm, she'll show her heels to anything, even steam-ships. West o' Saint Tommy, even wi' a full load o' black cattle, she could snap her fingers at the whole Navy, and wi' the fair winds coming south, like we are now, she's gone before they see her. Only risky time is on the coast itself, afore we load up. If they was to catch us there, wi' the Government wind pinning us on the coast, they could impound us, empty an' all, 'cos o' the law as lays down that if you're rigged and fitted for slavin', like we are, they can pinch you even wi'out a black aboard. Used to be that even then they couldn't touch ye, if ye had the right papers—Greek, say, or Braziliano." He laughed. "Why, I've sailed on a ship that had Yankee, Gyppo, Portugee, an' even Rooshian papers all ready for inspection, as might serve. But it's different now—ye don't talk, ye run."[18]

He and the clerk and the other man—I think he was a Norwegian—harked back a good deal to the old days, when the slave-ships had waited in turn at the great African barracoons to ship their cargoes, and how the Navy had spoiled the trade by bribing the native chiefs not to deal with slavers, so that all the best stretches of coast nowadays were out of court, and no niggers to be had.

"Mind you," says Kirk, winking, "show 'em the kind o' goods we got here, an' they'll spring you a likely cargo o' Yorubas or Mandingos, treaty or not—an' if sometimes you have to fight for 'em, as we did two trips back, well, it comes cheaper, don't it? An' Cap'n Spring, he's got a grand nose for a tribal war, or a chief that's got too many young bucks of his own people on his hands. He's a caution, he is, an' worth every penny the owners pay him. Like to guess 'ow much?"

I said I had no idea.

"Twenty thousand pound a trip," says Kirk. "There now! An' you wonder I ship on a slaver!"

I knew slavers made huge profits, of course, but this staggered me. No wonder old Morrison had an interest in the trade—and no doubt paid a subscription to the Anti-Slavery Society and thought it well worthwhile. And he wasn't laying out overmuch in trade goods, by the look of this cargo—you never saw so much junk, although just the kind of stuff to make a nigger chief happy, no doubt. There were old Brown Bess muskets that probably hadn't been fired in fifty years, sackfuls of condemned powder and shot, rusty bayonets and cheap cutlasses and knives, mirrors and looking glasses by the dozen, feathered hats and check trousers, iron pots and plates and cauldrons, and most amazing of all, a gross of Army red coats, 34th Foot; one of 'em had a bullet-hole and a rusty stain on the right breast, and I remember thinking, bad luck for someone. There was a packet of letters in the pocket, which I meant to keep, but didn't.

And there was case after case of liquor, in brown glass bottles; gin, I suppose you'ld call it, but even to sniff the stuff shrivelled the hairs off your arse. The blacks wouldn't know the difference, of course.

We were searching through all this trash, I counting and calling out to the clerk, who ticked the manifest, and Kirk and his fellow stowing back, when Looney, the idiot steward, came down to gape at us. He squatted down, dribbling out of the corner of his mouth, making stupid observations, till Kirk, who was bundling the red coats, sings out to him to come over. Kirk had taken two of the brass gorgets off the officers' coats—they must have been d----d old uniforms—and winking at us he laid the gorgets on the deck, and says:

"Now, Looney, you're a sharp 'un. Which is the biggest? If you can tell, I'll give you my spirits tomorrow. If you can't, you give me yours, see?"

I saw what he was after: the gorgets were shaped like half-moons, and whichever was laid uppermost looked bigger—children amuse themselves with such things, cut out of paper. Looney squinted at them, giggling, and pointing to the top gorget, says:

"That 'un."

"Ye're sure?" says Kirk, and taking the gorget which Looney had indicated, placed it *beneath* the other one—which now looked bigger, of course. Looney stared at it, and then said:

"That un's bigger now."

Kirk changed them again, while his mates laughed, and Looney was bewildered. He gaped round helplessly, and then kicking the gorgets aside, he shouted:

"You make 'em bigger an'—an' littler!"

And he started to cry, calling Kirk a dirty b - - - - - d, which made us laugh all the more, so he shouted obscenities at us and stamped, and then ran over to a pile of bags stowed beyond the cargo and began to urinate on them, still swearing at us over his shoulder.

"Hold on!" cries Kirk, when he could contain his mirth. "That's the niggers' gruel you're p - - - - - g on!"

I was holding my sides, guffawing, and the clerk cries out:

"That'll make the dish all the tastier for 'em! Oh, my stars!"

Looney, seeing us amused, began to laugh himself, as such idiots will, and p - - - - d all the harder, and then suddenly I heard the others' laughter cut off, and there was a step on the ladder, and there stood John Charity Spring, staring at us with a face like the demon king. Those pale eyes were blazing, and Looney gave a little whimper and fumbled with his britches, while the piddle ran across the tilting deck towards Spring's feet.

Spring stood there in a silence you could feel, while we scrambled up. His hands clenched and unclenched, and the scar on his head was blazing crimson. His mouth worked, and then he leaped at Looney and knocked the cowering wretch down with one smashing blow. For a moment I thought he would set about the half-wit with his boots, but he mastered himself, and wheeled on us.

"Bring that—that vermin on deck!" he bawled, and stamped up the ladder, and I was well ahead of the seamen in rushing to Looney and dragging him to the scuttle. He yelled and struggled, but we forced him up on deck, where Spring was stamping about

556

in a spitting rage, and the hands were doubling aft in response to the roars of the Yankee first mate.

"Seize him up there," orders Spring, and with me holding Looney's thrashing legs, Kirk very deftly tied his wrists up to the port shrouds and ripped his shirt off. Spring was calling for the cat, but someone says there wasn't one.

"Then make one, d - - n you!" he shouted, and paced up and down, casting dreadful glances at the imploring Looney, who was babbling in his bonds.

"Don't hit us, cap'n! Please don't hit us! It was them other b - - - - - ds, changin' things!"

"Silence!" says Spring, and Looney's cries subsided to a whisper, while the crew crowded about to see the sport. I kept back, but made sure I had a good view.

They gave Spring a hastily made cat, and he buttoned his jacket tight and pulled his hat down.

"Now, you b - - - - r, I'll make you dance!" cries he, and laid in for all he was worth. Looney screamed and struggled; each time the lashes hit him he shrieked, and between each stroke Spring cursed him for all he was worth.

"Foul my ship, will you?" Whack! "Ruin the food for my cargo, by G - d!" Whack! "Spread pestilence with your filth, will you?" Whack! "Yes, pray, you wharfside son-of-a-b - - - h, I'm listening!" Whack! "I'll cut your b - - - - y soul out, if you have one!" Whack! If it had been a regulation Army cat, I think he'd have killed him; as it was, the hastily spliced yarn cut the idiot's back to bits and the blood ran over his ragged trousers. His screams became moans, and then silence, and then Spring flung the cat overboard.

"Souse him and let him hang there to dry!" says he, and then he addressed the unconscious victim. "And let me catch you at your filthy tricks again, you scum, so help me G - d I'll hang you —d'ye hear!"

He glared at us with his madman's eyes, and my heart was in my mouth for a moment. Then his scar faded, and he said in his normal bark:

"Dismiss the hands, Mr Comber. Mr Sullivan, and you, super-cargo, come aft. Mrs Spring is serving tea."

There were a few curious glances at me as I followed Spring and the Yankee mate—I was new to the crew, of course—and as we went down the ladder to his cabin, Spring looked me over. "Go and put on a jacket," he growled. "G-d d--n you, don't you know anything?" so I scudded off smartly, and when I came back they were still waiting. He examined me—and in a flash of memory I thought of waiting with Wellington to see the Queen, and being fussed over by flunkeys—and then he threw open the door.

"I trust we don't intrude, my dear," says he. "I have brought Mr Sullivan to tea, and our new supercargo, Mr Flashman."

I don't know what I expected—the Queen of Sheba wouldn't have surprised me, aboard the *Balliol College*—but it wasn't the mild-looking, middle-aged woman sitting behind a table, picking at a sampler, who turned to beam at us pleasantly, murmured something in greeting, and then set to pouring tea. Presently Comber came in, smoothing his hair, and the grizzled old second mate, Kinnie, who ducked his head to me when Spring made us known to each other. Mrs Spring handed over cups, and we stood round sipping, and nibbling at her biscuits, while she beamed and Spring talked—she had little to say for herself, but he paid her as much respect as though it had been a London drawing-room. I had to pinch myself to believe it was real: a tea-party aboard a slaver, with this comfortable woman adding hot water to the pot while a flogged man was bleeding all over the deck above our heads, and Spring, his cuff specked with the victim's gore, was laying it off about Thucydides and Horace.

"Mr Flashman has had the beginning of an education, my dear," says he. "He was with Dr Arnold at Rugby School."

She turned a placid face in my direction. "Mr Spring is a classical scholar," says she. "His father was a Senior Fellow."

"Senior Tutor, if you please, my dear," says Spring. "And it's my belief he achieved that position by stealing the work of better men. Scholarship is merely a means to an end these days, and *paucis carior est fides quam pecunia.** You remember Sallust, Mr Comber? No? There seems to be little to choose between the ignorance of Rugby and that of Winchester College." (Oho, thinks

---

* Few do not set a higher value on money than on good faith.

I, Winchester, that accounts for a lot.) "However, if we have some leisure on this voyage, we may repair these things, may we not, Mr Flashman?"

I mumbled something about being always eager to learn.

"Aye," says he, "*pars sanitatis velle sanari fuit,** we may hope. But I imagine Seneca is yet another among the many authors with whom you are not acquainted." He munched on a biscuit, the pale blue eyes considering me. "Tell me, sir, what *do* you know?"

I stole a glance at the others; Kinnie had his head down over his cup, and Sullivan, the big, raw-boned Yankee, was gazing bleakly before him. Comber was looking nervous.

"Well, sir," says I, "not very much . . ." And then, like a fool, I added, toady-like: "Not as much as a Fellow of Oriel College, I'm sure."

Comber's cup clattered suddenly. Spring says, very soft: "I am not a Fellow, Mr Flashman. I was dismissed."

Well, it didn't surprise me. "I'm very sorry, sir," says I.

"You well may be," says he. "You well may be. You may come to wish that I was in my rightful place, sir, instead of here!" His voice was rising, and his scar going crimson. He set his cup down with a force that rattled the table. "Herding with the carrion of the sea, sir, instead of . . . of . . . d - - n your eyes, man, look at me! You think it a matter for contempt, don't you, that a man of my intellect should be brought to this! You think it a jest that I was flung into the gutter by jealous liars! You do! I see it in your . . ."

"No, no indeed, sir!" cries I, quaking. "I was expelled myself . . . I don't . . ."

"Hold your confounded tongue!" he bawled. "You can't do right for doing wrong, can you? No, by G - d! Well, I warn you, *Mister* Flashman—I'll remind you of another text from Seneca, whom you don't b - - - - y well read, d - - n your ignorance! *Gravis ira regum semper*† Mr Comber will construe it for you—he's heard it before, and digested it! He'll tell you that a captain is to be feared as much as a king!" He thumped the table. "Mrs

* The wish to be cured is itself a step towards health.
† The anger of kings is always severe.

559

Spring, you'll excuse me!" And he burst past me, slamming the door behind him.

He left me shaking, and then we heard his voice on deck, bawling at the man at the wheel, and his feet stamping overhead. I felt the sweat starting on my forehead.

"May I give you some more tea, Mr Sullivan?" says Mrs Spring. "Mr Comber, a little more?" She poured for them in silence. "Have you been to sea before, Mr Flashman?"

God knows what I said; it was too much for me, and it's quite likely I answered nothing at all. I know we stood about a little longer, and then Sullivan said we must be about our duties, and we thanked Mrs Spring, and she inclined her head gravely, and we filed out.

Outside, Sullivan turned to me, glanced up the ladder, sighed, and rubbed his jaw. He was a youngish, hard-case sailor, this one, with a New England figurehead and a slantendicular way of looking at you. At last he says:

"He's mad. So's she." He thought for a moment. "It don't matter, though. Much. Sane or silly, drunk or dry, he's the best d----d skipper on this coast, or any other. You follow me?"

I stood there, nodding.

"Well and good," says he. "You'll be in Mr Comber's watch —just tail on to the rope and keep your eyes open. And when the skipper starts talkin' Latin, or whatever it is, just shut up, d'ye hear?"

That was one piece of advice which I didn't need. If I'd learned one thing about the *Balliol College*, it was that I had no wish to bandy scholarship with John Charity Spring—or anything else, for that matter.

By now you will have some idea of what life at sea was like when Uncle Harry was a boy. I don't claim that it was typical—I've sailed on many ships since the *Balliol College*, and never struck one like it, thank G-d—but although it was often like cruising in an asylum, I'll say one thing: that ship and crew were d - - - d good at their work, which was kidnapping niggers and selling them in the Americas.

I can say this now, looking back; I was hardly in a position to appreciate their qualities after that first day of flogging and tea parties. All I could think of then was that I was at the mercy of a dangerous maniac who was h - - l bent on a dangerous criminal expedition, and I didn't know which to be more scared of—him and his Latin lectures or the business ahead. But as usual, after a day or two I settled down, and if I didn't enjoy the first weeks of that voyage, well, I've known worse.

At least I had an idea of what I was in for—or thought I had —and could hope to see the end of it. For the moment I must take care, and so I studied to do my duties well—which was easy enough—and to avoid awakening the wrath of Captain J. C. Spring. This last wasn't too difficult, as it proved: all I had to do in his presence was listen to his interminable prosing about Thucydides and Lucan, and Seneca, whom he particularly admired, for he dearly loved to display his learning. (In fact, I heard later that he had been a considerable scholar in his youth, and would have gone far had he not assaulted some dignitary at Oxford and been kicked out. Who knows? he might have become something like Head at Rugby—which prompts the thought that Arnold would have made a handy skipper for an Ivory Coast pirate.)

At any rate, he lost no opportunity of airing his Latinity to Comber and me, usually at tea in his cabin, with the placid Mrs Spring sitting by, nodding. Sullivan was right, of course; they were both mad. You had only to see them at the divine service which

Spring insisted on holding on Sundays, with the whole ship's company drawn up, and Mrs Spring pumping away at her German accordion while we sang "Hark! the wild billow", and afterwards Spring would blast up prayers to the Almighty, demanding his blessing on our voyage, and guidance in the tasks which our hands should find to do, world without end, amen. I don't know what Wilberforce would have made of that, or my old friend John Brown, but the ship's company took it straight-faced—mind you, they knew better than to do anything else.

They were as steady a crowd as I've ever seen afloat—hard men, and sober, who didn't say much but did their work with a speed and efficiency that would have shamed an Indiaman. They were professionals, of course, and a good cut above your ordinary shellback. They respected Spring, and he them—although when one of them, a huge Dago, talked back to him, Spring smashed him senseless with his bare fists inside a minute—a man twice his size and weight. And another, who stole spirits, he flogged nearly to death, blaspheming at every stroke—yet a couple of hours later he was reading aloud to us from the *Aeneid*.

Mind you, if it was a tolerable life, it was damned dull, and I found my thoughts turning increasingly to Elspeth—and other women—as the days grew longer. But it was Elspeth, mostly; I found myself dreaming about her soft nakedness, and that silky golden hair spilling down over my face, and the perfume of her breath—it was rough work, I tell you, knowing there wasn't a wench in a hundred miles, nor likely to be. And from that my thoughts would turn to Morrison, and how I might get my own back when the time came: that at least was a more profitable field of speculation.

So we ran south, and then south by east, day after day, and the weather got warmer, and I shed my coat for a red striped jersey and white duck trousers, with a big belt and a sheath knife, as like Ralph Rover as ever was, and the galley stopped serving duff and the cask-water got staler by the day, and then one morning the wind had a new smell—a heavy, rotten air that comes from centuries of mangrove growing and decaying—and that afternoon we sighted the low green bank far away to port that is the coast of Africa.

We sighted sails, too, every now and then, but never for long. The *Balliol College*, as Kirk told me, drew wind like no other ship on the ocean—the best fun was stand up in her forechains as she lay over, one gunwale just above the crests, thrashing along like billy-be-damned, with mountains of canvas billowing above you —Dick Dauntless would have loved it, I'll be bound, and I enjoyed it myself—or at night, when you could lean over and watch the green fire round her bows, and look up at that African sky that is purple and soft like no other in the world, with the stars twinkling. G-d knows I'm no romantic adventurer, but sometimes I remember—and I'd like to run south again down Africa with a fair wind. In a private yacht, with my youth, half a dozen assorted Parisian whores, the finest of food and drink, and perhaps a German band. Aye, it's a man's life.

That land we had sighted was the Guinea Coast, which was of no interest to us, because as Kirk assured me it was played out for slaving. The growing sentiment for abolition at home, the increasing number of nations who joined with England in fighting the trade, the close blockade of the coast by British and Yankee patrol ships, who burned the slave stations and pounced on the ships— all these things were making life more difficult in the blackbird trade in the '40s. In the old days, the slavers had been able to put in openly, and pick up their cargoes, which had been collected by the native chiefs and herded into the great pens, or barracoons, at the river mouths. Now it wasn't so easy, and speed and secrecy were the thing, which was why fast ships like the *Balliol College* were at an advantage.

And of course clever slavers like Spring knew exactly where to go for the best blacks and which chiefs to deal with—this was the great thing. Your slaver might easily dodge the patrols on the way in and out—for it was a huge coast, and the Navy couldn't hope to watch it all—but unless he had a good agent ashore, and a native king who could keep up a supply of prime nigs, he was sunk. It's always amused me to listen to the psalm-smiting hypocrisy of nigger-lovers at home and in the States who talk about white savages raping the Coast and carrying poor black innocents into bondage—why, without the help of the blacks themselves we'd not have been able to lift a single slave out of

563

Africa. But I saw the Coast with my own eyes, you see, which the Holy Henriettas didn't, and I know that this old wives' tale of a handful of white pirates mastering the country and kidnapping as they chose, is all my eye. We couldn't have stayed there five minutes if the nigger kings and warrior tribes hadn't been all for it, and traded their captured enemies—aye, and their own folk, too—for guns and booze and Brummagem rubbish.

Why my pious acquaintances won't believe this, I can't fathom. *They* enslaved *their* own kind, in mills and factories and mines, and made 'em live in kennels that an Alabama planter wouldn't have dreamed of putting a black into. Aye, and our dear dead St William Wilberforce cheered 'em on, too—weeping his pious old eyes out over niggers he had never seen, and d - - ning the soul of anyone who suggested it was a bit hard to make white infants pull coal sledges for twelve hours a day. Of course, he knew where his living came from, I don't doubt. My point is: if he and his kind did it to their people, why should they suppose the black rulers were any different where their kinsfolk were concerned? They make me sick, with their pious humbug.

But it's all by the way; the main thing is that Spring had a good black king to work with, a horrible old creature named Gezo, who lorded it over the back country of Dahomey. Now that the Windward Coast wasn't the place any more, and the slavers were concentrating round the corner in the White Man's Grave, stretches like Dahomey and Benin and the Oil rivers were where the real high jinks were to be found. The Navy lay in all the time at places like Whydah and Lagos, and your sharp captains like Spring were as likely as not to use the lonelier rivers and lagoons, where they could load up at their leisure, provided no one spotted 'em coming in.[14]

After our first landfall we bore away south, and came eastabout to Cape Palmas, where you could see the palm trees that gave it its name down by the water's edge, and so along the Ivory Coast and Gold Coast past Three Points to Whydah, where we put into the open roads. Spring had the Stars and Stripes at the masthead, and was safe enough, for there wasn't a Yankee in port. There were two British naval sloops, but they wouldn't come near us —this was where the slavers scored, Kirk told me; the Yanks wouldn't let any but their own navy search an American ship, so our blue-jackets would interfere only with Portuguese and Spaniards and so on.

We lay off, looking at the long yellow beach with the factories and barracoons behind it, and the huge rollers crashing on the sand, and it was as hot as hell's kitchen. I watched the kites diving and snatching among the hundreds of small craft plying about between ships and shore, and the great Kroo canoes riding the surf, and tried to fan away the stench that rose from all the filth rotting on the oily water. I remembered what Kinnie had said:

"Oh, sailor, beware of the Bight o' Benin.

There's one as comes out for a hundred goes in."

You could smell the sickness on the wind, and I wondered why Spring, who was talking at the rail with Sullivan and scanning the shore with his glass, had put in here. But presently out comes a big Kroo canoe, with half a dozen niggers on board, who hailed us, and for the first time I heard that queer Coast lingo which passes for a language from Gambia to the Cape.

"Hollo, Tommy Rot," cries Spring, "where Pedro Blanco?"[15]

"Hollo, sah," sings out one of the Kroos. "He lib for Bonny; no catch two, three week."

"Why he no lib for come? Him sabby me make palaver, plenty plenty nigras. Come me plenty good stuff, what can do, him lib Bonny?"

"Him say Spagnole fella, Sanchez, lib for Dahomey ribber. Him make strong palaver, no goddam bobbery. You take Tommy Rot, sah, catch Rum Punch, Tiny Tim, plenty good fella, all way ribber. Make good nigra palaver wid Spagnole fella, no Inglish Yankee gunboat."

Spring cursed a bit at all this; it seemed he had been hoping to meet one Pedro Blanco at Whydah, but the Krooboy Tommy Rot was telling him instead he should make for a river where a Spaniard named Sanchez would supply him with slaves. Spring didn't like it too much.

"Blanco bobbery b------d," says he. "Me want him make palaver King Gezo one time."

"Palaver sawa sawa," bawls the Kroo. "Sanchez lib for Gezo,

lib for you, all for true."

"He'd better," growls Spring. "All right, Tommy Rot, come aboard, catch Tiny Tim, ten fella, lib for ship, sabby?"

We took on a dozen of the Kroos, grinning, lively blacks who were great favourites among the Coast skippers. They were prime seamen, but full of tricks, and went by ridiculous names like Rum Punch, Blunderbuss, Jumping Jack, Pot Belly and Mainsail. Each one had his forehead tattooed blue, and his front teeth filed to points; I thought they were cannibals, but it seems they carried these marks so that they would be recognised as Kroos and therefore wouldn't be taken as slaves.

With them aboard, the *Balliol College* stood out from Whydah, and after two days sniffing about out of sight of land we put in again farther east, on to a long low rotting coast-line of mangrove crawling out into the sea among the sunken sandbars. It looked d ---- d unpleasant to me, but Spring at the wheel brought her through into a lagoon, beyond which lay a great delta of jungle-covered islands, and through these we came to what looked like a river mouth. We inched through the shoals, with everyone hauling and sweating at the sweeps, and the Kroos out ahead in canoes, while three men either side swung the lead incessantly, chanting "Three fathom, two and a half, two and Jesus saves, two and a half, two and Jesus saves, three fathom!"

And then, round the first bend, was a clearing, and huge stockades between river and jungle, and huts, and presently a fat Dago in a striped shirt with a hankie round his head and rings in his ears comes out in a small boat, all smiles, to meet a great storm of abuse from Spring.

"You're Sanchez, are you? And where the h -- l's my cargo? Your barracoons are empty, you infernal scoundrel! Five hundred blacks I signed for with that thieving blackguard, Pedro Blanco, and look yonder!" He flung out an arm towards the empty stockades, in which the only sign of life was a few figures idling round a cooking-fire. "D --- l a black hide in sight apart from your own! Well, sir?"

The Dago was full of squealing apologies, waving his arms and sweating. "My dear Captain Spring! Your fears are groundless. Within two days there will be a thousand head in the barracoons.

Pedro Blanco has taken order. King Gezo himself has come down country—especially on your behalf, my good sir. He is at Dogba, with his people; there has been much fighting, I understand, but all quiet now. And many, many nigras in his slave train—strong young men, hardy young women—all the best, for you, captain!" He beamed around greasily.

"You're sure?" says Spring. "Two days? I want to be out of here in three—and I want to see King Gezo, d'you hear?"

Sanchez spread his sticky hands. "There is no difficulty. He will be coming west from Dogba to Apokoto tomorrow."

"Well..." growls Spring, quieting down. "We'll see. What's he got for us. Sombas?"

"Sombas, Fulani, Adja, Aiza, Yoruba, Egbo—whatever the captain requires."

"Is that so? Well, I'll have six hundred, then, 'stead of five. And no sickly niggers, see? They're not going to be auctioned off with their arses stuffed with tar, mind that! I want sound stock."[16]

Sanchez took his leave, full of good wishes, and the *Balliol College* was made fast, as close to the bank as she could be warped. Men were sent aloft to hang her topmasts with leaves and creepers, so that no patrol vessel out at sea might spot us, and Sanchez sent men aboard to unload the cargo. This meant work for me, making sure they pinched nothing, and by the time the last bale was out and under the guard of Sanchez's native soldiers, I was running with sweat. It was a hellish place; green jungle all around, and steam coming off the brown oily surface of the water as though it were a bath; clouds of midges descended as soon as the sun dropped, and the heat pressed in on you like a blanket, so that all you could do was lie stifling, with your chest heaving and the perspiration pouring off you. Three days, Spring had said; it was a wonder to me that we had survived three hours.

That night Spring called a council in his cabin, of all his officers; I was there, as supercargo, but you can be sure I was well out of the running. I don't suppose I've listened to a more interesting discussion in my life, though, unless it was Grant and Lee meeting in the farmhouse, or Lucan and my old pal Cardigan clawing at each other like female cousins at Balaclava. Certainly, for technical knowledge, Spring's little circle was an eye-opener.

"Six hundred," says Spring. "More than I'd bargained for; it'll mean fifteen inches for the bucks, and I want two bucks for every female, and no d - - - - d calves."

"That's an inch under the old measure, cap'n," says Kinnie. "Might do for your Guineas, but it's tight for Dahomeys. Why, they're near as big as Mandingos, some of 'em, an' Mandingos take your sixteen inches, easy."

"I've seen the Portugoosers carry Mande's in less than that," says Sullivan.

"An' had twenty in the hundred die on 'em, likely."

"No fear. They put bucks in with wenches—reckon they spend all their time on top of each other, an' save space that way."

Spring didn't join in their laughter. "I'll have no mixing of male and female," he growled. "That's the surest way to trouble I know. I'm surprised at you, Mr Sullivan."

"Just a joke, sir. But I reckon sixteen inches, if we dance 'em regular."

"I'm obliged to you for your opinion. Dance or not, they get fifteen inches, and the women twelve."[17]

Kinnie shook his head. "That won't do, sir. These Dahomey b - - - - - s takes as much as the men, any day. Sideways packin's no use either, the way they're shaped."

"Put 'em head to toe, they'll fit," says Sullivan.

"You'll lose ten, mebbe more, in the hundred," says Kinnie. "That's a ten thousand dollar loss, easy, these days."

"I'll have no loss!" cries Spring. "I'll not, by G - d! We'll ship nothing that's not A1, and the b - - - - - s will have fresh fruit with their pulse each day, and be danced night and morning, d'ye hear?"

"Even so, sir," insisted Kinnie. "Twelve inches won't. . . ."

Comber spoke up for the first time. He was pale, and sweating heavily—mind you, we all were—but he looked seedier than the others. "Perhaps Mr Kinnie is right, sir. Another inch for the women. . . ."

"When I want your advice, Mr Comber, I'll seek it," snaps Spring. "Given your way, you'd give 'em two feet, or fill the b - - - - y ship with pygmies."

"I was thinking of the possible cost, sir. . . ."

"Mr Comber, you lie." Spring's scar was going pink. "I know you, sir—you're tender of black sheep."

"I don't like unnecessary suffering, and death, sir, it's true . . ."

"Then, by G - d, you shouldn't have shipped on a slaver!" roars Spring. "D - - nation, d'you want to give 'em a berth apiece? You think I'm cruising 'em round the b - - - - y lighthouse for a lark? Forty pieces a pound, Mr Comber—that's what an ordinary buck will fetch in Havana these days—perhaps more. A thousand dollars a head! Now, take note, Mr Comber, of what your extra inch can mean—a forty thousand dollar loss for your owner! Have you thought of that, sir?"

"I know, sir," says Comber, sticking to his guns nervously. "But forty dead gives you the same loss, and. . . ."

"D - - nation take you, will you dispute with me?" Spring's eyes were blazing. "I was shipping black pigs while you were hanging at your mother's teat—where you ought to be this minute! D'ye think I don't take as much thought to have 'em hale and happy as you, you impudent pup! And for a better reason— I don't get paid for flinging corpses overboard. It's dollars I'm saving, not souls, Mr Comber! Heaven help me, I don't know why you're in this business—you ought to be in the b - - - - y Board of Trade!" He sat glaring at Comber, who was silent, and then turned to the others. "Fifteen and twelve, gentlemen, is that clear?"

Kinnie sighed. "Very good, cap'n. You know my views, and . . . ."

"I do, Mr Kinnie, and I respect them. They are grounded in experience and commercial sense, not in humanitarian claptrap picked up from scoundrels like Tappan and Garrison. *The Genius of Universal Emancipation*, eh, Mr Comber?[18] You'll be quoting to me in a moment. Genius of Ill-digested Crap! Don't contradict me, sir; I know your views—which is why I'm at a loss to understand your following this calling, you d - - - - d hypocrite, you!"

Comber sat silent, and Spring went on: "You will take personal responsibility for the welfare of the females, Mr Comber. And they won't die, sir! We shall see to that. No, they won't die, because like you—and Mr Flashman yonder—they haven't read Seneca, so they don't know that *qui mori didicit servire dedidicit.*[*] If they did, we'd be out of business in a week."

I must say it sounded good sense to me, and Comber sat mumchance. He was obviously thankful when the discussion turned to more immediate matters, like the arrival of King Gezo the next day at Apokoto, which lay some miles up river; Spring wanted to meet him for a palaver, and said that Kinnie and Comber and I should come along, with a dozen of the hands, while Sullivan began packing the first slaves who would be arriving at the barracoons.

I was all in favour of getting off the *Balliol College* for a few hours, but when we boarded the Kroos' big canoe at the bank next day, I wasn't so sure. Kinnie was distributing arms to the hands, a carbine and cutlass for each man, and Spring himself took me aside and presented me with a very long-barrelled pistol.

"You know these?" says he, and I told him I did—it was one of the early Colt revolvers, the type you loaded with powder and ball down the muzzle. Very crude they'd look today, but they were the wonder of the world then.

"I picked up a dozen of these last winter in Baltimore," says he. "American army guns—Gezo would give his very throne for 'em, and I intend to use them in driving a very special bargain with him. Are you a good shot? Well, then, you can demonstrate them for him. Get Kinnie to give you a needle gun and cutlass as well."[19]

"D'you think . . . we'll need them?" says I.

He turned the pale eyes on me. "Would you rather go unarmed —into the presence of the most bloodthirsty savage in West Africa?" says he. "No, Mr Flashman—I don't expect we shall need to use our weapons; not for a moment. But I fear the Greeks even when I'm bearing gifts to 'em, sir, d'you see?"

Well, that was sense, no doubt of it, so I took my needle carbine and bandolier, buckled on the cutlass and stuck the Colt in my belt, and stood forth like Pirate Bill; as we took our places in the canoe, it looked like something from a pantomime, every man with his hankie knotted round his head, armed to the teeth, some of 'em with rings in their ears, and one even with a patch over his eye. It struck me—what would Arnold say if he could

* Who has learned to die, has learned how not to be a slave.

look down now from his place at the right hand of God? Why, there, he would say, is that worthy lad, Tom Brown, with his milk-and-water wife in the West Country, giving bread and blankets to needy villagers who knuckle their heads and call him "squire": good for you, Brown. And there, too, that noble boy Scud East, lording it over the sepoys for the glory of God and the profit of John Company—how eminently satisfactory! And young Brooke, too, a fearless lieutenant aboard his uncle's frigate *Unspeakable*—what a credit to his old school! Aye, as the twigs are bent so doth the trees grow. But who is this, consorting with pirates and preparing to ship hapless niggers into slavery, with oaths on his lips? I might have known—it is the degraded Flashman! Unhappy youth! But just what I might have expected!

Aye, he would have rejoiced at the sight—if there's one thing he and his hypocritical kind loved better than seeing virtue rewarded, it was watching a black sheep going to the bad. The worst of it is, I wasn't there of my own free will—not that you ever get credit for that.

These philosophical musings were disturbed by the tender scene between Mr and Mrs Spring as he prepared to board the canoe. Unlike the rest of us, he was dressed as usual—dark jacket, round hat, neck-cloth all trim—how the devil he stood it, in that steaming heat, I can't figure. Well, at the last minute, Mrs Spring leans over the ship's side crying to him to take his comforter "against the chill of the night". This in a country where the nights are boiling hot, mark you.

"D--nation!" mutters Spring, but out he climbed, and took the muffler, crying good-bye, my dear, good-bye, while the men in the canoe grinned and looked the other way. He was in a fine temper as we shoved off, kicking the backside of the cabin boy —who had been ordered to come along—and d--ning the eyes of the man at the tiller.

Just as we pushed out into mid-stream came another diversion —from the jungle on the landward side of the stockade came a distant murmuring and confused sound. As it grew nearer you could hear that it was a great shuffling and moaning, with the occasional shout and crack of a whip, and a dull chanting in cadence behind it.

"It's the slave train!" bawls Spring, and sure enough, presently out of the jungle came the head of a long line of niggers, yoked two by two with long poles, shuffling along between their guards. They were a startling sight, for there were hundreds of 'em, all naked, their black bodies gleaming in the sunshine and their legs covered with splashes of mud up to the thigh. They moaned and chanted as they walked, big stalwart bucks with woolly heads, jerking and stumbling, for the yokes were at their necks, and if a man checked or broke his stride he brought his yoke-fellow up short. The sound they made was like a huge swarm of bees, except when one of the guards, big niggers in kilts and blouses carrying muskets, brought his whip into play, and the crack would be followed by a yelp of pain.

"Easy with those kurbashes, d--n you!" yelled Spring. "That's money you're cutting at!" He leaned eagerly over the thwart, surveying the caravan. "Prime stuff, 'pon my soul, Mr Kinnie; no refuse there. Somba and Egbo, unless I'm mistaken."

"Aye, sir, good cattle, all of 'em," says Kinnie.

Spring rubbed his hands, and with many a last glance, gave the order to give way. The men at the sweeps hauled, and the big canoe pushed forward up river, Mrs Spring fluttering her handkerchief after us from the *Balliol College*'s rail.

Once round the first bend, we were in another world. On either side and overhead the jungle penned us in like a huge green tent, muffling the cries and shrieks of the beasts and birds beyond it. The heat was stifling, and the oily brown water itself was so still that the plash of the sweeps and the dripping of moisture from the foliage sounded unnaturally loud. The men pulling were drenched in sweat; it was a labour to breathe the heavy damp air, and Kirk was panting under his breath as he accompanied the rowers with "Rock an' roll, rock an' roll, Shenandoah sail-or! hoist her high, hoist her dry, rock an' roll me ov-er!"

It must have been three or four hours, with only a few brief rests, before Spring ordered a halt at a small clearing on the water's edge. He consulted his watch, and then his compass, and announced:

"Very good, Mr Kinnie, we'll march from here. No sense in risking our craft any nearer these gentlemen than we have to.

Cover her up and fall in ashore."

We all piled out, and the huge canoe was manhandled in under the mangroves which hung far out from the water's edge. When she was hidden to Spring's satisfaction, with a guard posted, and he had ensured that every man was properly armed and equipped, he led the way along a track that seemed to me to run parallel with the river—although the jungle was so thick you couldn't see a yard either side. The air was alive with mosquitoes, and in the shadows of that little green tunnel we stumbled along, slapping and cursing; it was a poor trail, and when Spring asked me what I thought of it, I answered, h - - lish. He barked a laugh and says:

"Truer than you know. It's made of corpses—some of the thousands that result from the Dahomeyans' yearly festival of human sacrifice.[20] They build up the path with 'em, bound together with vines and cemented with mud." He pointed to the dense thickets either side. "You wouldn't make a mile a day in there—nothing but ooze and roots and rotting rubbish. Sodden wet, but never a drop of water to be had—you can die of thirst in that stuff."

You may guess how this cheered up the journey, but there was worse ahead. We smelled Apokoto long before we saw it; a rank wave of corruption that had us cursing and gagging. It was a stink of death—animal and vegetable—that hit you like a hot fog and clung in your throat. "Filthy black animals," says Spring.

The town itself was bigger than I had imagined, a huge stockaded place crammed with those round grass lodges which are beehive shaped with an onion topknot. All of it was filthy and ooze-ridden, except for the central square which had been stamped flat and hard; the whole population, thousands of 'em, were gathered round it, stinking fit to knock you flat. The worst of the reek came from a great building like a cottage at the far side, which puzzled me at first because it seemed to be built of shiny brown stones which seemed impossible in this swampy jungle country. Kirk put me wise about that: "Skulls," says he, and that is what they were, thousands upon thousands of human skulls cemented together to make the death-house, the ghastly place where the human sacrifices—prisoners, slaves, criminals, and the like—were herded before execution. Even the ground directly before it was paved with skulls, and the evil of the place hung over that great square like an invisible mist.

"I seen as many as a hundred chopped up at one time before that death-house," says Kirk. "Men, women, an' kids, all cut up together. It's like a Mayday fair to these black heathen."

"They seem amiable enough just now," says I, wishing to God I were back at the ship, and he agreed that as a rule the Apokoto folk were friendly to white traders—provided they had trade goods, and looked as though they could defend themselves. It was plain to see now why Spring had us heavily armed; I'd have been happier with a park of artillery as well.

"Aye, they're savage swine if you don't mind your eye," says Kirk, rolling his quid, "an' Gezo's the most fearsome b - - - - - d of the lot. He's the man to set upon your landlord, by G - d! An' wait till you see his warriors—you're a military man, ain't you?—well, you never seen nothin' like his bodyguard, not nowheres. You just watch out for 'em. Best fighters in Africa, they reckon, an' probably the on'y nigger troops anywhere that march in step —an' they can move in dead silence when they wants to, which most niggers can't. Oh, they're the beauties, they are!"

We had to wait near an hour before Gezo put in an appearance, in which time the sun got hotter, the reek fouler, and my mind uneasier. I've stood before the face of savage kings often enough, and hated every minute of it, but Gezo's little home-from-home, with its stench of death and corruption, and its death house, and its thousands of big, ugly niggers to our little party, was as nasty a hole as I've struck; I found myself shivering in spite of the heat haze, but took heart from the fact that all our fellows seemed quite composed, leaning on their muskets, chewing and spitting and winking at the niggers. Only Spring seemed agitated, but not with fear; he fidgeted eagerly from time to time, snorting with impatience at the delay, and took a turn up and down. Then he would stop, standing four square with his hands in his pockets, head tilted back, and you could feel he was working to contain himself as he waited.

Suddenly everything went dead quiet; the chatter of the crowd stopped, everyone held their breaths, and our fellows stiffened and shifted together. Utter silence lay over that vast place, broken only by the distant jungle noises. Spring shrugged and muttered: "High time, too. Come on, you black b - - - - - d."

The silence lasted perhaps a minute, and then out of the street beside the death house scampered a score of little figures, either dwarves or boys, but you couldn't tell, because they were grotesquely masked. They swung rattles as they ran, filling the air with their clatter, and crying out a confused jumble of words in which I managed to pick out "Gezo! Gezo!" They scattered about the square, prancing and rattling and questing, and Spring says to me:

"Chasing away bad spirits, and finding the most propitious place for his majesty to plant his fat posterior. Aye, as usual, on the platform. Look yonder."

Two warriors were carrying forward a great carved stool, its feet shaped like massive human legs, which they planked down on the dais of skulls before the death house. The masked dancers closed in, whisking away round the stool, and then scattered back to the edge of the square. As they fell silent a drum began to beat from beyond the death house, a steady, marching thump that grew louder and louder, and the crowd began to take it up, stamping and clapping in unison, and emitting a wordless grunt of "Ay-uh! ay-uh!" while they swayed to the rhythm.

"Now you'll open your eyes," says Kirk in my ear, and as he said it I saw emerging from the street by the death house a double file of warriors, swinging along in time to the steady cadence of the drum, while the chanting grew louder. "Ha!" cries Spring, eagerly. "At last!"

They marched out either side of the square in two long lines, lithe, splendid figures, swaying as they marched, and it was something in the manner of that swaying that struck me as odd; I stared harder, and got the surprise of my life. The warriors were all women.

And such women. They must have been close on a man's height, fine strapping creatures, black as night and smart as guardsmen. I gaped at the leading one on the right as she approached; she came sashaying along, looking straight before her, a great ebony Juno naked to the little blue kilt at her waist, with a long stabbing spear in one hand and a huge cleaver in her belt. The only other things she wore were a broad collar of beadwork tight round her throat, and a white turban over her hair, and as she passed in front of us I noticed that at her girdle there hung two skulls and a collection of what looked like lion's claws. The others who followed her were the same, save that instead of turbans they wore their hair coiled together and tied with ropes of beads, but each one carried a spear, some had bows and quivers of arrows, and one or two even had muskets. Not all were as tall as the leader, but I never saw anything on Horse Guards that looked as well-drilled and handsome—or as frighteningly dangerous.

"None o' your sogers could throw chests like them," says Kirk, licking his lips, and then I felt Spring's hand grip my wrist. To my surprise his pale eyes were shining with excitement, and I thought, well, you old lecher, no wonder you left Mrs Spring at home this trip. He pointed at the black, glistening line as they marched past.

"D'you realise what you're seeing, Flashman?" says he. "Do you? Women warriors—Amazons! The kind of whom Herodotus wrote, but he knew nothing of the reality. Look at them, man —did you ever see such a sight?"

Well, they were likely big wenches, certainly, and they bounced along very jolly, but when I watch a wobbling buttock I prefer it to be unobscured by a dangling skull. And I'm no hand with women who look as though they'd rather kill and eat me than grapple in the grass. But Spring was all for 'em; his voice was husky as he watched.

"D'you know what they call themselves? Mazangu—the fair ones. You see how every company leader wears a spotless turban —they call 'em Amodozo. Doesn't that name bring back an echo from your school-days—think, man! Who was the leader of the Amazons in Africa—Medusa! Amodozo, Medusa. Mazangu, Amazons." His face was alive with a delight I'd never seen before. "These are the cream of the Dahomeyan army—the picked bodyguard of the king. Every voyage I've made, I vowed I'd bring back half a dozen of them, but I've never been able to make this black Satan part with even one. He'll part this time, though." He rounded on me. "You've a gift of languages, have you not? On this voyage we'll learn it—we'll find out everything there is to know about 'em, study them, their history, their customs.

The real Amazons! By the holy, I'll make those smug half-educated Balliol sons-of-b - - - - - s sit up, won't I though? They'll find out what real scholarship is!"

I suppose I've been in some queer places, with some d - - - - d odd fellows, but nothing queerer than watching those big black fighting sluts march by while a classically-educated slaver skipper babbled to me about anthropological research. I thought it had been lust that excited him, at the sight of all those black boobies quivering, and it was lust, at that—but it was scholarly, not carnal. Well, if he thought I was going to huddle up with those female baboons, studying present infinitives, he was dead wrong.

"They've got both tits," I said. "Thought Amazons only had one."

He snarled his contempt. "Even Walter Raleigh knew better than that. But he was wrong about what mattered—so was Lopez Vaz, so was Herodotus. Not South America, not Scythia—here! Africa! I shall make a name—a great name, with my work on these women. Despise John Charity Spring, will they?" He was shouting again, not that anyone could hear much, above that drumming. "I'll show them, by G-d, I will! We'll keep one, perhaps two. The others will fetch a handy price in Havana— what? Think of the money they'll pay for black fighting women in New Orleans! I could get two—no, three thousand dollars a head for creatures like those!"

I never interrupt an enthusiast, especially one with a temper like a wild dog's. Presently he fell silent, but he never took his eyes off those women, who were halted now in a great circle round the square. Two other companies of them had filed in and taken station close to the death house, and now in their wake came a gross black figure, under a striped umbrella, at the sight of whom they raised their spears in salute and stamped, while the mob round the square roared a welcome.[21]

King Gezo of Dahomey was bitter ugly, even by nigger standards. He must have weighed twenty stone, with a massive belly hanging over his kilt of animal tails, and huge shoulders inside his scarlet cape. He had a kind of wicker hat on his head, and under it was a face that would have shamed a gorilla—huge flat nose, pocked cheeks, little yellow eyes and big yellow teeth.

He waddled to his stool, plumped down, and opened the palaver in a croaking voice that carried harshly all over the square.

At first we were ignored, although he could be seen squinting our way every now and then. He palavered with elders of the town, and then with several folk who were summoned forward from the crowd; one of them evidently displeased him, because he suddenly screamed an order, and two of the Amazons beside his throne stepped forward, drawing their cleavers, and without ceremony laid into the victim right and left, and literally slashed him to pieces. The crowd hollo'ed like mad, Gezo surged about on his stool, and those two harpies hacked away at the dismembered corpse, spattering the skull platform with blood. When they were done, slaves came forward to clear up—they had to sweep what was left of the body off the stage.

No doubt this was for our benefit, for we were now beckoned forward. Gezo was even more horrifying at close range, with those yellow eyeballs rolling at you, but he was civil enough to Spring, laughing hoarsely and chattering at him through one of his officials, who spoke fair Coast English.

They palavered for a while about the slaves who had been sent down to our ship, and then Gezo in high good humour ordered stools to be set for all our party, and we squatted down at the edge of the dais, while servants brought dishes of food—I expected it would turn my stomach, but it was not bad: stew, and fruit, and native bread, and a beer that was powerful and not unlike a German lager. Gezo gorged and talked, spluttering out food as he squealed and barked at Spring, and occasionally drinking beer from a gaudy china mug on which was inscribed, of all things, "A Present for a Good Boy from Scarborough". I remember thinking how odd it was that this shoddy article should obviously be a prized possession, while the local cups from which we drank were really fine pieces, of metal beautifully carved.

All told it was as pleasant a meal as one could have in the presence of a terrifying ogre, with the blood still sticky before his feet, and the foul stench of the death house all around. Another distraction was the Amazons, who ringed the dais; one of the white-turbanned leaders stood close by me and I took close stock of her. She had the flat face, broad nose, and thick lips usual on this part of the Coast, but with that splendid shape, and a fine black satin thigh thrust out and almost touching me as I sat, I thought, by gum, one could do worse. They had men only once a year, Spring had said, and I decided that being the man would be interesting work, if you survived it. I gave her a wink, and the sullen face never altered, but a moment later she raised the fly whisk that dangled from her wrist and brushed away an insect buzzing round my head. I could see she fancied me; black or white, savage or duchess, they're all alike.

Meanwhile the meal finished, and presently Gezo beckoned Spring to draw his stool closer; they grunted away at each other through the interpreter, and I heard Spring suggest the purchase of six of the Amazon women. This threw Gezo into a great passion, but Spring let it rage, and then whispered to the interpreter again. There was much conferring, and Gezo barked and screamed, but less loud each time, I thought, and at last Spring turned to me.

"Show him your pistol," says he, and I handed it over. Gezo pawed over it excitedly, rasping questions at Spring, and finally it was given back to me, and Spring says:

"Fire it for him—all five shots as fast as you can. Into the side of the death house will do."

I stood up, all eyes on me, Gezo chattering and bouncing up and down on his stool. I drew a bead on one of the skull bricks and fired; it kicked like blazes, but I thumbed back the hammer smartly and loosed off the next four shots in quick time. Five gaping holes were smashed in the wall, with splinters flying all over the place, the mob roared, Gezo beat his fists on his knees with excitement, and even the Amazons put up their knuckles to their mouths; my own pipsey-popsey with the white turban stared at me round-eyed.

Then Spring called up one of our seamen, who carried a case, and when he opened it there were the five other Colt pistols; Gezo slobbered and squealed at the sight of them, but Spring wouldn't hand them over—he had more guts than I'd have had with that blood-stained maniac mowing and yelling at me. They whispered away again, and then Gezo rolled his eyes shifty-like at the Amazons, summoned my girl, and mumbled orders to her. She didn't bat an eyelid, but snapped a command to six of her wenches. They grounded their spears like guardsmen, put by their cleavers, and then stood forward. Gezo yammered at them, one of them said something back, Gezo yelled at them, and from the ranks of all the other Amazons there was something like a gasp and a murmur, which rose to a growl; they didn't like what was happening, and Gezo had to stand up and bawl at them until they were quiet.

I didn't like the look of this; you could feel the anger and hatred welling up all round us. But Spring just snapped shut the case, handed it to Gezo, and then turned to us.

"Mr Kinnie," says he, "the palaver is finished. Form up round these six women; we're getting out of here." Then he tipped his hat to Gezo, who was sitting back on his stool, looking d - - - - d peevish, and clutching his case. Our fellows had turned to face the crowd, who were milling closer beyond the ranks of the Amazons; it was beginning to look ugly, but Spring just marched ahead, bulldog fashion, the Amazons stepped back smartly to let him go, and with our six black beauties in our midst we followed after. Two of the girls hesitated, looking round over their shoulders, but my Amazon lady, standing beside Gezo's throne, shouted to them, and they dropped their heads meekly and marched on with us.

By jove, it was a long minute's walk to the gate of the stockade, through the double file of those black Amazon furies, their faces sullen with anger and grief at the sale of their fellows, while the great crowd of townsfolk roared in protest behind them. But the discipline of those women warriors was like iron; the king had said, and that was that—mind you, if Gezo had run for president at that moment, he wouldn't have had my money on him, but even so, no one in that whole town was bold enough to gainsay him.

We were moving d - - - - d smartly by the time we reached the stockade, a tight knot of men with our needle guns at the ready, and the women being jostled along in the middle. Spring was first at the gate, where he stopped and hurried us through, I stood close by him; his jaw was tight and he was as near scared as I ever saw him.

"Hurry, b - - - t you!" he shouted. "D - - n that Gezo, to haggle so long, and d - - n those women—I didn't think they'd raise such a bother about the business. Straight ahead, Mr Kinnie, and keep those six sluts close, d'you hear?" Then to me: "Come on!"

"Wait!" say I—it was instinctive, believe me; I'd no wish to linger, not with that growling mob behind me. But I'd noticed the little ferrety cabin boy was missing. "Where the h - - l is he?"

"Back there!" snaps Spring. "He's senseless with nigger beer—Gezo wanted him—wanted a white slave! Come on, d - - n you, will you stand there all day?"

I'm not shocked easy, but that took me flat aback—for about the tenth part of an instant. If Spring wanted to trade his cabin boy to a nigger king, it was all one to me; I was into the fringe of the jungle a yard ahead of him, and then we were running, with the others in front of us, the Amazons being driven along, one of 'em wailing already. Behind us the hubbub of the town was cut off by the dense foliage; we hustled down the path, but you don't run far in that climate, and soon we had to slow down to a trot.

"Well enough, I think," says Spring. He stopped for a moment to listen, but there was nothing except the jungle noises and the sobbing of our own breathing. "I didn't like that," says he, addressing no one in particular. "By G - d, I didn't! If I'd known they were so d - - - - d jealous of their fighting wenches... Phew! It's the last time I deal with Gezo, though. *Quid violentius aure tyranni?** For a moment I'd a notion he would change his mind —and keep the pistols, which would have been short shrift for us." He laughed, and the mad pale eyes blinked. "On, there, Mr Kinnie! Mr Comber, keep a sharp eye on the prisoners! Back to that boat in double time, my lads, before his majesty thinks better of his bargain!"

We pushed on down the narrow trail, and we must have been half-way to ⁀the river when Spring stopped again, listening. I strained my ears; nothing. Just the chickering of the forest beasts and birds. Spring called to the fellows to be quiet, and we all listened. Spring turned his head from side to side, and then I heard Kirk say: "Wot the h - - l we standing here for? If there's anything to hear, then the sooner we're in that boat the better."

"There's nuthin' behind us," says another, uneasily.

* What is more dangerous than having the ear of a tyrant?—Juvenal.

"Silence!" snaps Spring. He was peering through the foliage at the side of the path. I found my heart racing, and not just with exertion—if we were pursued, they couldn't have outflanked us, through that swamp and jungle, surely. We would have heard them—and then I remembered Kirk saying: "They can move in dead silence when they wants to."

"For G - d's sake!" I whispered to Spring. "Let's get on!"

He ignored me. "Mr Kinnie," he called softly. "D'you hear anything to port?"

"No, cap'n," sings back Kinnie, "there's noth—"

The end of that word was a horrid scream; in terror I stared down the path, and saw Kinnie stagger, clawing at the shaft in his throat before tumbling headlong into the mangrove. Someone yelled, a musket banged, and then Spring was thrusting forward, bawling:

"Run for it! Keep on the path for your lives. Run like h - - l!"

His order was wasted on me—I was running before he had started thinking, even; someone screamed in front of me, and a black shadow leaped on to the path—it was an Amazon, swinging a machete; one of the seamen caught it on his musket, and dashed the butt into her face. She went down, shrieking, and as I leaped over her my foot landed on her bare flesh; I stumbled, but went careering on. The vision of those two naked black fiends slashing a man to death was before my eyes, and the crash of shots and yelling behind me urged me on. I fairly flew along that trail.

And by gum, I wasn't alone. They say sailors are poor runners, but that landing party from the *Balliol College* could move when they wanted to; we stampeded along that twisting path, elbowing each other aside in our panic to get away from the horror in the jungle on either side. They were screaming their war cries now, those terrible black sows; once a spear flashed past in front of my face, and I believe a couple of arrows buzzed above our heads, and then I tripped and fell headlong, with the others trampling over me.

I thought I was done for, but when I scrambled to my feet I saw we were on the edge of the clearing by the river. The fleetest of our party was tearing aside the branches where our canoe was hidden, the man who had been left on guard was on one knee, aiming his musket; it banged, and I turned to see an Amazon fall shrieking not ten yards from me, her cleaver bouncing along to land at my feet. Instinctively I grabbed it, and then a flying body knocked me sideways. Some of our fellows were firing from the water's edge; as I scrambled up I saw an Amazon on her knees, clutching her side with one hand as she tried vainly to hurl her spear with the other. Close by me was Spring, bawling like a madman; he had his pepper-pot revolver in one hand, firing back towards the path, and by G - d, with the other he was trying to drag along one of the Amazons he'd bought. The man's dedication to scholarly research was incredible.

They were leaping through the edge of the jungle now, howling black devils, and if you believe that even the worst of young women has charms, you are in error. As I fled for the boat, I saw the man who had been on guard spin round with an arrow in his shoulder; before he could regain his feet three of them were on him, and while two held him down, throat and ankle, the third carefully pulled up his shirt, and with the utmost delicacy disembowelled him with her machete. Then I was at the boat, a needle gun was in my hands, and I was firing at another who was leaping across the clearing; she went cartwheeling into the river, and then Spring was beside me, dashing down his empty gun and drawing his cutlass.

"Shove off!" he bawled, and I made a leap for the thwart, missed, and came down in the shallows. Spring jumped over me, and I felt someone drag me upright; it was Comber. For a moment we were shoulder to shoulder, and then an Amazon was on us. Her spear was back to thrust into my breast, and in that split second I saw it was my white-turbanned wench of the fly whisk, her teeth bared in a ghastly grin. And you may think me fanciful, but I'll swear she recognised me, for she hesitated an instant, swung her point away from me, and drove it to the haft into Comber's side. And as I threw myself headlong over the gunwale the ridiculous thought flashed through my mind: bonny black cavalry whiskers, they can't resist 'em.

"D - - nation!" Spring was roaring. "I lost that confounded slut!" And as the boat shot away from the bank he seized a needle gun, almost crying with rage, and blazed away. I pulled myself up by the thwart, and the first thing I saw was a bloody hand gripping the edge of the boat. It was Comber, clinging on for dear life as we wallowed out into the stream, with the dark red blood staining the water around him. For a second I wondered whether I should try to haul him in or bash his fingers loose, for he was encumbering our way, but then Spring had leaned over and with one titanic heave had dragged him over the thwart.

We were ten yards from the bank, and it was lined with shrieking black women, hurling their spears, bending their bows, leaping up and down in a frenzy of rage. Why none of them took to the water after us I don't know, unless it was fear of crocodiles; we cowered down to escape their missiles, and then a voice was screaming from the bank:

"Help, cap'n! Cap'n, don't leave me—for Jesus' sake, cap'n! Save me!"

It was Kirk; he was in the shallows, being dragged back by half a dozen of those black witches. They hauled him on to the bank, screaming and laughing, while we drifted out into midstream. Some bold idiot had seized a sweep, and Comber, bleeding like a butchered calf, was crying:

"Help him, sir! We must turn back! We must save him!"

Spring thrust him away, threw himself on to the sweep with the sailor, and in spite of the arrows that whistled over the boat, the two of them managed to drive us still farther away towards the opposite mangrove shore. We were beyond the spears now, and presently the arrows began to fall short, although one of the last to reach the boat struck clean through the hand of the seaman at the oar, pinning him to the timber. Spring wrenched it clear and the fellow writhed away, clutching his wound. And then Holy Joe Comber was at it again:

"Turn back, sir! We can't leave Kirk behind!"

"Can't we, by G-d?" growls Spring. "You just watch me, mister. If the b-----d can't run, that's his look-out!"

Spoken like a man, captain, thinks I; give me a leader you can trust, any day. And even Comber, his face contorted with pain, could see it was no go; they were swarming on the bank, and had Kirk spreadeagled; we could see them wrenching his clothes off, squealing with laughter, while close by a couple of them had even started kindling a fire. They were smart house-wifely lasses those, all right.

Kirk was yelling blue murder, and as we watched, my girl in the white turban knelt down beside him, and suddenly his voice rose into a horrible, blood-chilling shriek. Several of the Amazons prancing on the bank indicated to us, by obscene gestures, what she was doing to him; Comber groaned, and began to spew, and Spring, swearing like a lunatic, was fumbling to load one of the needle guns. He bawled to the rest of us to follow suit, and we banged away at them for a moment, but it was too dangerous to linger, and with Kirk's screams, and the gloating shrieks of those she-d - - - ls, drifting downstream after us, we manned the sweeps and rowed for all we were worth. With the current to help us we drove along hard, and I was finally able to choke down my panic and thank my stars for another delivery. Of the half dozen of us in the boat, I was the only one without even a scratch; Spring had a machete cut on his left arm, but not a deep one, and the others' wounds were mild enough, except for Comber's. But if Spring was only slightly injured in the flesh, his ambition had taken a nasty jar. He d - - - - d Gezo's eyes for a treacherous hound, and called the Amazons things that would have made a marine blush, but his chief fury, voiced over and over again as we rowed downstream was:

"I lost that black slut. All these years, and I lost the sow! Even that single one—she would have done! My G - d, I could have used that woman!"

I was pondering that I could have used my white-turbanned Hebe, for a different and less academic purpose—but then I thought of Kirk, and discovered that any *tendre* I might have cherished for the lady had died. And as I think back now, strapping lass though she was, I can't say that the old flame rekindles. She was a shrew if ever I saw one.

With the danger safely past, I was soon in good fettle again. As I've said before, there's nothing so cheering as surviving a peril in which companions have perished, and our losses had been heavy. Five men had died in our hasty retreat from Apokoto; apart from Kinnie, Kirk, and the guard on the boat, two others had been cut down by Amazons on the path, and of course the cabin boy had been left behind deliberately by Spring, not that he was any great loss. (It will give you some notion of the kind of men who manned the Coast slavers, when I tell you that not a word of protest was said about this; nobody had liked the little sneak anyway.)

For the rest, it looked as though Comber was a goner. My wench had shovelled her spear well in under his short ribs, leaving a hole like a hatchway; Murphy the surgeon, when he had sobered up, announced that there was nothing he could do but clean and stitch it, which he did, "but for what may have come adrift inside," says he, "I can't answer." So they put Comber in his berth, half-dead, with Mrs Spring to nurse him—"that'll carry the poor s - d off, even if his wound doesn't," says Murphy.

Then we went to work. There were upwards of a thousand niggers in the barracoons on the morning after our Apokoto exploit, and Spring was in a sweat to get our cargo loaded and away. It was the possibility of naval patrols sniffing us out that worried him; Sullivan's suggestion, that Gezo might take it into his head to come down and make a clean sweep of us, he dismissed out of hand. As Spring saw it, the Amazons and not Gezo had been responsible for the attack; now they had rescued their six wenches, and Gezo still had his pistols, he wouldn't want to offend us further. He was right; Sanchez, who was an astonishing good plucked 'un, for a Dago, actually went up to talk to Gezo a day later, to see that all was well, and found the black rascal full of alarm in case Spring was going to wash his hands of the Dahomey trade. Sanchez reassured him, and dropped a hint that if Gezo would even now part with an Amazon it would make for friendly relations, but Gezo was too windy of provoking his bodyguard. He just clutched his case of pistols and begged Sanchez to tell Spring that he was still his friend, *sawa sawa*, and hoped they would continue to do good business together—all this, mark you, while Kirk and one of the men who'd been caught on the path were strung up in front of the death house, with those black she-fiends working on them before a cheering crowd. They were still alive, Sanchez said, but you wouldn't have known they were human beings.

So honour was satisfied, both sides, but Spring and Sanchez took no chances. The *Balliol College*'s nets were rigged, and her twelve and nine-pounders shotted, while Sanchez's pickets guarded the jungle trails and the river. All remained peaceful, however, and the business of loading the slaves went ahead undisturbed.

With our second mate dead and our third apparently dying, I found myself having to work for a living. Even with men who knew their business as well as these, it's no easy matter to pack six hundred terrified, stupid niggers into a slave deck; it's worse than putting Irish infantry into a troopship.

First Spring and Murphy went through the barracoons, picking out the likeliest bucks and wenches. They were penned up in batches of a hundred, men and women separate, a great mass of smelling, heaving black bodies, all stark naked, squatting and lying and moaning; the sound was like a great wailing hum, and it never stopped, day or night, except when the tubs of burgoo were shoved into the pens, and they shut up long enough to empty the gourds which were passed round among them. What astonished me was that Spring and Murphy were able to walk in among them as though they were tame beasts; just the two of them in that mass of cowed, miserable humanity, with a couple of black guards jerking out the ones selected. If they'd had a spark of spirit the niggers could have torn them limb from limb, but they just sat, helpless and mumbling. I thought of the Amazons, and wondered what changed people from brave, reckless savages into dumb re-signed animals; apparently it's always the way on the Coast. Sulli-

notion of what a sailing-ship was like in the forties; people who travel P.O.S.H. in a steam packet can't imagine, for one thing, the h - - - ish continual din of a wooden vessel—the incessant creaking and groaning of timber and cordage, like a fiend's orchestra playing the same discordant notes, regular as clockwork, each time she rolled. And, by G - d, they rolled, far worse than iron boats, bucketing up and down, and stinking, too, with the musty stale smell of a floating cathedral, and the bilges plashing like a giant's innards. Oh, it was the life for a roaring boy, all right, and that was only the start of it. I didn't know it, but I was seeing the *Balliol College* at her best.

One morning, when I was sufficiently recovered to hold down the gruel that Looney brought me, and strong enough to kick his backside into the bargain, comes Captain Spring to tell me I'd lain long enough, and it was time for me to learn my duties.

"You'll stand your watch like everyone else," says he, "and in the meantime you can start on the work you're paid for—which is to go through every scrap of that cargo, *privatim et seriatim*, and see that those long-shore thieves haven't bilked me. So get up, and come along with me."

I followed him out on deck; we were scudding along like a flying duck with great billows of canvas spread, and a wind on the quarter deck fit to lift your hair off. There was plenty of shipping in sight, but no land, and I knew we must be well out of the Channel by now. Looking forward from the poop rail along the narrow flush deck, it seemed to me the *Balliol College* didn't carry much of a crew, for all her size, but I didn't have time to stop and stare, with Spring barking at me. He led me down the poop ladder, and then dropped through a scuttle by the mizzen mast.

"There you are," says he. "Take a good look."

Although I've done a deal more sailing than I care to remember, I'm no canvas-back, and while I know enough not to call the deck the floor, I'm no hand at nautical terms. We were in what seemed to be an enormous room stretching away forward to the foremast, where there was a bulkhead; this room ran obviously the full breadth of the ship, and was well lighted by gratings in the deck about fifteen feet above our heads. But it was unlike the interior of any ship I'd ever seen, it was so big and roomy; on either side,

van told me he reckoned it was the knowledge that they were going to be slaves, but that being brainless brutes they never thought of doing anything about it.

Those who were selected were herded out of the barracoons into a long railed place like a sheep pen, all jammed together with three black guards either side, armed with whips and pistols. There was a narrow gate at the other end, just wide enough to let one slave through at a time, and the two biggest guards were stationed there. As each nigger emerged they seized him and flung him face down beside an iron brazier full of glowing coals, and two of Sanchez's Dago pals clapped a branding iron on his shoulder. He would squeal like blazes, and the niggers in the pen would try to crowd back out the other end, but the guards lashed them on, and another would be hauled out and branded the same way. The screaming and weeping in the pen was something to hear; everyone who could was on hand to watch, and there was much merriment at the antics of the niggers, blubbering before they were burned, and hopping and squealing afterwards.

Spring was there for the branding of the wenches, to see that it was done lightly, just below the ankle on the inside, in the case of the better-looking ones. "Who the d - - - l wants a young wench with scars on her backside?" he growled. "Even if we ain't selling fancies, the less marking the better; the Legrees tell me the Southern ladies don't want even their field women burned these days.[22] So have a care with those irons, you two, and you, doctor, slap on that grease with a will."

This was to Murphy, who sat beyond the brazier with a huge tub of lard between his feet. As each branded nigger was pulled forward one of the black guards would thrust the burned shoulder or ankle under Murphy's nose; he would take a good look at it and then slap a handful of the lard on the wound, crying either, "There's for you, Sambo", or "That'll pretty you up, acushla"; he was half full of booze, as usual, and from time to time would apply himself to his bottle and then cry encouragement to the niggers as they came through, or break into a snatch of raucous song. I can see him now, swaying on his stool, red face glistening, shirt hanging open over the red furze on his chest, plastering on the grease with his great freckled hand and chanting:

"Al-though with lav-ish kind-ness
The gifts of Go-od are strewn,
The heath-en in his blind-ness
Bows down to wood and sto-one."

When he was done with them the heathens were pushed through
a series of wooden frames set up close by the *Balliol College's*
gangplanks. One was six feet by two, another slightly smaller, and
a third smaller still. By means of these the slaves were sized, and
sent up one of three gangplanks accordingly; the biggest ones
were for the bottom of the slave deck, the middle-sized for the
first tier of shelves, and the smallest for the top tier, but care was
taken to separate men and women—a tall wench or a little chap
could have got in among the wrong sex, and Spring wouldn't have
that. He insisted that the women should be berthed forward of the
first bulkhead and the men all aft of it, and since they would be
chained up they wouldn't be able to get up to high jinks—I didn't
see why they shouldn't, myself, but Spring had his own reasons,
no doubt.

Once up the planks, though, the really hard work began. I
didn't know much about it, but I had to work with the hands who
stowed the slaves, and I soon picked up the hang of it. As each
slave was pushed down the hatch, he was seized by a waiting
seaman and forced to lie down on the deck in his allotted place,
head towards the side of the ship, feet towards the centre, until
both sides of the deck were lined with them. Each man had to go
in a space six feet by fifteen inches, and now I saw why there had
been so much argument over that extra inch; if they were jammed
up tight, or made to lie on their right sides, you could get ever so
many more in.

This was the hard part, for the slaves were terrified, stupid, and
in pain from their branding; they wriggled and squirmed on the
deck and wouldn't be still, and the hands had to knock them about
or lay into the most unruly ones with a rope's end. One huge buck,
bawling and with tears streaming down his face, made a dash for
the hatch, but Sullivan knocked him flat with a hand-spike, threw
him into place, and terrified the others by shaking a cat-o'-nine-
tails at them, to let them see what they might hope to get if they

589

misbehaved.

When they were placed, a shackle was clapped round each right ankle, and a long chain threaded through it, until they were all stowed, when the chain was made fast to the bulkheads at either end. Soon there were four lines of niggers flat on the deck, with a space up the middle between them, so that the seamen could stand there to pack the later arrivals into the shelves.

It's not that I'm an abolitionist by any means, but by the end of that day I'd had my bellyful of slaving. The reek of those musky bodies in that deck was abominable; the heat and stench grew by the hour, until you'd have wondered that anything could survive down there. They howled and blubbered, and we were fagged out with grabbing brown limbs and tugging and shoving and nudging them up with our feet to get the brutes to lie close. They fouled themselves where they lay, and before the job was half done the filth was indescribable. We had to escape to the deck every half hour to souse ourselves with salt water and drink great draughts of orange juice, before descending into that fearful pit again, and wrestle again with wriggling black bodies that stunk and sweated and went everywhere but where you wanted them. When it was finally done, and Sullivan ordered all hands on deck, we climbed out dead beat, ready to flop down anywhere and go to sleep.

But not with John Charity Spring about. He must go down to inspect, and count the rows, and kick a black body into place here and tug another one there, before he was satisfied. He d - - - - d our eyes for letting 'em soil the deck, and ordered the whole place hosed down, niggers and all; they dried where they lay in no time, of course, and the steam came out of the hatches like smoke.

I looked down at it just before the hatch gratings went on, and it was an indiscribable sight. Row upon row of black bodies, packed like cigars in a box, naked and gleaming, the dark mass striped with glittering dots of light where the eyes rolled in the sooty faces. The crying and moaning and whimpering blended into a miserable anthem that I'll never forget, with the clanking of the chains and the rustle of hundreds of incessantly stirring bodies, and the horrible smell of musk and foulness and burned flesh.

My stomach doesn't turn easy, but I was sickened. If it had been left to me, then and there, I'd have let 'em go, the whole boiling lot of them, back to their lousy jungle. No doubt it's a deplorable weakness in my character, but this kind of raw work was a thought too much for me. Mind you, sit me down in my club, or at home, and say, "Here, Flash, there's twenty thou for you if you'll say 'aye' to a cargo of black ivory going over the Middle Passage", and I ain't saying I'ld turn you down. Nor do I flinch when someone whips a black behind or claps on a brand—but enough's enough, and when you've looked into the hold of a new-laden slaver for the first time, you know what hell is like.[23]

I mentioned this to Sullivan, and he spat. "You think that's hell, do you? First blackbird voyage I made, as a young hand, we took three hundred coons from the Gallinas, and we were setting out for Rio when a Limey sloop tacks on to us. It was a Portuguese flag we carried, with a yaller-black Dago skipper in command; he saw sure enough they were going to take us." He looked at me with his head on one side. "Can you guess what that Christian Angolese son-of-a-b - - - h did? G'wan, have a guess."

I said I had heard of slave cargoes being thrown overboard, so that when the Navy came up all the evidence had gone. Sullivan laughed.

"There wasn't time for that, our skipper figures. But we were carryin' palm oil as well as slaves, and had a good deal of trade powder left over. So he set the ship on fire, an' we took to the boats. Navy couldn't get near her, so she just burned out an' sank—with three hundred niggers aboard. I wouldn't care to guess how many of 'em were lucky enough to drown." He laughed again, without any mirth at all. "And you think that's hell, down there? I guess you also think that Mr J. C. Spring is a real tough skipper!"

Well, I did, and if there were bigger swine afloat in the earlies I'm only glad I never met them. But Sullivan's story gave me the shudders all right, for it reminded me that the next stage of our voyage was the notorious Middle Passage, with all the dangers of pursuit and capture, to say nothing of hurricane and shipwreck.

"D'you think there's any chance of . . . of that happening with us?" says I, and Sullivan snorted.

"I'll say this for Spring—he don't lose ships, or cargoes. He believes in keeping the sharks hungry. Any Navy coaster that comes up with us is in for a h--l of a chase—less'n she's a steamer an' catches us in a flat calm."

Here was a fearful thought. "What then?" says I.

"Then—why, we fight her," says he, and left me prey to a nausea that had nothing to do with the heat or the slave-stench or my weariness. Having lately been at grips with fighting nigger women, I could see myself shortly assisting in a running sea-battle against the Royal Navy—just what was needed to liven up the cruise. And by jove, it nearly came to that, too, and on our very first hour out from that abominable coast.

We dropped down river early the next morning, to catch the ebb tide, I believe, and it seemed a piece of lunacy to me to try those shoals and islands in the half light. However, Spring knew his business; he took the wheel himself, and with only the fore-topsail spread we drifted slowly between the green banks, the leadsmen chanting quietly, and the first hint of dawn beginning to lighten the sky over the black jungle mass astern. It was a queer, eery business, gliding so silently along, with only the mumble of the slaves, the creak of rope and timber, and the gurgle of water to break the stillness, and then we were clear of the last banks and the sun shot a great beam of light ahead of us across the placid surface of the sea.

It was all very beautiful, in its way, but just as Sullivan was roaring the watch up to set more sail the idyll was marred by the appearance round the southern headland of a small, waspish-looking vessel, standing slowly out on a course parallel to our own. It happened that I saw her first, and drew my commander's attention to her with a sailor-like hail of: "Jesus! Look at that!"

Spring just stared for a moment, and then says: "Foresail and main-tops'l, Mr Sullivan," before getting his glass out for a look.

"White ens'n," says he presently, without any emotion. "Take a look, mister. Twenty-gun sloop, I'd say."

Sullivan agreed, and while my bowels did the polka the two of them just stood and watched her as though she'd been a pleasure steamer. I didn't know much about sailing, as you're aware, but even I could see that she was moving more briskly than we were, that there was nothing but light airs stirring the surface, and that she wasn't more than two miles away. It looked to me as though the *Balliol College*'s voyage was over before it had rightly begun which merely shows how ignorant I was.

For an hour, while my gorge rose steadily, we watched her; we were doing no more than creep out from the coast, and the sloop did the same, only a little faster, and converging gradually all the time on our course. I could see that eventually we would be bound to meet, if we held our courses, and I had an idea that in light wind the sailing advantage would be all with the smaller vessel. But Spring seemed unconcerned; from time to time he would turn and survey the coast behind us, and the sky, converse shortly with Sullivan, and then go back to watching the sloop, with his hands stuck deep in his pockets.

He was waiting confidently, I now know, for a wind, and he got it just when I had finally given up all hope. The sails flapped, Spring barked an order, and at a shout from Sullivan the hands were racing aloft; in the same moment the boom of a shot sounded over the water, and a pillar of spray rose out of the sea a few hundred yards from our port bow.

"Burn your powder, you useless son of a Geordie coaster skipper, you!" bawls Spring from the wheel. "Look alive, Mr Sullivan!" And he sent out a perfect volley of orders as the *Balliol College* heeled gently and lifted to the first puffs of wind, and then I found myself tailing on a rope with the others, hauling for dear life and wondering what the d - - - l would happen next.

If I were a nautical man, no doubt I could tell you, but I'm not, thank God; the mysteries of ship handling are as obscure to me today as they were fifty years ago. If I were Bosun McHearty I daresay I could describe how we jibed with our futtock gans'ls clewed up to the orlop bitts, and weathered her, d'ye see, with a lee helm and all plain sail in the bilges, burn me buttocks. As it was, I just stuck like a shadow to a big Portugal nigger of the deck watch, called Lord Peabody, and tailed on behind him with the pulley-hauley, while Spring and Sullivan bawled their jargon, the men aloft threw themselves about like acrobats, and the *Balliol College* began to surge forward at greater speed. There was another shot from the sloop, and an ironic cheer from our fellows —why I couldn't imagine, for our pursuer was soon cracking along famously, and I could make out her ensign plainly, and the figures on her deck, all far too close for comfort. I saw, in the intervals of scampering about after Peabody, and hauling on the ropes, that she would be able to fire in earnest soon, and I was just commending my soul to God and wondering if I could turn Queen's Evidence, when Spring let loose another volley of orders, there was a tremendous cracking and bellying of sails overhead, and the *Balliol College* seemed to spin round on her heel, plunge over with a lurch that brought my breakfast up, and then go bowling away across the track of the sloop.

I don't understand it, of course, but in the next hour Spring executed a similar manoeuvre half a dozen times, while the wind freshened, and although the sloop copied our movements, so far as I could see, she always somehow finished up farther away—no doubt any yachtsman could explain it. The hands cheered and laughed, although you could hardly hear them for the fearful howling that was coming from below decks, where the slaves were spewing and yelling in terror at the bucketing of the ship. And then we were standing out to sea again, and the sloop was away off our quarter, still flying along, but making no headway at all.

Only then did Spring hand over the wheel and come to the stern rail, where he delivered a catechism to the distant Navy vessel, calling them lubberly sons of dogs and shaking his fist at them.

"There's where the tax-payer's money goes!" he roared. "That's what's supposed to defend us against the French! Look at them! I could sail rings round 'em in a Blackwall coal lighter! *Quo, quo, scelesti ruitis,** eh? I tell you, Mr Sullivan, a crew of All Souls dons could do better on a raft! What the blazes are they letting into the Navy these days? He'll be some rum-soaked short-haul pensioner, no doubt—either that or a beardless brat with a father in the Lords and some ladylike Mama whoring round the Admiralty. My stars, wouldn't I like to put them all to sea under Bully Waterman,[24] or let 'em learn their trade in an opium clipper with a Down East Yankee skipper and a Scotch owner— you hear that, you Port Mahon bumboatman, you? You ought to be on the beach!"

It was fine stuff, but wasted since the sloop was miles away; by

* Where are you hastening, fools?

594

afternoon she was just a speck on the horizon, and the coast of Africa had vanished behind us. The ease of our escape, I was told, all came of Spring knowing his weather, for standing away from the Slave coast was evidently a most unchancy business, and many slavers had been caught in the calms that so often beset them there. But some of the deltas and river mouths could be relied on to give you wind, and Spring knew all about this; it was also true that he was a first-rate seaman with a prime crew, and together they were probably a match for anything. We did sight another patrol vessel on the following day, but we were tearing along at such a rate that she never came near us, and Spring didn't even interrupt his dinner.

It was blowing fairly stiffish now, and the slaves had an abominable time. For the first few days they just lay howling and weeping in their sea-sickness, but Spring insisted that the huge coppers and tubs in which their pulse porridge was made should be kept at work, and by flogging one of the bucks down on the slave deck in the sight of his fellows he terrified them into eating, ill as they were. Murphy was constantly at work, especially among the women, to make sure that none died, and twice a day the hoses were turned on to scour out the filth which would otherwise have bred an epidemic in no time.

About the fourth day, the wind dropped, the slaves stopped spewing, and the cooks who tended the mess tubs became the hardest-worked men on the ship. One thing the *Balliol College* didn't stint to its human cargo, and that was food—which was good business, of course. Spring also insisted that lime juice be issued, and the slaves forced to drink it—they hated it, but when they saw it was that or the cat they swilled it down fast enough. They were still in a fearful funk, of course, since they had no idea of what the ocean was like, and couldn't seem to get used to the rolling of the ship; when they weren't eating or sleeping they just lay there in their long black rows, wailing and rolling their eyes like frightened sheep. There was no spirit in them at all, and I began to see why the slavers thought of them not as humans, but as animals.

Every day they went through a curious exercise which was called dancing. They were brought up on deck in batches, and forced to caper about for half an hour, leaping up and down and trotting round the deck. This of course was just to keep them in trim; they didn't like that, either, at first, and we had to smarten them with rope's ends to get them moving. But after the first few times they began to enjoy it, and it was the most ludicrous sight to see them skipping and shuffling round the deck, clapping their hands and even crooning to themselves, the bolder spirits grinning and rolling their eyes—they were just like children, forgetting the misery of their condition, and sky-larking about, quite delighted if the hands cried encouragement to them. One of the fellows had a fiddle, on which he would play jigs and reels, and the niggers would try to out-do each other in capering to the music.

The men got over their fears faster than the women, who danced with much less jollity, although everyone on the ship was always on hand to watch them. You couldn't have called any of 'em pretty, with their pug faces and great woolly mops of hair, but they had fine shapely bodies, and none of us had seen a proper woman for near on six weeks. The sight of those naked black bodies shuffling and swaying got me into a fever the first time I saw it, and the others were the same, licking their lips and muttering when was Murphy the surgeon going to set about his business?

I understood what this meant when we were all ordered to report and strip down for Murphy in his berth, where he examined us carefully to see that none of us had pox or crabs or yaws or any of the interesting diseases that wicked sailormen are prone to. When we were pronounced clean Spring had us each pick out a black wench—I thought this was by way of seaman's comforts, but it turned out that the more black wenches who could be got pregnant by white men, the better the traders liked it, for they would produce mulatto children, who being half-white were smarter and more valuable than pure blacks. The Cuban dealers trusted Spring, and if he could guarantee that all his female slaves had been bulled by his crew, it would add to their price.

"I want all these wenches pupped," says he, "but you'll do it decently, d'you hear, *salvo pudore*,* in your quarters. I'll not have Mrs Spring offended."

* Without offending modesty.

It may sound like just the kind of holiday for a fellow like me, but it was no great fun as it turned out. I picked out a likely enough big wench, jet black and the liveliest dancer of the lot, but she knew nothing, and she reeked of jungle even when she was scrubbed down. I tried to coax some spirit into her, first by kindness and then by rope's end, but she was no more use than a bishop's maiden aunt. However, one has to make do, and in the intervals of our laborious grappling I tried to indulge my interest in foreign languages, which apart from horses is the only talent I can boast. I can usually make good use of a native pillow partner in this way, provided she speaks English, but of course this one didn't, and was as stupid as a Berkshire hog into the bargain. So it was no go as far as learning anything was concerned, but I did succeed in teaching her a few useful English words and phrases like:

"Me Lady Caroline Lamb. Me best rattle in *Balliol College*."

The hands thought this a great joke, and just for devilment I also taught her a tag from Horace, and with immense work got her perfect in it, so that when you pinched her backside she would squeak out:

"*Civis Romanus sum. Odi profanum vulgus.*"

Spring almost leaped out of his skin when he heard it, and was not at all amused. He took the opportunity to upbraid me for not having sent her back to the slave-deck and taken another wench, for he wanted them all covered; I said I didn't want to break in any more of 'em, and suggested that if this one learned a little English it might add to her value; he raised his voice and d - - - - d my impudence, not realising that Mrs Spring had come up the companion and could hear us. She startled him by suddenly remarking:

"Mr Flashman is a constant heart. I knew it the moment I first saw him."

She was mad, of course, but Spring was much put out, because she wasn't meant to know what was going on with the black women. But he let me keep Lady Caroline Lamb.

So it was a pleasant enough cruise to begin with, for the weather blew just enough to give us a good passage without being too

* I am a Roman citizen. I hate vulgar profane persons.

rough for the niggers; their health remained good, with no deaths in the first week, which greatly pleased Spring; the work was light above deck, as it always is in a fast ship with a favourable wind, and there was time to sit about watching the flying fish and listening to the hands swapping yarns—my respect for them had increased mightily over our encounter with the British sloop, which had confirmed my earlier impression that these were no ordinary packet rats with the points knocked off their knives, but prime hands. And I've learned that no time is wasted which is spent listening to men who really know their work.

However, as always when I feel I can loaf for a spell, something happened which drove all other thoughts out of my head—even my daydreams about Elspeth, and how I might contrive to come home respectably before too long, and scupper old Morrison, too, if possible. What happened was little enough, and not unexpected, but in the long run it certainly saved my liberty, and probably my life.

On the seventh day out from Dahomey, Murphy came to me and said I must go directly to Comber, who was dying. Since we sailed he'd been stowed away in a little cubby off the main cabin aft, where there was a window and Mrs Spring could tend to him.

"It's all up with him, poor lad," says Murphy, fuming with liquor. "His bowels is mortified, I'm thinkin'; maybe that jezebel's spear wuz pizened. Any roads, he wants to see you."

I couldn't think why, but I went along, and as soon as I clapped eyes on him I could see it was the Union Jack for this one, no error. His face was wasted and yellow, with big purple blotches beneath the eyes, and he was breathing like a bellows. He was lying on the berth with just a blanket over him, and the hand on top of it was like a bird's claw. He signed feebly to me to shut the door, and I squatted down on a stool beside his cot.

He lay for a few moments, gazing blankly at the sunbeams from the open window, and then says, in a very weak voice:

"Flashman, do you believe in God?"

Well, I'd expected this, of course; his wasn't the first deathbed I'd sat by, and they usually get religious sooner or later. There's nothing for it but to squat down on your hunkers and let them babble. Dying people love to talk—I know I do, and I've been in extremis more often than most. So to humour him I said certainly there was a God, not a doubt about it, and he chewed this over a bit and says:

"And if there is a God, and a Heaven—there must be a Devil, and a Hell? Must there not?"

I'd heard that before, too, so playing up to my part as the Rev. Flashy, B.D., I told him opinion was divided on the point. In any event, says I, if there was a Hell it couldn't be much worse than life on this earth—which I don't believe for a minute, by the way.

"But there is a Hell!" cries he, turning on me with his eyes shining feverishly. "I know it—a terrible, flaming Hell in which the damned burn through all Eternity! I know it, Flashman, I tell you!"

I could have told him this was what came of looking at the pictures in Bunyan's *Holy War*, which had blighted my young life for a spell when I first struck it. But I soothed him by pointing out that if there was a Hell, it was reserved for prime sinners only, and he probably wasn't up to that touch.

He rolled his head about on the pillow, biting his lip with distress and the pain of his wound.

"But I am a sinner," he gasped. "A fearful sinner. Oh, I do fear I am beyond redemption! The Saviour will turn from me, I know."

"Oh, I'm not sure, now," says I. "Slaving ain't that bad, you know."

He groaned and closed his eyes. "There is no such sin on my conscience," says he fretfully, which I didn't understand. "It is my weak flesh that has betrayed me. I have so many sins—I have broken the seventh commandment . . ."

I couldn't be sure about this; I had a suspicion it was the one about oxen and other livestock, which seemed unlikely, but with a man who's half-delirious you can never tell.

"What is it that's troubling you?" I asked.

"In that—that village . . ." he said, speaking with effort "Those . . . those women. Oh, God . . . pity me . . . I lusted after them . . . in my mind . . . I looked on them . . . as David looked on Bathsheeba. I desired them, carnally, sinfully . . . oh, Flashman . . . I

599

am guilty . . . in His sight . . . I . . ."

"Now, look here," says I, for I was getting tired of this. "You won't go to Hell for that. Leastways, if you do, it'll be a mighty crowded place. You'll have the entire human race there, including the College of Cardinals, I shouldn't wonder."

But he babbled on about the sin of lechery for a bit, and then, as repentant sinners always do, he decided I was right, and took my hand—his was as dry as a bundle of sticks.

"You are a good fellow, Flashman," says he. "You have eased my mind." Why he'd been worried beat me; if I thought that when I go I'll have nothing worse on my conscience than slavering over a buxom bum, well, I'll die happy, that's all. But this poor devil had obviously been Bible-reared, and fretted according.

"You truly believe I shall be saved?" says he. "There is forgiveness, is there not? We are taught so—that we may be washed clean in the blood of the Lamb."

"Clean as a whistle," says I. "It's in the book. Now, then, old fellow . . ."

"Don't go," says he, gripping my hand. "Not yet. I'm . . . I'm dying, you know, Flashman . . . there isn't much time . . ."

I said wouldn't he like Mrs Spring to look in, but he shook his head.

"There is something . . . I must do . . . first. Be patient a moment, my dear friend."

So I waited, wishing to blazes I was out of there. He was breathing harder than ever, wheezing like an old pump, but he must have been gathering strength, for when he opened his eyes again they were clear and sane, and looked directly at mine.

"Flashman," says he, earnestly, "how came you aboard this ship?"

It took me aback, but I started to tell him (a revised version, of course), and he cut me off.

"It was against your will?" He was almost pleading.

"Of course. I wouldn't have . . ."

"Then you too . . . oh, in God's name tell me truthfully . . . you detest this abomination of slavery?"

Hollo, thinks I, what's here? Very smartly I said, yes, I detested it. I wanted to see where he was going.

"Thank God!" says he. "Thank God!" And then: "You will swear to me that what I tell you will be breathed to no one on this accursed vessel?"

I swore it, solemnly, and he heaved a great sigh of relief.

"My belt," says he. "On the chest yonder. Yes, take it . . . and cut it open . . . there, near the buckle."

Mystified, I examined it. It was a broad, heavy article, double welted. I picked out the stitches as he indicated, with my knife, and the two welts came apart. Between them, folded very tight, was a slender oilskin packet. I unfolded it—and suddenly thought, I've been here before: then I remembered slitting open the lining of my own coat by the Jotunschlucht, with de Gautet lying beside me, groaning at the pain of his broken toes. Was that only a few months ago? It seemed an eternity . . . and then the packet was open, and I was unfolding the two papers within it. I spread the first one out, and found myself gaping at a letterhead design which showed an anchor, and beneath it the words:

"To Lieutenant Beauchamp Millward Comber, R.N. You are hereby required and directed . . ."

"Good G - d!" says I, staring. "You're a naval officer!"

He tried to nod, but his wound must have caught him, for he groaned and gasped. Then: "Read on," says he.

". . . to report yourself immediately to the Secretary of the Board of Trade, and receive from him, or such subordinate official as he may appoint, instructions and directions whereby you shall assist, in whatsoever capacity the Secretary shall deem most fitting, against those persons engaged in the illicit and illegal traffic in human slaves between the Guinea, Ivory, Grain, Togo, Dahomey, Niger and Angola Coasts and the Americas. You are most strictly enjoined to obey and carry out all such instructions and directions as though they had proceeded from Their Lordships of the Admiralty or others your superior officers in Her Majesty's service." It was signed "Auckland".

The other paper, which was from the Board of Trade, was really no more than a sort of passport, requesting that all officials, officers, and other persons in H.M. service, and of foreign governments, should render to Lieutenant Comber all assistance of which he might stand in need, etc., etc., but in its way it was equally impressive, for it was signed not only by the President, Labouchere, but also countersigned by my old pal T. B. Macaulay, as Paymaster, and some Frog or other for the French merchant marine.

I goggled at these things, hardly understanding, and then looked at Comber; he was lying with his eyes shut, and his face working.

"You're a spy," says I. "A spy on the slavers!"

He opened his eyes. "You . . . may call it that. If it is spying to help to deliver these poor creatures . . . then I am proud to be a spy." He made a great effort, gasping with pain, and turned on his side towards me. "Flashman . . . hear me . . . I'm going . . . soon. Even if you don't . . . see this as I do . . . as God's work . . . still, you are a gentleman . . . an Army officer. Why, you are one of Arnold's people . . . the paladins. For God's sake, say you will help! Don't let all my work . . . my death . . . be in vain!"

He was in a desperate sweat, straining a hand out towards me, his eyes glittering. "You must . . . in honour . . . and, oh, for these poor lost black souls! If you'd seen what I've seen . . . aye, and had to help in, God forgive me . . . but I had to, you see, until I had done my work. You must help them, Flashman; they cannot help themselves. Their minds are not as ours . . . they are weak and foolish and an easy prey to scoundrels like Spring . . . but they have souls . . . and this slavery is an abomination in God's sight!" He struggled to get farther up. "Say you will help . . . for pity's sake!"

"What do you want me to do?"

"Take those letters." His voice was weakening, and I could see blood seeping through his blanket; he must have opened his wound in his exertion. "Then . . . my chest . . . there under the canvas shirt . . . packet. Copy of Spring's accounts . . . last voyage. I took some of them . . . completed them this trip. Letters, too . . . evidence against him . . . and others. For God's sake get them to the Admiralty . . . or the American Navy people . . . oh, dear God!"

He fell back, moaning, but by then I was ferreting through his chest, snatching out a slender packet sewn in an oilskin cover. I slipped it and the letters quickly out of sight in my pocket, and bent over his cot.

"Go on, man! What more? Are there any others like yourself —agents, officers, or what?"

But he just lay there, coughing weakly and breathing in little moaning gasps. I closed the chest and sat down to see if he would revive again, and after a moment he began to mumble; I leaned close, but it was a moment before I could make out what he was saying—in fact, he was singing, in a little whisper at the back of his throat; it was that sad little song, "The Lass so good and true", that they call "Danny Boy" nowadays. I knew at once, without telling, that it was the song his mother had used to sing him to sleep, for he began to smile a little, with his eyes closed. I could have kicked the brute; if he'd spent less time making his soul and belly-aching to me about hell fire, and minded his duty, he would have had time to tell me more about his mission. Not that I cared a button for that, but all knowledge is useful when you're in the grip of folk like Spring. But he was going to slip his cable with all the good scandal untold, by the looks of it.

Sure enough, when his whispered song died away, he began muttering, "Mother . . . Sally . . . yes, Mother . . . cold . . ." but nothing to make sense. It was maddening. Of course, my generation were preoccupied with their mothers, which sets me apart; mine died when I was little, you see, and I never really knew her, which may account for a deal. It crossed my mind, in that moment, what will I have to say in the last few seconds before I slip over the edge of life? Whose name will be on my repentant lips? My father's?—now there would be a cheery vision to carry over to the other side, all boozy face and rasping voice. Elspeth's? I doubt it. Some of the other ladies?—Lola, or Natasha or Takes-Away-Clouds-Woman or Leonie or Lady White Willow or . . . no, there wouldn't be time. I'll have to wait and see. Which reminds me, young Harry East, when they pulled what was left of him into the dooli at Cawnpore, muttered, "Tell the doctor", and everyone thought he meant the surgeon—but I knew different. He meant Arnold, which as a dying thought has one advantage, that the Devil, if you meet him later, will be an improvement.

So I speculated, as Comber's breathing slackened, and then I saw the shadow of death cross his wasted face (there is such a shadow, down from the temple and across to the chin, seen it scores of times) and he was gone. I pulled the blanket over his head, went through his jacket pockets and chest, but found nothing worth while except a pencil case and a good clasp knife, which I appropriated, and then went topsides to tell Spring.

"He's gone at last, is he?" was his charitable comment. "Aye, *omne capax movet urna nomen.** We need not pretend he is a great loss. Blackwall fashion was about his style[25]—a sound enough seaman, but better fitted for an Indiaman than our trade. Very good, you can tell the sailmaker to bundle him up; we'll bury him tomorrow." And he continued to survey the horizon through his glass, while I slipped away to think over the momentous news I'd learned from the dying Comber. Obviously the fact that he had been an Admiralty man working against the slavers was of the first importance, but for the life of me I couldn't see what use it might be to me. For all that I'd soothed his passing moments out of an uncommon civility, I didn't mind a snap whether his precious evidence ever reached government hands or not. In fact, it seemed to me that if an information was laid against the *Balliol College* and her master, those who had sailed with him would land in the dock as well, and they included H. Flashman, albeit he wasn't aboard willingly. Yet my knowledge, and Comber's, might be valuable somehow, provided I kept them safe from prying eyes.

So it seemed to me at the time anyway, so I took a leaf out of Comber's book, and in the privacy of my berth sewed his two letters into my belt. I hesitated a long while over the packet, for I knew the secrets it contained would be fatally dangerous to whoever shared them; if Spring ever found out it would be a slit throat and a watery grave for me. But curiosity got the better of me in the end; I opened it carefully so that it could be re-sealed, and was presently goggling my way through the contents.

It was prime stuff, no question: all Spring's accounts for 1847 copied out in minute writing—how many niggers shipped, how many sold at Roatan and how many at the Bay of Pigs, the names of buyers and traders; a full description of deals and prices and orders on British and American banks. There was enough to hang old John Charity ten times over, but that wasn't the best of it;

* Every name is shaken in death's great urn.

Comber had been at his letters, too, and while some of them were in cypher, quite a few were in English. They included one from the London firm which had supplied the trade goods for our present voyage; another from New York lawyers who seemed to represent American investors (for Comber had annotated it with a list of names marked "U.S. interests, owners") and—oh, b----y rapture!—a document describing the transfer of the *Balliol College* from its American builders, Brown & Bell, to a concern in London among the names of whose directors was one J. Morrison. I almost whooped at the sight of it—what Spring was thinking of to keep such damaging evidence aboard his vessel I couldn't fathom, but there it was. I found Morrison mentioned in one other letter, and a score of names besides; it might not be enough to hang him, or them, but I was certain sure he would sell his rotten little soul to keep these papers from the public gaze.

I had him! The knowledge was like a warm bath—with these papers at my command I could, when I got home again, turn the screw on the little shark until he hollered uncle. No longer would I be the poor relation; I would have evidence that could ruin him, commercially and socially, and perhaps put him in the dock as well, and the price of my silence would be a free run through his moneybags. By gad, I'd be set for life. A seat in the House? It would be a seat on the board, at least, and grovelling civility from him to me for a change. He'd rue the day he shanghaied me aboard his lousy slave ship.

Chuckling happily, I sewed it all up again in its oilskin, and stitched this carefully into the lining of my coat. There it would stay until I got home and it could be employed in safety to my enrichment and Morrison's confusion. I reflected, as I went back on deck later, that it all came from my act of Christian kindness in listening by Comber's deathbed and comforting his last moments. There's no doubt about it; virtue isn't always just its own reward.

Comber wasn't buried the next day, because one of the slaves died during the night, and when the watch found him at dawn they naturally heaved the body overside to the sharks. For some reason this sent Spring into a passion; he wasn't having a white man buried at sea on the same day as a black had been slung over, which seemed to be stretching it a bit, but a lot of the older hands agreed with him. It beats me; when I go they can plant me in with the whole population of Timbuctoo, but others see things differently. Spring, now, was mad about little things like that, and when eventually we did come to bury Comber on the morning after, and his body had been laid out on a plank by the rail, all neatly stitched up in sail-cloth, our fastidious commander played merry h - - l because no one had thought to cover it with a flag. This on a Dahomey slaver, mark you. So we all had to wait with our hats off while Looney was despatched to get a colour from the flag locker, and Spring stamped up and down with his Prayer Book under his arm, cursing the delay, and Mrs Spring sat by with her accordion. She was wearing a floral bonnet in honour of the occasion, secured with a black scarf for mourning, and her face wore its usual expression of vacant amiability.

Looney came back presently, and you wouldn't believe it, he was carrying the Brazilian colours. We were wearing them at the moment, this being the Middle Passage,[26] so I suppose he thought he'd done right, but Spring flew into a towering passion.

"D - - n your lousy eyes!" cries he. "Take that infernal Dago duster out of my sight—would you bury an Englishman under that?" And he knocked Looney sprawling and then kicked him into the scuppers. He cursed him something fearful, the scar on his head bright crimson, until one of the hands brought a Union Jack, and then we got on with the service. Spring rattled through it, the shotted corpse went over with a splash, Mrs Spring struck up, we all sang "Rock af Ages", and the "amen" hadn't died away before Spring had strode to the unfortunate Looney and kicked his backside again so hard that he went clean down the booby hatch to the main deck. I've often thought how instructive it would have been for our divinity students to see how the offices for the dead were conducted aboard the *Balliol College*.

However, this was just another incident which I relate to show you what kind of a lunatic Spring was; I suppose it stands out in my mind because the next few weeks were so uneventful—that may seem an extraordinary thing to say about a slave voyage on the Middle Passage, but once you are used to conditions, however remarkable, you start to twiddle your thumbs and find life a bore. I had little to do beyond stand my watches, help dance the slaves, and continue the instruction of Lady Caroline Lamb. She took to following me about, and had to be made to wear a cotton dress that the sailmaker ran up, in case Mrs Spring caught sight of her—as though she'd never seen naked black wenches before, by the hundred. Lady Caroline Lamb didn't care for this, and whenever she was in my berth she used to haul the dress off, and sit stark by the foot of my cot, like a black statue, waiting to be educated, one way or the other.

One other thing I should mention, because it turned out to be important, was the behaviour of Looney. Whether Spring's hammering had driven him even more barmy I can't say, but he was a changed man after Comber died. He'd been a willing, happy idiot, but now he became sullen, and started if anyone spoke to him, and took to muttering to himself in corners. I cuffed him smartly to make him stop it, but he wouldn't; he just blubbered and mowed and shuddered if Spring's name was even mentioned. "He's the Devil!" he whined. "The b----y Devil! He bashed us, for nowt. He did, the ----." And he would crawl away, whimpering obscenities, to find a place to hide. Even Sullivan, who was softer with him than most, couldn't prevail on him to do his duties aft as steward, and the cook's Chinese mate had to serve in Spring's cabin.

So we ran westward, and then north-west, for about a month if I remember rightly, until one morning I learned that we were out of the Atlantic and into the Caribbean. It all looked alike to me, for the weather had continued fine the whole way and I'd never worn more than my jersey, but now a change came over the ship. Each day there was gun drill at the long nines and twelves, which struck me as ominous, and you could sense a growing restlessness among the hands: where men off watch had been content to loaf before, they now kept watching the horizon and sniffing the wind; either Spring or Sullivan was always at the after rail with the glass; whenever a large sail was sighted Spring would have the guns shotted and their crews standing by. As the weather grew even hotter, tempers got shorter; the stench from the slave-deck was choking in its foulness, and even the constant murmuring and moaning of the cargo seemed to me to have taken on a deeper, more sinister note. This was the time, I learned, when slave mutinies sometimes broke out, as more of them died—although only five perished all told in our ship—and the others became sullen and desperate. You'd been able to feel the misery and fear down on the slave-deck, but now you could feel the brooding hatred; it was in the way they shuffled sulkily round when they were danced, heads sunk and eyes shifting, while the hands stood guard with the needle-guns, and the light swivel pieces were kept armed and trained to sweep the decks if need be. I kept as well away from those glowering black brutes as I could; even the sharks which followed the ship didn't look more dangerous—and there were always half a dozen of them, dark sinuous shapes gliding through the blue water a couple of fathoms down, hoping for another corpse to come overside.

I wasn't the only one in a fine state of nerves on the last week's run along the old Spanish Main; apparently even Spring was apprehensive, for instead of running up north-west to the Windward Passage and our intended destination—which was somewhere on the north side of Cuba—he held almost due west for the Mosquito Coast, which if anything is a more God-forsaken shore than the one we had left in Africa. I saw it only as a far distant line on our port beam, but its heavy air lay on the ship like a blanket; the pitch bubbled between the planks, and even the wind seemed to have come from a blast furnace door. By the time we stood into the bay at Roatan, which you'll find on the map in the Islas de la Bahia, off the Honduras Coast, we were a jittery, sun-dried ship, and only thankful that we'd come safe through with never a Yankee patroller or garda costa in sight.[27]

We dropped anchor in that great clearing-house of the African slavers, where Ivory Coast brigs and schooners, the Baltimore clippers and Angola barques, the Gulf free-traders and Braziliano pirates all rode at their moorings in the broad bay, with the bumboats and shorecraft plying among them like water-beetles, and even the stench of our own slave-deck was beaten all to nothing by the immense reek of the huge barracoons and pens that lined the shore and even ran out into the sludgy green waters of the bay on great wooden piers. One never dreams that such places exist until one sees and hears and smells them, with their amazing variety of the scum of the earth—blacks and half-breeds of every description, Rio traders with curling mustachios and pistols in their belts and rings in their ears, like buccaneers from a story-book; Down Easter Yankees in stove-pipe hats with cigars sticking out of faces like flinty cliffs; sun-reddened English tars, some still wearing the wide straw hats of the Navy; packet rats in canvas shirts and frayed trousers; Scowegians with leathery faces and knives hanging on lanyards round their necks; Frog and Dago skippers in embroidered weskits with scarves round their heads, and niggers by the hundred, of every conceivable shape and shade —everyone babbling and arguing in half the tongues on earth, and all with one thing in common: they lived by and on the slave trade.

But best of all I remember a big fellow all in dirty white calicos and a broad-brimmed Panama, holding on to a stay in one of the shore-boats that came under our counter, and bawling up red-faced in reply to some one who had asked what was the news:

"Ain't ye heard, then? They found gold, over to the Pacific coast! That's right—gold! Reckon they're pickin' it up fast as they can shovel! Why, they say it's in lumps big as your fist—more gold'n anyone's ever seen before! Gold—in California!"[28]

We landed all our slaves at Roatan, herding them down into the big lighters where the Dago overseers packed them in like sheep, while Spring conducted business aft of the mizzen-mast with half a dozen brokers who had come aboard. A big awning had been rigged up, and Mrs Spring dispensed tea and biscuits to those who wanted it—which meant to Spring himself and to a wizened little Frenchman in a long taffeta coat and wideawake hat, who perched on a stool sipping daintily from his cup while a nigger boy stood behind fanning the flies off him. The other brokers were three greasy Dagoes in dirty finery who drank rum, a big Dutchman with a face like a suet pudding who drank gin punch, and a swarthy little Yankee who drank nothing at all.

They had all made a quick tour of the slave-deck before it was cleared, and then they bickered and bid with Spring, the Dagoes jabbering and getting excited, the other three mighty calm and business-like. In the end they divided the six hundred among them, at an average price of nine dollars a pound—which came to somewhere between seven and eight hundred thousand dollars for the cargo. No money changed hands; nothing was signed; no receipts were sought or given. Spring simply jotted details down in a note-book—and I daresay that after that the only transactions that took place would be the transfer of bills and orders in perfectly respectable banks in Charlestown, New York, Rio and London.

The niggers we landed would be resold, some to plantation owners along the Main, but most of them into the United States, when smugglers could be found to beat the American blockade and sell them in Mobile and New Orleans at three times what we had been paid for them. When you calculate that the trade cargo we'd given to King Gezo, through Sanchez, had been worth maybe a couple of thousand pounds—well, no wonder the slave trade throve in the forties.[29]

I said we sold all our slaves, but in fact we kept Lady Caroline Lamb. Spring had decided that if I persevered with her instruction in English, she would be worth keeping as an interpreter for later voyages—such slaves were immensely valuable, and we had actually made our last trip without one. I didn't mind; it would help pass the time, and I felt somehow that it was a feather in my cap.

To her Spring also added about a dozen mustee and quadroon girls sent aboard by the brokers, who wanted them shipped to America where they were destined for the New Orleans brothels. Spring agreed for a consideration to take them as far as Havana, where we were to load cargo for our homeward trip. These yellow wenches were quite different from the blacks we had carried, being graceful, delicate creatures of the kind they called "fancy pieces", for use as domestic slaves. I'd have traded twenty Lady Caroline Lamb's for any one of them, but there was no chance of that. They weren't chained, being so few and not the kind who would make trouble anyway.

We didn't linger in Roatan. Slaves from the barracoons came aboard with a load of lime and scoured out the slave-deck, and then we warped out of the bay to cleaner water, and the pumps and hoses washed out the shelves for twenty-four hours before Spring was satisfied. As one of the hands remarked, you could have eaten your dinner off it—not that I'd have cared to, myself. After that we made sail, due north for the Yucatan Passage, and for the first time, I think, since I'd first set foot on that d----d ship, I began to feel easy in my mind. It was no longer a slaver, I felt—well, give or take the few yellows we were carrying— we had turned the corner, and now there was only Havana and the run home. Why, in two or three months, or perhaps even less, I would be in England again, the Bryant affair—how trivial it seemed now!—would be blown over, I would be able to see Elspeth—by jove, I would be a father by then! Somebody would be, anyway—but I'd get the credit, at least. Suddenly I began to feel excited, and the Dahomey Coast and the horrors of that jungle river were like a nightmare that had never truly happened. England, and Elspeth, and peace of mind, and—what else? Well, I'd see about that when the time came.

I should have known better, of course. Whenever I'm feeling up
to the mark and congratulating myself, some fearful fate trips me
headlong, and I find myself haring for cover with my guts
churning and Nemesis in full cry after me. In this case Nemesis
was a dandy little sloop flying the American colours that came up
out of the south-west when we were three days out of Roatan and
had Cuba clear on our starboard bow. That was nothing in itself;
Spring put on more sail and we held our own, scudding north-east.
And then, out from behind Cape San Antonio, a bare two miles
ahead, comes a brig with the Stars and Stripes fluttering at her
peak, and there we were, caught between them, unable to fly and
—in my case, anyway—most unwilling to fight.

But not John Charity Spring. He turned the *Balliol College* on
her heel and tried to race the sloop westward, but on this tack she
came up hand over fist, and presently from her bow-gun comes a
plume of smoke, and a shot kicked up the blue water off our port
bow.

"Clear for action!" bawls he, and with Sullivan roaring about
the deck they ran out the guns while the little sloop came tearing
up and sends another shot across our bows.

Now, in my experience there is only one way to fight a ship, and
that is to get below on the side opposite to the enemy and find a
snug spot behind a stout bulkhead. I was down the main hatch
before the first crash of our own guns, and found myself on the
slave-deck with a dozen screaming yellow wenches cowering in
the corners. I made great play ordering them to keep quiet and
settle down, while overhead the guns thundered again, and there
came a hideous crash and tearing somewhere forward where one of
the Yankee's shots had gone home. The wenches shrieked and
I roared at them and waved my sheath-knife; one of them ran
screaming across the tilting deck, her hands over her face, and
I grabbed hold of her—a fine lithe piece she was, too, and I was
taking my time manhandling her back to her fellows when
Sullivan stuck his head through the hatch crying:

"What the h--l d'ye think you're about?"

"Preventing a slave mutiny!" says I.

"What? You skulking rascal!" He flourished a pistol at me.
"You shift your d---d butt up here, directly, d'ye hear?" So

reluctantly I dropped the wench and went cautiously up the ladder again, poking my head out to see what was what.

I'm no judge of naval warfare, but by the way the hands were serving the port guns we were in the thick of a d - - - - d hot running fight. The twelve-pounders were crashing and being reloaded and run out again like something at Trafalgar, and although from time to time there was the shuddering crack of a shot striking us, we seemed to be taking no great harm; the deck watch were tailing onto a line while Sullivan was yelling orders to the men aloft. He bawled at me, so I scrambled out and tailed on to the line, and out of the corner of my eye I saw the sloop running across our bows, her broadside popping away like fury, and the scream and crash of shot just overhead sent me diving for the scuppers. I fetched up against the rail with a crash, wondering why the blazes I'd been fool enough to come out from cover just because Sullivan told me to—instinct, I suppose—and then there was a rending crackle from overhead, something hit the deck with an almighty crash, and somebody fell on top of me. I pushed him off, and my hand came away sticky with blood. Horrified, I watched as the body rolled into the scuppers; it had no head, and blood was pouring out of the neck stump like a fountain.

All this had happened in a matter of minutes. I climbed unsteadily to my feet and looked around. A great tangle of cordage and splintered timber lay between the main and mizzen masts; looking up I saw that our main top mast had come away, and for a moment I felt the ship floundering and rolling helplessly. Someone was shrieking beneath the wreckage, and Sullivan was jumping forward with an axe and a dozen men at his heels to try to clear the tangle away. Beyond them Spring was at the wheel, hat jammed down as usual, but his orders were lost in the crash of one of our port guns.

What happened in the next five minutes I barely remember; I know that we were hit again, and for a time you could hardly see across the deck for acrid powder smoke. I crouched beside the rail, palpitating, until the clearing party came dragging their mass of wreckage and I had to jump away as they bundled it overside. Our guns had stopped firing, and presently I was aware the Yankee wasn't firing either, so I chanced a look.

Somehow, after that brief holocaust, a semblance of order had been restored. The gun crews were standing by their pieces, Sullivan was by the mizzen, volleying commands to the topmen, and Spring was at the wheel. The Yankee sloop was astern, limping, with her foresail all askew, but the brig was ploughing along like thunder; in our injured condition even I could see she would be with us in no time at all. And then, no doubt, she would batter us to pieces—or take us, with slaves aboard, and that would be prison, and possibly the gallows. I felt the bile coming up in my throat.

And then I heard Spring's voice, raised in a bellow of anger.

"You'll do as you're d----d well told, mister. Now, get those yellows up on deck, with their shackles on! Lively, d--n you, d'ye hear?"

Sullivan, his hat gone, seemed to be protesting, but Spring silenced him with another bellow, and presently the hands were driving up the yellow girls, fastening leg irons about their ankles and herding them together by the mizzen mast. Spring and Sullivan were by the wheel, the latter pointing to the brig, which was overhauling us fast.

"We'll have her shooting us up in five minutes!" he was shouting. "We can't run, skipper; we can't fight! We're crippled, d--n it!"

"We can fight, mister!" Spring's scar was flaming. "We've settled the sloop, haven't we? What's that but a measly brig? D'ye want me to strike to her?"

"Look at her!" cries Sullivan. "She's got thirty guns if she's got one!" I always knew he was a sensible chap.

"I'll fight her, though," says the idiot Spring. "I haven't made this cruise to be towed into New Orleans by that pack of longshore loafers! But we'll make that nigger rubbish safe first—and if we fight and fail there won't be a black hide aboard to show against us. Now—get the chain into 'em!"

Sullivan looked as though he would burst. "It won't do! They're too d----d close—they'll see 'm drop, won't they?"

"What if they do? No niggers, no felony—they can make what they like of the ship, with the d----d equipment law, but they can't lay a hand on you or me! Now, I'm telling you, mister—

get that chain rove through!"

I made nothing of this, until four of the hands came running aft, dragging a massive chain, which they laid by the starboard rail. Then they herded the wenches over, and began to pass the chain between their legs, above the shackles, so that it linked them all together. They made the chain fast with rope to the end slaves in the line, then forced the girls to lie flat with their feet up, and by main force lifted the chain until it lay along the rail.

"Steady, there!" bawls Spring. "Now—hold it, so, till I give the word."

I don't bilk at much: I watched them blowing sepoys from the ends of guns at Cawnpore with a keen interest, and I ate my dinner at Peking an hour after the massacre, but I confess that Spring's method of disposing of incriminating evidence made me gulp. The wenches screamed and writhed in terror; once that chain was pushed over they would be hurtled across the rail by its weight, and in the sea they would sink like stones. And then, if the *Balliol College* was taken—well, what slaves do you mean, captain? I'd heard of it being done,[30] and I remembered Sullivan's story of the Dago who set his ship on fire. But for all Spring's confidence, I couldn't believe it would wash; the Yankee brig must have half a dozen glasses trained on us; they could swear to murder done and seen to be done, and then it was the gallows for certain.

Funk-stricken though I was, I could think at least. Spring obviously hoped he could fight the Yankee off, and save his liberty and his slaves at the same time; he'd only push 'em over in the last extremity. I was sure Sullivan was right; we couldn't hope to fight the brig. Somehow that madman had to be stopped, or he'd have all our heads in the noose.

If there's one thing that will make my limbs work in a crisis, it is the thought of self-preservation. I'd no notion of what I intended, but I found myself, unheeded in the excitement, walking across to the chest of arms that had been broken out by the main mast. Two of the hands were loading and priming pistols and passing them out; I took a couple, one a double-barrelled piece, and thrust them into my belt. Then, seeing all eyes were fixed either on the pursuing brig or the line of squealing unfortunates

615

shackled by the rail, I dropped down the main hatch on to the slave deck.

I still didn't know what I was going to do; I remember thinking, as I stood there in an agony of uncertainty, this is what comes of dabbling in politics and playing vingt-et-un with spinsters. I had some frenzied notion of making my way aft through the main bulkhead door, which was open now that the slave-deck was in a wholesome condition, finding Mrs Spring in the main cabin, and appealing to her; I knew it was a lunatic thought, but I found myself scampering through anyway, pulling up by the after companion, swithering this way and that, cursing feebly to myself and racking my brains over what to do next.

Spring's bellowing almost directly overhead had me jumping in alarm; squinting up the companion I could just see his head and shoulders, facing away from me, as he stood at the wheel. He was roaring to the gun crews, urging them to their stations, and by the sound of his voice he was having his work cut out. Like Sullivan, they were ready to strike, and then I heard the mate's voice, shouting at Spring, and suddenly cut off by the crack of a pistol shot.

"Take that, d - - n you!" shouts Spring. "Stand away from him, you there! Get to those tackles, or by G - d you'll get the next round!" His hand came into view, holding a smoking pistol, and thinks I, if he's daft enough to turn a gun on Sullivan there's no stopping him except by the same way.

That was it, of course, as I'd known all along. Here was I, armed, and there was the back of his head not fifteen feet away. And, by G - d, if ever a man needed a bullet in the skull it was J. C. Spring, Fellow of Oriel. But I daren't do it—oh, it wasn't that I shrank from the dirty deed for Christian reasons; I'd killed before, and anyone who stands between me and safety gets whatever I can give him, no holds barred. But only if it's safe—and this wasn't. Suppose I missed? Something told me that Spring wouldn't. Suppose the crew raised objections? Well, if they didn't the Yankee Navy would—they'd be just the kind of idiots to consider it murder. One way and another, I couldn't risk it, and I stood there sweating in panic, torn between my terrors.

Suddenly there was a patter of feet from the main bulkhead,

and here came the idiot Looney, trying to buckle on a cutlass as big as himself. And to my amazement he was grinning foolishly to himself as he hurried towards the companion.

"What the blazes are you doing?" cries I.

"I'm goin' to kill them b-----ds!" cries he. "Them's is firin' on us!"

"You numskull!" And then suddenly a great light dawned, and I saw the safe way out. "You don't want to kill them! It's the captain that's doing this! That d---l Spring, up there!"

I pointed to the companion way, down which our skipper's dulcet voice could be clearly heard. "He's your man, Looney! He's the man to kill!"

He stood gaping at me. "Whaffor?" says he, bewildered.

"He's just killed Mr Sullivan!" I hissed at him. "He's gone mad! He's killed Sullivan, your friend!" And some guardian angel prompted my next words. "He's going to kill you next! I heard him say so! 'I'm going to settle that b-----d Looney'; that's what he said!"

The loose idiot face just stared for a moment, while I shook his arm; from far astern came the boom of a gun, and from overhead there was a crash of breaking timber and shouts and running feet.

"It's *him* they're trying to kill! Not you! Not me! He's the Devil, remember! He just killed Sullivan! He'll kill you—and all of us"

Suddenly his face changed; I'll swear a light of understanding came into his eyes, and to my consternation he began to weep. He stared at me, choking:

"'E killed Mr Sullivan? 'E done that?"

By gum, I know a cue when I hear one. "Shot him like a dog, Looney. In the back."

He gave a little whimper of rage. "'E shouldn't 'ave! Why 'e done that?"

"Because. he's the Devil—you know that!" I've done some fearful convincing in my time, but this topped everything. "That's why the Yankees are shooting at us! You've got to kill him, Looney, or we're all done for! If you don't, he'll kill you! He hates you—remember how he flogged you, for nothing! You've got to kill him, Looney—quickly!"

I was thrusting a pistol at him as though it had been red hot, and suddenly he grabbed it out of my hand, just as our own stern-chasers thundered overhead in reply. His face contorted with rage—wonderful, beatific sight—and he plunged past me to the ladder.

"'E killed Mr Sullivan! The b - - - - - d! I'll do for 'im!"

It was splendid. Thank God he was an idiot, and hated Spring like poison. I reckon it had taken me all of sixty seconds to turn him to murder, which was a considerable feat of persuasion; now all I had to do was make sure he didn't flinch from the act.

"Up you go, Looney! Good lad! It's him or you! Quick, man quick!" I thrust at his backside as he swung on to the ladder. "Jam it into his back and give him both barrels! He killed Sullivan! He's the Devil! Sick 'im, boy!"

I probably could have spared my breath; the thought of Sullivan —the only person Looney cared for—dead at Spring's hand, had probably completed the turning of that idiot brain. He fairly flung himself up the ladder, scrambled half-way through the hatch, mouthing hideous oaths; he thrust out the pistol, and with an incoherent scream let fly with both barrels together.

Before the echo of the shots had died I was tearing down to the main bulkhead, and up the main hatch. As my head came clear I looked aft; Spring was writhing on the deck beside the wheel, his hat gone, his hands beating at the planks. Looney was struggling in the grip of one of the hands, yelling that he'd killed the Devil. Sullivan was sprawled face down in the scuppers, and the after rail was a milling scene of men running every which way, while another shot from the brig's bow-chasers came whistling overhead to tear through the mainsail. She was close up now, and turning to port to show her starboard guns, like grinning teeth; there was a yell of alarm from the men aft, and then hands were hauling at the flag lanyard; with Spring gone, everyone knew what had to be done.

I was not backward, either. I strode over to the men at the rail who were still gripping the chain, and in my parade ground voice ordered them to bring it inboard, smartly. They obeyed without a second's pause, and when I ordered them to free the slaves' ankle-irons they did that, too, falling over each other in their hurry.

I lent a hand myself, patting the yellow sluts on the shoulder and assuring them that all was well now, and that I would see they came to no harm. I trusted this would go a little way to ensuring that I came to no harm myself, and as the Yankee brig ran up on our port beam I began to rehearse in my mind the scheme I had formed for getting old Flash safely out from under this time.

·By and large I'm partial to Americans. They make a great affectation of disliking the English and asserting their equality with us, but I've discovered that underneath they dearly love a lord, and if you're civil and cool and don't play it with too high a hand you can impose on them quite easily. I'm not a lord, of course, but I've got the airs when I want 'em, and know how to use them in moderation. That's the secret, a nice blending of the plain, polite gentleman with just a hint of Norman blood, and they'll eat out of your hand and boast to their friends in Philadelphia that they know a man who's on terms with Queen Victoria and yet, by gosh, is as nice a fellow as they've ever struck.

When they came aboard the *Balliol College*, raging angry and full of zeal, I bided my time while they herded us all forward, and didn't say a word until the young lieutenant commanding them had ordered us all under hatches. They were pushing us to the companion, and being none to gentle about it, when I stepped smartly out of the line and said to him, very rapidly and civilly, that I wanted to see his commander on a most urgent matter.

He stared down his Yankee nose at me and snaps: "Goddam your impudence. You'll do your talking in New Orleans—much good may it do you. Now, git below!"

I gave him a cool stare. "Believe me, sir," says I, in my best Cherrypicker voice, "I am in most solemn earnest. Please—do nothing untoward." I tilted my head slightly towards the *Balliol College* hands who were being pushed below. "These people must not know," I said quietly, "but I am a British naval officer. I must see your commander without delay."

He stared at me, but he was sharp. He waited till our last man was down the companion, and then demanded an explanation. I told him I was Lieutenant Comber, Royal Navy, on special service from the Board of Admiralty—which, I assured him, I could prove with ease. That settled it, and when one of his men had collected my traps from below, I was hustled off under guard, the Yankee officer still eyeing me suspiciously. But he had other things to think about—there was Spring, shot through the back and unconscious, being taken down on a stretcher; Mrs Spring was under guard in the cabin; there were three corpses on our deck, including Sullivan's; Looney was below with the other prisoners, raving in a voice you could have heard in Aldershot; there was blood and wreckage on the deck, and a dozen weeping nigger girls huddled by the rail. I made the most of them, drawing the lieutenant's attention to them and saying:

"Take care of those poor people. They must suffer no more than they have done. Miserable souls, they have come through hell today."

I left him not knowing what to think, and allowed myself to be conducted aboard the U.S.S. *Cormorant* by my Leatherneck escort. And there it was plain sailing all the way, as I knew it must be. Captain Abraham Fairbrother, a very spry young gentleman, didn't believe a word I said, at first, but once I had slit open my belt and laid Comber's papers before his bulging eyes he hadn't a leg to stand on. It was all so impressively official, and my own bearing and manner, although I say it myself, were so overwhelming, that the poor soul took it all in like a hungry fish. Why shouldn't he? I would have done.

Of course I had to tell him a tremendous tale, but that sort of thing has never presented me with difficulty, and barring the fact that I wasn't Comber, the whole thing was gospel true, which always makes lying easier. He shook his fair young head in amazement, and vowed that it beat everything he had ever heard; he was full of venom against slavers, I discovered, and so naturally he was all admiration for me, and shook my hand as though it was a pump handle.

"I feel it an honour to welcome you aboard, sir," says he. "I had no notion that such a thing ... that such people as yourself, sir, were engaged in this work. By George, it's wonderful! My congratulations, sir!" And believe it or not, he actually saluted.

Well, I fancy I can carry off this sort of situation pretty well, you know. Modest and manly, that's Flashy when the compliments are flying, with a touch of a frown to show that my mind is really on serious matters. Which it was, because I knew I hadn't got farther than the first fence so far, and would have to tread delicately. But Captain Fairbrother was all eager assistance: what could he do to serve me? I confess I may have given him the impression that the entire slave trade could expect its coup de grace when once I'd laid my report before the British and American governments, and he was itching to help oil the wheels.

Have you noticed, once you have succeeded in convincing a man of something incredible, he believes it with an enthusiasm that he wouldn't dream of showing for an obvious, simple fact? It had been like that with Looney; now it was so with Fairbrother. He simply was all over me; I just had to sit back and let him arrange matters. First, I must be delivered to Washington with all speed; the bigwigs would be in a positive lather to see me —I doubted that, myself, but didn't say so. Nothing would do but he must carry me to Baltimore in his own brig, while the sloop could take the *Balliol College* into New Orleans with a prize crew —there, observes Mr Fairbrother darkly, the miscreants would meet with condign punishment for slavery, piracy, and attempted murder. Of course, I would give evidence eventually, but that could wait until Washington had been thrown into transports by my advent there.

Washington, I could see, was going to present problems; they wouldn't be as easy to satisfy as Captain Fairbrother, who was your genuine Northern nigger-lover and violently prejudiced in my favour. He was one of these direct, virtuous souls, bursting with decency, whose very thought was written plainly on his fresh, handsome face. Arnold would have loved him—and young Chard could have used a few of him at Rorke's Drift, too. Brainless as a bat, of course, and just the man for my present needs.

I impressed on him the need for not letting any of the *Balliol College* crew know what I truly was, and hinted at dangerous secret work yet to come which might be prejudiced if my identity leaked out. (That was no lie, either.) He agreed solemnly to this, but thought it would be an excellent plan to take some of the freed slaves to Washington, just for effect; "tangible evidence, sir, of your noble and heroic endeavours in the great crusade against this vile traffic". I didn't object, and so about six yellows and

Lady Caroline Lamb were herded aboard and bedded down somewhere in the bowels of the brig. Fairbrother wondered about Mrs Spring, whose presence on the *College* shocked and amazed him; they had caught her hurling Spring's log, papers, and accounts out of the cabin window, whereby much valuable evidence had been lost (that's all you know, I thought). Still, she was a woman. . . .

"Take her to New Orleans, is my advice," says I. "There are not two more diabolical creatures afloat than she and her fiend of a husband. How is he, by the way?"

"In a coma," says Fairbrother. "One of his own pirates shot him through the back, sir—what creatures they are, to be sure! He will live, I dare say—which is no great matter, since the New Orleans hangman will, if the fellow survives, have the duty of breaking his neck for him."

Oh, the holy satisfaction of the godly—when it comes to delight in cruelty I'm just a child compared to them. His next remark didn't surprise me, either.

"But I am inconsiderate, Mr Comber—here have I been keeping you in talk over these matters, when your most urgent desire has surely been for a moment's privacy in which you might deliver up thanks to a merciful Heavenly Father for your delivery from all the dangers and tribulations you have undergone. Your pardon, sir."

My urgent need was in fact for an enormous brandy and a square meal, but I answered him with my wistful smile.

"I need hardly tell you, sir, that in my heart I have rendered that thanks already, not only for myself but for those poor souls whom your splendid action had liberated. Indeed," says I, looking sadly reflective, "there is hardly a moment in these past few months that I have not spent in prayer."

He gripped my hand again, looking moist, and then, thank God, he remembered at last that I had a belly, and gave orders for food and a glass of spirits while he went off, excusing himself, to splice the binnacle or clew up the heads, I shouldn't wonder.

Well, thinks I, so far so good, but we mustn't go too far. The sooner I could slip out of sight, the better, for while the *Balliol College* crew were alive and kicking there was always the risk that I would be given away. I didn't want to get the length of the British Embassy in Washington, for someone there might just know me, or worse still, they might know Comber. But for the moment, with the brig heading east by north, and the *Balliol College* making north under guard to Orleans, it was all sunshine for Harry—provided I didn't trip myself up. I was meant to be Navy, and Fairbrother and his officers were Navy also, so I must watch my tongue.

As it turned out, by playing the reserved Briton and steering the conversation as often as possible to India, about which they were curious, I passed the thing off very well. I had to talk some slavery, of course, and there was a nasty moment when I was almost drawn into a description of our encounter with the British sloop off Dahomey, but I managed to wriggle clear. It would have been easier, I think, with Englishmen, for Yankee bluebacks are deuced serious fellows, more concerned with their d----d ratlines and bobstays than with interesting topics like drink, women and cash. But I was very pious and priggish that voyage, and they seemed to respect me for it.

However, there was a human side, I discovered, even to the worthy Bible-thumping Fairbrother. I had made a great thing, the second day, of visiting the freed slaves and giving them some fatherly comfort—husbandly comfort would have been more like it, but with those sharp Yankee eyes on me I daren't even squeeze a rump. Lady Caroline Lamb was there, eyeing me soulfully, but I patted her head sternly and told her to be a good girl. What she made of this I can only guess, but that evening, when I was settling down in the berth I had been allotted aft, I was startled by a rapping on my door. It was Fairbrother, in some consternation.

"Mr Comber," says he, "there's one of those black women in my berth!"

"Indeed?" says I, looking suitably startled.

"My G-d, Mr Comber!" cries he. "She's in there, now—and she's stark naked!"

I pondered this; it occurred to me that Lady Caroline Lamb, following her *Balliol College* training, had made her way aft and got into Fairbrother's cabin—which lay in the same place as my berth had done on the slaver. And being the kind of gently-reared fool that he was, Fairbrother was in a fine stew. He'd probably never seen a female form in his life.

"What shall I do?" says he. "What can she want? I spoke to her—she's the big, very black one—but she has hardly any English, and she just stays there! She's kneeling beside my cot, sir!"

"Have you tried praying with her?" says I.

He goggled at me. "Pray? Why, I...I don't know. She looks as though..." He broke off, going beetroot red. "My G-d! Do you suppose that slaver captain has been...using her as...as a *woman?*"

Humanity never ceases to amaze me. Here was this fine lad, old enough to vote, in command of a hundred men and a fighting ship which he could handle like a young Nelson, brave as a bull, I don't doubt—and quivering like a virgin's fan because a buxom tart had invaded his cabin. It's this New England upbringing, of course; even a young manhood spent in naval service hadn't obliterated the effect of all those sermons.

"Do you suppose she has been...degraded?" says he, in a hushed voice.

"I fear it is more than likely, Captain Fairbrother," says I. "There is no depth unplumbed by their depravity. This unfortunate young woman may well have been trained to concubinage."

He shuddered. "Monstrous...terrible. But what am I to do?"

"I find it difficult to know what to advise," says I. "The situation is...unique in my experience. Perhaps you should tell her to go back to the quarters she has been allotted."

"Yes, yes, of course. I must do that." He hesitated, pulling at his lip. "It is frightful to think of these ignorant young creatures being...misled...in that way."

"We must do what we can for them," says I.

"Indeed, indeed." He cleared his throat nervously. "I must apologise, Mr Comber, for disturbing you...I was startled, I confess...totally unexpected thing...yes. However, I shall do as you advise. My apologies again, sir. Thank you...er, and good night."

He fairly fled into his cabin, that good pious lad, and I listened in vain thereafter for the sound of his door re-opening. Not that I expected it. Next day he avoided my eye, and went red whenever the slaves were mentioned. He probably still does, but I'll wager his conscience has never been quite strong enough to make him regret his lost innocence.

We made capital speed to Baltimore, which is just another port at the far end of the uninviting Chesapeake Bay, and from there, after Fairbrother had reported to his commodore, and the importance of my presence had been duly emphasised, we were taken by train to Washington, about forty miles off. I was getting fairly apprehensive by now, and looking sharp for a chance to make myself scarce—although what I would do then, in a strange country without any means of support, I couldn't imagine. I knew the longer I kept up my imposture, the more chance there was of being detected, but what could I do? Fairbrother, who had wangled leave from his commander to be my personal convoy to the capital, stuck like a leech; he was looking for a share of the glory, of course. So I just had to sit back and see what came—at worst, I decided, I could make a bolt for it, but in the meantime I would carry the thing through with a wide eye and a bold bluff front.

Washington is an odd place. You could see the Jonathans had designed it with an eye to the future, when they envisaged it as the finest city in the world, and even then, in '48, there were signs of building on every hand, with scaffolding about even in the middle of the city, and the outer roads all churned mud with the autumn rain, but fringed with fine houses half-completed. I got to know it well in the Civil War time, but I never liked it—sticky as Calcutta or Madras in summer, and yet its people dressed as though they'd been in New York or London. I could always smell fever in the air there, and why George Washington ever chose the site beats me. But that's your rich colonial Englishman all over—never thinks twice about other people's convenience.

But sticky or not, the officials who lived there were d----d sharp men, as I discovered. Fairbrother delivered me at the Department of the Navy, where a white-whiskered admiral heard my tale and d----d his stars at every turn; then he handed me on to a section much like our Board of Trade, where several hard-faced civilians took up the running and I went through the thing again. They didn't seem to know what to make of me at all, at first, or what precisely they ought to do; finally, one of them, a fat little fellow called Moultrie, asked me exactly what could I contribute to the anti-slave trade campaign apart from giving evidence against the crew of the *Balliol College*? In other words, what was so remarkable about me that Washington was being troubled with me at all? Where was the important report that had been talked about by Captain Fairbrother?

Since it didn't exist, I had to invent it. I explained that I had gathered an immense amount of detail not only about the slave-traders, but about those in Britain and America who were behind them, supplying them with funds and ships, and organising their abominable activities under the cover of legitimate commerce. All this, I explained, I had committed to paper as opportunity arose, with such documents as I had been able to obtain, and I had ear-marked useful witnesses along the way. I had consigned one report to a reliable agent at Whydah, and another to a second agent at Roatan—no, I dare not disclose their names except to my own chiefs in London. A third report I would certainly write out as soon as I could—a rueful smile here, and a reminder that life for me had been fairly busy of late.

"Yes, yes, sir," says he, "this is excellent, and very well, in its way. Your prudence about the disposal of your earlier reports is commendable. But from what you say you are obviously in possession of information which must be of the first importance to the United States Government—information which Her Majesty's ministers would obviously communicate to us. You have names, you say, of Americans who are behind the slave trade—who, at least, are involved in it at a safe remove from slaving operations. Now, sir, here we have the root of the thing—these are the men we must bring to book. Who are those men?"

I took a deep breath, and tried to look like a man in mental struggle, while he and his two fellow-inquisitors waited, and the secretary sat with his pen poised.

"Mr Moultrie," says I, "I can't tell you. Please, sir—let me explain." I solemnly checked his outburst. "I have many names

—both in my mind and in my reports. I don't know much about American public affairs, sir, but even I recognise some of them as —well, not insignificant names. Now if I were to name them to you—now—what would they be but names? The mass of evidence that would—that will—lead to their proven involvement in the traffic in black souls, is already on its way to England, as I trust. Obviously it will be communicated to you, and these people can be proceeded against. But if I were to name names now, sir" —I stabbed a finger on the table—"you could do nothing; you would have to wait on the evidence which has been assembled. And while I trust your discretion perfectly, gentlemen—it would be an impertinence to do otherwise—we all know how a word once spoken takes wings. Premature disclosure, and consequent warning, might enable some of these birds to escape the net. And believe me, gentlemen . . ." I gritted my teeth and forced moisture into my eyes " . . . believe me, I have not gone through the hell of those Dahomey raids, and watched the torture of those poor black creatures on the Middle Passage—I have not risked death and worse—in order to see those butchers escape!"

Well, it wasn't a bad performance, and it took them pretty well aback. Moultrie looked d----d solemn, and his pals wore the alarmed expression of men in the presence of a portent they didn't understand. Then Moultrie says:

"Yes . . . I see. You are in no doubt, sir . . . of the consequence . . . that is, the importance, of some of those implicated? Do you suggest that . . . when all is known . . . there would be a, er, a political scandal, perhaps?"

I gave my mirthless laugh. "I may indicate that best, sir, by assuring you that among the Britons whom I know to be involved in the traffic—and whose complicity can be proved, sir—are two peers of the realm and one whose name was, until lately, to be found among Her Majesty's Ministers. And I believe, sir, that the American names include men of comparable stature. The profits of the slave trade, sir, are immense enough to tempt the highest. Judge whether a scandal may be expected."

He was regarding me round-eyed. "Mr Comber," says he, "your knowledge makes you a very dangerous young man."

"And therefore," says I, smiling keenly, "you would say—a

very endangered young man? I am used to risk, sir. It is my trade."

I was almost believing it myself by now, so I wasn't surprised that they took it in. So much so, that being Yankees, and no fools, they made me go through my whole yarn again—from the Channel to Whydah, Gezo's village, our escape, the voyage west, Roatan, and all the rest—in the hope of my slipping out some information unawares. But since I didn't have any they were wasting their time. Finally they conferred while I cooled my heels, and announced that they would discuss matters with the British Ambassador, and in the meantime I would hold myself ready to go to New Orleans to testify against the *Balliol College*.

I didn't fancy this, at all, but again there was nothing to be done at the moment. So I bowed, and later that day I was hailed to the Ambassador's house—a very decent old stick, and a pleasant change from those yapping Jonathan voices. I was a shade wary in case he, or any of his people, might by a chance in a thousand be acquainted with the real Comber, but all was well. I told my story for a fourth time, and that evening, when he bade me to dinner with him, I went through it yet again for the entertainment of his guests. And I'll swear I didn't put a foot wrong—but there was one man at that table with as keen a nose for a faker as I have myself. How or when he saw through me I shall never understand, but he did, and gave me one of the many nasty moments in my life.

There were about a dozen at the dinner, and I didn't even notice him until the ladies had withdrawn, and Charterfield, our host, had invited me to regale the gentlemen with my adventures on the Slave Coast. But he seemed to take an even closer interest in my story than the others. He was an unusually tall man, with the ugliest face you ever saw, deep dark eye sockets and a chin like a coffin, and a black cow's lick of hair smeared across his forehead. When he spoke it was with the slow, deliberate drawl of the American back-countryman, which was explained by the fact that he was new to the capital; in fact, he was a very junior Congressman, invited at the last moment because he had some anti-slavery bill in preparation, and so would be interested in meeting me. His name will be familiar to you: Mr Lincoln.[31]

Let me say at once that in spite of all the trouble he caused me at various times, and the slight differences which may be detectable in our characters, I liked Abe Lincoln from the moment I first noticed him, leaning back in his chair with that hidden smile at the back of his eyes, gently cracking his knuckles. Just why I liked him I can't say; I suppose in his way he had the makings of as big a scoundrel as I am myself, but his appetites were different, and his talents infinitely greater. I can't think of him as a *good* man, yet as history measures these things I suppose he *did* great good. Not that that excites my admiration unduly, nor do I put my liking down to the fact that he had a sardonic humour akin to my own. I think I liked him because, for some reason which God alone knows, he liked me. And not many men who knew me as well as he did, have done that.

I remember only a few of his observations round that table. Once, when I was describing our fight with the Amazons, one of the company exclaimed:

"You mean to say the women fight and torture and slay on behalf of their menfolk? There can be no other country in the world where this happens."

And Lincoln, very droll, inquires of him: "Have you attended many political tea parties in Washington lately, sir?"

They all laughed, and the fellow replied that even in Washington society he hadn't seen anything quite to match what I had described.

"Be patient, sir," says Lincoln. "We're a young country, after all. Doubtless in time we will achieve a civilisation comparable with that of Day-homey."

I spoke about Spring, and Charterfield expressed amazement and disgust that a man of such obvious parts should be so great a villain.

"Well, now," says Lincoln, "why not? Some of the greatest villains in history have been educated men. Without that education they might have been honest citizens. A few years at college won't make a bad man virtuous; it will merely put the polish on his wickedness."

"Oh, come, now," says Charterfield, "that may be true, but you must admit that virtue more often goes hand in hand with learning than with ignorance. You know very well that a nation's criminal class is invariably composed of those who lack the benefits of education."

"And being uneducated, they get caught," says Lincoln. "Your learned rascal usually goes undetected."

"Why, at this rate, you will equate learning with evildoing," cries someone. "What must your view be of our leading justices and politicians? Are they not virtuous men?"

"Oh, virtuous enough," says Lincoln. "But what they would be like if they had been educated is another matter."

When I had finished my tale, and had heard much congratulation and expressions of flattering astonishment, it was Lincoln who remarked that it must have been a taxing business to act my part among the slavers for so long. Had I not found it a great burden? I said it had been, but fortunately I was a good dissembler.

"You must be," says he. "And I speak as a politician, who knows how difficult it is to fool people."

"Well," says I, "my own experience is that you can fool some people all the time—and all the people some times. But I concede that it's difficult to fool all the people all the time."

"That is so," says he, and that great grin lit up his ugly face. "Yes, sir, Mr Comber, that is indeed so."

I also carried away from that table an impression of Mr Lincoln's views on slaves and slavery which must seem strange in the twentieth century since it varies somewhat from popular belief. I recall, for example, that at one point he described the negroes as "the most confounded nuisance on this continent, not excepting the Democrats".

"Oh, come," says someone, "that is a little hard. It is not their fault."

"It was not my fault when I caught the chicken pox," says Lincoln, "but I can assure you that while I was infected I was a most unconscionable nuisance—although I believe my family loved me as dearly as ever."

"Come, that's better," laughs the other. "You may call the nigras a nuisance provided you love them, too—that will satisfy even the sternest abolitionist."

"Yes, I believe it would," says Lincoln. "And like so many

satisfactory political statements, it would not be true. I try to love my fellow man, with varying success, the poor slaves among the rest. But the truth is I neither like nor dislike them more than any other creatures. Now your stern abolitionist, because he detests slavery, feels he must love its victims, and so he insists on detecting in them qualities deserving unusual love. But in fact those qualities are not to be found in them, any more than in other people. Your extreme anti-slaver mistakes compassion for love, and this leads him into a kind of nigra-worship which, on a rational examination, is by no means justified."

"Surely the victim of a misfortune as grievous as slavery does deserve special consideration, though."

"Indeed," says Lincoln, "special consideration, special compassion, by all means, just such as I received when I had the chicken pox. But having the chicken pox did not make me a worthier or better person, as some people seem to suppose is the case with victims of slavery. I tell you, sir, to listen to some of our friends, I could believe that every plantation and barracoon from Florida to the river is peopled by the disciples of Jesus. Reason tells me this is false; the slave being God's creature and a human soul, is no better than the rest of us. But if I said as much to Cassius Clay[32] he would try to prove me wrong at the point of his bowie knife."

"You have worked too long on your anti-slavery bill," laughs Charterfield. "You are suffering from a surfeit."

"Why, sir, that is probably so," says Lincoln. "I wish I had ten dollars for every time I have fought a client's case, never doubting its justice and rightness, pursuing it to a successful verdict with all my powers—and finished the trial feeling heartily sick with that same worthy client. I would not confess it outside this room, but you may believe me, gentlemen, there are moments, God forgive me, when I become just a little tired of nigras."

"Your conscience is troubling you," says someone.

"By thunder, there is no lack of people determined to make my conscience trouble me," says Lincoln. "As though I can't tend to my own conscience, they must forever be running pins into it. There was a gentleman the other day, a worthy man, too, and I was ill-advised enough to say to him much what I've said tonight: that nigras, while deserving our uttermost compassion and assistance, were nevertheless, a nuisance. I said they were the rock on which our nation had been splitting for years, and that they could well assume the proportions of a national catastrophe— through no fault of their own, of course. I believe I concluded by wishing the whole parcel of them back in Africa. He was shocked: 'Strange talk, this', says he, 'from the sponsor of a bill against slavery'. 'I'd sponsor a bill to improve bad drains', says I. 'They're a confounded nuisance, too.' A thoughtless remark, no doubt, and a faulty analogy, but I paid for it. 'Good God,' cries he, 'you'll not compare human souls with bad drains, surely.' 'Not invariably,' says I, but I got no further, because he stalked off in a rage, having misunderstood me completely."

"You can hardly blame him," says the other, smiling.

"No," says Lincoln. "He was a man of principle and conscience. His only fault lay in his inability to perceive that I have both commodities also, but I didn't buy mine ready-made from Cincinnati, and I don't permit either to blind me to reality, I hope. And that reality is that the slave question is much too serious a matter for emotion, yet I very much fear that emotion will override reason in its settlement. In the meantime, I pray to God I am wrong, and continue to fight it in my own way, which I believe to be as worthy as polemical journalism and the underground railroad."

After that the talk turned to the great California gold strike that I had first heard of at Roatan, and which was obsessing everyone. The first rumours had spoken of fabulous wealth for the taking; then word had spread that the first reports had been greatly exaggerated, and now it was being said that the first reports had been true enough, and it was the rumours of disappointment that were false. Thousands were already heading west, braving the seas round Cape Horn or the perils of starvation, weather and Indian savages on the overland trails. Most of the men at that dinner agreed that there was obviously gold in quantity along the Pacific streams, but doubted if many of the enthusiastic seekers would find quite as much as they expected.

"You are the cynic, Abraham," says one. "What will the Tennessee wiseacres say of the New El Dorado?"

When the laugh died down, Lincoln shook his head. "If they are real Tennessee wiseacres, Senator, they won't 'say nuthin'.' But what they'll do—if they're *real* wiseacres—is buy themselves up every nail, every barrel-stave, every axe-handle, and every shovel they can lay hold on, put 'em all in a cart with as many barrels of molasses as may be convenient, haul 'em all up to Independence or the Kansas, and *sell* them to the fortunate emigrants at ten times their value. That's how to make gold out of a gold strike."

"Well, you can handle a team, surely?" cries the merry Senator. "Why not make your fortune out of axe-handles?"

"Well, sir, I'll tell you," says Lincoln, and everyone listened, grinning. "I've just put the return on axe-handles at one thousand per centum. But I'm a politician, and sometime lawyer. Axe-handles aren't my style; my stock-in-trade is spoken words. You may believe me, words can be obtained wholesale a powerful sight cheaper'n axe-handles—and if you take 'em to the right market, you'll get a far richer return for 'em than a thousand per centum. If you doubt me—ask President Polk."

They guffawed uproariously at this, and presently we went to join the ladies for the usual ghastly entertainment which, I discovered, differed not one whit from our English variety. There was singing, and reading from the poetic works of Sir Walter Scott, and during this Lincoln drew me aside into a window alcove, very pleasant, and began asking me various questions about my African voyage. He listened very attentively to my replies, and then suddenly said:

"I tell you what—you can enlighten me. A phrase puzzled me the other day—in an English novel, as a matter of fact. You're a naval man—what does it mean: to club-haul a ship?"

For a moments my innards froze, but I don't believe I showed it. This was the kind of thing I had dreaded: a question on nautical knowledge which I, the supposed naval man, couldn't have answered in a thousand years.

"Why," says I, "let's see now—club-hauling. Well, to tell you the truth, Mr Lincoln, it's difficult to explain to a landsman, don't ye know? It involves . . . well, quite complicated manoeuvres, you see . . ."

"Yes," says he, "I thought it might. But in general terms, now ... what happens?"

I laughed, pleasantly perplexed. "If I had you aboard I could easily tell you. Or if we had a ship model, you know ..."

He nodded, smiling at me. "Surely. It's of no consequence. I just have an interest in the sea, Mr Comber, and must be indulging it at the expense of every sailor who is unlucky enough to— lay alongside me, as you'd call it." He laughed. "That's another thing, now, I recall. Forgive my curiosity, but what, precisely, is long-splicing?"

I knew then he was after me, in spite of the pleasant, almost sleepy expression in the dark eyes. His canny yokel style didn't fool me. I gave him back some of his own banter, while my heart began to hammer with alarm.

"It's akin to splicing the mainbrace, Mr Lincoln," says I, "and is a term which anyone who is truly interested in the sea would have found out from a nautical almanac long ago."

He gave a little snorting laugh. "Forgive me. Of course I wasn't really interested—just testing a little theory of mine."

"What theory is that, sir?" asks I, my knees shaking.

"Oh—just that you, Mr Comber—if that is your name— might not be quite so naval as you appear. No, don't alarm yourself. It's no business of mine at all. Blame my legal training, which has turned a harmless enough fellow into a confounded busybody. I've spent too long in court-rooms perhaps, seeking after truth and seldom finding it. Maybe I'm of an unusually suspicious nature, Mr Comber, but I confess I am downright interested when I meet an English Navy man who *doesn't* smother his food with salt, who *doesn't*, out of instinct, tap his bread on the table before he bites it, and who *doesn't* even hesitate before jumping up like a jack-rabbit when his Queen's health is proposed. Just a fraction of a moment's pause would seem more natural in a gentleman who is accustomed to drinking that particular toast sitting down." He grinned with his head on one side. "But all these things are trivial; they amount to nothing—until the ill-mannered busybody also finds out that this same English Navy man *doesn't* know what club-hauling and long-splicing are, either. Even then, I could still be entirely mistaken. I frequently am."

"Sir," says I, trying to sound furious, with my legs on the point of giving way, "I fail to understand you. I am a British officer and, I hope, a gentleman . . ."

"Oh, I don't doubt it," says he, "but even that isn't *conclusive* proof that you're a rascal. You see, Mr Comber, I can't be sure. I just suspect that you're a humbug—but I couldn't for the life of me prove it." He scratched his ear, grinning like a gargoyle. "And anyway, it's just none of my business. I guess the truth is I'm a bit of a humbug myself, and feel a kind of duty to other humbugs. Anyway, I'm certainly not fool enough to pass on my ridiculous observations and suspicions to anyone else. I just thought you might be interested to hear about the salt, and the bread, and so forth," said this amazing fellow. "Shall we go and listen to them laying it off about the Last Minstrel?"

It was touch and go at this point whether I launched myself head first through the open window or not; for a moment it seemed that the wiser course might well be headlong flight. But then I steadied. I cannot impress too strongly on young fellows that the whole secret of the noble art of survival, for a single man, lies in knowing exactly when to make your break for safety. I considered this now, with Lincoln smiling down at me sardonically, and decided it was better to brazen things through than to bolt. He knew I was an impostor, but he could hardly prove it, and for some whimsical reason of his own he seemed to regard the whole thing as a joke. So I gave him my blandest smile, and said: "I confess, sir, that I have no idea what you're talkng about. Let us by all means rejoin the company."

I think it puzzled him, but he said nothing more, and we turned back into the room. I kept a bold front, but I was appalled at being discovered, and the rest of that evening passed in a confused panic for me. I recall that I was dragooned into singing the bass part in a group song—I believe it was "'Tis of a sailor bold, but lately come ashore", which no doubt caused Mr Lincoln some ironic amusement—but beyond that I can remember little except that eventually we all took our leave, and Fairbrother carried me off to quarters at the Navy Department, where I spent a sleepless night wondering how I could get out of this latest fix.

They would send me back to New Orleans, assuming that the

prying bumpkin Lincoln kept his suspicions to himself—which seemed likely—and it was imperative that I should take French leave before there was any risk of my confronting the *Balliol College* crew at their trial. Washington was no place to try to decamp, so that left Baltimore or New Orleans. I favoured the former, but as it turned out there was no opportunity, for when the Navy Department finally finished with me on the following morning, I was sent back with Fairbrother to his brig, and he took me straight aboard. We sailed within a few hours, so there was nothing to do but resign myself to sitting out the voyage, and make plans for escaping when we reached Louisiana. What I would do when I slipped away, I didn't know; if my own mother wit couldn't get me back to England hale and sound, I wasn't the man I thought I was. When you've come safe through an Afghan rising and a German revolution, with all manner of cut-throats on your tail, you regard evasion from the United States as a pretty smooth course, even if they set the traps after you for slave-running and impersonation, as Fairbrother and his superiors eventually would do. I fancied I could manage passably well, if I minded my step—oh, the optimism of youth. If I'd known what lay along the path to England, home and beauty, I'd have surrendered then and there, told Fairbrother the whole truth, and taken my chance in a slavery trial any day. Thank God I've never had the gift of second sight.

The closer we got to New Orleans, the worse my prospects of successful desertion looked, and by the time we dropped anchor at the big bend in the Mississippi River off Customs House levee, I was well in the dumps. Having nothing to unload, you see, except me, the brig stood well out in midstream, so my notion of slipping down a gangplank to the quay was quite out of court. We hove to at night, with the whole splendid panorama of lights twinkling on either bank, the glow of Algiers to port and the French Quarter to starboard, but it was lost on me. Fairbrother was to take me ashore personally in the morning, so my only hope must be to give him the slip when we landed.

I already had a good idea of what my first moves would be when I had won free, so I set about my preparations. First I went through the clothes which I hadn't worn since I first boarded the *Balliol College*, and which had been bundled up in my valise. There was a superb coat by Gregg of Bond Street, in fine plum broadcloth, now foully creased, but I borrowed an iron from the steward, waved away his offers of help, and working secretly in my cabin, soon put it to rights and sponged out the stains it had taken. I had two good pairs of trousers, excellent boots from Todd, a smart grey embroidered waistcoat, several shirts which were beyond redemption, and a fine neckercher of black China silk. That was my wardrobe; the coat and neckercher at least could be counted on for what I had in mind.

My other valuables consisted of a ruby pin and an old-fashioned gold and silver chain with seals which had belonged to my grandfather Paget. They could pawn for a tidy sum, but I hoped this would be unnecessary, as I had a more immediate use for them. For the rest, I had eleven gold sovereigns, which would tide me over the beginning at least.

Having completed my inventory, I packed everything carefully in my valise, and next morning when Fairbrother took me ashore I stood forth in the clothes he had lent me; since I should be staying ashore when he had presented me to the proper authorities it was natural that my valise should go with me in the boat.

We were rowed to the Algiers side by four bluejackets, Fair-brother sweating in full fig, and as we neared the bank my spirits rose. The levee and wharves were positively teeming with people, there was a forest of shipping along the bank, with small craft scudding about everywhere, half-naked negroes toiling at the derricks as cargo was swung ashore, folk bustling about every which way on the jettys, nigger children playing and squealing among the piles, ship's officers and cargo bosses bawling above the hubbub—a tremendous confusion of thousands of busy people, which was just what I wanted.

At need I had been prepared to bolt for it, but I didn't have to. While I was handed ashore at the levee, and one of the men swung up my valise, Fairbrother stopped a moment to give orders to the coxswain. I picked up my baggage, took three steps, and in that moment I was lost in the throng, jostling my way quickly along the wharf. I didn't even hear a shout from the boat; in two minutes I was striding along through the heaps of cargo and cotton bales, and when I glanced back there wasn't a glimpse of Fairbrother and his men to be seen. They would be gaping around, no doubt, swearing at my carelessness at having got lost, and would start a hunt for me, but it would be an hour or so before they began to suspicion that my disappearance wasn't accidental. Then the fun would begin in earnest.

Now, I had considered carefully the possibility of trying to board an outgoing ship immediately, and had dismissed the notion. When Fairbrother and his navy friends eventually decided I had slipped my cable, there would be a tremendous hue and cry, and the first places they would look for me would be on departing ships. I couldn't be sure of finding a vessel that would be out and away before that happened; anyway, I hadn't much passage money. So I had determined to lie low in New Orleans until I could see what was best to be done, and then carefully pick my best passage home, perhaps from another port altogether.

So now, when I had put a quarter of a mile between myself and the spot where the boat touched, I halted on the levee, waited till I spotted a likely-looking craft among the hundreds that were putting in and out along the bank, and asked its rower to carry me over to the north shore. He was a big, grinning nigger with brass rings in his ears who chattered unceasingly in a queer mixture of French and English, and in no time at all he set me down on the levee from which you walked up to the Vieux Carré, the old French Quarter which is the very heart of New Orleans. I paid him in English shillings, which didn't bother him at all; provided it's gold or silver, the Orleanais don't care whose head is on it.

There is no city quite like New Orleans ("Awlins" as its inhabitants called it then; outsiders called it "Nawlins"). I loved it at first sight, and I believe that setting aside London, which is my home, and Calcutta, which has a magic that I cannot hope to explain, I still think more kindly of it than of any other place on earth. It was busy and gay and bawdy and full of music and drink and pleasure; nowhere else did eyes sparkle so bright, voices sound so happy, colours look so vivid, food taste so rich, or the very air throb with so much excitement. In the unlikely event that there is a heaven for scoundrels like me, it will be built on the model of the Vieux Carré, with its smiling women, brilliant clothes, and atmosphere of easy indulgence. The architecture is also very fine, spires and gracious buildings and what not, with plenty of shade and places to lounge and sit about while you watch the ivory girls sauntering by in their gorgeous dresses. Indeed, it was sometimes not unlike a kind of tropical Paris, but without those bloody Frogs. New Orleans, of course, is where they civilised the French.

The first thing I did was to find a barber, and let him remove the fine black beard which I had sprouted in the past two or three months. I kept my whiskers, of course—where would Flash be without his tart-catchers?—but had my hair trimmed fairly short to suit the role I intended to play. Then I passed on to a good tailor, and laid out most of my cash on a new finely-frilled shirt, in the Southern style, a silver-topped cane, and a curly-brimmed white stove-pipe hat.

Finally, I sought out a printer, in one of the back streets, spun him a tale, and placed an order for a gross of cards in the name of Count Rudi von Starnberg, which was my new identity. It warmed me to think of how Rudi would have delighted in this, evil throat-cutting b - - - - - d that he was. I had the printer, who was all eagerness to oblige such a distinguished gentleman, run me off half a dozen of the cards then and there for immediate use, and promising to send round for the remainder next day, when they would be ready, bade him good morning. I had no intention of collecting them, of course, and doubtless they are still there. It occurred to me that if Rudi ever visited America he might find himself billed for them, which would have been most satisfactory.

Now I was ready to face the United States in all my glory—an immaculately dressed Austrian nobleman, speaking French and English with the accent of Vienna, and as different as you could wish from some English scoundrel calling himself Comber who had vanished, bearded and nautically attired, some hours before. True, I had little cash and no place of abode, but you would never have imagined that from a glance at the splendid gentleman who now strolled at ease through the Vieux Carré, stopping to refresh himself with wine and water at one of the wayside cafés, glancing over a newspaper, and generally spying out the land. I spent a few hours getting the sense of the place, dined extremely well at a Creole eating place where they had the good sense not to smother everying in garlic, and then went to work.

What I did, in my quest for quarters for the night, was to test a theory suggested to me years before by old Avitabile, the Italian soldier of fortune who had been governor of Peshawar. "When you're like-a light in the pocket, boy, in a strange town, you got to find a whore-house, see, an' wheedle-wheedle your way roun' the madame, you know? Do I got to tell you? No, sir. Your shoulders an' moustaches—jus' like-a mine—it's like-a fall under a log. You charm, you talk, you tell any goddam lies—but you get that madame into bed, boom-boom-boom—why, she's glad to lodge you for a week, ne' mind for a night! Didn't Avitabile travel clear from Lisbon to Paris, an' I didn't pay onc night's lodging, not-a one, you bet. Goddam it, does a gentleman got to stay in hotels?"

Well, if he could do it, so could I, and towards evening I set out to find a likely bawdy house. This, in New Orleans, was child's play; there may have been establishments in the Vieux Carré which were not bordellos, but precious few. All I had to do was find one with a susceptible·madame, and take my ease for a few days.

It took me all evening, and four false starts. What I did in each case was to select a good-class house, send my card up to the proprietress by the nigger porter, and then address myself to the arch-harpy herself. I had a story all ready, and even now I must say it sounds not half bad. I explained that I was an Austrian gentleman in search of his sister, who had eloped with a profligate Englishman and been abandoned by him during a visit to the United States. Since then we had heard nothing of her, except an unconfirmed report that she had somehow found her way into . . . into, er, an establishment such as madame was conducting. We were beside ourselves with grief and horror, and here was I, the son of the family, on a tragic quest to find the erring creature and bring her back to the bosom of her distracted but unforgiving parents. Her name was Charlotte, she was a mere eighteen, blonde and of exquisite beauty . . . could madame render me any assistance in tracing her? Money, of course, was of no object, if only I could rescue my dear wilful sister from the dreadful plight into which she had fallen.

This, of course, was purely introductory, to let me sum up the madame and see if she was likely game. The first four weren't —beaky, sharp-eyed old harridans whom I wouldn't have galloped for a pension, anyway. But they swallowed the story—no doubt it sounded well, coming from six-foot Harry with his curly whiskers and melancholy brown eyes, to say nothing of his well-cut clobber and light cavalry airs. Three of them even went the length of making fruitless inquiries among their staffs; the fourth, I'm afraid, didn't fully understand me—she said she had never heard of my sister, but she would undertake to procure her for me for seventy-five dollars. As with the others, I bade her a courtly good-night, thanked her profusely, and withdrew.

At the fifth knocking-shop, I struck pure gold. It was a splendid establishment, all plush and crystal, with a nigger band playing wild music, and in the saloons off the main hall the finest of trollops on view, willowy creatures of every colour from cream to jet black, with beautiful gowns cut away so that their breasts were bare, and strutting like duchesses. It was plain to see that outside New Orleans, fornication was still in its infancy.

However, I had no time for these distractions. My business was with the madame, and as soon as I was ushered upstairs into her private apartment, I knew I was home. She was nearing fifty, a stately buxom piece who must have been a rare beauty and was still handsome, running to fat but well laced up in a green velvet gown which looked as though it must burst asunder at any moment. She was painted and powdered and jewelled like a May Day cuddy, with an ostrich plume in her red-dyed hair, and a big peacock fan which she used to disclose her fine bust and shoulders; it was this, and the quizzy gleam in her eye as she sized me up and down, that convinced me I need look no farther. Here was one who fancied Flashy, no error. The fact that she appeared to have been at the bottle already that evening may have helped; she swayed a mite too much as she walked, even for a retired strumpet. She was all affability—and to my astonishment, when she invited me to take a seat and state my requirements, her voice was purest Bow Bells. "Honnered to 'ave a gentleman of the nobility calling at hower little hestablish'nt," says she, simpering and pressing my hand warmly. "'Ow may we be of service, pray?" Well, thinks I, if I can't charm this one flat on her back, I've lost my way with women.

It took me exactly three-quarters of an hour by her fine grandfather clock, which I thought quite smart work on first acquaintance. Ten minutes disposed of my mythical sister, of whom my plump hostess had naturally never heard, although she expressed touching dismay ("Why, the wicked villain!" and "Ow, yore pore mama!"). Another ten were spent in idle gossip, after which she suggested some refreshment, and I sipped a very reasonable Moselle while she fluttered her eyelids and shoved her tits at me. After half an hour we were quite intimate, and I was murmuring in her ear and tweaking her bottom while she giggled and called me a great sauce; with forty minutes gone I was unbuttoning her dress at the back—I have uncanny skill at this —and in a trice I had her standing in her corset. Before she could

643

turn round I had impaled her, and was subsiding into a chair with her on my lap. She gave one protesting squeal of "Oh, Lor'", and then lay back against me—God, what a weight she was! I thought my thigh-bones would crack, but I bulled away for all I was worth, and the baggage revelled in it, plunging and writhing until I thought we must go over, chair and all. The clock chimed the three-quarters, I remember, just as we finished.

This broke the ice splendidly, of course, and to cut a longish and damned tiring story short, I didn't spend only the night at Mrs Susie Willinck's establishment, but the best part of a week. Avitabile was absolutely right, you see; if you manage to get round a madame, you're made. But I must say in honesty that I doubt if many madames are as susceptible as Susie was. She proved to be one of those rare creatures who are even jollier and nicer —and randier—than they look, give her a man who was handsome and impudent and made her laugh and was a good mount, and she would do anything for him—so it followed naturally that she took to me from the start. Of course, the fact that I was English helped —she found that out smartly enough, on the first night, the shrewd old strumpet, but instead of being furious at the way I'd imposed on her, she just shook with laughter and called me a bonny young rascal and hauled me on to the sofa again. I had to tell her my name was Comber, and that I was on the run from the American Navy—which was true, in its way, although she naturally took it that I was a deserter. She didn't care; I was something new, and a lusty rogue, and that was enough for her.

Mind you, I earned my keep. I've always been able to keep pace with most women, but this one, when roused, was like a succubus gone berserk. She had a knack of getting astride of me, pinning me down with her weight, and going to work in her own way; it was fearful, for the randy trollop would tease and plague me for close on an hour, until I was nearly bursting, and by the time she was done I would be ecstatically ruined, and certain sure I'd never be able to present arms again. On the other hand, she could be as soft as mush, and cry over me afterwards, which was rather disturbing. At first I put it down to her fondness for port, but in fact it was just that she was a genuinely sentimental soul—where lively young men were concerned, anyway.

Mind you, I wasn't complaining, either way; I realised I was uncommon lucky to have found just the billet I was looking for, and I'll say this for Susie, although she was like a wild beast in bed, she was damned good to me during my stay with her. I soon recognised that it wasn't just that she was unusually partial to Adam's arsenal; she was one of these large-hearted females who can't go to bed with a man without conceiving an affection for him, and wanting to cherish and own him, even. She was as soft in that way as any woman I can remember, which was remarkable, for she knew men, and was far too worldly-wise to have any illusions about me. She must have seen I was a wrong 'un from the minute she laid eyes on me, and especially when she realised I was only romping her for the sake of a few nights' lodging. But although she knew I was the kind of heartless scoundrel who would use her shamelessly and then slide out when it suited me, she couldn't help liking me, apparently. She knew after the first couple of days that she was growing too fond of me, and it frightened her, so that she wished me away at the same time as she wanted me to stay.

This ain't Flashy's vanity, by the way; she admitted it herself, when I'd been there about four days and spoke about moving on.

"I orter be thankful," says she. "You're as big a villain as the rest—worse, prob'ly. I know you'll just break my heart in the end, if you stay."

Thinking back to the previous night, it struck me that whatever was in danger of breaking belonged to me, and it wasn't my heart. "Oh, come, now, it's short acquaintance to be talking like that," says I.

"You would, though," says she, smiling kind of wry. "I know your sort, an' what's worse, I know me. I was a fool even to let you in the 'ouse. You'd think, with all I've seen, an' the rotten swine I've known, that I'd 'ave more sense; I've been 'ere before. You men—you don't care a button; it's just another rattle to you, an' thanks ever so, dearie, an' good-night. But I like you too much as it is, an' I know what comes of that. Another two days an' you'd be bored, an' a flabby ol' faggot like me can't 'old a man against the kind of merchandise there is in this 'ouse—little yellow sluts with hard titties—humph!" She shook her head. "The trouble is—it'd hurt. I spose you think that's funny, from an' ol' bag like me."

"No," says I, "but since I'm not staying anyway, you needn't worry. I'll tell you this much—I may not love you, Susie, but I like you, and you're a damned sight better in bed than any of your fellow girls would be."

"Gammon!" says she, hitting me with her fan, but she looked pleased. She didn't believe me for a moment, of course, but for once I wasn't buttering her. It's one of the great truths, that young pieces aren't in it where love-making is concerned, compared with their mothers and aunts who have been about long enough to enjoy it. For the real thing, give me a well-fleshed matron every time, with her eyes wide open and a mind of her own. But women, of course, will never credit this.

The difficulty about my leaving, of course, was that the best way to get out of New Orleans was by the river, and that meant running the gauntlet of the Navy people who might be looking for me. Thanks to Susie, whose acquaintances were legion, there was no trouble about getting a passage to England, and it was arranged that I should go two days later, on a packet bound for Liverpool. One advantage to it was that she would weigh anchor at night, when I'd have a good chance of slipping aboard unnoticed.

There was the question of my fare, and here Susie turned up trumps. She would advance me the cash—not, she said, that she expected it back. I protested at this, and she laughed and chucked me under the chin.

"I've heard that, an' all," says she. "If I'd a guinea for every dollar I've given to stake a man out of town, I'd be a rich woman, an' never once did I see a penny of it back. Oh, I know—you're full o' good intentions now, when you need the cash, but come next week you'll 'ave forgotten all about it."

"I'll pay it back, Susie," says I. "I promise."

"Ducky," says she, "I'd rather not—honest. I don't want to hear from you no more—really, I don't."

"Why ever not?"

"Oh, hold your tongue!" snaps she, and turned away, dabbing at herself. "There—now! Me face'll be all to do up again. Go on, let me alone!" And she went off, sniffing. Which, I must admit, I found very gratifying.

You may think I've dwelt on my meeting with Susie at some length, but there's reason for it. For one thing, it may be a valuable pointer to young men who come after, and who find themselves adrift in a strange town. Secondly, it had a bearing on my life many years on, as my later memoirs will show. And she was unique, too: among all the women I've known she must be about the only one that I never had hard feelings with, on either side. And she could touch me, somehow—at least I remember thinking, the night I left, that in all the journeys I'd set off on before, never a woman had been at such pains to see I had everything packed and ready, and that my clothes were brushed, and my money safe, and the rest of it. She fussed over me in a way that none of the others—wife, aunts, mistresses, whores, legions of them—had ever done. It's strange, and no doubt significant, that the warmest leave-taking I remember should be from a bawdy-house.

I set out about ten, with a nigger carrying my valise, and Susie hustled me away. "Give us a kiss, dearie. Now, be off with you. 'Ave a glass in the Cider Cellars for me." She was absolutely crying, the soft old slut. "An' take care of yourself you—you big scallawag, you!"

We slipped out of the side gate into the alley. It was one of those lazy, warm nights, with many stars, and above the hum of the town I could hear a distant steamboat whistle on the river, where my ship, the *Anglesey Queen*, would be lying. We set off down the dark lane together, and just as we reached its end a dark shadow loomed up before us and I was aware of others suddenly coming in at my back. I stopped dead, and the figure in front of me, a tall man in a broad-brimmed hat, said:

"Hold it right there, mister. Hands away from your sides. Now, don't make a move, because you're covered front and rear!"

I must have heard the same sort of thing barked at me in a dozen different languages, and it has never failed to paralyse me on the spot. My first thought was that these must be American Navy men, and my heart froze inside me. How the devil had they traced me? Could I bolt?—but there wasn't a hope. They knew their business too well—one a couple of yards dead ahead, and two others on my flanks, slightly behind me. But if I couldn't bolt I could bluff.

"Wer ruft mich?" I demanded, trying to sound angry. "Was wollen sie?"

"Don't come your Dutch on me, Mr Comber," says the big one, and that settled it. They were Navy men, and I was done for.

"You, nigger, gimme that bag," he went on. "Billy, take him down to the levee and let him go. And now, mister, you step ahead right lively. Do as you're told and you won't get hurt; try to run and you're a dead man."

Sick with fear I started forward, with the big man and his mate right behind me, down a side-street and then, at their direction, into a maze of alleys until I had no earthly idea where I was. Why were they taking me out of the main ways, and why had they taken the nigger to the levee before letting him go? My G - d, were they going to murder me?—and at that instant the big fellow growls:

"Stop right there," and came up beside me.

At this my nerve broke. "What d'you want with me? What are you going to do? In God's name, if you're the Navy, I can explain, I can—"

"We ain't the Navy," says he, shortly. "And we ain't gonna hurt you." And amazingly he added: "You're the last man on God's earth I'd want to hurt."

I gaped at him, trying to make out the shadowy face beneath the hat brim, but he went on:

"I've got a black bag here, and I'm gonna put it over your head, so you don't see where you're goin'. Now, don't fret ye'self; do as you're told an' you'll come to no harm."

He slipped the bag over my head, and I choked in its coarse muffled folds, panicking, but he took my arm and said:

"Straight ahead now. Easy does it."

We walked for three hundred and sixty eight paces through innumerable turns, and then stopped. I heard a gate creak, and when we went forward there was gravel beneath my feet. Then up stone steps, and a door opened, and we were in a house. Forward up stairs—thickly carpeted, too. I was suffocating with dread and astonishment by the time we had passed down a well-carpeted corridor, and I heard knuckles knock on a door and a voice call: "Enter!" I was pushed forward, the bag was whipped from my head, and as the door closed behind me I found myself blinking in the light of a great, well-furnished library. Behind a big oak desk a little bald-headed man was standing eyeing me benevolently over his spectacles, and waving a hand to an empty chair.

"Pray be seated, Mr Comber. And before you assail me with angry protests—which you're perfectly entitled to do, I confess—allow me to extend my most sincere and heartfelt apologies for the rather . . . er . . . cavalier manner of my invitation. Now, won't you be seated, sir, please? No one intends you the least harm—quite the contrary, I assure you. Sit down, sir, do."

"Who the blazes are you?" I demanded. He was obviously friendly, and a kindly-looking little fellow in his old-fashioned neckercher and breeches, with bright grey eyes that peered eagerly at me. "And what's the meaning of this?" Now that I was half-past fear I was prepared to be angry.

"There, now, that's exactly what I mean to tell you, if you'll only be seated," says he soothingly. "That's better. A glass of port?—no, perhaps brandy would be better. Settling for the nerves, eh?—though I don't think yours are nerves that need much settling, young man, from all I've heard."

Well, I'll always take brandy when it's kindly offered, so I fastened on the glass and gulped a mouthful down. And as he went back to his desk I took stock of the richly-furnished room, with its fine carpet and dark panelling, and found myself reassured, if bewildered.

"Now, then," says he, "that feels better, eh? Well, Mr Comber, I owe you an explanation as well as an apology, so you shall have it." He was American, but well-educated, and when you took a closer view of him you saw that he wasn't quite such an old Cheeryble as he looked. "Let me begin by astonishing you. I have been waiting to make your acquaintance these past few days. Indeed, if you hadn't left tonight to board the *Anglesey Queen* —there, there, sir, all shall be made plain presently—I was preparing to come and call on you. Oh, yes, I much wanted to meet you. We have kept a very close eye on you indeed, sir, since you arrived in Washington, although I confess we lost you for a moment when you gave the good Captain Fairbrother the slip." He chuckled. "Very neat, that. Of course, we quite understood. Quite understood. Didn't we?"

This was bewildering, but I had my nerve back. "Did you? If you understand so much, you won't mind enlightening me. Who or what are you—are you American government?"

He smiled. "No—not exactly. Although we have great influence, and many highly-placed friends, in that same government —that government which, I'm afraid, has been rather embarrassing you lately with insistent questions. Naturally—you're in possession of what I believe one senior official called dangerous information, and Washington wants it. But you want to take it straight home to England—perfectly right, sir. So you gave them the slip, and behold you tonight preparing to set sail secretly for Liverpool."

He hadn't quite got hold of the wrong end of the stick, you see, but very nearly. His only mistake lay in believing that I was Comber, and in deducing the wrong reason for my attempted flight from New Orleans. A flight which, rot him, he was putting in severe jeopardy.

"Then would you kindly tell me," says I, "why you have hauled me here at gun-point, instead of letting me catch my ship? In heaven's name, sir, I must get aboard her—"

"You would never have got aboard her," says he. "The Navy Department want you, Mr Comber, as a witness against those slaver friends of yours, and the U.S. Government, I know, wish to question you further about—those certain names you have in your head. Slave-trade names, I believe." And suddenly he wasn't a genial little buffer any more; his mouth was like a rat-trap. "Believe me, Mr Comber, the levee is well-watched; they know which way you'll try to go."

"And by what right would they try to stop me?" says I, brazening. By George, if they ever found out I wasn't Comber, they'd have right enough. Maybe they *had* found out—but if they had my omniscient little friend evidently hadn't.

"Oh, no right at all," says he. "But governments can generally arrange diplomatic reasons for delaying departures. I suppose they might hold on to you for a few weeks—until your ambassador pressed them into letting you go home. By then, Washington would hope, you might have let slip those names they want to know about."

I saw I must play Comber's part for all I was worth, so I smiled grimly. "They have no hope of that; those names are for my chiefs in London, and no one else. And if you think—whoever you are—that you can get them out of me—"

"My dear Mr Comber." He held up a hand. "I'm not interested. My concern with the slave trade lies in quite another direction —the same direction, I believe, as your own. That is why you are here. That is why my agents have traced you, even into the house of ill fame where you took refuge." Well, thinks I, I hope they didn't trace too close, or they must have got an eyeful. "Thus we knew of the passage home its proprietress arranged for you—I take it she is an English anti-slavery agent ... but there, the less said, the better. Thus we were able to intercept you tonight."

"You know a lot," says I. "Now, look here; I've heard everything but what I want to know. Who are you, and what d'you want with me?"

He looked at me steadily. "You have heard, I am sure, of the underground railroad."

Six months earlier I wouldn't have known what he meant, but when you've been in the company of slavers, as I had been, you recognise the phrase. Spring had mentioned it; I'd heard it spoken about, low-voiced, in Susie's brothel.

"It's a secret society for stealing slaves, and helping them to escape, isn't it? To Canada."

"It is an organisation for saving souls!" snaps he, and once again he didn't look half amiable. "It is an army that fights the most horrible tyranny of our time—the blasphemous iniquity of black slavery! It is an army without colours, or ranks, or pay— an army of dedicated men and women who labour secretly to release their black brethren from bondage and give them liberty. Yes, we steal slaves! Yes, we run them to free soil. Yes, we die for doing it—like them we are hunted with dogs, and tortured and hanged and shot if we are caught by the brutes who own and trade in human flesh. But we do it gladly, because we are marching in Christ's army, sir, and we will not lay down our weapons until the last shackle is broken, the last branding iron smashed, the last raw-hide whip burned, and the last slave free!"[33]

I gathered he was an abolitionist. By gad, he was in a fine sweat about it, too, but now he sat back and spoke in a normal voice.

"Forgive me. As though I need to say such things to you. Why, you take a thousand risks for our one, you put your life in the hazard in the nethermost hell of this foul traffic. Oh, we know all about you, Mr Comber—as you yourself said in a certain Washington office, 'Walls have ears.' The underground railroad has ears, certainly, and it heard your name in Washington, and the heroic work you did in bringing the *Balliol College* and that scoundrel Spring to book. Which reminds me of a privilege I had promised myself tonight, but have overlooked." He got to his feet. "Mr Comber, may I have the honour to shake your hand?"

And blow me, he seized my fist and pumped it hard enough to start water out of me. I didn't mind, but the thought occurred to me, here I was again being congratulated on my dauntless devotion, when all the time it had been frantic poltroonery. But it had done the trick, which just goes to show: we also serve who only turn and run.

"Thank you, sir, thank you," says he. "You have made me a happy man. Now, may I tell you how you may make me happier still?"

I wasn't sure about this, but I sat down again and listened.

I couldn't decide whether this little blighter was going to turn out well for me or not.

"As you know, we of the underground railroad rescue slaves wherever we can—from plantations, markets, pens, wherever they may be—and send them north secretly to the free states beyond the Ohio river and the Mason–Dixon line. Alone, they could never hope to make the journey, so we send with them our agents, who pose as slave-owners and slave-dealers, and convoy the unfortunates to safety. It is perilous work, as I have said, and our roll of martyrs grows longer every day. This is a savage country, sir, and while there are many in government who love and assist our work, government itself cannot condone or protect us, because we break the law—man's law, not God's. We are criminals, sir, in the eyes of our country, but we are proud of our crimes."

He was almost away again, but checked himself.

"Now, all slaves are important to us, however lowly, but some are more important than others. Such a one is George Randolph. Have you heard of him? No, well you shall. You have heard of Nat Turner, the slave who led a great rebellion in Virginia, and was barbarously executed by his tormentors? Well, Randolph is such another—but a greater man, better educated, more intelligent, with a greater vision. Twice he has tried to organise insurrection, twice he has failed; three times he has escaped; twice he has been recaptured. He is a fugitive at this moment—but we have him safe, and God willing they shall never take him again."

Comber would have applauded, so I said, "Oh, bravo!" and looked pleased.

"Bravo indeed," says he, and then looked solemn. "But all is not done. Randolph must be taken in safety to Canada—what a blow that will be in our cause! Why, sir, think of what such a man can do, when he is on free soil. He can talk, he can write, he can go abroad, not only in Canada but in England, in our own free states—I tell you, sir, the burning words of such a man, striking the ears of the civilised world, will do more to rekindle the fire against slavery than all our white journalists and orators can accomplish. The world will see a man like themselves, and yet greater—a man fit for a chair in our finest universities, or to sit in the highest councils of a nation—but a black man, sir, with the whip-marks on his back and the shackle-scars on his legs! They will understand, as they have never understood, what slavery is! They will feel the whip and shackles on their own bodies, and they will cry out: 'This infamy shall not be!' "

Well, it seemed to call for something, so I said:

"Capital. First-rate. This news will be welcomed with joy in England, I'm sure, and as soon as I am home again you may rely..."

"But Mr Comber," says he, "this is still to be achieved. George Randolph is not in Canada yet—he is still here, a hunted runaway. The journey to freedom lies ahead of him."

"But is that difficult? For your splendid organisation? I mean, you have shown me, tonight, how far-reaching it is. Why, you know as much about me as I do myself—almost. Your agents..."

"Oh, we have many agents; our intelligence system is extensive. We have an eye at every window in this land, sir, and an ear at every door; information is no difficulty. But most of our spies are black; most are still slaves. Collecting intelligence is one thing, but running slaves to Canada is quite another. Here we need white agents, dedicated, resolute, and bold, and these are pitifully few. Many are willing, but only a handful are able. And even then, they have become too well known. Of the gallant young men who ran our last three convoys one is dead, one in jail, and the third in Canada, unable to return because he would certainly be arrested. I have not one that I can send with Randolph, sir, not one that I could trust. For with a cargo of such importance, I cannot risk sending any but the hardiest, the bravest, the least suspected. Do you see my plight, sir? Every day that Randolph hides in New Orleans his danger grows—the enemy has spies also. I must get him out, and quickly. Can you understand?"

I understood all right, but ass that I was, I didn't see what it had to do with me. I suggested sending him by sea.

"Impossible. The risk is too great. Ironically, his safest route is the one that would appear most dangerous—up the Mississippi to the free states. One slave in a coffle may pass unnoticed— my one fearful problem is the white agent to go with him. I tell you, Mr Comber, I was at my wits' end—and then, in answer to my prayers, I had word of you from Washington, and that you would be coming to Orleans."

I absolutely said: "Christ!" but he was in full spate.

"I saw then that God had sent you. Not only are you a man dedicated to fighting the abomination of slavery, but you are one who scorns danger, who has come unscathed through perils ten times greater than this, who has the experience, the intelligence —nay, the brilliance—and the cold courage such an enterprise requires. And, above all this, you are not known!" He smacked his fist on the table excitedly. "If I had all the world to choose from, I should have asked for such a man as you. You, who I had never heard of ten days ago. Mr Comber, will you do this for me —and strike yet another, greater blow above all those you have surely struck already?"

Well, of all the appalling nonsense I had ever heard, this beat everything, even Bismarck. By George, they were two of a kind— the same fanatic gleam in the eye, the same fierce determination to thrust a hapless fellow-human into the stew, head first, to further their own lunatic schemes. But Bismarck had had a pistol to my head; this idiot hadn't. I was on the point of telling him straight what I thought of his revolting suggestion, laughing right in his eager little face, and I suddenly checked—I was Comber. How would *he* have refused—my God, he probably wouldn't, the reckless fool. I had to go very canny.

"Well, sir? Well—is this not such a crusade as your heart desires?"

There was a fine, short answer to that, but I daren't give it. "Sir," says I, "this is a startling proposal. Oh, you honour me, indeed you do. But sir, my duty is to my country—I must return at once—"

He laughed exultantly. "But of course, and you shall! You may do this thing and be in England *faster* than if you wait here to catch a packet home. Listen, sir—you would go upriver by steamboat, as a slave-trader, with a coffle for—Kentucky, let us say. But you sail straight on to Cincinnati—why, you will be there in six days, pass Randolph to our agent there, and continue to Pittsburgh. You may be in New York in a week or a little more from now, sir, and a sailing there will have you home far more speedily than a boat from Orleans—if you could even get one here. Remember, the Navy are watching for you."

"But, sir," I protested, cudgelling fearfully for excuses, "consider the danger, not to me, but to my own mission—the information I hold, if I went astray, would be lost to my own government, and yours—"

"I have thought of it," cries he. Of course, he would, rot his measly little soul. "You may commit it to paper here, sir, this very night, under seal, and I swear upon my honour it shall go straight to London. No one in Washington, no one at all, shall see it. You have my word. But, Mr Comber," he went on earnestly, "there is no risk of that. You will come through without the slightest danger—no slave-catcher will give *you* a second glance. They know *us*, sir, but not you. And you will be serving the cause dear to your heart; I implore you, sir, say you will aid us in this."

Well, I knew the cause dear to my heart, if he didn't. "Sir," says I. "I am sorry. Believe me, I would aid you if I could, but my duty must come above my personal inclination."

"But you will be doing that duty, don't you see? Better than if you refuse—for if you do, why then, I could only apologise for bringing you here, and—send you back to the Navy Department. I should be reluctant—it would delay you still further, for they would keep you here for the trial of Spring and his pirates. But that would plainly be my only course."

So there it was. Blackmail, the pious little scoundrel. Oh, he was twinkling solemnly; he thought, you see, that all I had to fear from being delivered back to the clutches of the Navy and the U.S. Government was delay and more inconvenient questioning. He didn't know that if I appeared at the *Balliol College* trial my true identity must appear, and it would be into the dock for Flashy with the rest of the crew. Then it would be prison—my God, they might even hang us. Against that, the risk—which he said was no risk—of running a fugitive nigger to Ohio. He had me, the little serpent, but he didn't know *how* he had me, and he mustn't find out.

Well, if I refused him, I was done for, that was sure. So presumably, I must accept. I tried to think straight, tried to reason, tried to see a way out, but couldn't. My innards quailed at what he had proposed, but it was only a risk against a certainty. And *he* didn't think the risk was much at all—not that I put any faith in that. What could I do, though? I've been trapped so often, between two loathsome choices, and it's in my coward's nature to choose what seems the less dangerous. That was all I could do now, at this moment, and see what turned up. Yes, that was it: I must accept, and be ready to fly at the first hint of danger. If I must take this lout Randolph north, well, there it was. If things went adrift, I'd slide out somehow. I'd deny him, if I had to. But if all went well—and the chances were they would —why, I'd be half way home, with Spring and the U.S. Navy and the rest far astern. Looking back, I can only say it seemed the lesser of two evils. Well, I've been wrong before.

When you have to bow the knee, do it with grace.

"Very well, sir," says I, looking solemn, "I must accept. I must combine duty—" and I forced myself to look him in the eye "—with the desire of my heart, which is to assist you and your worthy cause."

Comber couldn't have said it better, and the little monster was all over me. He wrung my hand, and called me a saviour, and then he got business-like again. He called in another chap, a long-faced zealot, this one, and introduced me "—our own names," he added to me, "I think it wiser not to divulge to you, Mr Comber. I choose to be known as Mr Crixus, which you will no doubt consider appropriate, ha-ha."[34]

And then it was all joy and good fellowship and be damned, they were so delighted, and my mind was in a turmoil, but I couldn't for the life of me see a way clear. Crixus bustled about, calling in two other chaps who I suspected were the men who had brought me, and told them the glad news, and they shook hands, too, and blessed me, full of solemn delight. Yes, they said, all was ready, and the sooner things were started the better. Crixus nodded eagerly, rubbing his hands, and then beamed at me:

"And now I promise myself another little pleasure. I told you, Mr Comber, that George Randolph was in hiding. He is—in this house, and it shall now be my privilege to present to each other two of the greatest champions of our cause. Come, gentlemen."

So we filed out, downstairs, and came to the back of the house, and into a plain room where a young nigger was sitting at a table, writing by the light of an oil lamp. He looked up, but didn't rise, and one sight of his face told me that here was a fellow I didn't like above half.

He was about my age, slim but tall, and a quadroon. He had a white man's face, bar the thickish lips, with fine brows and a most arrogant, damn-you-me-lad expression. He sat while Crixus poured out the tale, turning his pencil in his hand, and when he had been told that here was the man who would pilot him to the promised land, and Crixus had got round to presenting me, he got up languidly and held out a fine brown hand. I took it, and it was like a woman's, and then he dropped it and turned to Crixus.

"You are in no doubt?" says he. His voice was cold, and very precise. A right uppity white nigger, this one was. "We cannot afford a mistake this time. There have been too many in the past."

Well, this took me flat aback; for a moment I almost forgot my own fears. And Crixus, to my astonishment, was all eagerness to reassure him.

"None, George, none. As I have told you, Mr Comber is a proved fighter on our side; you could not be in better hands."

"Ah," says Randolph, and sat down again. "That is very well, then. He understands the importance of my reaching Canada. Now, tell me, exactly how do we proceed from here? I take it the *modus operandi* is as we have already discussed it, and that Mr Comber is capable of falling in with it precisely."

I just gaped. I don't know what I had expected—one of your woolly-headed darkies, I suppose, massa-ing everyone, and pathetically grateful that someone was going to risk his neck to help him to freedom. But not your Lord George Bloody Randolph, no indeed. You'd have thought he was doing Crixus a favour, as the old fellow went through the plan, and our runaway sat, nodding and occasionally frowning, putting in his points and pursing his lips, like a judge on the bench. Finally he says:

"Very well. It should answer satisfactorily. I cannot pretend that I welcome some of the ... er ... details. To be chained in a gang of blacks—that is a degradation which I had hoped was behind me. But since it must be—" he gave Crixus a pained little smile "—why, it must be endured. I suppose it is a small price to pay. My spirit can sustain it, I hope."

"It can, George, it can," cries Crixus. "After all you have suffered, it is a little thing, the last little thing."

"Ah, yes—always the last little thing!" says Randolph. "We know about the camel, do we not, and the final feather. Do you know, when I look back, I ask myself how I have borne it? And this, as you say, is a trifle—why should it seem so bitter a trifle? But there." He shrugged, and then turned in his chair to look at me—I was still standing, too.

"And you, sir? You know the gravity of what lies before us. Your task should not be hard—merely to ride on a steamboat, in rather greater comfort than I shall be. Are you confident of . . ."

"Yes, yes, George," says Crixus. "Mr Comber knows; I talked to him in the library."

"Ah," says Randolph. "In the library." He looked about him, with a little, crooked smile. "In the library."

"Oh, now, George," cries Crixus, "you know we agreed it was safer here. . . ."

"I know." Randolph held up a slim hand. "It is of no importance. However, I was speaking to Mr Comber—yes, you will have been told, sir, how vitally important is this journey of ours. So I ask again, do you trust yourself entirely to carry it through—simple though it should be?"

I could have kicked the black bastard off his chair. But caught as I was, in the trap Crixus had sprung on me, what was there to do but cram down my resentment on top of my fears—I was an overloaded man, believe me—and say:

"No, I've no doubts. Play your part on the lower deck, and I'll play mine in the saloon—George."

He stiffened just a little. "You know, I believe I prefer Mr Randolph, on first acquaintance."

I nearly hit him, but I held it in. "D'you want me to call you Mr Randolph on the steamboat?" says I. "People might talk—don't ye think?"

"We shall be on the steamboat soon enough," says he, and there our discussion ended, with Crixus fidgetting nervously as he ushered me out, and telling Randolph to get some sleep, because we must soon be off. But when the door had closed I let out my breath with a whoosh, and Crixus says hurriedly:

"Please, Mr Comber—well, I know what you may be thinking. George can be ... difficult, I guess, but—well, we have not endured what he has endured. You saw his sensitivity, the delicacy of his nature. Oh, he is a genius, sir—he is three parts white, you know. Think what slavery must do to such a spirit! I know he is very different from the negroes with whom you are used to dealing. Dear me, I sometimes myself find it ... but there. I remember what he means to our cause—and to all those poor, black people." He blinked at me. "Compassionate him, sir, as you compassionate them. I know, in your own loving heart, you will do so."

"Compassion, Mr Crixus, is the last thing he wants from me," says I, and I added privately: and it's the last thing he'll get, too. Indeed, as later I tried unsuccessfully to sleep under that strange roof, I found myself thinking that I'd find Master Randolph's company just a little more than I could stomach—not that I need see him much. My God, thinks I, what am I doing? How the devil did I get into this? But even as my fears reawoke, it came back to the same thing: almost any risk was preferable to letting the U.S. authorities get me, unmask me, and—. After all, this would be the quicker way home, and if things went adrift, well, Master Randolph could shift for himself while Flashy took to the timber. He would be all right; he was a genius.

If ever you have to run slaves—which seems unlikely nowadays, although you never can tell what may happen if we have the Liberals back—the way to do it is by steamboat. The *Sultana*, bound for Cincinnati by way of Baton Rouge, Vicksburg, Memphis and Cairo, beat the old *Balliol College* all to nothing. It was like cruising upriver in a fine hotel, with the niggers out of sight, mind and smell, no pitching or rolling to disturb the stomach, and above all, no John Charity Spring.

The speed and sureness with which Crixus and his minions organised our departure had almost banished my first fears. I had woken on a resolve to run from the house and take my chance with the Navy, but they kept far too close a watch on things for that, and by the afternoon I was glad of it. Crixus spent four hours drilling me in the minutest details of the journey, about cash, and passage tickets, and how the slaves would be fed en route, how I might answer casual inquiries and take part in river gossip without appearing too out of place, and by the end of it I realised how little chance I would have stood as a fugitive on my own account. The main thing was to talk as little as possible; there were enough Englishmen on the river in those days to make an extra one nothing out of the ordinary, but since I was meant to be a new-fledged slave trader it was important that I shouldn't make any foolish slips. My story would be that I had recently forsaken African blackbirding in favour of river dealing—I had all the expert knowledge for that, at any rate.

Really, it was astonishing how easy it was. In mid-afternoon, with a broad-brimmed planter's hat, my long-tailed coat, and half-boots, I joined my coffle in the cellars of Crixus's house. There were six of them, in light ankle irons, with Randolph in the middle, looking damned miffed, which cheered me considerably. The other five, by the way, were free niggers in Crixus's employ, and like him devoted to the underground railroad. There was much hand-shaking and God-blessing, and then we were conducted through what seemed like miles of cellars to a deserted yard, from which it was a short step to the levee.

I had my heart in my mouth as I strode along, trying to look like Simon Legree, with my gang of coons shuffling behind; I had protested to Crixus that if the Navy were on the look-out for me the waterfront would be a deuced dangerous place, but he said not at the steamboat wharves, and he was right. We pushed through the crowds of niggers, stevedores, boatmen, passengers and bummarees without anyone giving us a glance; there were coffles by the score, with fellows dressed like me shepherding and spitting and cursing, bawling to each other and chewing on big black cigars; old ladies with hat-boxes and parasols and men with carpet-bags and stove-pipe hats were hurrying for their boats; niggers with carts were loading piles of luggage; the big twin smoke-stacks were belching and the whistles squealing; it was like the Tower of Babel with the scaffolding about to give way. I pushed ahead until I found the *Sultana*, and within an hour we were thrashing upstream, close inshore, on the slow bend past what is now called Gretna—and with the great jam of ships and rafts and scuttling small boats along its levee, anything less like the real Gretna you never saw. My niggers were stowed down on the main deck at water-level, where the baggage and steerage people go, and I was reclining in my state-room up on the texas deck, smoking a cigar and deciding that things had turned out not so badly after all.

You see, it had gone so well and naturally in the first hour that I was beginning to believe Crixus. The purser fellow had accepted my ticket, in the name of James K. Prescott, without a blink, and bawled to one of his niggers to come an' take the gennelman's coffle and see 'em disposed forrard, thankee sir, straight ahead there to the stairway, an' mind your head. And with the boat so crowded with passengers I felt security returning; this looked like an easy trip to the point where one Caleb Cape, trader and auctioneer, would meet me at Cincinnati and take my coffle, and I would steam on up the Ohio, free as a bird.

In the meantime I set out to enjoy the trip as far as possible. The *Sultana* was a big fast boat, and held the New Orleans–

Louisville record of five and a half days; she had three decks from the texas to the water-line, with the boiler deck in the middle.[35] This was where the main saloon and state-rooms were, all crystal chandeliers and gilding and plush, with carved furniture and fine carpets; my own cabin had an oil painting on the door, and there were huge pictures in the main rooms. All very fine, in a vulgar way, and the passengers matched it; you may have heard a great deal about Southern charm and grace, and there's something in it where Virginia and Kentucky are concerned—Robert Lee, for instance, was as genteel an old prig as you'd meet on Pall Mall —but it don't hold for the Mississippi valley. There they were rotten with cotton money in those days, with gold watch-chains and walking-sticks, loud raucous laughter, and manners that would have disgraced a sty. They spat their "terbacker" juice on the carpets, gorged noisily in the dining saloon—the sight of jellied quail being shovelled down with a spoon and two fingers, and falling on a shirt-front with a diamond the size of a shilling in it, is a sight that dwells with me still, and I ain't fastidious as a rule. They hawked and belched and picked their teeth and swilled great quantities of brandy and punch, and roared to each other in their hideous plantation voices.

Theirs weren't the only manners to cause me concern, either. That first evening I went down to the main deck to see that my slaves were being properly housed and fed, as a good owner should, and to enjoy the sight of the precious Master Randolph regaling himself on pulse and pone. A slave's life didn't suit him one little bit; he had taken his place in the coffle that afternoon with a very ill grace, and much self-pitying nobility for Crixus's benefit. When he and his fellows were herded off to their passage quarters he had still been damned peaked and sulky, and now he was sitting with a bowl of hash from the communal copper, sniffing at it with disgust.

"How d'ye like it, George?" says I. "You and the other niggers feeding well?"

He gave me a glance of sheer hate, and seeing there was no one else at hand, he hissed:

"This filth is inedible! Look at it—smell it, if you can bear the nauseating stuff!"

663

I sniffed the bowl; it would have sickened a dog. "Capital stew!" says I. "Eat it down, heartily now, or I shall begin to fear I have been spoiling you, my boy. Now, you other niggers, are you all pitching into your vittles, hey? That's the spirit."

The other five all cried: "Yes, massa, shore 'nuff, mighty fine, massa." Either they had more acting gumption than Randolph or else they liked the awful muck. But he, all a-quiver with indignation, whispers fiercely:

"Capital stew, indeed! Could you bear to eat this foulness?"

"Probably not," says I, "but I'm not a nigger, d'ye see." And without another glance at him I strolled off to my own dinner, resolving to describe it to him later. I never believe in neglecting the education of my inferiors.

It was worth describing, too. Mississippi food, once you get outside Orleans, tends to be robust and rich, and I wolfed my stewed chicken, prime steak and creamed chocolate with all the more relish for the thought of Randolph squatting on the main deck grubbing at his gristle. I had champagne with it, too, and a very passable brandy, and finally topped the whole thing off with a buxom little cracker girl in my cabin. Her name was Penny or Jenny, I forget which; she had dyed gold hair which went vilely with her yellow satin dress, and she was one of your squealing hoydens, but she had tremendous energy and high pointed breasts of which she was immensely proud, which made up for a lot. Most of the women on the boat were noisy, by the way; the respectable ones clacked and squawked to each other interminably, and the mistresses and whores, of whom there seemed to be a great number, were brassy enough to be heard in San Francisco. Penny (or Jenny) was one of the quieter ones; she didn't scream with laughter above once a minute.

I was lying there, drowsy and well satisfied, listening to her prattling, when a nigger waiter comes up with a message that I was wanted on the main deck—something to do with my coffle, he said. Wondering what the devil was what, I went down, and to my rage and concern discovered that it was that confounded George up to his nonsense again.

The overseer was swearing and stamping over in the corner where my slaves were, with Randolph standing in front of him looking as arrogant as Caesar.

"What's the matter with it, damn ye?" the overseer was shouting, and then, seeing me:

"Say, look here, Mist' Prescott—here's this jim-dandy nigger o' yours don' like this yere 'commodation. No suh, 'pears like 'taint good enough for him. Now, then!"

"What's this I hear, George?" says I, pushing forward. "What are you about, my boy? Turning up your nose at the quarters —what's wrong with them, sir?"

He looked me straight in the eye, with as much side as old Lord Cardigan.

"We have been given no straw to make beds for ourselves. We are entitled to this; it is covered in the money you have paid for our passage."

"Well, — me drunk, will ye hear that, now?" cries the overseer. "Entye—entitt—ent-what-the-hell-you-say! Don' you give me none o' your shines, ye black rascal! Beds, by thunder! You'll lay right down where you're told, or by cracky you'll be *knocked* down! Who're you, that you gotta have straw to keep yore tender carcass offen the floor? 'Tother hands is layin' on it, ain't they? Now, you git right down there, d'ye hear?"

"My master has paid for us to have straw," says Randolph, looking at me. "The other slaves over yonder have it; only our coffle goes without."

"Well, there *ain't* no more goddamed straw, you no-good impident son-of-a-bitch!" cries the overseer. "So now! I never heerd the like—"

I could have felled that bloody ass Randolph on the spot— perhaps I should have done. Couldn't the fool understand that he must behave as a slave, even if he didn't feel like one? How the devil he ever existed on a plantation was beyond me—it must have taken a saint or a lunatic to put up with his insolent airs. All I could do was play the just master, kindly but firm.

"Come, come, George," I said sternly. "Let us have no more of this. Lie down where you are told directly—what, is this how you repay my kind usuage, by impertinence? Have you forgotten yourself altogether, that you speak back to a white man? Lie down at once, sir, this instant!"

He stared at me; I was urging him with my eyes, and he had just wit enough to obey, but with no great humility, plumping down on the deck and folding his arms stubbornly round his knees. The overseer growled.

"I'd take the starch outer *that* jackanapes right smart, if he was mine. You be 'vised, Mist' Prescott, an' give that uppity yaller bastard a good dressin' down, or he'll have the whole passel on 'em as bad as hisself. Beds, by Christ! An' sassin' back to me! That's the trouble with all these fancy house-niggers, with bein' roun' white folks they start thinkin' *they* white, too. Peacocky high-an'-mighties, every last dam' one of them. He'll have bin brought up 'mong white ladies, I don't doubt; too much dam' pettin' when he's young. You trim him up smart, Mist' Prescott, like I say, or he'll be a heap o' trouble to ye."

He stumped off, muttering to himself, and Randolph sneered softly to himself.

"The gentleman is not without perception," says he. "He, at least, was not brought up among white ladies; white sows, perhaps." He glared up at me. "We are entitled to straw to lie on —why did you not insist that he provides it? Isn't it enough that I am chained up like a beast in this verminous place, fed on nauseating slops? Aren't you meant to protect me—you, who neglect me to the mercies of that uncouth white scum?"

I wondered if the fellow was insane—not for the way he spoke to me, but for the purblind stupidity with which he overlooked the position he was in, the role he was meant to be playing. He was five days away from freedom, and yet the idiot insisted on drawing attention to himself and provoking trouble. Ordinarily I'd have taken my boot to him, but he so mystified me that I was alarmed. I glanced round; the overseer was out of sight.

"Come over by the rail," says I, and when we were standing apart:

"Look—haven't you got sense enough to keep your mouth shut and your head down? Where the hell do you think you are— the House of Lords? D'ye think it matters whether you get straw or not—or whether I've paid for it or not? D'ye expect me to take your side against a white man—it'd be the talk of the boat in five minutes, you fool. Just you forget your lofty opinion of yourself for once, and talk humble, and don't be so damned particular, or you'll never see Ohio this trip!"

"I need no advice from you!" he flashed back. "You would be better remembering the duty you have promised to do, which is to take me north in safety, than to spend your time in gorging with white-trash sluts."

It took my breath away—not just the insolence, but the discovery of how fast news travels among niggers. And there was just a note in his indignation that made me decide to put my anger aside and be amused instead.

"What's the matter, Sambo?" says I. "Jealous?"

If looks could kill there'd have been a corpse at his feet.

"I have no words to express my contempt of you, or of the slatterns you . . . you associate with," says he, and his voice was shaking. "But I will not have you endanger my freedom, do you hear? What kind of guardian are you? That swine of an overseer might have provoked me beyond endurance—while you were at your beastliness. It is your task to see me to Canada—that is all that matters."

There was no piercing this one's arrogance, I saw, not by reason or taunts. So I put my hands on my hips and stuck my face into his.

"All that matters, you black mongrel! I'll tell you what matters —and that is that you keep your aping airs to yourself, touch your forelock, and say 'Yes, massa' whenever I or any white man talks to you. That way you might get to Canada—you just might." I shook my fist at him. "If you haven't the brain in that ape skull of yours to see that kicking up the kind of shines you've been at today is the surest way of setting us all adrift—if you can't see that, I'll teach it to you, by God! I'll follow that overseer's advice, Mr Randolph, and I'll have you triced up, Mr Randolph, and they'll take a couple of stone of meat off you with a raw-hide, Mr Randolph! Then maybe you'll learn sense."

If you think a quadroon can't go red with rage, you're wrong.

"You wouldn't dare!" he choked furiously. "To me! Why, you . . . you . . ."

"Wouldn't I, though? Don't wager your big black arse on that, George, or you'll find you've only half of it left. And what would you do about it, eh? Holler 'I'm a runaway nigger, and this man is smuggling me to Canada?' Think that over, George, and be wise."

"You . . . you scoundrel!" He mouthed at me. "This shall be reported, when I reach Cincinnati—the underground railroad shall hear of it—what manner of creature they entrust with—"

"Oh, shut up, can't you? I don't give a fig for the railroad—and if you weren't a born bloody fool you wouldn't even mention their name. 'When you reach Cincinnati,' no less. You won't reach Cincinnati unless I please—so if you can't be grateful, Randolph, just be careful. Now, then, take off your airs, close your mouth, and get back there among your brothers—lively now! Cross me or that overseer again, and I'll have the cat to you—I swear it. Jump to it, nigger!"

He stood there, sweat running down his face, his chest heaving with passion. For a moment I thought he would leap at me, but he changed his mind.

"Some day," says he, "some day you shall repent this most bitterly. You heap indignities on me, when my hands are tied; you insult me; you mock my degradation. As God is my witness you will pay for it."

There was no dealing with him, you see. It was on the tip of my tongue to yell for the overseer, and have him string Master George up and raw-hide the innards out of him, just for the fun of hearing him howl, but with this kind of quivering violet you couldn't be certain what folly he mightn't commit if he was pushed too far. There was a spite and conceit in that man that passed anything I've ever struck, so I lit a cigar while considering how to catch him properly on the raw.

"I doubt if I'll pay for it," says I. "But supposing I did—it's something *you* can never hope to emulate." I blew smoke at him. "*You'll* never be able to pay for this trip, will you?"

I turned on my heel before he had a chance to reply and strode off, leaving him to digest the truth which I guess he hated more than anything else. That would boil his bile for him, but I wasn't so certain that my threats would have the desired effect on his conduct. Well, if they didn't, I'd carry them out, by God, and he could get to Canada with a new set of weals to show on his lectures to the Anti-Slavery Society.

What beats me, looking back, is the stupidity of his ingratitude. Here was the railroad—and for all he knew, myself—in a sweat to save his black hide for him, but would he show a spark of thanks, or abate his uppity pride one jot? Not he. He thought he had a *right* to be assisted and cosseted, and that we had a *duty* to put up with his airs and ill humour and childishness, and still help him for his own sweet sake. Well, he'd picked the wrong man in me; I was ready to drop the bastard overboard just to teach him the error of his ways—indeed, I paused on the ladder going up to reflect whether I could get away with selling him to a trader or in one of the marts on the way north. He would fetch a handy sum to help me on my way home—but I saw it wouldn't do. He'd find a way to drag me down, and even if he didn't, the underground railroad would hear of it, and I'd developed too healthy a respect for Mr Crixus and his legions to wish them on my tail with a vengeance. No, I'd just have to carry on with the plan, and hope to God that Randolph wouldn't get us into some fearful fix with his wilful white-niggerishness.

It's an interesting thought, though, that within a few short weeks I'd found myself engaged in running niggers *into* slavery, and running 'em *out* again, and all the hundreds of black animals on the *Balliol College*, with every reason to resist and mutiny and raise cain, hadn't given a tenth of the trouble I was getting from this single quadroon, who should have been on his knees in gratitude to me and Crixus and the others. Of course, he was civilised, and educated, and full of his own importance. Lincoln was right; they're a damned nuisance.

One consolation I had on that first night was that it didn't look as though our trip would be a long one, and I could look forward to being shot of Master George Randolph within a week. We thrashed up and down the river in fine style—I say up and down because the Mississippi is the twistiest watercourse you ever saw, doubling back and forth, and half the time you are steaming south-east or south-west round a bend to go north again. It's a huge river, too, up to a mile across in places, and unlike any other I know, in that it gets wider as you go up it. There was nothing to see as far as the banks were concerned except mud flats and undergrowth and here and there a town or a landing place, but the river itself was thick with steamboats and smaller vessels, and great lumber rafts piled high with bales and floating lazily down the muddy brown waters towards the gulf.

It's a slow, ugly river, and the ugliness isn't in what you can see, but what you can feel. There's a palling closeness, and a sense of rot and corruption; it's cruel river, to my mind at any rate, both in itself and its people. Mind you, I may be prejudiced by what it did to me, but even years later, when I came booming down it with the Union Army—well, they boomed, and I coasted along with them—I still felt the same oppressive dread of it. I remember what Sam Grant said about it: "Too thick to drink and too thin to plough. It stinks." Not that he'd have drunk it anyway, unless it had been pure corn liquor from Cairo down.

She's a treacherous river, too, as I realised on the morning after we had boarded the *Sultana*, and she ran aground on a mud bank on the Bryaro bend, not far below Natchez. The channels and banks are always shifting, you see, and the pilots have to know every twist and stump and current; ours didn't, we stuck fast, and a special pilot, the celebrated Bixby, had to be brought down from Natchez to get us afloat again.[36] All of which consumed several hours, with the great man strutting about the pilot house and making occasional dashes out to the texas rail to peer down at the churning wheel, and scampering back to roar down his tube: "Snatch her! Hard down! Let her go, go, go!" while the Mississippi mud churned up in huge billows alongside and you could feel the boat shuddering and heaving to be off. And when she finally "snatched", and reared off the shoal into the water, Bixby was half over the rail again, yelling to the nigger leadsman, and the scream of the whistles all but drowned their great bass voices singing out: "Eight feet—eight and a half—nine feet—quarter-less-twain!" And then as she surged out; "Mark twai-ai-ain!" and the whole ship roared and cheered and stamped and Bixby clapped his tall hat on his head and resumed his kid gloves while they pressed cigars on him and offered him drinks from their flasks. It was quite fun, really, and I'd have enjoyed it if I hadn't been so anxious to get ahead, for I like to see a man who's *good* at something, *doing* it, and throwing on a bit of extra side, just for show. As I've said, I don't have many kindly memories of the Mississippi, but the best are of the steamboats riding tall, and the swaggering pilots, and the booming voices ringing "De-eep four!" and "Quarter-twa-ain!" across the brown waters. I'll never hear them again—but they wouldn't sound the same today anyway.

However, after Mr Bixby's performance we steamed on to Natchez, and there any slight enjoyment I'd been getting from our cruise came to an abrupt end. From now life on the Mississippi was to be one horror after another, and I was to regret most bitterly the day I'd clapped eyes on her dirty waters.

I had no inkling of anything wrong until we were away and steaming up river again, and I sauntered down to see my coffle getting their evening meal—and no doubt, I thought, to discuss the menu with Black Beauty himself. I was considering a few taunts to add sauce to his diet, and wondering if it was wise to stir up his hysteria again, but the sight of his face drove them clear out of my mind. He looked strained and ugly, and quite deaf to the sneering abuse that the overseer gave him as he received his hash from the copper. He shuffled off with his bowl, glancing round at me, and I followed him out of eyeshot round the bales to the rail, where we could be alone.

"What's the matter?" says I, for I knew something had shaken him badly. He looked left and right up the rail.

"Something dreadful has happened," says he in a low voice. "Something unforeseen—my God, it can undo us utterly. It is the most terrible chance—a chance in a thousand—but Crixus should have anticipated it!" He beat his fist on the rail. "He should have seen it, I tell you! The fool! The blind, incompetent blunderer! To send me into this peril, to—"

"What the hell is it?" I demanded, now thoroughly terrified. "Spit it out, in God's name!"

"A man came aboard at Natchez. I was watching, when the passengers came up the plank, and by God's grace he did not see me. He *knows* me! He is a trader from Georgia—the very man who sold me to my first master! The first time I escaped, he was among those who brought me back! Don't you see, imbecile— if he should catch sight of me here, we are finished! Oh, he knows all about George Randolph—he will know me on the instant.

671

He will denounce me, I will be dragged back to—oh, my God!"
And he put his head in his hands and sobbed with rage and fear.

He wasn't the only one to be emotionally disturbed, I can tell
you. *He* would be dragged back—by George, he would have
company, unless I looked alive. I stood appalled—this was what
my very first instinct had told me might happen, when Crixus
had proposed this folly to me. But he had been so sure it would
all be plain sailing, and in my cowardice I had allowed myself to
be persuaded. I could have torn my hair at my own stupidity
—but it was too late now. The damage was done, and I must try
to think, and see a way out, and quieten this babbling clown
before panic got the better of him.

"Who could have thought that it would happen?" he was
chattering. "Not a soul in Mississippi or Louisiana knows me
—not a soul—and this fiend from Georgia has to cross my path!
What is he doing here? Why didn't Crixus *see* that this could
happen? Why did I let myself be driven into this calamity?"
He jerked up his head, glaring through his tears. "What are you
going to do?"

"Shut up!" says I. "Keep your voice down! He hasn't seen
you yet, has he?" I was trying to weigh the chances, to plan
ahead in case we were discovered. "Perhaps he won't—there's no
reason why he should, is there? He'll be travelling on the boiler
deck or the texas—there's no reason why he should come down
here, unless he has niggers with him, by God! Has he?"

"No—no, there were no new coffles came aboard at Natchez.
But if he should, if—"

"He won't, then. Even if he did, why should he see you, if you
lie low and keep out of sight? He's not going to go peering into
the face of every nigger just for fun. Look, what's his name?"

"Omohundro—Peter Omohundro of Savannah. He is a terrible
creature, I tell you—"

"Look, there's nothing to do but sit tight," says I. It was a nasty
shaker, no error, but common sense told me it wasn't as bad as he
made out it was. I don't need any encouragement to terror, as a
rule, but I can count chances, and there wasn't a damned thing to
be done except watch out and hope. The odds were heavy that
Omohundro wouldn't come anywhere near him; if he did, thinks I,

then Master Randolph 'can look out for himself, but in the meantime the best thing to do is get some of his almighty cockiness back into him.

"You keep out of sight and keep quiet," says I. "That's all we can do—"

"All! You mean you intend to do nothing! To wait until he sees me?"

"He won't—unless your vapourings attract attention!" I snapped. "I'll watch out for him, never fear. At the first hint that he may come down here, I'll be on hand. You've got the key to your irons hidden, haven't you? Well, then, you stay behind the bales and keep your eyes open. There isn't a chance in a million of his seeing you, if you are careful."

That calmed him down a little; I believe that he had been more angry than frightened, really, which in itself was a relief to me. He blackguarded Crixus some more, and threw in a few withering remarks about my own shortcomings, and there I left him, with a promise to return later and report any developments. I won't deny I was rattled, but I've had a lot worse perils hanging over me, and when I considered the size of the boat, and the hordes of folk aboard, white and nigger, I told myself we should be all right.

The first thing was to get a sight of Omohundro, which wasn't difficult. By discreet inquiry I got him pointed out to me by a nigger waiter: a big, likely-looking bastard with a scarred face and heavy whiskers, one of your tough, wide-awake gentlemen who stared carefully at whoever was talking to him, spoke in a loud, steady way, and laughed easily. I also discovered that he was travelling only as far as Napoleon, which we ought to reach on the following evening. So that was all to the good, as I told Randolph later; he wasn't going to have much time for prying about the boat. But I didn't sleep much that night; even the outside risk of catastrophe is enough to keep me hopping to the water closet, and reaching for the brandy bottle.

Next day passed all too slowly; we lost time at Vicksburg, and I became fretful at the realisation that we wouldn't reach Napoleon and get rid of Omohundro before midnight. The man himself did nothing to set my bowels a-gallop; he spent the morning loafing about the rail, and sat long after luncheon with a group of Arkansas planters, gossiping. But he never stirred off the boiler deck, and I became hopeful again. With evening and darkness coming, it looked as though we were past the most dangerous time.

I kept an eye on him at dinner, though, and afterwards, when he went into the saloon and settled himself with the planters to booze and smoke the evening away, I was glad of a chance offered me to stay on hand. Through Penny-Jenny I had made the acquaintance of two or three fellows on the boat, and one of them, a red-faced old Kentuckian called Colonel Potter, invited me to make up a game of poker. He was one of your noisy, boozy sports, full of heavy humour and hearty guffaws; he fumbled at Penny's thighs under table, slapped backs, twitted me about the Battle of New Orleans, and generally played Bacchus. With him there was a pot-bellied planter named Bradlee, with a great fund of filthy jokes, and a young Arkansan called Harney Shepherdson, who had a yellow whore in tow. Just the kind of company I like, and I was able to watch Omohundro at the same time.

He left his friends after a while, and during a pause in our game he approached our table. Potter welcomed him boisterously, pressed him to sit down, introduced us all round, called for another bottle, and said would Omohundro take a hand.

"No, thankee, colonel," says he. "Matter of fact, I'm taking the liberty of intrudin' on your little party in the hope I can kindly have a little word with your friend here—" he indicated Bradlee, to my relief "—on a matter of business. If the ladies will forgive, that is; I'm due off at Napoleon in an hour or two, so hopin' you won't mind."

"Feel free, suh; help y'self," cries Potter, and Omohundro turns to Bradlee.

"Understand you have some niggers below, suh," says he, and my innards froze at the words. "Couple of Mande's 'mong 'em, accordin' to my friends yonder. Now, while I'm not on a buyin' trip, you understand, I never miss a Mande if I can help it. Wonder if you feel inclined to talk business, suh, an' if so, I might take a look at 'em."

I leaned back, hoping no one would notice how the sweat was beginning to pump off me, as I waited for Bradlee's answer.

"Always talk business, anytime," says he. "Got to warn you though, suh, my niggers don't come cheap. Could be askin' a right nice price."

"Could be payin' one, for the right kind of cattle," says Omohundro. "Be deeply 'bliged to you, suh, if I might take a look at 'em for myself; be much beholden to you."

Bradlee said it was fine with him, and heaved himself up, with his apologies to the table. I was shuddering by this time; I must get down to the main deck before them, and get Randolph out of sight somehow. I was on the point of jumping to my feet and making my excuses, when Potter, the interfering oaf, sings out:

"Say, why'nt you take a look at Mr Prescott's coffle while you about it, suh? He got some right prime stock there, ain't you, though? Purtiest set o' niggers I seen in a while—it's so, suh, I assure you. Reckon Mr Prescott's got good taste in mos' things —eh, honey?" And he set Penny squealing with a pinch.

What possessed him to stick his oar in, God knows; just my luck, I suppose. I found Omohundro's eyes on me.

"That so, suh? Well, I ain't rightly buyin', like I said, but if—"

"Nothing for sale, I'm afraid." I strove to sound offhand, and he nodded:

"In that case, your servant, ladies, colonel, gentlemen," and he and Bradlee went off towards the staircase, leaving me floundering. I had to get away, so I started to my feet, saying I must fetch something from my cabin. Potter cried that we were just about to go on with the game, and Penny squeaked that without me to guide her she couldn't tell the little clover leaves from the other black things on the cards, but by that time I was striding for the staircase, cursing Potter and with panic rising in my chest.

I saw Omohundro and Bradlee disappear downwards just ahead of me, so I hung back, and then slipped down the spiral staircase in their wake. By the time I reached the main deck they were already over at the far port rail, where Bradlee's coffle lay, calling for the overseer to bring another light. It was pretty dim on the main deck, with only a few flare lamps which cast great black shadows among the bales and machinery; the various coffles of niggers were scattered about, nesting among the cargo, with my own crew up forward, away from the rest.

I lurked in the shadows, debating whether to go and warn Randolph, and decided not to; you never knew what that highstrung gentleman might do if he thought there was danger close by. It seemed best to lurk in the shadows unobserved, keeping an eye on Bradlee and Omohundro, and ready to intervene—God alone knew how—if they decided to take an interest in my coffle. The truth was I just didn't know what to do for the best, and so did nothing.

Peeping over a box I watched while Omohundro, by the light of the overseer's lantern, examined a couple of Bradlee's slaves, walking round them prodding and poking. I couldn't hear what was said, what with the churning of the great paddle wheel and the steady murmur and crooning of the slaves, but after about five minutes Omohundro shook his head, I heard Bradlee laugh, and then the three of them moved slowly amidships, where Omohundro stopped to light a cigar. From where I lurked among the bales I began to hear their voices.

"... and of course I don't blame you, pricin' high," Omohundro was saying. "Reckon your figure is about right, these days, but that wouldn't leave any margin of profit. Still, I'm right sorry; good bucks you have, suh, an' well schooled."

"Guess I can train a nigger," says Bradlee. "Yessir, I jus' about think I can. Whup seldom, but whup good, my ol' dad used to say, an' he was right. Guess I ain't laid a rawhide on a nigger o' mine this las' twelve-month; don't have to. They got a respect for me, on 'count they know if I *do* trim one of 'em up, he'll *stay* trimmed."

"That's the style with 'em," chips in the overseer. "On'y way, otherwise they git spoiled. Breaks my heart to see good niggers spoiled, too, by soft handlin', like the coffle that Englishman brung aboard."

"How's that?" says Bradlee. "I hear they's prime; so Potter sayin'."

"Oh, prime enough—just now. But he don't know how to handle 'em, an' he in a right way to ruinin' 'em, to my way o' thinkin'. Shame, it is." And then to my horror, he added: "Care to see 'em, gennelmen?"

My heart stopped beating, and then Omohundro said:

"Reckon not; he ain't sellin', so he tell me."

"No?" chuckles the overseer. "I guess he'll be glad 'nough to, come a year or so. Leastways with one of 'em—the uppitiest yaller son-of-a-bitch you ever see. First-rate nigger, too—clean, straight, smart, an' talks like a college p'fessor—oh, you know *his* sort, I reckon. All frills an' goddam' lip."

"Uh-huh," says Bradlee. "Educated, likely, an' spoiled to hell an' gone. Got no use for 'em, myself."

"That kind of fancy fetches a good price, though, once the tar's been taken out of 'em," says Omohundro. "Make valets, butlers, an' so forth—ladies in Awlins an' Mobile payin' heavy money for 'em." He paused. "Think the Englishman knows what this feller's worth?"

"How could he?" says Bradlee. "He tells me he spent all his time in Afriky slave ships, till now. He don't know the value of talkin' niggers."

Shut up, shut up about my bloody niggers, I found myself whispering. Mind your own business and get upstairs where you belong, can't you. And they would have done but for that benighted swine of an overseer.

"Talkin' niggers is right—this one of Prescott's sure can handle his gab. Highest-falutin' smart-assed buck in creation, answers back sassy as be damned. An' what you think Mist' Prescott do, gennelmen, hey? Why, he jus' pats and smooths him! Yessir. Makes a body sick to listen."

"The English is soft on niggers. Ev'yone know that," says Bradlee. "I'd like to see the buck'd talk back to *me*; I'd just about like to hear *that*."

"Well, suh, you don't have to stir more'n twenty feet to see him," cries the infernal clod. "Here, gennelman, step across this ways—I see Mist' Omohundro kinda interested anyway, that right, suh?"

I should have strode out then and there, I know, and done something, anything, to keep them away from my coffle. I might have talked them away, or damned their eyes for going near my blacks, or made some diversion. But my consternation had reached the point where I had lost my nerve altogether; I hesitated, and then the overseer was up forward, barking at my niggers to rise and let the white men have a look at them. I waited, helpless, for the blow to fall.

"Where that George?" the overseer was shouting. "Here, you George, ye black varmint, step out when I calls ye!"

It was like watching a play I had seen before, and a bloody tragedy at that. Randolph, unsuspecting, stood up among his fellows, blinking in the light.

"That one?" says Bradlee. "Well, he don't look so dam' pert, eh, Omohundro? Good clean buck, too, quadroon, I reckon—why, what's the matter with you, boy? You seen a ghost?"

Randolph was staring, with his hand to his mouth, at Omohundro, who was stooping to peer at him.

"What's that? Wait, though—hold on a minute! What's your name, boy? I seen you before somewheres, ain't I—yes! By God, I have!" His voice rose in a shout of amazement. "You're George Rand—"

In that moment Randolph was on him like a tiger, carrying the big man to the deck, and then falling himself as his shackles tripped him. He was up in an instant though, agile as a cat, smashing a fist into Bradlee's face before the overseer, swearing in astonishment, managed to close with him. They reeled against the bales, locked together, and then Randolph jerked his knees up, and the overseer staggered away yelping, clutching his groin.

"Get him!" bawls Omohundro. "He's a runaway—Randolph! Stop him, Bradlee!"

Hobbled by his irons—he hadn't time to get at his hidden key—Randolph half hopped, half ran for the rail, with Bradlee clutching at his shirt, trying to drag him back. Omohundro got a hold, too, but stumbled and fell, cursing; as they tried to grapple him Randolph broke away, and before his irons finally tripped him he had covered half a dozen yards which brought him to the big box where I was crouching. He saw me as he fell, and shouted:

"Help! Help me, Prescott! Fight them off!"

Such an appeal, addressed to Flashy, meets a prompt response. I ducked back behind cover just as Omohundro came crashing over the bales, clutching at Randolph's feet. The quadroon kicked free, scrambled on to the rail, and was trying to roll over it when he must have realised that he would fall plumb in the path of the great thirty-foot paddle wheel; he shrieked, rearing up on the rail, the overseer's pistol banged, and I saw Randolph's body arch and his face contort with agony. He fell, outwards, and the huge wheel blades came churning down on him as he hit the water.

I daresay that if I had had a few minutes for quiet reflection it would have occurred to me that the safest course would be to stand my ground, playing the innocent trader amazed at the news that there had been a runaway in his coffle, and brazen it out that way. But I hadn't those few minutes, and I'm not sure I'd have acted any differently anyway. The overwhelming feeling that I had when I saw Randolph's body fall, with Omohundro and Bradlee roaring bloody murder and the whole deck in uproar, was that here was no place for Flashy any longer. I was skipping away between the bales before the echo of the shot had died; Omohundro's bellow to me to stop merely assisted my flight. I crossed the deck in half a dozen strides, and launched myself over the starboard rail in a fine flat dive; there was no wheel on that side, I knew, and when I surfaced in the warm Mississippi water with all the breath knocked out of me the *Sultana* was already a hundred yards away upriver.

Even today I can't feel anything but irritation and dislike for George Randolph. If he had only had the sense to keep his mouth shut and act humble for once, he'd never have been confronted by Omohundro that night; the odds are he'd have reached Canada without fuss and embarked immediately on a happy life as a professor at some liberal university, or the leader of a nigger minstrel troupe, or something equally useful. Instead his pride and folly had bought him a bullet in the belly and a grave in the Mississippi mud, as far as I could see; more important, he had put me in a highly dangerous and embarrassing position.

My wits must have been cleared by the water, for I had the immediate presence of mind not to swim for the Arkansas shore, a mere hundred yards away, but to strike out instead across the stream for the Mississippi bank, which was almost three-quarters of a mile off. I'm a strong swimmer, and the water was warm, so I made it easily enough; by the time I climbed out across a mud bank and plumped down among some willows, the *Sultana* had stopped at the next bend, but after half an hour she started off again, doubtless to stop at the next landing and start the hue and cry.

I blasted Randolph bitterly at the thought that I was a hunted fugitive once more, in the middle of a strange land with only a few dollars in my pocket. The one consolation was that they would scour the Arkansas side first, and I would have time to get inland in Mississippi unmolested. And then whither? There could be no going back south, with the Navy still doubtless on the look-out for me, and it would be madness to try to continue north along the river on foot. But north I would have to go eventually, if I were to reach home again; in the meantime I must find some place to lie up undetected until all the hullaballoo had died down, and I could work cautiously upriver to the free states, and so to the Atlantic seaboard and a passage home.

It was a damned tall order and depressing prospect, and I had a grand old curse that night at my folly in being bullied into this fearful fix by Crixus. My one hope was that Mississippi was such a big place, where I assumed news travelled slowly and uncertainly, that I ought to be able to find a bolt-hole; I reasoned that itinerant strangers must be commonplace in the western states, so I might escape remark if I was careful how I went.

I slept that night among the cottonwoods, and struck due east before sunrise, as I wanted to get away from the river as quickly as possible. And so began three of the most dam' dismal days of my life, in which I skulked through woods and along by-roads, living the life of a vagrant, stopping only at the loneliest farms and places I could find to buy a meal out of the few dollars I had left. The one thing that cheered me was that none of the people I saw paid me any close attention, which confirmed my belief that they were used to all sorts of odd fellows trudging about the country; I tried to speak as American as I could, when I spoke at all, and must have made a passable job of it, for nobody appeared to take me for anything else.

However, I realised that this could not continue. Soon I would be destitute, and since I've never been any hand at petty theft or highway robbery, I came to the reluctant conclusion that I must try and find work. It's a last resort, of course, but it seemed to me if I could get some employment in an out-of-the-way spot I could lie up and save money for my eventual flight at one and the same time. I made one or two cautious inquiries, without success beyond an afternoon's labour splitting logs for my supper, and I was in despair by the fourth morning, when by sheer chance I lit on the very thing I was looking for.

I had slept in the woods, and spent my last few cents on bread and milk at a run-down store, when a burly chap on a grey horse comes cantering up, roaring for the storekeeper that he had come to settle his debt.

"What's the row then, Jim?" says the storekeeper. "Where you off to?"

"Headed west," cries Jim. "I seen my last load o' goddamned cotton, I can tell you that. It's Californey for me, my boy, an' a pisspotful of gold. There's your four dollars, Jake, an' much obliged to ye."

"Well, that beats all," says the storeman. "Californey, eh? Wisht I could go myself, by thunder. Say, but what's Mandeville goin' to do without a driver, in the middle o' pickin' time?"

"Do his goddamned drivin' his goddamned self," says the other cheerfully. "I guess I'll worry about him, won't I, all the way to the diggin's. I'm off to see the elephant! Yeh-hoo! It's Californey or bust!" And he waved his hat and thundered away, leaving the storeman scratching his head in wonder.

I didn't inquire at the store; the less said the better. But I met a nigger up the road, found where Mandeville's place was, and after a four-mile walk came to his imposing front gates. They were made of granite, no less, and the place was called Greystones, an impressive spread of cotton plantation with a fine white colonial house at the head of a tree-lined drive. It looked a likely spot for me, so I strode up and presented myself as a driver in need of work.

Mandeville was a broad, bull-necked man of about fifty with heavy whiskers on a coarse red face.

"Who told you I needin' a driver?" says he, standing four-square on his verandah and squinting down at me suspiciously. I said I had met his former employee on the road.

"Huh! That fool Jim Bakewell! Ups an' off in the middle o' pickin', cool as you please, to go to Californey. Ifn he ain't any better at diggin' than at drivin' he'll finish up cleanin' out privies, which is all he good for anyways. Triflin' useless bastard." He cocked his head at me. "Reckon you kin drive?"

"Anything that moves," says I.

"Oh, my niggers *move*," says he. "They *move*, ifn someone on hand to make 'em skip. You driven cotton-hands befo', I guess, by the look o' you." In the surprise of realising what "driving" meant, I overlooked the doubtful compliment. "Where you from, an' what your name?"

"Tom Arnold," says I. "From Texas, a while back."

"Uh-huh, the Texies. Well, no denyin', gotta have a driver. Dunno where I get one, this season, ifn I don't take ye. Ain't no slouch of a job, min'—you be th' only white driver on the place. Thirty dolla's a month, an' yo' keep. Satisfy ye, Tom?"

I said it would, and at that moment a nigger came round the house leading a fine white mare, and a lady came through the pillared front door, dressed for riding. Mandeville hailed her eagerly.

"Why, Annie dahlin', there you are! Fine, fine—jus' off a-ridin', I see. That's fine, fine." And then, seeing her eyes on me, he hurried to explain. "This here's Tom Arnold, honey; jus' hired him as a new driver, in room o' that no-good Bakewell. Right piece o' luck, I reckon, him turnin' up. Yes, suh."

"Is it?" said the lady, and you could see she doubted it. She was one of the tiniest women I've ever seen, somewhere under five feet, although well-shaped in a dainty doll-like way. But there was nothing doll-like about the sharp little face, with its pointed elfin chin, tight lips, and cold grey eyes that played over me with a look of bleak disdain. I became conscious of my bedraggled appearance and unshaven face; three days in the woods make a poor toilet.

"We may hope he is a better driver than Bakewell," says the lady coldly. "At the moment he looks as though he was more accustomed to being driven."

And without another word or glance at me she mounted her mare, Mandeville fussing to help her, and cantered off along the drive with the nigger groom trotting at her heels. Mandeville waved after her, his red face beaming, and then turned back to me.

"That Mrs Mandeville," says he, proudly. "She the lady o' my plantation. Yessuh, Mrs Mandeville." Then his eyes slid away and he said he would show me my quarters and instruct me in my duties.

As it turned out, these were easy enough; slave-driving is as pleasant an occupation as any, if you must work. You ride round the cotton rows on horse-back, seeing that the niggers don't let up in filling their baskets, and laying on the leather when they slack. Greystones was a fair-sized place, with about a hundred niggers working the great snowy fields that stretched away from behind the house to the river, and they were a well-drilled pack by the time I'd done with 'em, I can tell you. I vented the discontent I felt at America on them, and enjoyed myself more than I'd done since my Rugby days, when lacing fags was the prime sport.

Although I had a couple of black drivers to help me, I became quite expert with my hide—you could make a sleepy nigger jump his own height with a well-placed welt across his backside, squealing his head off, and if any of them were short-weighted at the end of the day you gave them half a dozen cuts for luck. Mandeville was delighted with the tally of cotton picked, and told me I was the best overseer he'd ever had, which didn't surprise me. It was work I could take a hearty interest in.

After the first few days he left me alone to the job, for he frequently had business in Helena, about fifty miles away on the other side of the Mississippi river, or in Memphis, over the Tennessee border, and would stay away for nights at a time. He always went alone, leaving his wife in the house, which seemed damned indiscreet to me. I didn't realise, fortunately for my self-esteem, that while a Southern planter wouldn't have dreamed of leaving his wife unchaperoned in a house while there was a white man there, he'd never think twice if that man was a hired servant living in a cottage fifty yards away. However, she kept out of my way in those early days, and I out of hers.

Knowing me, you may think that strange. But all my thoughts at this stage were on my own plight; Greystones seemed to be just the kind of out-of-the-way spot I required; it was isolated in the woodland and marsh, and was seldom visited, but even so I had my heart in my mouth every time hoofbeats sounded on the drive, and I kept well out of sight when one of Mandeville's neighbours called. It didn't seem likely that if there was a search going on for me, it would reach this far from the river, and there was nothing to connect the steamboat fugitive with Mandeville's new driver, but even so I kept a sharp eye open at first for any hint of danger. As the days passed, and none appeared, I began to feel easier.

Another reason why I kept out of Annette Mandeville's way was that I disliked her, and she me, apparently. I had guessed two things from our first brief meeting: one was that she was an unpleasant, arrogant little piece, and the other that she had her big, powerful husband on a string. He was more than twice her age, of course (she couldn't have been above two-and-twenty), and I've noticed that there are few things that a middle-aged man will go in such awe of as an imperious young wife; he'll face a wounded buffalo, or go headlong into a sabre charge, but he'll turn pale and stutter at the thought of saying, "I'd rather not, dearest." Well, I can understand it, when the wife holds the purse, or is bigger than he, or can get the law on him. But even without these things Mandeville went in awe of her.

And she knew it, and enjoyed using her power to torment him. She wasn't just spoiled and petulant—she was cruel, in a subtle way, and I say it who am a recognised authority. I saw enough of them together to judge the pleasure she took in fretting and hurting him with her ready sneers and icy disdain; the more eager he was to please her, this man who was so coarse and masterful in other things, the more she seemed to delight in making him uneasy and bewildered.

Much of this I learned from Mandeville himself—not that he dreamed he was instructing me. But he loved to talk, and there not being another white man on the place, he took to inviting me up to the house at night, after his wife had retired, for a booze and prose; he was a decent enough fellow, I suppose, in his rough way, and greatly given to foxing himself on corn toddy, and nothing pleased him more than to yarn away about his niggers and his horses, and—when he was well maudlin—about his wife. And this most often after she had set him down, which she did most days.

"Yes, suh," this infatuated idiot would say, smiling blearily at his glass, "I'm a lucky man, an' she a won'erful li'l lady. Yes suh, 'deed she is. Well, you kin see that, Tom; you a travelled man, I guess, you kin see she is. Course, she git a li'l short, time to time —like today, now—but it ain't nuthin' at all. My own fault, I guess. Y'see, the truth is, although this here's a pretty fair spread at Greystones, tain't altogether what she bin used to. No-suh. She come from one o' the best French families in N'Awlins —the Delancy's, likely you heard o' them, gotta tre-mendous big estate out to Lake Pontchartrain. Trouble is, ol' man Delancy, he a bit stretched, an' I helped him out over a couple o' deals. Five years ago, that was, when I married Annie. Here, Jonah, light a see-gar for Mist' Arnold; fill your glass, suh."

By now he would be well launched, convincing himself for the thousandth time, against all reason.

"Ye-es, five years ago. Happiest day o' my life, suh. But I'll admit—you take a gel who's bin brought up a real lady, who's got real blood, bin to convent, had a half-dozen yaller maids waitin' on her, an' who's used to livin' in the top so-ciety in N'Awlins —well, I do her pretty good here, I reckon, but it ain't the same. Not much society, even in Memphis, an' the local folks ain't 'xactly the kin' o' bucks an' belles she used to meet at home. So it's natural she gits these fits an' starts now an' then. But you 'ppreciate that, Tom. An' no denyin', either, me bein' older'n she is, a little, she get kinda bored. I don' talk quite her way, you see, an' I ain't got her—tastes, so to speak. So she get a mite res'less, like I say. An' boy, don' she dress me down then!" And he would giggle drunkenly, as though at some good joke which he thoroughly enjoyed. "Say, you oughta hear her when she got a real head o' steam. My stars! Course, tain't often."

Not more than twice a day, and three times on Sundays, I would say to myself. Serve the clown right for marrying out of his class.

"Say, but don' get me wrong! Here, have 'nuther drink. Don' get me wrong—she a real lovin' gel. Yes-suh. She the lovin'est little creatur' you ever did see. When I say she sometimes bored, don' think I mean she goin' short! Ho-ho, I guess not!" And he would nudge me, winking ponderously, with a lewd leer. "I tell you, I'm 'bout wore out pilin' inter that li'l darlin'! Fact. She cain't seem t'get enough o' me. 'Do it again, Johnny lover, do it again.' That what she say. An' don' I do it? Oh, I should say not! I should jus' 'bout reckon not. An' don' she know how to rouse a man on, hey? Why, I see some men—like Parkins, down at Helena, an' young Mackay, who got the Yellowtree place—they jus' itchin' for her, jus' at the sight of her. Why, I could see you fancy her you'self—no, don't fret you'self, don't fret. I don't mind one li'l bit. It's only natural, ain't it? I don't take no offence, cos I know she never think o' no one but me. 'Do it again, Johnny lover.' That what she say. Talk 'bout your nigger wenches—pish!'"

It was from drunken meanderings such as this that I formed my conclusions about the Mandevilles—an obvious one being that they didn't bed together, and probably never had. Well, that could explain a lot about Madame Annette's behaviour, and in other circumstances I would probably have set myself to supply her want, for she was a trim little half-pint, bar her shrew face. But she was so damned unpleasant that the thought didn't cross my mind; when we met she either looked straight through me or treated me as though I were no better than the blacks. If I hadn't needed the work I'd have taken the rough side of my tongue to her, and as it was I gave her back sneer for sneer as far as I dared, so that before long we hated each other as cordially as man and woman can. And mind you, I don't like this sort of thing; it ain't usual to find a woman who isn't prepared to be civil to me, and I'd grown my whiskers long again, and a rakish little black imperial, too.

However, I had my own affairs to attend to. I was working quietly away towards the day when I'd have enough saved to be able to move off north again. I reckoned two or three months would see me set and ready, and by that time all the haroosh caused by my flight from the *Sultana* would have died down, and I'd be able to take the road in safety.

So I laboured away, whopping niggers, mounting the occasional black wench in my quarters, and counting my dollars every fortnight, and never gave a thought to Annette Mandeville. Which was foolish of me; equally foolish was the way in which I allowed a sense of security to grow on me as the weeks passed and no hue and cry came to disturb the peace of Greystones. Picking time passed and with less to do I got restless, and impatient to be up and away for England; I suppose that made me more thoughtless and short-tempered than usual, all of which was to lead to my undoing.

It was the approach of Christmas that finally broke my patience, I think. I suppose everyone's thoughts turn home then, whether they really wish they were there or not. I had only Elspeth to miss —and the baby I'd never seen. Not that I've any use for brats, mind you, but any excuse will do for a self-pitying weep when you're alone in your quarters in a foreign land, with two inches left in the bottom of the corn bottle, and the rest gurgling in your belly and making you feel sick and miserable. I imagined Elspeth, fair and radiant, bending over a crib and shaking a rattle at its occupant, and looking adoringly across at me with that lovely pink bloom on her cheeks, and myself toasting my arse at the nursery fire with my coat tails pulled back, and a fine helping of duff and brandy inside me, quite the proud papa, while waits sang in the street outside. Instead, here I was, half-foxed and croaking to myself in a draughty shack, with no Elspeth, but a black slut snoring open-mouthed in the corner, and in place of waits the eternal caterwauling of the field hands as they sang one of their morbid chants. I sat there blubbering boozily, trying to put the home picture out of my mind, and telling myself it was all a sham —that Elspeth would be back in the saddle with one of her gallants by now, and old Morrison would ruin Christmas anyway by whining about the cost of geese and holly. It was no good; I was homesick, bloody homesick, and the thought of Morrison was an added incentive. By God, I'd make the old scoundrel skip when I got back and flourished Spring's papers under his ugly nose. The thought cheered me up, and when I had finished the bottle, been sick, and thrashed the nigger girl for snoring, I felt more like myself again.

But I was still chafing to be away, and with only two weeks of my enforced sojourn to go I was in a thoroughly ill humour and ready to take my spite out on anyone—even Annette Mandeville or her soused clown of a husband. Not that I was seeing much of either of them by now, for Mandeville was absent more and more, and Annette kept to the house. But she had her eyes open too, as I was to discover to my cost.

I mentioned a black girl in my quarters; she was the least ugly and smelly of the field women whom I had taken as a carnal cook —a bedfellow-cum-housekeeper, that is. She was little use as either, but one has to make do. Anyway, it happened that one evening, after a long day down by the river where the slaves were cutting a ditch, I came home to find her whimpering and groaning on her mattress, with a couple of nigger girls tending her and looking mighty scared.

"What's this?" says I.

"Oh, massa," says the wenches, "Hermia she pow'ful sick; she real po'ly, she is."

And she was. Someone had flogged her until her back was a livid mess of cuts and bruises.

"Who the devil's done this?" roars I in a great rage, and it was

Hermia herself who told me, between her wails.

"Oh, Massa Tom, it the Miz—Miz Annette. She done tell me I's ins'lent, en she'd trim me up good. I don' done nuthin' Massa Tom—but she git Hector to whup me, en oh I's hurtin', hurtin' suthin' awful, massa. Hector he lay on 'til I's swoondin' —en ain't done nuthin'. Oh, Massa Tom, whut ins'lent mean?"

Well, I knew Annette was hard on the niggers, who went in terror of her, and I'd no doubt this silly slut had offended her in some way. So I gave no thought to it, but turned Hermia out, since she was of no use for anything in her present state. Next day I picked another wench to take her place, and went off to the fields in due course—and when I came home there she was, beaten black and blue, just as Hermia had been, again on Miz Annette's orders.

Now I can take a hint as fast as the next man, but I confess I didn't see all the way through this one, which was foolish of me. I took it that the spiteful little harridan was bent on denying me female companionship, but it never occurred to me why. Which shows what a modest chap I am, I suppose. In any event, I had to do something about it, for I was seething with anger at her malice, and since Mandeville was away in Memphis, I went straight up to the house to have it out with the mistress.

She was obviously just back from a canter round the plantation, for she was still in her grey riding suit, issuing orders to Jonah in the hall. When he had gone, I tackled her straight.

"Two of the field girls have been flogged, on your instructions," says I. "May I be permitted to ask why?"

She didn't even look at me. "What concern is it of yours?" says she, taking off her gloves.

"As your husband's overseer, I'm responsible for his slaves."

"Under his authority—and mine," says she, and started off upstairs without another word. I wasn't having this, so I strode after her.

"By all means," says I, "but I find it strange that you undertake to discipline them yourself. Why not leave the matter to me— since it's what I'm paid for?"

We were at the head of the stairs by now, but she kept right on towards her room. I kept pace with her, fuming, and suddenly she snapped at me:

"What you are paid for is to obey orders, not to question what I do. Your place is in the fields—not in this house. Be so good as to leave, at once!"

"I'm damned if I do! You've had the tar whaled out of two of those girls, and I want to know why."

"Don't be impertinent!" She wheeled on me, her face screwed up with fury. "How dare you follow me in this way? How dare you take that tone? Get out, before I call the servants to throw you into the fields! Not another word!" And she flounced into her room—but she left the door open.

"Now listen to me, you vicious brat, you!" I was in a fine fury by now. "If you won't tell me, I'll tell you! You had them thrashed because they were *my* girls, didn't you? You thought—"

"Your girls!" She spat it at me. "Your girls! Since when could a penniless beggar like you talk of *your* girls! *My* slaves, do you hear? And if I choose to punish them, I shall do it—" she was fairly hissing the words "—as I choose, and you will keep your place, you mongrel!"

I think the only reason I didn't strike her was that she was so tiny, snarling up at me, that I was frightened of breaking her. And even in my anger I saw a better way of hurting her—always Flashy's forte, as Tom Hughes has testified.

"Well, now," says I, holding myself in, "I don't think the word 'mongrel' is one that comes at all well from a Creole lady." I let it sink in and added: "I don't have to worry about *my* finger-nails."

It was quite false, of course; I don't suppose she had a drop of black blood in her. But it struck her like a blow; she stood glaring, her face chalk-white, unable to speak, so I carried on, amiably:

"You whipped those girls because I was bedding them, and no doubt you'll be prepared to go on whipping until you've half-killed every wench on the plantation. Well, see if I care—they ain't my property. See if your husband cares, though; he mayn't like having his investment wasted. He'll maybe ask you why you did it. 'Because your overseer's covering 'em,' you'll say—using a lady-like term, I'm sure. 'And why not?' he'll say, 'what's that to you?' Why, he may even wonder—"

And there I stopped, for there, and only there, the light dawned.

As I say, I'm over-modest; she had been so damned uncivil to me, you see, that it honestly hadn't crossed my mind that she fancied me. Usually, of course, I'm ready to accept that every woman does —well, they do—but she was such a shrew-faced pip-squeak, and so unpleasant. . .

I stared at her now, and noted with interest that from white her witch-face had turned flushed, and her breathing was slow and thick. Well, well, thinks I, what have we here; let's see if our manly charms have truly captivated this unlikely creature after all. And purely by way of scientific experiment I leaned forward, picked her up with my hands at her waist—it was like lifting a puppet—and kissed her.

She didn't struggle or kick or cry out, so I kept at it, and very slowly her mouth opened, and she gave a little sob, and then she took my lip in her teeth and began to bite, harder and harder, until I pulled her free, holding her at arm's length. Her eyes were shut, and her face tight set; then she motioned me to set her down, and she stood against me. Her head touched my top weskit button.

"Wait," said she, in a little whisper, and quickly closing the door she vanished into her dressing-room. I could have laughed, but instead I began peeling off my coat, reflecting that the road to fornication is truly often paved with misunderstanding. I was sitting on the bed, removing my boots, when she re-entered, and she was a startling sight, for she was stark naked except for her riding boots. That took me aback, for it ain't usual among amateurs; something to do with her French upbringing, no doubt. But it was the rest of her that took the eye; I'd known she was well-shaped, but in the buff she was an undoubted little nymph. Scientific research be damned, says I, reaching out for her, and she came with her mouth open and her eyes shut, straining at me.

"You silly little popsy," says I. "Why didn't you let me know before?" And so to work, which proved none too bad, bar one unexpected and painful surprise. I was settling into my stride when I discovered why she had kept her boots on, for she suddenly clapped her legs round me, and so help me, those boots were spurred. Hair brushes (that was dear Lola) I was used to, but being stabbed in the buttocks is an arse of a different colour, if you'll forgive the pun, and it was fortunate the bed was a wide one or we'd have flown off it. There was no untangling her, for she clung like a limpet, and I could only wrestle away, yelping from time to time, until we were done. I was stuck like a Derby winner.

Then she pushed me away, slipped off the bed, and picked up a robe. She put it on, without looking at me, and then she said:

"Now get out."

And without another word she went into her dressing-room and bolted the door.

Well, I'm not used to this kind of treatment, and in other circumstances I'd have kicked the door in and taught her manners, but in a house full of niggers you can't conduct an affair as though you were man and wife. So I dressed, staunching my wounds and muttering curses, and presently limped away, vowing that she'd had the last of me.

But of course she hadn't. Mandeville returned next day, and I kept well clear of the house, but come the end of the week he was off to Helena again, to meet some fellows on business. With only a week of my time left I should have gone about my business, ignoring Madame Annette, but human nature being what it is, I didn't. No woman tells me to get out with impunity, especially a haughty dwarf who was no great shakes in bed anyway. This is illogical, of course, but those of us who study immoral philosophy are guided by some contrary rules. At all events, I came sniffing round the day after he left—well, she was white, and interesting, and apart from her face she was a well-set-up piece in a miniature way.

To my surprise, she didn't either rebuff me or welcome me with open arms. We discussed the piece of plantation business which I'd made my pretext for coming, and when I assailed her she fell to with a will—but never a word, or a smile, or anything but a fierce, cold passion that almost scared me. It was damned spooky, when I think of it now, and afterwards, when I tried to engage her in sociable chat, she sat moody and withdrawn, hardly saying a word. And not a stitch on, mark you—not even her boots. I'd taken good care of that.

I gave up, half-puzzled and half-annoyed; I couldn't fathom her at all, and I still can't. My experience with women has been, I dare say, considerable and varied; I've had them fighting to get at me and running for dear life to escape, all ages, shapes and colours, in beds, haylofts, thickets, drawing-rooms, palaces, hovels, snow-drifts (that was in Russia, in the cold spell), baths, billiard rooms, cellars, camps, covered wagons, and even in the library of Corpus Christi College, Cambridge, which is probably a record of some sort. I've sometimes regretted that the flying machine was invented so late in my life, but things move so fast nowadays it's difficult to keep pace.

Anyway, my point is that only three women that I can recall out of that darling multitude have refused to be sociable afterwards, provided there was time, of course. My Afghan lotus-blossom, Narreeman, was one, but she had been constrained, as they say, and wanted to murder me anyway. Queen Ranavalona was another, but apart from being as mad as a hatter she had affairs of state to attend to, which is some excuse. Annette Mandeville was the third, and I believe she was neither mad nor murderous. But who's to say? I doubt if she'd have been an entertaining talker anyway; she didn't have much education, for all her careful upbringing.

She was avid enough, however, for pleasure itself, and since Mandeville seemed to be making a protracted stay in Helena I visited her on each of the next three days. This was foolishness, of course, for it increased the chances of detection, but when I voiced my doubts, remarking that I hoped none of the niggers would guess what brought me to the house, she laughed un-pleasantly and said:

"Who cares if the whole plantation knows? Not one of these black animals would dare breathe a word—they know what would happen to them."

I didn't like to think what that would be, knowing Madame Annette, but since she seemed so unconcerned I saw no reason why I should fret, and consequently grew careless. I had been in the habit of opening one of her bedroom windows, so that we might hear if anyone approached the house from the road, but on the third day I forgot, so that we never heard the pad of hooves across the turf.

We had just finished a bout; Annette was lying face down on the bed, silent and sullen as usual, and I was trying to win some warmth out of her with my gay chat, and also by biting her on the buttocks. Suddenly she stiffened under me, and in the same instant feet were striding up the corridor towards the room, Mandeville's voice was shouting:

"Annie! Hullo, Annie honey, I'm home! I've brought—" and then the door was flung open and there he stood, the big grin on his red face changing to a stare of horror. My mouth was still open as I gazed across her rump, terror-stricken.

"My God!" he cries. "Betrayed!"

Well, I'd heard the same sort of exclamation before, and I've heard it since, and there's no doubt it's unnerving. But I doubt if there's a man living who can move faster with his pants round his ankles than I can; I was off that bed and diving for the window before the last word had left his lips, and had the sash half up before I remembered it was a cool twenty-foot drop to the ground. I turned like a cornered rat just as he came for me, swinging his horse-whip and bawling with rage; I ducked the cut and slipped past him to the door, stumbing on the threshold. I glanced back in panic, but he was heading straight on for the bed, yelling:

"Filthy strumpet!" and raising his whip again, but Annette, who had sprung up into a kneeling position, just snapped:

"Don't you dare touch me! Drop that whip!"

And he did. He fell back before that tiny, naked figure, mouthing, and then he turned and hurled himself at me, with a face of apoplexy. I was afoot again by this time, dragging up my breeches and haring for the landing, and then a man's figure loomed up at the head of the stair. I heard Mandeville shout: "Stop him!" and although I tried to dodge the upraised riding crop I wasn't quick enough. Something smashed against my forehead, knocking me backwards; the white ceiling spun dizzily above me, and then I was falling into nothing.

I can't have been unconscious more than a few minutes, but when I came to my own leather belt was round my wrists, blood was caking one of my eye-lids, and there was an unholy pain in my brow. I was lying at the foot of the staircase, and a man was bestriding me, one of his booted feet planted on my ankle. There was a tremendous hubbub of voices, with Mandeville yelling blue murder and others trying to quieten him. I turned my head; two or three men were holding him back, and when he saw me conscious he waved his arms and shouted:

"You slimy bastard! You stinkin' hound! I'll have your heart's blood for this! I'll crucify you! Let me at him, boys, an' I'll tear his dirty innards out!"

They struggled with him, and one of them sings out:

"Get that feller outa here, Luke—quick now! afore he gits done a mischief! Damn ye, Mandeville, won't ye hold still!"

"I'll murder him! I'll butcher him 'sif he was a hog! Oh, turn me loose, boys! He's dishonoured me! He's bin an' tried to ravish my wife, my dear Annie, pore defenceless little critter! You got to let me at him!"

The man above me chuckled, leaned down and grabbed me by the waistband, and with surprising strength dragged me across the hall and threw me bodily through a doorway. Then he stepped into the room, shut the door, and growled:

"Now you just lie tʰ ʳe easy, friend, or it'll be the worse fer you."

He had a whip in one hand, and I guessed he was the fellow who had hit me. He was a tall, rangy chap, with a heavy moustache and bright grey eyes which surveyed me sardonically as he went on:

"Layin' still oughtn't to be no hardship fer you; I reckon you're a right smart hand at *layin'*. Mandeville seems to think so, anyways." And he nodded to the door, beyond which we could hear Mandeville still roaring.

I was getting my wits back, and they told me that this fellow wasn't unfriendly.

"For heaven's sake, sir!" I cried. "Cut me loose! I can explain, I promise you! Mandeville is mistaken, believe—"

"Well, now, I reckon he is. Leastways, 'bout his little lady gittin' ravished. I seen her, an' a less ravished-lookin' female I never clapped eyes on. Say, ain't she a sight when she's nekkid, though; mighty trim little tail." He laughed, and leaned down towards me. "Tell me, friend—what she like in the hay? I often fancied—"

"Cut me free! I assure you I can explain—"

"Well, can ye now? I would doubt that, I really would."

He laughed again. "An' if I was Mandeville, I wouldn't listen. I'd cut your goddamned throat here an' now, yessir. Hold on, though; sound like he's comin' to do it his own self."

I struggled on to my knees as the tumult in the hall increased; it sounded as though Mandeville's friends were still having to restrain him by main force. I knelt there, quaking, and pleading with Luke to cut me free, but he shook me off, and when I persisted he kicked me flat on my back.

"Didn't I tell ye to lay still? Any more out o' you an' I'll take this hide to ye." He laughed again, and I suddenly realised that his good humour was not at all friendly, as I'd supposed. He was just enjoying himself.

I didn't dare move after that, but lay shaking with dread, and then after what seemed an age the door opened and the others came in. Mandeville was in the lead, panting and dishevelled, but he seemed to have himself in hand for the moment. Not that that was any consolation; I hope I never see eyes glaring at me like that again.

"You!" says he, and it was like the growl of a beast. "I going to kill you! D'ye hear that now? Kill you for the sneakin' scum you are. Yes sir, I goin' to watch you die for what you done!" There was froth at the corner of his mouth; he was appalling. "But before I do, you goin' to tell these here gennelmen somethin' —you goin' to confess to 'em that you tried to rape my wife! That so, isn't it! You snuck up there, an' you tuk her unawares, an' try to ravish her." He paused, livid. "Now, then—you tell 'em it was so."

Terrified, I stared at the man, but I couldn't have spoken for the life of me, and suddenly he lost control and flung himself at me, kicking and clawing. The others hauled him back, and Luke says:

"It don't signify a damn thing, John! Hold him off, you fellows! You think you're goin' to get the truth out of him? Anyways, we know he tried to rape your good lady—don't we boys? We're all satisfied, I reckon."

He knew it was a lie, and so did they, but they chorused assent, and eventually it pacified Mandeville, at least to the point where his only interest lay in disposing of me.

"I ought to burn you alive!" he snarled. "I ought to nail you to a tree an' have the niggers geld you. In fact, that's just what I'll do! I'll—"

"Hold on there, John," says Luke. "This is jus' wild talk. You can't murder him thataway—"

"Why cain't I? After what he done?"

"Because word'd git out—an' it don't do to murder a man, even if he is a rapin', stinkin' skunk—"

"I'm not!" I cried. "I swear I'm not!"

"You shet up," says Luke. "Fact is, John Mandeville, while I don't deny he's got killin' comin' to him, I don't see how you can do it lessn you fight him, on the square."

"Fight him!" shouts Mandeville. "Damned if I do. He ain't deservin' anythin' but execution!"

"Well, now, ain't I a-tellin' you it cain't be done? Even ifn you hang him, or cut his throat, or shoot him—how you gonna be sure word ain't gonna git out?"

"Who's to tell, Luke Johnson? They's on'y us here—"

"An' niggers, with mighty long ears. No, sir, unless you fight him, which you ain't willin' to do, and cain't say as I blame you, for he don't deserve the consideration—well, then we got to study out some way of givin' him what's comin' to him."

They argued on, and I listened in horror as they discussed means of slaughtering me—for that was what they meant to do, not a doubt. God, the value men place on a rogered woman. I tried to intervene, pleading to be heard, but Mandeville smashed me in the face, and Luke stuck a gag in my mouth, and then they went on with their dreadful discussion. It was terrible, but all I could do was listen, until one of them motioned the others away, and they fell to talking in lowered voices, and all I could catch was snatches and words like "Alabama" and "Tombigbee river", and "very place for him", and "no, I reckon there ain't no risk—who's to know?", and then they laughed, and presently Mandeville came over to me.

"Well, Mr Arnold," says he, smiling like a hyena, "I got good news for you. Yes sir, mighty good. We ain't goin' to kill you —how you like that? No, sir, we value you a mite too high for that, I reckon. You're a sneakin' varmint that took advantage of a man's hospitality to try and steal his honour—we got suthin' better for you than jus' killin'. You like to hear about it?"

I wanted to stop my ears, but I couldn't. Mandeville smirked and went on.

"One of my friends here, he got a prime idea. His cousin a planter over to Alabama—quite a ways from here. Now my friend goin' over that way, takin' a runaway back to another place, and he ready to 'blige me by takin' you a stage farther, to his cousin's plantation. Nobody see you leave here, nobody see you git there. An' when you do, you know what goin' to happen to you?" Suddenly he spat in my face. "You goin' to be stripped an' put in the cane-fields, 'long with the niggers! You pretty dark now—I seen mustees as light as you—an' by the time you laboured in the sun a spell, you brown up pretty good I reckon. An' there you'll be, *Slave* Arnold, see? You won't be dead, but you'll wish you were! Ain't nobody ever goin' to see you, on account it a lonely place, an' no one ever go there—ifn they do, why you just a crazy mustee! Nobody know you here, nobody ever ask for you. An' you never escape—on account no nigger ever run from that plantation—swamps an' dogs always git 'em. So you safe there for life, see? You think you'll enjoy that life, *Slave* Arnold?" He stood up and kicked me savagely. "Now, ain't that a whole heap better'n jus' killin' you, quick an' easy?"

I couldn't believe my ears; I must be dreaming the whole ghastly thing. I writhed and tried to spit the gag out—tried to beg for mercy with my eyes, but it was useless. They laughed at my struggles, and then they tied my feet and threw me into a cupboard. Before they shut the door, Luke leaned over me with his friendly grin, and said softly:

"Reckon you'll count it a pretty dear ride you had, friend. Was she good? I hope for your sake she was, 'cos she's the last white woman you'll ever see, you dirty Texian bastard!"

I couldn't believe what I'd heard—I still find it incredible. That white men—civilised white men, could doom another white man to be dragged away to some vile plantation, herded with niggers, flogged to work like a beast—it couldn't be true, surely? All I'd done was rattle Mandeville's wife—well, if I ever caught a man doing the like to Elspeth, I'd want to kill him, probably, and I could understand Mandeville wanting to as well—but how could he doom me to the living hell of black slavery? It must be their ghastly idea of a joke—it couldn't be true, it just could not be!

But it was. How long I lay in that cupboard I don't know, but it was dark when the door opened and I was dragged out. They had brought my coat, and it was wrapped over my head, and then I felt the horror of fetters being clapped on my ankles. I tried to scream through my gag, and struggled, but they carried me away bodily, muttering and laughing, and presently I was flung on to the hard surface of a cart. I heard Luke say, "Take good care o' that valuable merchandise, Tom Little," and laughter, and then we were jolting away in the darkness.

I twisted in my bonds, half-crazed with the abomination of it, and then the jacket was pulled away, and in the dimness of the cart a woman's voice said:

"Lie still. There's no use struggling. Believe me, I tried struggling —once. It's no good. You must wait—wait and hope."

She pulled out the gag, but my mouth was too parched to speak. She laid her hand on my head, stroking it, and in the dark her voice kept whispering:

"Rest, don't struggle. Wait and hope. Lie still. Wait and hope."

Her name was Cassy, and I believe that without her I must have gone mad on that first night on the slave cart. The darkness, the close animal stench of the enclosed space in which we were cooped up, and most of all the horror of what lay ahead, reduced me to a croaking wreck. And while I lay shuddering and moaning to myself, she stroked my head and talked in a soft, sibilant voice—hardly a trace of nigger, more New Orleans Frenchy, like Annette's—telling me to be easy, and rest, and not to waste my breath on foolish raving. All very well, but foolish raving is a capital way of releasing one's feelings. However, she talked on, and in the end it must have soothed me, because when I opened my eyes the cart was stopped, and a little sunlight was filtering through cracks in the board roof, giving a dim illumination to the interior.

The first thing I did was to crawl about the place—it wasn't above four feet high—examining it, but it was as tight as a drum, and the doors appeared to be padlocked. I couldn't see a hope of escape. I was chained by the legs—the woman had managed to untie the cord at my wrists—and even if I had succeeded in breaking out, what could I have done against two armed men? They would doubtless be making for Alabama by back roads and trails, far from any hope of assistance, and even if, by some miracle, I got out and gave them the slip, they would easily run me down, hobbled as I was.

The horror of it overcame me again, and I just lay there and wept. There was no hope, and the woman's voice suddenly came to confirm my fears.

"It won't seem so bad after a while," she said. "Nothing ever does."

I turned to look at her, and for a moment a crazy thought struck me—that she, too, was white, and the victim of some fearful plot like my own. For she was no more like a nigger than

I was, at first glance. You have seen her head on old Egyptian carvings, both chin and forehead sloping sharply away from a thin curved nose and wide heavy lips, with great almond-shaped devil's eyes which can look strong and terrible in that delicate face. She was unusually tall, but everything about her was fine and fragile, from the high cheekbones and thin black hair bound tight behind her head to the slender ankles locked in slave fetters; even her colour was delicate, like very pale honey, and I realised she was the lightest kind of nigger, what they call a musteefino.[87] She reminded me of a Siamese cat, graceful and sinuous and probably far stronger than she looked.

Mind you, my thoughts weren't running in their usual direction; I was too powerfully occupied with my predicament for that, and I fell to groaning and cursing again. I must have babbled something about escape, because she suddenly said:

"Why do you waste your breath? Don't you know better by now—there's no escape. Not now, or ever."

"My God!" I cried. "There must be. You don't know what they're going to do to me. I'm to be enslaved on a plantation —for life!"

"Is that so strange?" said she, bitterly. "You're lucky you haven't been there before. What were you—a house slave?"

"I'm not a bloody slave!" I shouted. "I'm a white man."

She stared at me through the dimness. "Oh, come now. We stop saying that when we're ten years old."

"It's true, I tell you! I'm an Englishman! Can't you tell?"

She moved across the cart, peering at my face, frowning. Then: "Give me your hand," she says.

I let her look at my nails; she dropped my hand and sat back, staring at me with those great amber-flecked eyes. "Then what are you doing here, in God's name?"

You may be sure I told her—at length, but leaving out the juicy parts: Mandeville suspected me unjustly, I told her. She sat like a graven image until it was done, and then all she said was:

"Well, now one of you knows what it feels like." She went back to her corner. "Now you know what a filthy race you belong to."

"But, dear Christ!" I exclaimed. "I must get out of it, I must—"

"How?" Her lips writhed in a sneer. "Do you know how many times I've run? Three times! And each time they caught me, and dragged me back. Escape! Bah! You talk like a fool."

"But . . . but . . . last night ∴ . . in the dark . . . you said something about waiting and hoping . . ."

"That was to comfort you. I thought you were . . . one of us." She gave a bitter little laugh. "Well, you are, now, and I tell you there isn't any hope. Where can you run to, in this vile country? This land of freedom! With slave-catchers everywhere, and dogs, and whipping-houses, and laws that say I'm no better than a beast in a sty!" Her eyes were blazing with a hatred that was scaring. "You try and run! See what good it does you!"

"But slave-catchers can't touch me! If only I can get out of this cursed wagon! Look," I went on, desperately, "there must be a chance—when they open the doors, to feed us—"

"How little you know of slavery!" she mocked me. "They won't open the doors—not till they get me to Forster's place, and you to wherever you're going. Feed us!—that's how they feed us, like dogs in a kennel!" And she pointed to a hatch in the door, which I hadn't noticed. "For the rest, you foul your sty—why shouldn't you? You're just a beast! Did you know that was what the Romans called us—talking beasts? Oh, yes, I learned a lot about slavery, in the fine house I was brought up in. Brought up so that I could be made the chattel of any filthy ruffian, any beggar or ignorant scum of the levees—just so he was white!" She sat glaring at me, then her shoulders drooped. "What use to talk? You don't know what it means. But you will. You will."

Well, you may guess how this raised my spirits. The very fierceness of the woman, her bitter certainty, knocked what little fight I had out of me. I sat dejected, and she silent, until after a while I heard Little and his companion talking outside, and presently the hatch was raised, and a tin dish was shoved in, and a bottle of water. I was at the hatch in a flash, shouting to them, pleading and offering money, which set them into roars of laughter.

"Say, hear that now! Ain't that bully? What about you, Cass—ain't you got a thousand dollars to spare for ifn we let you go? No? Well, ain't that a shame, though? No, my lord, I'm sorry, but truth is me an' George here, we don't need the money anyways. An' I ain't too sure we'd trust your note o' hand, either. Haw-haw!"

And the cruel brute slammed down the hatch and went off, chuckling.

Through all this Cass never said a word, and when we had tried to eat the filthy muck they had given us, and rinsed our throats from the bottle, she went back to her corner and sat there, her head against the boards, staring into vacancy. Presently the cart started up, and for the rest of the day we jolted slowly over what must have been a damned bad road, while the atmosphere in the cart grew so hot and stifling that I was sure we must suffocate before long. Once or twice I bawled out to Little, pleading with him, but all I got was oaths and obscene jokes, so I gave up, and all the time Cassy sat silent, only occasionally turning to stare at me, but making no reply to my croaks and questions. I cursed her for a black slut, but she didn't seem to hear.

Towards sunset, the cart stopped, and immediately Cassy seemed to come to life. She peered through a crack in the side of the wagon, and then crawled over to me, motioning me to talk in whispers.

"Listen," she said. "You want to escape?"

I couldn't believe my ears. "Escape? I—"

"Quiet, in heaven's name! Now, listen. If I can show you how to escape—will you make me a promise?"

"Anything! My God, anything!"

The great almond eyes stared into mine. "Don't protest too easily—I mean what I say. Will you swear, by all that you believe to be holy, that if I help you escape, you will never desert me —that you will help me, in my turn, to gain my freedom?"

I'd have sworn a good deal more than that. With hope surging through me, I whispered. "I swear—I promise! I'll do anything. No, I'll never desert you, I swear it!"

She stared at me a moment longer, and then glanced towards the door.

"Soon now they will bring our food. When they do, you will be making love to me—do you understand?"

I couldn't follow this, but I nodded, feverish with excitement.

In a whisper she went on:

"When they see us, whatever they say, defy them. Do you understand me? Taunt them, swear at them—anything! Then leave the rest to me. Whatever I do or say, do nothing further."

"What are you going to do? What can I—"

"Quiet!" She started up. "They're coming, I think. Now—over there, where they'll see us."

And as footsteps came round to the back of the cart she sprawled into the middle of the floor, dragging up her dress, and pulling me down on top of her. Trembling, and for once not for the usual reasons, I clung to the pliant body, crushing my mouth down on hers and plunging like mad—gad, as I look back, what a waste of good effort it was, in the circumstances. I heard the hatch flung open, and in that moment Cassy writhed and began to sob in simulated ecstasy, clawing at me and squealing. There was an oath and commotion at the hatch, and then a cry of:

"Tom! Tom! Come quick! That damned Texian feller, he's screwin' the wench!"

More commotion, and then Little's voice:

"What you think you're doin', blast ye? Get offa her, this minute! Get off, d'ye hear, or I'll fill yore ass with buckshot!"

I bawled an obscenity at him, and then there was a rattling at the lock, the door was flung wide, to the gathering dusk, and Little glared in, his piece levelled at me. I decided I had defied him sufficiently, and rolled away; Cassy scrambled up into a re-clining position.

"Damn you!" bawls Little. "Don't you never get enough?"

I stayed mum, while he cursed at me, his pal staring pop-eyed over his shoulder. And then Cass, shrugging her shoulders petulantly and moving to display her fine long legs, remarked:

"Why can't you let us be? What's the harm in it?"

Little's piggy little eyes went over her; he licked his lips, still keeping his gun pointed at me.

"Harm in it?" His voice was thick. "You ol' Forster's wench, ain't you? Think you can rattle with everyone you please? Not while I'm around, my gel. You dirty nigger tail, you!"

She shrugged again, pouting, and spoke in a voice very unlike her own.

"Ifn massa say. Cassy don' mind none, anyways. This feller ain't bait for a gel like me—I used to real men."

Little's eyes opened wide. "Is that a fact?" His loose bearded mouth opened in a grin. "Well, think o' that, now. I didn't know you was thataway inclined, Cass—fancy yellow gel like you, with all them lady airs." He was thinking as he talked, and there was no doubting what those thoughts were. "Well, now—you just come out o' that cart this minute, d'ye hear? You—" this was to me—"keep yourself mighty still, lessn you want a bellyfull o' lead. Come on, my gel, git your ass outa that wagon—smart!"

Cassy slid herself to the tail of the cart, while they watched her closely, and dropped lightly to the ground. I stayed where I was, my heart hammering. Little motioned with his gun, and the other fellow slammed and locked the door, leaving me in darkness. But I could hear their voices, plain enough.

"Now, then, Cass," says Little. "You step roun' there, lively now. So—now, you jus' shuck down, d'ye hear?" There was a pause, and then Cassy's new voice:

"Massa gwine ter be nice to Cassy?—Cassy a good gel, please massa ever so much."

"By God, an' so ye will! Look at that, George—here, you hol' the gun! An' make yourself scarce. By gosh, I'm goin' to 'tend to this li'l beauty right here an' now! What you waitin' for, George—you get outa here!"

"Don' I get none o' her, then? Don' I even get to watch?"

"Watch? Why, how you talk! Think I'm a hog, or a nigger, that I'd do my screwin' with you watchin'? Get outa here, quick! You'll get your piece when I'm done. Here, gimme back that gun—reckon I'll keep it by, case her ladyship gits up to anythin'. But you won't, honey, will you?"

I heard George's reluctant footsteps retreating, and then silence; I strained my ears, but could hear nothing through the wagon side. A minute passed, and then there was a sudden sharp gasp, and a thin whining sound half-way between a sigh and a wail, and the sound of it made the hairs rise on my neck. A moment later, and Cassy's voice in sudden alarm:

"Mas' George, Mas' George! Come quick! Suthin' happen to

Mas' Tom—he hurt himself! Come quick!"

"What's that?" George's voice sounded from a little way off, and I heard his feet running. "What you say—what happened, Tom? You all right, Tom? What—"

The gunshot crashed out with startling suddenness, near the back of the wagon; there was a scream and a choking groan, and then nothing, until I heard the padlock rattle, the door was flung back, and there was Cassy. Even in the dusk I could see she was naked; she still had the musket in her hand.

"Quickly!" she cried. "Come out! They're both done for!"

I was out, fetters and all, in a twinkling. George lay spread-eagled at my feet, the top half of his face a bloody mash—she had given him the buckshot at point-blank range. I looked round and saw Little, crouched on his knees by the camp-fire, his head down; even as I started towards him he rolled over, with a little bubbling sob, and I saw the knife hilt sticking out of the crimson soaking mess that stained his shirt. He twitched for a moment, bubbling, and then was still.

Cassy was at the wagon, holding weakly to the door, her head hanging. I hopped over to her, grabbed her round the waist and swung her off her feet.

"Oh, you wonderful nigger!" I shouted, spinning her round. "You little black beauty, you! Bravo! Two at one stroke, by George! Well done indeed!" And I kissed her gleefully.

"Set me down!" she gasped. "In God's name, set me down!"

So I put her down, and she shuddered and sank to the ground, all of a heap. For a moment I thought she'd fainted, but she was a prime girl, that one. With her teeth chattering she grabbed up her dress, pulling it down over her head, which seemed a pity, for she cut a truly splendid figure in the firelight. I patted her on the shoulder, telling her what a brave wench she was.

"Oh, God!" says she, with her eyes tight shut. "Oh, horrible! I didn't know . . . what it was like . . . when I drew the knife from his belt and . . . " She put her face in her hands and sobbed.

"Serve him right," says I. "You've done him a power of good. And the other one, too—couldn't have done better myself, by jove, no, I couldn't! You're a damned good-plucked 'un, young Cassy, and you may tell 'em that Tom Arnold said so!"

706

But she sat there, shivering, so I wasted no more time but searched Tom's pockets for the keys to our fetters, and soon had us both loose. Then I went through their pockets, but apart from fifteen dollars there was nothing worth a curse. I stripped George's body, because it struck me that he was about my size, and his togs might come in handy. Then I looked to their guns—one musket, two pistols, with powder and ball—saw that the wagon horse was all to rights, and all the time my heart was singing inside me. I was free again, thanks to that splendid nigger wench. By gum, I admired that girl, and still do—she'd have made a rare mate for my old Sergeant Hudson—and while I heated up some coffee and vittles left by the late unlamented, I told her what I thought of her.

She was crouched by the fire, staring straight ahead of her, but now she seemed to shake herself out of her trance, for she threw back that lovely Egyptian head and looked at me. "You remember your promise?" says she, and I assured her I did—assured her twenty times over. I can see her now, those wonderful almond eyes watching me while I prattled on, praising her resource and courage—it was a strange meal that, a runaway slave girl and I, sitting round a camp fire in Mississippi, with two dead bodies lying by. And before it was done she had thrown off her fit of the shakes—after all, when you're new to it, killing is almost as disturbing as nearly being killed—and was telling me what we must do next. My admiration increased—why, she had thought it out all beforehand, in the wagon, down to the last detail.

It had been my remark about slave-catchers not touching a white man that had set her thinking, and shown her how she could make a successful run this time, with me to help her.

"We must travel as master and slave," says she. "That way no one will give us a second thought—but we must go quickly. It may be a week before Mandeville discovers that this wagon never reached Forster's place, and that these two men"—she gave a little shudder—"are missing. It might even be longer, but we dare not count on it—we dare not! Long before then we must be out of the state, on our way north."

"In that?" says I, nodding to the cart, and she shook her head.

"It can take us no farther than the river; we must go faster than it will carry us. We must go by steamboat."

"Hold on, though—that costs money, and these two hadn't but fifteen dollars between them. We can't get a passage on that."

"Then we'll steal money!" says she, fiercely. "We have pistols —you are a strong man! We can take what we need!"

But I wasn't having that—not that I'm scrupulous, but I'm no hand as a foot-pad. It's too risky by half, and so I told her.

"Risk!" she blazed. "You talk of risk, after what I have done this night? Don't you see—we have two murders on our hands— isn't *that* a risk? Do you know what will happen if we're caught— you will be hanged, and I'll be burned alive! And you talk of robbery as a risk!"

"Holding someone up will only increase the danger," says I, "for then we *would* be hunted, whereas if we go our way quietly there'll be no hue and cry until these two are found—if they ever are."

"Whoever we robbed could go the way these went," says she. "Then there would be no added danger." By God, she was a cold-blooded one, that. When I protested, she lost her temper:

"Why should we be squeamish over white lives? D'you think I care if every one of these filthy slave-driving swine is torn to pieces tomorrow? And why should you shrink from it, after what they would have done to you? Are they your people, these?"

I tried to convince her it wasn't principle, but pure lack of nerve, and we argued on, she waxing passionate—she hated with a lust for revenge that frightened me. But I wouldn't have it, and eventually she gave up, and sat staring into the fire, her hands clenched on her knees. At last she says, very quietly:

"Well, money we must have, however we come by it. And if you will not steal for it—well, there is only one other way. It does not add greatly to the risk, but... but I would do almost anything to avoid it."

Possibly I'm a natural-born pimp, for I jumped to the conclusion that she was thinking of whoring her way upriver, with me as her protector, but it was something far grander than that.

"We must go to Memphis," says she. "It is a town on the river, not more than fifty miles from here, so far as I can judge. That would be for the day after tomorrow—perhaps another day. That in itself is no great risk, for we have to go to the river anyway, and if God is kind to us none of Mandeville's friends, or people of Forster's, who would know me, will cross our path. And when we are there . . . we can find the money. Oh, yes, we can find the money!"

And to my astonishment she began to weep—not sobbing, but just great tears rolling down her cheeks. She dashed them away, and then fumbled inside her dress, and after a moment she produced a paper, soiled but very carefully-folded, which she passed to me. Wondering, I opened it, and saw that it was a bill of sale, dated February 1843, for one Cassy, a negro girl, the property of one Angel de Marmalade (I swear that was the name) of New Orleans, now duly sold and delivered to Fitzroy Howard, of San Antonio de Bexar. There was another scrap of paper with it which fluttered down—she made a grab, but not in time to prevent me seeing the words scrawled on it in a coarse, lumpy hand:

"Wensh Cassy. Ten lashys. Wun dollar," and a signature that was illegible.

She drew away, and spoke with her head turned from me.

"That was my second bill of sale. I was fourteen. I stole it from Howard, when he was drunk and I ran from him. They caught me, but he was dead by then, and when they auctioned me with his other . . . goods, they didn't bother to look for the old bill. I kept it—to remember. Just to remember, so that when I was free, and far away, I should never forget what it was to be a slave! No one ever found it!—they never found it!" Her voice was rising, and she swung her head round to stare at me, her eyes brimming. "I never thought it might serve to win my freedom! But it will!"

"How, in heaven's name?"

"You'll carry it to Memphis—you'll be Mr Fitzroy Howard! No one knows him this far north—he died in Texas four years ago—four years he's been screaming in Hell! And you'll *sell* me in Memphis—oh, I'll fetch a fine price, you'll see! A thousand, two thousand dollars—maybe three, for a choice mustee wench, fancy-bred, only nineteen, and schooled in a New Orleans brothel! Oh, they'll buy all right!"

Well, this seemed first-rate business to me, and I said so.

"Three thousand dollars—why, woman, what were you ever thinking of highway robbery for? Half that sum will see us rolling upriver in style—but wait though! If you're sold—how'll you get away?"

"I can run. Oh, believe me, I can run! The moment you have the money, you'll buy passages on a boat north—we'll have decided which one beforehand. Leave it to me to run at the right time—we'll meet at the levee or somewhere and go aboard together. You'll be what they call a nigger-stealer then, and I a runaway slave—but they won't catch us. What, Mr and Mrs Whatever-we-choose-to-call-ourselves, first-class passengers to Louisville? Oh, no, we'll be safe enough—if you keep our bargain."

Well, it had crossed my mind, of course, in the last two seconds, from the moment she'd reminded me of the nasty stigma of nigger-stealing, that it would be a sight safer to catch a different boat, all on my own, with the three thousand dollars, and leave Miss Cassy to fend for herself. But she was as quick as I was.

"If I didn't get out of Memphis," says she, slowly and intently, leaning forward to look into my face, "I'd give myself up—and tell them how we had run together, and you had killed two men back in Mississippi, and where the bodies were, and all about you. You wouldn't get far, Mr—what is your name, anyway?"

"Er, Flash—, er, Brown, I mean. But, look here, my dear girl, I promised not to desert you—remember? D'you think I'm the kind to break his word? I must say—"

"I don't know," says she, slowly. "I only tell you what will happen if you do. It may cost me my life, but it will certainly cost you yours, Mr Flash-er-Brown."

"I wouldn't dream of leaving you," says I, seriously. "Not for a moment. But, I say, Cassy—this is a top-hole plan! Why didn't you tell me before—it's absolutely splendid!"

She gazed at me, and took a deep breath, and then turned to gaze into the fire.

"You would think so, I suppose. Perhaps it seems a little thing to you—to be placed on a block, and auctioned like a beast to the highest bidder. To be pawed over and fumbled by dirty hands—stripped even, and gloated over!" The tears were starting again, but her voice never shook. "How could you even begin to imagine it? The hideous shame—the humiliation!" She swung round on me again—a habit of hers which I confess made me damned jumpy.

"Do you know what I was, until I was thirteen? I was a little Creole girl, in a fine house in Baton Rouge, with my papa and two brothers and two sisters, all older than I. Their mother was dead—she was white—and my mother, who was a slave mustee, was mother to them as well. We were the happiest family in the world—I loved them, and they loved me, or so I thought, until my father died. And then they sold us—my loving brothers sold me, their sister, and my mother, who had been more than a mother to them. They sold us! My mother to a planter—me to a bawd in New Orleans!"

She was shaking with passion. Something seemed called for, so I says:

"Pretty steep work, that. Bad business."

"I was a whore—at thirteen! I ran away, back to my family—and they gave me up! They put me in a cellar until my owner came, and took me back to New Orleans. You saw that other paper, with the bill of sale. Do you know what it is? It is a receipt from a whipping-house—where slaves are sent to be corrected! I was only thirteen, so they were lenient with me—only ten lashes! Can you understand what that did to me? Can you? For they make a spectacle of it—oh, yes! I was tied up naked, and whipped before an audience of men! Can you even begin to dream what it is like—the unbelievable, frightful shame of it? But how could I make you understand!" She was beating her fist on my knee by now, crying into my face. "You are a man—what would it do to you, to be stripped and bound and flogged before a pack of leering, laughing women?"

"Oh, well," says I, "I don't really know—"

"They cheered me! Do you hear that—cheered me, because I wouldn't cry, and one of them gave me a dollar! I ran back, blind with tears, with that receipt in my hand, and the she-devil who kept that brothel said: 'Keep it to remind you of what disobedience brings'. And I kept it, with the other. So that I shall never forget!"

She buried her head on my knee, weeping, and I was at a loss for once. I could think of one good way of comforting us both, but I doubted if she'd take kindly to it. So I patted her head and said:

"Well, it's a hard life, Cassy, there's no denying. But cheer up —there's a good time coming, you know. We'll be away to Memphis in the morning, raffle you off, collect the cash, and then, hey! for the steamboat! Why, we can have a deuced good time of it, I daresay, for I'm bound for the east coast, you know, and we can travel together. Why, we can—"

"Do you swear it?" She had lifted her head and was gazing up at me, her face wasted with crying. God, she was a queer one, one minute all cold steel and killing two men, and then getting the jumps over 'em—and from that she was plotting calmly, and suddenly raging with passion, and now imploring me with the wistful eyes of a child. By George, she was a handsome piece—but it wasn't the time or place, I knew. She was too much in a taking —I'll wager she had talked more that night than she'd done for years. But women have always loved to confide in me; I think it's my bluff, honest, manly countenance—and my whiskers, of course.

"You do promise?" she begged me. "You will help me, and never desert me? Never, until I'm free?"

Well, you know what my promises are; still I gave it, and I believe I meant it at the time. She took my hand, and kissed it, which disturbed me oddly, and then she says, looking me in the eyes:

"Strange, that you should be an Englishman. I remember, years ago, on the Pierrepoint Plantation, the slaves used to talk of the underground railroad—the freedom road, they called it—and how those who could travel it in safety might win at last to Canada, and then they could never be made slaves again. There was one old man, a very old slave, who had a book that he had gotten from somewhere, and I used to read to them from it—it was called *Nore's Epitome of Navigation*, all about the sea, and ships, and none of us could understand it, but it was the only book we had, and so they loved to hear me read from it." She tried to smile, with her eyes full of tears, and her voice was trembling. "On the outside there was a picture of a ship, with a Union Jack at its mast, and the old man used to point to it and say: 'Dat's de flag o' liberty, chillun; dat de ol' flag'. And I used to remember what I had once heard someone say—I can't recall where or when, but I never forgot the words." She paused a moment, and then said in a whisper almost: "'Whoever stands on British soil, shall be forever free'. It's true, isn't it?"

"Oh, absolutely," says I. "We're the chaps, all right. Don't hold with slavery at all, don't you know."

And, strange as it may seem, sitting there with her looking at me as though I were the Second Coming, well—I felt quite proud, you know. Not that I care a damn, but—well, it's nice, when you're far away and don't expect it, to hear the old place well spoken of.

"God bless you," says she, and she let go my hand, and I thought of making a grab at her, for the third time, but changed my mind. And we went to sleep on opposite sides of the fire, after I'd stoked it up and shoved Little's body into the bushes; deuce of a weight to move he was, too.

* * *

It took us two full days to Memphis, and the closer we got the more uneasy I became about the scheme we had undertaken. The chief risk was that we would be recognised by somebody, and if looking back I can say that it was only a chance in a thousand—well, that's still an uncomfy chance if your neck depends on it.

I was in high enough spirits when we set off from our camping place at dawn, for the glow of being free again hadn't worn off. It was with positive zest that I hauled the corpses of Little and George well into the thickets, and dumped them in a swampy pool full of reeds and frogs; then I tidied up the tracks as well as I could, and we set off. Cassy sat in the back of the cart, out of sight, while I drove, and we rolled along through the woods over the rutted road—it was more like a farm-track, really—until I came to a fork running north-west, which was the direction we wanted to go.

We followed it until noon without seeing a soul, which I now know was pretty lucky, but soon after we had cooked up a fry and moved on we came to a small village, and here something happened which damped my spirits a good deal, for it showed me what a small place even the American backwoods can be, and how difficult it is to pass through without every Tom, Dick and Harry taking an interest in you.

The village was dozing in the afternoon, with only a nigger or two kicking about, a dog nosing in a rubbish tip, and a baby wailing on a porch, but just the other side of town there was the inevitable yokel whittling on a stump, with his straw hat over his eyes and his bare feet stuck in the dust. I decided it was safe to make an inquiry, and pulled up.

"Hollo," says I, cheerily.

"Hollo, y'self," says he.

"Am I on the road to Memphis, friend?" says I.

He thought about this, chewing and polishing up one of those cracker-barrel witticisms which are Mississippi's gift to civilisation. At last he said:

"Well, if y'don't know for sartain, you're a damfool to be headin' along it, ain't you?"

"I would be, if I wasn't sure of direction from a smart man like you," says I.

He cocked an eye at me. "How come you're so sure?"

It's like talking before salt with the Arabs, or doing business with a Turk; you must go through the ritual.

"Because it's a hot day."

"*That* makes you sure?"

"Makes me sure you're thirsty, which makes me sure you'll take a suck at the jug I've got under my seat—and *then* you'll tell me the road to Memphis." I threw the jug at him, and he snapped it up like a trout taking a fly.

"Guess I might sample it, at that," says he, and sampled about a pint. "Jay-zus! That's drinkin' liquor. Ye-ah—I reckon you might be on the Memphis road, sure enough. Should git there, too, provided you don't fall in Coldwater Creek or git elected guv-nor *or* die afore you arrive." He threw the jug back, and I was about to whip up when he says:

"You f'm Nawth? You don't talk like ol' Miss, nor Arkinsaw, neether."

"No, I'm from Texas."

"You don't say? Long ways off, the Texies. Young Jim Noble, he went down there, 'bout two years back. Ever run across Jim?"

"I reckon not."

"No." He considered me, the sharp, sleepy little eyes peeping out under the frayed straw brim. "Would that be Tom Little's wagon your drivin'? Seems I know that broken spoke—an' the horse."

For a moment my blood ran cold, and I stopped my hand from going to the pistol in the back of my belt.

"Well, it *was* Tom Little's wagon," says I. "Still would be, if he hadn't loaned it me yesterday. When I take it back, it *will* be his again, I guess." If I'd stayed in that country, and learned to whittle with a Barlow knife, and chew tobacco, I'd have made a president.

"That a fact," says he. "First time I heerd o' Tom lendin' anything."

"Well, I'm his cousin," says I. "So he didn't mind lending it to me." And I whipped up and made off.

"Good for him," calls the yokel after me. "He might ha' told you the road to Memphis, while he was about it."

By George, it rattled me, I can tell you. When we were out of sight I conferred with Cassy, and she agreed we must press on as hard as we could go. With every loafer in the county weighing us up, the sooner we were clear the better. So we pushed on, and might have made it next day if I hadn't had to rest the horse— spavined old bitch she was. We had to sleep another night out, and the following morning we left the cart beside a melon patch, telling a nigger to mind it for us, and walked the last mile into Memphis town.

It was a fair-sized place, even in those days, for half the cotton in the world seemed to find its way there, but to my jaundiced eye it appeared to be made entirely out of mud. It had rained from first light, and by the time we had walked through the churned-up streets, and been splashed by wagons and by dam-fools who didn't look where they were going, we were in a sorry state. But the crowded bustle of the place, and the foul weather, made me feel happier, because both lessened the chance of anyone recognising us.

Now all that remained to be done was for me to sell a runaway slave and arrange for us to get out of town without any holes in our hides. Easy enough, you may think, for a chap of Flashy's capabilities, and I'll admit your confidence wouldn't be misplaced. But I wonder how many young chaps nowadays, in this civilised twentieth century, would know how to go about it, if they were planked down, near penniless and with their boots letting in, on a foreign soil, and asked to dispose of a fine-strung mustee woman whose depression and nervousness were growing steadily as the crisis approached? It takes thought, I tell you, and a strong grip on one's own gorge to keep it from leaping out.

The first thing was to find when the next sale was, and here we were lucky, for there was one in the market that very afternoon, which meant we could do our business and, God willing, be out by nightfall. Next I must inquire about steamboats, so leaving Cassy under the shelter of a shop porch, I ploshed down to the levee to make inquiries. It was pouring fit to frighten Noah by now, with a howling wind as well, and by the time I tacked up to the steamboat office I was plastered with gumbo to the thighs and sodden from there up. To add to my difficulties, the ancient at the office window, wearing a dirty old pilot cap and a vacant expression, was both stone deaf and three parts senile; when I bawled my inquiries to him above the noise of the storm he responded with a hand to his ear and a bewildered grin.

"Is there a boat to Louisville tonight?" I roared.

"Hey?"

"Boat to Louisville?"

"Cain't hear you, mister. Speak up, cain't ye?"

I dragged my collar closer and dashed the rain out of my eyes.

"Boat to Louisville—tonight?" I yelled.

"Boat to where?"

"Oh, for pity's sake! LOUIS!—" I gathered all my lung power "—VILLE! Is there a boat tonight?"

At last he beamed and nodded.

"Shore 'nough, mister. The new *Missouri*. Leaves at ten."

I thanked him forcibly and ploughed back up town. Now all that must be done was render myself and Cassy as respectable as possible and go to work with our hands on our hearts. The first part we managed, roughly, in the back room of a cheap apartment house which I hired for the day; my good coat, which had been thrown over my head when I left Greystones—a prodigious stroke of luck that, for it had Spring's precious papers sewn in the lining —was sadly soiled, but we made the best of it, and rehearsed the final details of our plan. I was in a sweat about how Cassy would slip away from her new owner, but this she brushed aside; what made her grit her teeth to stop them chattering was the thought of mounting the slave block and being sold, which seemed strange to me, since it had happened to her before, and didn't involve any pain or danger at all.

She was to run late that evening, make her way back to the apartment house, knock at my window, which was on the ground floor, and be admitted. I would have clothes for her by then, and we'd make our way to the levee and go aboard the *Missouri* as Mr and Mrs James B. Montague, of Baton Rouge, travelling north. In the dark it should be simple enough.

"If I do not come—wait," says she. "I will come in the end. If I don't come by tomorrow, I'll be dead, and you will be able to go where you will. But until then I hold you to your word—your pledged promise, remember?"

"I remember, I remember!" says I, jittering. "But suppose you can't run—suppose he chains you up, or something. What then?"

"He won't," says she, calmly. "Be assured, I can run. There is nothing hard about running—any slave can do it. But to stay free —that is the impossible part, unless you have a refuge, a protector. I have you."

Well, I've been called a few things in my time, but these were new. If she'd known me better she'd have thought different, no doubt, but she was desperate, and I was her only hope—a hellish pickle for a girl to be in, you'll agree. I strove to calm my fluttering bowels, and presently we set out for the slave market.

If you've never seen a slave auction, I can tell you it's no different from an ordinary cattle sale. The market was a great low shed, with sawdust on the floor, a block at one end for the slaves and auctioneer, and the rest of the space taken up with the buyers and spectators—wealthy traders on seats at the front, very much at ease, casual buyers behind, and more than half the whole crew just spectators, loafers, bumarees and sightseers, spitting and gossiping and haw-hawing. The place was noisy and stank like the deuce, with clouds of baccy smoke and esprit de corps hanging under the beams.

I'd been scared stiff that when I entered Cassy for sale there would be all sorts of questions, cross-examination, and the like, which I wouldn't be able to answer convincingly, but I had been fretting unduly. I believe if you entered a Swedish albino at a Memphis sale and swore he was a nigger, they'd stick him on the block, no questions asked. That auctioneer would have sold his own grandfather, and probably had. He was a small, furious, red-bearded man with a slouch hat, a big cigar, and a quart bottle of forty-rod in his coat pocket which he sucked at in between accusing his assistants of swindling him and bawling to everyone to give him some sellin' room.

When I entered Cassy he hardly glanced at her bill of sale, but spat neatly between my feet and asked me aggressively if I was an underground railroad agent who'd thought better of convoying a nigger to Canada and decided to sell her off for private gain.

The crowd round him all haw-hawed immensely at this, and said he was a prime case, which relieved my momentary horror at his question, and the auctioneer said he didn't give a damn, any-how, and where the hell was Eli Bowles's nigger's papers, because he hadn't got them, and they'd drive a man out of his mind in this country, what with their finickin' regulations, and would they get the hell out of his way so he could start the sale? No, he wouldn't put up Jackson's buck Perseus, because he was rotten with pox, and everyone knew it; Jackson had better put him out to stud over in Arkansas, where nobody noticed such things. No, he wouldn't take notes of hand from any but dealers he knew—he'd enough tarnation paper as it was, and his clerk just used it to confuse him and line his own pockets, and *he* knew all about it, and one of these days wouldn't he make that clerk's ass warm for him. And, strike him dumb, but his bottle was half empty and he hadn't even started the sale yet—would they git out from under his feet or did they want to be still biddin' their bollix off at two in the morning?

And more of the same, all of which was mighty reassuring. I left Cassy to be herded off with the other niggers, and got a place by the wall to watch the sale, which the little auctioneer conducted as if he was a ring-master, pattering away incessantly, and keeping up his style of irascible confusion all the time. The crowd loved it, and he was good, too, taking an occasional swill at his bottle and firing his comments at the lots while the bids came in.

"See this here old wench of Masterson's, who died last week. Masterson died, that is, not her. Not a day over forty, an' a prime cook. Well, y'only had to look at the belly Masterson had on him; that's testimony enough, I reckon. Yes sir, it was her fine cookin' that kilt him—now then, what say? Eight hunnert to start—nine, for the best vittles-slinger 'tween Evansville an' the Gulf." Or again: "This buck of Tomkins, he sired more saplin's than Methuselah—that's why they call him George, after George Washington, the father of his country. Why, 'thout this boy, the nigger pop'lation'd be only half what it is—we wouldn't hardly be havin' this sale today, but for this randy little hero. There was talk of a syndicate to send him back to Afriky to keep the numbers up—now then, who'll say a thousand?"

But there was someone there who knew more about raising prices than even he did, and that was Cassy. When she took the block, after a whispered conference with the auctioneer, he went on about how she spoke French, and could embroider and 'tend to growing children or be a lady's maid or governess and play the piano and paint—but it was all sham. He knew what she would be sold for, and the mob kept chorusing "Shuck her down! Let's get a look at her!" while she stood, very demure, with her hands folded in front of her and her head bowed. She was pale, and I could see the strain in her face, but she knew what to do, and presently when the auctioneer spoke to her she took off her shoes and then let down her hair, very carefully, so that it hung down her back almost to her waist.

That wasn't what they wanted, of course; they yelled and stamped and whistled, but the auctioneer got the bidding up to seventeen hundred before he nodded to her, and without a change of expression she shrugged her shoulders out of the dress, let it slip down, and stepped out as bare as a babe. By gad, I was proud of her as she stood there like a pale golden statue, in the dim light under the beams, with the mob goggling and roaring approval; the price ran up to twenty-five hundred dollars in less than a minute.

At that there were only two bidders left, a fancy-weskitted young dandy in a stove-pipe hat with his mouth open, and a grey-bearded planter in the front row with a red face and big panama hat, who had a little nigger boy behind his seat to fan him. I reckon Cassy got another thousand dollars out of those two, all on her own. She put one hand on her hip—twenty-seven hundred; then she put her hands behind her head—three thousand; she stirred her rump at the dandy—thirty-two hundred, and the planter shook his head, his face sweating. She looked straight down at him, grave-faced, and winked, the crowd yelled and cheered, and the dirty old goat slapped his thigh and bid thirty-four. The dandy swore and looked sulky, but that was the bottom of his poke, evidently, for he turned away, and Cassy was knocked down to the other, amidst whoops and cries of obscene advice to him; he'd better send his wife away to visit her folks in Nashville for a spell, they shouted, and when she came back she could give him a decent burial, for he'd have killed himself by then, haw-haw.

"Wish I'd a wench like *that* every day," says the little auctioneer, at paying-out time—you never saw such a heap of gold coin on one dirty deal table. "I'd make my fortune. Say, if you'd given me time to advertise proper, we'd ha' had four, mebbe five thousand. Where d'you git her, Mr—eh—Howard?"

"As you said, she was a lady's maid—at my academy for gentlewomen," says I gravely, and the crowd in his office roared and clapped me on the back and offered me swigs from their bottles; I was a card, they said.

I had no opportunity to see what happened to Cassy after she came down from the block; her buyer was obviously a local man, so presumably she wouldn't be taken far. For the hundredth time I found myself wondering how she was going to make her escape, and what I would do if she didn't come before steamboat time. I daren't leave without her, for fear she'd split. I would just have to wait, jumping at every shadow, no doubt. But in the meantime I had plenty to occupy myself with, and I set off for town, well-weighted down with my new-found wealth.

It was the deuce of a lot of cash to be carrying—or so I thought. I didn't know America well then, or I'd have realised that they don't think twice about carrying and dealing in sums that in England would be represented by a banker's draft. Odd, in such a wild country, but they like to have their cash about 'em, and don't mind killing in its defence.

The first thing I now did was to repair to the best tailor in town and buy myself some decent gear, and from there I made for a dressmakers, to do the like for Cassy. I've never numbered meanness with cash among my many faults, and I do like my women to have the very finest clothes to take off, and all the little vanities to go with 'em. There had been just north of three thousand dollars left when the auctioneer had taken his commission—a man could do worse than be a slave-knocker, it occurred to me—and I made a fine hole in them with my purchases; I spent probably twice on Cassy what I'd spent on myself, and didn't grudge it; the Creole woman who ran the shop was in a tremendous twitter, showing every gown she had, and the deuce of it was I could see Cassy looking peachy in every one.

In any event, I had two trunks full of gear which I ordered to be delivered to the levee, labelled to go aboard the *Missouri* that evening, and took only enough clothing away with me for us to look respectable when we went aboard. While I was doing my buying, I had the dressmaker send a nigger to buy the tickets— God, the tiny things that change one's life; if I'd gone in person, all would have been different. But there—he brought them back, and I stuffed them into the pocket of my new coat, and that was that.

The business of sitting back like a sultan, buying all the silks and satins in sight and gallantly chaffing Madame Threadneedle, had put me in excellent fettle, but as the afternoon wore away I began to feel less bobbish. My worries about Cassy's escape returned, and brandy didn't drive them away; I couldn't bring myself to eat anything, and finally I went back to my mean little room and busied myself removing Spring's papers from my old coat and stitching them into the waist-band of one of my new pairs of pants. After that I sat and chewed my nails, while seven o'clock went by, and then eight, and outside the rain pattered down in the dark, and I envisaged Cassy being overtaken in some ·dirty alley and hauled off to a cell, or being shot climbing a fence, or pulled down by hounds—give me leisure in my fearful moments and my imaginings can outrun Dante's any day.

I was standing staring at the candle guttering on its stand, feeling the gnawing certainty that she'd come adrift, when a scratching at the window had me leaping out of my skin. I whipped up the sash, and she slipped in over the sill, but my momentary delight was quickly snuffed when I saw the state she was in. She was plastered from head to foot with mud, her dress was reduced to a torn, sodden rag, her eyes were wild, and she was panting like a spent dog.

"They're after me!" she sobbed, slithering down against the wall; there was blood oozing through the mud from a cut on her foot. "They spotted me slipping out of the pen, and like a fool I ran for it! Oh, oh! I should have waited! They'll rouse the section . . . find us . . . oh, quick, let us go now—at once, before they come!"

She might, as she said, be an experienced runner, but she wasn't up to Flashy's touch. "Steady, and listen," says I. "Keep your voice low. How far behind are they?"

She sobbed for breath. "I . . . don't know. They lost me, when I . . . doubled back. Oh, dear God! But they know I've run . . . they'll scour the town . . . take me again . . ." She lay back against the wall, exhausted.

"How long since you last heard 'em?"

"Oh, oh . . . five minutes . . . I don't know. But they have . . . dogs . . . track us here..."

"Not on a night like this, they won't, and certainly not through a town." My mind was racing, but I was thinking well. Should I bolt and leave her? No, she'd talk for certain. Could we make the boat? Yes, if I could put her in order.

"Up," says I, and hauled her to her feet. She sagged against me, weeping, and I had to hold her up. "Now, listen, Cassy. We have time; they don't know where you are, and every hunt in Rutland couldn't nose you out here. We can't run until you're clean and dressed—we'd never get aboard the boat. Haste won't serve—

when Mr and Mrs Montague step out on to that street to go to the levee, they'll go nice and sedate." As I talked I was already sponging at her with the wet cloths I had ready. "Now, rest easy while I get you shipshape."

"I can't run any longer!" she sobbed. "I can't!" She tossed her head from side to side, crying with fatigue. "I just want to lie down and die!"

I went on towelling her, cleansing away the filth, whispering urgently all the while. We would make it, I told her, the boat was waiting, we were rotten with money, if we kept calm and went ahead without flinching we were bound to win free, I had bought her a wardrobe that would take Canada by storm—yes, Canada, I told her, the freedom road—an hour from now we would be steaming upriver, safe as sleep. I was trying to convince myself as much as her, as I sponged and dried away frantically, with one ear cocked for sounds of approaching pursuit.

It was tremendous work, because even when I had got her clean she just lay there, quite played out in mind and body, moaning softly to herself. I was almost in despair as I tried to haul clothes on to her; she just lay back in the chair, her golden body heaving —gad, she was a picture, but I'd no time to enjoy it. I struggled away, coaxing, pleading, swearing—"come on, come on, you can't give up, Cassy, not a staunch girl like you, you stupid black bitch," and finally I shook her and hissed in her ear: "All you have to do is stand up and walk, confound it! Walk! We can't fail now—and you'll never have to call anyone 'massa' again!"

That was what did it, I think, for she opened her eyes and made a feeble effort to help. I egged her on, and we got her into the long coat, and adjusted the broad-brimmed bonnet and veil, and I jammed the shoes on her feet, and gloved her, and stuck the gamp in her hand—and when she managed to stand, leaning against the table, she looked as much like the outward picture of a lady as made no odds. No one would know there wasn't a stitch on her underneath.

I had to half-lead, half-drag her out of the back way, and there was a feverish ten minutes while a nigger boy went and found a trap for us, and we waited crouched on the boardwalk against the wall, with the rain slashing down. But there was no sign of her pursuers; they must have lost her utterly, and presently we were rolling down to the levee through the mud and bustle of the Memphis waterfront, and there in the glare of the wharf lamps was the good ship *Missouri*, with her twin whistles blasting the warning of departure. I lorded it with the purser at the gangplank, explaining that I would take Madame directly to our state-room, as she was much fatigued, and he yes-sirred me all over the place, and roared up boys to escort us; everyone was too occupied with crying good-bye and stand clear and all aboard to notice that I was holding up the graceful veiled lady on my arm by main strength.

When I laid her on the bed she was either in a swoon or asleep from exhaustion and fright; I was so tuckered myself that I just collapsed in a chair and didn't stir until the whistles shrieked again and the wheel began to pound and I knew we'd done it. Then I began to slop the brandy down—lord, I needed it. The last-minute scare and hurry had been the final straw; the glass was chattering against my teeth, but it was as much exultation as nervous reaction, I think.

Cassy didn't stir for three hours, and then she could hardly believe where she was; not until I had ordered up a meal and a bottle of bubbly did she understand properly that we had got away, and then she broke down and cried, swaying from side to side while I comforted her and told her what a damned fine spunky wench she was. I got some drink into her, and forced her to eat, and at last she calmed, and when I saw her hand go up, shaking, and push her hair back, I knew she was in command of herself again. When they can think of their appearance, they're over the worst.

Sure enough, she went to the mirror, pulling the coat round herself, and then she turned to me and said:

"I don't believe it. But we are here." She put her face in her hands. "God bless you—oh, God bless you! Without you, I'd be—back yonder."

"Tut-tut," says I, champing away, "not a bit of it. Without you, we'd be in queer street, instead of jingling with cash. Have some more champagne."

She didn't answer for a moment. Then she says, in a very low voice. "You kept your word. No white man ever did that to me before. No white man ever helped me before."

"Ah, well," says I, "you haven't met the right chaps, that's all." She was overlooking, of course, that I hadn't any choice in the matter, but I wasn't complaining. She was grateful, which was first-rate, and must be promptly taken advantage of. I walked over to her, and she stood looking at me gravely, with the tears brimming up in her eyes. No time like the present, thinks I, so I smiled at her and set the glass to her lips, and slipped my free hand beneath her coat; her breast was as firm as a melon, and at my touch she gave a little whimper and closed her eyes, the tears squeezing out on to her cheeks. She was trembling and crying again, and when I pushed away the coat and carried her over to the bed she was sobbing aloud as she clasped her arms round my neck.

I blame myself. If there is one thing that can make me randier than usual, it is danger safely past, and with a creature like Cassy to occupy me I don't give a thought to anything else. She, for her part, was probably still so distraught that she was ready to abandon herself altogether—she said later that she had never willingly made love to a man before, and I believed her. I suppose if you've been a good-looking female slave, used to being hauled into bed by a lot of greasy planters whether you like it or not, it sours you against men, and when you meet a fine upstanding lad like me, who knows when to tickle rather than slap—well, you're grateful for the change, and make the most of it. But whatever the reasons, the upshot was that Mr and Mrs Montague spent that night and the rest of next day in passionate indulgence, never bothering about the world outside, and that was how I came adrift yet again.

Of course, a moralist would say that this was to be expected: he would doubtless point out that I had fornicated my way almost continuously along the Mississippi valley, and draw the conclusion that all my trials arose from this. I don't know about that, as a general statement, but I'll agree that if I hadn't made such a beast of myself in Cassy's case I would have avoided a deal of trouble.

What with sleeping and dallying, it was late on the next afternoon before I tumbled out to dress myself and take a turn on the promenade; it was a splendid sunny day, the good ship *Missouri* was booming along in great style, and I was in that sleepy, well-satisfied state where you just want to lean on the rail, smoking and watching the great river roll by, with the distant bank half hidden in haze, and the lumber rafts and river craft sweeping down, their crews waving, and the whistles tooting overhead. Cassy wouldn't come out, though; she decided that the less she was seen the better, until we were up among the free states, which was sensible.

Well, thinks I, you've had some bad luck, my boy, but surely it's behind you now. Charity Spring and his foul ship, the nosey-parkering Mr Lincoln, the Yankee Navy—they were all a long way south. I could smile at the ludicrous figure of George Randolph, although he had brought me catastrophe enough at the time; the abominable Mandeville and his shrew of a wife, the terror of the slave-cart, and the anxieties of Memphis—all by and done with. Up the Ohio to Louisville and then Pittsburgh, a quick trip to New York, and then it would be England again, and not before time. And Flashy the Vampire could go to work on his father-in-law—I was looking forward to that, rather.

I wondered, as I watched the brown water swirling by, what would become of Cassy. If she'd been a woman of less character I'd have been regretful at the thought of parting soon, for she was a fine rousing gallop, all sleek hard flesh like an athlete, except for her top hamper. But she was too much the spitfire, really; her present lazy compliance didn't fool me. I'd bid her farewell around Pittsburgh, where she'd be as safe as the bank, and could travel easily to Canada if she wanted. There, with her looks and spirit, she'd have no difficulty in getting a fortune somehow, I'd no doubt. Not that I minded, but she was a game wench.

Presently I went back to the state-room, and ordered up a dinner —the first full meal we had sat down to in style, and the first Cassy had had since she was a little girl, she told me. Although we were alone in the cabin, she insisted on putting on the finest dress I had bought her; it was a very pale coffee-coloured satin, I remember, and those golden shoulders coming out of it, and that strange Egyptian head of hers, with its slanting eyes, quite kept me off my food. That night she tasted port for the first time in her life; I recall her sipping it and setting down the glass, and saying:

"This is how the rich live, is it not? Then I am going to be rich. What use is freedom to the poor?"

Well, thinks I, it doesn't take long to get ambition; yesterday all you wanted was to be free. However, all I said was:

"What you want is a rich husband. Shouldn't be difficult."

She clicked her lips in contempt. "I need no man, from now on. You are the last man I shall be indebted to—I should hate you for it, but I don't. Do you know why? It is not just because you helped me, and kept your word—but you were kind also. I shall never forget that."

Poor little simple black girl, I was thinking, to mistake absence of cruelty for kindness; just wait till it serves my interest to do you a dirty turn, and you'll form a different opinion of me. And then she took me aback by going on:

"And yet I know that you are not by nature a kind man; that there is little love in you. I know there is lust and selfishness and cruelty, because I feel it when you take me; you are just like the others. Oh, I don't mind—I prefer that. I tell myself that it levels the score I owe you. And yet, it cannot quite level it, ever, because even although you are such a man as I have always taught myself to hate and despise—still, there were moments when you were kind. Do you understand?"

"Clearly," says I. "You're maudlin. It's the port, of course." Tell the truth, I was half-amused, half-angry, at the way she told me what she thought of me. Still, if the fool wanted to think I was kind, she was welcome. She was looking at me in her odd, solemn way, and do you know, it made me somehow uncomfortable; those big eyes saw far too much. "You're a strange chit," I told her.

"Not as strange as the man who buys a dress like this one for a runaway slave girl," says she, and blast me if the tears didn't start again.

Well, there you are; understand 'em if you can. So to cheer her up, and put an end to her foolish talk I came round and took her, across the table this time, with the crockery rattling all over the place, the wine splashing on the floor, and my left knee in a bowl of fruit. It was a fine frenzied business, and pleased me tremendously. When it was over I looked down at her, with the knives and forks scattered round her sleek head, and told her she should run away more often.

She reached over an apple and began to eat it, her eyes smouldering as she looked up at me.

"I shall never have to run again," she said. "Never, never, never."

That was all she knew. Our blissful little idyll was coming to an end, for next morning I made a discovery that turned everything topsy-turvy, and drove all thoughts of philosophy out of her head. I had determined to breakfast in the saloon, and leaving her in bed I took a turn round the deck to sharpen my appetite. It seemed to me that we ought to be making Louisville sometime that day, and seeing a bluff old chap leaning at the rail I inquired of him when we might expect to arrive.

He looked at me in amazement, removed his cigar, and says: "Gawd bless mah soul, suh! Did you say Louisville?"

"Certainly," says I. "When will we get there?"

"On this boat, suh? Never, 'pon my word."

"What?" I gazed at the man, thunderstruck.

"This boat, suh, is for St Louis—not Louisville. This is the Mississippi river, suh, not the Ohio. For Louisville you should have caught the J. M. White at Memphis." He regarded me with some amusement. "Do I take it you have boa'ded the wrong steamer, suh?"

"My God," says I. "But they told me—" And then I remembered my shouted conversation in the rain with that drivelling buffoon at the steamboat office; the useless old bastard had caught the word "Louis" only, and given me the wrong boat. Which meant that I was some hundreds of miles from where I wanted to be—and Cassy was as far from the free states as ever.

If I was dismayed, you should have seen her; she went blazing wild and hurled a pot of powder at my head, which fortunately missed.

"You fool! You blockhead! Hadn't you the sense to look at the tickets?" So much for all my kindness that she'd been so full of.

"It wasn't my fault," says I, trying to explain, but she cut me off.

"Do you realise the danger we are in? These are *slave* states! And we should have been close to Ohio by now! Your idiocy will cost me my freedom!"

"Stuff and nonsense! We can catch a boat from St Louis back to Louisville and be there in two days; where's the danger?"

"For a runaway like me? Turning south again, towards the people who may be coming up river to look for me. Oh, dear Lord, why did I trust an ape like you?"

"Ape, you insolent black slut? Blast you, if you had taken thought yourself, instead of whoring about these last two days like a bitch in heat, you'd have seen we were on the wrong road. D'you expect me to know one river from another in this lousy country?"

Our discussion continued on these lines for a spell, and then we quieted down. There was nothing to be done except wait through an extra two days in the slave states, and while Cassy was fearful of the prolonged risk, she said she supposed we could make Louisville, and then Cincinnati and Pittsburgh, safe enough. However, the shock didn't make our voyage any happier, and we were barely on speaking terms by the time we reached St Louis, where some more bad news awaited us. Although the river was thick with steamboats, traffic was so heavy that there wasn't a state-room, or even a maindeck passage, to be had for two days, which meant that we must kick our heels in a hotel, waiting for the *Bostona*, which would carry us up the Ohio.

We kept under cover for those forty-eight hours, except for one trip that I made down to the steamship office, and to buy one of the new Army Colt revolvers, just in case. At the same time I was able to take a look at the town, which interested me, because in those days St Louis was a great swarming place that never went to bed, and was full of every species of humanity from the ends of America and beyond. There were all the Mississippi characters, steamboat people, niggers, planters, and so on, and in addition the place was choc-a-bloc with military from the Mexican war, with Easterners and Europeans on their way to the Western gold fields, with hunters and traders from the plains, men in red shirts and buckskins, bearded to the eyes and brown as nuts, salesmen and drummers, clergymen and adventurers, ladies in all the splendours of the Eastern salons shuddering delicately away from the sight of some raucous mountain savage crouched vomiting in the muddy roadway with his bare backside, tanned black as mahogany, showing through his cutaway leather leggings. There were skinners with their long whips, sharps in tall hats with paste pins in their shirts, tall hard men chewing tobacco with their long coats thrown back to show the new five- and six-shooters stuck in their belts; there was even a fellow in a kilt lounging outside a billiard saloon with a bunch of yarning loafers as they eyed the white and yellow whores, gay as peacocks, tripping by along the boardwalk.

From the levee, crammed with bales and boxes and machinery, to the narrow, mud-churned streets uptown, it was all bustle and noise and hurry, and stuck in the middle was the church St Louis was all so proud of, with its Grecian pillars and pointed fresco— just like a London club with a spire stuck on top.

And I was sauntering back to the hotel, smoking a cigar, and congratulating myself that we would be on our way tomorrow, when I chanced to stop outside an office on one of the streets, just to cast an idle eye over the official bills and notices posted there. You know the way of it; you are just gaping for gaping's sake, and then suddenly you see something that shrivels the hairs right down to your backside. There it was, a new bill, staring me full in the face:

ONE HUNDRED DOLLARS REWARD!!

I will pay the above sum to any person or persons who will capture, DEAD or ALIVE, the Murderer and Slave stealer calling himself TOM ARNOLD, who is wanted for the brutal killings of George Hiscoe and Thomas Little, in Marshall County, Mississippi, and stealing away the female slave, CASSIOPEIA, the property of Jacob Forster, of Blue Mountain Spring Plantation, Tippah County, Mississippi.
The fugitive is six feet in height, long-legged and well built, customarily wears a Black Moustache and Whiskers, and has Genteel Manners. He pretends to be a Texian, but speaks with a Foreign Accent.
Satisfactory proofs of identity will be required.

ONE HUNDRED DOLLARS REWARD!!

Offered in the name and authority of

Joseph W. Matthews,
Governor of Mississippi.

I didn't faint away dead on the spot, but I had to hold on to a rail while the full import of it sank in. They had found the bodies, and assumed I had murdered them, and the traps were in full cry. But here—hundreds of miles away? And then I remembered the telegraph. They'd be looking in every town from St Louis to Memphis by now—you'd have thought, with killings happening every day in their savage country, that they wouldn't make such a row over another two: but of course it was the slave-stealing that had really stirred them up. Here was added reason for getting to the free states quickly; in Ohio they wouldn't give a damn how many nigger-beaters' throats I'd cut, especially in such a good cause—I'd learned enough in my brief unhappy experience of the United States to know that it was two countries even then, and they hated each other like poison. Yes, up there I'd be safe, and on trembling legs I hurried back to the hotel, to break the glad news that they were after us with a vengeance.

Cassy gasped and went pale, but she didn't cry, and while I was stamping about chewing my nails and swearing she got out a map which we had bought, and began to study it. Her finger was trembling as she traced the route down from St Louis to the Cairo fork, and then north-east up the Ohio river. At Louisville she stopped.

"Well, what now?" says I. "That's only a two-day journey, and we'll be beyond their reach, won't we?"

She took her head. "You do not understand. The Ohio river is the boundary between the slave states and the free, but even in the free states we are not safe until we have gone well upriver. See—" She traced again. "From Louisville to Cincinnati and far beyond that, we still have slave states on our right hand, first Kentucky and then Virginia. If we were to land on the Indiana or Ohio shores, we should be in free states, but I could still be retaken by the slave-catchers who are thick along the river."

"But—but—I thought the free state folk sheltered slaves, and helped them. Surely they can't take you off free state soil?"

"Of course they can!" There were tears in her eyes now. "Oh, if we could be sure of finding an abolitionist settlement, or an underground railroad station, all would be well, but how do we know? There are laws forbidding people in Ohio to aid runaways; slaves are caught and dragged back across the river daily by these bands of catchers, with their guns and dogs! And with the time we have lost here, notices of my running from Memphis will have reached the Kentucky shore—my name will have been added to the list of the other poor hunted creatures trying to escape north!"

"Well, what the blazes can we do?"

She traced on the map again. "We must stay aboard our steamboat all the way to Pittsburgh, if indeed the boats run so far in this weather.[88] If not, they will at least take us far enough up the Ohio to catch a train from one of the eastern Ohio towns into Pennsylvania. Once we are in Pittsburgh we can laugh at all the slave-catchers in the South—and you will be far beyond the reach of the Mississippi law."

Well, that was a comforting thought. "How long does it take?" says I.

"To Pittsburgh by boat? Five days." She bit her lip and began to tremble again. "Within a week from now I shall be either free or dead."

I wish she'd thought of some other way of putting it, and it crossed my mind that I might be a good deal safer parting company with her. On the other hand, a boat to Pittsburgh was the fastest way home, and if we kept to our cabin the whole way we should come through safe. They don't look for runaway slaves in state-rooms. They might look there for a murderer, though—and blast it, I hadn't even *done* the murders! Could I fob them off on her if the worst came to the worst? But it wouldn't—there must be a limit to the distance they could chase us.

It was in a fine state of the shakes that we boarded the *Bostona* the next morning, and I didn't know an easy moment until we had passed the Cairo fork that night and were steaming up the Ohio. I drank a fair amount, and Cassy sat gazing out towards the northern shore, but early on the second morning we reached Louisville without incident, and I began to breath again. Evening saw us at Cincinnati and Cassy was in a fever of anxiety for the boat to move off again; Cincinnati, although on the Ohio side, was a great place for slave-catchers, and she cried with relief when the side-wheel started at last and we churned on upriver.

But at breakfast time next day there was a rude awakening. The weather had grown colder and colder throughout our journey, and now when you looked overside there were great cakes of dirty brown and green ice riding down the current, and a powdering of snow lying on the Ohio bank. The fellows in the saloon were of opinion that the boat would go no farther than Portsmouth, if that far; the captain wouldn't risk her in this kind of weather.

And sure enough, down comes the captain presently, all gravity and grey whiskers, to announce to the saloon that he couldn't make Portsmouth this trip, on account of the ice, but would put in at Fisher's Landing, which was three miles short of the town, and set anyone ashore that wanted to go. The rest he would carry back to Cincinnati.

They raised a tremendous howl at this, waving their tickets and demanding their money back, and one tubby little chap in gold glasses cries out angrily:

"Intolerable! Fisher's Landing is on the Kentucky shore—how am I to be in Portsmouth tonight? There won't be a ferry running in this weather."

The captain said he was sorry; the Ohio side was out of the question, because the ice was thick all down the north channel.

"But I must be in Portsmouth tonight!" fumes the tubby man. "Perhaps you don't know me, captain—Congressman Smith, Albert J. Smith, at your service. It is imperative that I be in Portsmouth to support my congressional colleague, Mr Lincoln, at tonight's meeting."

"Well, I'm sorry, Congressman Smith," says the captain, "but if you were going to support the President, I couldn't land you in Ohio today."

"Infamous!" cries the little chap. "Why, I've come from Evansville for this, and Mr Lincoln has broken his journey home specially for this meeting, and is awaiting me in Portsmouth. Really, captain, when matters of such national importance as the slave question are to be discussed by eminent—"

"The slave question!" cries the captain. "Well, sir, you may land in Kentucky for me, let me tell you, and I hope they welcome you warmly!"

And off he stumped, red in the face, leaving the little chap wattling and cursing. I didn't have to be told the captain was a Southerner, but I was vastly intrigued to find my path crossing so close to Mr Lincoln's again. That seemed to me a good reason for turning back to Cincinnati, and giving Portsmouth a wide berth. He and his sharp eyes and embarrassing questions were the last things I wanted to meet just now.

But Cassy wouldn't have it; even landing in Kentucky was preferable to Cincinnati, and she pointed out that the farther I was upriver the safer I'd be. She was sure there must be a ferry running at Portsmouth; it was only a short walk along the shore, she said, and once across we could journey inland to Columbus and from there quickly to Pittsburgh.

If she didn't mind, I didn't, because I felt we must be beyond pursuit by now, but I noticed she hesitated at the gangplank, scanning the shore at Fisher's Landing, and her steps were slow as we walked over the creaking wooden stage. Suddenly she stopped, caught my arm, and whispered:

"Let us go back! I never thought to stand on this soil again—I feel evil hanging over us. Oh, we shouldn't have landed! Please, let us go back quickly, before it's too late!"

But it was too late even then, for the steamboat, having landed about a dozen of us, including the incensed Congressman, was already backing away from the stage, her whistle whooping like a lost soul. Cassy shuddered beside me, and pulled her veil more tightly round her face. Truth to tell, I didn't care for the look of the place much myself; just the stage, and a mean little tavern, and bleak scrubby country stretching away on both sides.

However, there was nothing for it now. The other passengers crowded round the tavern, asking about a ferry, and the yokel there opined that there might be one later that day, but with the ice he couldn't be sure. The others decided to wait and see, but Cassy insisted that we should push on along the bank; we could see Portsmouth in the distance on the far shore, and it did seem there would be a better chance of a ferry there.

So we set off together, carrying our bags, along the lonely little road that wound among the trees by the river. It was a cold, grey afternoon, with a keen wind sighing among the branches, and through the trunks the brown Ohio ran by, with the massive floes grinding and booming in the brown water. There was low cloud and a threat of snow, and a dank chill in the air that was not just the weather. Cassy was silent as we walked, but her words still sounded in my ears, and although I told myself we were safe enough by this time, surely, I found myself ever glancing back along the deserted muddy track, lying drear and silent under the winter sky.

We must have walked about an hour, and although it was still early afternoon it seemed to me to be growing darker, when we saw buildings ahead, and came to a tiny village on the river bank. We were nearly opposite Portsmouth by now, and already some lights were twinkling across the water. The river here seemed to be more choked with ice than ever, stirring and heaving but moving only gently downstream.

The keeper of the tavern that served the place laughed to scorn our inquiries about a ferry; however, in his opinion the ice would freeze again overnight, and then we could walk across. He couldn't give us beds, but we were welcome to couch down for the night, and in the meantime he could give us fried ham and coffee.

"We should have stayed at Fisher's Landing," says I, but Cassy just sank down wearily on a bench without replying. I offered her some coffee but she shook her head, and when I reminded her it was only for one night, she whispered:

"It is very near us now—I can feel the dark shadow coming closer. Oh, God! Oh, God! Why did I set foot on this accursed shore again!"

"What bloody shadow?" snaps I, for she had my nerves like fiddle strings. "We're snug enough here, girl, within spitting distance of Ohio! We've come this far, in God's name; who's going to stop us now?"

And as though in answer to my question, from somewhere down the road outside, came the yelping and baying of hounds.

Cassy started, and I own that my heart took a sudden leap, although what's a dog barking, after all? And then came the sound of footsteps, and men's voices, and presently the door was shoved open, and half a dozen or so rough fellows came in and bawled for the landlord to bring them a jug of spirits and some food. I didn't like the look of them by half, big tough-looking men with pistols in their belts and two of them carrying rifles; their leader was a tall, black-bearded villain with a broken nose who gave me a hard stare and a curt good day and then strode to the door to curse the dogs leashed up outside. I felt Cassy sink shuddering against me, and just caught her whisper:

"Slave-catchers! Oh, God help us!"

I fought down my instinctive desire to make a dash for the door; I'd made too many sudden dashes on this trip already. My throat was dry and my hands trembling, but I forced myself to drink my coffee, and even asked Cassy in a loud, steady voice if she required anything more to eat. Plainly we would have to get out of here as soon as possible, but we must not rouse an instant's suspicion, or we were done for.

The newcomers were talking so much by now that our silence went unnoticed, and almost their first words confirmed what Cassy had said.

"That nigger of Thompson's'll be hidin' up in Mason's Bottom," says one. "That's whar they always run afore they try the Portsmouth ferry. Well, he ain't gettin' no ferry tonight, for sure; he can lay out an' freeze an' the dogs kin pick him up in the mornin'."

"Too bad about the ferry, though," says the leader. "Kinda had a notion to go over tonight, to th' abolitionist meetin'."

"Since when you go to abolitionist meetin's, Buck?"

"Since I heerd that son-of-a-bitch of an Illinoy lawyer goin' to be speakin', that's since when. Precious Mr Goddam Congressman Lincoln. That's a bastard I get real discontented with, that is."

"You figurin' on takin' a few bad eggs along?" says the other, laughing.

"Could be. Could be, if things had looked right, I might have taken me a picket rail, a nice big bag o' feathers, an' mustered up some hot tar to boot. I reckon that's th' only way to discourage some o' these nigger-lovin' duffers."

"Discourage 'em a dam' sight better with a rope, or a good spread of buckshot," says a third, and other suggestions followed, most of them unrepeatable.

All this time I had felt Cassy trembling beside me, but now she suddenly whispered, in a shaking gasp:

"We must leave! I can't bear it any longer! Please, let us go—anywhere away from them!"

I knew she was near breaking—this same wench who'd killed

two men on a dark country road—so I helped her to her feet, and with a muttered good day led her towards the door. Naturally they turned to look at us, and the leader, Buck, says:

"Ain't no ferry movin' tonight, mister. Where you figurin' on goin'?"

"Er . . . Fisher's Landing," says I.

"No ferry there, either," says he. "You be best here tonight."

I hesitated. "I think we'll move on," says I. "Come, my dear."

And we were almost at the door when he said:

"Hold one one moment, mister." He was sitting forward on his stool, and there was a grin on his loose mouth that I didn't care for. "Pardon my askin'—but would your companion be a white lady?"

Sickened, I turned to face him. "And if she is not?" says I.

"Thought she warn't," says he, standing up. "Mighty fancy dressed, though, for a nigger."

"I like my women well dressed." I tried to keep my voice level, but it wasn't easy.

"Sure, sure," says he, hooking his thumbs in his belt. "Jus' that when I see nigger ladies, an' their wearin' veils, *an'* shiverin' like they had the ague—well, I get curious." He kicked his stool away and walked forward. "What's your name, wench?"

I saw Cassy's eyes flash behind her veil, and suddenly she was no longer trembling, which made up for me. "Ask my master," she said.

He gave a growl, but checked himself. "Right pert, too. All right, Mister—what's her name?"

"Belinda."

"Is it now?" Suddenly he reached forward, before I could stop him, and twitched away her veil, laughing as she started back. "Well, well, now—right pretty, as well as pert. You're a lucky feller, mister. An' what might your name be?"

"J. C. Stubbs," says I, "and I'll be damned if—"

"You'll be damned anyway, unless I'm mistaken," he snapped, his face vicious. "Belinda an' J. C. Stubbs, eh? Jus' you wait right there, then, while I have a little look here." And he pulled a handful of papers from his pocket. "I been keepin' an eye on you, this few minutes, Mr J. C. Stubbs, an' now I get a look at your little black charmer, I got me a feelin'—where is it, now?—yes, here we have it—uh, huh, Mr Stubbs, I got a suspicion you ain't Mr Stubbs at all, but that you're a Mr Fitzroy Howard, who offered a spankin' mustee gal named Cassy at Memphis a few days back, an'—"

He broke off with a shouted oath, because he was looking down the barrel of my Colt. There was nothing else for it; at the hideous realisation that we were caught I had snatched it from the back of my waist, and as he started back and his hand swept away his coat-tail I jammed the gun into his midriff with the violence of panic, and bawled in his face:

"Move, and I'll blow your guts into Ohio! You others, get your hands up—lively now, or I'll spread your friend all over you!"

I was red in the face with terror, and my hand was quivering on the butt, but to them I was probably a fearsome sight. Their hands shot up, a rifle clattered to the floor, and Buck's ugly face turned yellow. He fell back before me, his mouth trembling, and the sight of it gave me a sudden surge of courage.

"Down on the floor, damn you—all of you! Down, I say, or I'll burn your brains!"

Buck dropped to the boards, and the others followed suit. I hadn't the nerve to go among them to remove their weapons, and for the life of me I couldn't think what to do next. I stood there, swearing at them, wondering if I should shoot Buck where he lay, but I hadn't the bate for it. He raised his head to cry hoarsely:

"You ain't gonna run nowhere, mister! We'll get you before you're gone a mile—you an' that yaller slut! We'll make you pay for this—"

I snarled and mowed at them, brandishing my gun, and he cowered down, and then I backed slowly towards the door, still covering them—the Colt was shaking like a jelly. I couldn't think—there wasn't time. If we ran for it now, where would we run to? They'd overhaul us, with their filthy dogs—if only there was some way to delay them! A sudden inspiration struck me, and I glanced at Cassy; she was at my elbow, quivering like a hunted beast, and if she too was terrified at least it wasn't with the terror that is helpless.

"Cassy!" I snapped. "Can you use a gun?"

She nodded. "Take this, then," says I. "Cover them—and if one of them stirs a finger shoot the swine in the stomach! There—catch hold. Good girl, good girl—I'll be back in an instant!"

"What is it?" Her eyes were wild. "Where are you—"

"Don't ask questions! Trust me!" And with that I slipped out of the door, pulled it to, and was off like a stung whippet. I'd make quarter of a mile, maybe more, before she would twig, or they overpowered her, and that quarter mile could be the difference between life and death—but even as I was away with my first frenzied spring a dun-coloured, white-fanged horror came surging up at my side, teeth dragged at the tail of my coat, and I came down in a sprawling tangle of limbs with one of those damned hounds snarling and tearing at me.

By the grace of God I fell just beyond reach of its leash; I suppose the brute had gone for me because it knew a guilty fugitive when it saw one, and now it tore and frothed against its chain to be at me. I jumped up to resume my flight, and then I heard Cassy scream in the tavern, the Colt banged, somebody howled, and the door flew open. Cassy came out at a blind run, making for the thicket that bordered the river; I spared not a glance for the tavern door but went high-stepping after her for all I was worth, expecting a bullet between the shoulders at every stride.

As luck had it the thicket was only a dozen yards away, but by the time I had burst through it Cassy was well ahead of me. I suppose it was blind instinct that made me follow her, now that my own chance of a clear getaway had been scuppered by what-ever had gone amiss in the tavern—the stupid bitch could have held them longer than two seconds, you'd have thought—and there was nothing to do but shift like blazes. It was growing dusk, but not near dark enough for concealment, and she was running for dear life along the bank eastwards. I pounded down the slope, yelling to her, at my wits' end over where we were going to run to. Could we hide—no, my God, the dogs! We couldn't outstrip them along the bank—where then? The same thoughts must have been in Cassy's mind, for as I closed on her, and heard the din of shouting rise a hundred yards behind me, she suddenly checked, and with a despairing cry leaped down the bank to the water's edge.

"No! No!" I bawled. "Not on the ice—we'll drown for certain!"

But she never heeded. There was a narrow strip of brown water between her and the nearest floe, and she cleared it like a hunter, slipping and falling, but scrambling up again and clambering over the hummocks beyond. Oh, Christ, thinks I, she's mad, but then I looked behind, and there they were, running down from the tavern, with the dogs yelping in the background. I took a race down the bank and jumped, my feet flew from under me on the ice, and I came down with a sickening crash. I staggered up, plunging over the mass of frozen cakes locked like a great raft ahead of me, and saw Cassy steadying herself for a leap on to a level floe beyond. She made it, and I tumbled down the hummocks and leaped after her. Somehow I kept my footing, and slithered and slipped across the floe, which must have been thirty yards from side to side.

Beyond it there were great rough cakes bucking about in the current, but so close together that we were able to scramble across them. Once my leg went in, and I just avoided plunging headlong; Cassy was twenty yards ahead, and I remember roaring to her to wait for me—God knows why, but one does these things. And then behind me came the crack of a shot, and glancing over my shoulder I saw that our pursuers were leaving the bank and taking the ice in our wake.

God! It was a nightmare. If I'd had a moment to think I'd have given up the ghost, but fear sent me skipping and stumbling over the pack, babbling prayers and curses, sprawling on the ice, cutting my hands and knees to shreds, and staggering up to follow her dark figure over the floes. All round the ice was grinding and groaning fearfully; it surged beneath our feet, cracking and tilting, and then I saw her stumble and kneel clinging to a floe; she was sobbing and shrieking, and two more shots came banging behind and whistled above us in the dusk.

As I overtook her she managed to regain her feet, glaring wildly back beyond me. Her dress was in shreds, her hands were dark with blood, her hair was trailing loose like a witch's. But she went reeling on, jumping another channel and staggering across the rugged floc beyond. I set myself for the jump, slipped, and fell full length into the icy water.

It was so bitter that I screamed, and she turned back and came slithering on all fours to the edge. I grabbed her hand, and somehow I managed to scramble out. The yelping of the dogs was sounding closer, a gun banged, a frightful pain tore through my buttock, and I pitched forward on to the ice. Cassy screamed, a man's voice sounded in a distant roar of triumph, and I felt blood coursing warm down my leg.

"My God, are you hurt?" she cried, and for some idiot reason I had a vision of a tombstone bearing the legend: "Here lies Harry Flashman, late 11th Hussars, shot in the arse while crossing the Ohio River". The pain was sickening, but I managed to lurch to my feet, clutching my backside, and Cassy seized my hand, dragging me on.

"Not far! Not far!" she was crying, and through a mist of pain I could see the lights on the Ohio bank, not far away on our right. If only we could make the shore, we might hide, or stagger into Portsmouth itself and get assistance, but then my wound betrayed me, my leg wouldn't answer, and I sank down on the ice.

We weren't fifty yards from the shore, with fairly level ice ahead, but the feeling had gone from my limb. I looked round; Buck and his fellows were floundering across the ice a bare hundred yards away. Cassy's voice was crying:

"Up! Up! Only a little farther! Oh, try, try!"

"Rot you!" cries I. "I'm shot! I can't!"

She gave an inarticulate cry, and then by God, she seized my arms, stooped into me, and somehow managed to half-drag, half-carry me across the ice. There must have been amazing strength in the slim body, for I'm a great hulking fellow, and she was near exhaustion. But she got me along, until we fell in a heap close to the bank, and then we slithered and floundered through the ice-filled shallows, and dragged ourselves up the muddy slope of the Ohio bank.[39]

"Free soil," sobs Cassy. "Free soil!" And a bullet smacked into the bank between us to remind her that we were still a long way from safety. That shot must have done something to my muscular control, for I managed to hobble up the bank, with Cassy hauling at me, and then we stumbled forward towards the lights of Portsmouth. It was only half a mile away, but try running half a

mile with a bullet hole in your rump. With Cassy's arm round me
I could just stagger; we plunged ahead through the gloaming, and
there were figures on the road ahead, people staring at us and
calling out. Just before we reached them, we passed a tree, and my
eye caught the lettering on a great yellow bill that had been
stuck there. It read something about "Great Meeting Tonight,
All Welcome", and in large letters the names "Lincoln" and
"Smith". I was gasping, all in, but I remembered that the little
tubby man on the steamboat had been Smith, and he had said
Lincoln was speaking in Portsmouth. And I had sense enough to
realise that wherever Lincoln was there would be enemies of
slavery and friends to all fugitives like us. Two hours ago I'd been
wanting to avoid him like the pox, but now it was life or death,
and there was something else stirring in my head. I don't know
why it was, but I remembered that big man, and his great hard
knuckles and dark smiling eyes, and I thought, by God, get to
Lincoln! Get to him; we'll be safe with him. They won't dare touch
us if he's there. And as Cassy and I stumbled along the road, and
I heard voices calling out in concern: "Who are they? What is
it? Great snakes, he's bleeding—look, he's been shot," I managed
to find the breath to cry out:

"Mr Lincoln—where can I find Mr Lincoln?"

"Great snakes, man!" A face was peering into mine. "Who are
you? What's—"

"Slave-catchers!" cries Cassy. "Behind us—with guns and
dogs."

"What's that, girl? Slave-catchers! My stars, get them up—
here, Harry, lend a hand! John, you run to your uncle's—quick
now! Tell him slave-catchers come over the river—hurry, boy,
there's no time to lose!"

I could have cried out in relief, but as I turned my head I saw
in the distance figures clambering the bank, and heard the yelp
of those accursed dogs.

"Get me to Lincoln, for God's sake!" I shouted. "Where is he
—what house?"

"Lincoln? You mean Mr Abraham Lincoln? Why, he's up to
Judge Payne's, ain't he, Harry? C'mon, then, mister, it ain't that
far, ifn you can manage along. Harry, help the lady, there. This

way, then—best foot forward!"

Somehow I managed to raise a run, and by blessed chance the house proved to be not more than a few furlongs away. I was aware of a hubbub behind us, and gathered that Buck and his friends had run into various Ohio citizens who were disputing their progress, but only verbally, for as we turned into a wide gateway, and our helpers assisted us up a long pathway to a fine white house, I heard the barking again, and what I thought was Buck's voice raised in angry defiance.

We stumbled up the steps, and someone knocked and beat on the panels, and a scared-looking nigger put his head round the door, but I blundered ahead, pushing him back, with a man helping Cassy beside me. We were in a big, well-lit hall, and I remember the carpet was deep red, and there was a fine mural painted on the wall above the stairs. People were hurrying out of the rooms; two or three gentlemen, and a lady who gave a little shriek at the sight of us.

"Good God!" cries one of the men. "What is the meaning—? who are you—?"

"Lincoln!" I shouted, and as my leg gave way I sat down heavily. "Where's Lincoln? I want him. I've been shot in the backside—slave-catchers! Lincoln!"

At this there was a great hubbub, and women swooning by the sound of it, and I hobbled to the newel post of the stair and hung on—I couldn't sit down, you understand. Cassy, with a man supporting her, tottered past me and sank into a chair, while the nicely-dressed ladies and gentlemen gaped at us in consternation, two horrid, bleeding scarecrows leaving a muddy trail across that excellent carpet. A stout man in a white beard was confronting me, shouting:

"How dare you, sir? Who are you, and what—?"

"Lincoln," says I, pretty hoarse. "Where's Lincoln?"

"Here I am," says a voice. "What do you want with me?"

And there he was, at my shoulder, frowning in astonishment.

"I'm Fitzhoward," says I. "You remember—"

"Fitzhoward? I don't—"

"No, not Fitzhoward, blast it. Wait, though—Arnold—oh, God, no!" My mind was swimming. "No—Comber! Lieutenant

Comber—you must remember me?"

He took a pace back in bewilderment. "Comber? The English officer—how in the world—?"

"That's a slave girl," I gasped out. "I—I rescued her—from down South—the slave-catchers found us—chased us across river —still coming after us." And praise be to providence I had the sense to hit the right note. "Don't let them take her back! Save her, for God's sake!"

It must have sounded well, at least to the others, for I heard a gasp of dismay and pity, and one of the women, a little ugly battleship of a creature, bustles over to Cassy to take her hands.

"But—but, here, sir!" The stout chap was all agog. "What, a runaway girl? Septy, shut that door this minute—what's that? My God, more scarecrows! What the devil is this? Who are—?"

I looked to the door, and my heart went down to my boots. The old nigger was clinging to the handle as though to support himself, his eyes rolling, the people of the house were rustling back to the doorways off the hall, the stout man—who I guessed was Judge Payne—had fallen silent. Buck stood in the doorway, panting hard, his clothes sodden and mud-spattered, with his gun cradled in his left arm, and behind him were the bearded faces of his fellows. Buck was grinning, though, with his loose lower lip stuck out, and now he raised his free hand and pointed at Cassy.

"That's a runaway slave there, mister—an' I'm a warranted slave-catcher! That scoundrel at the stair there's the thievin' skunk that stole her!" He took a pace forward into the hall. "I'm gonna take both of 'em back where they belong!"

Payne seemed to swell up. "Good God!" says he. "What— what? This is intolerable! First these two, and now—is my house supposed to be a slave market, or what?"

"I want 'em both," Buck was beginning, and then he must have realised where he was. "Kindly sorry for intrudin' on you, mister, but this is where they run to, an' this is where I gotta follow. So— jus' you roust 'em out here to me, an' we won't be troublin' you or your ladies no further."

For a moment you could have heard a pin drop. Then Buck added defiantly:

"That's the law. I got the law on my side."

I felt Lincoln stiffen beside me. "For God's sake," I whispered. "Don't let them take us!"

He moved forward a pace, beside Judge Payne, and I heard one of the ladies begin to sob gently—the first sobs before hysterics. Then Lincoln says, very quietly:

"There's a law against forcing an entry into a private house."

"Indeed there is!" cries the judge. "Take yourself off, sir—this instant, and your bandits with you!"

Buck glared at him. "Ain't forcin' nuthin'. I'm recapturin' a slave, like I'm legally entitled to. Anyone gits in my way, is harbourin' runaways, an' that's a crime! I know the law, mister, an' I tell you, either you put them out o' doors for us, or stand aside— because if they ain't comin' out, we're comin' in!"

Judge Payne fell back at that, and the other people shrank away, some of the women bolting back to the drawing room. But not the ugly little woman who had her arm round Cassy's shoulders.

"Don't you move another step!" she cries out. "Nathan—don't permit him. They don't touch a hair of this poor creature's head in this house. Stand back, you bully!"

"But, my dear!" cries Payne in distress. "If what they say is true, we have no choice, I fear—"

"Who says it's true? There now, child, be still; they shan't harm you."

"Look, missus." Buck swaggered forward, limbering his rifle, and stood four-square, with his pals at his back. "You best 'tend to what your ol' man says. We got the law behind us." He glanced at Lincoln, who hadn't moved and was right in his path. "Step aside."

Lincoln still didn't move. He stood very easy and his drawl was steady as ever.

"On the subject of the law," says he, "you say she's a runaway, and that this man stole her. We don't know the truth about that, though, do we? Perhaps they tell a different tale. I know a little law myself, friend, and I would suggest that if you have a claim on these two persons, you should pursue it in the proper fashion, which is through a court. An Ohio court," he added. "And I'd further advise you, as a legal man, not to prejudice your case by

746

armed house-breaking. Or, for that matter, by dirtying this good lady's carpet. If you have a just claim, go and enter it, in the proper place." He paused. "Good night, sir."

It was so cool and measured and unanswerable that I could have wept with relief to hear him—but I didn't know much about slave-catchers. Buck just grunted and sneered at him.

"Oh, yeah, I know about the courts! I guess I do—I bin to court before—"

"I'll believe that," says Lincoln.

"Yeah? You're a mighty fancy goddam legal beanpole, ain't you though? Well, I'll tell you suthin', mister—I know about courts an' writs an' all, an' there ain't one o' them worth a lick in hell to me! I'm here—them dam' runaways is here—an' if I take 'em away nice an' quiet, we don' have to trouble with no courts nor nuthin'. An' afterwards—well, I reckon I'll answer right smart for any incon-venience caused here tonight. But I ain't bein' fobbed by smart talk—they're comin' with me!"

And he pushed the barrel of his piece forward just a trifle.

"You'll just take them," says Lincoln. "By force. Is that so?"

"You bet it's so! I reckon the courts won't worry me none, neither! We'll have done justice, see?"

I quailed to listen to him. God, I thought, we're finished; he had the force behind him. If he wanted to march in and drag us out bodily, the law would support him in the end. There would be protests, no doubt, and some local public outcry, but what good would that be to us, once they had us south of the river again? I heard Cassy moan, and I sank down, done up and despairing, beside the newel. And then Lincoln laughed, shaking his head.

"So that's your case is it, Mr—?"

"Buck Robinson's my—"

"Buck will do. That's your style, is it, Buck? Brute force and talk about it afterwards. Well, it has its logic, I suppose—but, d'ye know, Buck, I don't like it. No, sir. That's not how we do things where I come from—"

"I don't give a damn how you do things where you come from, Mr Smart," Buck spat out. "Get out of my way."

"I see," says Lincoln, not moving. "Well, I've put my case to you, in fair terms, and you've answered it—admirably, after your own lights. And since you won't listen to reason, and believe that might is right—well, I'll just have to talk in your terms, won't I? So—"

"You hold your gab and stand aside, mister," shouts Buck. "Now, I'm warnin' you fair!"

"And I'm warning you, Buck!" Lincoln's voice was suddenly sharp. "Oh, I know you, I reckon. You're a real hard-barked Kentucky boy, own brother to the small-pox, weaned on snake juice and grizzly hide, aren't you? You've killed more niggers than the dysentery, and your grandma can lick any white man in Tennessee. You talk big, step high, and do what you please, and if any 'legal beanpole' in a store suit gets in your way you'll cut him right down to size, won't you just? He's not a *practical* man, is he? But you are, Buck—when you've got your gang at your back! Yes, sir, you're a practical man, all right."

Buck was mouthing at him, red-faced and furious, but Lincoln went on in the same hard voice.

"So am I, Buck. And more—for the benefit of any shirt-tail chawbacon with a big mouth, I'm a who's-yar boy from Indiana myself, and I've put down better men than you just by spitting teeth at them.[40] If you doubt it, come ahead! You want these people—you're going to take them?" He gestured towards Cassy. "All right, Buck—you try it. Just—try it."

The rest of the world decided that Abraham Lincoln was a great orator after his speech at Gettysburg. I realised it much earlier, when I heard him laying it over that gun-carrying bearded ruffian who was breathing brimstone at him. I couldn't see Lincoln's face, but I'll never forget that big gangling body in the long coat that didn't quite fit, towering in the centre of the hall, with the big hands motionless at his sides. God knows how he had the nerve, with six armed men in front of him. But when I think back to it, and hear that hard, rasping drawl sounding in my memory, and remember the force in those eyes, I wonder how Buck had the nerve to stand up in front of him, either. He did, though, for about half a minute, glaring from Lincoln to Cassy to me and back to Lincoln again. Twice he was going to speak, and twice thought better of it; he was a brawny, violent man with a gun in his hands, but speaking objectively at a safe distance now, he has my sympathy. As a fellow bully and coward, I can say that Buck behaved precisely as I should have done in his place. He glared and breathed hard, but that was his limit. And then through the open door came the distant sound of raised voices, and a hurrying of many feet on the road.

"I doubt if that's the Kentucky militia," says Lincoln. "Better be going, Buck."

Buck stood livid, still hesitating; then with a curse he swung about and stumped to the door. He turned again there, dark with passion, and pointed a shaking finger.

"I'll be back!" says he. "Don't you doubt it, mister—I'll be back, an' I'll have the law with me! We'll see about this, by thunder! I'll get the law!"

They clattered down the steps, Buck swearing at the others, and as the door closed and the exclamations started flying, Lincoln turned and looked down at me. His forehead was just a little damp.

"The ancients, in their wisdom, made a great study of rhetoric," says he. "But I wonder did they ever envisage Buck Robinson? Yes, they probably did." He pursed his lips. "He's a big fellow, though—likely big fellow, he is. I—I think I'd sooner see Cicero square up to him behind the barn than me. Yes, I rather think I would." He adjusted his coat and cracked his knuckles. "And now, Mr Comber—?"

I've been wounded several times, all of them damned painful, but you may take my word for it that a ball in the bum is the worst. By the time that ham-fisted sawbones had hauled it out I was weak and weeping, and my immediate recuperation wasn't eased by the fact that Judge Payne and Lincoln agreed that Cassy and I must be spirited out of the house without delay, in case Buck and his friends returned with an officer and a warrant. With two men to support me and my buttocks in a sling I was helped about half a mile to another establishment, where I gathered the folk were red-hot abolitionists, and put to bed face down.

Of course I had already given a rough account of what had happened, in answer to the questions they fired at me after Buck had gone. The Judge wasn't concerned with anything but the events of the last few hours, and was full of praise for my daring and endurance, while his wife, the ugly little woman, and the other females made much of Cassy, and called her a poor dear, and clucked over her cuts and bruises. They were all stout anti-slavers, of course, as I'd guessed they would be, and would you believe it, while that blasted doctor was probing and muttering over my bottom, the women downstairs actually sang "Now Israel may say and that truly", with harmonium accompaniment. This to celebrate what Judge Payne called our deliverance, and the others cried "Amen", and were furious in their wrath against these vile slave-traffickers who hounded poor innocents with dogs and guns—"and she such a sweet and refined young thing—oh, my land, the pity of her poor bruised limbs." You ought to see her with a knife sometime, thinks I, or stripping for the buyers. And for me they had nothing but blessings and commiseration for my torn arse, which the Judge called an honourable scar, taken in the defence of liberty. Lincoln stood in the background, watching under his brows.

But when they had taken us to the new house, and I had been tucked up in bed, he came along, very patient, and begged our hosts for a little time alone with me.

"I'm afraid the good people of Portsmouth will have to do without me this evening," says he. "They might find my presence in public somewhat embarrassing. Anyway, one successful speech in a day is quite enough." So they left us, and he sat down beside the bed, with his tall hat between his feet.

"Now, sir," says he, pointing that formidable head of his at me, "may I hear from you at some length? I last parted from a respectable British naval officer in Washington; tonight I meet a wounded fugitive running an escaped slave across the Ohio. I'm not only curious, you understand—I'm also a legislator of my country,[41] a maker and guardian of its laws which, on your behalf, I suspect I have broken fairly comprehensively this night. I feel I'm entitled to an explanation. Pray begin, Mr Comber."

So I did. There was no point in lying. much; I hadn't time for invention, anyway, and he would have seen through it. So from New Orleans on I told him the truth—Crixus. my escape with Randolph, what happened on the steamboat. the Mandevilles, the slave cart and Cassy, Memphis, and our eventual flight. I kept out the spicy bits, of course, and Mandeville's barbarous treatment of me I explained by pretending that Omohundro had turned up at Greystones with searchers and identified me—that was how they treated underground railroad men in the south, I said. He listened attentively, saying nothing, the bright eyes never leaving my face. When I had finished he sat silent a long while, studying. Then he said:

"Well," and then a long pause. "That's quite a story." Another pause. "Yes, sir, that is quite a story." He coughed. "Haven't heard anything to touch it since last time I was in the Liberal Club. There's—nothing you wish to add to it—at all? No detail you may have, uh, overlooked?"

"That is all, sir," says I wondering.

"I see. I see. No, no, I just thought—oh, a balloon flight over Arkansas, or perhaps an encounter with pirates and alligators in the bayous of Louisiana—you know—"

I demanded, did he not believe me?

"On the contrary, I don't doubt it for a moment—more or less, anyway. No, I believe you, sir—my expressions of astonishment are really a tribute to you. In America, as in most other places, it's only the truth that we find hard to believe. No—it's not what you've told me, but what you haven't told me that I find downright fascinating. However, I shan't press you. I would hate to force you off the path of veracity—"

"If you doubt me," says I stiffly, "you may ask the girl Cassy."

"I already have, and she confirms a great part of your story. Remarkable young woman, that; she has much character." He cracked his knuckles thoughtfully. "Very beautiful, too; very beautiful. Had you noticed? Yes, I guess the Queen of Sheba must have looked something—'black but comely', wasn't it? However —I was also going to add that your narrative of Randolph fits very well with what I read in the papers about his escape from the steamboat—"

"His escape?"

"Oh, yes, indeed. He turned up, in Vermont of all places, about two weeks ago, and is now in Canada, I understand. The liberal sheets were full of his exploits." He smiled. "I don't hold it against you that there was no mention of you in his very full relation. No mention of anyone, much, except George Randolph. But from all I've heard of him, that is consistent. Extraordinary fellow, he must be. He should be grateful to you, though—up to a point, at least."

"I doubt it," says I.

"Is that so? Well, well, I've no doubt you've noticed that even when gratitude costs nothing, folks are often reluctant to show it. They'll even pay hard money to avoid giving it where it's due. Strange, but human, I suppose." He was silent a moment. "You're sure there's nothing further you wish to tell me, Mr Comber?"

"Why, no, sir," says I. "I can think of nothing—"

"I doubt that very much," says he, drily. "I really and truly do —you've never seen the day when you couldn't think of something. But do you know what I think, Mr Comber—speaking plain, as man to man? I look at you, fine bluff British figurehead, well-spoken, easy, frank, splendid whiskers—and I can't help remembering the story they tell in Illinois about the honest Southern gentleman—you ever hear that one?"

I said I hadn't.

"Well, what they say about the honest Southern gentleman—he never stole the Mississippi river. No, don't take any offence. It's as I said in Washington—I don't know about you, except what my slight knowledge of humanity tells me, which is that you're a rascal. But again, I don't *know*. The trouble with people like you—and me, I guess—is that nobody ever finds us out. Just as well, maybe. But it lays a burden on us—we don't meet with regular punishments and penalties for our misdeeds, which will make it all the harder for us to achieve salvation in the long run." He frowned at the carpet. "Anyway, I'm a lawyer, not a judge. I don't really believe that I want to know all about you. It's enough for me that you brought that girl across the Ohio river today. I don't know why, for what reason, or out of what strange chance. It's sufficient that she's here, and will never wear chains again."

Well, since that was what counted most with him, I was all for it; his talk about suspecting me for a rascal had been downright unnerving. It seemed a good time to butter him a bit.

"Sir," says I eagerly, "all my efforts on that poor unfortunate girl's behalf, the hardships of the flight, the desperate stratagems to which I was forced, the wound taken in her defence—wound, did I say? Scratch, rather—why, all these things would have been without avail had you not championed us in our hour of direst need. That, sir, was the act of a Christian hero, of a sublime spirit, if I may say so."

He stood looking at me, with his head cocked on one side.

"I must have been mad," says he. "Mind you, I quite enjoyed it there, for a moment—" he laughed uncertainly—"at least, now that it's over, I think I did. Do you realise what I allowed myself to do? You, sir, are in a way to being as highly successful a slave stealer as ever I heard of—at least, Arnold Fitzroy Prescott or whatever his name is—he's one. He's also an accessory to two murders—that's what they'd call it, although I'd say it was moral self-defence, myself. But a Southern jury certainly wouldn't agree. In the eyes of the law you're a deep-dyed criminal, Mr Comber—and I, the junior Congressman from Illinois, a pillar of the community, a trusted legislator, a former holder of the United States commission, a God-fearing, respected citizen—it's all there in my election address, and the people believed it, so it must be true—I allowed myself, in a moment of derangement, moved by pity for that girl Cassy's distress—I allowed myself, sir, to aid and abet you. God knows what the penalty is in Ohio for harbouring run-away slaves, assisting slave-stealers, resisting a warranted slave-catcher, and offering to disturb the peace by assault and battery, but whatever it is, I'm not in a hurry to answer for it, I can tell you."

He scratched his head ruefully and began to fidget about the room, twitching at the curtains and tapping the furniture with his foot, his head sunk on his chest.

"Not that I regret it, you understand. I'd do it again, and again, and again, in spite of the law. Fine thing for a lawyer—humph! But there's a higher thing than the law, and it belongs in the conscience, and it says that evils such as slavery must be fought until the dragon is dead. And in that cause I hope I'll never stand back." He stopped, frowning. "Also, if there's one thing can get my dander good and high, it's a big mouthed Kentuckian hill rooster with his belly over his britches and a sass-me-and-see-what-happens look in his eye. Yes, sir, big-chested bravos like our friend Buck Robinson seem to bring out the worst in me. Still—I don't imagine we'll hear much more from his direction, and if we do, Judge Payne is fortunately a man of considerable influence—or Mrs Payne is, I'm never sure which—and by the time the good judge has come out from under the bedclothes and scrambled into his dignity again, I don't think I'll have much to fret over. Any-way, I can look after myself and lose no sleep. But you, Mr Comber, would be better a long way from here, and as quickly as may be."

Now he was talking most excellent sense; I twisted round from my prone position to cry agreement, and gave my backside a nasty twinge.

"Indeed, sir," says I. "The sooner I can reach England—"

"I wasn't thinking of quite so far as that; not just yet awhile. I know you're all on fire to get home, which is why you say you slipped away in New Orleans in the first place. Pity you allowed yourself to be . . . uh . . . distracted along the way. However, since you did, and have broken federal laws in the process, it puts a different complexion on things. For me, you could go home now, but it's not that simple. The way I see it, my government—my country—needs you; they still want you down in New Orleans to give evidence against the crew of—the *Balliol College*, wasn't it? Your testimony, as I understand it, can put those gentlemen where they belong—"

"But, Mr Lincoln, there is evidence enough against them without me," I cried, all a-sweat again.

"Well, perhaps there may be, but a little more won't hurt, if it makes certain of them. After all, that was why you sailed with them, why you risked your hide as an agent, wasn't it?" He was smiling down at me. "To bring them to book, to strike another blow against the slave trade?"

"Oh, of course, to be sure, but . . . well . . . er . . ."

"You're perhaps reluctant to go back to New Orleans because you feel it may be unsafe for you, after . . . recent events?"

"Exactly! You're absolutely right, sir . . ."

"Have no fear of that," says he. "No one is going to connect the eminently respectable Lieutenant Comber, R.N., with all those goings on far away up the river. That was the work of some scoundrel called Arnold FitzPrescott or Prescott FitzArnold or someone. And if anyone did connect them, I can assure you there would be no lack of influence working on your behalf to keep you out of trouble—there are enough sympathetic ears in high places in the federal government to see to that at need. Provided, of course, that you are doing your duty by that same government—and, incidentally, by your own."

By George, this was desperate; I had to talk him out of it somehow, without raising more suspicions of me than he had already.

"Even so, Mr Lincoln, I'm sure it would be best if I could proceed home directly. The case against the *Balliol College* can surely be proved without my help."

"Well, I daresay, but that's not the point any longer. This is quite a delicate situation, you know. See here: I've stood up for you tonight—and for that girl—helped you both to break my country's laws, and broken 'em myself, in a just, fine cause which

755

I believe to be in my country's true interest. And if it ever got out—which I pray to the Lord it won't—there is enough anti-slavery sentiment in our federal government to ensure that it would all be winked at, and no more said. But they're not going to wink if I, a Congressman, help a witness in an important case to avoid his duty. That's why I'm bound to send you back to Orleans. Believe me, you have nothing to fear there—you can say your piece in the witness box, and then go home as fast as my distant influence and that of grateful friends will send you."

Aye, and wait till the *Balliol College* scoundrels denounce me as Flashman, their fellow-slaver, posing as a dead man, thinks I; we'll see how much influence is exerted on my behalf then. I made a last effort.

"Mr Lincoln," says I, "believe me that nothing would give me more satisfaction than to accede to your request—"

"Capital," says he, "because that's what you're going to do." He regarded me quizzically. "Why you should be reluctant beats me—I begin to wonder if there's an outraged husband waiting for you in Orleans, or something of that order. If so, tell him to go to blazes—I daresay you've done that before."

There was one I could cheerfully have consigned to blazes, as I lay there going hot and cold, chewing my nether lip. I have damnable luck, truly—how many poor devils have had to try and wriggle clear in arguments with folk like Lincoln and Bismarck? He had me with my short hairs fast in the mangle, and I daren't protest any longer. What the devil was I to say, with those dark caverns of eyes smiling down at me?

"I doubt if it's anything as simple as an outraged husband, though," says he. "However, you don't choose to tell me, and I don't choose to press you. I owe you that much, on behalf of Randolph and the girl Cassy—in return you owe it to me to go to Orleans." He stood beside the bed, that odd quirk to his mouth, watching me. "Come, Mr Comber, it isn't very much, after all —and it's in the cause dear to your heart, remember."

There was nothing else for it, and I tried to keep the despair out of my voice as I agreed.

"So that's settled," says he cheerily. "You can go south again, but by a safe eastern route. I'll speak to Judge Payne, and see that a hint reaches Governor Bebb. We'll arrange for a U.S. marshal to accompany you. You'll be safe that way, and you won't run the risk of straying again." He was positively benign, the long villain; I could have sworn he was enjoying himself. "The trouble with you jolly tars is you don't seem to find your way on land any too well."

He talked a little more, and then picked up his hat, shook hands, and went over to the door.

"Good luck in New Orleans, Mr Comber—or whatever your name is. In the unlikely event that we ever meet again, try and find out for me what club-hauling is, won't you?" He pulled on his gloves. "And God bless you for what you did for that girl."

It was some consolation to think that I'd fooled Mr Lincoln some of the time, at least; he believed I had a spark of decency, apparently. So I thought it best to respond with a few modest and manly phrases about saving an innocent soul from bondage, but he interrupted me with his hand on the door.

"Keep it for the recording angel," says he. "I've a feeling you're going to need it."

And then he was gone, and I was not to see him again until that fateful night fifteen years later when, as President of the United States, he bribed and coerced me into ruining my military reputation (which mattered something) and risking my neck (which mattered a great deal) in order to save his Union from disaster (which didn't matter at all—not to me, anyway). But that's another tale, for another day.

That night in Portsmouth he left me in a fine frustrated fury. After all my struggling and running and ingenuity, I was going to be shipped back to New Orleans—and inevitably a prison cell, or worse. I couldn't even run any more, what with my behind laid open, and there would be a marshal to see that I got safe into the clutches of the American Navy, too. By George, I was angry; I could have broken Lincoln's long neck for him. You'd have thought, after all I'd done for his precious abolitionist cause —albeit against my will and better judgment—that he'd have had the decency to let me go my ways, and given me a pound or two out of the poor box to boot. But politicians are all the same; there's no trusting them whatever, not only because they're knaves, but because they're even more inconsistent than women. Selfish brutes, too.

At least, though, I was still alive, and fairly full of sin and impudence, when I might easily have been dead or chained on an Alabama plantation, or rotting at the bottom of the Mississippi or the Ohio. For the future, although it looked pretty horrid, I would just have to wait and see, and take my chance—if it came.

I was allowed up next day, and sat in state on the edge of a chair, with my wounded cheek over the edge, and various people came to see me—abolitionists, of course, who wanted to shake the hero's hand, and in the case of the older ladies of the community, to kiss his weathered brow. They came secretly, because like all towns thereabouts Portsmouth was split between pro-slavers and abolitionists, and my whereabouts was known only to a safe few. They brought me gingerbread and good wishes, and one of them said I was a saint; normally I'd have basked in it, as I'd done on other occasions, but the thought of Orleans took the fun out of it.

One of my visitors I even assailed with a thrown boot; he was a small boy, I suspect a child of the house, who came in when I was alone and asked: "Is it right you got shot up the ass, mister? Say, can I see?" I missed him, unfortunately.

Another glum thing was that Cassy left that evening. She isn't one of my prime favourites, looking back—too strong-willed and high strung—but I hate to lose a good mistress just when I'm getting the taste of her. However, they said it wasn't safe for her to remain so near the Ohio, and an underground railroad man was to take her to Canada. We didn't even have the chance of a lusty farewell, for when she came to say good-bye the ugly Mrs Payne was on hand to see fair play, with Cassy looking uncommonly demure and rather uncomfortable in a drab brown gown and poke bonnet. I gathered she hadn't realised that I'd done my level best to desert her on the far bank of the Ohio, for she thanked me very prettily for all my help, while Mrs Payne stood with her hands in her muff, nodding severe approval.

"Cassiopeia is quite recovered from her ordeal," says she, "and looks forward with the liveliest anticipation to reaching Canada. There our friends will see to it that she is provided with shelter and such employment as fits her station. I have no doubt that she will prove a credit to all of us her benefactors, and especially to you, Mr Comber."

Cassy's face was like a mask, but I saw her eyes glint in the shadow of the bonnet.

"Oh, I don't doubt it," says I. "Cassiopeia is a very biddable child, are you not, my dear?" I patted her hand. "There, there —just be a good girl, and mind what Mrs Payne and her kind friends tell you. Say your prayers each night, and remember your . . . er . . . station."

"There," says Mrs Payne. "I think you may kiss your deliverer's hand, child."

I wouldn't have been surprised if Cassy had burst out laughing, or in a fit of rage, but she did something that horrified Mrs Payne more than either could have done. She bent down and gave me a long, fierce kiss on the mouth, while her chaperone squawked and squeaked, and eventually bustled her away.

"Such liberties!" cries she. "These simple creatures! My child, this will *never*—"

"Good-bye," says Cassy, and that was the last I ever saw of her —or of the two thousand dollars we had had between us. I've never been able to recall for the life of me where it was stowed when we got off the steamboat at Fisher's Landing, but I know I didn't have it on my person, which was careless of me. Ah, well, I've no doubt she put it to good use—and it had been paid for her anyway.

However, money was the least of my concerns just then. Unless there was some unexpected turn of events in the next few weeks I could see the American republic would be paying my board and lodging for some time to come. I had nightmares about it, in which I was in a place like the Old Bailey, but with great stained-glass windows, and a hanging judge in scarlet on the bench, and Spring and his mates all chained up, leering, in the dock, and a voice droning out, "Call Beauchamp Comber, R.N." And I saw myself creeping into the witness box, goaded on by Lincoln and a U.S. marshal, and Spring bawling out: "That's not Comber—Comber's dead! That's the notorious Flashy, *monstrum horrendum*, come to impose on your worships like the bloody liar he is!" And then consternation, and I was dragged to the dock and chained to the others, and the judge said it would be twice as bad for me as for them, and upon conviction I would be shot in the other buttock and then hanged. At which there was great cheering, and I pleaded with them that I had been led astray and that it all came of playing vingt-et-un with D'Israeli, and they said that made it worse still, and then the faces and voices faded, and I would find myself awake, boiling with sweat and my wound aching like be-damned.

In the end, it wasn't quite like that, as you shall see. Have you noticed that things are never quite as bad or good as you expect them to be—at least, not in the way that you expect? So it was now, when my rump had healed enough for me to travel, and Judge Payne brought along the marshal, and with much hand-clasping and cheek-kissing and hallelujahs I was despatched on my way to continue God's work, as Payne put it.

I won't bother you with the journey, which was by coach and rail through Columbus, Pittsburgh and Baltimore, and then by packet down to Orleans. Sufficient to say that the marshal, a decent enough fellow called Cottrell, watched over me like a mother over a chick, very friendly, very careful, and that no official notice of our passage seemed to be taken, until we came to New Orleans.

There I was delivered into the care of Captain Bailey, U.S.N., a very bluff gentleman who shook me cordially by the hand, and said they were glad to see me, hey, and a fine commotion there had been when Captain Fairbrother had lost me, by thunder, yes, but here I was, safe and sound, so all was well that ended well.

"Mind you, Mr Comber, in these days I don't ask too many questions," says he. "I'm a sailor; like you, I do my duty. The past few months are a closed account to me, sir—one hears all about outlandish things like underground railroads and what not, but that's nothing to the point. What I know is that facing me now is a brother officer in the service of a friendly power, who is going to give evidence on behalf of the U.S. Navy against slave-runners. Capital work." And he rubbed his hands. "More than that— not my concern, sir. Not my concern at all. If anyone has been working for the underground railroad—which is an illegal organisation, of course—well, that's not our province, is it?

That's for Washington, or state governments, to worry about."
He grew confidential. "You see, Mr Comber, we're a strangely
divided country here—some for slave-holding, others against.
Now the government recognises it, officially, as you know, but a
lot of very important people—some in the government itself—
are against it. We have the strange position where federal government people, who may detest slavery, nevertheless are bound to
enforce the law against things like underground railroading. So,
often as not, a great many people frequently have to follow the
example of your good Lord Nelson, and turn a blind eye to a great
many things. Such as what you've been doing between your ... er
... departure from Captain Fairbrother and this moment, sir." He
frowned at me. "Do I make myself clear, sir?"

"I think so, sir," says I.

"Ye-es," says he. Then suddenly: "Look here, Comber, between
these four walls, I heard from circles in Washington that you've
been slave-stealing. Well, fine. I approve of that; so does half the
government. But it couldn't approve officially—my God, no!
Officially, it should arrest you and heaven knows what besides.
But we can't, even if we wanted to. We need your evidence in this
case, you're a damned important agent, by all Washington
accounts, and we can't, for the love of mercy, have an international
incident with the British." He shook his head. "I could wish you
had let well alone, young man—and yet, by God, from what I hear
from the friends of a certain Northern Congressman, you did a
capital piece of work, sir!" He beamed at me, winking. "So—there
it is. Washington is concerned at all costs to keep your name
and ... er ... recent activities quiet. You just make your statement
in court, put on your hat, and take the first packet out from this
port. You take me?"

If only it could be that simple, thinks I. But I made one last
effort to wriggle free.

"Is my evidence so necessary, sir?" says I. "Surely these
Balliol College people can be convicted ..."

"Convicted?" says he. "Why, we're a long way short of that at
the moment. You know the procedure, sir—when a slave-trading
ship is captured, she must first of all be *adjudged* to be a slaver.
You know how it is in your own mixed commission courts at

Surinam and Havana and so forth—they hear evidence and pronounce themselves satisfied that she *was* carrying slaves. You must have seen it a score of times. And *then*—when the ship has been confiscated and condemned—then her master and crew may be charged with slave-trading, and on conviction, they can be hanged—although they seldom are. Jail terms sometimes, fines, etc. But with us it's not quite the same, as you'll see."

I was hanging on every word, hoping and praying that he would point out some loophole to me.

"Here, in New Orleans, a court of adjudication will pronounce on the *Balliol College*, and according to that, her master and crew may be charged with slave-trading, and possibly—since Spring fought against ships of the U.S. Navy—with piracy. But none of these charges can even be brought, sir, unless the court of adjudication finds that the *Balliol College* was indeed a slaver. So far, then, we follow the same course as the mixed courts at Havana and elsewhere. But here, sir, there are much more powerful interests involved—this is New Orleans, remember, a long way from Washington, and New Orleans holds no grudge against slave-traders like Spring. To secure the confiscation and condemnation of the *Balliol College* as a slave ship, the case must be proved to the hilt and beyond. Now do you see why your evidence is vital?" He tapped his desk. "This is not just a criminal—a legal case, Mr Comber. It's a political one, sir. See here," he grew confidential again. "This man Spring. No ordinary blackbirder, that. Why, when he was brought in by Fairbrother's people—what happened? The fellow was wounded—I tell you, sir, there was a bail bond posted faster than you could sneeze, a surgeon in attendance, more lawyers running about than you'd think existed. Why, sir? Because there's money, and power, and political influence behind this damned trade—that's why! There's his ship—how many hundreds of thousands of dollars investment d'you think she represents—and not just dollars, either, but pounds sterling and pesos and francs? They couldn't find any papers on her, because that damned wife of Spring's heaved them all overside—so what happens now, but Spring's counsel enter papers to show she's registered in Vera Cruz, Mexico, of all places, and her owner is some bloody Dago with a name as long as your leg—Mendoza y

Cascara, or something. Mexico, Lord save us! If there's one place we don't need complications with, it's Mexico—and they know it. But they can prove she's Mexican-owned—for all she's Baltimore built, with an English skipper."

I could make little of this, but one thing seemed clear.

"But if she was carrying slaves when they took her—and had slave gear aboard—"

"Slave gear doesn't matter—the equipment treaty doesn't hold up in New Orleans, sir. Mixed commission trials, yes, but not here. The slaves, sir—they're the thing!"

"Well, then—"

"Precisely. That's where we've got them. There were slaves aboard, and for all the treasure and effort that will be poured in on their side, I don't see how they can get round it. Mind you, sir, the shifting and lying and trickery that goes on at a slave ship adjudication is something you must see to believe. It wouldn't surprise me if Spring claimed they were all his sons and daughters, wearing chains because they're perverted creatures. I've seen excuses just as wild. And in New Orleans—well, you can't tell. I would to God," he added, "that Fairbrother had had the sense to take the *Balliol College* to Havana—she'd have been nailed there, fast enough, and we'd have been spared all this. But with your evidence, Mr Comber, I don't see how we can go wrong. Oh, they'll fight; they've got Anderson, who's as sharp a mind as ever took a brief—or bribed a witness. He'll try every trick and dodge going, and the adjudicator will be leaning his way, remember. But when you take the stand—well, sir, where will they be then?"

Where *they* would be was of small interest to me; where was Flashy going to be? I gulped and asked:

"Do they ... er ... do they know about ... that I'll be giving evidence?"

"Not yet," says he, smiling happily. "You see, an adjudication isn't a trial—we don't have to come and go with the other side much beforehand, officially, although I can tell you that the politicking that's been done in this case—offers of settlement, God knows what—has been amazing. Whoever is behind Spring, they're people who matter. They want him and his ship clear —probably frightened of what he'll divulge *if* he's ever brought to trial. Oh, it's a fine, dirty business, Mr Comber—the slime and corruption doesn't end on the slave deck, I can tell you. No, they don't know about you, yet—but I'll be surprised if a little bird doesn't tell 'em pretty soon. Lucky, in a way, that you didn't turn up until now—court sits the day after tomorrow, and if you hadn't been here we'd have had to go in without our best witness."

Lucky, I thought—just another few days lost up north and they might have started and got it over, and I'd have been spared my appearance and inevitable unmasking. I couldn't see anything for it, now—unless I got the chance to run again, but Bailey, for all his amiability, was no less watchful than the marshal had been. Even at the Navy office there was a damned little American snotty keeping me company wherever I went, and on the following day, when I was taken down to the building where the adjudication court sat, and was introduced to the counsel representing the U.S. Navy, the snotty and a petty officer were trailing at my heels.

The counsel was a lordly man from Washington with a fine aristocratic beak and silver hair falling to his shoulders. His name was Clitheroe, and he talked to the air a yard above my head; to hear him, the business would be over in a couple of hours at most, and then he would be able to get back to Washington and direct his talents to something worth while. He talked briskly for a moment or two about my part in the proceedings—"decisive corroboration" was the expression he used—and then consigned me to the care of his junior, a quiet, dark little fellow called Dunne, who had said very little, and now took me apart into a side room, instructing my escort to wait while he had a private word with me.

Now what followed is gospel true, and you will just have to believe me. If it runs counter to your notions of how justice is done in the civilised world, I can't help it; nothing in my experience leads me to believe that things are any different in England or France, even today. This is what happened.

Dunne talked to me for about five minutes, around and about the case, but all very vague, and then begged to be excused for a moment. He went out, leaving me alone, and then the door opened and in comes a prodigious fat man, with a round face and spectacles, for all the world like some Friar Tuck in a high collar. He closed the door carefully, beamed at me, and says:

"Mr Comber? Delighted to meet you, sir. My name is Anderson—Marcellus Anderson, sir, very much at your service. You may have heard of me—I represent the defendants in the case in which you are to be a distinguished witness."

My jaw dropped, and I must have glanced at the door through which I had come from Clitheroe's office, for he gave a fat man's chuckle and slid into a chair, observing:

"Have no fears, sir; I shall not detain you above a moment. The admirable Clitheroe, and your, ha-ha, watchdog, Captain Bailey, would grudge me even that long, no doubt, but Mr Dunne is a safe man, sir—he and I understand each other." He regarded me happily over his spectacles; Mr Pickwick as ever was.

"Now, very briefly, Mr—er—Comber, when we heard that you were to testify, my client, Captain Spring, was mystified. Indeed, sir—do you know, he even seemed to doubt your existence? However, you will know why, I dare say. I made rapid inquiry, obtained a description of you, and when this was conveyed to my client—why, sir, a great light dawned upon him. Oh, he was thunderstruck, and I needn't go into distressing detail about what he said—but he understood your, ha-ha, position, and the steps you had taken to safeguard yourself when the *Balliol College* was arrested some months ago."

He took off his glasses and polished them, regarding me benignly.

"Rash, sir, very rash—if you'll forgive me for saying so. However, it's done. Now Captain Spring was incensed at what he considered—justifiably, I think—to be a disloyalty on your part. Yes, indeed, and it was his first instinct to denounce you the moment you took the stand. However, sir, it occurred to me—it's what I'm paid for—that there might even be advantage to my client in having Lieutenant—" he paused— "Beauchamp Millward Comber as a witness for the plaintiff. If his evidence was—oh, shall we say, inconclusive, it might do the defendant more good than harm. Do you take me, sir?"

I took him all right, but without giving me a chance to reply he went on.

"It amounts to this, sir. If my client is cleared, as I feel bound to tell you I believe he will be—for we have more shots in our locker than friend Clitheroe dreams of—then we have no interest in

765

directing attention to the antecedents of Lieutenant Comber. If Captain Spring is *not* cleared—" he shook his head solemnly "—then when the crew of the *Balliol College* are arraigned for slave-trading and so forth, their number will be greater by one than it is at present."

He stood up quickly. "Now, sir, Mr Dunne will be impatient to speak to you again. When we meet again, at the hearing, it will be as strangers. Until then, I have the honour to bid you a very good day."

"Wait . . . wait, for God's sake!" I was on my feet, my mind in a turmoil. "Sir . . . what am I to do?"

"Do, sir?" says he, pausing at the door. "Why, it is not for me to tell a witness how he shall give evidence. I leave that to your own judgment, Mr . . . er . . . Comber." He beamed at me again. "Your servant, sir."

And then he was away, and two shakes later Dunne was back, aloof and business-like, describing to me the form and procedure of an adjudication court, all of which went straight by me. Well, I've been in some fearful dilemmas, but this beat everything. The Navy expected my evidence to follow the lines of the statements I'd made in Washington, months back. If it did, Spring would cut me down in open court and I'd be for the dock myself. If it didn't—if I lied myself hoarse—Spring would keep his mouth shut, but the Navy . . . my God, what would they do to me? What could they do? They couldn't arrest me, surely . . . no, but they could investigate and question, and God alone knew what might come of that. The tangle was so terrible that I couldn't think straight at all—there was nothing for it but to be carried along on the tide, and do what seemed safest at the time. I wondered if I should confess to Bailey, telling him who I really was and admitting my imposture, but I daren't; I'd have been putting a rope round my own neck for certain.

There aren't many blank periods in my memory, but the rest of that terrible day is one; I cannot remember the night that followed, but I recall that on the next morning, the day of the adjudication, a strange recklessness had come over me. I was beyond caring, I suppose, but I remember I stood muttering to myself before a mirror as I brushed my hair: "Come on,

Flashy, my boy, they haven't got you yet. Remember Gul Shah's dungeon; remember Rudi's point at your throat in the Jotunberg cellar; remember the Ghazis coming at you on the road above Jugdulluk; remember the slave cart in Mississippi; remember de Gautet drawing a bead on you. Well, you're still here, ain't you? Your backside is better enough for you to run again, if need be—bristle up the courage of the cornered rat, put on a bold front, and to hell with them. Bluff, my boy—bluff, shift and lie for the sake of your neck and the honour of Old England."

And with these thoughts in my head and a freezing void in my bowels I was escorted to the adjudication court.

It was held in a great white room
with brown panelling, like a lecture theatre, with tiers of crescent-
shaped benches to one end for the spectators, a little rostrum and
desk for the adjudicator and his two assessors at the other, and
in between, right beneath the rostrum, were three great tables.
At one sat Clitheroe and Dunne, and on a bench behind were just
myself and—to my astonishment—two of the prettiest yellow girls
you ever saw, all in New Orleans finery, with an old female in
charge of them. They were giggling to each other under the
broad brims of their bonnets, and when I sat down they looked
slantendicular and giggled more than ever, whispering in each
other's ears until the old biddy told them to leave off. My escort
left me and went to sit on the first of the public benches, beside
Captain Bailey, who was in full fig; he nodded to me and smiled
confidently, and I gave him back a terrified grin.

At the centre table were a few clerks, but the far table was
empty until just before the proceedings began. By that time the
public benches were crowded with folk—nearly all men, and
consequential people at that, talking and taking snuff and calling
out to each other; I felt plenty of eyes on me, although most were
directed at the two yellow girls, who preened and simpered and
played with their gloves and parasols. Who the blazes they might
be, I couldn't imagine, or what they were doing here.

And then a door behind the far table opened, in rolls Anderson,
and to a rising buzz of chatter and comment, John Charity Spring
entered and took his seat, with Anderson puffing at his elbow.
The last time I had seen him he had been rolling on his own deck
with Looney's bullet in his back; he looked a trifle paler now, but
the beard and tight-buttoned jacket were as trim as ever, and when
the pale eyes looked across directly into my own, I saw his lips

twitch and the scar on his forehead began to darken. He stared at me fixedly for a full minute, with his hands clenched on the table before him, and then Anderson whispered in his ear, and he sat back, looking slowly about the court. He didn't look like a prisoner, I'll say that for him; if anyone looked guilty you may have three guesses who it was.

Then the adjudicator came in and we all stood up; he was a little, sharp-faced man, who smiled briefly to Clitheroe and Anderson, shot quick, accusing glances at everyone else, and told the nigger boy behind his chair to mind what he was about, and fetch some lime juice directly. Everyone fell silent, the two assessors sat either side of the adjudicator, and the clerk called out the case for hearing of the barque *Balliol College*, reputedly owned and registered in Mexico, master John Charity Spring, a British citizen; the said barque taken by U.S. brig *Cormorant*, in latitude 85 west 22.30 north or thereabouts, on such and such a day, and then carrying aboard her certain slaves and slaving equipment, in contravention of United States law—

Anderson was on his feet at once. "May the adjudicator take note that the *Balliol College* was not and is not an American vessel, and that her master is not an American citizen."

"Nevertheless," says Clitheroe, rising, "may the adjudicator note that the ownership is disputed, and recall the case of the ship *Butterfly*, condemned in similar circumstances.[42] Further, it will appear that the *Balliol College* was carrying slaves intended for trans-shipment to the United States, which is a clear violation of American law, and that when challenged by a United States ship of war, such challenge being proper and lawful, the *Balliol College* fired upon her challenger, which is piracy under American law."

"If these things are proved, sir," says Anderson, beaming.

"As they will be manifestly proved," says Clitheroe.

"Proceed," says the adjudicator.

The clerk read on that the *Balliol College* had resisted arrest, that an attempt had been made to dispose of the slaves aboard her by drowning them, and that the plaintiff, Abraham Fairbrother, U.S. Navy—it was news to me that the case was undertaken in his name—sought the confiscation and condemnation of the *Balliol College* as a slave-trading vessel.

769

That done, Clitheroe and Anderson and the adjudicator went into a great wrangle about procedure which lasted most of the morning, and had everyone yawning and trooping out and in, and fidgeting, until they had it settled. It was beyond me, but the result was that the business was conducted in a most informal way —more like a discussion than a court. But this, apparently, was the case with these adjudications; they had evolved a strange procedure that was all their own.[48]

For example, when they were at last ready to begin, it was Anderson who got up and addressed the adjudicator, not Clitheroe. I didn't know that it was common for the defendant to show his innocence, rather than the other way about. And for the life of me I couldn't see that Spring had a leg to stand on, but Anderson went ahead, quite unruffled.

The plaintiff's case, he said, such as it was, rested on the hope that he might show the *Balliol College* to be, de facto, American-owned, or part American-owned. Secondly, that it was carrying slaves for America in contravention of American law. Thirdly, that in such illicit carriage, it resisted arrest by an American ship of war, such resistance amounting to piracy.

"Unless I mistake the plaintiff's case," says he, easily, "everything rests on the second point. If the *Balliol College* was *not* carrying slaves for the United States, and so breaching American law, it is immaterial whether she is American-owned or no: further, if she was *not* carrying slaves, her arrest was illegal, and such resistance as she showed cannot be held against her master or crew. The plaintiff must show that she was a slave-trading ship, carrying slaves illegally." He beamed across the court. "May I hear counsel on the point?"

Clitheroe rose, frowning slightly, very austere. "That is the essence of the plaintiff's case, sir," says he. "We shall so demonstrate." He picked up a paper. "I have here the sworn deposition of Captain Abraham Fairbrother, U.S. Navy, commander of the brig *Cormorant*, who effected the capture."

"Deposition?" cries Anderson. "Where is the gentleman himself?"

"He is at sea, sir, as you well know. I have already had a word to say—" and he looked hard at Anderson "—on the point of delays engineered, in my opinion, by the defendant's counsel, in the knowledge that the witness would be compelled to resume his duties afloat, and would therefore be unable to appear in person."

Anderson was up like a shot, protesting innocence to heaven, with Clitheroe sneering across at him, until the adjudicator banged his desk and told them sharply to mind their manners. When the hubbub and laughter on the public benches had subsided, Clitheroe went ahead with Fairbrother's statement.

It was a fair, truthful tale, so far as I could see. He had challenged the *Balliol College*, which had been flying no flag, she had sheered off, he had fired a warning shot, which had been replied to, an action had been fought, and he had boarded. A dozen or so slaves had been found aboard, recently released from their shackles—as he understood it this had been done by Lieutenant Comber, R.N., who was aboard the ship ostensibly as one of the crew, although in fact he was a British naval officer. Lieutenant Comber would testify that it had been the intention of the master of the *Balliol College* to drown these slaves, and so remove all evidence.

There was a great humming in the court at this, and many glances in my direction, including a genial smile from Anderson and a glare from Spring. The adjudicator banged his desk for quiet, and Clitheroe went on to describe how the *Balliol College* crew had been arrested, and the ship brought into New Orleans for adjudication. He sat down, and Anderson got up.

"An interesting statement," says he. "A pity that we cannot cross-examine the deponent, since he isn't here. However, may I point out that the statement takes us no further so far as the status of the coloured people on board the *Balliol College* is concerned. Negroes were found—"

"And slave shackles, sir," says Clitheroe.

"Granted, sir, but the precise relation of one to the other is not determined by the statement. No doubt my friend, having delivered the statement which is the basis of his case, will call witnesses in due course. May I now enter my client's answer to the statement?"

Clitheroe nodded, the adjudicator snapped: "Proceed," and at Anderson's request one of the clerks swore Spring in to testify. Then Anderson said:

"Tell us, Captain Spring, of your voyage in the *Balliol College* prior to and including the events in question."

Spring glanced at the adjudicator, came to his feet, and leaned his hands on the table. The harsh grating voice took me back at once—I could smell the *Balliol College* again, and feel the hot sun beating down on my head.

"I sailed from Brest, in France, with a cargo of trade goods for the Dahomey coast," says he. "There we exchanged them for a general cargo of native produce, largely palm oil, which I conveyed to Roatan, in the Bay Islands. Thence I was proceeding in ballast for Havana, when I was intercepted by an American brig and sloop, who without justification that I could see, ordered me to heave to and fired upon me. I resisted, and my ship was presently boarded by these Navy pirates, who seized my ship, my person, and my crew!" His voice was rising, and the red scar burning. "We were carried in chains to New Orleans—I myself had been grievously wounded in defence of my ship, and I have since been held here, my ship confined, and myself and my owners deprived of its use, with subsequent loss to ourselves. I have protested in the strongest terms at this illegal detention, for which an account-ing will be demanded not only of the person involved, but of his government." And in true Spring fashion he growled: "*Qui facit per alium facit per se** holds as good in American law as in any other, I dare say. That I was carrying slaves in contravention of this country's enactments I emphatically deny—"

"My dear sir, my dear captain." This was Anderson. "May I anticipate my friend's question: if this is so, why did you not heave to when required, and permit a search of your vessel? Then all might have been easily resolved."

Spring made noises in his throat. "Do I have to tell an American court, of all places? I responded to a signal to heave to, from an American vessel, in precisely the manner in which an American captain would have replied to a similar demand from a British naval ship. In short, sir, I defied it."

There was a great shout of laughter from the public benches, and feet drummed on the floor in applause. The little adjudicator hammered his desk, and when all was fairly quiet Anderson asked:

*What a man does through another, he does himself.

"As the British captain of a Mexican vessel you saw no reason to heave to—quite so. You know, Captain Spring, it has been suggested that your vessel is not Mexican owned. I believe my friend may wish to pursue the matter?" And he invited Clitheroe with a cocked eyebrow.

So Clitheroe set about Spring—he threw names at him, American, British and French; he pointed out that the *Balliol College* was Baltimore-built and originally Yankee-owned; he put it to Spring that the papers now set before the adjudicator, showing Mexican ownership, were forgeries and makeshift. Why, he demanded, if Spring were an honest merchantman, had his wife thrown the ship's papers overboard?

"When I am attacked by pirates, sir," says Spring, "I do not permit my papers to fall into their hands. How do I know that they might not be falsified and tampered with to be used against me? Here is a whole trumped-up business anyway—to suggest that I am a slaver, without a rag of proof, and to badger me with nonsense about my papers!" He pointed to the adjudicator's desk. "My papers are there, sir—certified, vouched copies! Look at them, sir, *litera scripta manet,** and get on to the point of your inquisition, if it has one!"

It seemed to me he was playing the bulldog British skipper a thought too hard for safety, but the public were with him, crying, "hear, hear" until the adjudicator had to call them to order. Clitheroe shrugged and smiled.

"By all means, captain, since you desire it. I pass from the matter of ownership, which is secondary, to the heart of the matter. Since you are fond of tags, let's see if you remain quite so *rectus in curia*† when I ask—"

The adjudicator hammered his desk again. "I'll be obliged if you'll both speak English," cries he. "Most of us are familiar with the classics, but not on that account will I permit this adjudication to be conducted in Latin. Proceed."

Clitheroe bowed. "Captain Spring, you say you brought palm oil from Dahomey to Roatan—an unusual cargo. Why then was your ship rigged with slave shelves?"

*The written letter remains (as evidence).
†Upright in the court.

773

"Slave shelves, as you call them, are a convenient way of stowing palm oil panniers," says Spring. "Ask any merchant skipper."

"And they're also convenient for stowing slaves?"

"Are they?" says Spring. "May I point out that the shelves were not rigged when my ship was seized—when you say I was running slaves."

"I shall come to those same slaves, if you please," says Clitheroe. "There were, according to the affidavit we have heard, negroes aboard your ship—about a dozen women. They were found on deck, with slave shackles beside them. Evidence will be given that they had been chained, and that you had been preparing to cast them overboard, to destroy the evidence of your crime." He paused, and there wasn't a sound in court. "You are on oath, Captain Spring. Who were those women?"

Spring stuck out his jaw, considering. Then he answered, and the words hit the court like a thunderclap.

"Those women," says he deliberately, "were slaves."

Clitheroe gaped at him. There was a gasp from the public benches and then a great tumult, hushed at last by the adjudicator, who now turned to Spring.

"You admit you were carrying slaves?"

"I've never denied it." Spring was quite composed.

"Well—" The adjudicator looked about him. "Permit me, sir, but I have been in error. I thought that was what your counsel had been vigorously denying on your behalf."

Anderson got to his feet. "Not precisely, sir. May I suggest that my client be allowed to stand down for the moment, while the court digests his statement and reflects upon it? In the meantime, perhaps my friend will continue with his case."

"Frankly, sir," says Clitheroe, "it seems my case is made. I move for an order of confiscation and condemnation against the *Balliol College*, proved to be a slave-trader on her own master's word."

"Not quite proved," says Anderson. "If I may invite my friend to provide the corroboration which he doubtless has at command?"

Clitheroe looked at the adjudicator, and the adjudicator shrugged, and Clitheroe shuffled his papers and muttered to Dunne. For the life of me I couldn't fathom it; Spring appeared to have thrown away, with those words, his case, his ship, his liberty—

perhaps even his neck. It made no sense—not to the public or the adjudicator or to me. The one thing I prayed for now was that my evidence wouldn't be needed.

Clitheroe didn't like it; you could see, by the way he shot looks across at Anderson, that he smelled a rat. But Anderson sat smug and smiling, and presently Clitheroe shrugged ill-humouredly and picked up his papers.

"If the adjudicator wishes, I shall continue," says he. "But I confess I don't see the point of it."

The adjudicator peered at Anderson, thoughtfully. "Perhaps it would be as well, Mr Clitheroe."

"Very well." Clitheroe looked at his papers. "I shall call and examine the former slaves Drusilla and Messalina."

At this the yellow girls popped up, with little squeaks of surprise—and I realised that these tarts must be two of the women we had been shipping to Havana. Well, here were the two final nails for Spring's coffin, but he never batted an eyelid as they were brought forward, fluttering nervously, to the table, and sworn in by the clerk. The fellows on the public benches were showing great interest now, nudging and muttering as the little beauties took their stand, like two butterflies, one pink and one yellow, and Clitheroe turned to the adjudicator.

"With permission I shall examine them together, and so save the court's valuable time," says he. "As I understand it, both you young ladies speak English?"

The young ladies giggled, and the pink one says: "Yassuh, we both speak English, Drusilla'n' me."

"Very good. Now, if you will answer for both, Messalina. I believe you were in a place called Roatan—the Bay Islands, you might call it, a few months ago. What were you doing there?"

Messalina simpered. "We wuz in a who'-house, suh."

"A what?"

"A who'-house—a knockin'-shop, suh." She put her gloved hand up to her mouth, and tittered, and the public slapped their thighs and guffawed. The adjudicator snapped for silence, and Clitheroe, looking uncomfortable, went on:

"You were both—employed in a . . . whore-house. I see. Now then, you were taken on a ship, were you not?" They both nodded, suppressing their giggles. "Do you see here any of the men who were on that ship?"

They looked round, nervously, at the adjudicator, and then further afield. A voice near the back of the public benches called out: "Not me, honey. I was at home," and a great hoot of mirth broke out and had to be quieted, the adjudicator threatening to clear the room if there was unseemly behaviour. Then Messalina timidly pointed to Spring, and then they both looked round at me, and giggled, and whispered, and Messalina finally said:

"That one, too—with the nice whiskers. He was awful kind to us."

"I'll bet he was," says the voice again, and the adjudicator got so angry he swore, and said that was the last warning. Clitheroe gave me a look, and said:

"I see—these two men. Captain Spring and Mr Comber. They and others took you on a ship—where to, do you know?"

"Oh, to Havana, ev'yone said. An' then we was goin' on to here, by 'nother ship, to Awlins, right here."

"I see. Did you know where you were going to, in New Orleans?"

They giggled and conferred. "Miz Rivers' who'-house, so ev'yone reckon."

"I see, first to Havana, and then to Mrs Rivers' . . . er, establishment, in New Orleans." Clitheroe paused. "There is, I am told, such an establishment."

There was some haw-hawing from the public, and a cry of "He ain't foolin' '', but the adjudicator let it go.

"Now, girls," says Clitheroe, "when you were in Roatan, what were you?"

"Please, suh, we wuz whores," giggled Drusilla.

"Yes, yes, but what else? Were you free?"

"Oh, no, suh, we wuz slaves. Warn't we, Drusie? Yassuh, we'z slaves a'right."

"Thank you. And as slaves you were sent aboard the ship, to be taken to Havana, and thence sold to Mrs Rivers' . . . ah . . . whorehouse in New Orleans. But by the favour and mercy of God, the ship was captured by the United States Navy and—" Clitheroe leaned forward impressively "—you were brought to New Orleans

776

and *there set free.* Is this not so?"

"Oh, yassuh. We's set free, sho' nuff." Messalina smiled winningly at him.

"Fine. Splendid. You were liberated from that unspeakable servitude, and you are now free women." Clitheroe was enjoying himself. "Since when I don't doubt you have been happy in your new-found land of adoption and blessed free estate. You are both safe in New Orleans?"

"Oh, yassuh. We's fine, at Miz' Rivers' who'-house."

Even the adjudicator didn't try to stop the peal of laughter and applause that this provoked, and Drusilla and Messalina smiled around happily and preened themselves under all this male attention. But Clitheroe just sat down, red in the face, and Anderson got up and waited for the noise to subside.

"A very moving story," says he, and everyone roared again. "Tell me, Drusilla and Messalina—I don't doubt for a moment that every word you have told us is true, and I accept it as true—but tell me, you first, Messalina dear: where were you born?"

"Why . . . Baton Rouge, suh."

"And you, Drusilla?"

"N'Awlins, suh."

"Indeed. Very interesting. And how did you come to be at Roatan?"

Messalina had been taken by a wealthy planter visiting Cuba; she had been his mistress, but he had tired of her and sold her. ("Silly bastard," says the unseen voice.) Drusilla had been one of a party taken on a cruise by wealthy degenerates, who had sold their doxies at various places in the Caribbean.

"So you are both American-born? I see—and both born slaves?"

"Yassuh."

"The other girls on the ship with you—were they also American-born? You don't know—of course not. And they have not been cited as witnesses in this case, and can't be called now, accordingly." Anderson glanced knowingly across the court at Clitheroe, who was looking like a man who sees a ghost. "May I refresh the court's memory by referring to the enactment of 1820"—he rattled off a string of numbers while he leafed through a large tome. "Here we have it. Briefly it defines as piracy and illegal slave-trading—" he paused impressively "—the transportation for enslavement of any coloured person *who is not already a slave under American law.*"

In the hush that followed Anderson closed the book with a snap like a pistol shot.

"There we have it, sir. Captain Spring, as he has admitted, freely and openly, was carrying slaves—American slaves, born slaves, and in so doing he was in no way contravening any United States law. No more than a man breaks the law when he carries a slave across the Mississippi River. He was not *running* slaves, or slave-trading in the illicit sense, or—"

Clitheroe was on his feet, raging. "This is an outrageous twisting of the truth—why, just because these two happen to be American-born—why, they were only chosen to testify because they spoke English well—half of their fellow-captives on the *Balliol College*, I am certain, were not American-born, and were therefore—"

"Then it's a pity you didn't bring them here today," says Anderson. "You should choose your witnesses more carefully."

"Sir, this is monstrous!" cries Clitheroe. "In the name of justice, I demand to be allowed to call another—"

"In the name of justice you'll keep us here till kingdom come!" cries Anderson. "Really, sir, are we to be detained while this distinguished counsel rakes the whole of Louisiana for some witness who will suit his book? He has entered his witnesses before this court—let him abide by what they say. If they let him down, so much the worse for him, and so much the better for justice!"

There was no doubt whose side the spectators were on. They cheered and stamped and drowned out everyone until the little adjudicator had to shout for silence. And after several minutes, when all was quiet, he remarked:

"You had ample time to consider who you should call, sir. I'll hear the witnesses you have named."

"I protest!" cries Clitheroe, his white hair flung back. "I protest—but very well, sir—you shall hear my last witness, who will prove my case for me!" And as my heart shot into my mouth he turned and boomed:

"Beauchamp Millward Comber, Royal Navy!"

I suppose I took the oath, but I don't remember it. Then Clitheroe was taking me through my antecedents, my commissioning by the Board of Trade, my shipping aboard the *Balliol College* —all of which I had to invent, on the spur of the moment, and it wasn't made any easier by the unseen voice growling: "Goddam' limey spy!"—and so to the business he wanted to get his teeth into.

"You can, I think, testify, that when the *Balliol College* reached Dahomey, she took aboard not palm oil, as the defendant claims— but a human cargo. Slaves! Is this not so?"

But Anderson, bless his honest fat face, was on his feet. "This is quite improper, sir! I demand that the witness be instructed to ignore the question. We are not here concerned with what the British master of a Mexican ship was doing many thousands of miles from our shore. Such a case, if any there were, would be for a British or Mexican court, or a mixed commission of the type to which the United States does not subscribe. I demand—nay, insist—that no irrelevant observations, such as might prejudice my client's position, be permitted. We are here to determine the status of the *Balliol College* at the time of her seizure—" and he went bounding on to cite a great string of precedents—*Bright Despatch, Rosalinda, Ladies' Delight,* heaven knows what.

It sounded a near thing to me; I stood there with my palms sweating, and if that adjudicator had been an honest man I'd have been sunk. But someone had been to work, I've no doubt, for he shook his head, and snapped:

"I take the point of defendant's counsel. We are not concerned with the Captain's past history—"

"Or his ship's?" bawls Clitheroe. "What about *Mendon, Uncas,* any number I could name, sir—why, slavers have been condemned before ever they had taken a black on board, simply on a question of intent! This—"

"May I make a point, sir?" says Anderson. "I respectfully suggest that it would ill become an American court to deny to a British master the very rights which we insist upon for our own captains where British justice is concerned. We demand that our captains be not interfered with unless they expressly break British law; it cannot be argued that what Captain Spring was doing thousands of miles away, in a Mexican ship, is any concern of ours."

"Humbug—" Clitheroe was beginning, but Anderson added quickly:

"The court would hardly wish to set a precedent of which foreign governments, particularly the British, might take note."

That clinched it. The adjudicator glanced at me: "You will ignore that question, sir. Mr Clitheroe, I must ask you to confine yourself to the matter in hand. Proceed, sir."

"I protest again, most emphatically," says Clitheroe. "Very well, then—Mr Comber, were these negroes who were carried from Roatan for Havana—were they chained, sir?"

"Most of the time, not," says I, which was true.

"But chains were placed upon them when the American brig challenged the *Balliol College?*"

"Yes." I tried not to catch Spring's eye.

"Why were they chained, sir?"

"To prevent their possible escape, I imagine. I was below decks at the time."

He gave me an odd look. "Was there not another reason? Was it not so that a length of anchor chain could be rove through their shackles, so that they could be brutally hurled into the deep and drowned?" He looked at his papers. "I quote from your own statement to the Navy Department."

Up came Anderson. "May I point out that this ... statement, supposedly made by the witness, is not in itself evidence. We are concerned with what he says now, not what he said then."

I could feel the sweat starting out on my brow. How to balance the tightrope? Talk for your life, Flash, thinks I, so I looked perplexed, and said, addressing the adjudicator:

"Sir, I have reflected much on this matter in the past few months. That the slaves were shackled, and the anchor chain passed between those shackles, is true—I myself released them later. But in strict justice I must add that the shackling was performed by the late Mr Sullivan, mate of the *Balliol College*, and it was followed by a most violent altercation between Sullivan and Captain Spring."

Clitheroe's eyes narrowed, and I saw Bailey, who was behind him, sit up suddenly.

"Are you saying," says Clitheroe, "that Spring was objecting to this shackling?"

"I can't say, sir." God, I was treading warily. "What was the cause of their altercation, I do not know." I took a deep breath. "But I do know that Mr Sullivan had served aboard slave ships in the past—and I don't believe he was quite right in the head, sir."

Clitheroe was staring at me in frank disbelief. "But this is totally out of accord with your earlier statement, sir. What?—" he scrabbled over a page "—here we have you referring to Spring as 'an unhuman beast', a 'callous murderer', a—"

"This is infamous!" roars Anderson. "I have protested already —sir!" He swung on Clitheroe. "Is that statement, that rubbish you hold in your hand, and read out to vilify my client—is it signed, sir!"

"It is not signed, sir, but—"

"Then take it away, sir! Remove it! It is a scandal, a disgrace! I appeal to the adjudicator!"

"We will hear the witness," says the adjudicator. "Not what you say he once said, Mr Clitheroe. You must not lead the witness, sir—as you should know." Someone had greased his palm, right enough.

Clitheroe was in a quandary; Bailey, I could tell from his face, was in a fury. Clitheroe turned back to me, and his face was ugly.

"Very well," says he. "I now put the matter to you in different terms. Can you say, from your own knowledge, that there were slaves being carried on board the *Balliol College* in contravention of American law—that is to say, non-American slaves, and that an attempt was made to dispose of them by casting them overside— whoever gave the order."

I was ready enough for that. "Two hours ago, sir, I would have been able positively to answer your question as to the slaves. However, you must see, in the light of what we have heard from the last two witnesses, that I cannot in conscience answer positively now. The distinction about American-born slaves is new to me, sir; I cannot say whether the others were also American or not."

He gave a snort of impatience. "Was there not, on the *Balliol College*, an African woman—brought from Africa, sir, and carried to Baltimore with the others by Captain Fairbrother. A woman named—" he looked at his paper "—Lady Caroline Lamb, who spoke no English, and had been carried from Dahomey as a slave? Who could not possibly have been American, whatever the others were."

"I remember the woman perfectly," says I. "As to her status, I confess I am reluctant—now—to be too definite, since she was certainly not among those shackled by Mr Sullivan." (That was true, too; how had he overlooked her? She must have been in my cabin. Ah well, it's an ill wind.)

"Reluctant?" Clitheroe threw down his papers in disgust. Behind him I could see Bailey muttering with rage. "Reluctant? On my word, Mr Comber—I find this most extraordinary. Are you here, sir, to testify against that man—" and he flung out a hand at Spring "—or are you not? Damme, sir—I beg the adjudicator's pardon—what does this mean? Your whole tone, your attitude, the burden of your evidence, is so far from what you led us to believe it would be, that I could almost wonder—" His glance flickered to Anderson, but he thought better of it. Before he could go on, I plucked up my courage and got in first.

"I have answered your questions to the best of my ability, sir," says I. "If I am scrupulous, I must say I find it hard that I should be blamed for that."

He looked as though he would burst. "Scrupulous, by all that's holy! I don't ask you to be scrupulous—I ask for the truth! What did you sail aboard this damned slaver for, if not to bring him to justice, eh? Answer me that, sir?"

When in difficulty, bluster; it was the only weapon I had left, and I seized it, now that his loss of composure had given me the chance.

"I sailed in the performance of my duty to my chiefs, sir, as you well know. That duty I have done—or will do, as soon as I am permitted. If you look in my statement, sir, you will see that I was reluctant from the first to appear in this case, and that I appeared only because your Navy Department assured me it was necessary. I had assumed, wrongly, I fear—" and I took my whole courage in my hands, and tried to sound furious "—that such a simple case would be easily concluded without my intervention being called for."

He went white, and then red, and his breath came out in a great shudder. He looked at me with pure hate, and when he spoke, it was with great care.

"Indeed, sir? Very high-minded, and high-handed, are we not? Very well, Mr Comber, let us examine this, if you please. Your duty, sir, you have told us, is to your chiefs—you are an agent against the slave trade—although one would hardly suspect it from your conduct today. As such, I understand you obtained possession, during this voyage, of papers belonging to the master of the *Balliol College*—" out of the tail of my eye I saw Spring stiffen in his seat. "Will you tell us, sir, whether or not there was evidence in those papers—as to the ownership of the vessel, for example—to prove that she was engaged illegally in the slave trade, in contravention of American law? You are on oath, sir— remember that!"

My heart lurched, because I had seen the way out. I held my breath a moment, to make my face red, and let it out slowly. I drew myself up, and glared at him with all the venom I could muster.

"This, sir," says I, "is intolerable. It is precisely why I did not wish to appear. You are well aware, sir, that there are facts which I am in duty bound not to disclose—facts of the highest import— it is all explained in that statement, sir—which I cannot in honour convey to anyone except to my chiefs at home. I was promised immunity from this—" brazening it for all I was worth, I rounded on Bailey. "Captain Bailey, I appeal to you. This is entirely unworthy—I am badgered, sir, on the very grounds which it was promised to me would be inviolate. I will not endure it, sir! The counsel's questions must lead inevitably to the point which I was assured would not be touched. I . . . I . . ." There's nothing like a good stammer for conviction. "I was a fool to be coerced into this! I should have known . . . incompetence! . . . harm done!"

There was tumult in the court; even Bailey was looking bewildered now; the adjudicator was at a loss. Anderson, clever man, had the good sense to look amazed; Spring was looking worried. Clitheroe, stuck between rage and astonishment, looked to Bailey, and then to me.

"On my word!" This was the adjudicator, darting his nose at me. "What is this, sir? This outburst is quite—"

"Sir," says I, "I most humbly beg your pardon. I intended no disrespect to you, or to this august court." I hesitated. "I found myself placed in an intolerable position, sir—if an explanation is necessary, I beg that you will ask counsel for the plaintiff."

There was a moment's silence, in which the adjudicator looked at Clitheroe, and Clitheroe stood with his face white and his mouth set. Then he shook his head.

"I see no advantage to the court in . . . examining this witness further," says he, and he sat down.

Anderson jumped up, and began to address the adjudicator, but I was too bemused by my own eloquence to listen. The next thing I knew there was an adjournment, and I was hustled off to Bailey's office, with Clitheroe and Dunne, and the first two rounded on me like bears. But I snatched the ball from their hands, and laced into them for all I was worth—it was my only chance, I knew, to play the mystery as I had done in the Washington Navy Department, and play it as furiously as I could.

"If you so mishandle your case, sir, that you can't get a condemnation order that a child could obtain, is that my fault? The wrong slaves called as witnesses—this fellow Anderson permitted to shut me up on the very point where I could have given conclusive testimony! And then—the impudence to break the solemn assurance I was given in Washington, by questioning me in a way which, if I'd been fool enough to answer, must have elicited the names I am duty bound to conceal! And you dare to raise your voice to me, sir? Do you think I'll see my work ruined—two years of it—" Well, why not lay it on hard? "—simply because some fool of a lawyer can't win a case which in itself is nothing— nothing, sir, I tell you—compared with what I and my people are trying to do? Oh, this is too much!"

How I managed to lose my temper so badly for so long, when my innards were quaking, I am far from sure. They didn't take it lying down, either—especially Bailey, who was half-convinced my indignation was sham. But he couldn't be sure, you see; there was just enough mystery, as a result of all the bloody lies I'd told in Washington, to make him wonder.

"Your conduct, sir, gives me the gravest suspicions," says he. "I don't know—this is a deplorable affair! But we'll go into this, sir, believe you me; we'll get to the bottom—"

"Then you'll do it in your own good time, sir!" says I, looking him in the eye. "Not in mine. I'm sick and tired of this whole sorry business. I was promised protection, sir—"

"Protection?" cries he, looking ugly. "You have forfeited all claim to that. My department's protection is withdrawn, you may take that as read—"

"Thank God!" I exclaimed. "For all the good it's been to me, I'm better without it. I intend to place myself, at once, under the protection of my ambassador in Washington. At once, do you hear? And whoever tries to hinder me will do so at his peril!"

For a moment he looked as though he was believing me, and then we were summoned back to the court, and I sat red-faced, squeezing myself to keep it up, while Clitheroe and Anderson bandied away at each other, and finally Anderson challenged him on some point or other, and Clitheroe made a speech, and concluded it by moving for the confiscation and condemnation of the *Balliol College*. There was much palaver over the matter of Spring's resisting arrest, and Anderson stuck to the point about an innocent merchantman being entitled to protect himself, etc., and finally the adjudicator took off his spectacles and asked did their cases rest? They nodded, and he put his spectacles back on, and everyone stood up.

The adjudicator talked for about half an hour, while our legs creaked, and I couldn't for the life of me stop my hands trembling, for there was no telling which way he was going. He reviewed the evidence, Spring's and the girls and my own, and then came to his peroration. It was short, and decisive.

"It rests with the plaintiff, Abraham Fairbrother, to show that the *Balliol College* was carrying slaves in contravention of United States law. There are grounds for believing that she was, in view of her equipment and other circumstances related in evidence. It may also appear that grounds could exist for charges to be brought

785

in connection with damage done to United States property by Captain Spring. On the other hand, it may be that, after the conclusion of this court, the owners of the *Balliol College* may hold that an action lies against the United States government for unlawful detention.[44] These are matters outside the scope of this adjudication. The activities of the *Balliol College*, prior to her arrest, may also be matters for a mixed commission court of the British or other governments.

"It is precisely for the attention of such court, if it be called, that I have mentioned the conclusion of this adjudication that grounds exist for believing that the *Balliol College* was carrying slaves in contravention of United States law. But I cannot hold that the grounds have been proved conclusively to the satisfaction of this adjudication. The motion for confiscation fails."

I pulled myself together and shot Clitheroe as baleful a look as I could manage, for Bailey's benefit. The adjudicator turned to Spring.

"You are free to go. As I understand it, your vessel is in the river, is it not, under a prize crew? Hear our order that this prize crew be withdrawn forthwith, and that such stores, water and wood as may be required in reason for your departure shall be left aboard, and in accordance with custom, clearance be granted for your departure this very day, or such date thereafter as you find fitting."

"Thank you, sir," says Spring. "I thank the court. I shall leave anchorage today."

The adjudicator banged his desk and scuttled out, and at once there was a great rush from the public benches to Spring's table, and he was being clapped on the back, and fellows were shaking Anderson's hand and hurrah-ing. Clitheroe walked out of the court without a word, and Bailey, after a lowering look at me, followed him. The two yellow girls, giggling and ogling, tripped away with their chaperone or bawd or whatever she was.

And suddenly I was standing alone. But I doubted, somehow, if this happy state would endure for long. My escort had gone with Bailey, but in spite of our violent exchanges, they would be expecting me at his office, or at least back at the Navy place where he had housed me. And then, for all my fine talk, they would keep a tight grip on me—for what? Interrogation, no doubt, and at best a convoy to Washington and my embassy, and God knew what would come of that. My buttock ached at the thought of sliding out again, but I knew I daren't stay. For one thing, the longer I was in this blasted country the greater the chance of my activities on the Mississippi being brought home to roost.

I looked about me. The spectators were all streaming out now, by the entrances at the back of the room. Half a dozen steps and I was among them—once outside, I could easily find my way to Susie's brothel, and this time, surely, she would be able to see me safe away; at least she could hide me until I grew a beard, or—.

And then it struck me, all in a moment, the dazzling thought. It was fearful, at first, but as I considered it, on the steps leading down to the street, it seemed the only safe way. It was the answer, surely—and I found my legs taking me off to one side, behind a pillar, where I thought some more, and then I stepped out into the busy street, and walked across to the far side, and took refuge beneath a tree, waiting.

It was ten minutes before I saw what I wanted, and my heart was in my mouth in case Bailey or my escort would come on the scene, but they didn't. And then I was rewarded, and I set off, walking quickly, along the street, and into another, and there I overtook the figure ahead of me.

"Captain Spring," says I. "Captain Spring—it's me."

He swung round as if stung, as near startled as I'd ever seen him.

"The devil!" he exclaimed. "You!"

"Captain," says I, "in God's name, will you give me a passage out of here? You're leaving, on the *College*, aren't you? For pity's sake, take me with you—out of this blasted—"

"What?" cries he, his scar beginning to jump like St Vitus dance. "Take you? Why the devil should I? You—"

"Listen, please, captain," says I. "Look, I played up today, didn't I? I could have sworn you to kingdom come, couldn't I? But I didn't—I didn't! I got you off—"

"You got me off!" He tilted back his hat and glared at me. "You saved your own dirty little neck, you Judas, you! And you've the nerve to come crawling to me?"

"I'll buy my passage!" I pleaded. "Look, I'm not just begging—I can buy it with something you want."

"And what would that be?" But he stepped aside with me into a doorway, the pale eyes fixed on me.

"You heard in court—I got Comber's papers—the things he'd filched from you. Well—" I forced myself not to notice the darkening scar on his brow "—I've still got 'em. Are they price enough?"

His face was like flint. "Where are they?" he growled.

"In a safe place—a very safe place. Not on me," I lied, praying he'd believe it. "But I know where they are, and unless I say the word—well, they could get into the wrong hands, couldn't they? You'd be clear and away before that, of course, but your owners wouldn't like it. Morrison, for one."

"Where are they?" he demanded, and his hands came up, as though to seize me. But I shook my head.

"I'll tell you," says I, "in Liverpool or Bristol—not before. They'll be safe until then, on my word."

"Your word!" he sneered. "We know what that's worth! You perjured rascal. Look at you!" He laughed softly. "*Post equitem sedet atra cura.** Your friends in the American Navy are looking for you, I don't doubt."

"If they find me, they find those papers," says I. "But if you take me with you, I swear you'll have 'em." And welcome, I thought privately. Even when I'd handed them over, the knowledge of what was in 'em would still be in my head, and I'd use it to squeeze old Morrison dry. "You'll have them, captain," I repeated. "I promise."

"By God I will," says Spring. "I'll see to that." He stood considering me, "What a worthless creature you are—what shreds of loyalty have you, you object?"

"Plenty—to myself," says I. "Just as you have, Captain Spring."

His scar went pink; then he laughed again. "Well, well. You've picked up some Yankee sauce over here, I believe. Perhaps you're right, though. Horace reminds me, why should I sneer at you?

* Dark care sits behind the horseman (A guilty man cannot escape himself).

788

*Mutato nomine de te fabula narratur."** He looked up and down the street. "I'll take you. But you tell me those papers are safe, do you? For if they're not—by God, I'll drop you overside with a bag of coal on your feet, if we're within ten feet of the Mersey. Or Brest, which is where I'm going. Well?"

"You have my word," says I.

"No," says he. "But I've got your carcass, and I'll settle for that. Now, then—are these damned Yankees close behind you? Then step lively, Mr Flashman!"

Strange, I thought, how long it was since anyone had called me by my proper name. For the first time in months I felt I was almost home again. With Elspeth, and the youngster, too. Aye, and my dear papa-in-law—I was looking forward to presenting my account to him.

* Change the name, and the story is told of yourself.

[EDITOR'S POSTSCRIPT. On this optimistic note the third packet of the Flashman Papers comes to an end. How far the optimism was justified may be judged from the fact that, instead of describing his return in gloating detail, Flashman concluded this portion of his memoirs by attaching to the last page of manuscript a clipping, cracked and faded with age, from a newspaper (probably, from its type face and extreme column width, the *Glasgow Herald*) dated January 26, 1849. The news it contains was, of course, unknown to him when he left New Orleans homeward bound. It reads, in part:

"It is with deep regret that we impart to our readers news of the death of Lord Paisley. This untimely event occurred last week at the home of his daughter, Mrs Harry Flashman, in London, where he had been residing for some time past. Those who knew him, either as John Morrison of Paisley and this city, where he was formerly Deacon of Weavers in the Trades' House of Glasgow, or by the title to which he was raised by a gracious sovereign only in November last, will be united in mourning his sudden melancholy demise . . ."]

NOTES

1. The great Chartist Demonstration of Monday, April 10, 1848, was, as Flashman says, a frost. Following the numerous Continental revolutions, there were those who feared that civil strife would break out in Britain, and in addition to extra troops brought to the capital, the authorities enlisted 170,000 special constables between April 6 and 10 to deal with disturbances. Peel, Gladstone, Prince Louis Napoleon (later Napoleon III), about half the House of Lords and an immense number of middle-class volunteers were among the "specials". In the event, only about twenty to thirty thousand Chartists demonstrated, instead of the half million expected, and there was little violence apart from the fight between the butcher's boy and the French agitator, which happened as Flashman describes it. (Foreign agitators and hooligan elements were a frequent embarrassment to the Chartists, since they discredited the movement). Of the two (not five) million signatures to the great petition, about one-fifth are said to have been bogus—"Punch" noted caustically that if they had all been genuine, the Chartist procession should have been headed by the Queen and seventeen Dukes of Wellington. (See Halevy's *History of the English People in the Nineteenth Century*, vol. 4, pp. 242–6.)
2. From this and other allusions it is obvious that Flashman spent at least part of the 1843–47 period (the "missing years" so far untouched by his memoirs) in Madagascar and Borneo. He is known to have been both military adviser to Queen Ranavalona and chief of staff to Rajah Brooke of Sarawak; it now seems probable that he held these appointments between 1843 and 1847. Other evidence suggests that he may also have taken part in the First Sikh War of 1845–6.
3. Lord John Russell was then Prime Minister; Lansdowne was Lord President of the Council.
4. Berlins: articles, particularly gloves, knitted of Berlin wool.
5. Attendance money. A charge introduced on the railway about this time, which amounted to a kind of cover or service charge. It appears to have been levied for as small a service as asking a railway servant the time of day. Flashman's memory may be playing him false when he speaks of a railway book-stall; it was more probably a railway library.
6. Frances Isabella Locke (1829–1903) was to become famous in later years as Mrs Fanny Duberly, Victorian heroine, campaigner, and "army wife" extraordinary. She left celebrated journals of her service in the Crimea and the Indian Mutiny. (See E.E.P. Tisdall's *Mrs Duberly's Campaigns.*)
7. Lord George Bentinck (1802–48), one of the foremost sporting figures of his day, and leader of the Protectionist Tory opposition in the Commons. Handsome, arrogant, and viciously aggressive in political argument, Bentinck was widely respected as a guardian of the purity of the turf, although after his death his former friend Greville alleged

790

that he was guilty of "fraud, falsehood, and selfishness" and "a mass of roguery" in his racing conduct. Bentinck resigned his leadership of the opposition early in 1848, but was still the power in his party at the time of his meeting with Flashman at Cleeve. He died suddenly only a few months later, on September 21, 1848.

Disraeli, who then succeeded him as Tory leader in the Commons, was not to become Prime Minister for another twenty years. Flashman's view of him in 1848 fairly reflects the feeling of many Tories—"they detest D'Israeli, the only man of talent", wrote Greville in that year. His extravagances of dress and speech, his success as a novelist, and his Jewish antecedents combined to render him unpopular—Flashman, like Greville, insists on spelling him D'Israeli, although Disraeli himself had dropped the apostrophe ten years earlier. The nickname Codlingsby is a pun on Coningsby, perhaps his best novel, published in 1844. (See Charles Greville's Memoirs, January 7–September 28, 1848.)

8. Surplice had just beaten Shylock in the Derby, and on the following day the Jewish Disabilities Bill failed in the House of Lords.

9. With revolution everywhere on the Continent in 1848, it was confidently expected that Ireland would erupt, and there was a small abortive rising in the summer. John Mitchel, a leading agitator, was sentenced in May to fourteen years' transportation.

10. Jane Eyre by Charlotte Brontë was published in the autumn of 1847. Varney the Vampire, or The Feast of Blood by Malcolm Rymer was an outstanding horror story even in a decade which was unusually rich in novels of ghouls, vampires, and Gothic spine-chilling.

11. Miss Fanny's excuse was not very flattering to her fiancé, whose position with the Eighth Hussars was that of paymaster.

12. The Black Joke schooner had a career befitting its romantic name, being in turn a slaver, a Royal Navy tender, and an opium smuggler in the China Seas.

13. Under the Anglo–Dutch treaty of 1822 a ship fitted out for slaving (with shackles, slave shelves, unusually large cooking facilities, etc.,) could be condemned as a slaver even if she was not carrying slaves. (See W. E. F. Ward's The Royal Navy and the Slavers.)

14. What Flashman says of the background to the slave trade in the 1840s is accurate enough, but obviously he does not give more than a hint of the complicated system of treaties and anti-slavery laws by which the civilised nations fought the traffic. (See Ward.) Virtually all were prepared to pay at least lip service to the anti-slave trade cause, but only Britain mounted a continuous major campaign against the slaving vessels on the high seas and along the African coast, although at the time of Flashman's voyage the United States Navy was also lending its assistance. But there was no consistency about the various national laws against the trade, and the slavers were quick to take advantage of the numerous loopholes. What is sometimes not appreciated is the distinction that was drawn by governments between slavery and actual slave trading: for example, Britain prohibited the trade as early as 1807, but did not abolish slavery within the Empire until 1833; the United States prohibited the trade in 1808, but continued to practise slavery in her slave states until the Civil War. In this topsy-turvy situation, with huge private interests involved in the traffic, slave trading flourished into the second half of the century.

15. Pedro Blanco was a leading slave-broker who specialised in collecting Africans for sale to slaving ships. His usual scene of operations was farther north, on the Sierra Leone coast. Flashman's description of Whydah and the Kroos corresponds very closely with contemporary accounts.

16. With epidemics an ever-present danger on the Middle Passage, slaver captains took every precaution against shipping diseased or weakly slaves. However, they had no scruples about marketing those who fell ill on the voyage, and were at pains to disguise their disabilities. Spring is here referring to a particularly revolting means of hiding the symptoms of dysentery.

17. Spring was giving considerably less space to his slaves than that allowed by the Wilberforce Committee in 1788, when the famous plan of the slaving ship *Brookes* gave the following figures: Males, six feet by sixteen inches; females, five feet by sixteen inches; boys, five feet by fourteen inches; girls, four feet six by twelve inches. This, as F. George Kay points out in *The Shameful Trade*, meant that five men were packed into a space equivalent to two modern single beds, and lay there for perhaps twenty hours a day over a period of several weeks. Parliament was prepared to accept a death rate of two per cent.

18. *The Genius of Universal Emancipation*, a newspaper published from 1821 to 1839 by Benjamin Lundy, an early American abolitionist. William Lloyd Garrison, perhaps the greatest of anti-slavery journalists, worked with Lundy before founding his own paper, *The Liberator*, in 1831 which ran until the end of the Civil War. Arthur and Lewis Tappan were dedicated New York abolitionists.

19. The revolvers, by Flashman's description, were probably early Colt Patersons of 1836 (single-action muzzle-loaders, five-shot, .40 calibre), although it is not impossible that they were Colt Walkers of the type produced for the Mexican War (six-shot, .44). The needle guns must be the Prussian Dreyse single-shot breech-loaders of 1840, which were the first bolt-action military weapons.

20. The Dahomeyans believed that human sacrifices were messengers to the gods, and despatched about 500 each year, about a tenth of whom were killed at the "annual custom", as the great ritual slaughter festival was called. The "grand custom", held only when a king died, involved much greater bloodshed.

21. King Gezo, a liberal ruler by Dahomeyan standards, made £60,000 a year from the slave trade, according to Royal Navy intelligence estimates, and also reorganised the army of Amazons, which had previously been composed of female criminals, unfaithful wives, etc. Gezo, by recruiting from all the unmarried girls of his kingdom, raised a force of about 4,000 fighting women, and there is ample evidence of their ferocity and discipline. Flashman's description of them is accurate. Gezo ruled Dahomey for 40 years, dying of small-pox in 1858.

22. Quite apart from Harriet Beecher Stowe's famous villain, there was a Southern slave trader called Legree in Spring's time.

23. Methods of slave-packing varied according to a ship's accommodation, but Flashman's account gives a vivid impression of what a hideous business it was. His details of branding, sizing, and dancing are accurate; even so, it appears that Spring, despite his insistence on close packing, was a more humane skipper than most on the Middle Passage. Conditions on the *Balliol College* compare favourably with those on other slave ships of which contemporary records exist, and which tell appalling tales of human cargoes thrown overboard, epidemics, mutinies, and unspeakable cruelties. Even the sailors' stories which Flashman retells give only a pale impression of the reality. Figures compiled by Warren S. Howard in his *American Slavers and the Federal Law* indicate that on average one-sixth of slaves shipped died on the Middle Passage. The *Balliol College*'s low mortality rate was not unique, however, in 1847 only three slaves died out of 530 aboard the barque *Fame*, running to Brazil.

24. Captain Robert Waterman of the *Sea Witch*, one of the great Yankee tea clippers. His passages from China to New York broke all records in the mid-1840s.
25. Blackwall fashion: competent but leisurely sea-faring, as opposed to the tough life aboard the packets.
26. One of the slaver's common ruses was to fly whatever colours seemed safest, according to their position at sea. In fact American colours were most common on the Middle Passage.
27. Although Spain had banned the slave trade, Cuba continued to operate a large unofficial slave market, and cargoes were smuggled in as circumstances permitted. Possibly these did not appear favourable to Spring, and he determined to run to Roatan, a popular clearing house.
28. On January 24, 1848, James W. Marshall found gold at Coloma, California. News of his discovery led to the great rushes of '48 and '49.
29. Prices varied enormously from year to year, but the figures quoted generally by Flashman are above average. Possibly 1848 was a good year from the seller's point of view.
30. Slaves certainly were thrown overboard on the approach of patrol vessels (see the case of the *Regulo* which drowned over 200 in the Bight of Biafra, and the reported case of the clipper captain who was said to have murdered over 500 by dropping them with his anchor chain, both quoted in Kay).
31. Abraham Lincoln was 39 at this time, and the physical description tallies closely with his first known photograph, taken in 1846. When he met Flashman he was in the middle of his only term as a U.S. Congressman, although he already had a successful career in local politics and as a lawyer behind him. As a Congressman he was not especially distinguished, and his bill to abolish slavery in the District of Columbia was never brought in.
32. Cassius Clay (1810–1903), a fighting Kentuckian and fervent abolitionist, who later became President Lincoln's minister to Russia.
33. The underground railroad was a truly heroic organisation which ran more than 70,000 slaves to freedom. Founded in the early 1840s by a clergyman, its agents included the famous John Brown of the popular song, and the extraordinary little negress, Harriet Tubman, herself a runaway. She guided no fewer than nineteen convoys of escaped negroes out of the slave states, including infants who had to be drugged to escape detection, and is reputed never to have lost any of her many hundred "passengers".
34. The true identity of "Mr Crixus" can only be guessed at. Obviously he had adopted the name from the Gaulish slave who was a chief lieutenant to Spartacus in the Roman gladiators' rebellion of 73 B.C.
35. The *Sultana's* record for the trip was five days and twelve hours exactly, set in 1844. Although often exaggerated, the performance of the Mississippi steamboats was extraordinary, and reached a peak with the run of Captain Cannon in the "good ship *Robert E. Lee*" in 1870, when the 1218 miles from New Orleans to St Louis was covered in three days eighteen hours fourteen minutes. Normally a big side-wheeler could easily maintain an average of over 12 m.p.h. upstream.
36. Mr Bixby was later head pilot of the Union forces in the Civil War. His other claim to fame is that he taught the craft of steamboat piloting to Mark Twain.
37. Mustee, a shortened form of musteefino or musterfino: loosely, a half-caste, but particularly one who was very pale skinned. Strictly speaking, the child of one black and one white parent is a mulatto; the child of a mulatto and a white is a quadroon (one quarter black); the child of a quadroon and a white is a mustee (one eighth black). It is

a curious feature of colour prejudice that *any* admixture of coloured blood, however small, is deemed sufficient to make the owner a negro.

38. Thanks to Flashman's vagueness about dates, it is impossible to say in exactly which week he and Cassy were contemplating their journey up the Ohio. It must surely have been early spring in 1849, in which case Flashman must have spent longer on the Mandeville plantation than his narrative suggests; he was there for cotton-picking, which normally takes place in September and October, but can extend into early December.

39. There can be little doubt that Harriet Beecher Stowe, who was living in Cincinnati at the time, must have heard of Cassy and Flashman crossing the Ohio ice pursued by slave-catchers, and decided to incorporate the incident in her best-selling *Uncle Tom's Cabin*, which was published two years later. She, of course, attributed the feat to the slave girl Eliza; it can be no more than an interesting coincidence that the burden Eliza carried in her flight was a "real handsome boy" named Harry. But it seems quite likely that Mrs Stowe met the real Cassy, and used her, name and all, in that part of the book which describes life on Simon Legree's plantation.

Incidentally, Mrs Stowe timed Eliza's fictitious crossing for late February (which she calls "early spring"); this provides a further clue to the time of Flashman's crossing in similar weather conditions.

40. A "who's-yar" (usually spelled hoosier): an Indianan, supposedly deriving from the rustic dialect for "who's there?", although this is much disputed. In fact, although Lincoln spent most of his youth in Indiana, he himself was a Kentuckian by birth.

41. But not for much longer. Lincoln's term in Congress ended on March 4, 1849, which can only have been a few days after his meeting with Flashman in Portsmouth; it is curious that their conversation contains no mention of his impending retirement.

42. The *Butterfly*, a newly-built slave ship, was captured before she had even reached Africa, let alone taken on slaves. After a fierce legal battle she was condemned.

43. From Flashman's account of the adjudication, it is obvious that he has greatly simplified the procedure of the court; no doubt after half a century only the highlights remained in his mind. Procedure in slave-ship cases varied greatly from country to country, and did not remain consistent, and many such cases were never even printed. So bearing in mind that what he is describing was a form of preliminary hearing, and not a slave-ship trial proper, one can only take his word for what happened in the *Balliol College* adjudication.

As to Flashman's allegations of corruption and pressure exerted in slave-ship cases, one cannot do better than quote the words of a contemporary skipper, Captain C. E. Driscoll (see Howard), who boasted flatly: "I can get any man off in New York for a thousand dollars."

44. The owners of a ship arrested as a slaver, but subsequently acquitted, might well be in a strong position to claim damages from the arresting party. For this reason there was some reluctance in the late 1840s, especially among American Navy officers, to capture suspected slaveships, for fear of being sued.